MIS COMPANION CD

With this new international edition, we are proud to offer a unique and excitin...
technology, to enhance students' learning experience: the MIS Companion CD ...

The MIS Companion CD allows students to experience FREE training in Microsoft Office Excel 2003 and Microsoft Office Access 2003 along with additional coverage of MIS concepts using MIS Interactive Labs. The MIS Companion CD is a unique, free tool on CD at the front of every copy of this book. Integration of the CD can be found throughout the text; please look for the CD icon. There are also questions based on the CD material at the end of every chapter.

Excel 2003 and Access 2003 training

The MIS Companion CD gives students the chance to get hands-on training and practice with Access 2003 and Excel 2003 tasks, ranging from the beginning through advanced levels. Lecturers can now cover these software skills in their introductory MIS course by utilzing this Companion CD to help their students absorb and practise these skills. In addition, the tool also gives students the opportunity to learn and practise Access and Excel tasks independently.

MIS interactive labs

This CD also includes 15 robust interactive labs that reinforce key MIS-related concepts, enabling students to learn real-world computer-based activities in a simulated environment. These labs are designed to provide students with various options in absorbing concepts through reading, observation, step-by-step practice and hands-on application. Some of the exciting topics addressed in these labs include presentation software, networking basics, online privacy, project management and web design.

Table of contents for lab integration

The following table of contents illustrates which labs are best for reinforcing some of the content coverage in each chapter of this book. Use this list as a guide to match each MIS lab with its corresponding chapter.

Assessment options for instructors

Beyond the exciting MIS Companion CD for student training, Course Technology offers assessment options to further enhance student learning. SAM (Skills Assessment Manager) is the worldwide leader in online assessment and is proven to be the most effective tool to assess and train students in Microsoft Office tasks, Computer Concepts, Windows, the Internet and more. SAM is a hands-on, simulated computer assessment and training tool that gives students the feeling of working live in the computer application.

Want More? SAM 2003

Inject a wider breadth of applications, as well as additional Excel, Access and Computer Concepts coverage into your MIS course with SAM 2003! Visit http://samcentral.course.com to learn more.

Please contact your Course Technology Sales Representative for more information regarding these assessment options.

Management
Information Systems

Management
Information Systems

Effy Oz

The Pennsylvania State University, Great Valley

Andy Jones

Staffordshire University

LRC Stoke Park
GUILDFORD COLLEGE

COURSE TECHNOLOGY
CENGAGE Learning

Australia • Brazil • Japan • Korea • Mexico • Singapore • Spain • United Kingdom • United States

COURSE TECHNOLOGY
CENGAGE Learning™

Management Information Systems
Effy Oz and Andy Jones

Publishing Director: John Yates

Commissioning Editor: Tom Rennie

Development Editor: Alice Rodgers

Content Project Editor: Leonora
    Dawson-Bowling

Manufacturing Manager: Helen Mason

Senior Production Controller: Maeve Healy

Marketing Manager: Rossella Proscia

Typesetter: ICC Macmillan Inc., India

Cover design: Adam Renvoize

Text design: Deisgn Deluxe, Bath, UK

Copyright © 2008 Cengage Learning EMEA

For product information and technology assistance,
contact **emea.info@cengage.com**.
For permission to use material from this text or product,
and for permission queries, email **clsuk.permissions@cengage.com**.

Products and services that are referred to in this book may be either trademarks and/or registered trademarks of their respective owners. The publishers and authors make no claim to these trademarks.

British Library Cataloguing-in-Publication Data
A catalogue record for this book is available from the British Library.

Adapted from *Management Information Systems,* 5th Edition, published by Course Technology, a division of Cengage Learning, Inc. © 2006.

ISBN: 978-1-84480-758-1

Cengage Learning EMEA
High Holborn House
50-51 Bedford Row
London WC1R 4LR

Cengage Learning products are represented in Canada by Nelson Education Ltd.

For your lifelong learning solutions, visit **www.cengage.co.uk** and **www.course.cengage.com**.

Printed by C&C Offset Printing Co Ltd, China
1 2 3 4 5 6 7 8 9 10 – 10 09 08

To Narda, my best friend and beloved wife: It has been a great journey together, and it is only the beginning.

EFFY OZ

To Sue and all my family especially the two extremes of the age range, the lovely Lexie and my Mum (who will no doubt be showing this to everyone she meets).

ANDY JONES

Brief contents

Contents

Part five
Planning, acquisition
and controls 397

11 Systems planning and development 403

12 Choices in systems acquisition 441

13 Risks, security and disaster recovery 475

About the authors

Effy Oz is a Professor of Management Science and Information Systems at Pennsylvania State University, Great Valley. He received his MBA from the Hebrew University and his DBA from Boston University. Professor Oz has published and presented numerous academic and professional articles and authored best-selling textbooks in the areas of management information systems, e-commerce, and IT ethics. He serves on the editorial boards of Encyclopaedia of Information Systems as well as several academic journals. His writing draws both on his research and industry experience as an executive.

Andy Jones is Principal Lecturer and Group Head of Applied Computing at Staffordshire University and has taught introductory information systems for many years. He is also the Award Manager for Staffordshire University's Applied IT Degree Scheme and an external examiner for Leeds Metropolitan University, Sheffield Hallam University, The University of Hertfordshire and City University, Hong Kong. Two of his key research areas include open/distance learning and training methods for IT and he monitors various diplomas and degrees at APIIT, Malaysia and TMC, Singapore.

Acknowledgements

For this international edition, thanks are due to Tom Rennie, Alice Rodgers, Leonora Dawson-Bowling and Lea Paoli for guiding me through this process as painlessly as possible.

I would also like to thank all of the case study contributors who have helped to make this a truly international and diverse text (see p. xxvii).

The publisher would also like to thank Shelley John at CNET Networks UK for her generous efforts in coordinating the inclusion of the silicon.com case study material.

In addition to CNET Networks UK and their contributors, we are grateful to the following for permission to reproduce copyright material:

Alamy
Amazon.com
Amazon.co.uk
American Power Conversion Corp
Arsenal Football club
ASDA
Auction LotWatch
AXA Winterthur
BT Group plc
Center Parcs
Choices Hotel International, Inc
ConSentry Networks
CV Screen Ltd
Department for Business, Enterprise and Regulatory Reform
Deutsche Post AG
Dow Jones & Company
Dundas
GeoSim
Emirates Airline
Fedex
Forrester Research
Google Inc
IRIS www.iris.co.uk/hrmanager
i-com software (WStore)
istockphoto.com
Microsoft Corporation
Moodle
NASA
NetSuite Inc
OnOneMap Limited
PEFA.com
Pöyry (Beijing) Consulting Company Limited
Rackspace Ltd
Radar-soft.com
Royal Caribbean Cruises
Screwfix
Simon & Schuster, Inc
Skype
Sling Media, Inc
Somerfield
The British Computer Society
Travelocity
UpMyStreet
Unilever
University of Edinburgh
VerChip
vtiger Systems
Yahoo!
Zoho

In some instances we have been unable to trace the owners of copyright material, and we would appreciate any information that would enable us to do so.

Lecturer feedback at key stages of this international edition's development has been crucial and I would like to thank the following reviewers for their constructive comments and suggestions:

Lynette Barnard, Nelson Mandela Metropolitan University
Dimitar Christozov, American University in Bulgaria
Mike Herman, University of Hertfordshire
Alan Hogarth, Glasgow Caledonian University
Scott Raeburn, Napier University
Bjarne Rerup Schlichter, University of Aarhus
Lynn Snape, Anglia Ruskin University
Carina de Villiers, University of Pretoria

Andy Jones
Staffordshire University

Preface

The goal of *Management Information Systems* is to provide a real-world understanding of information systems (ISs) for business and computer science students studying in the United Kingdom, Europe, Middle East and Africa. This new international edition provides students with a firm foundation in business-related information technology (IT) on which they can build successful careers regardless of the particular fields they choose. They may find themselves formulating strategic plans in executive suites, optimizing operations in businesses or on factory floors, fine-tuning plans for their own entrepreneurial ventures, designing ISs to optimize their organization's operations, working as consultants, augmenting business activities on the Web, or creating valuable new information products in any number of industries.

The fundamental principle guiding this book is that ISs are everywhere in business. Information systems are pervasive because information is the single most powerful resource in every business function in every industry. Knowledge of IT is not always explicitly stated as a job requirement, but it is an essential element of success in virtually any position. Not everyone in business needs to have all the technical skills of an IT professional, but everyone needs a deep-enough understanding of the subject to know how to use IT in his or her profession.

Management Information Systems provides students with the proper balance of technical information and real-world applications within an international setting. No matter what field they undertake, students will enter the business world knowing how to get information to work for them. They will know enough about IT to work productively with IT specialists, and they will know enough about business applications to get information systems to support their work in the best way possible.

Approach

Part Cases show IS principles in action

In this international edition Part Cases were carefully prepared to integrate all the IT principles that arise in business, to give students an opportunity to view IS issues in action and to solve business problems related to IT just as they arise in the real world. The cases are built around companies that range in size from the entrepreneurial start-up to the corporate giant, reflecting a wide variety of industries. These cases were created to show students how the full range of business functions operate within virtually every business setting. The Part Cases are integrated into the text in four ways:

- *The Case:* Each part of the text (made up of between two and three chapters) opens with the Part Case: the story of a business, including the business's IS challenges, the characters involved and the issues. Everyone in business knows that almost every business problem has a human element; this aspect of managing IT-related challenges is realistically represented in each case.

- *The Business Challenge:* The presentation of each case is immediately followed by a succinct statement of the business challenge of the case and the ways the information in each chapter in the case will help the reader meet that challenge.

- *Case Instalments:* Each chapter opens with an instalment of the Part Case that focuses and expands on an aspect of the original story that relates most closely to the chapter content.

- *Case Revisited sections:* Each chapter ends with a Case Revisited section, which includes a concise summary of the challenge in the case instalment; a section called 'What Would You

Do?', a series of questions that asks the readers to play a role in the case and decide how they would handle a variety of challenges inherent in the case; and 'New Perspectives', a series of questions that introduces a wide variety of 'what ifs' reaching beyond the original scope of the case and again asking the students to play different roles to meet business challenges.

Emphasis on the real world

Management Information Systems is not afraid to warn about the limitations of ISs. The text also explains the great potential of many information technologies, which many organizations have not yet unleashed. Of course, this book includes chapters and features that provide a thorough, concise – and refreshingly clear – grounding in the technology of information systems, because all professionals in successful organizations are involved in making decisions about hardware, software and telecommunications. But, through current, detail-rich, real-world case studies throughout the book, and a dedication to qualifying each presentation with the real-world factors that may affect business, this book stays close to the workplace in its presentation.

Attention to new business practices and trends

Large parts of the text are devoted to discussing innovative uses of information technology and its benefits and risks. Contemporary concepts such as supply chain management systems, data warehousing, business intelligence systems, knowledge management, web-based electronic data interchange, and software as a service are explained in plain, easy-to-understand language.

Illustration of the importance of each subject to one's career

Business students often do not understand why they have to learn about information technology. The reason many students are frustrated with introductory MIS courses is that they do not fully understand how information technology works or why it is important for them to understand it. One of the primary goals of this book is for its entire presentation to make the answers to these questions apparent. First, all subjects are explained so clearly that even the least technically oriented student can understand them. Technology is never explained for technology's sake, but to immediately demonstrate how it supports businesses. For instance, networking, database management and the web technologies (Chapters 5 through 7), often confusing topics, are presented with clear, concise and vivid descriptions to paint a picture of technology at work. In addition, each chapter includes a feature titled 'Why you should . . .', which explains to students how being well-versed in that chapter's aspect of IT is important to their careers.

Emphasis on ethical thinking

The book puts a great emphasis on some of the questionable and controversial uses of information technology, with special treatment provided in the 'Ethical and Societal Issues' boxes. The students are required to weigh the positive and negative impacts of technology and to convincingly argue their own positions on important issues such as privacy, free speech and professional conduct.

Emphasis on critical thinking

Critical thinking is used throughout the text as well as in the book's many features. For instance, the students are put in the midst of a business dilemma relating to the running case of each chapter and required to answer 'What would you do?' questions. The questions motivate students to evaluate many aspects of each situation and to repeatedly consider how quickly IT evolves.

Organization

Management Information Systems is organized into five parts, followed by a glossary and an index.

Part one: The information age

Part One of the book includes three chapters. Chapter 1, 'Business information systems: an overview,' provides an overview of information technology (IT) and information systems (ISs) and a framework for discussions in subsequent chapters. Chapter 2, 'Strategic uses of information systems', discusses organizational strategy and ways in which ISs can be used to meet strategic goals. Chapter 3, 'Business functions and supply chains', provides a detailed discussion of business functions, supply chains and the systems that support management of supply chains in various industries. Together, these three chapters address the essence of all overarching ideas that are discussed at greater depth in subsequent chapters.

Part two: Information technology

To understand how ISs enhance managerial practices, one must be well versed in the technical principles of information technology, which are covered in Part Two. Chapters 4, 'Business Hardware and Software', and 5, 'Business networks and telecommunications', provide a concise treatment of state-of-the-art hardware, software and networking technologies in business. Chapter 6, 'Databases and data warehouses', covers database management systems and data warehousing, which provide the technical foundation for a discussion of business intelligence and knowledge management in Chapter 10.

Part three: Electronic commerce

Part Three is devoted to networked business and its use of the Internet. Chapter 7, 'The web-enabled enterprise', is fully devoted to a thorough discussion of relevant web technologies for business operations. Chapter 8, 'Challenges of global information systems', highlights cultural and other challenges in planning and use of the Web and international information systems.

Part four: Managers and information systems

Part Four is devoted to managerial issues as they relate to information systems and provides a view of state-of-the-art business intelligence. Chapter 9, 'Managers and their information needs', introduces the information needs of managers at the different levels of responsibility and describes the organization of the information systems unit in corporations and the responsibilities of information systems professionals. As set out in Chapter 10, 'Business intelligence and knowledge management', electronic decision aids have been integrated into other systems in recent years, but understanding of their fundamentals is important. Business intelligence applications, such as data mining and online analytical processing, are fast becoming essential tools in a growing number of businesses. Plenty of examples are provided to demonstrate their power.

Part five: Planning, acquisition and controls

Part Five is devoted to planning, acquisition and controls of information systems to ensure their successful and timely development and implementation, as well as their security. Chapter 11, 'Systems Planning and Development', discusses how professionals plan information systems. It details traditional and agile methods of software development. Chapter 12, 'Choices in Systems Acquisition', presents alternative acquisition methods to inhouse development: outsourcing, purchased applications, end-user systems development and software as a service. Chapter 13, 'Risks, Security and Disaster Recovery', discusses the risks that information systems face and ways to minimize them, as well as approaches to recover from disasters.

New features of this international edition

The original text by Effy Oz is a well written and clear guide to the subject. The fact that it is entering its sixth edition is obvious evidence of this. This new text seeks to add to the original by including more case studies and examples from around the world, particularly the United Kingdom, Europe, Middle East and Africa. However, the underlying principles of the original text remain the same and, building on the success of the original text, this new international edition of *Management Information Systems* includes a uniquely effective combination of new and established features:

Boosted chapter case studies

This new international edition provides the dedicated Case Studies which introductory information studies lecturers and students have been searching for – with over 45 end-of-chapter case studies included using a wide range of international settings and organizations (see the case study matrix on p. xxv–xxvi).

Unique silicon.com case studies

In addition to the boosted case study offering, unparalleled insight into the working realities of information systems is provided through new silicon.com Case Studies at the end of every chapter. In conjunction with the UK's leading website for IT and business decision-makers – silicon.com – these cases provide unique learning features and use exciting real-world examples such as Arsenal FC and Amazon. Drawing across a range of organizations and settings, each case study ties all of the preceding chapter material together and cements the key themes and concepts.

Updated part case studies

This new edition highlights again the well-received, powerful pedagogical tool: five Part Cases (using fictional organizations) that clearly incorporate a wide array of challenges that dramatize how information technology is integrated into everyday business.

New industry snapshots

Replacing the old 'Point of Interest' feature, new Industry Snapshots provide dozens of real-world examples throughout the text.

New managerial chapter

There is a new chapter, 'Managers and their information needs', which brings together the ideas and technology from the previous chapters to show how information systems can help managers at all levels in an organization to achieve their objectives.

Refocused technical material

In response to extensive reviewer feedback, the two chapters on hardware and software in the original text have been combined into a more focused chapter on 'Business hardware and software' (Chapter 4).

Strong foundation in strategic ISs in business functions

In addition to a complete chapter on strategic uses of ISs (Chapter 2), strategic thinking is an underlying theme throughout the book. Current examples are used to illustrate how information systems can give businesses a strategic advantage.

Up-to-date coverage of web technologies and web-enabled commerce

Reflecting the use of web technologies in so many business activities, the book integrates the topic seamlessly throughout the text, just as it has become integrated into business in general. But the text goes beyond the well-worn discussions of the topic (and the handful of sites everyone knows about) to tell the students what works about e-commerce and what doesn't work.

Thorough discussion of supply chain management systems

As SCM systems are becoming pervasive in the business world, supply chains and their management are discussed both in a dedicated chapter (Chapter 3) and throughout the text. Related technologies, such as RFID, are clearly explained. In text and diagrams, the importance of these systems is underscored.

Current real-world examples reflect a wide variety of organizations

This international edition incorporates more applications, cases and projects in the full range of business functions and industries throughout the book. Reacting to demands from lecturers, the widest possible range of international examples has been used, ranging from public sector organizations and SMEs through to multinational corporations.

Coverage of global issues

In addition to international examples throughout, an entire chapter, Chapter 8, is devoted to discussing challenges of global information systems, from legal discrepancies through cultural issues to time zone issues. The chapter also discusses how the challenges can be met successfully.

New aspects of ethical and societal issues

The coverage of Ethical and Societal Issues in *Management Information Systems* builds on the strong foundation started in the original editions. However, new issues have emerged, such as phishing and offshoring, which are discussed in this edition.

New hands-on reinforcement of material

This new international edition continues to provide a large selection of assignments at the ends of chapters, mainly assignments that require the use of relevant software and the Web. In addition to the hands-on exercises in each chapter, students and instructors will find a host of additional new hands-on work available at the Student Companion Website, which is discussed later in this Preface.

Case studies

Chapter	Page No.	Title	Organization	Country/Region
1	40	IT strategy as part of business strategy	Unilever	Global
1	41	The personal touch	FedEx	Global
1	44	Analysis: CRM – get involved	Various	United Kingdom
2	78	Screwfix	Screwfix	United Kingdom
2	81	Royal Mail Group	Royal Mail Group	United Kingdom
2	83	Offshoring – how to get it right	Various	Global
3	119	Banking on IT	Bank of Ireland	Ireland
3	121	DHL – moving in the right direction	DHL	Global
3	123	How to avoid an ERP disaster	Various	Global
4	169	Captivating	Metropolitan South Africa	South Africa
4	171	Making the fleet greener	Aberdeenshire Council	United Kingdom
4	172	Inside the transformation of Arsenal FC	Arsenal FC	United Kingdom
5	210	Mobile phone banking in Africa on the rise	Various	Africa
5	212	WiMAX by the sea	Brighton Metranet	United Kingdom
5	213	VoIP takes hold with small businesses	Various	Global
6	243	Coping with growth	TÜV NORD Group	Germany
6	244	Children at risk...	Various	United Kingdom
6	246	Tesco	Tesco	United Kingdom
6	248	Information overload	Various	Global
7	291	Ocado: an Internet supermarket	Ocado	United Kingdom

Contributors

The following lecturers kindly contributed case studies to this international edition:

Patricia Britten, University of Buckingham
Alan Hogarth, Glasgow Caledonian University
Scott Raeburn, Napier University
Martin Rich, Cass Business School

As part of the silicon.com case study feature, the following people kindly agreed to contribute material for use as case studies:

Stewart Baines
Elizabeth Biddlecombe
Danny Bradbury
George Colony
Ron Condon
Dan Ilett
Andy McCue
Anthony Plewes
Will Sturgeon

Walk-through tour

Part Cases provide an overarching background of a business and its challenges, and introduce topics covered in the part's chapters in a real-life setting.

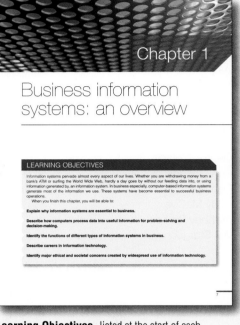

Learning Objectives, listed at the start of each chapter, are clear and succinct.

Business Challenges highlight the issues of the case and point to how the information in each part chapter contributes to meeting those challenges.

Each chapter is preceded by an **opening case,** which is an instalment of the **Part Case** and relates to the challenges and solutions discussed in the chapter.

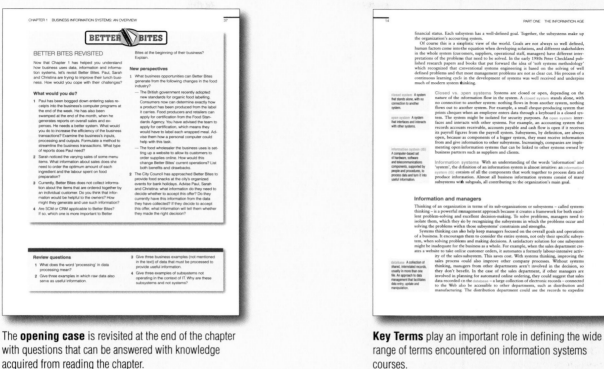

The **opening case** is revisited at the end of the chapter with questions that can be answered with knowledge acquired from reading the chapter.

Key Terms play an important role in defining the wide range of terms encountered on information systems courses.

Industry Snapshots provide dynamic real-world examples to illustrate key concepts.

Why you should . . . explains why professionals must understand the issues, concepts and technologies discussed in the chapter.

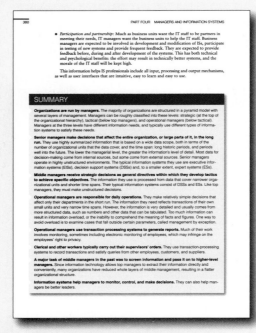

Ethical and Societal Issues present both sides of an IT-related issue that is ethically controversial or has a controversial impact on society.

The **Summary** lists the most important points of the chapter.

Review Questions help ensure that all the material discussed in the chapter is properly understood.

Discussion Questions address thought-provoking issues not specifically covered in the chapter but related to it.

Tutorial Activities, Companion CD Questions and **Video Questions** provide plenty of interactive assignments to help internalize and practise learned material.

From Ideas to Application: Real Cases include two or three recent actual cases of businesses and their IT challenges and solutions. Each case is followed with several critical thinking questions.

silicon.com Case Studies provide unique insights into the latest challenges facing information management professionals.

STUDENT COMPANION WEBSITE

Visit the *Management Information Systems* companion website at **www.cengage.co.uk/oz** to find valuable teaching and learning material including:

For students

- Videos – Twelve topical video clips, linked to chapters throughout the book, can be found on this website. Questions to accompany the respective video clips are featured at the end of each corresponding chapter in the book. These exercises reinforce the concepts taught and provide the students with more critical thinking opportunities.
- Glossary of Key Terms – Students can view a PDF file of the glossary from the book.
- Part Case Resources – Gain access to a multitude of online resources tied to the five Part Opening Cases.
- Part Case Projects – Unique hands-on projects associated with the five Part Cases have been created to allow for first-hand participation in the businesses introduced in each Part. For each Part Case, there is a selection of hands-on projects that asks the user to become a 'character' in the cases and perform small tasks to help meet business needs. The solution files for these activities are available to instructors at www.cengage.co.uk/oz, via the password-protected Instructor Downloads page for this textbook.
- 'Bike Guys' Business Cases – For more examples of MIS concepts in action, we have supplied the popular 'Bike Guys' cases from the Third Edition of the original text.
- Test Yourself on MIS – Brand new quizzes, created specifically for this site, allow users to test themselves on the content of each chapter and immediately see what answers were answered right and wrong. For each question answered incorrectly, users are provided with the correct answer and the page in the text where that information is covered. Special testing software randomly compiles a selection of questions from a large database, so students can take quizzes multiple times on a given chapter, with some new questions each time.
- Hands-On Exercises – Also created just for this Student Companion Website, a selection of exercises asks users to apply what they have learned in each chapter and further explore various software tools. The solution files for these activities are also available to instructors at www.cengage.co.uk/oz.
- Useful Web Links – Access a repository of links to the home pages of the primary websites relative to each chapter for further research.

For lecturers

- The Instructor's Manual – The text's authors have created this manual to provide materials to help instructors make their classes informative and interesting. The manual offers several approaches to teaching the material, with a sample syllabus and comments on different components. It also suggests alternative course outlines and ideas for term projects. For each chapter, the manual includes teaching tips, useful website addresses, and answers to the Review Questions, Discussion Questions, and Thinking about the Case questions.
- Solutions – We provide instructors with solutions to Review Questions and Discussion Questions as well as for quantitative hands-on work in each chapter.
- ExamView® – This objective-based test generator lets the instructor create paper, LAN or web-based tests from testbanks designed specifically for this Course Technology text. Instructors can use the QuickTest Wizard to create tests in fewer than five minutes by taking advantage of Course Technology's question banks – or create customized exams.
- PowerPoint Presentations – Microsoft PowerPoint slides are included for each chapter. Instructors might use the slides in a variety of ways, including as teaching aids during classroom presentations or as printed handouts for classroom distribution. Instructors can add their own slides for additional topics introduced to the class.
- Figure Files – Figure files allow instructors to create their own presentations using figures taken directly from the text.

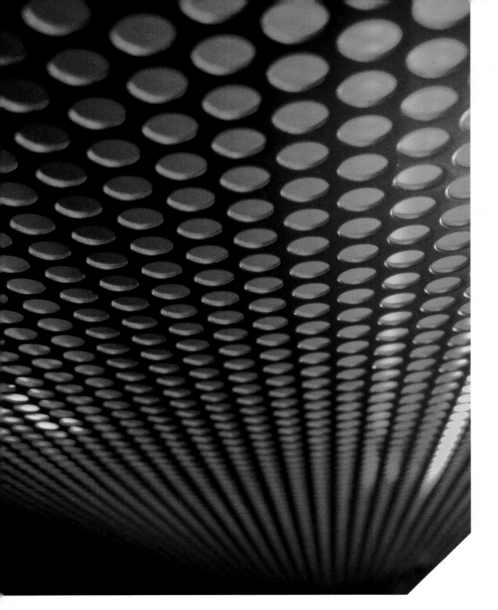

PART ONE

The information age

BETTER BITES

'Maybe we should start our own business.' As soon as Paul said it, his two friends put down their coffee and stared at him. Paul Clermont, Sarah Odell and Christina Healy were second-year hotel and restaurant management degree students and they were looking over the business and travel news and lamenting the sluggish job outlook in their chosen field. They had always joked about starting a business together, but this time Paul was serious. With few prospects in the job advertisements, the three friends were worried that travel and entertainment wouldn't pick up by the time they graduated. They'd begun their job searches in the autumn but weren't interested in the available positions. So, like many other young people, they considered heading out on their own and becoming entrepreneurs.

'Well, you know that I've always wanted to open a restaurant eventually, Paul,' said Sarah. 'I love being a chef. But aren't we getting ahead of ourselves? How could we get enough cash together to rent a place and staff it? Rental space is really expensive locally and we don't have the funds to pay anyone right now. We still have student loans to pay off when we graduate.'

'What about a pushcart in the university concourse?' suggested Christina. 'We could start small and take turns manning it ourselves. That'd keep our labour costs and store rental low. Besides, you're always complaining about the greasy food at that burger place, Sarah. We could offer better alternatives to burgers and fries. The student concourse has been improved recently with new benches and tables, too. It'd be a perfect spot to open a small lunch business. All we would need is permission from the University Director of Services.'

'We'd still need a business plan to get a loan for start-up,' Paul advised. He was excited about organizing a new firm, but knew they needed a detailed plan. 'We have to think everything through carefully and show people that we know what we're doing, or we'll never get off the ground.'

Sarah laughed. 'You're good with facts and figures,' she said to Paul. 'Must be the business and finance modules you took. With my restaurant management background, I'd love to develop the new menu. That's the fun, creative part of this for me. Christina, you have so many contacts through your student union experience. That could come in handy down the road, don't you think?'

'Looks like we each have some strengths that could help us get started,' observed Christina. 'So, what do you think? Shall we try it?'

The three friends stood up and raised their coffee cups in a formal toast to the new business – Better Bites.

Assessing business needs

When Paul, Sarah and Christina agreed to start their business, they had no clear idea of the amount of work involved. They each had certain skills to contribute – innate skills and skills they had polished in their modules – and they were excited about becoming entrepreneurs. But as they continued to meet to sketch out their plans, they quickly realized they'd need to collect quite a lot of information and allocate responsibilities:

- They needed facts and figures on the local lunch business to draft a business plan.
- They needed to negotiate an agreement with the university to set up their cart and rent the cart itself.
- They needed to ensure that they met health and safety regulations.
- They needed to plan a menu and price items and then track which offerings generated the most revenue.
- They needed to advertise their business and print menus.
- They needed a system to record food inventory, plastic serving utensils, paper wraps and serviettes – both costs and quantities.

Keeping track of so much information could be a headache, but computer systems would provide part of the solution. The three friends had grown up using computers in their classes, surfing the Web for fun and sending emails and instant messages to their families to keep in touch. But this was different. For the first time they were seeing computers as a critical tool for their success. Computer systems could track and store information they collected, help them calculate financial information, create forms and documents and even assist in future planning and forecasting. The entrepreneurs knew they needed to become proficient in information systems so that they could concentrate on their real business – running the lunch cart and attracting customers. They were determined not to take short-cuts and if information systems could help them, they would use them.

Formulating a plan

Paul Clermont had gained some restaurant experience through his family. His uncle owned a small French restaurant in the city that was open for lunch and dinner. Paul thought his uncle might be persuaded to allow the three entrepreneurs to use the kitchen early in the morning to prepare their cold sandwiches – for a small fee. So the three met with Paul's uncle, Philippe, and convinced him that they were serious about their business and would not interfere with his; he was adamant that they had to leave the kitchen spotless and be out of the way by 10.00 each morning. They also agreed on a rental fee to compensate Philippe for use of his facilities.

Sarah and Christina had participated in the University's Future Chefs lunch programme, in which cooking and nutrition students prepared and served hot lunches to paying staff members – to simulate a restaurant experience. Sarah loved selecting main dishes and their accompaniments and hoped some day to become a chef. Christina liked the organizational aspects of planning and wanted to concentrate on management.

Sarah began thinking about Better Bites' menu. She thought that limiting their food to cold sandwiches, drinks and side dishes simplified food preparation and storage – they would only need to keep items cold, not cook them on the spot. She discussed the menu with Paul and Christina and decided that wraps and small side dishes would work well for the cart – they weren't too bulky and would

be healthy, lighter alternatives to burgers or pizza, which were sold nearby. Sarah also had heard about a computer application that could track and print calorie and nutritional information; that program would be useful for their menu later.

Christina, with her student union experience, had attended University Council meetings where she had heard of the Business Start-up Scheme. Local venture capitalists would consider loaning funds for small, student-lead enterprises.

Writing a business plan

Once Paul, Sarah and Christina had their initial plans set, they turned to the task of writing a business plan. They knew a business plan would be the key to obtaining the seed capital from the University Business Start-up Scheme. The plan would be scrutinized in every detail to be sure that the three students were worth the risk and were reliable. A good plan would also need to catch the interest of the lender – to generate excitement so that it would stand out from the other loan applicants. So, they began work, fleshing out the sections of the plan to provide an overview of their business.

The Executive Summary provided a general synopsis of who the three entrepreneurs were, what business they planned to start, when they planned to start their operations, why they were qualified to own the business, why there was a need for it and where they planned to place their lunch cart. It also explained their enduring interest in the restaurant industry and their eagerness to bring their ideas to life in the new business.

The Introduction stated the general concept of the business, its purpose and general objectives and gave an overview of the lunch business in the area. They also included general information on their own backgrounds – education, experience and training.

The Marketing section outlined the target market, the business's main competitors and plans for advertising, pricing, food and supply procurement and preparation and location of the pushcart. They also included information and statistics on the growing trend towards more healthy alternatives to fast food and the lack of healthy, organic lunch options near campus. Finally, they mentioned their autumn start-up date, the start of the academic year and how they would then take into account the leaner times during the vacation period. Christina ensured that the fact that the university intended to move towards two-year degrees with teaching over the summer was mentioned in this section.

The Financial section detailed equipment and kitchen rental fees, the pushcart leasing fee, and initial food and supply purchase costs. The partners explained their plan to staff the cart themselves and so avoid additional labour costs. They included a budget forecast, the estimated total lunch business market in the area and the percentage they thought they could capture with their new business, the need for start-up capital and a plan for spending the funds.

The curriculum vitae (CV) section completed the plan, listing all three partners' backgrounds, experiences and references.

Ruth Phillipson from the Business Start-up Scheme reviewed their plan and was impressed with the work the three had done. She met with Paul, Sarah and Christina and discussed their completed business plan. She told them she thought they had provided critical information overall, but she requested more details on foot traffic counts at the student concourse and nearby lunch business competitors to be sure the cart could generate enough customers to be profitable. Also, she asked for more specifics on pricing details versus the competition and the point at which the three projected to break even on their business and begin earning a profit. Those details would help Ruth determine whether the business was a good risk and when the loan would be paid off.

Paul, Sarah and Christina did additional research and recorded the details in the revised plan. Then they provided Ruth with this additional information. Their hard work paid off. The loan was approved – they were in business! The three partners were excited but realized they needed to get started immediately to open their business in only four short months.

Business challenges

In the next three chapters, you will learn what Paul, Sarah and Christina need to know to get started: how to harness information technology to help build and grow their lunch business.

- In Chapter 1, 'Business Information Systems: An Overview', you will learn what your role in information technology might be, which types of information systems you would need whether you are running a large or small business and what information you need, in what form you need it, where you might find it and how to process it. You will also learn what computer-based information tools you need to build a business and some of the major ethical and societal concerns about acquiring, using, storing and reporting potentially sensitive information.

- In Chapter 2, 'Strategic Uses of Information Systems', you will learn how to use information strategically, how to initiate strategic moves and how to deal with competitive challenges.

- In Chapter 3, 'Business Functions and Supply Chains', you will learn how you might best use information technology to help manage a business, whether you need to order inventory and track sales, generate financial statements, or automate payroll systems. You will also learn how all the various business information systems work together.

Chapter 1

Business information systems: an overview

LEARNING OBJECTIVES

Information systems pervade almost every aspect of our lives. Whether you are withdrawing money from a bank's ATM or surfing the World Wide Web, hardly a day goes by without our feeding data into, or using information generated by, an information system. In business especially, computer-based information systems generate most of the information we use. These systems have become essential to successful business operations.

When you finish this chapter, you will be able to:

Explain why information systems are essential to business.

Describe how computers process data into useful information for problem-solving and decision-making.

Identify the functions of different types of information systems in business.

Describe careers in information technology.

Identify major ethical and societal concerns created by widespread use of information technology.

BUSINESS SYSTEMS AND INFORMATION

Paul Clermont, Sarah Odell and Christina Healy couldn't believe what they had accomplished in the five months since they obtained their small-business loan for their lunch pushcart business, Better Bites. They'd made so many decisions and solved so many problems, it was hard to keep track of them all.

Solving problems and making decisions

Paul rented a pushcart to place in the middle of the student concourse. Christina investigated a new PC, software and printer and the partners selected a desktop system that would fill their current computing needs and still allow for growth. Paul and Sarah worked on the food service side of the business. Paul's uncle, Philippe, had referred them to a food wholesaler who gave them a small discount because he could deliver Better Bites' supplies directly to Paul's uncle's restaurant.

Sarah developed her own recipes for wraps that would offer healthier alternatives to the cheeseburgers and pizza offered locally. She, Christina and Paul arose at dawn three weeks before opening to do practice runs in the kitchen and work out a smooth production process. By the fourth practice run, they thought they had a good system – the wraps and side orders were prepared and packaged for storage in the cart. Best of all, they were out of Philippe Clermont's kitchen by the 10.00 deadline.

Generating business information

Christina and Paul worked up a simple printed menu for the cart and used the calorie-counting application to generate nutrition information for their customers. Key advantages of their food were the freshness of their ingredients and their health-conscious menu, so they made sure the menu highlighted those features. They set prices a bit higher than the burger and pizza places down the street because their ingredients were completely fresh – without preservatives or additives.

Christina designed and arranged for advertisements to run in the university newspaper, both the paper and Web versions, two weeks before they opened for business. She also prepared simple flyers to hand out on campus.

Paul set up Better Bites' computer programs: a word-processing program to create basic business stationery and forms; a spreadsheet to record and track sales and profits; and a database to manage food inventory and supplies.

Managing data

After the business had been operating for a month, sales started to pick up. Whoever was staffing the pushcart wrote out a receipt for all items in an order and placed the receipt in a small plastic folder to be entered into the business's computer later. But as the lunch customers multiplied, Better Bites' owners realized that they were falling behind on their paperwork for the business. It was becoming inefficient to handwrite the many sales receipts and later record them into the spreadsheets.

As the backlog in sales receipts grew, Paul had to spend more and more time on weekends inputting sales data so that they could order supplies from the wholesaler on Mondays. He also was bogged down at the end of the month, when he prepared Better Bites' loan and rental payments and expenses.

Gathering useful information from customers

Sarah noticed that some of the items on the lunch menu sold better than others – the chicken pesto salad was a big hit, but the roast beef sold less

well – and she was surprised by the many requests for additional side dishes. And they needed to consider adding some seasonal menu items to keep the customers coming back. Paul, Sarah and Chris needed to consider the costs and profits of adding or dropping menu items, or re-pricing items. Also, several times the partners had had to place emergency calls to restock depleted ingredients and supplies. They had to find a better way to track all the data and forecast their needs so that they wouldn't run short of items or throw away unused ingredients. Dissatisfied customers meant lost sales and fewer profits. So, they thought that they could generate some reports on customer-ordering preferences.

The purpose of information systems

People require information for many reasons and in varied ways. For instance, you probably seek information for entertainment and enlightenment by viewing television, watching films, browsing the Internet, listening to the radio and reading newspapers, magazines and books. In business, however, people and organizations seek and use information specifically to make sound decisions and to solve problems – two closely related practices that form the foundation of every successful company.

What is a problem? A *problem* is any undesirable situation. When you are stuck in the middle of nowhere with a flat tyre, you have a problem. If you know that some customers do not pay their debts on time, but you don't know who or how much they owe, you have a problem. You can solve both problems with the aid of information. In the first case, you can call a breakdown and recovery company, which might use a computerized tracking system to send the breakdown van closest to your location; in the second case, simple accounting software can help.

An organization or individual that finds more than one way to solve a problem or a dilemma must make a *decision*. The problem '2 + 2 = ?' does not require decision-making because it has only one solution. However, as a manager, you might face a dilemma such as 'Which is the best way to promote the company's new car?' There are many potential ways to promote the new car – television advertising, radio advertising, newspaper advertising, Web advertising, car shows, direct mail, or any combination of these methods. This dilemma calls for decision-making.

Both problem-solving and decision-making require information. Gathering the right information efficiently, storing it so that it can be used and manipulated as necessary and using it to help an organization achieve its business goals – all topics covered in this book – are the keys to success in business today. The purpose of information systems is to support these activities. As a future professional, you need to understand and apply these information fundamentals to succeed.

Data, information and information systems

We use the words 'data', 'information' and 'system' almost daily. Understanding what these terms mean, both generally and in the business context, is necessary if you are to use information effectively in your career.

Data vs. information

The terms 'data' and 'information' do not mean the same thing. The word data is derived from the Latin *datum*, literally a given or fact, which might take the form

data Facts about people, other subjects and events. These may be manipulated and processed to produce information.

Industry **SNAPSHOT**

A paperless society?

The Information Age was supposed to reduce the amount of paper that offices use. The emergence of the Web was supposed to reduce paper use even further. As can be seen from the graph in Figure 1.1 this is certainly not the case. About 95 per cent of the world's information is still printed or written on paper. Environmentalists are interested in such figures because a growing percentage of this paper becomes waste.

Electronic storage of data and the electronic display and distribution of information are not a substitute for paper-based media; a business just wants more information to improve business decisions.

Figure 1.1 Co-existence of media

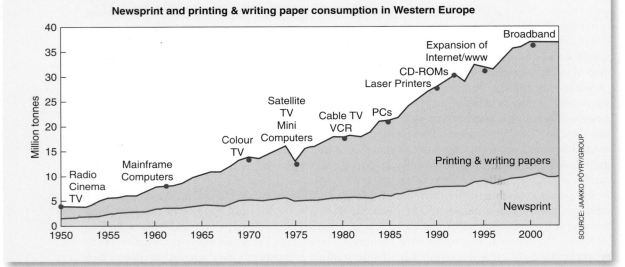

information The product of processing data so that they can be used in a context by human beings.

of a number, a statement, or a picture. Data are the raw material in the production of information. Information, on the other hand, is facts or conclusions that have meaning within a context. Raw data are rarely meaningful or useful as information. To become information, data are manipulated through tabulation, addition, subtraction, division, or any other operation that leads to greater understanding of a situation.

Data manipulation

Here's a simple example that demonstrates the difference between data and information. Assume that you work for a car manufacturer. Last year, the company introduced a new vehicle to the market. Because management realizes that keeping a loyal customer base requires continuously improving products and services, it periodically surveys large samples of buyers. It sends out questionnaires that include 30 questions in several categories, including demographic data (such as gender, age and annual income); complaints about different performance areas (such as ease of handling, braking and the quality of the sound system); features that satisfy buyers most; and courtesy of the dealer's personnel.

Reading through all this data would be extremely time-consuming and not very helpful. However, if the data are manipulated, they might provide highly useful information. For example, by categorizing complaints by topic and totalling the number of complaints for each type of complaint and each car model, the company might be able to pinpoint a car's weaknesses. The company then can pass the resulting information along to the appropriate engineering or manufacturing unit.

Also, the company might already have sufficient data on dealers who sold cars to the customers surveyed, the car models they sold and the financing method for each purchase. But with the survey results, the company can generate new information to improve its marketing. For instance, by calculating the average age and income of current buyers and categorizing them by the car they purchased, marketing executives can better target advertising to groups most likely to purchase each car. If the majority of buyers of a particular type of car do not ask for financing, the company might wish to drop this service option for that car and divert more loan money to finance purchases of other cars. In this way, the company generates useful information from data.

Generating information

In the examples just cited, calculating totals and averages of different complaints or purchasers' ages reveals trends associated with customers. These calculations are processes. A process is any manipulation of data, usually with the goal of producing information. Hence, while data are raw materials, information is output. Just as raw materials are processed in manufacturing to create useful end-products, so raw data are processed in information systems to create useful information (see Figure 1.2). Some processes, however, produce yet another set of data.

process Any manipulation of data, usually with the goal of producing information.

Sometimes, data in one context are considered information in another context. For example, if an organization needs to know the age of every person attending a concert, then a list of that data is actually information. But if that same organization wants to know the average price of tickets each age group purchases, the list of ages is only data, which the organization must process to generate information.

Figure 1.2 Input–process–output

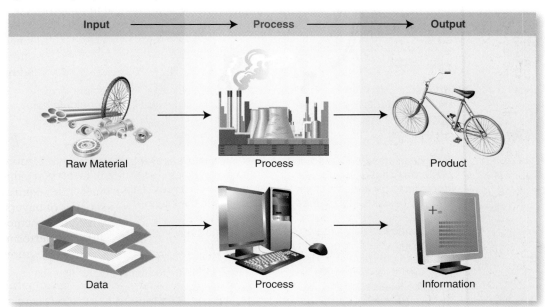

Input	Process	Output
Raw Material	Process	Product
Data	Process	Information

Information in context

Information is an extremely important resource for both individuals and organizations, but not all information is useful. Consider the following story. Two people touring in a hot-air balloon encountered unexpected wind that soon blew them off course. When they managed to lower their balloon, they shouted to a farmer on the ground, 'Where are we?' The farmer answered, 'You are right above a cornfield!' The balloonists looked at each other and one groaned, 'Some information! Highly accurate and totally useless!' To be useful, information must be relevant, complete, accurate and current. And in business, information must also be obtained economically, that is, cost-effectively. Figure 1.3 lists characteristics of useful information.

system An array of components that work together to achieve a common goal or multiple goals.

What is a system?

Simply put, a **system** is an array of components that work together to achieve a common goal, or multiple goals, by accepting input, processing it and producing output in an organized manner. Consider the following examples:

● A sound system consists of many electronic and mechanical parts, such as a laser head, an amplifier, an equalizer and so on. This system uses input in the form of electrical power and sound recorded on a medium such as a CD or DVD and processes the input to reproduce music and other sounds. The components work together to achieve this goal.

Figure 1.3 Characteristics of useful information

Relevant	Information must pertain to the problem at hand. For example, the total number of years of education might not be relevant to a person's qualifications for a new job. Relevant information might be that the person has so many years of education in mechanical engineering and so many years of experience. The information must also be presented in a way that helps a person understand it in a specific context.
Complete	Partial information is often worse than no information. For example, marketing data about household incomes might lead to bad decisions if not accompanied by vital information on the consumption habits of the targeted population.
Accurate	Erroneous information might lead to disastrous decisions. For example, an inaccurate record of a patient's reaction to penicillin might lead a doctor to harm the patient while believing that she is helping him.
Current	Decisions are often based on the latest information available, but what was a fact yesterday might no longer be one today. For example, a short-term Investment decision to purchase a stock today based on yesterday's stock prices might be a costly mistake if the stock's price has risen in the interim.
Economical	In a business setting, the cost of obtaining information must be considered as one cost element involved in any decision. For example, demand for a new product must be researched to reduce risk of marketing failure, but if market research is too expensive, the cost of obtaining the information might diminish profit from sales.

● Consider the times you have heard the phrase 'to beat the system'. Here, the term 'system' refers to an organization of human beings – a government agency, a commercial company, or any other bureaucracy. Organizations, too, are systems; they consist of components – people organized into departments and divisions – that work together to achieve common goals.

Systems and subsystems   Not every system has a single goal. Often, a system consists of several subsystems – components of a larger system – with subgoals, all contributing to meeting the main goal. Subsystems can receive input from, and transfer output to, other systems or subsystems.

> **subsystem** A component of a larger system.

Consider the different departments of a manufacturing business. The marketing department promotes sales of the organization's products; the engineering department designs new products and improves existing ones; the finance department plans a clear budget and arranges for every unused penny to earn interest by the end of the day. Each department is a subsystem with its own goal, which is a sub-goal of a larger system (the company), whose goal is to maximize profit.

Now consider the goals of a manufacturing organization's information system, which stores and processes operational data and produces information about all aspects of company operations. The purpose of its inventory control subsystem is to let managers know what quantities of which items are available; the purpose of its production control subsystem is to track the status of manufactured parts; and the assembly control subsystem presents the bill of material (a list of all parts that make up a product) and the status of assembled products. The entire system's goal is to help deliver finished goods at the lowest possible cost within the shortest possible time.

Figure 1.4 shows an example of a system found in every business: an accounting system. An accounting system consists of several subsystems: accounts payable records information about money that the organization owes to other organizations and individuals; accounts receivable records sums owed to the organization and by whom; a general ledger records current transactions; and a reporting mechanism generates reports reflecting the company's

Figure 1.4   Several subsystems make up this corporate accounting system

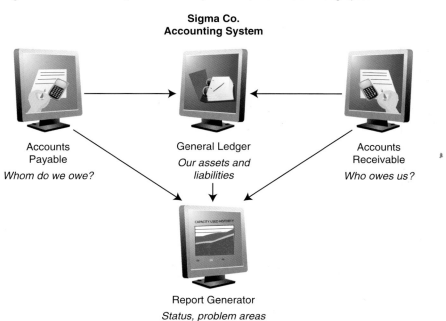

Sigma Co.
Accounting System

Accounts
Payable
Whom do we owe?

General Ledger
*Our assets and
liabilities*

Accounts
Receivable
Who owes us?

Report Generator
Status, problem areas

financial status. Each subsystem has a well-defined goal. Together, the subsystems make up the organization's accounting system.

Of course this is a simplistic view of the world. Goals are not always so well defined, human factors come into the equation when developing solutions, and different stakeholders in the whole system (customers, suppliers, operational staff, managers) have different interpretations of the problems that need to be solved. In the early 1980s Peter Checkland published research papers and books that put forward the idea of 'soft systems methodology' which recognized that conventional systems engineering is based on the solving of well defined problems and that most management problems are not as clear cut. His process of a continuous learning cycle in the development of systems was well received and underpins much of modern system thinking.

closed system A system that stands alone, with no connection to another system.

open system A system that interfaces and interacts with other systems.

Closed vs. open systems Systems are closed or open, depending on the nature of the information flow in the system. A closed system stands alone, with no connection to another system: nothing flows in from another system, nothing flows out to another system. For example, a small cheque-producing system that prints cheques when an employee enters data through a keyboard is a closed system. The system might be isolated for security purposes. An open system interfaces and interacts with other systems. For example, an accounting system that records accounts receivable, accounts payable and cash flow is open if it receives its payroll figures from the payroll system. Subsystems, by definition, are always open, because as components of a bigger system, they must receive information from and give information to other subsystems. Increasingly, companies are implementing open information systems that can be linked to other systems owned by business partners such as suppliers and clients.

information system (IS) A computer-based set of hardware, software and telecommunications components, supported by people and procedures, to process data and turn it into useful information.

Information systems With an understanding of the words 'information' and 'system', the definition of an information system is almost intuitive: an information system (IS) consists of all the components that work together to process data and produce information. Almost all business information systems consist of many subsystems with subgoals, all contributing to the organization's main goal.

Information and managers

Thinking of an organization in terms of its sub-organizations or subsystems – called systems thinking – is a powerful management approach because it creates a framework for both excellent problem-solving and excellent decision-making. To solve problems, managers need to isolate them, which they do by recognizing the subsystems in which the problems occur and solving the problems within those subsystems' constraints and strengths.

Systems thinking can also help keep managers focused on the overall goals and operations of a business. It encourages them to consider the entire system, not only their specific subsystem, when solving problems and making decisions. A satisfactory solution for one subsystem might be inadequate for the business as a whole. For example, when the sales department creates a website to take online customer orders, it automates a formerly labour-intensive activity of the sales subsystem. This saves cost. With systems thinking, improving the sales process could also improve other company processes. Without systems thinking, managers from other departments aren't involved in the decision, so they don't benefit. In the case of the sales department, if other managers are involved in planning for automated online ordering, they could suggest that sales data recorded on the database – a large collection of electronic records – connected to the Web also be accessible to other departments, such as distribution and manufacturing. The distribution department could use the records to expedite

database A collection of shared, interrelated records, usually in more than one file. An approach to data management that facilitates data entry, update and manipulation.

packaging and delivery, thanks to the information that appears on a computer monitor rather than a piece of paper. The manufacturing units could use the order records for planning resources such as labourers and inventory. Figuratively, by applying systems thinking, effective managers view their areas of responsibility as puzzle pieces. Each piece is important and should fit well with adjacent pieces, but the entire picture should always be kept in view.

One of an information system's most important contributions to the sound workings of an organization is the automation of information exchange among subsystems (such as departments and divisions). Consider the earlier example: customer orders taken via a website by the sales department could be automatically routed to the manufacturing and distribution units and processed by their own information systems for their specific purposes. In fact, such information exchanges make up a major portion of all interactions among business subsystems.

The information map of a modern business – that is, the description of data and information flow within an organization – shows a network of information subsystems that exchange information with each other and with the world outside the system. In an ideal organization, no human would need to retrieve information from one IS and transfer it to another. The organization would capture only new raw data, usually from its operations or from outside the organization. Then, data captured at any point in the system would automatically become available to any other subsystem that needs it. Thus, systems thinking is served well by information technology (IT), a term that refers to all technologies that collectively facilitate construction and maintenance of information systems. Systems thinking is the basic reasoning behind equipping organizations with enterprise software applications. Enterprise software applications are systems that serve many parts of the organization by minimizing the need for human data entry and

information map The description of data and information flow within an organization.

information technology (IT) Refers to all technologies that collectively facilitate construction and maintenance of information systems.

Why you should…
be well versed in information systems

You might be surprised at how much information technology (IT) knowledge your prospective employer will expect of you when you are interviewed for your next job, even if the position you seek is not in the IT area. Today's corporations look for IT-savvy professionals and with good reason. Information is the lifeblood of any organization, commercial or nonprofit; it is essential to sound problem-solving and decision-making, upon which business success is built. In fact, the main factor limiting the services and information that computers can provide within an organization is the budget.

Because of rapid changes in technology, information systems, unlike many other business components, are quickly changing in form and content. A computer considered fast and powerful today will be an outdated machine in 18–24 months. In 12–24 months, a better program will surpass one that is considered innovative right now. The dynamic nature of information technology is like a moving target. A professional who does not stay informed is of diminishing value to an organization. All knowledge workers, professionals, scientists, managers and others who create new information and knowledge in their work, must be familiar with IT.

Managers must at all times maintain a clear picture of their organizations and the outside business environment. They must know what resources are available to them and to their competitors. Information technology provides excellent tools for collecting, storing and presenting facts. But to be truly effective, those facts must be manipulated into useful information that indicates the best allocation of various resources, including personnel, time, money, equipment and other assets. Regardless of the operations being managed, information systems (ISs) are important tools. Successful professionals must know which ISs are available to their organizations and what ISs might be developed in the future.

Industry **SNAPSHOT**

Looking for more skilled graduates

Sandra Smith, IS director at Toshiba UK, says companies and technology leaders take it as an absolute given that graduates will come to the workplace equipped with basic IT skills, including the ability to use word processing, spreadsheet and presentation tools. But most companies need that little bit extra.

'Businesses need graduates to have an appreciation and enthusiasm for how IT enables the modern business world, such as the Internet, email, mobile communications and databases. But unless they're going to work in IT, I don't think it's necessary that graduates are particularly expert with the details of the technology', she says.

'It's more important that graduates are aware of the possibilities of technology and know how to research and present their findings. I'm not sure it's

an IT skill – but problem-solving, mental energy, planning and lateral thinking always seem to be in short supply. You can't put good systems in without them, that's for sure.'

SOURCE: http://www.vnunet.com/computing/analysis/2138557/skills-imperative-graduates

Companies like Toshiba look for more than just basic IT skills in today's graduates.

ensuring timely, useful information for the organization's entire supply chain, including taking customer orders, receiving raw materials, manufacturing and shipping, and billing and collection. In the service sector, companies often use document management systems, enabling workers from many departments to add information and signatures to a document from request to approval, or from draft to a final document. You will learn about these systems throughout this book.

The benefits of human–computer synergy

It is important to remember that computers can only carry out instructions that humans give them. Computers can process data accurately at far greater speeds than people can, yet they are limited in many respects – most importantly, they lack common sense. However, combining the strengths of these machines with human strengths creates synergy.

Some people call synergy the '2 + 2 = 5' rule. Synergy (from the Greek 'work together') occurs when combined resources produce output that exceeds the sum of the outputs of the same resources employed separately. A computer works quickly and accurately; humans work relatively slowly and make mistakes. A computer cannot make independent decisions, however, or formulate steps for solving problems, unless programmed to do so by humans. Even with sophisticated artificial intelligence, which enables the computer to learn and implement what it learns, the initial programming must be done by humans. Thus, a human–computer combination allows the results of human thought to be translated into efficient processing of large amounts of data. For example, when you use a Web search engine to find

synergy From Greek 'to work together.' The attainment of output, when two factors work together, that is greater or better than the sum of their products when they work separately.

Figure 1.5 Qualities of humans and computers that contribute to synergy

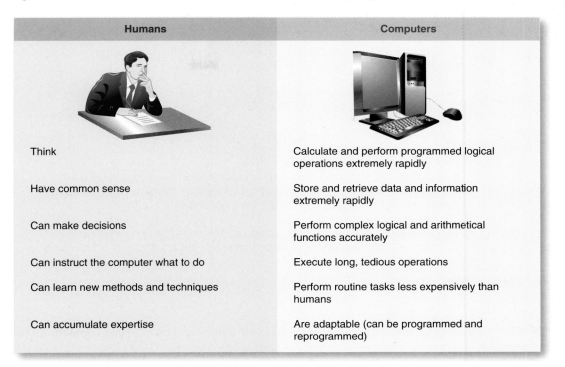

Humans	Computers
Think	Calculate and perform programmed logical operations extremely rapidly
Have common sense	Store and retrieve data and information extremely rapidly
Can make decisions	Perform complex logical and arithmetical functions accurately
Can instruct the computer what to do	Execute long, tedious operations
Can learn new methods and techniques	Perform routine tasks less expensively than humans
Can accumulate expertise	Are adaptable (can be programmed and reprogrammed)

articles about a topic, you, the human, enter a keyword or a series of keywords. By clicking the Search button you shift control to a computer program that quickly finds the articles for you. A human programmed a computer to perform an extremely fast search in a huge database of Web links; another human entered keywords and triggered the program; and the computer performed the matching of keywords with the links at a speed that is way beyond the capability of any human. The result is an efficient search that takes only seconds, which no human would be able to complete in a lifetime. Figure 1.5 presents qualities of humans and computers that result in synergy. It is important to notice not only the potential benefits of synergy, but also what computers should not be expected to do independently.

Information systems in organizations

In an organization, an information system consists of data, hardware, software, telecommunications, people and procedures as summarized in Table 1.1. An information system has become synonymous with a computer-based information system, a system with a computer at its centre to which peripheral equipment is connected. That is how this term is used in this book. In a computer-based information system, computers collect, store and process data into information, according to instructions people provide via computer programs.

Several trends have made the use of information systems (ISs) very important in business:

- The power of computers has grown tremendously while their prices have dropped.
- The variety and ingenuity of computer programs have increased.
- Quick and reliable communication lines and access to the Internet and the Web have become widely available and affordable.

Table 1.1 Components of an information system

Data	Input that the system takes to produce information
Hardware	A computer and its peripheral equipment: input, output and storage devices; hardware also includes data communication equipment
Software	Sets of instructions that tell the computer how to take data in, how to process it, how to display information and how to store data and information
Telecommunications	Hardware and software that facilitate fast transmission and reception of text, pictures, sound and animation in the form of electronic data
People	Information systems professionals and users who analyse organizational information needs, design and construct information systems, write computer programs, operate the hardware and maintain software
Procedures	Rules for achieving optimal and secure operations in data processing; procedures include priorities in dispensing software applications and security measures

- The fast growth of the Internet has opened opportunities and encouraged competition in global markets.
- An increasing ratio of the global workforce is computer literate.

In this environment, organizations quickly lag behind if they do not use information systems and skills to meet their goals. Moreover, they must continuously upgrade hardware, software and the skills of their employees to stay competitive.

The four stages of processing

All information systems operate in the same basic fashion whether they include a computer or not. However, the computer provides a convenient means to execute the four main operations of an information system:

- Entering data into the IS **(input)**.
- Changing and manipulating the data in the IS **(data processing)**.
- Getting information out of the IS **(output)**.
- Storing data and information **(storage)**.

input Raw data entered into a computer for processing.

transaction A business event. In an IS context, the record of a business event.

transaction processing system (TPS) Any system that records transactions.

A computer-based IS also uses a logical process to decide which data to capture and how to process them. This process will be discussed later.

Input The first step in producing information is collecting and introducing data, known as input, into the IS. Most data an organization uses as input to its IS are generated and collected within the organization. These data result from transactions undertaken in the course of business. A transaction is a business event: a sale, a purchase, the hiring of a new employee and the like. These transactions can be recorded on paper and later entered into a computer system, directly recorded through terminals of a transaction processing system (TPS), such as a till, or captured online when someone transacts through the Web. A TPS is any system that records transactions. Often, the same system also processes the transactions,

Ethical and Societal **ISSUES**

The not-so-bright side

New technology almost always improves lives. But new technology often also has undesirable effects. This was true of the labour-saving machines that prompted the industrial revolution (introducing 16-hour workdays and child labour under harsh conditions) and it is also true about information technology. Think of the bliss of IT: it makes our work more productive because a few keystrokes on a computer keyboard prompt the computer to calculate and print what would otherwise take many human hours. It educates us via technologies such as multimedia classes delivered online. It opens new economic opportunities such as trading with overseas consumers via the Internet. It makes the world smaller by letting people work and socialize together over great distances via networks such as the Web. It democratizes the business community by making important business tools affordable to both rich and start-up companies. And it puts at our fingertips information on practically every imaginable subject. So, what's the dark side? There are quite a few dark sides, which we will discuss in the following chapters. Here is a sample of the main issues and the questions they raise.

Consumer privacy The ability to inexpensively and quickly collect, maintain, manipulate and transfer data enables every individual and organization to collect millions of personal records. When visiting a commercial website, chances are the site installs a little file, a 'cookie', on your computer's hard disk. This file helps track every click you make on that site, so companies specializing in consumer profiling can learn your shopping and buying habits. When you collect a prescription, the chemist collects details about you. Before you send a warranty card for a newly purchased product, you are asked to answer some questions that have nothing to do with the warranty but much to do with your lifestyle. All these data are channelled into large databases for commercial exploitation. Your control of such data is minimal. While consumers, patients and employees might consent to the collection of information on one aspect of their lives by one party and on another

aspect by another party, the combination of such information might reveal more than they would like. For example, a firm can easily and inexpensively purchase *your* data from a chemist and several consumer goods companies, combine the data into larger records and practically prepare a dossier about you: your name, age and gender; your shopping habits; the medicines you take (and through this information, the diseases you might have); the political party to which you contributed; and so on.

Civil rights advocates argue that IT has created a Big Brother society where anyone can be observed. US business leaders oppose European-style legislation to curb collection and dissemination of private data because this limits target marketing and other economic activities. Business leaders ask, 'How can we target our products to consumers who are most likely to want them if we have no information about those consumers?' Are you willing to give up some of your privacy to help companies better market to you products and services you might be interested in? Do you accept the manipulation and selling of your personal data?

Employee privacy IT helps employers monitor their employees, not only via the ubiquitous video camera, but also through the personal computers they use. Employers feel it is their right to monitor keystrokes, email traffic, the websites employees visit and the whereabouts of people whose wages they pay while on the job. So, while IT increases productivity, it might violate privacy and create stress. Which is more important: your employer's right to electronically monitor you, or your privacy and mental well-being?

Freedom of speech The Web opens opportunities for many activities that people consider undesirable, such as the broadcast of violent and pornographic images and the dissemination of illegally copied digitized work. Almost anyone can become a publisher. If someone posts slurs about your ethnic group on a website, do you want the government to step in and ban such postings? And if one government legislates, can it impose its law on a network that crosses many national borders?

The problem is not only at international level. Playground bullying has now gone hi-tech. 'Bullies are increasingly using the Internet to terrorise teenagers outside of school, a survey suggests. More than 10 per cent of UK teenagers said they had been bullied online, while 24 per cent knew a victim, the MSN/YouGov survey found.'

Online annoyances Email is so popular because it allows easy and inexpensive transfer of ideas and creative work within seconds. However, more and more of us find our email boxes clogged with unsolicited messages, popularly called spam. Spam now makes up about 80 per cent of all email. Do you accept this? And if you own a new small business and want to advertise via email (because it is the least expensive advertising method), wouldn't you want the freedom to do so? While surfing the Web you encounter pop-up windows and pop-under windows. Your computer contracts spyware. Sometimes special software hijacks your browser and automatically takes you to a commercial site that you do not care for. Are these annoyances legitimate, or should they be stopped by legislation?

IT professionalism IT specialists play an increasing role in the lives of individuals and the operations of organizations. The information systems they develop and maintain affect our physical and financial well-being tremendously. Are IT specialists professionals? If they are, why don't they comply with a mandatory code of ethics as other professionals (such as doctors and lawyers) do? There are professional bodies, such as the British Computer Society, the Council of European Professional Informatics Societies and the Computer Society South Africa, with their clearly defined codes of conduct and good practice, but membership is not mandatory for anyone undertaking, for example, the development of a financial accounting system.

We will discuss these and other ethical and social issues throughout this book. As you will see, these issues are not easy to resolve. The purpose of these discussions is to make you aware of issues and provoke your thoughts. Remember that the purpose of education is not only to develop skilled professionals, but also to remind professionals of the impact of their work on the welfare of other people and to make professionals socially responsible.

SOURCE: http://news.bbc.co.uk/1/hi/technology/4805760.stm

summarizing and routing information to other systems; therefore, these systems are transaction *processing* systems, not just transaction *recording* systems.

Input devices (devices used to enter data into an IS) include the keyboard (currently the most widely used), infrared devices that sense bar codes, voice recognition systems and touch screens. Chapter 4, 'Business Hardware and Software', describes these and other means to input data. The trend has been to shorten the time and ease the effort of input by using devices that allow visual or auditory data entry.

data processing The operation of manipulating data to produce information.

Processing The computer's greatest contribution to ISs is efficient data processing, which is essential to a robust IS. The computer's speed and accuracy let organizations process millions of pieces of data in several seconds. For example, managers of a national retail chain can receive up-to-date information on inventory levels of every item the chain carries and order accordingly; in the past, obtaining such information would take days. These astronomic gains in the speed and affordability of computing have made information the essential ingredient for an organization's success.

output The result of processing data by the computer; usually, information.

Output Output is the information an IS produces and displays in the format most useful to an organization. The most widely used output device is the video display, or video monitor, which displays output visually. Another common output device is the printer, used to print hard copies of information on paper. However, computers can communicate output through speakers in the form of music or speech

Industry **SNAPSHOT**

Do it yourself – save labour (perhaps), please the customer (definitely)

Over the past few years there has been an increase in the number of supermarkets offering self-checkout systems. One of the market leaders is NCR Fastlane. A study commissioned by National Cash Registers (NCR) reported that 33 per cent of customers would choose one retailer over another if it offered self-checkout. From other studies it can be seen that such systems return greater user satisfaction. In addition to this there are possibilities for some savings on checkout staff, although experience has shown that these savings are not as high as they might be because there must be some staff on hand to deal with customer difficulties and to prevent theft. On this last point, the technology can help in that the latest systems compare the expected weight of the item (obtained from the bar code) with the actual weight of the item placed on the conveyor belt.

When self-checkout systems were first introduced, it was expected that the target market would be young professionals, comfortable with using new technology. However, experience has shown that older people like the fact that they can go through their shopping at their own pace, checking prices as they go. Also those people who have had to drag their children round the store find it useful to occupy them in helping out at the checkout point. There are signs that the similar systems have scope for use in different retail outlets. For example, Vodafone has recently launched the Quickphone kiosk, a machine for vending mobile phones.

SOURCE: 'Learning from the Supermarkets', Bill Waterson, UK Head of Retail, Fujitsu Services and 'Self-Checkout Systems: Creating Value Across the Retail Store', Kelly Matthews and Meredith Whalen, IDC White Paper, October 2004

A customer using a self-checkout system at a Tesco supermarket.

PHOTO SOURCE: © DAVID WILLIAMS/ALAMY

and also can transmit it to another computer or electronic device in computer-coded form, for later interpretation.

Storage One of the greatest benefits of using IT is the ability to maintain the storage of vast amounts of data and information. Technically, storing a library of millions of volumes on optical discs is not inconceivable. In fact, some universities are moving to do just that.

> **storage** The operation of storing data and information in an information system.

Computer equipment for information systems

Figure 1.6 illustrates the five basic components of the computer system within an IS:

- Input devices introduce data into the IS.
- The computer processes data through the IS.
- Output devices display information.
- Storage devices store data and information.
- Networking devices and communications lines transfer data and information over long distances.

Figure 1.6 Input, process, output, storage and networking devices

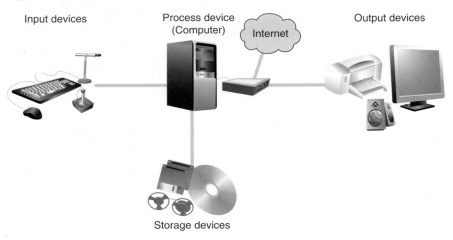

In addition to communication that takes place between computer components, communication occurs between computers over great distances (called **telecommunications**). Communications technology lets users access data and other electronic resources of many computers, all connected in a network. This way, a computer's power might be augmented with the power of an entire network.

telecommunications
Communications over a long distance, as opposed to communication within a computer, or between adjacent hardware pieces.

From recording transactions to providing expertise: types of information systems

There are many different types of information systems – for different types of organizations, for different functions within organizations, for different business needs and at different management levels of an organization. Business enterprises differ in their objectives, structures, interests and approaches. However, ISs can be generally categorized according to the level of a system's complexity and the type of functions it serves. ISs in business range from the basic transaction processing system that records events such as sales to sophisticated expert systems, such as computer programs that provide advice and reduce the need for the expensive services of a human expert. In recent years the capabilities of these applications have been combined and merged. It is less and less likely that you will find any of the following applications as stand-alone systems with a single capability. Managers and other professionals plan, control and make decisions. As long as a system supports one or more of these activities, it may be referred to as a **management information system (MIS)**.

management information system (MIS) A computer-based information system used for planning, control, decision-making or problem-solving.

Transaction processing systems

Transaction processing systems (TPSs) are the most widely used information systems. The predominant function of TPSs is to record data collected at the boundaries of organizations, in other words, at the point where the organization transacts business with other parties. TPSs include tills, which record sales; automatic teller machines (ATMs), which record cash withdrawals, deposits and transfers; and purchase order systems, which record purchases. A typical example would be the purchase of petrol at a pump, using a credit card. The purchase is recorded by the petrol company and later at the credit card processing bank. After these data are collected, the IS either automatically processes the data immediately or stores them for later access on demand.

Supply chain management systems

The term 'supply chain' refers to the sequence of activities involved in producing a product or service. In industries that produce goods, the activities include marketing, purchasing raw materials, manufacturing and assembly, packing and shipping, billing, collection and after-the-sale services. In service industries, the sequence might include marketing, document management and monitoring customer portfolios. Information systems that support these activities and are linked to become one large IS providing information on any stage of a business process are called supply chain management (SCM) systems.

supply chain management (SCM) The coordination of purchasing, manufacturing, shipping and billing operations, often supported by an enterprise resource planning system.

Often, such systems are called enterprise resource planning (ERP) systems, because the information they provide supports planning of shipping resources such as personnel, funds, raw materials and vehicles. However, ERP is a misnomer for the systems, because they mainly serve managers in monitoring and modifying business processes as they occur and not only for planning. The term 'supply chain', too, is somewhat misleading. Business processes do not always take the form of a sequence. There are processes that take place in parallel. This is true in manufacturing, where two or three teams work on different parts of a product and in services, where two or three different people peruse a document online and add their input to it within a certain period of time rather than sequentially. In the production of goods and services, some modules of SCM systems provide support to the major processes. These components include human resources (HR) information systems and cost accounting systems.

enterprise resource planning (ERP) system An information system that supports different activities for different departments, assisting executives with planning and running different interdependent functions.

SCM systems are the result of systems thinking and support systems thinking. They eliminate the need to reenter data that have already been captured somewhere else in the organization. An SCM is an enterprise application because the systems that support each business process are connected to each other to form one large IS. Technically, anyone with access to the system can know the status of every part of an order the business received: whether the raw materials have been purchased, which sub-assemblies are ready, how many units of the finished product have been shipped and how much money has been billed or collected for this order. HR managers can tell which workers are involved in any of the processes of the order. Accountants can use their module of the system to know how much money has been spent on this order and what the breakdown of the cost is into labour, materials and overhead expenditures.

enterprise application An application that fulfils a number of functions together, such as inventory planning, purchasing, payment and billing.

Customer relationship management systems

Customer relationship management (CRM) systems help manage an organization's relationships with its customers. The term refers to a large variety of information systems, from simple ones that help maintain customer records to sophisticated ones that dynamically analyse and detect buying patterns and predict when a specific customer is about to switch to a competitor. Many CRM systems are used by service representatives in combination with a telephone. When a customer telephones, the representative can view the entire history of the customer's relationship with the company: anything that the customer has purchased, deliveries made, unfulfilled orders and other information that can help resolve a problem or help the customer find the goods or service he or she is seeking. The main goals of CRM systems are to increase the quality of

customer relationship management (CRM) A set of applications designed to gather and analyse information about customers.

customer service, reduce the amount of labour involved in serving customers and learn as much as possible about the preferences of individual customers.

CRM systems are often linked to Web applications that track online shopping and process online transactions. Using sophisticated applications, a company can learn what makes a customer baulk just before submitting an online order, or what a customer prefers to see displayed on Web pages. Online retailers such as Amazon.co.uk, and Lastminute.com use applications that construct different Web pages for different customers, even when they search on the same keywords. The pages are constructed to optimally suit the individual customer's interests as inferred from previous visits and purchases. CRM systems provide important data that can be accumulated in large databases and processed into business intelligence.

business intelligence (BI) Information gleaned from large amounts of data, usually a data warehouse or online databases; a BI system discovers not-yet-known patterns, trends and other useful information that can help improve the organization's performance.

data warehouse A huge collection of historical data that can be processed to support management decision-making.

Business intelligence systems

ISs whose purpose is to glean from raw data relationships and trends that might help organizations compete better are called business intelligence (BI) systems. Usually, these applications consist of sophisticated statistical models, sometimes general and sometimes tailored for an industry or an organization. The applications access large pools of data, usually historical transaction records stored in large databases called data warehouses. With proper analysis models, BI systems might discover peculiar buying patterns of consumers, such as combinations of products purchased by a certain demographic group or on certain days; products that are sold at greater cycles than others; reasons for customer's churns, that is, customers leaving a service provider for a competitor; and other valuable business intelligence that helps managers quickly decide to change a strategy.

PHOTO SOURCE: VTIGER SYSTEMS INDIA PRIVATE LIMITED

Vtiger CRM is an example of an Open Source CRM product designed mainly for small and medium businesses.

Industry **SNAPSHOT**

CRM at DHL

DHL, wholly owned by Deutsche Post World Net, is the leading global delivery network dealing with overland express, air freight and international express delivery. It has approximately 285,000 employees who are dedicated to servicing 120,000 destinations in 220 countries. The company prides itself on its dedicated staff and is unusual in the logistics business in that two-thirds of its world-wide offices are owned by the company whereas most of its competitors make significant use of third parties. This means that DHL staff can help to achieve better transit time, efficient billing, easy tracking and so on. All of these can be considered to be part of customer relations, and to this end DHL make use of a CRM system called salesforce.com. This gives a holistic view of customers across the globe, enabling staff to give customers up-to-date information about the service that they are receiving from DHL, to resolve queries and problems, to enhance the service given to customers and so on.

The use of salesforce.com as the CRM platform involved a number of significant factors including

- the delivery of intensive staff training – If the company was to get maximum benefit from the system then the users (customer relations staff) needed to know how to use it properly.

- the importing of data from other sales systems – It would have been a shame to lose all the valuable data gathered over the previous years concerning customer profiles.

- integration with DHL Global Mail's other systems – The CRM system is just one of many IT systems within the company. It is vital that it interacts with these to ensure effective and efficient use of data in the whole of the organization.

The system aims to provide each customer with support via a single point of contact for all service-related issues. As Steve Garnett, SVP and general manager EMEA at salesforce.com says, 'an integrated approach to CRM worldwide and a single, 360 degree view of the customer regardless of geographic location was urgently required. This investment will undoubtedly support DHL Global Mail's long-term strategic goal to be the number one mail supplier on a worldwide level.'

SOURCE: www.crminfoline.com/crm-articles/crm-dhl.htm and http://www.salesforce.com/company/news-press/press-releases/2005/03/050301.jsp

DHL's IT service centre in Prague, which manages and supports the IT infrastructure within DHL Europe from a single state-of-the-art headquarters.

PHOTO SOURCE: DEUTSCHE POST AG

Decision support and expert systems

Professionals often need to select one course of action from many alternatives. Because they have neither the time nor the resources to study and absorb long, detailed reports of data and information, organizations often build information systems specifically designed to help make decisions. These systems are called decision support systems (DSSs). While DSSs rely on models and formulae to produce concise tables or a single number that determines a decision, expert systems (ESs) rely on artificial intelligence techniques to support knowledge-intensive decision-making processes.

Decision support systems help find the optimal course of action and answer 'What if?' questions. 'What if we purchase raw materials overseas?' 'What if we merge our warehouses?' 'What if we double our shifts and cut our staff?' These questions seek answers such as, 'This is how this action will impact our revenue,

decision support system (DSS) Information system that aids managers in making decisions based on built-in models. DSSs comprise three modules: data management, model management and dialog management. DSSs may be an integral part of a larger application, such as an ERP system.

expert system (ES) A computer program that mimics the decision process of a human expert in providing a solution to a problem. Current expert systems deal with problems and diagnostics in narrow domains. An ES consists of a knowledge base, an inference engine and a dialog management module.

or our market share, or our costs.' DSSs are programmed to process raw data, make comparisons and generate information to help professionals glean the best alternatives for financial investment, marketing strategy, credit approval and the like. However, it is important to understand that a DSS is only a decision aid, not an absolute alternative to human decision-making.

Many environments are not sufficiently structured to let an IS use data to provide the one best answer. For instance, stock portfolio management takes place in a highly uncertain environment. No single method exists to determine which securities portfolio is best, that is, which one will yield the highest return. Medical care is another unstructured environment. There might be many methods of diagnosing a patient's illness on the basis of his or her symptoms. Indeed, a patient with a particular set of symptoms might receive as many different diagnoses as the number of doctors he or she visits.

Using ESs saves a company the high cost of employing human experts. After gathering expertise from experts and building a program, the program can be distributed and used repeatedly. The expertise resides in the program in the form of a knowledge base consisting of facts and relationships among the facts. You learn about DSS and ES in detail in Chapter 10.

Geographic information systems

geographic information system (GIS) Information system that exhibits information visually on a computer monitor with local, regional, national or international maps, so that the information can easily be related to locations or routes on the map. GISs are used, for example, in the planning of transportation and product distribution, or the examination of government resources distributed over an area.

In some cases, the information that decision-makers need is related to a map. In such cases, special ISs called geographic information systems (GISs) can be used to tie data to physical locations. A GIS application accesses a database that contains data about a neighbourhood, city, county, country or even the entire world. By representing data on a map in different graphical forms, a user is able to understand promptly a situation taking place in that part of the world and act upon it. Examples of such information include population levels, the number of police officers deployed, probabilities of finding minerals, transportation routes and vehicle allocation for transportation or distribution systems. Thus, when a supermarket chain considers locations for expansion, executives look at a map that reflects not only geographic attributes but also demographic information such as population growth by age and income groups. GISs are often used to manage daily operations but also in planning and decision-making. They also have been used to provide service via the Web, such as helping residents find locations of different services on a city map or plan travel routes. Some GISs that support operations use information from global positioning system (GPS) satellites, especially to show the current location of a vehicle or person on a map or to provide directions.

Information systems in business functions

ISs serve various purposes throughout an organization in what are known as functional business areas – in-house services that support an organization's main business. Functional business areas include, but are not limited to, accounting, finance, marketing and human resources. As mentioned before, in a growing number of organizations these systems are modules of a larger enterprise system, an SCM or ERP system. Chapter 3, 'Business Functions and Supply Chains', discusses business functions and their systems in detail.

Accounting

In accounting, information systems help record business transactions, produce periodic financial statements and create reports required by law, such as balance sheets and profit-and-loss statements. ISs also help create reports that might not be required by law, but that help managers understand changes in an organization's finances. Accounting ISs contain controls to ascertain adherence to standards, such as double entry.

Finance

While accounting systems focus on recording and reporting financial changes and states, the purpose of financial systems is to facilitate financial planning and business transactions. In finance, information systems help organize budgets, manage cash flow, analyse investments and make decisions that could reduce interest payments and increase revenues from financial transactions.

Marketing

CD TASK

Marketing's purpose is to pinpoint the people and organizations most likely to purchase what the organization sells and to promote the appropriate products and services to those people and organizations. For instance, marketing information systems help analyse demand for various products in different regions and population groups in order to more accurately market the right product to the right consumers. Marketing ISs provide information that helps management decide how many sales representatives to assign to specific products in specific geographical areas. The systems identify trends in the demand for the company's products and services. They also help answer such questions as, 'How can an advertising campaign affect our profit?' The Web has created excellent opportunities both to collect marketing data and to promote products and services by displaying information about them. That is why organizations conduct so much of their marketing efforts through ISs linked to the Web.

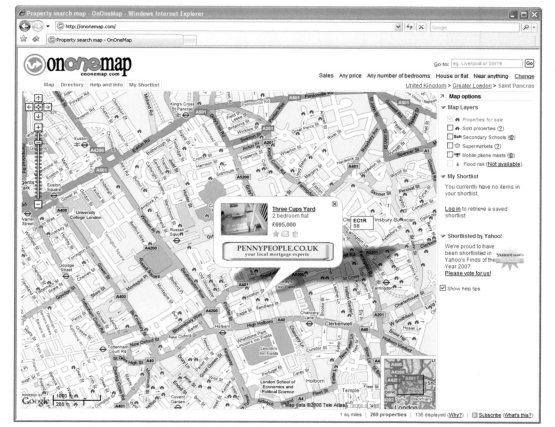

PHOTO SOURCE: © ONONEMAP LIMITED. MAP DATA © 2007 TELE ATLAS

Geographic information systems help associate information with locations and regions.

Human resources

Human resource (HR) management systems mainly help in record-keeping and employee evaluation. Every organization must maintain accurate employee records. Human resource management systems maintain such records, including employees' pictures, employee marital status and tax information and other data that other systems such as payroll might use.

Performance evaluation systems provide essential checklists that managers can use to assess their subordinates. These systems also offer a scoring utility to quantify workers' strengths and weaknesses.

HR management systems have evolved to serve many purposes: recruiting, selection, placement, benefits analysis, online benefits information for employees to access through an intranet, requirement projections (how many employees with certain skills will be required in so many months?) and other services.

CD TASK

Web-empowered enterprises

The most exciting intersection of IT and business in recent years is networked commerce – buying and selling goods and services via a telecommunications network – or as it is popularly called, e-commerce. The development of the Web and the opening of the Internet to commercial activities spawned a huge surge in business-to-business and business-to-consumer electronic trade. Now, every individual and small business can afford to use a network for business: the Internet.

> **e-commerce** Business activity that is electronically executed between parties, such as between two businesses or between a business and a consumer.

The Internet is a vast network of computers connected across the globe that can share both information and processing. The Web is capable of displaying text, graphics, sounds and moving images. It has enticed thousands of businesses to become involved in commercial, social and educational initiatives. Almost every brick-and-mortar business has extended its operations to the Web. Chapter 7, 'The Web-Enabled Enterprise', discusses Web technologies and how they are used in business activities. Because of its great impact on the use of information technology, the Web's impact on the use of information systems is discussed throughout the book.

Careers in information systems

The IT industry is made up of people in a wide variety of activities, but there has been a blurring of the edges between IT professionals and business professionals. It is worthwhile having a general idea of the subdivision of IT-specific jobs but everyone associated with the business will have a need for IT skills if 'only' as a user of IT systems. More organizations are realizing that there is scope for 'power-users' who are able to adapt and develop IT applications in order to gain the maximum advantage from the information that the business possesses.

Seventy-eight different IT jobs have been defined by the UK government-backed Skills Framework for the Information Age (SFIA). The range of jobs is divided into six broad categories, namely

- Strategy and planning, e.g. business systems strategy, technical strategy
- Development, e.g. systems development, implementation
- Business change, e.g. business change management
- Service provision, e.g. operations, user support
- Procurement and management support, e.g. supply management, resource management
- Ancillary skills, e.g. education and training, sales.

Industry **SNAPSHOT**

E-Christmas boom

The volume of online sales continues to grow year on year and a good metric is the amount of Christmas shopping carried out online. British consumers spent GB £7.66 billion online in the ten-week run-up to Christmas 2006, a 54 per cent increase on the 2005 figure. Germany had an increase in Internet traffic generally of 63 per cent in the first week of December while the French retail giant PPR saw a growth of Internet traffic of 73 per cent. Outside Europe, things are looking up for South African online shopping, with a massive 837 per cent increase from 2004 to 2006. Airline ticket purchases made up the majority of this increase, but flowers and groceries also showed significant increases of 113 per cent and 20 per cent respectively.

SOURCE: Interactive Media in Retail Group Index, 'Internet Retail Sales Leading Europe's Christmas Season', The *WWW.theaplahmarketer.com*, 6 December 2006 and 'MWEB online Christmas Shopping Up By 800 per cent in two years', ICTWorld, 24 January 2007

Consumer spending online continues to rise.

PHOTO SOURCE: © MARK GODDARD

The British Computer Society (www.bcs.org) has many case studies of real people employed in the industry categorized using the SFIA definitions. The job titles below are only indicative – an employer in an advertisement can call the job anything they like. It is the job description that is important. Salaries are also very variable. A useful site checking the current situation of IT salaries in the UK can be found at http://www.computingcareers.co.uk/it-salary-checker/. A similar annual survey for South Africa can be found at http://www.itweb.co.za/surveys/salary/2007/.

Systems developer

The term *programmer* may also be used but the more generic term *systems developer* is now more widely used. This recognizes the fact that much of what modern programmers do is higher-level programming, that is using pre-existing building blocks of code to create the desired application. That is not to say the job is any less skillful, just more efficient. Why should a programmer spend time writing a routine to sort a set of records into alphabetical order when someone has already written this function? The systems developer simply calls up the routine and then spends useful time on the specific processing of that set of records. Similar arguments can be made for elements of the user interface. There are predefined routines to produce, for example, a calendar on the screen so that the user can pick a date for their train ticket. Once again, the predefined piece of code can be called up and then the programmer can concentrate on the next part of the transaction, checking the database for availability.

Systems analyst

systems analyst An IT professional who analyses business problems and recommends technological solutions.

Many IT professionals start their careers as programmers, or *programmer/analysts* and then are promoted to systems analysts, positions that require a broad range of skills. A programmer/analyst is partly involved in the analysis of business needs and ISs, but the greater part of the job involves setting up business applications. A systems analyst is involved in designing new ISs and in updating and maintaining existing ISs. A big part of this job includes developing alternative system plans based on (1) analysing system requirements provided by user input, (2) documenting development efforts and system features and (3) providing adequate specifications for programmers.

To succeed, systems analysts must possess excellent communication skills to translate users' descriptions of business processes into system concepts. They must understand a wide range of business processes and ways in which IT can be applied to support them. Since analysts often deal with systems that serve more than one organizational unit, they must also understand organizational politics and be shrewd negotiators.

Most importantly, systems analysts must always keep in mind that they are agents of change and that most people resist change. Unlike many other occupations, theirs often involves the creation of new systems or the modification of existing ones. Because new or modified systems often affect human activities and organizational cultures, systems analysts must be able to convince both line workers and managers that change will benefit them. Thus, these IS professionals must possess good persuasive and presentation skills.

Job DESCRIPTION

Systems analyst

Analyses, documents and proposes solutions for large and/or complex business areas and prepares functional specifications. Assists in the preparation of user and system test plans.

Duties and responsibilities

- Collecting, understanding and transmitting the business requirements for the project, and translating these into functional specifications and detailed test plans.
- Analyse and document business processes.
- Document workflows and results of business analysis and obtain sign-off from client on the specifications.
- Provide the link between the customer, development team and any third party regarding software functionality, throughout the development lifecycle.
- Design and execute the test scenarios and test scripts.
- Day-to-day management of change requests in relation to the project plans to ensure agreed deadlines are met.
- Weekly reports to be produced for the project manager showing progress against outstanding milestones, status, resource requirements, issues, risks and dependencies.

Skills/attributes required

- Demonstrable evidence of analysing and documenting complex business processes.
- Demonstrable experience writing requirements specifications for information systems.
- A proven track record in software development.
- End-to-end experience of the project lifecycle.
- Proven experience interacting directly with end users.
- Results orientated with good communication and interpersonal skills.

SOURCE: © CV Screen Ltd

Senior systems analysts often advance to become project leaders. In this capacity, they are put in charge of several analysts and programmers. They seek and allocate resources, such as personnel, hardware and software, which are used in the development process, and they use project management methods to plan activities, determine milestones and control use of resources.

Database administrator

The **database administrator (DBA)** is responsible for the databases and data warehouses of an organization – a very sensitive and powerful position. Since access to information often connotes power, this person must be astute not only technologically but politically as well. He or she must evaluate requests for access to data from managers to determine who has a real 'need to know'. The DBA is responsible for developing or acquiring database applications and must carefully consider how data will be used. In addition, the DBA must adhere to government and corporate regulations to protect the privacy of customers and employees.

database administrator (DBA) The individual in charge of building and maintaining organizational databases.

A growing number of organizations link their databases to the Web for use by employees, business partners and customers. Attacks on corporate databases by hackers and computer viruses have made the DBA's job more difficult. In addition to optimizing databases and developing data management applications, this person must oversee the planning and implementation of sophisticated security measures to block unauthorized access but at the same

Job DESCRIPTION

Oracle database administrator

Responsible for supporting the Oracle databases and ensuring their performance, availability and security.

Duties and responsibilities

- Responsible for ensuring availability and performance of the databases that support the system.
- Work with the team to ensure that the associated hardware resources allocated to the databases are adequate and to ensure high availability and optimum performance.
- Proactively monitor the database systems to ensure secure services with minimum downtime.
- Responsible for providing trend analysis to the service management team to enable them to make informed decisions regarding resource management.
- Responsible for problem escalation to Oracle development team and third parties as appropriate.

- Responsible for improvement and maintenance of the databases to include rollout and upgrades.
- Responsible for implementation and release of database changes as submitted by the development team.

Skills/attributes required

- Proven Oracle database administration experience.
- Experience of managing multiple RDBMS on large systems.
- Experience of working in a team that delivers a high-availability service.
- Practical experience in monitoring and tuning a database to provide a high-availability service.
- Experience of other database systems, preferably SQL Server.
- Practical experience in managing the internal and external MS SQL database security.
- Oracle Certification, preferably OCP.

SOURCE: © CV Screen Ltd

time to allow easy and timely access to authorized users. The DBA is also highly involved in the implementation of SCM systems, because they access corporate databases.

Data administrator

Many organizations have realized that they need to look at data from a strategic point of view. A data administrator (DA) needs to understand the data that the company owns or has access to and the ability to consider this valuable resource in relation to the needs of senior management in the organization. If the DA does not instigate the development of new systems aimed at giving the company a competitive edge, he or she will certainly be charged with ensuring that these developments take place.

Network administrator

network administrator
The individual who is responsible for the acquisition, implementation, management, maintenance and troubleshooting of computer networks throughout the organization.

Among the many IT areas, the one that has seen the most exciting developments in recent years is networks and telecommunications. Not surprisingly, this area has also seen the greatest increase in corporate allocation of IT resources in many organizations. The emergence of new technologies, such as Voice over Internet Protocol and Wi-Fi, which are discussed in Chapter 5, is expected to sustain this trend for some years, allowing specialized professionals to be in great demand and to command high salaries.

The **network administrator** is responsible for acquiring, implementing, managing, maintaining and troubleshooting networks throughout the organization and the links with the

---

Job DESCRIPTION

Network administrator

Responsible for the operation and administration of the company's internal networks, servers, email and network security systems and for the development of the company website and database.

Duties and responsibilities

- Administration and maintenance of company's internal systems.
- Configuration and set-up of all new server systems required internally for the company's activities.
- Firewall administration and overall responsibility for company IT security.
- Administration of email servers for company-wide email.

- Providing telephone and desktop support to internal users.
- Forecasting any needed improvements, budgeting for and implementing any changes.

Skills/attributes required

- Good working knowledge of the following operating systems: Windows 2000 Server, Windows 2003 Server, Exchange, Citrix.
- Strong working knowledge of major networking components, network operating systems and basic computer hardware components.
- Hands-on knowledge of the procedures used in the installation, modification, maintenance and repair of IT hardware and software.

SOURCE: © CV Screen Ltd

outside world. He or she is also often involved in selecting and implementing network security measures such as firewalls and access codes.

Webmaster

The rapid spread of the Web, intranets and extranets has increased the responsibility and stature of the organizational Webmaster. A Webmaster is responsible for creating and maintaining the organization's website and its intranet and extranet pages. Webmasters are increasingly involved in creatively deciding how to represent the organization on the Web. These decisions involve elements of marketing and graphic design. Since many organizations use the Web for commerce, Webmasters must also be well versed in Web transaction software, payment-processing

CD TASK

Webmaster The person who is in charge of constructing and maintaining the organization's website.

Job **DESCRIPTION**

Webmaster

The Webmaster implements web pages, maintains content and oversees day-to-day management of the company website, and assures quality and filing integrity of web pages.

Duties and responsibilities

- Responsible for the design of company web pages, including graphics, animation and functionality.
- Develop web page infrastructure and application related to pages with more advanced graphics and features.
- Monitor web server and site technical performance.
- Implement search engine optimization strategies.
- Promote client websites online to increase prominence within their web community where possible.
- Management of Pay Per Click (PPC) campaigns to achieve optimum ROI (return on investment) for individual active search terms for each of the major search engines.
- Work closely with the Operations Director to set and ensure marketing campaigns achieve budgeted commercial targets.
- Circulate efficient and accurate reporting, detailing results of each web marketing campaign and possible improvement.

- Advise Director on the improvement, results, competition and new directions in technology to assist with marketing of the brand.
- Maximize online affiliate opportunities and revenue generation for the brand (with possibility of widening affiliate advertising schemes).
- Ensure regular communication and email contact with affiliates and act as main point of contact.
- Source and manage new revenue-generating online marketing opportunities.

Skills/attributes required

- Proven website management experience.
- You will have strong web design skills which will include the ability to edit HTML and JavaScript skills.
- A thorough knowledge of search engine optimization (SEO) techniques.
- Experience of running and evaluating online marketing campaigns, which will include the management of Pay Per Click (PPC) campaigns.
- A flexible attitude with proven experience of working in a small team.
- Excellent communication skills and attention to detail.

SOURCE: © CV Screen Ltd

software and security software. The demand for Webmasters is expected to grow as long as corporate use of the Web continues to grow.

Chief security officer

Because of the growing threat to information security, many organizations have created the position of chief security officer (CSO), or chief information security officer (CISO). In most organizations the person in this position reports to the chief information officer (CIO) (see next section), but in some the two executives report to the same person, usually the chief executive officer (CEO). The rationale is that security should be a business issue, not an IT issue. A major challenge for CSOs is the misperception of other executives that IT security is an inhibitor rather than an enabler to operations.

Job DESCRIPTION

Chief technology officer

Plans, directs, manages and oversees the activities and operations of the IT department; administers the IT budget, staff and physical facilities of the department.

Duties and responsibilities

- Develop information technology strategy in support of the company's mission and core objectives.
- Direct, control and motivate the staff of the information technology department.
- Develop an annual business plan and operating budget for the department and monitor the implementation of these to ensure that the financial targets are met.
- Negotiate service level agreements with both internal and external customers and service providers and monitor service delivery to ensure the agreed targets and standards are met.
- Accountable for the management, mentoring and career development of all IT staff.
- Define and seek approval for the level of IT resources required to meet these goals and prioritizes and schedules major projects.
- Direct the preparation and implementation of policies, procedures and standards relating to information and telecommunications systems.
- Responsible for researching and evaluating new technologies.
- Direct, attend and participate in staff meetings and related activities; attend workshops to keep up to date with information technology issues.

Skills/attributes required

- Proven senior IT management experience.
- A proven track record of driving and defining complex IT strategy.
- Budgetary experience of £3 million or more.
- Exceptional communication skills are essential in order to explain complex IT concepts to non-technical colleagues.
- Experience of managing multiple IT disciplines, e.g. software development, technical support, systems architecture and so on.
- A broad understanding of computer systems, applications and operating systems.
- Educated to degree level in computer science or related field.
- In-depth experience of negotiating with and managing third parties.

SOURCE: © CV Screen Ltd.

Chief information officer and chief technology officer

The fact that a corporation has a position titled chief information officer (CIO) reflects the importance that the company places on ISs as a strategic resource. The CIO, who is responsible for all aspects of an organization's ISs, is often, but not always, a corporate vice president. Some companies prefer to call this position chief technology officer (CTO). However, you might find organizations where there are both a CIO and a CTO and one reports to the other. There is no universal agreement on what the responsibility of each should be. Yet, in most cases when you encounter both positions in one organization, the CTO reports to the CIO.

A person who holds the position of CIO must have both technical understanding of current and developing information technologies and business knowledge. As Figure 1.7 shows, the CIO plays an important role in integrating the IS strategic plan into the organization's overall strategic plan. He or she must not only keep abreast of technical developments but also have a keen understanding of how different technologies can improve business processes or aid in the creation of new products and services.

chief information officer (CIO) The highest-ranking IS officer in the organization, usually a vice president, who oversees the planning, development and implementation of IS and serves as leader to all IS professionals in the organization.

chief technology officer (CTO) A high-level corporate officer who is in charge of all information technology needs of the organization. Sometimes the CTO reports to the chief information officer, but in some companies this person practically serves as the CIO.

Figure 1.7 Traits of a successful CIO

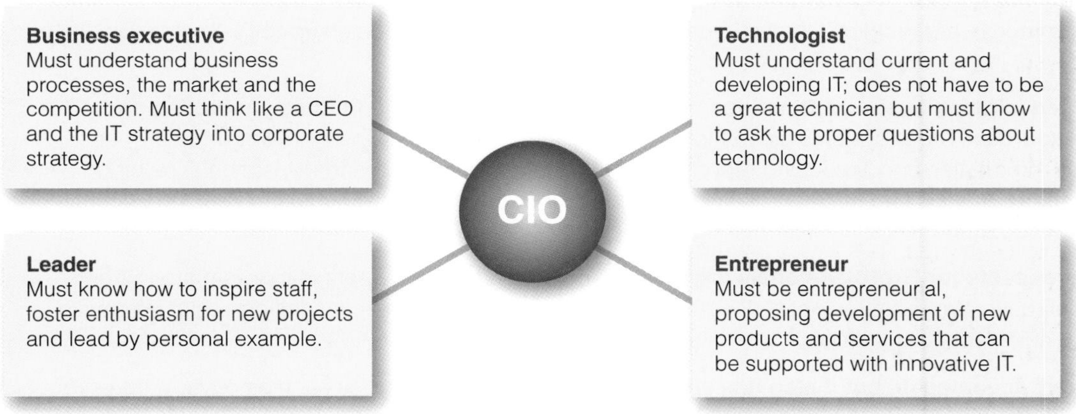

Business executive
Must understand business processes, the market and the competition. Must think like a CEO and the IT strategy into corporate strategy.

Technologist
Must understand current and developing IT; does not have to be a great technician but must know to ask the proper questions about technology.

CIO

Leader
Must know how to inspire staff, foster enthusiasm for new projects and lead by personal example.

Entrepreneur
Must be entrepreneurial, proposing development of new products and services that can be supported with innovative IT.

SUMMARY

Computer-based information systems pervade almost every aspect of our lives. Their ability to help solve problems and make decisions makes them indispensable in business and management. Computer-based information systems take data as raw material, process the data and produce information as output. While data sometimes can be useful as they are, they usually must be manipulated to produce information, facts, statistics and other items useful for reporting and decision-making.

A system is a set of components that work together to achieve a common goal. An information system (IS) consists of several components: hardware (the computer and its peripheral equipment), software (programs that run the computer), data, people and procedures. The components' common goal is to produce the best information from available data.

Often, a system performs a limited task that produces an end result, which must be combined with other products from other systems to reach an ultimate goal. Such a system is called a subsystem. Several subsystems might make up a system. Sometimes, systems are also classified as closed or open. A stand-alone system that has no contact with other systems is called a closed system. A system that interfaces with other systems is an open system.

Data processing has four basic stages. In the input stage, data are collected and entered into the computer. The computer then performs the next stage, data processing, which is the manipulation of data into information using mathematical, statistical and other tools. The subsequent stage, output, displays or presents the information. We often also want to maintain data and information for later use. This activity is called storage.

Any information system that helps in management may be referred to as a management information system (MIS). MISs use recorded transactions and other data to produce information for problem-solving and decision-making.

There are several different types of information systems. They include transaction processing systems (TPSs), supply chain management (SCM) systems, customer relationship management (CRM) systems, business intelligence (BI) systems, decision support systems (DSSs) and expert systems (ESs) and geographic information systems (GISs). Often, some or all of these systems are linked to each other or to other information systems.

Enterprise application systems, such as SCM or ERP systems, are information systems that tie together the different functional areas of a business, such as order entry, inventory management, accounting and finance and manufacturing. Such systems allow businesses to operate more efficiently by avoiding reentry and duplication of information. The systems can provide an up-to-the-minute picture of inventory, work in progress and the status of an order to be fulfilled.

ISs are used in many business functions, most commonly accounting, finance, marketing and human resources. These systems aid in the daily operations of organizations by maintaining proper accounting information and producing reports, assisting in managing cash and investments, helping marketing professionals find the most likely buyers for their products and services and keeping accurate employee records and assisting with their performance evaluations.

The job prospects for IT professionals are bright. Among the typical careers in this field are systems analyst, database administrator, network administrator, Webmaster, chief security officer, chief information officer and chief technology officer.

IT has many advantages, but it also has created societal concerns. Issues such as privacy, free speech on the Web, spam and web annoyances are viewed by many people as serious ethical issues. And while IT professionals increasingly affect our lives through the systems they develop and maintain, they are not required to adhere to any code of ethics as other professionals are. These and related issues are discussed throughout the book.

BETTER BITES REVISITED

Now that Chapter 1 has helped you understand how business uses data, information and information systems, let's revisit Better Bites. Paul, Sarah and Christina are trying to improve their lunch business. How would you cope with their challenges?

What would you do?

1   Paul has been bogged down entering sales receipts into the business's computer programs at the end of the week. He has also been swamped at the end of the month, when he generates reports on overall sales and expenses. He needs a better system. What would you do to increase the efficiency of the business transactions? Examine the business's inputs, processing and outputs. Formulate a method to streamline the business transactions. What type of reports does Paul need?

2   Sarah noticed the varying sales of some menu items. What information about sales does she need to order the optimum amount of each ingredient and the labour spent on food preparation?

3   Currently, Better Bites does not collect information about the items that are ordered together by an individual customer. Do you think that information would be helpful to the owners? How might they generate and use such information?

4   Are SCM or CRM applicable to Better Bites? If so, which one is more important to Better Bites at the beginning of their business? Explain.

New perspectives

1   What business opportunities can Better Bites generate from the following changes in the food industry?

— The British government recently adopted new standards for organic food labelling. Consumers now can determine exactly how a product has been produced from the label it carries. Food producers and retailers can apply for certification from the Food Standards Agency. You have advised the team to apply for certification, which means they would have to label each wrapped meal. Advise them how a personal computer could help with this task.

— The food wholesaler the business uses is setting up a website to allow its customers to order supplies online. How would this change Better Bites' current operations? List both benefits and drawbacks.

2   The City Council has approached Better Bites to provide food snacks at the city's organized events for bank holidays. Advise Paul, Sarah and Christina: what information do they need to decide whether to accept this offer? Do they currently have this information from the data they have collected? If they decide to accept this offer, what information will tell them whether they made the right decision?

Review questions

1   What does the word 'processing' in data processing mean?

2   Give three examples in which raw data also serve as useful information.

3   Give three business examples (not mentioned in the text) of data that must be processed to provide useful information.

4   Give three examples of subsystems not operating in the context of IT. Why are these subsystems and not systems?

5 How do TPSs and DSSs differ?

6 What is a problem? Give an example of a business problem and discuss how a computer-based information system could solve it.

7 What is synergy? How is synergy accomplished when a person uses a computer?

8 'An information system consists of hardware and software.' Why is this statement inadequate?

9 When does one need to make a decision?

10 How can a DSS help make decisions?

11 Note the word 'support' in decision support systems. Why are these applications not called decision-*making* systems?

12 Who is considered a knowledge worker? Will you have a career as a knowledge worker? Explain.

13 What is the most prevalent type of information system? Why is this type of IS so ubiquitous?

14 TPSs are usually used at the boundaries of the organization. What are boundaries in this context? Give three examples of boundaries.

15 Among IT professionals, the greatest demand is for network administrators and analysts. Why?

Discussion questions

1 No longer the domain of technical personnel, information systems are the business of every professional. Why?

2 Assume that computers can recognize voices easily and detect their users' exact meaning when talking. Will the necessity for written language be reduced to zero? Why or why not?

3 Information systems cannot solve some business problems. Give three examples and explain why technology cannot help.

4 An increasing number of knowledge workers must know how to use information systems. Why?

5 Often, computer illiteracy is likened to reading illiteracy. Is this realistic? Is computer illiteracy as severe a handicap as reading illiteracy?

6 Think of two examples of fully web-based businesses. What made the Web so attractive for these entrepreneurs?

7 We will soon stop talking of e-commerce and simply speak of commerce. Why?

8 'Help wanted' advertisements do not use the term 'computer specialists'; rather, they use the term 'information system professionals' or 'information technology professionals'. Why?

9 How do traditional commerce and web-based commerce differ?

10 What changed the average citizen's life more the industrial revolution or the information revolution? How and why?

11 Information technology might bring people together, but it also isolates them. Explain the latter claim and give an example.

12 Give two examples of phenomena that are a social concern because of information technology. Explain.

13 What irritates you about the Web? What would you do to minimize this irritation?

14 Do you foresee an IT-related societal or ethical concern that is not a current concern? Explain.

15 If you chose a career in IT apart from CIO or CTO, which position would you choose and why?

Tutorial activities

1 Recall what you did yesterday from the moment you got up until the moment you went to bed. How many times did you use a computer or receive data or information from someone who used a computer? (Do not forget ATMs, tills, automated kiosks, etc.) Consider the inputs, processing and outputs associated with each interaction and write a two-page essay on society's dependency on computers.

2 Contact a business organization and ask permission to observe a business process. Pinpoint the segments in the process that a computer-based information system could aid. Write a report detailing your observations and suggestions.

3 Observe activities in a supermarket: shoppers looking down aisles for specific products; queues forming at the tills; workers sticking new prices to items on the shelves. Prepare a list of shoppers' and workers' activities that could be carried out with less use of human time and more accuracy if they were aided by IT. Explain how you would change those activities.

4 Scientists are researching a contagious disease. They found that, on average, each person who is infected transmits the disease to three other people within one year. Currently, there are 3,000 infected people in the country. Use Excel or another spreadsheet application to find out (1) how many people will contract the disease each year over the next decade and (2) how many infected people will there be each year if no medication is administered. (Do not worry: there is a medication for this disease.) 'Currently' means in the first year of your calculation. Calculate for the next nine years. Explain why this is a modelling problem. What is your model in the spreadsheet?

5 Use a CV template in your word-processing program to type your CV. If you don't have a lot of direct work experience, remember to include all types of work, whether it's babysitting, mowing the lawn, or whatever.

6 Use your word-processing application to prepare a list: what information that you currently receive through other means could you receive through your computer? The list should include text, images, audio and animated information. Would you prefer to receive this information on the computer or as you do now?

7 Form a team with two other students. Each team member should play the role of a vice president in charge of a business function: human resources, accounting, marketing, finance and so on. Each vice president should enumerate information he or she needs to perform his or her function. Now list information that two or more of the functions must share and data produced by one function that another function uses.

8 Team up with another two students. Brainstorm and try to think of a new business opportunity that you would like to pursue in which you will not need IT. You should be able to convince the rest of the class that IT cannot improve the operations of this business.

Companion CD questions

1 Use Excel to create a simple financial spreadsheet for Better Bites' business plan.

2 Use presentation software to create a presentation in support of Better Bites' application to the bank for a business loan.

Video questions

1 The video segment mentions Jef Raskin. Who was he? What were some of his inventions? What are his theories about design?

2 Do you agree with Buxton's contention that devices should be designed by humanists rather than engineers? Why or why not?

From ideas to application
REAL CASES

Case study 1.1

IT strategy as part of business strategy

BY ALAN HOGARTH

The information systems function, after years of being seen as a prime candidate for outsourcing, is now once again viewed as an essential and core department in most large organizations. The main reason for this change of view is the need for information systems (IS) or information technology (IT) strategy to be part of an organization's wider business strategy. Due to the global nature of business it is now essential that organizations plan their IT strategy in conjunction with their business strategy. One organization which has recognized the importance of this approach is Unilever.

The consumer goods giant – producer of such brands as Sunsilk, Dove, Bertolli and Lipton – recently had to take a careful look at its strategy due to the first profit warning in the corporation's history. Global Chief Information Officer (CIO) of Unilever, Neil Cameron, says that, 'Having achieved that [strategy revision] and consolidated the organization, for 2006 the agenda [was] execution.' The company's plan was to cut 700 million euros from costs through streamlining and simplification of their systems by 2007 in a strategy titled 'One Unilever'.

According to Cameron, in Europe Unilever used to operate two systems: one for their food products and one for personal systems, but now the organization operates as one. Cameron affirms that, 'We have worked very hard over the last two years to get the basics right, and now they are, we can look at execution and delivering benefits.' IT strategy is now closely aligned to the business strategy in both global and regional terms, and business processes and information have to run as a single entity. Cameron further states that, 'The success of the systems convergence programme means we are now using the things we invested in. This has meant company-wide changes

including the IT organization has changed significantly too. We are now driving efficiencies and implementing programmes to unify the businesses geographically.'

Unilever operates in nearly 100 countries, has 365 manufacturing sites and employs around 223,000 people. So any efficiency it can gain from its convergence programme will have significant benefits by way of reducing resource costs. The company is looking at information and back-to-business programmes centred upon its global customers, for example Wal-Mart, and also at improving customer-centred systems at regional and local levels for customers such as Sainsbury, which have a local presence but do not operate in a global marketplace. Cameron is justifiably proud of his function's achievements when he states that 'Business and technology innovations which provide things like improvements in our supply chain, reductions in cost and speeding up customer response times are fundamentally changing our business. In the UK there have been a huge number of changes to systems, including manufacturing, basic HR and supporting accounts over the past year. This has brought lots of opportunities for Unilever UK. But we must make sure we support that.'

However, Cameron does recognize that there is still a lot of work to be done. For example, Unilever is selling the majority of its European frozen food business,

Unilever's recently refurbished UK headquarters in London.

including its Bird's Eye branded business. This could throw up complex requirements for IT, according to Cameron. 'If it is a trade sale, then we just have to support the buyer until they are ready to move to their own systems. But if it is bought by a private equity business we have to provide the services for it, and work out charges as well as segregating it from the rest of the business.'

The sale is part of Unilever's focus on growth, says Cameron. 'We have to focus on the business and where the growth is going to come from. The sale will be better for the business in the long term.' Systems are being standardized and consolidated with suppliers. In the UK for example, desktop supply, implementation and support are part of a standardized global deal with Dell and Unisys. Cameron says, 'These are good people to work with. Unisys handles Dell's services, and we will be transferring support to there. Global deals like this put us in great shape for execution, as well as improving efficiency and reducing costs.' Unilever also struck a deal recently for a seven-year contract with IBM to outsource financial transactional services. The contract covers more than 20 European countries and is part of the streamlining programme. The deal is that IBM will provide financial services including general accounting from its centres in Portugal, Poland and India.

Not only does IT support the sales end of Unilever, it also continues to support scientific research and product innovation. Cameron says 'We are supporting product Research and Development from an IT perspective.' He is very enthusiastic when he further adds that, 'It is very interesting and challenging working with the scientists, and trying to add something. The process goes the whole way from research and innovation concepts all the way through to product launch. Trying to get the balance right is important and the support comes from IT.'

'We are working very hard at innovation and science at the molecular level – for example V-shots have to taste of something – and there are huge scientific issues. We are doing some grid computing work on this, but frankly some of the scientists we have are much better at doing this than we are.'

Unilever has recognized not only the need to align its IT strategy with its business strategy but has also rationlized its IT systems by streamlining two systems into one more efficient and effective system. Consequently this has resulted in more efficient and successful business processes.

Thinking about the case

1   Why would Unilever seek to rationalize their IT systems?

2   What benefits would an organization expect due to such a rationalization?

3   Why is it important nowadays for organizations to align their IT strategy with their business strategy?

4   How important is it for Unilever's IT systems to be centred on its customers?

5   How might outsourcing functions such as 'financial transactions' aid in the streamlining of Unilever's IT systems?

SOURCE: CIO Magazine online at: http://www.cio.co.uk/mis100/companyprofile/index.cfm?companyid=8

Case study 1.2

The personal touch

'The information about a package is as important as the delivery of the package itself.'   FREDERICK W. SMITH, FOUNDER AND CHAIRMAN OF FEDEX

With bases from Brussels to Hong Kong, FedEx is an organization that never sleeps and for which every minute counts. On the peak days between Christmas and New Years' Eve, it typically ships more than 8 million packages. On a normal day the company transports more than 6 million packages, using over 600 aircraft and 71,000 trucks across 220 countries and territories. Inevitably, some packages miss their delivery time, some miss their destination and some are damaged. When that happens, FedEx's 4,000 customer service reps are the people customers call.

Prompt, efficient customer service is extremely important for staying in this highly competitive global shipping industry, let alone doing so with a satisfactory profit. Incoming telephone calls at FedEx's 46 call centres across the globe never stop and FedEx reps never have an idle moment on shift. Sitting in front of computer monitors in a cluster of cubicles with headsets on, these agents barely have time to stretch their limbs.

A caller in London complains that her package hasn't arrived, which is a common complaint. Another in Pretoria asks if he can change his pickup time. A third caller in Oslo is confused about signature: is he supposed to sign for the delivery or will the package just be dropped at his doorstep? The reps are confident and friendly. They welcome any question or complaint even if they have heard it a thousand times before. The words 'I am sorry' are uttered often. They are careful not to give the customers a feeling of being rushed, but try to resolve complaints quickly. Time is money.

Several years ago FedEx installed software that reps at the call centres can use to provide faster service. Many of the callers are already registered in the company's database. One of the most frequent requests is to send a FedEx worker to pick up a package. Using the software, a rep can handle such a request in 20 seconds. All she needs to do is enter a name, which leads to a post code, which in turn leads to a tracking number. That number uniquely identifies the package. Some complaints are more complex. For example, a FedEx driver misunderstood a note a caller had left for him and therefore misdelivered a package. A complaint like that takes no more than 10 minutes to resolve.

An experienced and efficient rep can handle about 10 callers in 45 minutes. Ideally, though, nobody would call. If FedEx had its way, at least six of the ten callers would use their computers to go to FedEx's global website and solve their problem by themselves. Six of ten, because about 60 per cent of FedEx's clients have a computer connected to the Internet. Like other companies, FedEx tries to save labour by directing callers to its website. Yet, many people prefer to use the phone and talk to a human helper.

Every time a customer decides to use the company's website instead of telephoning, the company saves up to €1.42. Efforts to divert callers to the site have been fruitful. In 2005, FedEx call centres received 470,000 calls per day, 83,000 fewer than in 2000. This difference in calls translates into a saving of €43.73 million per year. The company's website handles an average of 60 million requests per month to track packages. Operating the website does costs money. Each of these requests costs FedEx €0.02, amounting to €16.4 million per year. However, if all these requests were made by phone, the cost would exceed €1.03 billion per year. As it is impossible to divert all callers to the website, the company must maintain call centres. The annual costs of these call centres is €248 million. This cost might decrease over the years, as more and more customers use the website, but there will probably always be call centres, because FedEx does not want to lose frustrated customers.

Many people are still uncomfortable doing business at a website. The cost of a customer who is frustrated by the company website is incalculable. Experience shows that people are willing to encounter one or two obstacles with the website, but then they stop trying.

Since its establishment in the United States in 1971 as Federal Express Corp., the company was keen on information technologies, but over the years it used an increasing number of disparate systems for different business purposes, such as air freight, ground freight, special logistic operations and custom shipping of critical items. These discrepancies were compounded by expansion into major new territories, such as Europe and Asia in 1984 and the Middle East in 1989. By 1999, customer information was scattered across computer systems implemented over 14 years. To periodically test service, executives pretend to be customers. They discovered that customers who used more than one FedEx business were not treated consistently. For example, when claiming damages, a customer had to fill out 37 fields on a claims form, such as tracking number, ship date, pickup location and destination, even though FedEx systems already held data for 33 of those fields. The official change of 'Federal Express' to 'FedEx' started an important move: all the company units were to share the same information systems.

Meanwhile, FedEx's customer service centres were redesigned around a PC-based software desktop. If reps could pull up historical data on customers whenever they called – not just their shipping histories, but their preferences and even images of their paper bills – FedEx could provide better, faster service, both to individual customers and to businesses that sold goods through catalogues.

In 2000, management purchased customer relationship management software called Clarify. A new policy

FedEx Express employees in the company hub at Charles de Gaulle International Airport in Paris, France, help customers reach major European markets.

was established: systems and customer service experts are equally responsible for the call centres. Using PCs, reps can pull up historical data on customers whenever customers call. Customer records that are immediately available to reps include shipping histories, preferences and images of the paper bills. Customers are happier now than they were just a few years ago. So are the reps. Turnover of service reps has decreased 20 per cent.

Productivity is important, but so is the reps' service quality. They must be polite, provide customers with correct appropriate information and try not to give customers a reason to call again. Typically, callers are either determined to speak to a human or they know the help they need is too complex to be available at the company's website. Therefore, callers require more time than in the past. The company periodically evaluates the reps' performance based on clearly stated goals that take all these factors into consideration. Typically, 32 per cent of the reps' performance rating is based on the quality of their response and 17 per cent on their efficiency. The other 51 per cent is based on attendance, adherence to scheduled breaks and compliance with regulations.

Interestingly, customers are not interested in friendliness, but in quick and accurate information. FedEx constantly follows customer reactions to different help styles. Managers discovered then when reps' time is not limited, they tend to speak with customers beyond the time required to solve the problem. Customers perceive them as too talkative and they get a bad impression about FedEx. Thus, reps are encouraged to get off the phone as soon as the problem is resolved rather than try to be 'nice'.

The professionals who work for the vendor of Clarify, the CRM software, spend time with reps to see how well the software serves them. They discovered that reps often move quickly from one window of information to another and that sometimes they took extra time to find a window that 'disappeared'. The software engineers decided to modify Clarify so it interacts with Java code. This enables the reps to switch between windows and different applications of Clarify quickly during a call without reentering customer data. For instance, if a customer needs directions to pick up a package, the rep can click the tab of the mapping application. Relying on the customer's account data, the application picks up the customer's post code. Combining it with the code of the pickup centre, the software immediately produces directions, which the rep can read to the customer.

While great improvements have already been accomplished both in service speed and quality,

FedEx executives continue to look for ways to improve. They refuse to discuss what their next step is because it might be copied immediately by competitors, but they do reveal that their goal is to bring call centres to the point where a rep never has to put a customer on hold.

Experts expect a single 'nervous system' for all types of customer calls by 2010. Software will accept all customer calls from the customer's PC, phone or handheld device. Special software involving artificial intelligence techniques will screen all incoming calls, evaluate the problem complexity and decide whether to direct the calls to other software for resolution or to invite a human rep to intervene.

FedEx has already developed systems that integrate sales and marketing data. The FedEx Europe, Middle East, India and Africa division has developed a data warehouse that is fed data from more than 20 sources, not just CRM but also human resource (HR) systems and external sources. Immediate access is available to senior management to enable them to detect early warning signs of customer dissatisfaction. They can analyse customer activity to see if they are using competitors for their deliveries, what their preferred delivery destinations and types of service are, complaints received and so on. So customers who have the potential to become ex-customers can be targeted.

Thinking about the case

1 What is CRM in general? Give examples of *different* CRM applications.

2 Enumerate and explain the various ways in which the CRM application discussed here (Clarify) saves costs or helps in other ways.

4 Which metrics would you use to measure *before* and *after* performance regarding the information technologies implemented in this case? Consider cost, service quality, cycle time and any other performance factor and provide a specific metric (i.e., ratio, product, or absolute value).

4 As a customer, would you prefer more, or less, mechanized service in lieu of human help?

5 As an executive for FedEx or a similar company, what else would you implement using software and the Internet?

SOURCE: D. Gage, 'FedEx: Personal Touch', Baseline (www.baselinemag.com), 13 January, 2005; www.fedex.com/us, 2005; www.fedex.com/us/about/overview/worldwide/emea.html?link=4, 2007

silicon.com

Case study 1.3
Analysis: CRM – get involved

BY RON CONDON

Work with all parts of the business if you want a successful rollout . . .

Whatever the size of your business, if you're looking to roll out CRM, you must involve all parts of the organization, says Ron Condon. Recent developments, though, do favour smaller players.

When the dot-com bubble burst at the beginning of the decade, a lot of customer relationship management projects came to a grinding halt or just faded away. No wonder then that by 2002, research companies such as Gartner were saying that barely half of CRM implementations had been completed or had delivered any real benefit.

In the heady days of the boom, many companies had been seduced by the prospect of being able to track their customers' every move – and thereby gain some deep, new understanding of their own business.

Retailers especially began to construct huge data warehouses and even small corner shops started launching their own loyalty card schemes. According to those technology companies pushing the concept, CRM would give companies exciting new insights into the way shoppers think.

One example that did the rounds for a while was the close connection between the sales of beer and nappies. Analysis of customer data, it was claimed, had revealed the phenomenon of working dads popping into the supermarket on a Friday night to get the beers – and to do their paternal duty by picking up the weekly nappy supply.

Unfortunately, no other great insights emerged and the beer–nappy theory turned out to be an urban myth anyway. CRM had hit the buffers, and the whole area seemed to go quiet, with some big

supermarkets such as Asda and Safeway canning their loyalty card programmes. The rewards just didn't seem to be worth the trouble and the huge expense.

But the failure of so many CRM projects cannot be blamed purely on bad timing. Giles Hutchins, head of the CRM practice with consultants Atos Origin, says: 'A lot of CRM projects were run out of the sales or marketing department, where they just wanted to capture their customer information. But CRM needs to be an overarching application across the organization, not just the front office.'

The failure to integrate it with other areas of the organization meant that CRM could only deliver limited benefits. Without links into other aspects of the business – finance, order processing, supply chain, distribution, complaints handling – the CRM system was just a glorified contact management application.

Part of the problem was that companies concentrated just on technology without seeing that a customer-centric approach to business was going to require changes in processes, procedures and also in the way people in back-office functions operated. According to Paul Brewer, head of business development for BT's CRM practice, technology should account for just 30 per cent of a CRM implementation – with people and processes taking the lion's share of the budget.

As with any system that is going to touch the whole organization, a CRM project needs board-level backing and sponsorship, plus cooperation

Beer and nappies – a CRM-inspired myth?

and input from all departments. It also has to be underpinned by real business goals, such as a greater choice of sales channels, better product availability, ability to offer better, faster service and the ability to identify the most valuable customers.

In other words, no matter what the size of the organization, CRM has to be part of an overall business strategy with a clear model of where the business wants to get to. According to Juliet Armstrong, a partner at consultancy The Berkeley Partnership, development of that strategic model will help to involve senior management from the whole business – channel management, supply chain, product development, marketing and HR – and force them to decide overall priorities at an early stage. It also stops CRM being just an IT or sales project, but one that the whole organization will use.

That in turn sets the stage for greater integration between systems. Armstrong makes the point that new integration technologies based on web services, XML and common object models now make it far easier to create the seamless flow of information that is needed. 'The challenge of integrating new technologies with legacy systems was unachievable with the tools that were available in the late 1990s', she says.

In addition, most of the big CRM applications have created open APIs to allow an interchange of information with other systems. For instance, Salesforce.com, which began life very much as a sales automation service, now reports that more than 40 per cent of all its transactions come via its API – in other words, through other applications.

For complex integration projects, where the CRM system needs to interact with three or more other applications, point-to-point links via the API can start to get messy. In those cases, Atos Origin's Hutchins recommends going for some kind of enterprise application integration (EAI) tool from the likes of BEA, IBM or Tibco.

But Berkeley's Armstrong counsels against trying to make everything integrate regardless of cost. 'Consider any integration on a cost–benefit basis but also look at the impact on business process of implementing the resultant workaround [of not doing an integration]. Usually it's best to create a strategic target architecture and justified road map to achieve that architecture. This clearly explains the reasons for integration or business process workarounds at each phase of delivery.'

Despite the far-reaching nature of a fully integrated CRM system, most practitioners advise a phased introduction, so that some success can be won early on. Hutchins says: 'Start small and adopt a phased approach. Keep phase one succinct, so you can ensure success and buy-in for the completion of the project.'

Armstrong agrees: 'Each phase should have a clear business case and consider the wider impact on customers and the business – such as customer marketing and employee training. Importantly, each phase must minimize risk to the business and consider operational data requirements.'

She also notes that any integration should take into account the need to comply with the raft of corporate governance and financial regulations. With so many applications transmitting or sharing information, the company must be able to maintain an audit trail and ensure back-up and recovery if things go wrong. This may well influence the choice of integration mechanism.

She advises: 'Synchronous message-based integration is appropriate for order management solutions but unsuitable for transferring financial data in an auditable fashion. An ETL tool is likely to be more effective.'

The availability of so much technology to help tie different applications together means that smaller companies could have an advantage in the CRM stakes. While big companies, especially the High Street banks, are struggling to integrate huge legacy systems, smaller companies are less weighed down by past investments and can make the most of a newer, more streamlined approach.

Thinking about the case

1 There is a recommendation that the introduction of a CRM system should be phased. It would seem reasonable to introduce those aspects that are simplest and/or give the greatest benefits. Draw up a shortlist of CRM subsystems that best fit these criteria.

2 Are there any disadvantages to a phased approach to CRM system implementation?

Strategic uses of information systems

Executives know that information technology is not merely a resource to support day-to-day operations. Clever use of IT can significantly change an organization's long-term strategic position in national and global markets. Often, applying information systems to long-term planning completely changes the way a firm conducts its business. Some systems even change the product or service that a firm provides. Today, information systems are an accepted and integral part of strategic planning for nearly al organizations.

When you finish this chapter, you will be able to:

Explain what business strategy and strategic moves are.

Illustrate how information systems can give businesses a competitive advantage.

Identify basic initiatives for gaining a competitive advantage.

Explain what makes an information system a *strategic* information system.

Identify fundamental requirements for developing strategic information systems.

Explain circumstances and initiatives that make one IT strategy succeed and another fail.

USING INFORMATION STRATEGICALLY

The information systems that Better Bites had in place had succeeded so far: the business had been operating for a year and it was profitable. Paul Clermont, Sarah Odell and Christina Healy had begun to enjoy running their pushcart lunch business. Handling the food concessions for the city's major holiday celebrations had helped carry them through the summer, when there weren't as many students on campus. Now the three entrepreneurs were looking for ways to expand and increase their profits even more. An opportunity presented itself at a City Council meeting.

Looking at expansion

Christina regularly attended Council meetings to keep in touch with the local business community. She was always looking for new opportunities. After one meeting, the manager of a local shopping centre approached her with a proposal: the shopping centre manager wanted to draw more foot traffic and he thought that some small food vendors would provide a fun atmosphere and encourage shoppers to linger. He was thinking of a couple of pushcarts – would Better Bites be interested? Christina checked with her partners and they decided to expand their operations to the shopping centre.

However, the increased sales from operating three carts meant that Paul, Sarah and Christina needed to ramp up their production – and quickly. They were having trouble handling their increased cooking and food preparation load – they were in Paul's uncle's kitchen earlier and earlier to finish in time. They seriously needed to consider renting kitchen space for themselves. And they also needed to hire additional staff to help prepare the sandwiches and staff the carts – it was simply too much for Paul, Sarah and Christina to cover three carts by themselves.

A new line of business?

Customers began lining up at the shopping centre lunch carts in droves. To keep their clientele

happy, Better Bites experimented with new crisp varieties – handing them out to waiting customers and getting their immediate feedback. Sarah tried parsnip crisps and baked tortilla chips in different flavours, in addition to the all-natural potato crisps they originally offered. Customers loved the new tortilla crisps and they could be made from wraps that hadn't been used the previous day, so their additional cost was minimal. With the great customer reception of the crisp line, Paul, Sarah and Christina were now considering producing and packaging the crisps for sale to other retail establishments – in other words, becoming a food manufacturer. They would definitely need to move to new kitchen facilities, but they reasoned they could use the new kitchen space around the clock eventually, if needed. The additional crisp revenue

A local shopping centre provided the first opportunity for Better Bites' expansion and introduced new strategic challenges for Paul, Sarah and Christina.

could help them cover the cost of the equipment and new space. They'd also need their own pots and pans, ovens and packaging equipment. None of this would be cheap, so they'd need to watch expenses and revenues closely in their spreadsheets.

Charting a strategy with information systems

Paul and Christina also investigated the option of using only organic ingredients, to appeal even more to the health-food market. They called organic suppliers and surfed the Web to gather data to plug into their spreadsheets. Doing this research helped them avoid what could have been a costly mistake – going organic would raise their prices 33 per cent and would not be a good strategic move for them right now.

New competition on the block

After Paul, Sarah and Christina had made these important decisions, they received some bad news. Word of Better Bites' success had evidently spread – a local Subwich franchise had located a shop near to the University concourse to attract some of their business. The three partners were very worried about competing with a national franchise, which had much greater financial resources than they did.

To help retain loyal customers, they decided to implement a frequent buyer programme, where current customers could get a free sandwich after the purchase of ten. The three partners registered repeat customers in their database and issued cards to be punched. They hoped this additional programme would help them stay competitive with Subwich, but they knew they'd need to remain on their toes.

Strategy and strategic moves

The word 'strategy' originates from the Greek word *strategos*, meaning 'general'. In war, a strategy is a plan to gain an advantage over the enemy. Other disciplines, especially business, have borrowed the term. As you know from media coverage, corporate executives often discuss actions in ways that make business competition sound like war. Business people must devise decisive courses of action to win – just as generals do. In business, a strategy is a plan designed to help an organization outperform its competitors. Unlike battle plans, however, business strategy often takes the form of creating new opportunities rather than beating rivals.

Although many information systems are built to solve problems, many others are built to seize opportunities. And, as anyone in business can tell you, identifying a problem is easier than creating an opportunity. Why? Because a problem already exists; it is an obstacle to a desired mode of operation and, as such, calls attention to itself. An opportunity, on the other hand, is less tangible. It takes a certain amount of imagination, creativity and vision to identify an opportunity, or to create one and seize it. Information systems that help seize opportunities are often called strategic information systems (SISs). They can be developed from scratch, or they can evolve from an organization's existing ISs.

> **strategic information system** Any information system that gives its owner a competitive advantage.

In 1979 Michael Porter of Harvard Business School presented a framework for businesses to consider their strategic position in a competitive environment. He defined five forces that can affect the marketplace which can therefore be used to give a qualitative analysis of the business' position. Figure 2.1 shows diagrammatically how the forces potentially affect a business initiative. Any change in one or more of the forces may lead the business to re-asses what it is doing. In all cases, information systems can be helpful in analysing the situation, alerting us to subtle changes and trends and generally giving us market intelligence.

- Supplier bargaining power – An information system can help to analyse the relative costs of goods and materials from suppliers, investigate trends in prices and volumes and look for the best deal from our suppliers.

Figure 2.1 Porter's five forces model

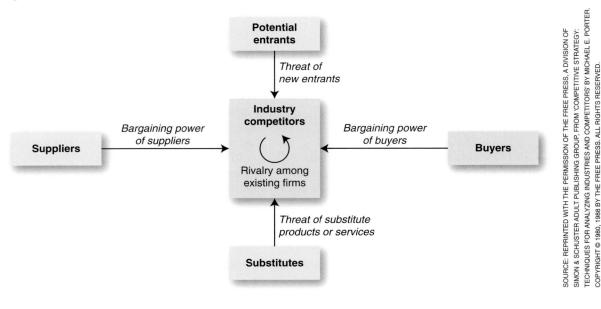

- Competitive rivalry – An information system can help analysis of our competitors, the prices they are charging, their customer base and so on.

- Buyer bargaining power – The more we know about our customers the easier it is to hold on to them. An information system that holds details of previous purchases will enable us to pitch our sale price at the right level.

- Threat of substitutes – More complicated than keeping an eye on companies in direct competition, we need sophisticated analysis that enables us to identify potential substitute products early and react accordingly.

- Threat of new entrants – Any profitable market will lead to new firms joining. We need an information system to give us early warning about these new competitors and strategic information to enable us to maintain our share of the market.

In a free-market economy, it is difficult for a business to do well without some strategic planning. Although strategies vary, they tend to fall into some basic categories, such as developing a new product, identifying an unmet consumer need, changing a service to entice more customers or retain existing clients, or taking any other action that increases the organization's value through improved performance.

Many strategies do not, and cannot, involve information systems. But increasingly, corporations are able to implement certain strategies – such as maximizing sales and lowering costs – thanks to the innovative use of information systems. In other words, better information gives corporations a competitive advantage in the marketplace. A company uses strategy to maximize its strengths, resulting in a competitive advantage. When a business uses a strategy with the intent to *create* a market for new products or services, it does not aim to compete with other organizations, because that market does not yet exist. Therefore, a strategic move is not always a competitive move. However, in a free-enterprise society, a market rarely remains the domain of one organization for long; thus, competition ensues almost immediately. So, we often use the terms 'competitive advantage' and 'strategic advantage' interchangeably.

competitive advantage
A position in which one dominates a market; also called strategic advantage.

You might have heard statements about using the Web strategically. Business competition is no longer limited to a particular country or even a region of the world. To increase the sale of

Industry **SNAPSHOT**

IT and business strategy at board level

SOURCE: NCC Benchmark of IT Strategy 2006, National Computer Centre

A 2006 study by the National Computer Centre of 288 IT decision-makers in medium- to large-sized UK organizations found that the IT function is becoming more widely represented at company board level. Nearly 85 per cent of those surveyed now have IT representation at the top level compared to only 61 per cent in 2001. On the other hand 54 per cent of the respondents where IT is not represented on the board cited lack of involvement and commitment of senior managers as the cause of a poor IT strategy. The study's authors concluded that 'IT strategy is becoming a much bigger component of business strategy. This means the business drivers and consequent abilities to apply these through technology is becoming a critical issue for the business and the IT professional.'

The IT function's presence at board level is growing but, as the chapter 9 silicon.com case study illustrates, this growth remains unsatisfactorily slow for many businesses.

PHOTO SOURCE: © MAARTJE VAN CASPEL

goods and services, companies must regard the entire world as their market. Because thousands of corporations and hundreds of millions of consumers have access to the Web, augmenting business via the Web has become strategic: many companies that utilized the Web early on have enjoyed greater market shares, more experience with the Web as a business enabler, and larger revenues than latecomers. Some companies developed information systems, or features of information systems, that are unique, such as Amazon's 'one-click' online purchasing and Priceline's 'name your own price' auctioning. Practically any web-based system that gives a company competitive advantage is a strategic information system.

Achieving a competitive advantage

Consider competitive advantage in terms of a for-profit company, whose major goal is to maximize profits by lowering costs and increasing revenue. A for-profit company achieves competitive advantage when its profits increase significantly, most commonly through increased market share. Table 2.1 lists eight basic initiatives that can be used to gain competitive advantage, including offering a product or service that competitors cannot provide or providing the same product or service more attractively to customers. It is important to understand that the eight listed are the most common, but not the only, types of business strategies an organization can pursue. It is also important to understand that strategic moves often consist of a combination of two or more of these initiatives and other steps. The essence of strategy is innovation, so competitive advantage is often gained when an organization tries a strategy that no one has tried before.

For example, Dell was the first PC manufacturer to use the Web to take customer orders. Competitors have long imitated the practice, but Dell, first to gain a web audience, gained

CD TASK

Table 2.1 Eight basic ways to gain competitive advantage

Initiative	Benefit
Reduce costs	A company can gain advantage if it can sell more units at a lower price while providing quality and maintaining or increasing its profit margin.
Raise barriers to market entrants	A company can gain advantage if it deters potential entrants into the market, enjoying less competition and more market potential.
Establish high switching costs	A company can gain advantage if it creates high switching costs, making it economically infeasible for customers to buy from competitors.
Create new products or services	A company can gain advantage if it offers a unique product or service.
Differentiate products or services	A company can gain advantage if it can attract customers by convincing them its product differs from the competition's.
Enhance products or services	A company can gain advantage if its product or service is better than anyone else's.
Establish alliances	Companies from different industries can help each other gain advantage by offering combined packages of goods or services at special prices.
Lock in suppliers or buyers	A company can gain advantage if it can lock in either suppliers or buyers, making it economically impractical for suppliers or buyers to deal with competitors.

more experience than other PC makers on this e-commerce vehicle and still sells more computers via the Web than its competitors. Figure 2.2 indicates that a company can use many strategies together to gain competitive advantage.

Initiative 1: Reduce costs

Customers like to pay as little as possible while still receiving the quality of service or product they need. One way to increase market share is to lower prices and the best way to lower prices is to *reduce costs*. For instance, if carried out successfully, massive automation of any business process gives an organization competitive advantage. The reason is simple: automation makes an organization more productive and any cost savings can be transferred to customers through lower prices. We saw this happen in the car industry. In the 1970s, Japanese car manufacturers brought robots to their production and assembly lines and reduced costs – and subsequently prices – quickly and dramatically. The robots weld, paint and assemble parts at a far lower cost than manual labour. Until their competitors began to employ robots, the Japanese had a clear competitive advantage because they were able to sell high-quality cars for less than their competitors.

CD TASK

In the service sector, the Web has created an opportunity to automate what until recently was considered an activity that only humans could perform: customer service. An enormous trend towards automating online customer service began with companies such as FedEx, which initially gave customers an opportunity to track their parcels' status by logging on to a dedicated, private network and database. The same approach is now implemented through the Web. Many sites today include answers to FAQs (frequently asked

Figure 2.2 Many strategic moves can work together to achieve a competitive advantage

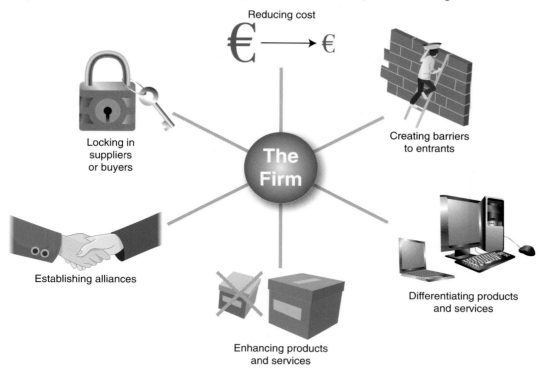

questions). Others have special programs that can respond to customer questions. Online service gives businesses two major benefits: it changes service from being labour-intensive to technology-intensive, which is much less expensive; and it provides customers easy access to a service seven days a week, 24 hours a day. It cuts the costs not only of expensive human labour but also of telephone and postal charges. Companies that are the first to adopt advanced systems that reduce labour enjoy competitive advantage for as long as their competitors lag behind.

Initiative 2: Raise barriers to market entrants

The smaller the number of companies competing within an industry, the better off each company is. Therefore, an organization might gain competitive advantage by making it difficult, or impossible, for other organizations to produce the product or service it provides. Using expertise or technology that is unavailable to competitors or prohibitively expensive is one way to bar new entrants.

Companies *raise barriers to entrants* in a number of ways. Obtaining legal protection of intellectual property such as an invention or artistic work will bar competitors from freely using it. Microsoft and other software powerhouses have gained tremendous strategic advantages by copyrighting and patenting software. On the Web, there are numerous examples of such protection. Priceline.com holds a patent for online reverse ('name your own price') auctioning, which has prevented competitors from entering its business space. Amazon.com secured a patent for one-click online purchasing, which enables customers to enter delivery and credit-card information once, so all subsequent orders do not have to go through a verification web page. Although the software is quite simple, Amazon obtained a patent for it in 1999 that won't expire until 2017. Amazon successfully sued Barnes & Noble (B&N) when

CD TASK

it implemented the same technology on BN.com. Now B&N pays Amazon for its use. More recently, Amazon obtained a patent for its techniques used to decide what types of items a user might like to buy in the future. Exclusive use of the methods might give the company additional strategic advantage in online shopping. Protecting any invention, including hardware and software, with patents and copyrights provides an excellent barrier to potential entrants.

Another barrier to potential new market entrants is the high expense of entering that market. The pension fund management industry is a prime illustration. State Street Corporation is one of its most successful examples. The company maintains operations in 26 countries covering all major investment centres, including London, Frankfurt, Paris and Johannesburg. In the 1980s, State Street committed massive amounts of money to developing ISs that helped make the company a leader in managing pension funds and international bank accounts. The huge capital allocation required to build a system to compete successfully with State Street keeps potential entrants out of the market. Instead, other pension management corporations rent State Street's technology and expertise. In fact, State Street derives about 70 per cent of its revenues from selling its IS services. This company is an interesting example of an entire business refocusing around its ISs.

Initiative 3: Establish high switching costs

switching costs
Expenses that are incurred when a customer stops buying a product or service from one business and starts buying it from another.

Switching costs are expenses incurred when a customer stops buying a product or service from one business and starts buying it from another. Switching costs can be explicit (such as charges the seller levies on a customer for switching) or implicit (such as the indirect costs in time and money spent adjusting to a new product that does the same job as the old).

Often, explicit switching costs are fixed, non-recurring costs, such as a penalty a buyer must pay for terminating a deal early. In the mobile telephone service industry, you can usually get an attractive deal, but if you cancel the service before a full year or more has passed, you have to pay a hefty penalty. So although another company's service might be more attractive, you might decide to wait the full contract period because the penalty outweighs the benefits of the new company's service. When you do decide to switch, you might discover that the telephone is not suitable for service with any other telephone company. The cost of the telephone itself, then, is another disincentive to switch.

A perfect example of indirect switching expenses is the time and money required to learn new software. Once a company trains its personnel to use one word-processing or spreadsheet program, a competing software company must offer a very enticing deal to make switching worthwhile. The same principle holds for many other applications, such as database management systems and web page editors and graphical software. Consider Microsoft's popular MS Office suite; you can purchase the significantly less expensive Sun Microsystems' StarOffice, a software suite that is equivalent to MS Office. Better yet, you can download free of charge the entire suite of OpenOffice.org. Yet, few organizations or consumers who are accustomed to MS Office are willing to switch to StarOffice or OpenOffice.org.

Manufacturers of laser and ink-jet printers sell their printers at cost or below cost. However, once you purchase a printer, you must replace a depleted ink or toner cartridge with one that the printer manufacturer sells, or take a risk with non-original cartridges. As a cartridge customer, you face high costs if you consider switching to another brand. Even if comparable cartridges from another manufacturer are less expensive, you cannot use them; and if you decide to use those cartridges, you will lose your investment in the printer, because you must buy a new one. Thus, establishing high switching costs often locks in customers. Locking in customers by any means is a way to accomplish a strategic advantage and is discussed later.

Initiative 4: Create new products or services

Clearly, *creating a new and unique product or service* that many organizations and individuals need gives an organization a great competitive advantage. Unfortunately, the advantage lasts only until other organizations in the industry start offering an identical or similar product or service for a comparable or lower price.

Examples of this scenario abound in the software industry. For instance, Lotus Development Corporation became the major player early on in the electronic spreadsheet market after it introduced its Lotus 1-2-3 program. When two competitors tried to market similar products, Lotus sued for copyright infringement and won the court case, sustaining its market dominance for several years. However, with time, Microsoft established its Excel spreadsheet application as the world leader, not only by aggressive marketing but also by including better features in its application.

CD TASK

Another example of a company creating a new service is eBay, the firm that dominates online auctions. The organization was the first to offer this service, which became very popular within only a few months. While other firms now offer a similar service (e.g., Amazon and Yahoo! Auctions), the fact that eBay was the first to offer it gave eBay a huge advantage: it quickly acquired a large number of sellers and bidders, a network that is so critical to creating a 'mass' of clients, which in turn is the main draw for additional clients. It also gave eBay a great advantage in experience and allowed it to open a gap that was difficult for competitors to close, even for giants such as Amazon. eBay is an example of an entire business that would be impossible without the Web and the information technologies that support the firm's service.

eBay's success demonstrates the strategic advantage of the first mover, an organization that is the first to offer a new product or service. By the time other organizations start offering the same product or service, the first mover has usually created some assets that cannot be had by the competitors: a superior brand name, a better technology or method for delivery, or a critical mass. A critical mass is a body of clients that is large enough to attract many other clients. In many cases, first movers simply enjoy longer experience, which in itself is an advantage over competitors.

first mover A business that is first in its industry to adopt a technology or method.

Being a first mover is not always a guarantee of long-term success, however. One example of how a first-mover strategic advantage can be lost within just a few months is in the web browser arena. Netscape Corporation (now part of AOL) dominated the web browser market, which was new in 1994. By allowing individual users to download its browser for free, it cornered up to 95 per cent of the market. The wide use of the browser by individuals moved commercial organizations to purchase the product and other software compatible with the browser. Netscape's dominance quickly diminished when Microsoft aggressively marketed its own browser, which many perceived as at least as good as Netscape's. Microsoft provided Internet Explorer free of charge to anyone and then bundled it into the Microsoft Windows operating system software distributed with almost all PCs. Even after the court-ordered unbundling, its browser still dominated. This dominance in turn has been threatened by free browsers such as Mozilla's Firefox and Avant Force's Avant Browser, which offer similar or better features, more flexibility and fewer security vulnerabilities.

Other first movers have lost market share because they neglected to improve the service they pioneered. Few web surfers remember Infoseek, the first commercial search engine. Google, which entered the search engine arena in 1998, improved the quality and speed of web searches, offering a clutter-free home page. The strategy of its two young entrepreneurs was simple: provide the best search engine and refrain from commercialising it for a while. Over a period of about three years Google established itself as the best search engine. In time, it started to capitalize on this prominence by selling sponsored links (the right side of the results of a user's search). Most importantly, the organization never stopped improving its search algorithms and periodically has offered new services. The strategy has succeeded so much that 'google it' has become synonymous with 'search for it on the Web'.

PHOTO SOURCE: COURTESY OF GOOGLE INC

A Google employee enjoying a unique working environment.

Initiative 5: Differentiate products or services

A company can achieve a competitive advantage by persuading consumers that its product or service is better than its competitors', even if it is not. Called 'product differentiation', this advantage is usually achieved through advertising. Brand-name success is a perfect example of product differentiation. Think of Levi's Jeans, Chanel perfume and Gap clothes. The customer buys the brand-name product, perceiving it to be superior to similar products. In fact, some products *are* the same, but units sold under a prestigious brand name sell for higher prices. You often see this phenomenon in the food, clothing, pharmaceutical and cosmetics markets.

Product and service differentiation impacts not only consumers but also businesses. For example, IBM's Global Services division has created a great brand name for itself as an IT consulting firm. Interestingly, while IBM lost the corporate world's perception that only IBM computers are reliable enough to support business operations ('Nobody ever got fired for buying IBM'), it has gradually differentiated itself as a reliable and knowledgeable consulting organization.

Initiative 6: Enhance products or services

Instead of differentiating a product or service, an organization might actually add to the product or service to increase its value to the consumer; this is called *enhancing existing products or services*. For example, car manufacturers might entice customers by offering a longer warranty period for their cars and estate agents might attract more business by providing useful financing information to potential buyers.

Since the Internet opened its portals to commercial enterprises in the early 1990s, an increasing number of companies have supplemented their products and services. Their websites provide up-to-date information that helps customers utilize their purchased products better or receive additional services. Companies that pioneered such Internet use reaped great rewards. For example, Charles Schwab gained a competitive advantage over other, older brokerage companies such as Merrill Lynch by opening a site for online stock transactions. Nearly half its revenue now comes from this site. All brokerage houses followed and allow customers to trade through a website.

Other companies use the Internet to maintain their competitive edge by continually adding to and enhancing their online services. Dell is not the only company that sells computers online, for example. Other, smaller companies provide a similar service and sell comparable products, with more flexibility in 'building your own computer online', often at lower prices. However, Dell maintains the popularity of its site through continuous enhancement of the services it offers. For example, it offers a buying guide centre that clearly explains what to look for in various types of products and explains topics of interest such as software security.

Industry **SNAPSHOT**

Online holiday brochures

The availability of electronic brochures on holiday company websites has lead to a significant saving in printing costs as well as giving customers an improved, faster service according to www.onlinetravelbrochures.com. Operators such as Page and Moy and TrekAmerica have seen a 90 per cent decline in requests for printed brochures because they have given the customer the ability to browse a full electronic version of their printed brochures. The major tour operators (such as Thomson) have their own specially designed websites giving views of the accommodation, description of the facilities and so on but this third-party web service gives the smaller operators a chance to compete without the need for a dedicated website design. It is also reported that the availability of the online brochures leads to the average user staying with the website a further five minutes, hence opening up sales and marketing opportunities.

SOURCE: European Travel Commission, New Media Review, Online Travel Market (http://www.etcnewmedia.com) 21 December 2006

Royal Carribean International is one of a growing number of companies that use electronic brochures.

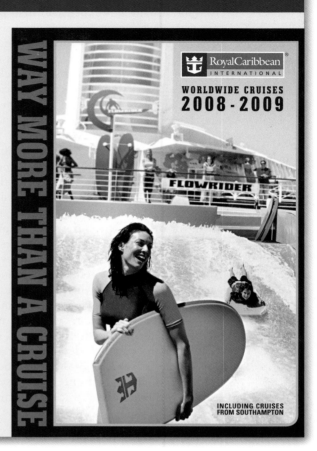

PHOTO SOURCE: COURTESY OF ROYAL CARRIBEAN CRUISES LTD

Why you should…

understand the notion of strategic information systems

Although devising strategic moves is mainly the responsibility of senior management, let us remember Napoleon's words: 'Every soldier carries a marshal's baton in his knapsack.' To paraphrase: every junior manager is a potential senior manager. Thus, it is incumbent on every professional to try to think strategically for his or her organization. In fact, employees at the lowest levels have proposed some of the most brilliant strategic ideas. In today's highly competitive market, strategy might determine an organization's rise or fall.

An increasing number of strategic moves are either possible only with the aid of ISs or have ISs at the centre of their strategy – that is, technology provides the product, service or method that gains the organization strategic advantage. The potential for new business models on the Web is still great. Thus, professionals must understand how to use technology in strategic moves. Understanding how strategic information systems are conceived and implemented might help you suggest good ideas for such systems in your organization and facilitate your promotion up the organizational ladder.

Initiative 7: Establish alliances

Companies can gain competitive advantage by combining services to make them more attractive (and usually less expensive) than purchasing services separately. These alliances provide two draws for customers: combined service is cheaper and one-stop shopping is more convenient. The travel industry is very aggressive in this area. For example, airlines collaborate with hotel chains and car-rental firms to offer travel and lodging packages and with credit-card companies that offer discount ticket purchases from particular airlines or the products of particular manufacturers. Credit-card companies commonly offer frequent flier miles which can be exchanged for flights or for other goods and services through alliances. In a similar manner, the leading UK supermarket chain, Tesco, runs a customer loyalty card which can accumulate points exchangeable for not just grocery vouchers but holidays, theatre tickets and so on. In all these cases, alliances create competitive advantages. For example, by forging alliances the Tesco group can negotiate special deals with the suppliers of the 'treats'. The alliances work both ways too so that, for example, by staying at the Singapore Marriot Hotel you can earn Tesco Clubcard points!

As Figure 2.3 indicates, by creating an alliance, organizations enjoy synergy: the combined profit for the allies from the sale of a package of goods or services exceeds the profits earned when each acts individually. Sometimes, the alliances are formed by more than two organizations. Consider the benefits you receive when you agree to accept a major credit card: discounts from several hotel chains, restaurant chains, flower delivery chains and other stores, as well as free insurance when renting a car and frequent flier miles, to name a few. Similarly, travel websites such as Lastminute.com offer you the opportunity to reserve accommodation and car rental at discounts while you make your airline reservations. The company has also established alliances with hotel chains, car rental companies and health spas.

What is the common denominator among these companies? They each have an information system that tracks all these transactions and discounts. A package of attractive propositions entices clients who need these services (and most businesses do). Would this offer be feasible without an IS to track transactions and discounts? Probably not.

Figure 2.3 Strategic alliances combine services to create synergies

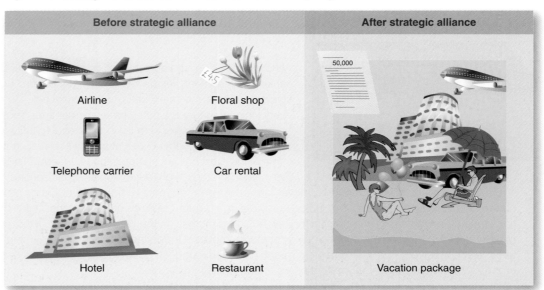

Industry **SNAPSHOT**

IT spending mismatch

According to statistics from the United Kingdom's National Computing Centre, gathered in August 2006, spending on IT increased from the previous year by 28 per cent to £3,891 per end user. However there is a sharp contrast between the spending from different sectors of industry. The finance sector reported a median spend of £9,864 per end user whilst the lowest-spending sectors of local government and health reported a relatively meagre spend of £2,189 and £1,713 per end user respectively.

Predictions for the future again show a contrast with the median level of spending growth at 1.9 per cent (compared to 1.6 per cent the previous year) but central government predicting a 'growth' rate of minus 2.5 per cent.

SOURCE: National Computer Centre press release 'No news is bad news for IT vendors', 1 November 2006

London's financial centre at Canrary Wharf – home to high levels of IT expenditure.

PHOTO SOURCE: © PEETER VIISIMAA

Growing web use for e-commerce has pushed organizations to create alliances that would be unimaginable a few years ago. Consider the alliance between Hewlett-Packard and FedEx. HP is a leading manufacturer of computers and computer equipment. FedEx is a shipping company. HP maintains inventory of its products at FedEx facilities. When customers order items from HP via its website, HP routes the order, via the Web, to FedEx. FedEx packages the items and ships them to customers. This arrangement lets HP dispatch ordered items within hours rather than days. The alliance gives HP an advantage that other computer equipment makers do not share. Again, it is a clever IS that enables this strategy.

CD TASK

On the Web, an obvious example of alliances is an *affiliate programme*. Anyone can place links to commercial sites on his or her personal website. When a visitor clicks through to a commercial site and makes a purchase, the first site's owner is paid a fee. Some online retailers have thousands of affiliates. The early adopters of such programmes, Amazon.co.uk, Buy.com, Priceline.co.uk and other large e-retailers, enjoyed a competitive advantage in gaining new customers. It is easy for any website holder to become an affiliate of Amazon.co.uk.

> **affiliate programme** An arrangement by which a website promotes sales for another website through a link to the seller's site, and for which the affiliate is compensated. There are various schemes of compensation to affiliates.

Another example is the collaboration between Amazon.com and other retailers who make use of Amazon's technology. Target Corp. is one of America's largest retailers. To extend its operation to the Web, it formed a strategic alliance with the giant online retailer. If you go to Target's site, you will notice the words 'Powered by Amazon.com'. Amazon provides Target with its proprietary search engine, order-fulfilment and customer-service systems and the patented one-click shopping application, which lets customers pay for merchandise selected from the Target, Marshall Field's and Mervyns' sites from one electronic shopping cart (Marshall Field's and Mervyns are Target subsidiaries). In return, Amazon collects a percentage of all sales from Target's retail sites, as well as annual fixed fees. Have we mentioned referrals? Next to the logos of Target and its subsidiaries, you also find Amazon's logo, which serves as a link to Amazon's site (where you also see the Target logo prominently displayed). There are countless small Internet-based businesses displaying the 'powered by Amazon' logo and linking to Amazon.com, Amazon.co.uk or one of its many subsidiaries. These small businesses are often niche sites (for football programmes, local history, etc.) and they make a small amount of money for every sale that is made on Amazon via a referral from the affiliated site.

Initiative 8: Lock in suppliers or buyers

Organizations can achieve competitive advantage if they are powerful enough to lock in either suppliers to their mode of operation or buyers to their product. Possessing bargaining power – the ability to influence buyers and suppliers – is the key to this approach. As such, companies so large that suppliers and buyers must listen to their demands use this tactic nearly exclusively.

A firm gains bargaining power with a supplier either when the firm has few competitors or when the firm is a major competitor in its industry. In the former case, the fewer the companies that make up a supplier's customer base, the more important each company is to the supplier; in the latter case, the more important a specific company is to a supplier's success, the greater bargaining power that company has over that supplier.

CD TASK

The most common factor in bargaining is purchase volume. Companies that spend huge amounts of money purchasing parts and services have the power to force their suppliers to conform to their methods of operation and even to shift some costs onto suppliers as part of the business arrangement. Consider Tesco, the UK's largest retailer and fourth largest in the world. Not only does the company use its great bargaining power to pressure suppliers to lower prices, but it also requires them to use information systems that are compatible with its own automated processes. The suppliers must use ISs that tell them when to deliver products to Tesco so that the giant retailer is never left understocked or overstocked. The company is currently working towards a requirement for its suppliers to use radio frequency identification (RFID) devices in packaging, to allow more accurate tracking of ordered, shelved and sold items. This great bargaining power and tight control of inventory enables Tesco to enjoy great cost savings, which it passes on to customers, which keep growing in numbers thanks to the competitive prices. Many suppliers are locked in with Tesco because of the sheer volume of business they have with the company: some sell a third to one-half of everything they produce to this single retailer.

One way to lock in *buyers* in a free market is to create the impression that an organization's product is significantly better than the competitors', or to enjoy a situation in which customers fear high switching costs. In the software arena, enterprise applications are a good example. This type of software helps organizations manage a wide array of operations: purchasing, manufacturing, human resources, finance and so forth. The software is expensive, costing millions of dollars. After a company purchases the software from a firm, it is locked in to that firm's services: training, implementation, updates and so on. Thus, companies that sell enterprise software, such as SAP and Oracle, make great efforts to improve both their software and support services to maintain leadership in this market.

Another way to lock in clients is to *create a standard*. The software industry has pursued this strategy vigorously, especially in the Internet arena. For example, Microsoft's decision to give away its web browser by letting both individuals and organizations download it free from its site was not altruistic. Microsoft executives knew that the greater the number of Internet Explorer (IE) users, the greater the user base. The greater the user base, the more likely organizations were to purchase Microsoft's proprietary software to help manage their websites. Also, once individual users committed to IE as their main browser, they were likely to purchase Microsoft software that enhanced the browser's capabilities.

Similarly, Adobe gives away its Acrobat Reader software, an application that lets web surfers open and manipulate documents created using different computers running different operating systems, such as various versions of Windows, the Mac operating system and UNIX. When the Reader user base became large enough, organizations and individuals found it economically justifiable to purchase and use the full Acrobat application (the application used to create the documents) and related applications. Using this strategy put Adobe's PDF (portable data format) standard in an unrivalled position.

Another company, Macromedia Inc., developed software called Flash to create web page animations. It offers the Flash player for download free of charge but sells the development tool. Like Adobe, Macromedia has created a symbiotic situation to augment its market: the more individuals who download the player, the more businesses who are willing to purchase the development tool. The more companies who engage Flash modules in their web pages, the more individuals who download the player, without which they cannot enjoy those animations.

Creating and maintaining strategic information systems

There might be many opportunities to accomplish a competitive edge with IT, especially in industries that are using older software, such as the insurance industry. Insurance companies were among the early adopters of IT and have not changed much of their software. This is why some observers say the entire industry is inefficient. Once an insurance company adopts innovative software applications, it might gain competitive advantage. As you'll learn later in the chapter, when JetBlue was established, it adopted the latest technologies and this was a major reason for its great competitive advantage.

Companies can implement some of the strategic initiatives described in the previous section by using information systems. As we mentioned at the beginning of the chapter, a strategic information system (SIS) is any information system that can help an organization achieve a long-term competitive advantage. An SIS can be created from scratch, developed by modifying an existing system, or 'discovered' by realizing that a system already in place can be used to strategic advantage. While companies continue to explore new ways of devising SISs, some successful SISs are the result of less lofty endeavours: the intention to improve mundane operations using IT has occasionally yielded a system with strategic qualities.

Strategic information systems combine two types of ideas: ideas for making potentially winning business decisions and ideas for harnessing information technology to implement the decisions. For an information system to be an SIS, two conditions must exist. First, the information system must serve an organizational goal rather than simply provide information; and second, the organization's IS unit must work with managers of other functional units (including marketing, finance, purchasing, human resources and so on) to pursue the organizational goal.

Creating an SIS

To develop an SIS, top management must be involved from initial consideration through development and implementation. In other words, the SIS must be part of the overall organizational strategic plan. There is always the danger that a new SIS might be considered the IS unit's exclusive property. However, to succeed, the project must be a corporate effort, involving all managers who use the system.

Table 2.2 presents questions that management should ask to determine whether to develop a new SIS. Executives meet to try to identify areas in which information can support a

Table 2.2 Questions to answer in a strategic information system idea-generating meeting

1 What would be the most effective way to gain an advantage?

2 Would more accessible or timely information to our employees, customers, or suppliers help establish a significant advantage? If so . . .

3 Can an information system be developed that provides more accessible and timely information?

4 Will the development effort be economically justified?
   - Can existing competitors afford to fund the development of a similar system?
   - How long will it take the competitors to build their own, similar system?
   - Can we make our system a moving target to the competition by constantly enhancing it, so that it always retains its superiority?

5 What is the risk of not developing such a system?

6 Are alternative means of achieving the same goals available, and if so, how do they compare with the advantages and disadvantages of a new SIS?

strategic goal. Only after completing the activities outlined in Table 2.2 will management be able to conceptualize an SIS that seizes an opportunity.

A word of caution regarding Question 4 in Table 2.2, the issue of economic justification of an SIS: an increasing number of researchers and practitioners conclude that estimating the financial benefits of information systems is extremely difficult. This difficulty is especially true of SISs. The purpose of these systems is not simply to reduce costs or increase output per employee; many create a whole new service or product. Some completely change the way an organization does business. Because so many fundamental business changes are involved, measuring the financial impact is difficult, if not impossible, even after implementation, let alone before. For example, if a bank is considering offering a full range of financial services via the Web, how can management know whether the move justifies the great cost of the special software? It is extremely difficult to estimate the success of such a bold approach in terms of how many new customers the bank would gain.

Reengineering and organizational change

Sometimes, to implement an SIS and achieve competitive advantage, organizations must rethink the entire way they operate. While brainstorming about strategic plans, management should ask: 'If we established this business unit again, from scratch, what processes would we implement and how?' The answer often leads to the decision to eliminate one set of operations and build others from the ground up. Changes such as these are called reengineering. Reengineering often involves adoption of new machinery and elimination of management layers. Frequently, information technology plays an important role in this process.

reengineering The process by which an organization takes a fresh look at a business process and reorganizes it to attain efficiency. Almost always, reengineering includes the integration of a new or improved information system.

Reengineering's goal is not to gain small incremental cost savings, but to achieve great efficiency leaps – of 100 per cent and even 1000 per cent. With that degree of improvement, a company often gains competitive advantage. Interestingly, a company that undertakes reengineering along with implementing a new SIS cannot always tell whether the SIS was successful. The reengineering process makes it impossible to determine how much each change contributed to the organization's improved position.

Implementation of an SIS requires a business to revamp processes – to undergo organizational change – to gain an advantage. For example, when General Motors Corp. (GM) decided to manufacture a new car that would compete with Japanese cars, it chose a different production process from that of its other cars. Management first identified goals that could make the new car successful in terms of how to build it and also how to deliver and service it. Realizing that none of its existing divisions could meet these goals because of their organizational structures, their cultures and their inadequate ISs, management established Saturn as an independent company with a completely separate operation.

Part of GM's initiative was to recognize the importance of Saturn dealerships in gaining competitive advantage. Through satellite communications, the new company gave dealers access to factory information. Clients could find out if, and exactly when, different cars with different features would be available.

CD TASK

Another feature of Saturn's SIS was improved customer service. Saturn embeds an electronic computer chip in the chassis of each car. The chip maintains a record of the car's technical details and the owner's name. When the car is serviced after the sale, new information is added to the chip. At their first service visit, many Saturn owners were surprised to be greeted by name as they rolled down their windows. While the quality of the car itself has been important to Saturn's success, the new SIS also played an important role. This technology was later copied by other car manufacturers.

Competitive advantage as a moving target

As you might have guessed, competitive advantage is not often long-lasting. In time, competitors imitate the leader and the advantage diminishes. So, the quest for innovative strategies must be dynamic. Corporations must continuously contemplate new ways to use information technology to their advantage. In a way, companies' jockeying for the latest competitive advantage is a lot like an arms race. Side A develops an advanced weapon, then side B develops a similar weapon that terminates the advantage of side A and so on.

In an environment where most information technology is available to all, SISs originally developed to create a strategic advantage quickly become an expected standard business practice. A prime example is the banking industry, where surveys indicate that increased IS expenditures did not yield long-range strategic advantages. The few banks that provided services such as ATMs and online banking once had a powerful strategic advantage, but now almost every bank provides these services.

A system can help a company sustain competitive advantage only if the company continuously modifies and enhances it, creating a moving target for competitors.

An Airline Reservation Systems (ARS) for travel agents is a classic example. American Airlines developed Sabre, an innovative IS, in the late 1970s to expedite airline reservations and sell travel agencies a new service. In 1976 United Airlines began installing its own ARS called Apollo into travel agencies themselves and American Airlines quickly followed. The cost savings in reducing call centre staff by getting the agents to make the booking themselves was too significant to ignore. Sabre surpassed Apollo in market share to take a dominant position, giving a return on investment (ROI) of more than 100 per cent in the late 1980s. The reservation system now encompasses hotel reservations, car rentals, train schedules, theatre tickets and limousine rentals. It later added a feature that let travellers use Sabre from their own computers. The system has been so successful that in its early years American earned more from it than from its airline operations. However, in the 1990s European airlines began developing their own reservation systems with Amadeus, owned jointly by Air France, Lufthansa, Iberia and SAS, being the market leader with a 27 per cent market share. Over the years the major players in the travel industry (airlines, traditional travel agents, tour operators, web-based travel companies) have been trying to get ahead of one another by the use of ISs and the fight goes on!

Industry SNAPSHOT

Keeping on track – A success story

TheTrainline was created by Virgin Trains in 1997 to sell rail tickets to UK destinations over the phone. In 1999 Virgin saw the potential of the Internet as a sales channel and launched TheTrainline website. The enhanced service to customers in the provision of timetable information as well as significant extra information on ticket prices and special deals was seen as an excellent way to gain competitive advantage.

The service was an immediate success and the company needed to add to its IT infrastructure to cope with demand. When the company formed alliances with other national rail companies such as Chiltern Railways and Southwest Trains as well as National Rail Enquiries, there was further growth in the company's IT support. The continued expansion of services and alliances lead to incremental growth in the IT systems but these were made in response to short-term business needs rather than a long-term, well planned strategy.

Robert Parkinson, Development Director, TheTrainline, says: 'We have grown very rapidly since the website's beginning and have become hugely successful. However, this has caused us to effect changes in an organic rather than structured fashion, which caused costs to rise. These issues are as a result of our success so are nice problems to have, but from a technical perspective they are genuine headaches.'

Therefore in 2002 the company commissioned Cap Gemini, the consultancy firm that originally created the website, to develop a plan for the migration from TheTrainline-evolved technology to a newer, more appropriate technology. The aim was to support growth, reduce maintenance costs and make site improvements easier. After considerable work on comparing alternative strategies, the company decided on a solution based around Microsoft .NET technology. System operation costs could be reduced by consolidating the number of servers from 180 machines to about 100 so there are fewer points of failure and hence increased reliability. However, the transition needed to be smooth and virtually imperceptible to the users. According to Parkinson, 'We chose this solution as it was worked out as the least risky and most cost-effective. It will enable us to transfer to the new platform gradually as we can neither afford nor countenance stopping our current system cold.'

However, it is not just in the web-based technology that TheTrainline is making strategic developments. The company have two contact centres based in Edinburgh and Dingwall, Scotland. These centres receive over 120,000 calls per week and sell train tickets worth more than £10 million per month. Although the centres were providing an essential personal service to customers, there was a need to investigate ways to make them operate more efficiently to reduce the cost per sale. One obvious way of reducing the costs is to reduce the one-to-one telephone conversations. The improvements made to the Internet-based service was one way but many customers still preferred to use the telephone. Traditional touch-tone technology is limited in the customer information that could be captured and certainly more appropriate for balance enquiries at a bank than for capturing complex travel requirements. However, something needed to be done, as 40 per cent of calls received an engaged tone, the average length of call was six minutes and 65 per cent of calls did not convert into a sale. In addition there was low morale and high turnover at the two sites.

Cable & Wireless, working with Cap Gemini, developed a system that enables a customer to use their telephone while minimizing the human operator's interaction. This is how it works:

- Calls are answered by an automated system that requests details of a planned journey (from/to, date, time, etc.). The customer responds naturally, as if speaking to a friend.

- Speech recognition software records the detail provided by the customer and feeds it into data format within the IT system.

- The 'demand' data then trigger automatic and virtually instant retrieval of all 'supply side' information (e.g. train times, seat availability, ticket prices) from rail industry databases.

- The data are sent to the screen of the appropriate sales agent and within a few seconds the customer call is patched through to that same agent, using Cable & Wireless's Intelligent Call

Manager (ICM) platform. The sale is confirmed person-to-person, payment details are taken and the transaction is completed.

Of course it was still important to make the automated part of the system friendly. A professional voice-over artist was commissioned to be the 'Voice of Virgin,' and the digitized recordings were embedded into the Cable & Wireless Advance Speech Recognition (ASR) system.

The system is even cleverer than that. Computer-telephony integration (CTI) checks the calling line identity (CLI) against a database of previous callers' CLIs. Returning callers are taken through a briefer menu than first-time callers and additionally the contact centre agent will have customer information displayed such as the caller's name, recent transactions and so on.

The benefits for TheTrainline have been huge:

● Overall operating costs have been reduced by 10 per cent, a saving of about a million pounds.

● Conversion rates for calls have increased with about 4,000 extra calls per week resulting in tickets being sold.

● Customer satisfaction has improved.

● Resource usage has improved, with CTI sharing the loading of calls and providing management reports.

According to Bill Hopkins, customer services director of TheTrainline, 'The improvement in TheTrainline contact centre infrastructure has led to significant benefits by improving the customer experience and in reducing our operating costs. As a consequence TheTrainline has been able to grow its business in a very competitive market place.'

SOURCE: http://www.cw.com/docs/why_cw/trainline.pdf 'Cable & Wireless contact centre puts TheTrainline back on track' and http://www.capgemini.com/resources/success-stories/capgemini_migration_strategy_will_help_thetrainline_to_reduce_maintenance_by_25/ 'Capgemini Migration Strategy Will Help TheTrainline to Reduce Maintenance by 25 per cent'

TheTrainline is the UK's leading independent retailer of train tickets with over 8.4 million registered users purchasing tickets for trips throughout the country.

We return again to Amazon as an example of how ISs help companies maintain competitive advantage. Management believes that it must add new features to its website to attract buyers over and over again. The company continuously improves its web pages' look and the online services it provides. Amazon has moved from merely selling books through the Web to providing best-seller lists, readers' reviews, authors' interviews; selling almost any consumer product imaginable including users' own unwanted items through its Marketplace. The constant improvements help the company maintain its dominant position in online retailing.

A line of JetBlue planes, illustrating the rapid growth the airline has enjoyed since it was established in 2000.

JetBlue: A success story

We usually expect entrepreneurs to enter a new and profitable industry, not an old, money-losing one. However, with the proper technology and management methods, it seems that some energetic people can gain strategic advantage where others have been hurting. The US airline industry has seen mainly bad times since the industry's deregulation in the 1970s. Things got worse in the beginning of the third millennium and even worse after the terrible events of September 11, 2001. In 2001, the industry lost US$7.7 billion, but JetBlue had a profit of US$38.5 million on revenue of US$320.4 million. It continued to be profitable in 2002, 2003 and 2004 along with only one other US airline, Southwest Airlines, while all other US carriers had losses. Its revenues grew from US$998.4 in 2003 to US$1.27 billion in 2004.

JetBlue was established in February 2000 by David Neeleman, who serves as its CEO. Two decades earlier, in 1984, Neeleman cofounded Morris Air, a small airline in Salt Lake City, Utah, which was the first airline to offer ticketless travel, a programme that was developed inside the company. With a college student he developed Open Skies, a computer program that integrates electronic ticketing, Internet reservations and revenue management. Revenue management tools help an airline plan the most profitable routes and ticket pricing. Morris Air was sold to Southwest Airlines, which enthusiastically adopted the e-ticket idea. Neeleman became an executive at Southwest but left in frustration, because he believed that an airline could achieve much more efficiency with information technology. Now JetBlue has gained a great strategic advantage over larger and older airlines. The company's success is the result of understanding customers' priorities and gaining great efficiencies through automating whatever IT can automate. Management also learned to break away from practices that inhibit efficiency and agility. In a highly competitive industry that traditionally has had a narrow profit margin, JetBlue managed to gain strategic advantage by *reducing cost* and therefore reducing the price to the customer; and *improving a service*, especially in terms of on-time departures and arrivals.

Massive automation

We usually think of manufacturing organizations when mentioning automation, but great benefits can also be gained by automating services. JetBlue uses Open Skies, the software that Neeleman developed. It is a combination reservation system and accounting system which also supports customer service and sales tracking. The company avoids travel agents. Booking a flight through a travel agent costs airlines US$20 per ticket. JetBlue saves office space rent and electricity by using reservation agents who work from home (telecommuting is discussed in Chapter 5) and use VoIP (Voice over Internet Protocol, also discussed in Chapter 5) for telephoning. The company pays a flat fee of US$25 per telephone line per month for these telecommuting agents. This reduces its handling cost per ticket to US$4.50.

Because all tickets are electronic, there is no paper handling or expense. JetBlue encourages customers to purchase their tickets online and more than 79 per cent of them do so, saving the company much labour. The cost of handling a ticket ordered via the Web is reduced

CD TASK

to only 50 cents, as opposed to US$4.50 paid to a reservation agent and a far cry from the US$20 a booking through a travel agent.

JetBlue automates other aspects of running an airline as well. Its maintenance workers use a maintenance information system from Dash Group to log all airplane parts and their time cycles, that is, when the parts must be replaced and where they can be found. The system reduces manual tracking costs.

Flight planning to maximize yield – the number of seats occupied on a flight – is executed on a flight-planning application from Bornemann Associates. It reduces planning costs and makes operations more efficient. JetBlue also uses an application that its team of 58 IT professionals developed in-house, called Blue Performance. It tracks operational data that is updated flight by flight. The company's intranet enables its 2800 employees to access the performance data. Managers have up-to-the-minute metrics, so critical in airline operations, which enable them to respond immediately to problems.

When on the ground, employees use wireless devices to report and respond to any irregular event, from weather delays to passenger injuries. The response is quick and the events are recorded in a database for later analysis.

CD TASK

When training pilots and other employees, no paper records are kept. An aviation training management system provides a database to track each employee's training record. It is easy to update and efficient for record retrieval.

Away from tradition

The company decided not to use the hub-and-spokes method of routing its airplanes, a method used by all major airlines. Instead of having its airplanes land in one or two hubs and undergo maintenance there before taking off for the next leg of a route, it simply uses the most profitable routes between any two cities. All flights are point to point – no hubs, no spokes.

JetBlue was the first airline to establish paperless cockpits. The Federal Aviation Authority (FAA) mandates that pilots and other air crew members have access to flight manuals. The manuals are the documents showing information about each flight, including route, weight and how the weight is spread on board, fuel quantity and even details such as how many pets are on board. Other airlines update their manuals and then print them after every update. All JetBlue flight manuals are centrally maintained and the pilots and first officers access and update the manuals on laptop computers that they carry into the cockpit. As soon as the data have been entered, employees have access to the information.

The laptops enable the pilots and first officers to calculate the weight and balance of their plane with a few keystrokes instead of relying on dispatchers at headquarters to do the calculations for them. JetBlue saves paper and time by having employees enter flight data. The company subscribes to SharePoint, a web-based portal that enables electronic updates to flight manuals. This cuts 15 to 20 minutes from preflight preparations for every flight. The result is a saving of about 4800 hours per year and planes that take off and land on time.

JetBlue continues to harness IT to maintain the strategic gap between it and its competitors. Management planned a paperless frequent flier programme, cockpit-monitoring cameras transmitting through satellites so that ground crews can monitor activity and biometric applications in airport terminals. Biometrics use physical characteristics of people, such as fingerprints and retina scans, for authentication and access to physical places and online information systems. Biometrics are more secure than access codes. The IT team is also developing a new reservation system that will have features no other airline reservation system has.

Enhanced service

Much of the technology that helps JetBlue employees provide better service is invisible to the customers, but it also has some more obvious winning features. JetBlue offers leather seats and individual real-time television on all its airplanes. Other airlines do not offer such seats on economy class and offer only recorded television programmes. The real-time TV service is offered under a contract with DirecTV.

Its use of IT technologies also placed the airline at the top of the list for on-schedule departures and arrivals, a service that is very important, especially to business travellers. Perhaps even better, JetBlue ranks at the top as having the fewest mishandled bags. Thanks to constant updates to the Open Skies system, the company has managed to maintain check-in time at less than one minute. When passengers arrive at JetBlue's terminal at JFK airport, they are directed by a large LCD display with a computer-generated voice telling them which window is available to serve them. Usually, checking baggage takes 45 seconds. When passengers arrive at their destination, they do not have to wait for their suitcases. Their electronically tagged suitcases wait for them at the baggage claim area.

Because of heightened security awareness, management decided to install hidden video cameras in the cabin and monitors in the cockpit. Technicians used the DirecTV wires to add the cameras and monitors. Customers are more comfortable knowing of this extra step to enhance their safety.

Impressive performance

The most important metric in the airline industry is cost per available seat-mile (CASM), which is how much it costs to fly a passenger one mile of the journey. JetBlue has been able to maintain the lowest or next-to-lowest CASM in its first three years of operations. While its competitors' CASM is 11 cents or higher, JetBlue's CASM is less than 7 cents. While its competitors fill only 71 per cent of seats, JetBlue fills 78 per cent.

Late mover advantage

Some observers cite the fact that JetBlue is a late competitor as an important factor in its success. The company is not burdened with antiquated information systems, or as IT professionals like to call them, legacy systems. This allowed its CIO, Jeff Cohen, to implement the latest available technologies: fast databases, VoIP, a slick website, laptop computers with the latest algorithms for fast calculation of routes and loads in the cockpit and other technologies. This situation illustrates the strategic advantage of the late mover.

late mover An organization that adopts a technology or method after competitors have adopted it.

JetBlue executives quip that while other airlines run on fuel, theirs runs on information technology. Cohen said that up to 40 per cent of the software the company was using was beta or new software. Beta software is software that the developer gives to potential adopters for trial use. Talk about being on the cutting – and possibly bleeding – edge! Yet, competitors have taken notice. Delta Airlines established a subsidiary called Delta Song. The organization mimics many of JetBlue's innovations, including live TV. Similarly, United Airlines created a nimble subsidiary airline called Ted to compete with JetBlue.

Ford on the Web: A failure story

Sometimes what seems to be a great, forward-looking strategic move ends up as a colossal failure. It might be because of lack of attention to details or simply because the innovator could not predict the response of customers or business partners. Such was the great initiative

Industry SNAPSHOT

A healthy IT strategy? – A not so successful story

'Securing Our Future Health: Taking A Long-Term View' – an independent review by Derek Wanless in 2002 for the UK Treasury, concluded that the government would need to devote more resources to health care in order to meet people's expectations. In particular, there should be a spending equivalent to 4 per cent of the National Health Service (NHS) turnover on business-related IT.

However, it seems, according to a British Computer Society (BCS) report in December 2006, this necessary spending is not leading to the benefits that are needed. Many NHS staff see the National Programme for Information Technology (NPfIT) as of little relevance rather than, as the NHS believes, a key enabler of essential business change.

The BCS Health Informatics Forum (BCSHIF) is made up of experts in the field of IT in health. It brings together IT experts, academics, users, suppliers and patients. According to the chair of BCSHIF, Dr Glyn Hayes, 'IT enables change, is sometimes a catalyst for change, but it is not an end in itself. This misconception has been a prime cause of large-scale IT project failure since computers first became commonplace. The problem has

been heightened by NPfIT's top-down nature; the patchy reflection of NHS requirements in the procurements in 2002; and the subsequent changes in those requirements to meet the Government's NHS reform programme. We believe that this is one reason why so many NHS staff have yet to see NPfIT as a key enabler of business change and it has thus discouraged the local ownership of NPfIT implementations.'

Dr Hayes added, 'Instead of the current monolithic systems intended to meet most of the needs of users in a local health community, we need a range and choice of more innovative and agile solutions contributing to a common purpose, encouraged within national standards to deliver functionality in whatever way suits the users and suppliers. This should not be interpreted as ruling out adoption of local server provider (LSP) products where they fit the business requirements.'

It seems that money alone will not make an IT strategy. There needs to be sensible spending with support at all levels of the organization, the involvement of users and 'joined-up thinking' in making IT work for you.

SOURCE: http://www.itpro.co.uk/news/100099/bcs-calls-for-major-changes-to-nhs-it-strategy.html, 'BCS calls for major changes to NHS IT strategy', Maggie Holland, ITPro

of Jacques Nasser, the former CEO of Ford Motor Company, the second largest US car manufacturer.

The ideas

When Nasser was appointed CEO of Ford in 1999, he regarded himself as an agent of change. He was eager to push the company into the Web, which was then at the height of its hype as a commercial vehicle. 'We are now measuring speed in gigahertz, not horsepower', he said at the 2000 North American International Auto Show in Detroit. The concept cars sported, among other innovations, mobile Internet access. Ford Motor Co., he said, would put the Internet on wheels.

Ford launched Wingcast telematics, devices that would be installed in the company's vehicles and enable drivers and passengers to access the Web. To this end the company formed an alliance with Qualcomm Inc., a telecommunications company and Yahoo!

CD TASK

Ford created a joint venture with General Motors Corp. and DaimlerChrysler to establish Covisint, a website that serves as an electronic market for parts suppliers who can bid online on requests for proposals posted by the car manufacturers. Although not announced this way, the manufacturers' hope was that suppliers would fiercely compete in an open bidding process and cut their prices dramatically, so the car companies could enjoy cost cuts. This was the business-to-business (B2B) part of Nassers's grand plan.

The business-to-consumer (B2C) idea was bolder: Ford wanted to push vehicle sales to the Web. Nasser wanted to bypass dealerships and retail the vehicles online directly to consumers. Consumers would go to the website, take a virtual test-drive, see images of a vehicle in all its available colours, order a vehicle, pay for it online and then have it driven to their door. Ford would not only provide a great service but also save the dealer fees. The company called the site FordDirect.com. A special organizational unit, ConsumerConnect, was established to build the website and handle the direct sales.

Hitting the wall

Apparently, buyers were not as enthusiastic about having web access in their vehicles as Nasser predicted. In June 2001, Ford eliminated the Wingcast project. The B2B effort, Covisint, works and now includes more manufacturers, such as the French company Renault and the Japanese company Nissan. The B2C initiative failed.

The failure was not the result of faulty technology. There are excellent web technologies that would support retail through the Web. There is no reason why a car cannot be selected, paid for and delivered (with the help of companies that specialize in such delivery from the manufacturer to the buyer) via the Web. The company failed because it did not carefully consider US state laws and its relationships with dealers.

Many US state laws do not permit cutting an agent out of the sale. State franchising laws did not allow Ford to bypass its dealers. Also, since Ford would still rely on dealers to sell cars to people who do not have access to the Internet or who like to sit in a physical car and test-drive it, it could not cut the relationship all at once. Ford still needed the collaboration of the dealers, if it could overcome the legal hurdles, in order for direct sales to take off.

The retreat

The circumstances convinced Ford to abandon its plan to sell directly to consumers. The ConsumerConnect unit was disbanded. FordDirect.com is now operated jointly by Ford and its 3900 Ford and Lincoln Mercury dealerships. The site helps consumers find the vehicles they want, but they then have to find a dealer close to their homes who can deliver the vehicle. Like any car dealer, the site also offers used cars for sale, which is not what Ford would like to do. The price tag of this failed experiment was reported to be a hefty portion of the US$1 billion Ford spent on its Internet initiative under Nasser's leadership.

Ford's management can find some solace in the continued operation of FordDirect.com. Although the grand plan did not materialize, the site is the origin point of 10,000 sales transactions per month. Ford reported that it sold 100,000 vehicles through the website in 2001 and that 60 per cent of those transactions would not even have started had the site not existed. The monthly sales through the website have increased since. In April 2005 the site generated sales of 22,500 new vehicles.

Some observers say that Ford's focus on the Internet was at times greater than on making cars. While other car manufacturers were making modest profits in the period from 2000 to 2001, Ford had losses. Nasser was forced to leave the company.

Ethical and Societal ISSUES

Size matters

At what point do the public and the courts start to consider a successful strategy as a predatory, unfair business practice that makes competition from other businesses impossible, even if their products are better? For instance, should a firm that takes bold entrepreneurial steps to become a business leader be curbed when it succeeds in becoming powerful? Several court cases against Microsoft, the software industry leader, have focused on these questions. However, the questions are not simply legal issues. They are also important because they impact the economy and, as a result, society.

Historical background In the 1970s, Microsoft was a small software company headed by its young president, Bill Gates, who established the company at age 19. The company was fortunate to find and buy an operating system from a small company in Seattle, Washington, for US$50,000. An operating system (OS) is the software program that 'mediates' between any computer program and the computer. Every application is developed with a particular operating system, or several operating systems, in mind. To a great extent, the operating system determines which applications a computer can run. Therefore, it is an extremely important program. We discuss operating systems and other types of software in Chapter 4, 'Business Hardware and Software'.

So, people who purchased a computer had to consider the OS to determine which applications they could run on their computer. After Microsoft bought the operating system, it entered into a contract with IBM, the most powerful computer manufacturer at that time. IBM needed an operating system for its new creation, the IBM PC and they chose Microsoft's DOS (Disk Operating System). While Microsoft did not make much money on the IBM deal, its executives realized the strategic potential of contracting with 'the big guy'.

Indeed, the strategy paid off. Soon, Compaq (now part of Hewlett-Packard) and many other manufacturers started to market IBM PC clones, cheaper computers that performed as well as IBM PCs and could run the same operating system and applications. Because Microsoft's contract with IBM allowed it to sell DOS to other parties, it made a fortune selling DOS to Compaq and others. Later, Microsoft developed Windows, an improved operating system and the success story repeated itself. To this day, the majority of buyers of personal computers also buy a copy of some version of Windows.

One major key to gaining a decent share of the new Internet market was the widespread use of web browsers. In the mid-1990s, more than 80 per cent of web surfers used Netscape's browsers. Netscape (now part of AOL) was a young, entrepreneurial company selling innovative products. Microsoft decided to increase its own browser's market share of about 15 per cent to a leading position. If a great number of people used its browser, Microsoft could expect hefty sales of related software, such as server management applications.

Controversial practices No one would deny that Microsoft's attempt to compete in the browser market was legitimate. While Netscape gave its browsers away to individuals and educational institutions but charged for-profit organizations, Microsoft gave its browser to everyone free of charge. Also, the company took advantage of Windows dominance; it started bundling its browser with Windows, practically forcing any PC maker who wanted to sell the machines with the operating system installed to also install Internet Explorer (IE). The great majority of new PC owners used IE without even trying any other browser.

The German headquarters of software giant Microsoft near Munich. Microsoft Germany is the largest European subsidiary of the U.S. corporation.

Within two years, a majority of web surfers were using IE. But Netscape, the US Department of Justice and many individuals considered Microsoft's tactics unfair. Microsoft used its muscle in the operating system market to compel sellers of personal computers to include a copy of Internet Explorer with Windows. Furthermore, the browser was inseparable from the newer Windows version, Windows 98. Since sellers had to include Windows on every machine and because it is practically the only operating system most buyers would accept, sellers had no choice but to succumb to the pressure. The US Department of Justice and the Attorneys General of several states filed lawsuits claiming Microsoft violated fair trade practices. Subsequently, legal authorities in other countries, such as the European Union (EU) and Taiwan, also either probed the company or sued it. In 2004, the EU's antitrust office fined Microsoft 497 million euros (US$665 million) for abusively wielding Windows' monopoly and for locking competitors out of the software market. Meanwhile, as competition in the digital audio and video media increased, Microsoft bundled its Media Player software with the Windows OS. In 2002, the US Department of Justice settled with Microsoft on this issue, requiring the company only to enable users to hide Media Player and set another application as the default player. The EU demanded that Microsoft sell Windows without Media Player.

It also demanded that the company allow all software developers access to information about Windows, so that they could develop applications that would compete well with Microsoft's own applications. The EU claimed that developers of nonproprietary software (software that is not owned by anyone and can be used free of charge) were denied access to the Windows information altogether. If the company did not stop these practices, the EU threatened it with additional fines reaching 5 per cent of the company's daily worldwide sales revenue until the company complied with the EU's demands.

Contrary to public perception, the United States, the European Union and many other countries do not outlaw monopolies. They only forbid unfair use of monopolistic power. Because anyone may compete in any market, it would be unfair to punish an entrepreneur for marketing unique products and mustering market power of any magnitude. Of concern in the eyes of US law, for example, are two issues: (1) have any unfair practices helped the company gain monopolistic power and (2) does the monopolistic situation serve customers well, or does it hurt them?

Up side, down side Microsoft argues that although it could charge higher prices for Windows, it has not, because it wants to make Windows affordable to all. Microsoft also argues that, unlike typical monopolists, it invests huge amounts of money in research and development, which eventually benefit society in the form of better and less-expensive products. Microsoft's rivals in the software industry claim that Microsoft's practices stifle true competition. Both claims are difficult to measure. Some observers argue that allowing the same company to develop operating systems and many applications is good for consumers: the applications are compatible with each other; all use the same interface of menus and icons. Others suggest that Microsoft should be broken into two organizations; one that develops operating systems and another that develops only applications and competes fairly in that market. And some organizations and individuals simply fear the great power that a single person, Bill Gates, holds in an industry that so greatly impacts our economy and society. What is your opinion? What would you do about this issue?

The bleeding edge

As you might often hear, huge rewards go to whoever first implements a new idea. Innovators might enjoy a strategic advantage until competitors discover the benefits of a new business idea or a new technology. However, taking such steps before competitors have tested a system involves great risk. In some cases, failure results from rushing implementation without adequately testing a market. But even with careful planning, pioneers sometimes get burned.

For example, several supermarket chains tried self-checkout stations in the mid-1990s. Consumers were expected to ring up their own purchases. By and large, investment in such devices failed not because the technology was bad, but because many consumers either preferred the human touch, or because they did not want to learn how to correct mistakes when the devices did not pick up the price of an item or picked it up twice. Recently, machines that are more user friendly and less error prone have been installed by several chains and consumers have been more willing to use them.

While it is tempting to take the lead, the risk of business failure is quite high. Several organizations have experienced disasters with new business ideas, which are only magnified when implementing new technology. When failure occurs because an organization tries to be on the technological leading edge, observers call it the bleeding edge. The pioneering organization 'bleeds' cash on a technology that increases costs instead of profits. Adopting a new technology involves great risk: there is no experience from which to learn, no guarantees that the technology will work well and no certainty that customers and employees will welcome it.

bleeding edge The situation in which a business fails because it tries to be on the technological leading edge.

Being on the bleeding edge often means that implementation costs are significantly more than anticipated, that the new technology does not work as well as expected, or that the parties who were supposed to benefit – employees, customers or suppliers – do not like using it. Thus, instead of leading, the organization ends up bleeding, that is, suffering from high cost and lost market share. For this reason, some organizations decide to let competitors test new technology before they adopt it. They risk losing the initial rewards they might reap, but if a competitor succeeds, they can quickly adopt the technology and even try to use it better than the pioneering organization.

Microsoft generally takes this approach. It seizes an existing idea, improves it and promotes the result with its great marketing power. For instance, the company did not invent word processing, but Word is the most popular word-processing application today. The company did not invent the electronic spreadsheet, but Excel is the most popular spreadsheet application. And Microsoft was not the first to introduce a PC database management application, but it sells the highly popular Access. The company joined the Internet rush late, but it developed and gave away Internet Explorer, a web browser that competed with the highly popular Netscape Navigator and now dominates the market (in part because it was given free to everyone, including for-profit businesses). You might call this approach competing by emulating and improving, rather than competing by being on the leading edge.

Sometimes, companies wait quite a long time to ensure that a technology has matured before they start using it, even at the risk of diminishing their strategic position. Although data warehousing – the organization and summarization of huge amounts of transactional records for later analysis – has been around since the mid-1990s, The Home Depot, Inc., decided only in 2002 to build a data warehouse. Home Depot is the world's largest home improvement retailer. It started the project years after its main rival in the United States, Lowe's, had implemented a well-functioning data warehouse, which it used effectively for strategic decision-making.

SUMMARY

Some ISs have become strategic tools as a result of strategic planning; others have evolved into strategic tools. To compete in the market, executives need to define strategic goals and determine whether new or improved ISs can support these goals. Rather than waiting complacently until a problem occurs, businesses actively look for opportunities to improve their position with information systems.

An IS that helps gain strategic advantage is called a strategic information system (SIS). To assure optimal utilization of IT for competitive advantage, executives must participate in generating ideas and champion new, innovative uses of information systems. In recent years, many of these ideas involved using the Internet.

A company achieves strategic advantage by using strategy to maximize its strengths, resulting in a competitive advantage.

Strategic advantage is often achieved by one or a combination of the following initiatives. Cost reduction enables a business to sell more units of its products or services while maintaining or increasing its profit margin. Raising barriers to potential entrants to the industry lets an organization maintain a sizeable market share by developing systems that are prohibitively expensive for competitors to emulate. By establishing high switching costs, a business can make buying from competitors unattractive to clients. Developing totally new products and services can create an entirely new market for an organization, which can also enjoy the advantage of being a first mover for that product and market. And if the organization cannot create new products or services, it can still enjoy competitive advantage by differentiating its products so that customers view them as better than a competitor's products. Organizations also attain advantage by enhancing existing products or services. Many new services are the fruits of alliances between companies: each contributes its own expertise to package services that entice customers with an overall value greater than that offered by the separate services individually. Locking in clients or suppliers, that is, creating conditions that make dealing with competitors infeasible is a powerful strategy to gain advantage.

In the software industry, creating standards often creates strategic advantage. A standard is an application used by a significant share of the users. To this end, many companies go as far as giving software away. When the standard has been established, the company enjoys a large sales volume of compatible and add-on software. Microsoft, the software giant, has been found guilty of using unfair trade practices in trying to establish standards and squash competitors.

Reengineering is the process of designing a business process from scratch to achieve hundreds of percentage points in improvement rates. Almost always, reengineering involves implementing new ISs.

Strategic advantages from information systems are often short-lived, because competitors quickly emulate the systems for their own benefit. Therefore, looking for new opportunities must be an ongoing process.

To maintain a strategic advantage, organizations must develop new features to keep the system on the leading edge. But they must be mindful of the bleeding edge, the undesirable results (such as huge ongoing costs and loss of customers) of being the first to use new technology with the hope of establishing a competitive advantage. Early adopters find themselves on the bleeding edge when the new technology is not yet fully reliable or when customers are uncomfortable with it.

BETTER BITES REVISITED

As you have seen in the continuing story of Better Bites, the three young entrepreneurs have gained experience, used information systems to research options and instituted changes to remain profitable and expand their business. They also face some new opportunities and challenges for the strategic direction of their business. The next section explores some of their strategic initiatives to see whether you think they can make improvements.

What would you do?

Through their alliance with the shopping centre owner, Better Bites has increased its business to three lunch carts. From the case at the beginning of the chapter, identify some strategic moves the three have already made to help them compete. Have any of their partners operated strategically? How? Be sure to consider these ways to gain a competitive advantage:

- Reduce costs.
- Raise barriers to entrants.
- Establish high switching costs.
- Create new products and services.
- Differentiate products and services.

- Enhance products or services.
- Establish alliances.
- Lock in suppliers or buyers.

Review the decision that Paul, Sarah and Christina made not to pursue organic labels for their food. Was this decision correct, in your opinion? What further information could they use to monitor the organic food market in the future?

New perspectives

Operating from a new kitchen space and becoming a crisp manufacturer offers Paul, Sarah and Christina the opportunity to rethink completely their food preparation processes – to reengineer. Think of some options the three can pursue in redesigning their food preparation for both their lunch business and crisp manufacturing. Consider how the changes can help them compete effectively.

With the Subwich franchise as a new competitor to the pushcart lunch business, Paul, Sarah and Christina need to monitor costs and profits closely and they need to keep making changes to remain competitive. They already have a loyal customer base. How can they use their existing information systems to compete effectively against Subwich? Suggest at least three ways to help them compete. Would a website help them at all? Why or why not?

Review questions

1 In what respect does business strategy resemble military strategy?

2 What should an information system achieve for an organization in order for it to be considered a strategic information system?

3 What strategic goal can an IS attain that does not involve wresting market share from competitors?

4 What conditions must exist in an organization planning an SIS?

5 Sometimes it is difficult to convince top management to commit funds to develop and implement an SIS. Why?

6 An SIS often offers a corporation short-lived advantages. How so?

7 What is reengineering? What does it have to do with IT?

8 Software developers have made great efforts to 'create a standard'. What does creating a standard mean in the software industry and why are companies doing it?

9 What should an organization do to sustain the strategic benefits of an IS?

10 Adobe encourages PC users to download its Acrobat Reader free of charge. Macromedia encourages people to download its Flash player free of charge. How does this eventually

help them strategically? If they give the application away, how does their generosity help them make money?

11 Referring to the list of strategic moves (see Figure 2.2), classify the initiatives of JetBlue.

12 What were the reasons for the failure of FordDirect.com?

13 The executives of well-established airlines are not less smart than those at JetBlue and yet, their larger companies have not done what JetBlue has done. Why?

14 What does the term 'first mover' mean?

15 Can a *late mover* have any strategic advantage with IT? What is the risk that a late mover takes?

16 What does the term 'bleeding edge' mean?

Discussion questions

1 Can an off-the-shelf computer program be used as an SIS? Why or why not?

2 The organizations that eventually use the systems, not consulting firms, develop more successful SISs. What might be the reasons for this?

3 You head a small company. You have an idea for software that can give your company an advantage over competitors. Since you do not have staff that can develop and implement the software, you decide to approach a software company. Other than the technical requirements, what should you desire of the software company?

4 Some argue that an SIS gives a company an unfair advantage and might even cause the demise of smaller, weaker companies that cannot afford to build similar systems. Is this good or bad for customers? Explain your opinion.

5 Why has the Web been the arena of so much competition in recent years?

6 ISs play a major role in almost every reengineering project. Why?

7 Accounting and payroll ISs have never become SISs. Why? What other types of ISs are unlikely to ever gain their owners' strategic advantage?

8 Ford's CEO envisaged a future in which consumers log on to a car manufacturer's

website, design their cars online, wait for the cars to be manufactured (design transformed into electronic blueprints) and have the car delivered to their door. Do you think we will see this in practice within the next decade? Why, or why not?

9 Give two examples of other products or services whose delivery time could be cut from days to minutes with the aid of IT.

10 What is the role of ISs in alliances such as airlines and credit-card issuers? Why would such alliances be practically infeasible without IT?

11 Many companies use new software that has not been tested by other companies. If you were a Chief Information Officer (CIO), would you use software that is still in beta (untested with live data) in your organization?

12 You are an executive for a large organization that provides services to local government. A software development firm approached you with an offer to implement new software that might give your organization a strategic advantage by reducing the service delivery cycle by several days. What would you do to avoid putting your organization on the 'bleeding edge' while still considering the new software?

13 When a software developer creates a *de facto* standard (i.e., not the official standard, but something so widely used that it becomes a standard), it has monopolistic power. Should governments intervene to prevent this practice? Explain your opinion.

14 Suppose you are a venture capitalist considering a proposal to invest a significant amount of money in a new online business. What questions would you ask the enthusiastic young people who have approached you for funds?

15 What are the potential risks of a single organization controlling much of the market of essential software?

Tutorial activities

1 Use a literature search program to find a news story on a strategic information system. Write a short report that explains: (a) the industry in which the business competes, (b) the function(s) of the system and (c) how the system gives the company strategic advantage. For (c), identify the type of strategic move that the organization made from the list provided in Figure 2.1. Suggest how the company might improve the system to maintain its advantage in the future, when competitors mimic the system. Alternatively, find a story on a new business model. In your write-up explain (a) the term 'business model', (b) the particular business model you found and (c) how information systems support this business model.

2   Prepare a brief essay that includes an example of each of the following strategic moves: raising barriers to entrants (*Hint*: intellectual property), establishing high switching costs, creating a new product or service (*Hint*: the Web) and establishing alliances. The examples do not necessarily have to involve IT. Do not use examples already presented in the text. You may use examples from actual events or your own suggestions, but the examples must be practical.

3   A publishing company is contemplating publishing electronic books on small CDs. To read the discs, users will need a device called an electronic book reader. At least two firms have developed e-book technologies that the publisher can adopt. The publisher hires you as a strategic consultant. Write a report explaining the strategic moves you suggest. What would you advise the company to do: try to develop its own e-book reader or purchase a licence for existing technology? Who should be the initial target audience for the product? What should be the company's major goal in the first two or three years: profit, market share, user base, technological improvement, or perhaps having the largest salesforce in this industry? Should the company give anything away? Prepare a detailed report enumerating and explaining your suggestions.

4   You are a software-marketing expert. A new software development firm has hired you to advise it on pricing and marketing strategies of its new application. After some research, you conclude that the firm can be successful either by selling at a high unit price (in which case, probably only businesses would purchase licences to use the application), or at a very low

price, which would be attractive to many individuals and companies. You estimate that by the end of the sixth year of the marketing effort, competing software will be offered, which will bring the number of units sold to zero. For alternative A, the price would be €400 per licence and you expect 500 adopters in the first year and an annual growth of adopters of 70 per cent. For alternative B, the price would be €30 and you expect 600,000 adopters in the first year and an annual growth of adopters of 4 per cent. Use a spreadsheet application to calculate revenue and tell the firm which strategy is expected to bring in greater revenue. Enter the prices and number of first-year adopters for each alternative only once, each in a single cell and use absolute referencing to those cells.

5   Use PowerPoint or other presentation software to present the ideas you generated in Question 1 or 2 above. Use the program's best features to make a convincing and visually pleasing presentation.

6   Do a library or web search of business journals and magazines such as the *Wall Street Journal*, *BusinessWeek*, *Forbes* or *Fortune*. Find a story on a business's strategic use of data, information, or information systems. (*Note*: The writer might not have identified the strategic use, but you might find that the use served strategic goals.) Prepare a report explaining the opportunity seized. Did the organization create a new product or service, improve one, or manage to capture a significantly greater market share of an existing product or service? How did the data, information or information system play a major role in the strategic move?

7   Consider the information provided in the 'Ethical and Societal Issues' box of this chapter. Prepare two extensive lists, pros and cons. The pros should aim to convince an audience why Microsoft, or a similar company, should be left alone to practise its business manoeuvres. The cons should aim to convince an audience why governments should intervene in how corporations such as Microsoft behave and explain what such interventions are meant to accomplish.

8   Brainstorm with your team to answer the question: 'Which information technology over the past two years has epitomized a unique product or service that was "ahead of the curve" for a significant amount of time?' This

might be a physical product using IT or an online service that was, or still is, unique. List the reasons each of the team members liked this product or service so much.

9 Some information technologies had a certain original purpose but were creatively used to serve additional purposes. For example, companies have used caller ID to retrieve customer records as soon as a customer telephones. This saves labour and increases service quality. You and your teammates are consultants who work with many businesses. Offering your clients original ideas will increase your success. Select an information technology or IT feature that can be used in ways not originally conceived. How can your clients (in manufacturing, service or any other business sector) use this feature to gain strategic advantage? Prepare a rationale.

10 Someone suggested that you and your teammates establish the first web cemetery for pets. Obviously, you cannot bury any pets there, but there might be other services you can offer. Prepare a written plan that describes what you would offer, what you would charge for different features and how you can sustain your strategic

position if traditional pet cemeteries go online. (*Note*: There might be some online pet cemeteries. Assume there are none.)

Companion CD questions

1 Clear the cookies from your computer. Visit Amazon.co.uk or another e-commerce site listed in this chapter. Browse the site and click on items you might buy and add them to your cart. Don't actually make a purchase. Open the cookie file on your computer. How many cookies did the site put on your computer?

2 How can Excel's goal seek function be used in strategic planning? Give an example.

Video questions

1 Do some research to determine how big the potential market for this product is. Who are its competitors (think about products that are designed to do similar things (e.g., prevent car theft) but may not be a direct competitor)?

2 Name three companies whose products or services might be potential strategic alliances with this product.

From ideas to application
REAL CASES

Case study 2.1

Screwfix

BY SCOTT RAEBURN

Screwfix is a retail phenomenon in Britain. At one point, the managers were told 'You can't sell screws over the Internet!' But they have – to the tune of £260 million in 2005/6. Admittedly, it is now screws, other building materials and tools, but Screwfix are the third largest online retailer in the UK after Amazon and Tesco.

The start back in 1981 was inauspicious. Jon Goddard-Watts bought a small company which sold

wood screws. The Woodscrew Supply Company sold its products through *Exchange & Mart*, a UK weekly magazine dedicated to advertising supplies for DIY and small business (as well as allowing individuals to sell their own goods). Over the next ten years or so, JGW and family added another two small businesses. The big change came in 1993, when the company became Screwfix Direct and set up a telephone ordering centre in Yeovil in southwest England. Turnover doubled every year from then until 1999. By then it had 470 staff, was handling 15,000 orders per week and had set up its first website. Professional managers had been brought in two years previously and had helped make the company 'e-commerce ready'.

The potential for growth in Internet sales made the company, selling a range of very basic products, part of the 'dotcom' boom. But like all growing companies, more investment was needed. The original founder and his family decided to sell to the highest bidder, a process won by the Kingfisher Group. JGW and family netted £60 million from the sale. Kingfisher were well known in the City as national and international retailers, with Woolworths, Comet and B&Q part of the group. Indeed many analysts at the time expected Screwfix Direct to become part of B&Q, a very large chain of DIY stores. But Screwfix Direct retained its independence within the Group and flourished via its telephone and online sales. David Cox, Screwfix CEO since 1997, said: 'This is a fantastic success story. Our takings have doubled every year for the last six years. With Kingfisher's resources behind us, we'll be able to expand even faster.'

Screwfix Direct continued to develop its product range, building experience in selling via the Internet and advertising to its target customers – DIY and small builders – in a range of innovative ways. One involved an ad campaign with posters in male toilets in motorway service stations. It's not recorded how successful this was, or indeed what their female customers thought.

By 2003 Screwfix Direct had 1 million customers and sales of £187 million. More importantly, the number of orders handled per week was growing inexorably,

having trebled since 1999. Those familiar with the map of the UK will realize that Yeovil (in the southwest of England) is not an ideal place to have a UK-wide distribution centre promising next working day delivery anywhere on mainland Britain. Getting the stock down there, well away from major ports and 30 miles from the nearest motorway was bad enough. Getting orders despatched to the bulk of the population in the southeast, Midlands and north of England was more difficult and costly. A distribution centre in Leicester in the East Midlands had been set up a couple of years earlier but now more was needed.

It was decided to create a new distribution centre at Stoke-on-Trent in the Midlands of England. Midway between Birmingham and Manchester and just off the M6 motorway in the west Midlands, it was much nearer its customer base. Such a move, however, meant that the warehouse staff in Yeovil would be redundant – Stoke is almost 200 miles away and relocation for most would not be an option. In mid-2004 the Yeovil warehouse closed down with the loss of 500 jobs. The Stoke distribution centre took over but had problems recruiting and training staff. This caused many problems and by September that year deliveries were being affected. Screwfix took the decision to close the main website and call centre for a week to control the flow of orders

After setting up their first website in 1999, Screwfix today holds in excess of 4 million customer records, carries out over 40 per cent of transactions online and employs 1 000 people at its head office and contact centre.

and allow the distribution centre time to catch up. By the end of September, the telephone sales and Internet sales operations were back to normal, as were deliveries of more than 50,000 parcels per week.

Meanwhile, the Yeovil warehouse was becoming Head Office. Parallel developments of a supplier web portal, financial management systems and sales intelligence systems were proceeding. The supplier portal, for example, was supplied by Yantra and made dealing with more than 300 suppliers in the Far East and Eastern Europe much easier. Screwfix Direct relies on global sourcing to maintain its cost advantage over competitors.

Since then, further software contracts have led to the development of a dispatch process which can integrate the dispatch of larger items direct from suppliers' factories around the country with smaller items which come direct from Screwfix distribution centres. Esker Software supplied a system which is now handling 80,000 dispatches per week and gathers much sales information. An interesting part of this system analyses daily sales data overnight and sends summaries by text message to executives early each morning. This system also alerts technical staff by text message if there is a major power failure and the UPS (uninterruptible power supply) is activated on the main systems.

The Logic Group managed the process of integrating and upgrading the network infrastructure of Screwfix. The company now has an integrated IP (Internet Protocol) network which handles both voice and data. This led to the contact centre for sales converting to IP telephony, further managing Screwfix's cost base downward. Vecta were contracted to develop software to provide higher-quality sales information over this network, this time to telephone sales staff. The target was a detailed sales report to an operator within two clicks while on the phone to a customer. Not only does this help sales directly, but the new software also provides information for both strategic business decisions and targeted sales campaigns, making best use of all the available data.

One of those strategic decisions was taken in late 2004, following the interruption to orders because of distribution centre problems. By March 2005, Screwfix CEO John Allan had announced the year-long trial of six 'trade counters' in various locations across the UK. As well as positioning Screwfix Direct to compete with a rival joinery firm which was moving into building supplies, this would spread the load by allowing customers to collect goods from a local store. The model chosen was the 'Argos' model, with a small front area containing catalogues and several sales terminals. Customers would select goods from the catalogue, pay at a terminal after local stock was checked by sales staff and the goods would be brought to a delivery counter by picking staff. These are now being rolled out across the UK, with 14 complete by mid-2006. Interestingly, the systems do not allow the customer to check stock as is done at Argos stores.

These changes necessitated an increase in the staff complement and Screwfix Direct now employs 1900 people. Coordinating these staff members across the Yeovil Head Office, the Stoke distribution centre and local trade counters needed more new software. Coda Financial Intelligence was contracted in 2006 to eliminate as much paper handling as possible. All invoices to Screwfix from suppliers are converted to electronic images, either by the supplier or by Image Integrators, a firm which specializes in document image processing. Invoices arrive at Head Office as images only, with paper copies safely stored off-site. The system is also used for HR and personnel records and many legal documents. The proposed next stage is Goods Received Note processing which will speed up payments to suppliers and reduce disputes.

So Screwfix, a firm which had never had retail outlets and grew spectacularly with telephone and Internet sales, is now becoming a traditional supplier to the building trade and DIY markets. As other traditional companies, such as B&Q, are moving into web sales to complement store-based retail, Screwfix has found itself moving into store-based retail. Recent figures suggest that telephone orders account for 57 per cent of sales, Internet orders for 38 per cent and the trade counters account for 5 per cent.

This is a good example of the 'last mile' problem – how do you get lots of small orders quickly to your customers spread around a large area? Perhaps the Tesco online grocery solution will be the future: web orders delivered from the nearest store rather than from a distribution centre. One interesting side-effect of this is that the price advantage of Screwfix goods is falling. Prices for at least some items sold by Screwfix have risen significantly in the past two years. If you take on a traditional business model, all the software in the world won't keep your costs down!

Case study questions

1   What was Screwfix's original USP (unique selling proposition)? What advantages did this give Screwfix?

2   In what ways did the strategic use of information systems allow Screwfix to expand its operations?

3   Why does Screwfix appear to need to modify its information systems frequently?

SOURCES: www.kingfisher.co.uk, May 2007; www.esker.co.uk, May 2007; www.the-logic-group.com, May 2007; www.bbc.co.uk, 2004; *The Times*, 5 March 2005; The *Independent*, 14 March 1999; *Financial Times*, 22 July 1999

Case study **2.2**

Royal Mail Group

BY PATRICIA BRITTEN

The Royal Mail Group is a public limited company wholly owned by the British Government. The head office is in London and the organization employs almost 193,000 people in the UK, which represents about 1 per cent of the population. It operates Britain's mail services and the Post Office network and has total revenues of around £8.8 billion per year. Royal Mail became a plc on 26 March 2001 under the Postal Services Act 2000 and since then has undergone a huge transformation, turning losses of £1 million a day to a profit of £355 million at the end of 2005.

The head of IT is David Burden, CIO (Chief Information Officer). David Burden says Royal Mail Group focused on two issues in 2005: improving the delivery of letters and rolling out chip and pin to about 15,000 post offices. Of the two, the organization's reputation really stands or falls on the delivery of 83 million items to 27 million addresses each working day. Prices charged are some of the lowest in Europe, but its reputation has taken a battering in recent years. However, there is no doubt that performance has improved over the past year.

Improved postal service

Between July and September 2005, 92 per cent of first class letters arrived the day after posting – one of its best performances for a decade. By the end of 2006 this performance had improved to 94.4 per cent on time delivery for first class post and 99.1 per cent for second class post. IT has contributed enormously to this improvement across a very complex delivery process. 'We collect from 113,000 red pillar boxes and there are probably about 70,000 collection points, including large businesses', says Burden. Mail goes through a process involving 72 mail centres, 1400 delivery offices and enormous physical transportation systems which include the use of 30,000 vehicles and 33,000 bicycles.

'We have put in new processes, computing systems and communication links. We also implemented new report processing last year so that every level of the organization can validate an issue before it goes up to another level. It uses a SAP data warehouse and lots of reporting tools from different vendors', says Burden.

Letter recognition

'The really clever stuff is the letter processing systems. We have been doing an enormous amount of work with address systems,' says Burden.

The new system – which replaced an optical character recognition device – first went live in 2004, but Burden's team continues to work on enhancements. It photographs the envelope, including handwritten letters to interpret the correct address. 'It is a very sophisticated image recognition system working against a database of 27 million addresses. It is one that is very specifically aimed at identifying defects in processing.' The beauty of the new online centrally hosted system is that it can identify the correct address even when someone makes a mistake, such as omitting the postcode.

'Previously if someone got the postcode wrong it would have gone to the wrong address. If someone misses out the postcode we can detect this and put it in. If it cannot do this, we can put it on one side and rectify it', explains Burden. What happens is that a

Royal Mail's traditional red pillar boxes mark the start of an increasingly sophisticated delivery process.

PHOTO SOURCE: © TRACY HEBDEN

sorting office's computer captures the data and sends them to the central image recognition system. 'If there is a problem, it is sent to one of three centres, where someone will resolve it', says Burden.

Chip and pin

Installing chip and pin technology in post offices has presented a different set of challenges. It required fairly substantial changes to the software systems. The organization installed new hardware at each site. 'As a result, the major challenge was the sheer scale of project', says Burden. The installation was complete in all 14,902 post offices by mid-2005.

A heavily outsourced operation, primarily to CSC, IT has also contributed to Royal Mail's drive to cut costs. 'We have been chopping back as always', says Burden. It has slashed IT operating costs by 10 per cent over the past 12 months. 'We keep very tight control and make sure that we do not have any inefficient use of IT.'

Overall, Royal Mail said that it was making more than £1 million per day – instead of losing more than £1 million per day before its renewal plan kicked in. However, Royal Mail faces many challenges to its profitability in the future.

Future challenges

The future challenges to Royal Mail's business come from the competitive and regulatory environment. Their market place is rapidly changing, with the UK postal market having been fully liberalized since January 2006, resulting in full competition from rival companies. The Postal Services Act also established a new regulatory regime with an independent regulator, Postcomm, and a consumer body, Postwatch. Royal Mail says it cannot compete on commercial terms because of the constraints on pricing imposed by the regulator. Royal Mail currently loses around 2 pence on every item handled. The amount of mail handled by rival companies in 2007 is forecast to be around 2.5 billion letters and packets (out of a total volume of 22 billion).

The postal services market is also a mature one, which has seen a decline of 2 per cent in volumes over the past year – a pattern repeated throughout Europe. This is thought to be due to the growth in electronic communications using the Internet, and the recent growth of broadband services is a key factor.

Operating losses at the Post Office have doubled to £4 million a week following the loss of government contracts to handle pensions and social security benefit payments. This has led to the decision to close many of the smaller branches (of which 7793 are rural), causing a public outcry from rural communities who depend on these retail outlets for many other services. Currently nearly 25 million customers make over 36 million visits a week to post offices.

This has put an emphasis on further improving both the efficiency and effectiveness of the services provided by Royal Mail. The modernization programme has resulted in many improvements to date, which include record quality of service, improved productivity, reduced absenteeism and substantial increases in pay for the workforce. Information technology has contributed greatly to this, but further modernization of the business is required. Overall, the technology currently lags behind that of their competitors and innovative new systems are required if they are to be ahead of the game. It is estimated that around £2 billion needs to be spent on modernizing the company and renewing its premises and equipment. Consequently, it was announced in July 2006 that the UK Government would provide a £1.2 billion investment facility to help achieve the next five-year modernization programme.

New services are being provided to meet these challenges, which range from new Post Office financial services, such as personal loans and 'two-in-one' credit cards, to electronic 'stamps', online shopping facilities and data tools to help companies improve their marketing performance.

Alan Leighton, Chairman, said: 'The changes the Group will now need to make are more stretching and challenging than the gains we made during the three-year renewal plan to 2005. New technology is vital for our future.' This represents both challenges and real opportunities for the application of IT systems.

Case study questions

1 Does the letter recognition system in the case give Royal Mail a competitive advantage? Is it an example of a strategic information system?

2 Do you consider that the information technology and computer systems in use by Royal Mail, as described in the case, are 'bleeding edge' or 'leading edge'? Justify your answer.

3 Which of the six strategic initiatives described in this chapter has Royal Mail chosen to adopt to achieve its goals?

4 Carry out Porter's five forces analysis of the Postal Services industry and assess whether the application of information technology could help to alter these forces.

SOURCES: An article by James Thompson in *MIS U.K.*, April 2005; Allan Leighton, Chairman's Statement, December 2006; and www.royalmailgroup.com

silicon.com

Case study **2.3**

Offshoring – how to get it right

BY ANDY McCUE

The debate about whether – and how – to send work overseas has moved out of the IT department and into the domain of top-level business executives and the board. Andy McCue speaks to the experts about best practices for all the various options.

Globalization has had a positive impact on the way businesses can source products, services and skills in order to gain competitive advantage, cut costs and drive top-line growth – but many boardrooms still don't have a centralized and consistent strategy for sending work offshore, instead relying on piecemeal and uncoordinated efforts.

The model for using lower-cost overseas locations such as India for software development and call centre work has become a mainstream and widely accepted business practice over the last decade, led largely by the financial services sector.

That trend is only set to grow, both in volume and in the types of services that will increasingly be sent offshore. A study conducted last year by management consultants McKinsey and Indian IT trade body Nasscom predicts around $110 billion of IT and business process outsourcing (BPO) services globally will be offshored by businesses by 2010.

But how does this globalization – 'the world is flat' vision of Thomas Friedman's book of the same title – affect a company's sourcing strategy?

Devise a strategy

Businesses over the past twenty years have focused on the supplier selection and contract negotiation elements of sourcing, but Gartner says leading-edge organizations are now firmly focused on sourcing strategy and sourcing management first.

Phanish Puranam, assistant professor of strategic and international management at the London Business School (LBS), says best practice is to operate from a portfolio perspective.

He says: 'People are increasingly looking at the whole portfolio of choices and saying "let's look at the whole range of options". A big trend has also been to centralize the services function so there is a common method for evaluating these decisions.'

But in many boardrooms a complete shift in mindset is needed as the sourcing situation becomes more complex, according to Phil Morris, founding director and COO at outsourcing advisers Morgan Chambers.

Morris says: 'The whole of the executive management needs to understand the impact of their response to the globalization phenomenon on their organization. Every executive needs to understand how different types of outsourcing can be woven into the organization to make it more competitive.'

One of the reasons for the need for a group-wide sourcing strategy is the range of services and processes that can now be offshored – aside from the obvious things such as software development and tech support.

Neil Hammond, head of IT at British Sugar, experienced the first wave of offshore outsourcing as head of IT strategy for Thomas Cook in the late 1990s when he offshored IT development work

The Bangalore headquarters of Infosys – a major IT company at the forefront of the offshore outsourcing boom.

to India. He says globalization and offshore outsourcing can no longer be ignored or sidelined by a business.

He says: 'It must be a factor in any significant sourcing decision, new business development or process improvement strategy.'

BPO on the rise

The current offshoring buzz is around BPO which at the top end is the outsourcing of an entire end-to-end process in HR or finance and at the lower end is basic call centre outsourcing.

Analyst Forrester predicts that over the next few years organizations will centralize activities such as customer service, marketing, HR, and finance and accounting (F&A) and move non-core processes such as low-level HR or payroll activities to low-cost offshore destinations.

British Sugar's Hammond says: '[Offshoring] has moved beyond IT development and call centres into areas such as back office transaction processing, engineering and architectural design, bespoke equipment manufacture, through to buying and operationalizing "shell" factories.'

Frances Karamouzis, VP of research at Gartner, says BPO adoption is just taking hold but that the pace of growth is picking up all the time.

She says: 'The core focus in terms of volumes is HR followed by F&A. Beyond that it's procurement or CRM and call centre work.'

KPO on the horizon

The future over the next five to ten years, however, appears to be around what industry experts are labelling knowledge process outsourcing, which refers to tasks such as financial analysis, legal work and research. There are already some examples of that in action.

LBS's Puranam says: 'Processes that would have been unthinkable a decade or so ago are now on the table and that's definitely the case in financial services companies.'

Equity analysis and research is offshored by many Wall Street and City of London organizations, for example. The number crunching is done in Mumbai or some other low-cost location and then sent back to the bank for review and analysis.

According to Gartner's Karamouzis, while the numbers in terms of headcount involved in KPO are smaller than IT or BPO offshoring, the value is higher in payback and return on investment.

She says: 'The per capita savings [for KPO] are around the 50 to 60th percentile. But the savings in absolute dollar amount also don't factor in productivity. You can get those [offshore] people to produce more in less hours and you can staff two or three people doing a deeper dive into the research', she said.

Pick a model

The other factor businesses need to address is the model they choose for offshoring. The most common option is to outsource the service or process to a third-party supplier, whether that be one of the traditional 'big six' consultancies, such as Accenture or IBM, or to one of the home-grown service providers in the offshore location, such as India's Infosys, TCS or Wipro.

Other options include going down the captive route, which means setting up a wholly owned unit of the business in the offshore country. Several high-profile companies have done this including GE, HSBC and Tesco.

Then there are joint ventures or 'build, operate, transfer' deals where a third-party supplier sets up the offshore operation, gets it up and running and then transfers it to the company using it. All these different models have their own pros and cons and the decision will depend on factors like the size of the company and the type of service being offshored.

The rule of thumb is that large global companies looking to offshore work that is a core competency or closely regulated are best suited to setting up their own captive operation, otherwise it is difficult to justify the business case.

Brand is also an issue that many companies fail to take into account when setting up their own captive offshore operation. In countries such as India, where there is stiff competition for staff and high attrition rates, the company's brand reputation is key to being able to attract and retain talent.

Morgan Chambers' Morris says: 'You need to understand how your brand will be perceived in the local market. If your brand doesn't stack up against Microsoft, Oracle, etc. you will suffer high attrition.'

Crunch the numbers

But none of this matters if the figures don't stack up. There are many good reasons for offshoring including filling skills gaps, freeing up resources and speeding up product development – but cost savings are still the chief motivation for sending work overseas.

In a recent Forrester survey of business and IT executives in European companies that use offshore providers, 45 out of 47 rated cost as the principal choice behind their decision.

The most important thing here is to be realistic about the level of savings once all the extra communication, management and travel time and resources have been factored into the basic return on investment equation, according to LBS's Puranam.

He says: 'Instead of 30 to 40 per cent savings the business case is now being made on more like 15 to 20 per cent.'

Beyond cost, British Sugar's Hammond says some of the issues to consider when offshoring are the management of a remote operation, ensuring you can gain access to sufficient technological and managerial expertise, and dealing with different cultural expectations and attitudes.

The lesson for boardrooms then is to look at offshore outsourcing within the context of a company-wide global sourcing strategy to ascertain which services and processes could be sent offshore and to make those decisions in a consistent framework. This means that while price is important, it is also a balance against other advantages such as access to talent, and quality and process improvements.

As Morgan Chambers' Morris says: 'Offshoring is not just a panacea on short-term labour arbitrage.'

Thinking about the case

1   The offshoring of manufacturing has been used for many years. Technology has helped to increase 'higher level' offshoring, such as call centres. What technology drivers are there to assist the extension of these functions to even higher levels such as knowledge processing?

2   The report suggests that while HR would remain as a home-based function 'low level' HR could be offshored. What do you understand by the term 'low level HR'?

Business functions and supply chains

In an economy that produces and consumes so much information, professionals must know how to use information systems in virtually every business activity. Managers must have an overall understanding of all elements of a system, so that they know what options are available to control quality, costs and resources. Modern information systems encompass whole business cycles, often called supply chains.

When you finish this chapter, you will be able to:

Identify various business functions and the role of ISs in these functions.

Explain how ISs in the basic business functions relate to each other.

Articulate what supply chains are and how information technology supports management of supply chains.

Enumerate the purposes of customer relationship management systems.

Explain the notion of enterprise resource planning systems.

CONTINUED GROWTH AND SPECIALISM

Something had to give: Better Bites' business expansion to more carts and to crisp manufacturing had worked so well that Paul Clermont was drowning in piles of sales receipts. He had employed a part-time assistant to help him input the receipts to the business's spreadsheet program, but that solution was no longer enough. The labour-intensive process simply had to go. Luckily, Paul, Sarah Odell and Christina Healy found a solution in a handheld personal digital assistant (PDA) with wireless mobile printer software. The sales staff serving from the carts keyed the customer's menu selections into the PDAs and printed a receipt. Later, the information was downloaded from the PDAs to the business's main accounting system. The time saved by automating the sales transactions allowed Paul to concentrate on bigger issues the partners faced: tracking sales, costs and profitability.

As part of his monthly sales analysis, Paul printed sales reports segregated by each of the three carts. When he did so, he noticed that sales from the University Concourse pushcart were dropping. Their Subwich competitor was drawing customers from the Concourse cart. Also, Paul noticed that business was even worse during colder months and bad weather. The partners needed to turn the situation around.

A new opportunity appears

Earlier Paul, Sarah and Christina had decided to find their own kitchen space to handle their increased food volume. When they were looking for rental space, they ran across a vacant shop unit in their local town. Instead of simply renting kitchen space, they decided they'd open a small restaurant with its own kitchen. That way, they could meet their Subwich competitor head on, offering dinners as well as lunches and not worrying about the change of seasons or weather. They could also use the restaurant's kitchen for crisp manufacturing when the restaurant was closed.

To handle the increased workload for the restaurant, the three entrepreneurs hired a full-time chef and kitchen staff. Sarah and the chef developed streamlined cooking procedures for both the meal and crisp operations and then trained the staff in the procedures. That freed Sarah to work on new restaurant recipes.

Advertising needs and promotions

To announce the opening of their new restaurant, Christina used a desktop publishing program to create flyers for their grand opening that could be handed out to pushcart customers or on campus. The flyers included a feedback form and those who returned the forms received discount coupons for a free beverage with the purchase of a sandwich. They hoped these special offers would attract new customers. Paul also suggested they produce radio commercials, reasoning that radio offered an affordable means of reaching their customers – college students, shoppers and commuters. They'd need professional help with that media project.

Moving forward

Better Bites had come a long way since its start, but the entrepreneurs still had decisions to make and changes to undergo. With the opening of the restaurant, the partners needed to revamp their computer systems to handle credit-card purchases. Better Bites also needed to automate and expand its employee systems. Paul had written cheques by hand when the business only had a small staff payroll to deal with. But the new chef and kitchen staff now made that system impractical. Finally, Sarah thought that their food inventory and preparation systems might benefit from automation. She had tracked

her inventory closely, but with the expansion, it was getting more and more difficult to keep up. Paul and Christina agreed that an inventory control system would be a good move, so they bought the Quick-Books program. This software could help them not only with inventory control but also with online credit verifications, sales and expenses, payroll and accounting as well as other needed functions, such as tracking sales taxes, invoicing and cheque printing. With this more comprehensive system, the three entrepreneurs believed they had made a great leap forward. It was clear to them that a well-run information system was an integral part of their business, simplifying their business as activities became more complex. They'd need to remain informed about technology as they looked to the future.

Effectiveness and efficiency

As we saw in TheTrainline 'Industry Snapshot' in the previous chapter, the use of technology enables the contact centre staff to deal with calls more efficiently and also every call has potential added value because of the extra information that the operator has in front of them. It is often said that the use of information technology makes our work more effective, more efficient, or both. What do these terms mean? **Effectiveness** defines the degree to which a goal is achieved. Thus, a system is more or less effective depending on (1) how much of its goal it achieves and (2) the degree to which it achieves better outcomes than other systems do.

CD TASK

effectiveness The measure of how well a job is performed.

Efficiency is determined by the relationship between resources expended and the benefits gained in achieving a goal. Expressed mathematically,

efficiency The ratio of output to input; the greater the ratio, the greater the efficiency.

$$\text{Efficiency} = \text{Benefits} \div \text{Costs}$$

One system is more efficient than another if its operating costs are lower for the same or better quality product, or if its product's quality is greater for the same or lower costs. The term 'productivity' is commonly used as a synonym for efficiency. However, **productivity** refers specifically to the efficiency of *human* resources. Productivity improves when fewer workers are required to produce the same amount of output, or, alternatively, when the same number of workers produces a greater amount of output. This is why IT professionals often speak of 'productivity tools', which are software applications that help workers produce more in less time. The closer the result of an effort is to the ultimate goal, the more effective the effort. The fewer the resources spent on achieving a goal, the more efficient the effort.

productivity Efficiency, when the input is labour. The fewer labour hours needed to perform a job, the greater the productivity.

Suppose your goal is to design a new car that reaches a speed of 60 miles per hour in five seconds. If you manage to build it, then you produce the product effectively. If the car does not meet the requirement, your effort is ineffective. If your competitor makes a car with the same features and performance, but uses fewer people and fewer other resources, then your competitor is not only as effective as you but also more efficient. ISs contribute to both the effectiveness and efficiency of businesses, especially when positioned in specific business functions, such as accounting, finance and engineering and when used to help companies achieve their goals more quickly by facilitating collaborative work.

One way to look at business functions and their supporting systems is to follow typical business cycles, which often begin with marketing and sales activities (see Figure 3.1). Serving customers better and faster, as well as learning more about their experiences and preferences, is facilitated by **customer relationship management (CRM)** systems. When customers place orders, the orders are executed in the supply chain. Customer relationship management continues after delivery of the ordered goods in the forms of customer service and more marketing. When an organization enjoys the support of CRM and supply chain management (SCM)

customer relationship management (CRM) A set of applications designed to gather and analyse information about customers.

Figure 3.1   Business activities consist of customer relationship management, supply chain management and supporting functions

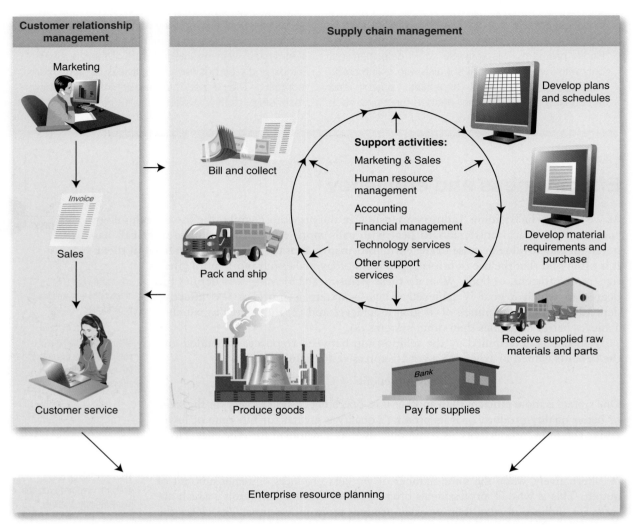

systems, it can plan its resources well. Combined, these systems are often referred to as enterprise resource planning (ERP) systems.

Figure 3.2 shows some of the most common business activities and their interdependence. For example, cost accounting systems are linked to payroll, benefits and purchasing systems to accumulate the cost of products manufactured by a company; and information from purchasing systems flows to both cost accounting and financial reporting systems. The following discussion addresses the role of information systems, one business function at a time.

Accounting

The purpose of accounting is to track every financial transaction within a company, from a few cents to multimillion euro purchases, from salaries and benefits to the sale of every item. Without tracking the costs of labour, materials and purchased services using a

Figure 3.2 Information systems in different business functions are interdependent

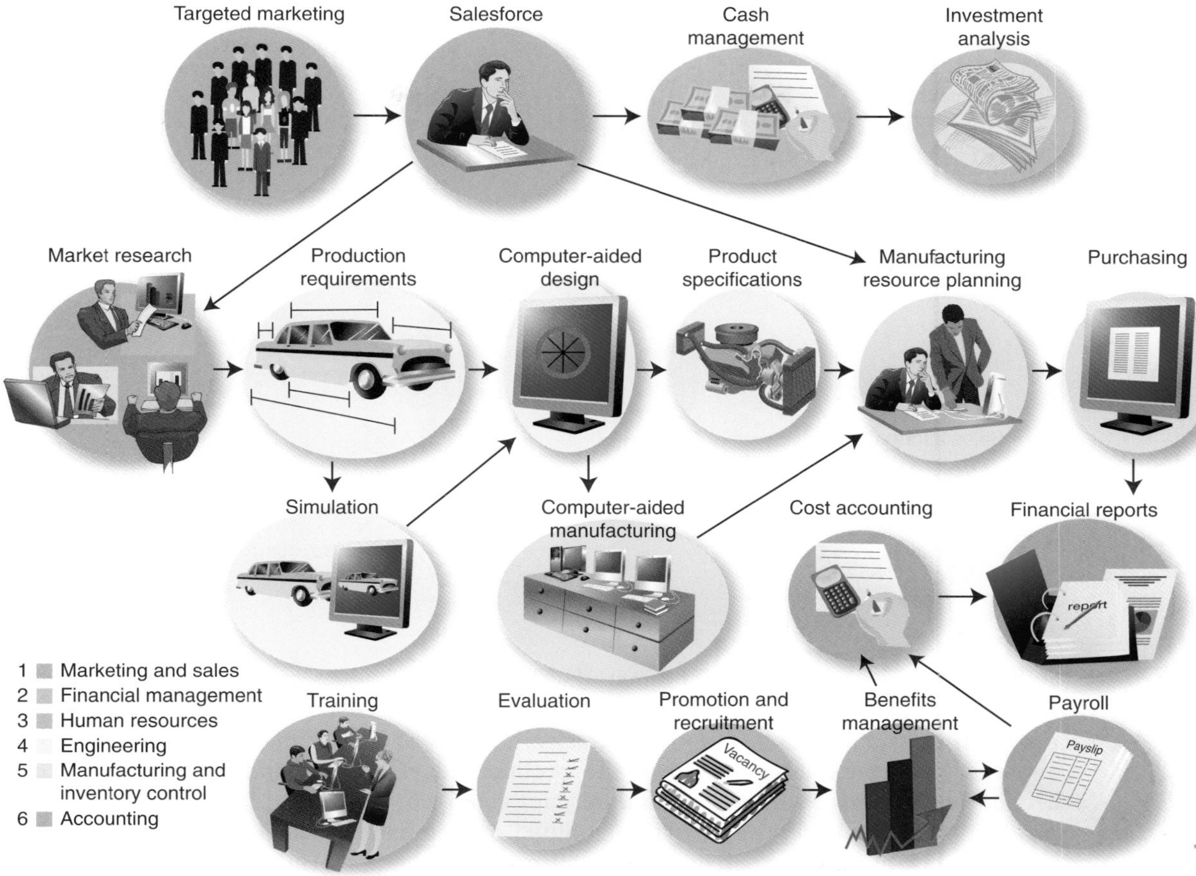

1 ▦ Marketing and sales
2 ▦ Financial management
3 ▦ Human resources
4 ▦ Engineering
5 ▦ Manufacturing and
      inventory control
6 ▦ Accounting

cost-accounting system, a company might discover too late that it sells products below what it costs to make them. Without a system of accounts receivable, managers might not know who owes the company how much money and when it is due. Without an accounts payable system, managers cannot know how much money the company owes each supplier and when payment is due. Without a system that records and helps plan cash flow, managers cannot keep enough cash in the bank to make payments on schedule. At the year's end, the company cannot present a picture of its financial situation – called a balance sheet – and a profit-and-loss report, unless it maintains a general ledger to record every transaction with a financial impact. General ledger, accounts receivable, accounts payable and cash-flow books conveniently lend themselves to computerization and can easily generate balance sheets and profit-and-loss statements from records (see Figure 3.3).

Typically, accounting ISs receive records of routine business transactions – such as the purchase of raw materials or services, or the sale of manufactured goods – from transaction processing systems (TPSs). Such a system automatically routes every purchase of raw materials or services to the accounts payable system, which uses it to produce cheques or transfer funds to a vendor's bank account. Whenever a sale is recorded, the transaction is routed to the accounts receivable system (which generates invoices) and other destinations. Totals of accounts receivable and accounts payable can be automatically transferred to a balance sheet. Data from the general ledger can be automatically compiled to generate a cash-flow report or a profit-and-loss report for the past quarter or year. Accounting ISs can generate any of these reports on demand, as well as at scheduled times.

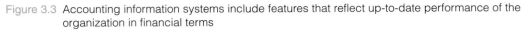

Figure 3.3 Accounting information systems include features that reflect up-to-date performance of the organization in financial terms

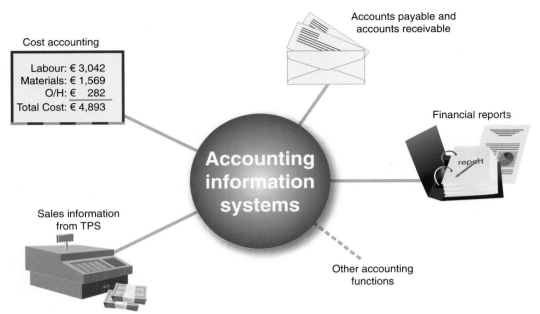

When a company develops and manufactures a new product that has never been available on the market, how can it determine a price that covers costs and generates a decent profit? It must maintain a system that tracks the costs of labour, materials, consulting fees and every other expense related to the product's development and manufacture. Cost-accounting systems, used to accumulate data about costs involved in producing specific products, make excellent use of IT to compile pricing data. ISs also help allocate costs to specific work orders. A work order is an authorization to perform work for a specific purpose. When interfaced with payroll and purchasing ISs, a cost-accounting system automatically captures records of everything spent (and originally recorded in the payroll and purchasing systems) and routes expenses to the appropriate work order. Because work orders are associated with specific products and services, the company now knows how much each product or service costs.

Why you should...

know about business functions and supply chains

Today's professionals are expected to be knowledgeable not only in their specific line of work but also in other areas, specifically information technology. In today's market, many employers look for generalists rather than specialists and focus on the techno-manager, a manager well versed in information technology.

Because many ISs serve multiple functions and interface with other systems, it is extremely important for a professional to be familiar with the way ISs facilitate work in areas outside his or her expertise. If you work for a commercial organization, you are bound to be part of a supply chain or work for a unit that supports a supply chain. Knowledge of systems in different business areas helps you cooperate with your peers and coordinate efforts that cross departmental boundaries. Because professionals often have opportunities to be promoted to positions in other disciplines, the more you know, the better your chances of being 'cross-promoted'.

Accounting ISs are also used extensively for managerial purposes, assisting in organizing quarterly and annual budgets for departments, divisions and entire corporations. The same systems help managers control their budgets by tracking income and expense in real time and comparing them with the amounts predicted in the budget. Budget applications are designed with proper controls, so that the system does not allow spending funds for a specific purpose beyond the amount that was budgeted for that purpose.

Finance

A firm's health is often measured by its finances and ISs can significantly improve financial management (see Figure 3.4). The goal of financial managers, including controllers and treasurers, is to manage an organization's money as efficiently as possible. They achieve this goal by (1) collecting payables as soon as possible, (2) making payments at the latest time allowed by contract or law, (3) ensuring that sufficient funds are available for day-to-day operations and (4) taking advantage of opportunities to accrue the highest yield on funds not used for current activities. These goals can be best met by careful cash management and investment analysis.

Cash management

Financial information systems help managers track a company's finances. These systems record every payment and cash receipt to reflect cash movement, employ budgeting software to track plans for company finances and include capital investment systems to manage investments, thus balancing the need to accrue interest on idle money against the need to have cash available. The information on expected cash receipts comes from sales contracts and the information on cash outlays comes from purchasing contracts, as well as payroll and benefits schedules. Systems that deal specifically with cash are often called cash management systems (CMSs). One common use for a CMS is to execute cash transactions in which financial

cash management system (CMS) Information system that helps reduce the interest and fees that organizations have to pay when borrowing money and increases the yield that organizations can receive on unused funds.

Figure 3.4 Financial information systems help manage cash and investment portfolios

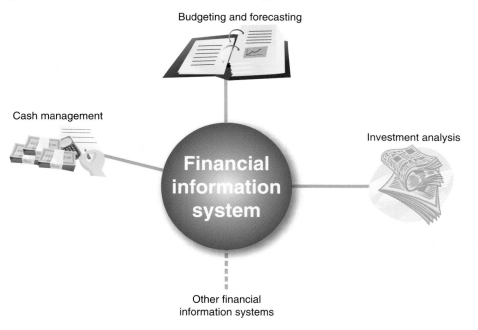

Budgeting and forecasting

Cash management

Investment analysis

Financial information system

Other financial information systems

electronic funds transfer (EFT) The electronic transfer of cash from an account in one bank to an account in another bank.

institutions transfer huge amounts of money using electronic funds transfer (EFT). EFT is the electronic transfer of cash from an account in one bank to an account in another bank.

Investment analysis and service

Every investor's goal is to buy an asset and later sell it for more than it cost. When investing in securities, such as stocks and bonds, it is important to know the prices of securities in real time, that is, *right now*. The ability of financial ISs to record millions of securities prices and their changes over long time periods, coupled with the ability to manipulate numbers using software, puts powerful analysis tools in investment managers' hands. Within seconds, an investment analyst can use a financial IS and chart prices of a specific stock or bond over a given period and then build models to estimate what might happen to securities prices in the future.

Even the smallest investment firm can provide clients with an inexpensive online service for buying and selling securities, providing on-demand statements listing the stocks they own (called a portfolio), periodic yield and the portfolio's current value. Clients serve themselves through the websites of brokerage firms to place buy and sell orders. Execution of orders takes only a few seconds.

Nearly instantaneously, ISs provide subscriber brokers and their clients with financial news, stock prices, commodity prices and currency exchange rates from multiple locations across the world. Consider what happens when a foreign currency's exchange rate fluctuates a fraction of a percentage. A brokerage house can make a significant profit within two minutes of buying and selling a large block of the foreign currency. A small fraction of a very large number is still big!

Financial managers need to consider many factors before they invest in a security. Some of the most important factors these managers must consider are (1) risk, measured as the variability (degree of change) of the paper's past yield; (2) expected return; and (3) liquidity, a measure of how fast an investment can be turned into cash. Special programs help calculate these factors and present the results in either tables or graphs to allow timely decision-making.

time to market The time between generating an idea for a product and completing a prototype that can be mass-manufactured; also called engineering lead time.

brainstorming The process of a group collaboratively generating new ideas and creative solutions to problems.

computer-aided design (CAD) Special software used by engineers and designers that facilitates engineering and design work.

rapid prototyping Using software and special output devices to create prototypes to test design in three dimensions.

Engineering

The time between generating an idea for a product and completing a prototype that can be mass-manufactured is known as engineering lead time or time to market. Engineering includes brainstorming (the process of a group of colleagues meeting and working collaboratively to generate creative solutions and new ideas), developing a concept, creating mock-ups, building prototypes, testing and other activities that require investments of time, labour and money. Minimizing lead time is key to maintaining a competitive edge: it leaves competitors insufficient time to introduce their own products first. ISs can contribute significantly to this effort. Over the past decade, car manufacturers have used engineering and other ISs to reduce the time from product concept to market from seven to two years.

IT's greatest contribution to engineering is in the area of computer-aided design (CAD) and rapid prototyping (creating one-of-a-kind products to test design in three dimensions). Engineers can use computers to modify designs quickly and store drawings electronically. With collaborative software, they perform much of this process over the Internet: engineers can conduct remote conferences while viewing and developing plans and drawings together. The electronic drawings are then available to make rapid prototypes.

Rapid prototyping allows a model of a product to be produced within hours, rather than days or weeks. The model required is often a mock-up to show only the physical look and dimensions of a product, without the electronics or other

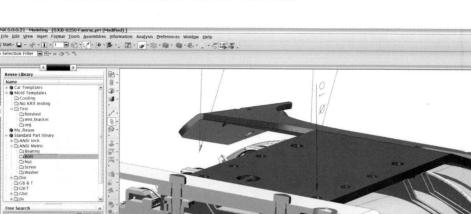

Computer-aided design systems significantly shorten the time needed to produce drawings and complete the design of new products.

components that are part of the full product. First, an image of the object is created on a computer. The computer is connected to a special machine that creates a physical, three-dimensional model by laying down hundreds or thousands of thin layers of liquid plastic or special resin. The model can be examined by engineers and marketing managers in the organization, or shown to clients.

When the prototypes are satisfactory, the electronic drawings and material specifications can be transferred from the CAD systems to computer-aided manufacturing (CAM) systems. CAM systems process the data to instruct machines, including robots, how to manufacture the parts and assemble the product (see Figure 3.5).

Until several years ago, car manufacturers needed four to five years to turn a concept into vehicles rolling out for sale. Now, thanks to CAD, CAM, rapid prototyping and collaborative engineering software, the lead time has been reduced to less than two years. The digital design of vehicles saves not only time but also the cost of cars crashed in tests. All the tests are performed with sophisticated software rather than with real cars.

Supply chain management

In its fundamental form, a supply chain consists of three phases: procurement of raw materials, processing the materials into intermediate and finished goods and delivery of the goods to customers. Processing raw materials into goods is manufacturing. Supply chain management (SCM) consists of monitoring, controlling and facilitating supply chains, as depicted on the right side of Figure 3.1. Supply chain management (SCM) systems are information technologies that support SCM. Such systems have been instrumental in reducing manufacturing costs, including the costs of managing resources and controlling inventory (see Figure 3.6). In retail, the manufacturing phase does not exist, so the term 'supply chain' refers only to the purchasing of finished goods and the delivery to customers of those goods. In the service industries the term is practically meaningless.

As is clear from the previous discussion, much of the data required for manufacturing processes can flow directly from CAD systems to CAM systems, as well

computer-aided manufacturing (CAM) Automation of manufacturing activities by use of computers. Often, the information for the activity comes directly from connected computers that were used for engineering the parts or products to be manufactured.

supply chain The activities performed from the purchase of raw material to the shipping of manufactured goods and collecting for their sale.

supply chain management (SCM) The coordination of purchasing, manufacturing, shipping and billing operations, often supported by an enterprise resource planning system.

Figure 3.5 Engineering information systems aid engineers in designing new products and simulating how they operate

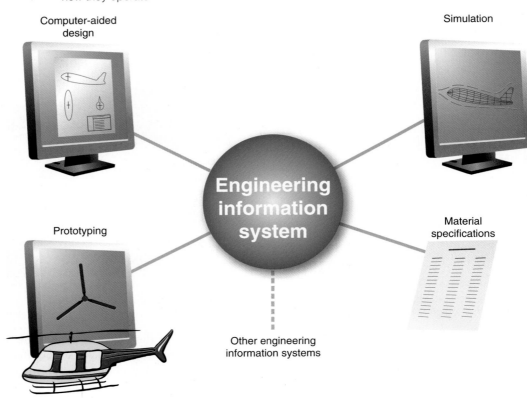

Figure 3.6 Manufacturing and inventory control information systems help reduce cycle times and the cost of maintaining inventory

as inventory control systems and other systems that support planning and execution of manufacturing. While CAM systems participate in physical activities such as cutting and welding, other information systems help to plan and monitor manufacturing.

Information technology helps in the following manufacturing activities:

- Scheduling plant activities while optimizing the combined use of all resources – machines, personnel, tooling and raw and interim materials.
- Planning material requirements based on current and forecasted demand.
- Reallocating materials rapidly from one order to another to satisfy due dates.
- Letting users manage inventories in real time, taking into consideration demand and the responsiveness of all work centres.
- Grouping work orders by characteristics of items ordered, such as colour and width of products.
- Considering the qualifications of each resource (such as qualified labour, set-up crews and specialized tools) to accomplish its task. For instance, people and raw materials can be moved from one assembly line to another to respond to machine breakdown or customer emergency, and design changes can be implemented quickly to respond to changes in customer wishes.

Material requirements planning and purchasing

One area of manufacturing that has experienced the greatest improvement from IS is inventory control, or material requirements planning (MRP). Traditional inventory control techniques operated according to the basic principle that future inventory needs are based on past use: once used up, inventory was replaced. By contrast, replenishment in MRP is based on *future* need, calculated by MRP software from demand forecasts. MRP programs take customer demand as their initial input. The main input to MRP programs is the number of product units needed and the time at which they are needed; the programs then work back to calculate the amounts of resources required to produce subparts and assemblies. The programs use long-range forecasts to put long-lead material on order.

Other important input to MRP applications includes a list of all raw materials and subcomponent demands (called the bill of materials, or BOM) and the economic order quantity of different raw materials. The economic order quantity (EOQ) of a specific raw material is the optimal quantity that allows a business to minimize overstocking and save cost, without risking under-stocking and missing production deadlines. A special program calculates EOQ for each item. It considers several factors: the item's cost, the discount schedule for large quantities, the cost of warehousing ordered parts, the cost of alternative uses of the money (such as the interest the money could earn had it not been spent on inventory) and other factors affecting the cost of ordering the item. Some MRP applications are tied to a purchasing IS, to produce purchase orders automatically when the quantity on hand reaches a reorder level. The purchase order includes the economic order quantity.

material requirements planning (MRP) Inventory control that includes a calculation of future need.

bill of materials (BOM) A list showing an explosion of the materials that go into the production of an item. Used in planning the purchase of raw materials.

economic order quantity (EOQ) The optimal (cost-minimizing) quantity of a specific raw material that allows a business to minimize overstocking and save cost without risking understocking and missing production deadlines.

Manufacturing resource planning

Manufacturing resource planning (MRP II) combines material requirements planning (MRP) with other manufacturing-related activities to plan the entire manufacturing process, not just inventory. MRP II systems can quickly modify schedules to

manufacturing resource planning (MRP II) The combination of MRP with other manufacturing-related activities to plan the entire manufacturing process, not just inventory.

accommodate orders, track production in real time and fix quality slippage. The most important input of MRP II systems is the master production schedule (MPS), which specifies how production capacity is to be used to meet customer demands and maintain inventories. Virtually every report an MRP II package generates starts with, or is based on, the MPS. Purchases of materials and internal control of manufacturing work flow, for example, start with the MPS, so the MPS directly affects operational costs and asset use.

MRP II systems help balance production economies, customer demands, manufacturing capacity and inventory levels over a planning horizon of several months. Successful MRP II systems have made a significant contribution to just-in-time (JIT) manufacturing, where suppliers ship parts directly to assembly lines, saving the cost of warehousing raw materials, parts and subassemblies.

Ideally, the ISs of manufacturing organizations and their suppliers would be linked in a way that makes them subsystems of one large system. The MRP II application of an organization that manufactures a final product would plan and dictate the items required, their quantities and the exact times they are needed at the assembly lines. Suppliers would deliver items directly to assembly lines just before they are incorporated into the final product (hence the term *just-in-time manufacturing*). Manufacturing organizations have not yet reached the point where JIT is accomplished with every product, but they have made great progress towards this ideal.

The Internet facilitates such system linking. Companies that were quick to link their systems to their suppliers' systems attained strategic advantages. One such company is Cisco Systems, a world leader in design and manufacturing of telecommunications devices. The company used to maintain many manufacturing plants. In 2001, it had sold all but two. The company's ISs are linked through the Internet to the ISs of its suppliers, some of whom purchased the very plants that Cisco sold. Through these systems managers can track orders. They can tell Cisco clients the exact status of their orders and the time of delivery. Cisco managers keep track of the products they order and know at what phase of manufacturing and delivery each item is – as if *they* were running the manufacturing plants. More than 80 per cent of what Cisco orders never passes through the company's facilities; the manufacturers deliver the products directly to Cisco's clients.

Monitoring and control

Information systems have been designed to control manufacturing processes, not just monitor them. Controlling processes is important to ensure quality. Most of the major car manufacturers use a combination of bar coding and wireless technology to ensure the quality of the assembly. Since each vehicle is assembled on a chassis, each chassis is tagged with a unique bar code. A bar-code sensor is installed at each stop of the assembly line. The sensor transmits wireless signals to computers and electronically controlled gates. The purpose of the system is to ensure that no assembly steps are skipped and that each vehicle passes a series of performance and quality tests along the way. If a step is missed, the gate does not let the vehicle leave the plant.

However, the use of ISs in monitoring and control is not limited to manufacturing. Care-Caller is a computer-based alarm processing system for use in nursing environments. It monitors routine nursing calls and emergency calls, routing the request for assistance to appropriate nursing staff who carry radio phones. These events can be recorded and used to produce management reports showing, for example, average response time, how often each patient pressed his or her button and when, and so on. However, the system also has an element of control. For example, in the case of an emergency, doors which are usually kept locked for security reasons can be automatically unlocked to allow fast access by the emergency response team.

Distribution

When the process of manufacturing products is complete, the next link in the supply chain is delivery to the customer. Distribution is performed either by the manufacturer or by a hired delivery company. The variables that affect the cost and speed of delivery are numerous: length of routes, sequence of loading and unloading, type of materials (e.g., perishable, hazardous or fragile), fuel prices, road tolls, terrain and restricted roads and many more. Therefore, the use of sophisticated software to give an optimal delivery time for every customer and the cost of labour and equipment use helps companies stay competitive. Figure 3.7 shows an example of such software.

Today's lorries are equipped with computers and satellite communication hardware and software. Each can receive real-time orders from a central distribution office, especially when routing changes are necessary, and transmits information about the truck, such as current location, the previous point of loading or unloading and the next point of loading or unloading. Lorry drivers rarely reach a shipping office. These systems allow them to be on the road doing productive work all the time, thanks to constant communication with the office.

Supply chain management software in transportation helps load lorries, ships and aeroplanes in an optimal manner both in terms of space utilization and sequence of unloading. Figure 3.8 provides a visual description of an optimal loading of boxes on a lorry before its dispatch.

Figure 3.7 A software tool for optimizing utilization of human resources and equipment in transportation

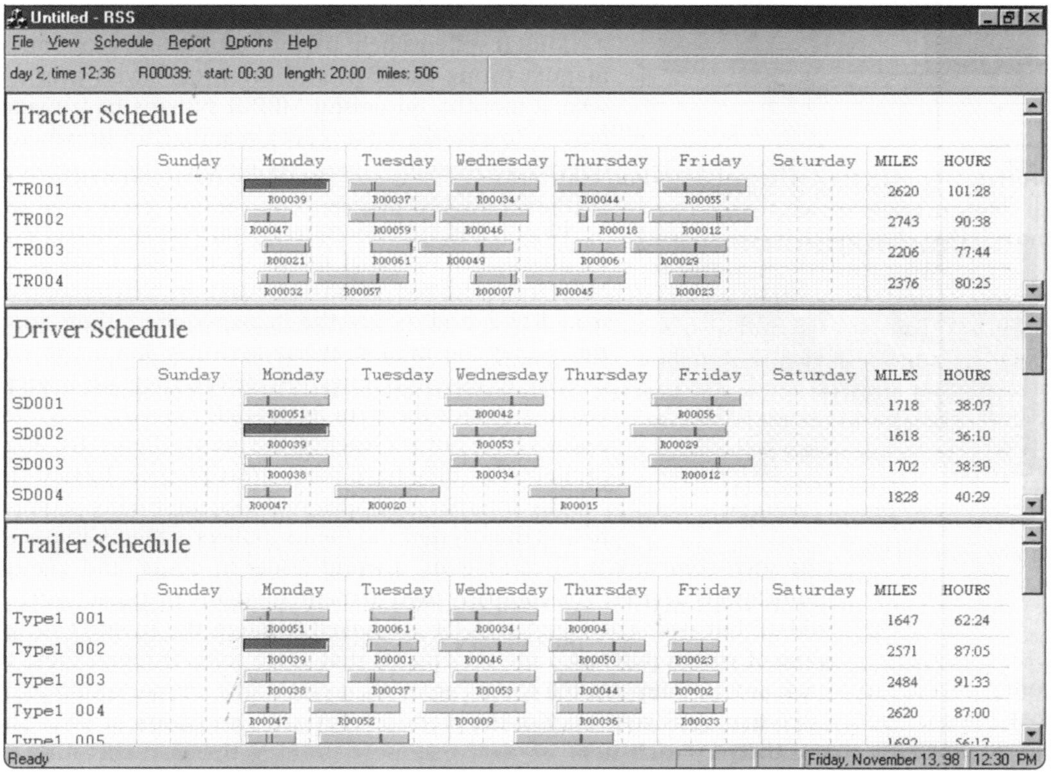

Untitled - RSS

File View Schedule Report Options Help

day 2, time 12:36   R00039: start: 00:30 length: 20:00 miles: 506

Tractor Schedule

	Sunday	Monday	Tuesday	Wednesday	Thursday	Friday	Saturday	MILES	HOURS
TR001		R00039	R00037	R00034	R00044	R00055		2620	101:28
TR002		R00047	R00059	R00046	R00018	R00012		2743	90:38
TR003		R00021	R00061	R00049	R00006	R00029		2206	77:44
TR004		R00032	R00057	R00007	R00045	R00023		2376	80:25

Driver Schedule

	Sunday	Monday	Tuesday	Wednesday	Thursday	Friday	Saturday	MILES	HOURS
SD001		R00051		R00042		R00056		1718	38:07
SD002		R00039		R00053		R00029		1618	36:10
SD003		R00038		R00034		R00012		1702	38:30
SD004		R00047	R00020		R00015			1828	40:29

Trailer Schedule

	Sunday	Monday	Tuesday	Wednesday	Thursday	Friday	Saturday	MILES	HOURS
Type1 001		R00051	R00061	R00034	R00004			1647	62:24
Type1 002		R00039	R00001	R00046	R00050	R00023		2571	87:05
Type1 003		R00038	R00037	R00053	R00044	R00002		2484	91:33
Type1 004		R00047	R00052	R00009	R00036	R00033		2620	87:00
Type1 005								1692	56:17

Ready

Friday, November 13, 98   12:30 PM

Figure 3.8　A graphical display of planned loading on a truck, as produced by shipping software

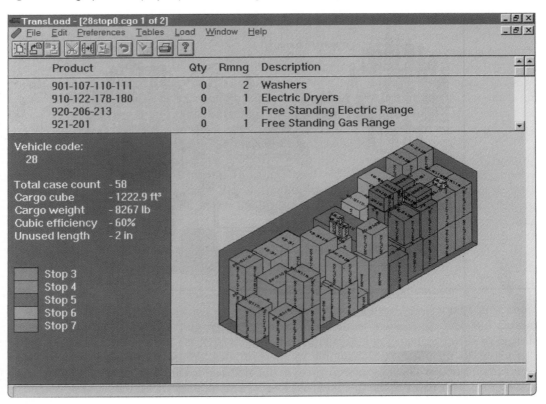

RFID in SCM

CD TASK

The most important development in hardware to support SCM has been a technology called **radio frequency identification (RFID)**. We discuss the technology itself in Chapter 5. RFID tags contain circuitry that allows recording of information about a product. When attached to a product, it contains an **electronic product code (EPC)**, which replaces the universal product code (UPC) with much more information. The tag can include the date of manufacturing, the plant in which the product was made, lot number, expiration date, destination and many other details that help track its movement and sale. The information can be read and also revised by special RFID transceivers (transmitter–receiver devices). Figure 3.9 shows an example of how RFID is used in a supply chain. Items with rewritable tags can contain the maintenance history of products, which helps in the maintenance of the items.

The same technology can also be used for other purposes: detection of items that should be recalled because of hazardous components, detection of counterfeit products and accurate condemnation of expired items, such as medicines and car parts. When a pattern of defects is discovered in a product, RFID helps pinpoint the plant at which it was produced and the particular lot from which it came. Only products from that lot are recalled and replaced or fixed. It does not take too long to find out the particular manufacturing phase in which the defect was caused. When the expiration date of an item arrives, a transceiver detects that fact and alerts personnel to remove it from a shelf. Packaging of medicines and other items contain RFID tags with unique identifiers. Transceivers can detect whether the products are genuine.

radio frequency identification (RFID) Technology that enables identification of an object (such as product, vehicle or living creature) by receiving a radio signal from a tag attached to the object.

electronic product code (EPC) A product code embedded in a radio frequency identification (RFID) tag. Similar to the older UPC.

Figure 3.9 RFID in the supply chain

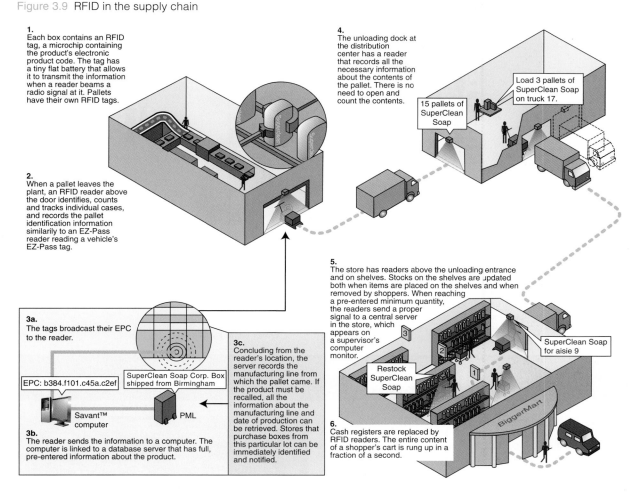

1.
Each box contains an RFID tag, a microchip containing the product's electronic product code. The tag has a tiny flat battery that allows it to transmit the information when a reader beams a radio signal at it. Pallets have their own RFID tags.

2.
When a pallet leaves the plant, an RFID reader above the door identifies, counts and tracks individual cases, and records the pallet identification information similarly to an EZ-Pass reader reading a vehicle's EZ-Pass tag.

3a.
The tags broadcast their EPC to the reader.

EPC: b384.f101.c45a.c2ef

Savant™ computer

SuperClean Soap Corp. Box shipped from Birmingham

PML

3b.
The reader sends the information to a computer. The computer is linked to a database server that has full, pre-entered information about the product.

3c.
Concluding from the reader's location, the server records the manufacturing line from which the pallet came. If the product must be recalled, all the information about the manufacturing line and date of production can be retrieved. Stores that purchase boxes from this particular lot can be immediately identified and notified.

4.
The unloading dock at the distribution center has a reader that records all the necessary information about the contents of the pallet. There is no need to open and count the contents.

15 pallets of SuperClean Soap

Load 3 pallets of SuperClean Soap on truck 17.

5.
The store has readers above the unloading entrance and on shelves. Stocks on the shelves are updated both when items are placed on the shelves and when removed by shoppers. When reaching a pre-entered minimum quantity, the readers send a proper signal to a central server in the store, which appears on a supervisor's computer monitor.

Restock SuperClean Soap

SuperClean Soap for aisie 9

BiggerMart

6.
Cash registers are replaced by RFID readers. The entire content of a shopper's cart is rung up in a fraction of a second.

Customer relationship management

No commercial organization can survive without selling its products or services. Thus, businesses seek to provide products that consumers want and to entice them to buy what the business produces. They exert marketing efforts to pinpoint demographic groups that are most likely to buy products, to determine features that consumers desire most and to provide the most efficient and effective ways to execute a sale when a consumer shows interest in the product or service. Because these efforts depend mainly on the analysis of huge amounts of data, ISs have become key tools for conceiving and executing marketing strategies. When marketing succeeds, ISs support the sales effort; to entice customers to continue to purchase, ISs support customer service (see Figure 3.10).

Customer relationship management (CRM) systems are designed to support any and all relationships with customers. Mostly, they support three areas: marketing, sales and customer service. Modern CRM systems can help capture the entire customer experience with an organization, from response to an online advertisement to automatic replenishment of products, to proactive service. With growing competition and so many options available to consumers, keeping customers satisfied is extremely important. Many executives will tell you that their companies do not make money (and might even lose money) on a first sale to a new customer because of the great investment in marketing. Thus, they constantly strive to

Figure 3.10 Customer relationship management systems help marketing, sales and customer sevice
departments target interested customers, learn from their experiences, and serve them better

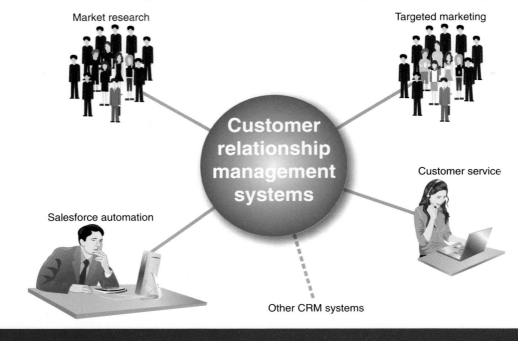

Market research

Targeted marketing

Customer relationship management systems

Customer service

Salesforce automation

Other CRM systems

Industry **SNAPSHOT**

Say it with flowers – using RFID

FloraHolland is the world's largest flower auction company. It houses flowers from 7000 growers in a warehouse the size of 100 football fields. It interacts with 4000 dealers and exporters and needs to move 100,000 trolleys of flowers around the warehouse. Each of the trolleys are fitted with RFID tags and RFID loops are embedded in the warehouse floor. The movement of the flowers is captured and this information is made available to the IT systems that handle the auctions. Data about the trolley number and the products on it are displayed on an LED screen on the auction floor, alerting buyers as to which products are heading to auction. Time is an important factor, as the flowers must be moved quickly to ensure they are fresh. Customers can receive an electronic processing history of the flowers to guarantee their quality, for example ensuring that they have not spent too much time out of cold storage en route to the auction. FloaraHolland can use the data to analyse their logistics and make improvements.

SOURCE: Claire Swedberg, 'Dutch Horticultural Company Sends Flowers via RFID', *RFID Journal*, http://www.rfidjournal.com/article/articleview/2793/1/1/

improve customer service and periodically contact anyone who has ever purchased something from them to ensure repeat sales and to encourage customer loyalty. Any information technology that supports these efforts is considered a CRM system, but in recent years the effort has been to combine applications that support all three areas – marketing, sales and customer service – to better understand what customers want, to ensure timely delivery and to be able to collect payment sooner.

CRM systems also provide an organization with an important element: all employees of the company who directly or indirectly serve a customer are 'on the same page'. Through their individual computers, all can have immediate access to the status of an order for an item or a resolution of a buyer's complaint, or to any other information that has to do with the customer. All who serve the customer are well informed and receive the information from the same source. This is especially important in a long, complex sales cycle, because it minimizes response time and improves the quality of service for customers.

Market research

Few organizations can sell their products and services without promotion; fewer still can promote successfully without market research. Market research systems help to find the populations and regions that are most likely to purchase a new product or service. They also help analyse how a new product fares in its first several months on the market.

Through interviews with consumers and retailers, market researchers collect information on what consumers like and dislike about products. When the researchers collect sufficient data, the marketing department uses statistical models to predict sales volumes of different products and of different designs of the same product. This critical information aids in planning manufacturing capacities and production lines. It is also extremely important for budgeting purposes.

Targeted marketing

To save resources, businesses use IT to promote to people most likely to purchase their products. This activity is often referred to as targeted marketing. Great advances in database technology enable even the smallest and poorest business to use targeted marketing. The principle of targeted marketing is to define the prospective customer as accurately as possible and then to direct promotional spending towards those people most likely to purchase your product. Perhaps the best evidence of how much companies use ISs for targeted marketing is the use of the Internet for mass communication of unsolicited promotional email, a practice called spamming. Many people loathe spamming, but it is certainly the least expensive method of advertising. Another controversial, but apparently effective, method is pop-up advertising, in which a small window pops up either in front of or behind a web browser's window.

targeted marketing Promoting products and services to the people who are most likely to purchase them.

To define their target markets, businesses collect data everywhere they can: from sales transactions and loyalty cards, or by purchasing databases with information about organizations and individuals. Using database management systems (DBMSs), special programs to build and manipulate data pools, a company can sort and categorize consumers by age, gender, income, previous purchase of a related product, or any combination of these facts and other demographic information. The company then selects those whose characteristics match the company's customer profile and spends its promotional effort and money to try to sell to those select customers.

The great amount of personal information that corporations collect and purchase lets them prepare electronic dossiers on the interests, tastes and buying habits of individuals. The information they possess lets them target 'a market of one', namely, an individual rather than a group. Online purchase transactions and online product registrations by consumers provide a wealth of information to corporations. Vendors sort the information to send promotional material by post or email only to those customers whose profiles indicate potential interest.

Telemarketing (marketing over the telephone) makes extensive use of IT. The telemarketer uses a PC connected to a large database. The database contains records of potential or existing customers. With a retrieved record displayed on the screen, a marketer dials the number by pressing a single key or clicking the mouse. The telemarketer speaks to the potential buyer while looking at that person's purchasing record with the organization or even other organizations. Charitable organizations use the same method to solicit donations.

Computer telephony integration (CTI) is a technique enabling a computer to use the digital signal coming through a telephone line as input in a computer system. It has been used often in marketing, sales and customer service. For example, some mail-order firms use caller ID to better serve their customers. Caller ID was originally intended to identify the telephone number from which a person calls, but mail-order businesses quickly found a new use for the gadget. They connect it to their customer database. When you call to order, a simple program searches for your number, retrieves your record and displays it on a PC monitor. You might be surprised when the person who receives your call greets you by name and later asks if you want to use the same credit card number you used in your last purchase.

Techniques such as data mining take advantage of large data warehouses to find trends and shopping habits of various demographic groups. For example, the software discovers clusters of products that people tend to purchase together and then the marketing experts promote the products as a combination and might suggest displaying them together on store shelves. You will learn more about data mining in Chapter 6.

With the proliferation of set-top boxes for digital televisions, several companies have developed applications that may allow television networks to transition from the wasteful and expensive 30-second commercial to more personal advertising. Relying on information provided by households through these interactive boxes, they can select and transmit to each subscriber commercials only for products in which the subscriber is interested. For example, you will not receive commercials about pet food if you do not have pets but will receive commercials about gardening if this is your hobby.

Use of information technology for targeted marketing has taken sophisticated forms on the Web. More than just targeting a certain demographic group, web technologies enable retailers to *personalize* marketing when shopping and buying are conducted online. Special software on online retailers' servers keeps track of every visit consumers make and captures their 'click streams' (the sequence of selections they make) and the amount of time they spend viewing each page. The retailer's software combines this information with information from online purchases to personalize the pages whenever consumers revisit the site. The reconstructed page introduces information about the products that the individual visitor is most likely to purchase. For example, two people with different purchasing records at Amazon.co.uk who revisit the company's home page will find that they are looking at slightly different versions of the page. Amazon's software custom-composes the elements for each person according to his or her inferred interests in products. The ones that the software concludes might be of the highest interest are displayed or linked on the page.

Customer service

Web-based customer service provides automated customer support 24 hours per day, 365 days per year. At the same time, it saves companies the cost of labour required when humans provide the same service. For example, letting customers pay their bills electronically not only provides convenience but also saves (both customers and companies) the cost of postage and paper and saves the company the time required for dealing with paper documents. Online billing costs only a small fraction of paper billing. The business research firm Gartner Group estimates the average invoice-to-payment cycle at 41 days, while online invoice and payment shortens the period by at least six days. Customers appreciate the discounts that many companies offer for accepting statements and paying bills online.

Ethical and Societal ISSUES

Consumer privacy

Consider the following scenario: you agree to give some financial information about yourself to one organization in exchange for credit. At a later date, you provide some medical information to another organization. In the meantime, your credit card company has enough information from your purchasing activity to know your culinary and fashion tastes better than you do. Finally, without your knowledge or consent, yet another organization gathers all this information and puts it in one big record that is practically a detailed personal dossier. Whenever you use your credit card, you provide information about you. Whenever you interact with an organization online, you provide information about you. Do you ever stop to think where the information goes?

Organizations collect huge amounts of personal information. Every time you pay with your credit card you leave a personal record; the few details of your purchase are often used to update an already hefty dossier about your buying habits. Every time you provide personal information at a website, you either help open a new dossier with an organization or help other organizations update their dossier about you. In their zeal to market more effectively, businesses often violate consumer privacy.

What is privacy? In the context of information, privacy is your right to control information about yourself. For example, you keep your privacy if you keep to yourself your university grades, medical background or the name of the person with whom you had dinner last evening. Someone who receives such information without your permission is violating your privacy.

Business arguments Business leaders argue that they must collect and use personal data. Without personal data, they would have to waste time and money to target likely buyers. They need to know the purchasing and payment habits of individuals because these details create credit histories that help make prudent decisions on consumer risks. This ability to purchase and manipulate large amounts of consumer information makes the business world more democratic than it used to be.

Small companies now have the same chances of targeting prospective buyers with good credit as big companies, creating more opportunities and more competition, which eventually benefit consumers.

Consumer arguments Consumers usually accept that they must divulge some private information to receive services, but many do not accept the mass violation of privacy. They resent unsolicited junk mail and email sent by companies who know much about them although they have never provided personal details to these companies. They hate telephone calls from salespeople who obtained their records from companies that were supposed to keep their records confidential. And they are frightened by the 'dossier phenomenon': it might be the greatest concern to consumers.

Losing control In many cases, you volunteer information in return for some benefit, such as receiving a discount or participation in a competition. In others, you simply cannot receive the service or product unless you agree to give certain personal details. In such cases, you give implicit or explicit informed consent to obtain information about yourself. However, once you provide information, you have little control over it. With some newer technology, such as RFID, you might not even be aware of who is collecting information about you and when it is collected. You have just stepped out of a supermarket with a cartful of groceries. All are RFID-tagged. The supermarket systems recorded your visit and detailed what you purchased. Can you be sure that nobody else has the proper device to read and record what you purchased?

The Eight Commandments of personal data collection and maintenance In a free, market-oriented society, not allowing organizations to collect personal data is inconceivable. What can businesses do to help protect privacy? They can try to adhere to these rules to avoid misuse:

Purpose. Companies should inform people who provide information of the specific, exclusive purpose for which the company maintains its data and use the data for another purpose only with the subjects' consent. For example, this practice could protect psychiatric patients from having their insurance companies sell information about their treatments.

Relevance. Companies should only record and use data necessary to fulfil their own purposes. For example, an applicant's credit record should not contain his or her political views because that information is irrelevant in credit considerations and would only be useful if sold.

Accuracy. Companies should ensure that the personal records they maintain are accurate. For example, many loan applicants have had terrible experiences because some of the data maintained by credit companies is erroneous. Careful data entry and periodic verification can enhance accuracy.

Currency. Companies should make sure that all data about an individual are current. If currency cannot be guaranteed, then data should be discarded periodically. Outdated information can create horribly negative repercussions. For example, a person who might have been unemployable due to past illness might not be able to get a job, even though he or she might be healthy now.

Security. Companies should limit access to data to only those who need to know. In addition to passwords, audit trails (which identify every employee who accesses a personal record and for what purpose) are also very effective tools for ensuring security.

Time limitation. Companies should retain data only for the time period necessary.

Scrutiny. Companies should establish procedures to let individuals review their records and correct inaccuracies.

Sole recording. When using a recording technology, a company should ensure that no other party can take advantage of the technology to record the same information. For example, if a supermarket records an individual's purchases using RFID technology, it must ensure that the RFID tags embedded in the packaging are disabled as soon as the customer leaves the store.

All of the above 'commandments' have been embodied into legislation in different parts of the world, for example the UK Data Protection Act. Of course, many consumers will still feel that their privacy is invaded even if every business is required to comply with the legislation. How can you protect your privacy? Do not furnish your name, passport (or any other identifying) number, address, or any other private information if you do not know how it will be used. If you do provide detailed information, indicate that you do not wish the data to be shared with any other organization or individual. You can usually check a box to this effect on paper or online forms. To avoid junk mail or junk email, again check the proper box on online forms. Do not fill out any online or paper forms with detailed data unless an opt-out option is available. Of course, many services we receive depend on our willingness to provide personal data, so at least some organizations must have personal information, but you can be selective. Always carefully weigh what you gain against the privacy you might lose.

Online customer service applications have become increasingly sophisticated. They help track past purchases and payments, update online answers to frequently asked questions (FAQs) about products and services and analyse customers' contacts with the company to maintain and update an electronic customer profile. The FAQ pages of many companies have been replaced with options for open-ended questions; instead of looking up a question that is similar to what you would ask, you can simply type in your question. Employing artificial intelligence software, the site will 'understand' your question and provide a short list of links where you can find an answer.

Sales force automation

Sales force automation equips travelling salespeople with information technology to facilitate their productivity. Typically, salespeople are equipped with notebook computers that store promotional information for prospective customers, software for manipulating this information and computerized forms. Many salespeople carry laptop computers or personal digital assistants (PDAs) with all the information they need and which allow them to connect to their organizational information systems through the Internet. Sales force automation can increase sales productivity significantly, making sales presentations more efficient and letting field representatives close deals on the spot, using preformatted contracts and forms.

Information technology lets salespeople present different options for products and services on the computer, rather than asking prospective customers to wait until the main office faxes or posts the information. At the end of the day or the week, salespeople can upload sales information to a computer at the main office, where it is raw input to the order-processing department, the manufacturing unit, or the shipping and invoicing departments.

Using PDAs that can establish a wireless connection to the Internet enables salespeople to check prices, check availability of the items in which a customer is interested and place an order away from the office. The salespeople can then spend much more time on the road, increasing time spent with prospective customers.

Human resource management

Human resource management (HRM) has become more complex due to the fast growth in specialized occupations, the need to train and promote highly skilled employees and the growing variety of benefits programmes. Human resource management can be classified into five main activities: (1) employee record management, (2) promotion and recruitment, (3) training, (4) evaluation and (5) compensation and benefits management (see Figure 3.11).

Text and pictures can be combined to store and retrieve employee records.

Figure 3.11 Human resource management information systems help managers optimize promotion and recruitment, training, evaluation and other activities

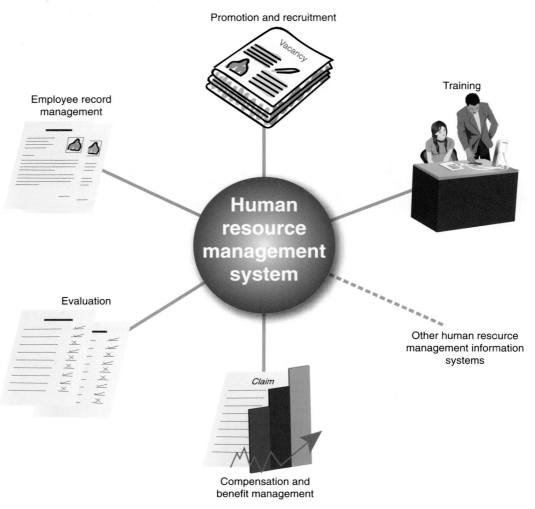

Employee record management

ISs facilitate employee record management. Human resource departments must keep personnel records to satisfy both external regulations (for example those required by law) and internal regulations, as well as for payroll and tax calculation and deposit, promotion consideration and periodic reporting. Many HR ISs are now held completely in digital form (including employees' pictures), which dramatically reduces the space needed to store records, the time needed to retrieve them and the costs of both.

Promotion and recruitment

To select the best-qualified person for a position, a human resource manager can search a database of applicants and existing employees' records for set criteria, such as a specific type and length of education, particular experience, specific talents and required licences or certifications. Automating the selection process significantly minimizes time and money spent on recruitment but does require that a current database be maintained.

Intranets (intra-organizational networks that support web applications) help HR managers post position vacancy announcements for employees to peruse and consider from their own PCs. This system is especially efficient in large organizations that employ thousands of workers and even more so at multisite organizations.

Many companies refuse to receive paper applications and curricula vitae (CVs). Some accept such documents via email, but others accept only forms that are filled out and submitted online. Using keywords, recruiting officers can then use special software to scour a database for the most-qualified candidates. HR consultants say that this process reduces the time spent on a typical search from several hours to several minutes. Some software companies sell automated recruiting and selection software to support such activities.

Industry **SNAPSHOT**

E-recruitment

A study conducted by the Institute for Employment Studies in 2003 found that organizations reported the following as being important factors in their decision to increase the use of e-recruitment:

- improve corporate image and profile

- reduce recruitment costs

- reduce administrative burden

- employ better tools for the recruitment team.

SOURCE: *e-Recruitment: Is it Delivering?* M. Kerrin and P. Kettley, IES Report 402, 2003. ISBN: 978-1-85184-329-9

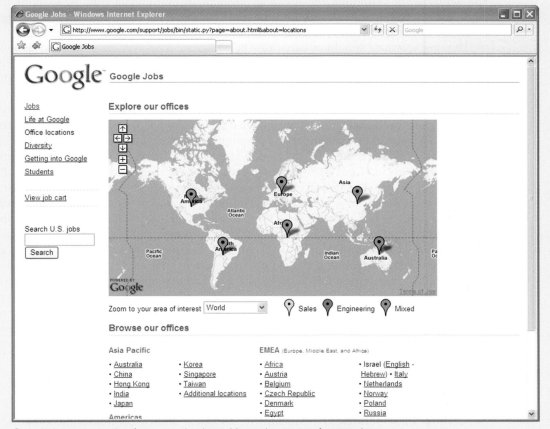

PHOTO SOURCE: ©2008 GOOGLE

Google is an example of an organization taking advantage of e-recruitment.

Some companies use the entire Web as a database for their search, which means they include in the search many people who have never applied for a job with them but have posted their CVs. Traditional recruitment methods often produce many candidates but, alas, often few (or none!) of these are suitable. The whole process can be very expensive and, worse still, a complete waste of money, and it would seem that the situation is potentially set to become worse. Demographics suggest that 35 million Europeans will disappear from the labour market in the next ten years. However, the Internet has created a significant number of 'always on' jobseekers, people who are not specifically looking for a particular job but are open to offers. Software exists that searches the Web for CVs and then matches qualified candidates with job openings. Across industries, as companies move from traditional recruiting to recruiting through the Web, the cost per hire is set to reduce significantly.

Training

One important function of human resource departments is improving employee skills. In both the manufacturing and service sectors, multimedia software training is rapidly replacing training programmes involving classrooms and teachers. Such applications include interactive, three-dimensional simulated environments. Some applications contain full-blown virtual reality components. For example, one such application trains workers to handle wrought iron that must be hammered manually. The worker wears special goggles and holds a hammer in one hand and a piece of metal in the other, over an anvil. The worker 'sees' the metal piece through the goggles, 'hears' the hitting sound through earphones and receives a programmed, realistic jolt every time he 'hits' the metal. This safely prepares the employees for the dangerous work instead of putting them at risk of injury before they have enough experience to do the actual work. Although the initial investment in multimedia training systems might be high, human resource managers find the systems very effective. Surgeons train using similar systems to operate on virtual patients rather than risk injuries to human patients.

Training software simulates situations in which an employee must act and includes tests and modules to evaluate a trainee's performance. In addition to the savings in trainers' time, there are other benefits. The trainee is more comfortable because he or she controls the speed at which the sessions run. The software lets the trainee go back to a certain point in the session if a concept is missed. Also, the software can simulate hazardous situations, thereby testing employee performance in a safe environment. And if training in a real environment involves destruction of equipment or consumption of materials, virtual reality training applications accomplish the same results in skill enhancement without destruction or waste.

Developments in IT enable organizations to reduce training costs dramatically. BUPA is the UK market leader in health and care services. Some staff spend a great deal of time travelling and need to be contactable via email. A solution was found in the issuing of Blackberry PDAs but naturally these people needed training in order to get the most out of the technology. The initial solution was to set up two-and-a-half-hour classroom-based training sessions but this proved problematical and expensive. BUPA commissioned Tata Interactive Systems, an international e-learning developer, to devise an alternative strategy for the delivery of this necessary learning. In addition BUPA introduced a learning management system (LMS) which enables the monitoring of all training programmes and the engagement of the employees with those programmes. The e-learning programme reduced the training time by an hour and also saved, on average, one and a half hours travelling time per employee with an associated reduction in training costs for the company. Staff are pleased with the flexible approach and they are also able to access refresher training at any time that they need it.

Evaluation

Supervisors must periodically evaluate the technical ability, communications skills, professional conduct and general behaviour of employees. While objective factors are involved in evaluation – such as attendance rates and punctuality – employee evaluation is often very subjective. Assessing performance and effort levels and their relative weights of importance, varies significantly, depending on who is evaluating. A supervisor might forget to include some factors altogether or might inappropriately weigh a particular aspect of performance. Subjectivity is particularly problematic when several employees are being considered for a promotion and their evaluations are compared to determine the strongest candidate. By helping to standardize the evaluation process across employees and departments, evaluation software adds a certain measure of objectivity and consistency.

In an evaluation, a supervisor provides feedback to an employee, records the evaluation for official records and future comparison and accepts input from the employee. Software helps managers standardize their employee evaluations by providing step-by-step guides to writing performance reviews, a checklist of performance areas to include in the evaluation (with the option to add or remove topics), scales to indicate how strong the employee is in each area and the ability to select the relative importance each factor should hold in the overall evaluation. Performance areas include written and oral communication, job knowledge and management skills, with each topic subdivided into basic elements to assist the supervisor in creating an accurate evaluation. A typical application guides the user through all necessary factors and includes a help guide. When the evaluator finishes entering data, the application automatically computes a subtotal for each category and a weighted grade, which can then be electronically stored as part of the employee's record.

Compensation and benefits management

ISs help HR officers manage compensation (salaries, hourly pay, commissions and bonuses) efficiently and effectively. Programs can easily calculate weekly, monthly and hourly pay according to annual salaries and can include tax tables to assist in complying with compensation regulations. This same system can also automatically generate pay cheques or direct deposits, which are the electronic transfer of funds from the firm's bank account to the employee's.

Special software helps the HR department manage benefits, such as health insurance, life insurance, retirement plans and sick leave days. To optimize benefits, some companies use special software, incorporating expert systems (ISs that emulate human expertise) that determine the optimal health and retirement plans for each employee based on factors such as marital status, age, occupation and other data.

Using intranets, many organizations allow their employees to access the benefits database directly and make changes to their preferences, such as selecting another health-care insurance programme, or adding a family member as a beneficiary in a life insurance plan. When the company engages a third party for managing pension funds or other benefits, employees can go directly to the website of that company, not involving their own company resources at all. By making the changes directly from their PCs, employees reduce the amount of work of the HR staff and decrease the company's overhead costs.

Inter-organizational supply chain management systems

According to IBM, companies that implemented SCM systems have reduced inventory levels by 10–50 per cent, improved the rate of accurate deliveries by 95–99 per cent, reduced unscheduled work stoppages to 0–5 per cent, reduced cycle time (from order to collection) by 10–20 per cent and reduced transportation costs by 10–15 per cent.

Figure 3.12 A shared supply chain management system

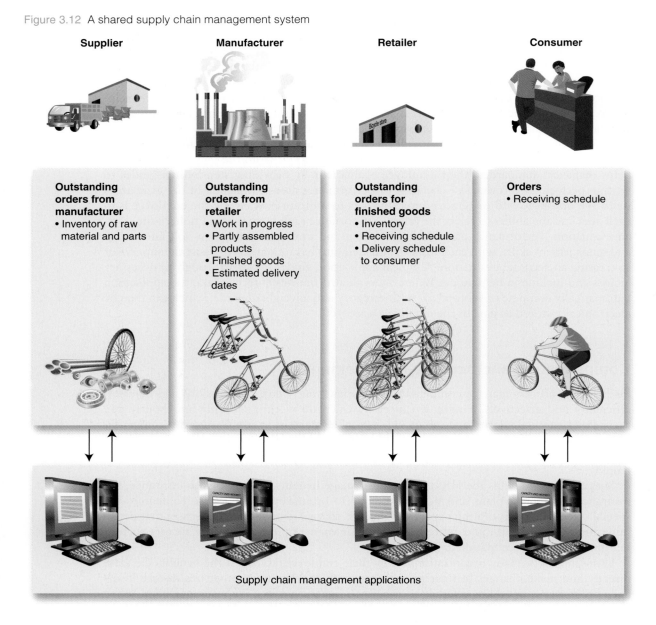

Several enterprise applications, such as ERP systems, also serve as SCM systems. As Figure 3.12 illustrates, many such systems enable managers not only to monitor what goes on at their own units or organization, but also to follow what goes on at the facilities of their suppliers and contractors. For example, at any given point in time managers can know the status of the following: an order now being handled by a contractor, by order number; the phase of manufacturing the produced units have reached; and the date of delivery, including any delays and their length. When purchasing parts, managers use the systems for issuing electronic purchase orders and they can follow the fulfilment process at the supplier's facilities, such as when the parts were packed, when they were loaded onto lorries and when they are estimated to arrive at the managers' floor or the floor of another business partner who needed the parts.

SCM applications streamline operations throughout the chain, from suppliers to customers, lowering inventories, decreasing production costs and improving responsiveness to suppliers and clients. Harnessing the global network, managers can supervise an entire supply chain regardless of the location of the activity – at their own facilities or another organization's, at the same location or thousands of miles away. Older SCM systems connected two organizations. New ones connect several. For example, a distributor can reorder products from Organization A and simultaneously alert Organization B, the supplier of Organization A. The systems let all parties – suppliers, manufacturers, distributors and customers – see the same information. A change made by any organization that affects an order can affect a corresponding change in scheduling and operations in the other organization's activities.

Companies that have adopted SCM systems have seen improvement in three major areas: reduction in inventory, reduction in cycle time (the time it takes to complete a business process) and, as a result, reduction in production cost. Companies can reduce their inventory by communicating to their suppliers through a shared SCM system the exact number of units of each item they need and the exact time they need them. In ideal situations, they do not need to stockpile any inventory, saving warehouse costs. The management consulting firm Aberdeen Group estimates that companies using SCM systems through the Internet reduce purchase order processing cycles by 70–80 per cent and pay 5–10 per cent less for the items they purchase.

The importance of trust

SCM systems accomplish the greatest efficiencies when all businesses in the chain link their systems and share all the information that is pertinent to planning production and shipment. For example, Nissan UK has a 750 acre site near Sunderland, currently the UK's biggest car plant with flexible production technology that allows different car models to be produced on the same line. The majority of the parts used come from the UK and almost all the rest come from Europe. Key components are sourced from suppliers who are located in Sunderland and are categorized as 'Synchro Suppliers' whose systems are closely linked with Nissan's production control system. It is reported that 97 per cent of parts are delivered on time and over 98 per cent of cars are completed within two hours of their allotted time slot. The inventory of parts has been reduced by 45 per cent since 2001, leading to a reduction in manufacturing costs of 16 per cent. All of this can only happen if the suppliers and Nissan are willing and able to work together, particularly with regard to their ISs.

However, not all organizations are willing to collaborate with their business partners. One reason is the fear that when Organization A purchases from Organization B and has access to Organization B's demand figures, it might disclose the information to competitors in an attempt to stir more competition and enjoy favourable prices. Another fear is that if Organization B realizes that at a certain point in time Organization A is in dire need of its raw materials, Organization B might take advantage of the situation and negotiate higher prices.

The first type of fear can be found in the initial reluctance of suppliers to share information with large buyers such as Tesco. Only the bargaining power of Tesco and its insistence on sharing such information convinced suppliers to link their systems with those of Tesco. The second type of fear is still there between General Motors and its main tyre supplier, Goodyear. Goodyear could enjoy lower inventories if it had GM's demand schedule for tyres. It could then calibrate its own order for raw materials, such as rubber, and its manufacturing capacity to suit those of GM, save money and pass at least some of the savings to its client in the form of cheaper products. It could always replenish its client's inventory of tyres before GM ran out of them. Better yet, it could deliver the tyres directly to the assembly lines just when they are needed, saving both GM and itself warehousing costs. Yet, GM is guarding its production schedule as confidential.

SCM systems can be taken a step beyond the sale. The systems can be used for after-the-sale services. For example, Beckman Coulter is an international company with operations in over 130 countries and more than 10,000 employees. It makes blood analysers and other medical devices. After it sells a machine, the company uses the Internet to link the machine from the client's facility to a computer system in its head office. Software on the computer runs seven days per week, 24 hours per day to monitor the sold machine. When a problem occurs, the computer alerts a Beckman technician, who can repair the machine before it stops working. Beckman estimates that the system saves it US$1 million annually, because malfunctions are captured at an early stage, which avoids the higher cost of fixing a more damaged machine. The added benefit is increased customer satisfaction.

The musical chairs of inventory

So sensible use of ISs can help to reduce the inventory and hence the costs involved in maintaining that inventory. However, much of the trend took place in the 1981–1991 period. Since then the situation across business and industry as a whole has remained the same. Apparently, while large corporations have the resources to install and run SCM systems to cut their own inventory, the ratio of inventory to revenue in small enterprises is growing because they do not use such systems. And sometimes, the companies that suffer the inventory ripple effect are not small. They might be powerful and they might even own their own SCM system, but their system might not be linked to their buyers' systems, so they cannot plan their own production to reduce inventory.

For an example, let us return to the relationship between General Motors and Goodyear. The world's largest car manufacturer improved 'inventory turns' 55.2 per cent between 1996 and 2001. Inventory turns are the number of times a business sells (or turns over) its inventory per year. It is calculated by dividing the sales revenue by the average value of inventory. The greater the inventory turns number, the better. During the same period, Goodyear, GM's tyre supplier, experienced a 21 per cent decrease in inventory turns. The likely conclusion is that GM avoided purchasing tyres from Goodyear until it needed them at the assembly line, but Goodyear did not have enough information on when, exactly, those tyres would be required and therefore kept overstocks. Had the SCM systems of the companies been linked, Goodyear could reduce inventory and see its inventory turns rise rather than fall. It is also reasonable to assume that thanks to the cost savings, Goodyear would be able to sell tyres to GM at a lower price. GM and other companies have created a situation where the company tries to 'sit' with a lean inventory while, inadvertently, leaving another 'standing' with an overstock. In order for all involved in a supply chain to enjoy efficiencies, the musical chairs, or 'hot potato' situation, must stop.

Collaborative logistics

The Web enables organizations from totally different industries to streamline operations through collaboration. In recent years an increasing number of businesses found a new way to cut distribution costs: they combine goods for delivery with other businesses, sharing their own lorries or the vehicles of delivery companies. The collaboration reduces partially empty lorries, or empty vehicles between stops. To this end, the companies connect their SCM systems to the site of a company that specializes in optimization of logistics, such as UK-based company Translogistica. The company manages the site and uses sophisticated software to calculate the shortest routes between departure and arrival points and the best combination of loads from two or more companies to share trucks and routes. The SCM systems of subscribing companies provide daily data into the shared system. The IS takes into consideration the type of freight to ensure safety and adherence to regulations. For example, the software is designed not to combine chemicals with food. Therefore, typical allies of food manufacturers have been paper manufacturers, for instance. The cost savings have been impressive.

A group of companies operating in Northern Ireland and the Republic of Ireland from small to medium enterprises (SMEs) to global brand names worked with the European Logistic Users, Providers and Enablers Group (ELUPEG) and InterTradeIreland on a project to demonstrate how collaboration could bring down costs and improve competitiveness. Their prediction is not only massive savings but also a positive environmental contribution through better utilization of vehicles and reduced traffic congestion.

Another area where some companies have explored collaboration is warehousing. The principle here is the same: try to maximize the use of warehouse space and if you cannot use all of it, allow other businesses to use the extra space. The way to accomplish this, again, goes through the Web: a third party specializing in warehousing optimization combines warehousing needs and availability from member companies to offer optimal solutions.

Enterprise resource planning

A growing number of organizations elect to replace old, disparate ISs with enterprise applications that support all or most of the business activities we have described. As mentioned before, these systems are often referred to as enterprise resource planning (ERP) systems, although they are used not only for planning but also for managing daily operations. Designers of ERP systems take a systems approach to an enterprise. For example, the manufacturing resource planning (MRP) component of the system uses the information recorded on a sale to retrieve product specifications; the data are used to generate purchasing information such as items, quantities and the timetable for suppliers to deliver for the purchasing department. As products are manufactured, the system tracks the stages of the work in progress. When items are ready to be delivered, the distribution department can retrieve information on the items for its operations. The system keeps delivery information such as content and destination, along with billing information, to help produce delivery and billing documentation. The system also records financial transactions involved in such activities, such as payment made from a bank account. The accounting component records the transactions. In addition, ERP systems also provide human resource modules for payroll, employee benefits management and employee evaluation software. CRM components are also available and are tied to other components through orders applications and sales records.

> **enterprise resource planning (ERP) system** An information system that supports different activities for different departments, assisting executives with planning and running different interdependent functions.

ERP packages are quite complex. Because they are not tailored to the needs of specific clients, they often require adjustment and fine-tuning for specific organizations. Therefore, their installation and testing involve experts who are usually employees of the software vendor or professionals who are certified for such work by the vendor. The most visible software companies specializing in ERP systems are SAP and Oracle.

ERP applications represent a significant expense for a business. Installation and modifications represent further major spending. Installation often takes many months to complete. Implementation of ERP systems can fail because of formidable challenges: the gap between system capabilities and business needs, lack of expertise on the consultant's part and mismanagement of the implementation project. The business research firm Standish Group found that only 10 per cent of ERP implementation projects are completed as planned, on time and within budget. Fifty-five per cent are completed late or over budget (which usually means loss of business and revenue) and the other 35 per cent of such projects are cancelled because of difficulties. At Hewlett-Packard, one of the world's largest computer and IT equipment makers, a US$400 million loss in the third quarter of 2004 was blamed on poorly managed migration to a new ERP system.

SUMMARY

Effectiveness is the degree to which a task is accomplished. The better a person performs a job, the more effective he or she is. Efficiency is measured as the ratio of output to input. The more output with the same input, or the less input for the same output used in a process, the more efficient the process. ISs can help companies attain more effective and efficient business processes. Productivity is the measure of people's efficiency. When people use ISs, their productivity increases.

ISs have been integrated into almost every functional business area. In accounting and payroll, because of the routine and structured nature of accounting tasks, the systems automatically post transactions in the books and automate the generation of reports for management and for legal requirements.

Financial ISs help managers track cash available for transactions, while ensuring that available money is invested in short- or long-term programmes to yield the highest interest possible. Investment analysis ISs help build portfolios based on historical performance and other characteristics of securities.

Computer-aided design (CAD) systems help engineers design new products and save and modify drawings electronically. Computer-aided manufacturing (CAM) systems direct machines in manufacturing parts and assembling products.

Supply chain management systems optimize workload, speed and cost in the supply chains: procurement of raw materials, manufacturing and distribution of goods. ISs, especially MRP and MRP II systems, facilitate production scheduling and material requirements planning and shorten lead time between idea and product. Shipping ISs help speed up delivery and cut costs. RFID technology helps promote and operate supply chain management (SCM) systems. Radio frequency identification (RFID) tags carry product information that can be tracked and updated.

Customer relationship management (CRM) includes the entire cycle of relationships with customers, from marketing through sales to customer service. CRM ISs collect information about shoppers and customers and help target the most likely buyers of a product or service. Online customer service systems help customers help themselves via the Web 24 hours per day, seven days per week and save the company labour and telephone expenses. Salesforce automation allows travelling salespeople to spend more time with customers and less time in the office.

Human resource management systems expedite staff selection and record keeping. An increasing amount of recruiting is done via the Web. Managers often use evaluation software to help assess their subordinates' performance. Employees can use expert systems to choose health care and other benefits programmes that best suit their situation.

Companies can link their SCM systems to monitor the status of orders not only at their own facilities but also at those of their business partners, usually their suppliers. Such cooperation can create further efficiencies, but it requires a high degree of trust between organizations.

Rather than use disparate ISs for business functions, many organizations opt to install a single system that encompasses all their business processes, or at least the major ones. They employ enterprise resource planning (ERP) systems to support their supply chain management and customer relationship management.

BETTER BITES REVISITED

Better Bites has grown in the past two years from a single pushcart to a business with many sites, different products and more customers. The partners have noticed that their activities are becoming more specialized as the business grows and that they need information systems to support those activities. Help them sort through their systems.

What would you do?

Using the classifications in this chapter, identify the business functions within Better Bites. Which information systems do Paul, Sarah and Christina use now to streamline their operations? What other applications could they use?

Do you think that Better Bites should invest in an ERP system at this time? Why or why not? If not, which types of information systems mentioned in this chapter would be appropriate short of an ERP system?

New perspectives

A large snack-food manufacturer has noticed that Sarah's crisp line is very successful. The manufacturer is now proposing that Better Bites license its crisp business – the partners would get a percentage of the profits from the expanded sales and the manufacturer would have a new healthful crisp line to round out its snack-food product line. What information could the three entrepreneurs use to help them decide whether this opportunity would be a good idea? Suggest how they could obtain this information.

Review questions

1   What is a supply chain? What is the purpose of supply chain management systems?

2   What is the purpose of cost accounting ISs?

3   What is the relationship between CAD and CAM systems?

4   What are the concerns in cash management and how do cash management ISs help financial managers?

5   What is time to market? How have ISs affected time to market?

6   In brief, what is the purpose of customer relationship management systems?

7   What are the typical components of ERP systems?

8   Although technologically the full linking of the SCM systems of suppliers and buyers is feasible, many buyers are reluctant to do so. Why?

9   Why do the ERP installation and testing of systems require that experts be involved? Why does the implementation of so many ERP systems face severe challenges or totally fail?

10   What is EOQ? Which two problems do ISs that calculate EOQ help minimize?

11   What is JIT? How do MRP and MRP II systems help achieve JIT?

12   For the human resource managers of some organizations the entire Web is a database of job candidates. How so?

13   What information technologies play a crucial role in marketing?

14   Many sales reps have no offices, yet their productivity is great. Explain how that is possible.

15   What is RFID and what role does it play in SCM?

16   In the supply chain, distribution software helps mainly in two ways. What are they?

Discussion questions

1   You established a small shop that manufactures a single product that you sell by mail. You purchase raw materials from several vendors and employ five full-time employees. For which business functions would you certainly use software?

2 Which of the ISs you listed for Question 1 would you link to each other and for what purpose?

3 Why is it so important to have a quick response of online investment ISs? Give two examples of how such systems are critical.

4 Some experts say that ISs have great potential in manufacturing. Explain why. (*Hint*: business process reengineering.)

5 Over the past decade, banks and investment firms have offered many services that would be impossible without ISs. Describe three such services and explain how IT makes them possible.

6 CAD systems replace older, manual tools in engineering, but they also contribute by maintaining all information in electronic form. How does this facilitate the work of draftspeople and engineers? How do such systems help the transition from engineering a product to manufacturing it?

7 ISs in both the manufacturing and service sectors often help to *optimize*. Give two examples of what they optimize.

8 The Web has significantly cut the cost of collecting data about shoppers and buyers. Explain how.

9 Sellers of consumer products argue that targeted marketing serves not only them but also their consumers. How so?

10 If you had to evaluate your own colleagues, would you prefer to evaluate them in written, open-ended form, or would you prefer to use employee evaluation software? Why?

11 As an employee, would you prefer that your supervisor evaluate you with the aid of employee evaluation software or without it? Why?

12 Try to remember the last time you gave someone your personal data. What was the reason for asking for the data?

13 Some consumer advocates argue that organizations should pay a small fee to every individual whenever they sell data about him or her to another organization. Do you agree? Why?

14 Examine the list of precautions suggested in 'Ethical and Societal Issues' for ensuring minimum invasion of privacy when businesses use personal data. Which steps can be taken without, or with minimal added cost? Which steps would impose financial burdens on businesses? Why?

15 RFID tags are increasingly embedded in almost every type of good, from washing powder to clothing items. Consumer advocates fear that the technology might cause massive violation of privacy. Describe at least two ways in which this can happen. What controls or limitations would you impose on RFID tags and use to minimize the fears of invasion of privacy?

Tutorial activities

1 Choose three distinct but related business functions (e.g. inventory control, purchasing payroll, accounting, etc.). Write a short paper describing how interfacing the information systems of these three functions can improve an organization's performance.

2 Select a business process (possibly at a local firm) not mentioned in this chapter. Write an essay explaining how IS technology could make the process (1) more efficient and (2) more effective.

3 Write a three-page essay titled 'Factory of the Future'. Your factory of the future will not require anybody in the manufacturing organization to enter any data into information systems. All the necessary information will come from customers at one end and suppliers at the other end. There will also be no need to type in any data for payments and collections. Explain how all this will work.

4 Many companies use email to advertise their products. Your company is trying to sell a new product and is advised to use email. The profit on each unit sold is 200 euro. Developing the attractive email message, use of 2,750,000 email addresses and sending the message would cost 25,000 euro. Experience shows that 5 per cent of the initial recipients forward such messages to friends and family. Experience also shows that 2 per cent of all recipients actually click the web address included in the message and visit the commercial site. Of these visitors, 0.5 per cent end up purchasing the advertised item. Using Microsoft Excel or another spreadsheet, answer the following questions: (1) Would you generate a profit if you used this advertising opportunity? (2) Would you profit if you could email only 1,000,000 people?

5   Form a team and design an IS for a small business that sells manufactured parts to other businesses. The system must handle customer order processing, sales, salesperson commissions, billing and accounts receivable. Prepare a report describing the system's different components and their points of interface. What files are necessary? How will the business use data in each file? If you have command of Microsoft Access, create the tables for the above objects and populate each one with three to five records.

6   Assume that you and your teammates are about to start a web-based business for sporting goods. You wish to email information to potential customers. Determine the demographic characteristics of your target audience. Search the Web for companies that

sell consumer data that can serve you. Prepare a report about three such companies: their names, services and prices (if available).

Companion CD questions

1   Create a database with at least five records that could be used by a company such as TheTrainline.

2   Research systems that distribution companies can use to track products throughout the distribution process. List at least two such systems and summarize how they work.

Video questions

1   What practices used by Krispy Kreme might Better Bites be able to adopt for their business?

2   Use PowerPoint or another presentation program to create a figure showing what you think the supply chain looks like for Krispy Kreme.

From ideas to application
REAL CASES

Case study 3.1

Banking on IT

The Bank of Ireland employs over 18,000 people and has assets of 87 billion euro, making it the number one banking institution in the Republic of Ireland. It has been in existence since 1783 and in that time has had to adapt to many changing circumstances in the national and global economy. Like any business, it faces the need to maximize its use of resources and minimize its costs. To this end the Bank realized the need for an integrated approach to its business functions, particularly finance, human resources and procurement. Over the years, fragmented and disparate IT systems had developed to improve specific

A view from Trinity College, Dublin, showing the statue of Edmund Burke overlooking the original Bank of Ireland building.

business processes, often with multiple, non-integrated systems to handle similar problems in different parts of the organization. For example, various human resource systems existed, generally not linked to payroll which in itself was not standardized throughout the group. Significantly there was no group procurement system and therefore no way to properly monitor supplier contracts and spending budgets.

The Bank commissioned the company Systems Applications and Products in Data Processing (SAP) to analyse their requirements and develop an integrated set of IT solutions. SAP is the world's largest business software company with more than 38,000 customers worldwide from all aspects of business.

Hugo Flinn, then general manager for finance and business services at the Bank of Ireland, described their requirements. 'One of the key elements of our vision was to provide information more quickly and to enable faster action. The main business driver behind the project was to improve productivity in both finance and HR through the implementation of shared services. From a procurement point of view, we wanted a better way of buying.'

Integration was the key. The Bank decided that it was a better solution, and cheaper in the long run, to standardize processes across the group rather than build interfaces between the separate systems.

The group had about 30 non-integrated general ledgers, several payroll and HR systems and no overall system for procurement. Data often had to be input twice, a cardinal sin in an IT environment as this can easily lead to inconsistencies between the 'same' items of data. With the implementation of mySAP® Financials, a suite of financial applications, staff at all levels were provided with accurate, up-to-date and consistent information in a suitable time-frame without having to search other systems or even manual records. The Bank now has one general ledger, one payroll system and one accounts payable system with integrated accounts reporting.

There were similar problems in HR with multiple and often incompatible systems which sometimes duplicated the information, again leading to problems of incompatibility as well as wasting staff time. The application mySAP® HR solved these problems by integrating recruitment, organizational management, personnel administration, payroll and time management. In addition, the functionality was increased by empowering the employees. Employee Self-Service (ESS) enables employees to view, create and maintain information relevant to their job. One of the most obvious benefits of this system, for both employees and the Bank, was the ability of employees to file their own expense reports. 'One of the key benefits of the HR solution is that employees can answer an awful lot of questions themselves through ESS', says Flinn.

The third major problem area was procurement. The group did not have a coordinated system to deal with purchasing. This disparate approach meant that no-one had an overview of procurement procedure or costs. There was no easy way for orders to be consolidated across the group. If you are ordering one chair for your office in Dublin you will get a better price quote if you bundle it up with an order for 50 chairs in the new branch in Cork. Once again the Bank used a solution from SAP, mySAP® Supplier Relationship Management (mySAP® SRM) which aims to reduce costs, increase efficiencies in purchasing, monitor buying behaviour and collaborate with business partners. It gives employees access to an online catalogue which they can browse using a standard web browser enabling them to start the procurement process. The Bank can establish supplier arrangements and pricing policies as well as define the purchasing authorization rules. The feedback suggests that employees are very comfortable with this approach as it has many similarities to personal Internet shopping, which is becoming second nature to virtually everyone. 'We are seeing benefits from process efficiency and visibility', says Flinn. 'We have enabled management to challenge costs on a transaction-by-transaction basis. Plus, we are realizing benefits from better supplier management.'

Thinking about the case

1 Give three examples of HRM activities that require access to an employee record. How could an organization benefit from integrating these activities so that they can be done in a single S?

2 The Bank of Ireland decided to use the same developer (SAP) for the three functional areas described above, namely finance, HRM and procurement. Why do you think this decision was made? Would it have been better to look for separate solutions for each of the three areas?

3 What other developments in IT can you think of for the Bank of Ireland to improve its business functions?

SOURCE: Bank of Ireland. SAP® for banking solutions increase profitability and deliver greater control, http://www.sap.com/uk/company/success/casestudies/boi.pdf

Case Study **3.2**

DHL – moving in the right direction

BY PATRICIA BRITTEN

Whether it is delivering the goods by plane, rail, sea or road, customers increasingly demand end-to-end global supply chain management (SCM) services.

DHL International (UK) is a good example of a company that has continuously used new technologies to improve its business. These include track and trace equipment, wireless technologies and business intelligence software.

Integrating infrastructure

Logistics companies, such as DHL and its competitors, often have to deliver different IT systems, documents and processes for individual sectors, such as retail or automotive. These have to be provided across many different business divisions, including warehouse or vehicle fleet management, and third-party suppliers.

As a result, a key thrust is to simplify, standardize and integrate their IT infrastructures, while driving down costs and improving supply chain visibility.

Peter Redshaw, an analyst at Gartner, says: 'Individual segments of the supply chain, such as warehousing, are already highly efficient. But many segments are not coupled together properly and a fragmented supply chain means extra cost.'

Track and trace

Even companies such as DHL that focus purely on the delivery of packages have complex operations. For instance, customers increasingly demand the capability to track and trace the delivery of products via an Internet portal.

'Track and trace functionality, delivered via self-service websites, is also cheaper and more efficient than a telephone call to a customer service centre. As a result, logistics portals are increasing in popularity and importance', says Redshaw. 'While customers expect online services, most are not prepared to pay any extra for them – unless suppliers extend them out to third parties', says Jeff Woods, principal analyst at Gartner.

Wireless technologies are also transforming the ability of logistics employees, such as truck drivers, to send data to back-office systems in real time. Companies have recently moved aggressively to replace clunky handheld devices with PDAs (Personal Digital Assistants) that connect to corporate systems over GPRS (Global Position Receiving Satellite) networks.

The real challenge for logistics companies is to integrate information held on multiple systems to generate cross-selling opportunities. To this end, logistics companies have invested heavily in data analytics tools (also called business intelligence tools) in a bid to provide a single view of customers and boost conversion rates.

Radio frequency identification (RFID) is a general term used to describe a system that transmits the identity of an object wirelessly. It is a contact-less technology and is made up of three components – the tag, the reader and the host computer system. A feature of RFID is the ability to read many tags together at once and it is not required for the 'reader' to be physically present. Furthermore, data can also be written to the tag. None of these features are possible with bar codes.

A DHL RFID tag.

In warehouses tagging technology cannot currently compete with the cheap and highly efficient bar code technology. Woods said, 'I do not think RFID will replace bar code in structured warehouse environments and manufacturing facilities. The two will co-exist for a long time and the challenge for RFID comes not with when it replaces bar code but what processes it is suitable for.' Woods considered that 'RFID might make sense in environments where you are moving high volumes of pallets rapidly off a truck.'

There are, however, developments in RFID that are making tagging technology cheaper and more reliable. RFID equipment has steadily fallen in price as volumes increase and microchip unit costs fall. The tag has the ability to store several kilobytes of data in addition to the number identifier and could be viewed as a form of 'mass distributed database' that has the potential to become ubiquitous – billions of tags in daily use throughout the world on all objects produced, stored and moved.

When used in conjunction with allied track and trace technologies, RFID can remotely contact objects to determine their identity and track their position in real time. This improves the movement and control of assets, which is particularly important if these are of high value or require urgent delivery. Applications that could be of use to logistics companies such as DHL include real-time item location/item visibility and status, anti-theft/tamper evidence and authentication.

According to the IT consultancy company Accenture, early adopters stand to gain the most benefits from this new technology through accelerated learning and experience. Accenture also considers that 'companies that apply more strategic thinking to RFID will be able to develop more high-value, game-changing applications and higher performance capabilities that will help them differentiate themselves in the market place'.

Multiple projects

DHL International launched a new service in the UK in 2005 enabling customers to book online from its full product portfolio.

The UK was the first country to pilot the online booking system, before the logistics giant rolled it out globally. Tony Eccleston, DHL's UK and Ireland IT director, says UK customers can choose any domestic or international air, sea or freight delivery service.

The new service was just one of many projects DHL has rolled out since late 2003. These include upgraded handheld devices for couriers, analytics reporting tools

for executives and online track and trace capabilities for customers.

The projects were designed to deliver parcels more efficiently, while providing customers and its own executives, couriers and call centre agents with near real-time information. DHL upgraded the handheld devices to GPRS connectivity in 2004. But it is DHL's process reengineering and back-office integration with the devices that is delivering the real value.

Scanning information

Couriers use the device's bar code scanner to upload parcel information to DHL's main system – where it is matched with the pre-shipment electronic document. 'Previously there was a fair degree of paperwork when couriers arrived in the morning. We have automated this processing, which saves couriers between 45 minutes and one hour per day. It is a fantastic change for us as a business. Couriers can be out on the road for one hour longer, which has knock-on benefits for customer service.'

Once a parcel has been delivered, couriers key in the final details and upload them to the central system. Data is then transmitted into DHL's global network, providing instant information on shipment availability. A parcel is scanned seven to eight times through its life cycle. DHL's service centres poll the uploaded information every 15 minutes – enabling it to update customers about status and identify any operational problems more quickly. 'We can target an issue in our operations before it becomes a major issue.'

DHL has also introduced an online track and trace service. Once logged in, customers can use their parcel identifier number to track the progress of a parcel across DHL's network. 'Big customers are interested in exceptions where something potentially goes wrong. Customers are increasingly seeing more visibility in terms of track and trace', says Eccleston.

DHL were also investigating the use of RFID technology in innovative applications to further improve their track and trace capability.

Accessing data

The company's investment in web-based reporting tools and an integrated data warehouse aims to give its executives vital data. DHL established several new data feeds into a common data warehouse, including financial, transactional, sales and operational data.

The 'dashboard' reporting tools give executives a helicopter view of their respective performances against targets. 'Historically, we did not have an integrated view. We had a system where different people came to meetings with different numbers.'

Eccleston says he and his team have delivered 36 projects since the end of 2003. 'My own role is now changing to be much more cross-functional in terms of change management and the benefits realization of IT delivery. Our focus over the next 12 months is less on building new capability, it is more about driving the value from them', says Eccleston.

Of the company's overall goals, he says: 'If you look at DHL globally, we are either number one or number two in most markets. Our aim is to get to number one everywhere and clearly IT is essential to that.'

Case study questions

1 What were the business benefits to DHL of introducing the new technologies?

2 Why is integrating the new technologies with existing back-off systems so important?

3 One of the consultants in the case has stated that he does not think that RFID tagging will be commercially viable for logistics companies in the future. Do you agree with his opinion? Can you think of any applications that might justify its use in DHL?

SOURCES: An article in *MIS U.K.* by James Thompson, April 2005; www.accenture.com and www.rfidc.com

---

silicon.com

Case study **3.3**

How to avoid an ERP disaster

BY ANDY McCUE

Implementing an enterprise resource planning (ERP) system is one of the biggest IT headaches many organizations will face, and while the rewards of doing it right are high, the cost of failing is often disastrous.

Examples include MFI, which was thrown £46 million into the red as a result of technical problems with the rollout of a SAP-based supply chain system, which led to inventory shortages and incomplete orders being sent out, and more recently chocolate manufacturer Cadbury took a £12 million hit on profits as a result of a chocolate glut related to problems with the rollout of a new SAP-based ERP system.

The software itself is now rarely the cause of these kinds of problems, the root cause of which can more often be linked to the massive business and process change associated with implementing an ERP system.

Yorkshire Water – now saving £12 million per year thanks to a new SAP-based supply chain system.

Jenny Sener, director of IT at property services organization OCS Group, speaking at a SAP customer event, said: 'It's the change management and the process change. That's where the real challenges are. The technology works. Many organizations fundamentally underestimate the scale of process change.'

Alan Harrison, CIO at Yorkshire Water, which is now saving almost £12 million per year after spending £30 million implementing SAP since 2000, said getting the business to change the way it works is vital to a successful project.

He said: 'The business managers are leading the implementation. They are the people who can actually deliver business change.'

Dale Vile, research director at analyst Freeform Dynamics, said problems with the business and process change often come when organizations hand over the implementation of the system to someone else, which leads to misunderstanding of roles and responsibilities.

He said: 'The most critical imperative is to regard the implementation as your own. The biggest danger comes when organizations delegate responsibility to their implementation partner. Remain in the driving seat and don't put it in the hands of someone else.'

Chris Gibbons, general manager of the internal IS consulting division at WHSmith News, is in charge of a £30 million SAP rollout that has paid for itself within four years but he admitted there were difficulties in getting the business to change processes and the way it works.

He said: 'There were teething problems in the first year. It is difficult to get the business to change.'

Scope creep is another issue. ERP implementations often take years and businesses rarely stand still, with the result that requests for changes to the scope of the project can spiral out of control.

Yorkshire Water's Harrison said scope creep is why a lot of SAP rollouts get into trouble. 'Scope creep is something you have to sit on', he said.

Vile agreed that a big pitfall is often trying to do too much in one go. 'The change requests should be challenged against the business objectives – be led by the business objectives and what the software can do', he said.

The final key piece of best practice advice for a major SAP rollout is to make the system as 'vanilla' as possible – that is to say using the standard off-the-shelf package with as little customization as is feasible.

Vile said: 'The golden rule is only deviate from the standard functionality in areas that really matter.'

He said that once an organization has got the core system implemented it can then look to 'unlock value incrementally' and build things around the edges such as remote web interfaces and wireless working.

Thinking about the case

1   The report uses the phrase 'scope creep'. What do you understand by this term? Can you think of examples of development that you have been involved in, either as a developer or as a user?

2   The suggestion is that an off-the-shelf ERP package should not be customized. Do you agree with this advice? Do you see any problems with this approach?

PART TWO

Information technology

Trent Courier Services

Andrew Langston looked out of his office window and smiled when he saw another of his bike messengers pedal in from a delivery. Had it really been a decade since he began Trent Courier Services? He'd come a long way from his early days in the business, when he got a phone call, hopped on his bike, and made the deliveries himself.

During his university days in London, Andrew competed in the cycling club's races. A friend told him that he worked part-time for the local bicycle delivery service to keep in shape, so Andrew decided to sign up, too. He could use a little extra cash. That was how he'd learned the ropes of the messenger delivery business. His employer had been operating for a long time in the City of London, and working there gave Andrew a taste of a different career option. After graduation, Andrew had moved back to Stoke-on-Trent, his hometown, and started Trent Couriers. It was the best way he could think to combine his love of cycling with the need to earn a living. Besides, at the time, Stoke-on-Trent had only a handful of small messenger services.

It was slow going at first. With such a small business and few funds, he had to watch every penny. But timing had helped him survive. With the business boom in the 1990s, the pace of business transactions skyrocketed. Firms of all sizes needed additional services to carry out their day-to-day transactions, so deliveries needed to increase, too. 'Instant service' became the watchword of business in the Information Age. Meanwhile, traffic on Stoke-on-Trent's streets had grown heavier and heavier. Delays throughout the area became a frustrating fact of life. Andrew found he could zip by the cars in heavy traffic as if they were parked. He loved pumping his way up the hills and coasting down to deliver his packages safe and sound – and always on time. He was proud that he'd built his business on his reputation for reliability. Now, here he was, owner of a company with nearly 50 employees making deliveries by both bicycle and car. He'd met each challenge with the determination he'd had when he was racing. And as with his bicycle, he tried to keep his business running smoothly, although it didn't always run the way a well-oiled machine should.

Bumps in the road

There was the time that a quickly opened door of a parked car had flattened one of his first messengers and landed him in Accident and Emergency. With no way to communicate except a pager, Andrew didn't know where his messenger was until he regained consciousness and had the nurses telephone him. Andrew spent the afternoon worrying, calling local police stations, and trying to placate his customer about her missing delivery. Also, he remembered the time high winds had brought down trees all over the

city. No traffic – including his car messengers – could get through for a day. Trent Couriers had no system for traffic alerts then, so some messengers were stranded in the chaos. Mobile phones and emailed delivery notices had certainly helped him maintain better contact in the field. Now if a messenger didn't arrive on time, he knew it sooner and could check the problem out directly.

Early expansion and growth

Trent Couriers had expanded rapidly over its first few years as demand grew for its services. Businesses found it cheaper to use a delivery service than to waste their own employees' time running across the city to make deliveries. The price for the service was another advantage – customers could get same-day delivery at prices much lower than the large package delivery services could offer. So, Trent Couriers definitely had a niche to fill in Stoke-on-Trent's business community.

As Trent Couriers grew, Andrew gradually added staff to his payroll – both messengers and dispatchers – to handle repeat customers and routine route deliveries. The company served a variety of businesses: solicitors needing contracts signed or papers filed, architects sending plans to their clients, medical and pharmaceutical companies and suppliers to the ceramics industry who needed rush deliveries, public relations firms sending their copy to poster and sign suppliers, and other businesses needing quick deliveries to satellite offices, suppliers or clients.

Andrew set up routes within the city to handle his regular customers' needs. He also accepted requests for special deliveries from drop-off or call-in business. Standard delivery was two-hour service, with premium rates for faster service. If a business only needed same-day service, then it could opt for the economy rate. Trent Couriers made deliveries all year round, in any kind of weather. Regular service operated Monday to Friday, from 7 a.m. to 7 p.m. During the high-technology boom, Trent Couriers also added premium service delivery on Saturdays.

Moving beyond bikes

After a few years of building Trent Couriers' clientele, Andrew noticed that revenues began to plateau. His competitors were offering the same type of service, and there was only so much business to go around. He needed to think of some way to separate his business from the pack – and soon.

In looking over the customer feedback his messengers entered into their report forms, Andrew saw patterns emerging. Messengers said several of his customers that had satellite offices outside the conurbation and in nearby towns had requested expanded routes. He also had repeated enquiries to serve several pottery businesses in the area. Handling fragile ceramics and other one-of-a-kind, irreplaceable items definitely called for a safer delivery method than bicycles. So, Andrew had investigated the feasibility of adding van deliveries to his business and decided to make the move.

Maintaining a fleet and drivers took the business to an entirely new level, but it also allowed Trent Couriers to deliver a wider and more profitable range of services – deliveries no longer had to fit in a backpack or bike basket. Ultimately, adding a van service allowed Trent Couriers to double its size. It now made about 500 deliveries per day and generated revenue of roughly £500,000 annually.

With the addition of a van service, Andrew needed to develop new pricing scales and schedules. He used his financial information system to calculate all the costs that went into a delivery – such as van purchases and maintenance, fuel costs and driver wages. Then he added a profit margin. Next, he used a mapping system to compute delivery route mileage based on the post codes of sending and receiving parties. To cover the new territories, he added even more employees, especially to the central office staff to handle customer orders and other business functions. Finally, he set special rates for 'white glove' service for pottery companies and medical centres.

Customers come first

Still, even with the expansion, the key to Trent Couriers' success remained its service quality. Andrew insisted that each of his employees provide the same on-time deliveries and courteous service that he had when he biked the routes himself. Messengers were on the front lines, and they represented the company to customers, so their attitudes and hard work were critical to Trent Couriers. Over the years, he'd had some run-ins with messengers over slack work habits, and a few had quit or just didn't work out and were let go. Andrew had documented problems in employees' computerized personnel files when necessary. But overall, he considered his employees part of an extended family and valued their loyalty. Ongoing training for messengers and dispatchers was important to maintain service levels. Above all, he wanted all his employees to enjoy the work they did.

Increasing reliance on information systems

Throughout his expansions, Andrew had turned to information systems to increase his efficiency and handle growing amounts of data. Information technology had helped him in so many areas:

- Automating payroll and accounting services.
- Streamlining customer paperwork.
- Tracking equipment maintenance and supplies.
- Routing deliveries.
- Maintaining customer and messenger contact.
- Providing customized services on the Web.
- Handling customer and employee database files.

In fact, for a business that many considered low-tech, Trent Couriers has relied on very high-tech computer hardware and software.

Handheld computers had rescued quite a few new messengers who became lost in Stoke-on-Trent's back streets. They'd found their way by bringing maps up on their handheld's screen. So, information technology was certainly critical to his employees. A couple of years ago the company even added a website offering online ordering to handle increased customer demands. Customers were pleased with the new option. For his own work, there were the useful databases – without which Andrew wouldn't know who his customers were or what their needs were. He'd also lose track of his employees and their productivity. The company had certainly followed the digital wave. Looking back, he knew he wouldn't be able to sustain his business without these technologies.

Back to business

Andrew's thoughts were interrupted by Mary Thomas, his administrative assistant, who was knocking at the door.

'Andrew? Sorry to bother you. Time for our meeting with the tyre supplier. They want to discuss our upcoming needs for the year.'

'Maybe we can get a volume price break on our fleet this year', noted Andrew. 'We added two new vans, you know'. He had used the same tyre supplier since the addition of the firm's first motor vehicle. His business relationship was strong and long-lasting. He'd heard that the supplier had offered some quantity price breaks to other businesses, so he was going to pull the entire purchasing history of the supplier and use the information to squeeze out better discounts this year. Savings made could be ploughed back into the company to make it bigger and better.

Business Challenges

Throughout his business's expansion, Andrew Langston has had to meet several challenges – not the least of which was selecting and using information systems to keep his business competitive. Information systems have played a critical role in Trent Couriers' history. You explore how Andrew met those challenges in the chapters of Part Two:

- In Chapter 4, 'Business Hardware and Software', you learn how to evaluate Trent Couriers' hardware and software needs as it grows, adds employees and customers, and streamlines its business processes.

- In Chapter 5, 'Business Networks and Telecommunications', you learn about the strategies Trent Couriers uses to remain in constant contact with its messengers and customers – with the goal of improving its services.

- In Chapter 6, 'Databases and Data Warehouses', you learn the importance of one of business's most powerful tools – databases – and see how Trent Couriers uses database technology throughout its business operations.

Business hardware and software

Trent Courier Services

HARDWARE STREAMLINES PROCESSES

When Andrew Langston opened Trent Couriers and worked solo, he wrote every log sheet and customer slip by hand – he had no computers. As business picked up, Andrew hired Sarah Truesdale to be his bookkeeper and receptionist. Sarah organized the office and set up basic business applications – word-processing, spreadsheet and database programs – on the company's first PC. So, when Andrew received a delivery request, Sarah typed it in her daily log sheet, and Andrew pedalled off.

To handle his growing customer base, Andrew hired university students as part-time bike messengers. The messengers carried beepers so that the dispatcher could contact them. If they were beeped, they'd find the nearest pay phone or use a client's phone to get their new instructions. This way, Trent Couriers were continually circulating through the city, ready for the next order.

Tracking delivery data

The system for tracking delivery data evolved over time. In his first improvement, Andrew ordered no-carbon-required (NCR) forms. The couriers carried these forms in their backpacks and had customers fill them out with their delivery information. Customers kept a copy of the form, and the couriers took the originals back to the main office. Sarah input the customer information such as order number, address and type of service along with the facts of the delivery – start and end times, courier name and delivery address. From those inputs, Sarah would generate monthly hard-copy invoices to post to customers.

The NCR system worked well enough for a time, but the handwriting on the forms was often hard to make out, and the forms tended to smear in wet weather. Sarah was constantly questioning the couriers about the delivery details. To say the least,

inputting the data was tedious, but it became completely unmanageable when Andrew expanded his services to van deliveries. Too many orders flowed into the office for Sarah to input.

New hardware, new systems

Andrew and Sarah put their heads together to devise a new process for data input. Technology came to the rescue in the form of the increasingly popular handheld computers. Andrew and Sarah designed new forms containing two matching bar codes representing an order number; one bar code had adhesive and could be detached from the form. Regular clients were also issued with their own bar codes representing their identification information. Messengers were equipped with handheld computers with bar-code readers. When a

messenger arrived at a customer's site, he or she simply swiped the order bar code and then the client's bar code, instantly creating a new order and entering client data. Messengers then attached the removable order bar code to the customer's package. They pushed a button to record pickup date and time on the handheld and entered delivery site information. Once at the delivery site, the messenger again swiped the package's bar code and recorded delivery times. All of the data were immediately stored in the handheld computer's memory.

That delivery-process improvement required a corresponding upgrade in Trent Couriers' central office computer system. Andrew selected a powerful personal computer as a server, with networked client computer terminals for the dispatchers and office staff. Mary Thomas, Trent Couriers' new administrative assistant, was brought on board to assist Sarah with main office functions. Mary downloaded the delivery information from the messengers' handheld devices into the system, instantly capturing data. As an added service, some clients also requested delivery confirmation for legal documents and medical supplies, and that information was also noted in the downloads. If confirmation was needed, Mary would email or fax the client with the delivery facts.

Backing it up

To safeguard all of its client and delivery data, Trent Couriers needed to back up its hard drives. Andrew and Sarah decided that two backups would be stored off site at their houses. At first, Trent Couriers backed data up on magnetic tape drives, but retrieving information from them was time-consuming. So, as soon as rewritable CD drives came on the market, Andrew purchased one. Now Sarah and Mary could pop the CD in the drive and directly access data by customer, delivery dates or courier, making retrieval a breeze. Now they could provide much faster service to their customers.

Software steers a path to stability

Growth adds complexity. But the efficiency Andrew Langston found in information systems had helped him manage Trent Couriers' complexity repeatedly through the years.

When Andrew considered buying a new PC-based server system, he wanted to be sure that it could handle his needs. So, he listed the main business functions for which he needed software support:

- General word-processing software for letters and memos.
- Financial accounting and reporting software for tracking sales, invoicing, and paying taxes and licence fees.
- Human resource information software to track full-time and part-time workers' time sheets.
- Database management system software for recording employee and client information.
- Basic desktop publishing software for direct-mail pieces to send to prospective clients.

Andrew chose a software suite to handle most of the business functions because the pieces would work together well and share a common database. He also was able to purchase the financial, human resource and desktop publishing software off the shelf.

Finding efficient routes

Andrew and his long-time messengers knew Stoke-on-Trent like the backs of their hands. They set their own best routes. Now that Trent Couriers had more than 90 employees – some not native to the area – Andrew noticed that a few deliveries were delayed because messengers had taken the wrong route. Customers complained, and the problem needed to be solved to maintain Trent Couriers' reputation.

Luckily, Andrew ran across an article in *Computer Weekly* on a new routing program. The software could be loaded with a map and, given start and end points, could generate the shortest route and logical delivery territories. He was surprised how well the software could organize the routes to save time, fuel and – most importantly – money. It worked particularly well for the longer routes he'd added when service was extended beyond the city.

The software was also tied into global positioning system (GPS) satellites so that messengers could get instant route information beamed to them as they worked. The software was installed on both the dispatchers' system and the messengers' handheld computers.

Staffing challenges

Andrew also had trouble tracking his employees' availability for work. Sarah Truesdale and Mary Thomas had to make frequent manual changes to the schedule to ensure that routes had adequate coverage. Scheduling became increasingly complicated as the company grew and hired more part-time workers. Because many of those workers were university students, their availability changed from semester to semester, thus the entire schedule was revamped two or three times a year. Also, when someone called in sick, they had to scramble to line up a replacement. It was time to automate.

Sarah told Andrew about scheduling software that her friend, a nurse at a local hospital, had used at work. The employer simply input employees' available hours, and the program generated a schedule. Making changes was streamlined, too – the software could identify on-call employees or revise a worker's schedule quickly. Master schedules were posted at the end of the week for next week's work, and changes were generated as needed.

Using financial software for assessing performance

Andrew had always enjoyed the closeness of his small company. Employees worked hard to do their jobs well. To foster pride in efficiency, Andrew began a new program to track the number of deliveries and shortest delivery times for each messenger. The program also tracked any feedback he received – customer compliments and complaints or speeding tickets. He called the messengers together to alert them that beginning with next month's deliveries, he'd begin tracking their productivity under his new incentive program. At the end of the month, the two employees – a bicycle courier and a van courier – with the most deliveries, lowest delivery times per mile, fewest complaints, and most compliments would receive a bonus.

Andrew also evaluated the delivery territories to determine which were most profitable. He generated sales reports by region from the customer database. From those reports, he noticed that the Saturday delivery service in the city wasn't generating enough revenue to cover its cost. Therefore, he decided to research this particular service further and see if its elimination could cause loss of regular services. He also adjusted the number of couriers to add more service to his most profitable routes. Those changes would help boost the bottom line and keep Trent Couriers rolling smoothly.

---

hardware All physical components of a computer or computer system.

software Sets of instructions that control the operations of a computer.

input device A tool, such as a keyboard or voice recognition system, used to enter data into an information system.

central processing unit (CPU) The circuitry of a computer microprocessor that fetches instructions and data from the primary memory and executes the instructions. The CPU is the most important electronic unit of the computer.

Hardware components

Hardware, in computer terms, refers to the physical components of the computer. Software refers to the sets of instructions that direct the hardware to perform particular tasks. In corporate decision-making, managers should consider software first, not hardware. Businesses need to first consider the tasks they want to support and the decisions they want to make, and therefore the information they need to produce. To this end, they should look for the proper software first, and only then purchase the most appropriate hardware on which this software can run. When a new organization makes such decisions, it can indeed decide first on software. However, in a great majority of cases, organizations already have a significant investment in hardware and, therefore, must often consider adopting new software within the constraints of their existing hardware. That's why we discuss hardware before software.

Regardless of size, age, function or capability, all computers have the same basic components (see Figure 4.1) and operate according to the same basic principles. A computer must handle four operations: (1) accept data, (2) store data and instructions, (3) process data, and (4) output data and/or information. In recent

Figure 4.1 All computers have the same basic components

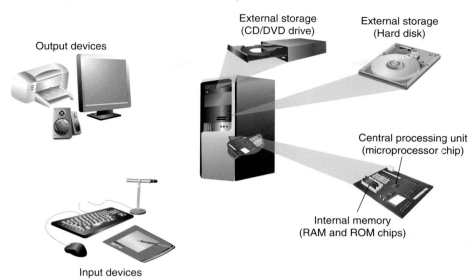

years, almost every computer has also been expected to support data communication over a network.

In general, every computer has these components:

Input devices receive signals from outside the computer and transfer them into the computer. The most common input devices are the computer keyboard and mouse, but some input devices accept voice, image or other signals.

The central processing unit, or CPU, is the most important part of any computer. The CPU accepts instructions and data, decodes and executes instructions, and stores results (output) in memory for later display. Some computers have several CPUs. The increase in the power of computers and decrease in their prices have been largely thanks to the ability of engineers to increase the complexity of the cicuitry without the need to increase their size.

Internal memory, also called main memory or primary memory, is located near the CPU and stores data and instructions just before and immediately after the CPU processes them. This includes programs currently running on a machine, intermediate results of arithmetic operations, intermediate versions of documents being word-processed, and data that represent the pictures displayed on a computer screen and the sounds played by the speakers. Two types form internal memory: most of it is RAM (random access memory), and the much smaller memory is ROM (read-only memory). The amount of RAM – often simply called memory – and the speed at which it operates are two of the properties that determine the power of a computer. The CPU and primary memory usually reside on a larger circuit board in the computer case called the *motherboard* or system board on smaller computers.

External memory, also called external storage, uses different types of media – such as magnetic disks, magnetic tapes, optical disks, DVDs and flash memory – to store data and information; however, unlike RAM, external memory allows for permanent storage. Thus, many external storage media are portable and can be moved from one computer to another.

Output devices, most commonly computer monitors and printers, deliver information from the computer to a person. There are also audio output devices such as speakers and digital audio players and specialized output devices such as Braille writers.

internal memory The memory circuitry inside the computer, communicating directly with the CPU. Consists of RAM and ROM.

RAM (random access memory) The major part of a computer's internal memory. RAM is volatile; that is, software is held in it temporarily and disappears when the machine is unplugged or turned off, or it may disappear when operations are interrupted or new software is installed or activated. RAM is made of microchips containing transistors. Many computers have free sockets that allow the expansion of RAM.

ROM (read-only memory) The minor part of a computer's internal memory. ROM is loaded by the manufacturer with software that cannot be changed. Usually, ROM holds very basic system software, but sometimes also applications. Like RAM, ROM consists of microchips containing transistors.

Table 4.1 Measuring amounts of digital data

1 KB (kilobyte) = 1,000 bytes
1 MB (megabyte) = 1,000,000 bytes
1 GB (gigabyte) = 1,000,000,000 bytes
1 TB (terabyte) = 1,000,000,000,000 bytes
1 PB (petabyte) = 1,000,000,000,000,000 bytes
1 EB (exabyte) = 1,000,000,000,000,000,000 bytes

CD TASK

external memory
Any non-RAM memory, including internal and external hard disks, flash memory and optical discs.

output device A device, usually a monitor or printer, that delivers information from a computer to a person.

bit Binary digit; either a zero or a one. The smallest unit of information used in computing.

byte A standard group of 8 bits.

supercomputer The most powerful class of computers, used by large organizations, research institutions and universities for complex scientific computations and the manipulation of very large databases.

parallel processing The capacity for several CPUs in one computer to process different data at the same time.

multiprocessing The mode in which a computer uses more than one processing unit simultaneously to process data.

The amount of data that computers process and store is measured in bits and bytes. A **bit** is a binary digit, a 0 or 1. A standard group of eight bits makes up a **byte**. Most characters (except for those in complex languages) can be represented by a unique byte. Therefore, when thinking of amounts of digital data, you can think of the number of bytes in terms of characters, such as letters, numerals and special marks. Computer memory and storage capacity are measured in kilobytes (K, thousands of bytes), megabytes (MB, millions of bytes), and gigabytes (GB, billions of bytes). Capacities of terabytes (millions of megabytes) and more are now a reality on the storage devices of many organizations (see Table 4.1).

Classification of computers

Computers come in a wide variety of sizes, from supercomputers to handheld personal digital assistants. Computers are classified by their power, which is determined mainly by the computer's processing speed and memory size. However, the lines between the classes are not clear. Furthermore, the names of the classes have changed over the years. In general, the more powerful the computer, the higher its price.

Supercomputers

Supercomputers are the most powerful computers at any given time. Usually, they are also the largest in physical size and most expensive. Universities, research institutions, government agencies and large corporations engaged in research and development are most likely to use them. Supercomputer manufacturers include IBM, Cray, Fujitsu, Hitachi and NEC. Supercomputers' RAMs consist of billions of bytes, and their processing speed is billions of instructions per second. The cost can be 1 million euro and up.

Supercomputers contain multiple processors that let them perform **parallel processing** (sometimes called **multiprocessing**), whereby several CPUs process different data at the same time. They can solve in a few minutes problems that used to take several hours or days to solve using smaller, conventional computers.

In lieu of one large supercomputer, some organizations link a 'cluster' of smaller computers via networks to create and enjoy similar computing power. This is properly known as **distributed computing**. Instead of a single machine with multiple processors, clustering uses the CPU power of multiple computers, with

Industry **SNAPSHOT**

Super Hector

A £113 million computer the size of two tennis courts and capable of performing 60 million calculations per second is due to be installed at Edinburgh University. Hector (High End Computing Terascale Resources) has an internal memory of 35 terabytes and disk storage of 700 terabytes. Some of the scientists and researchers who will be able to use this powerful machine are

- medical experts to develop new drugs by simulating the action of internal organs
- meteorologists to forecast climate change
- nano-scientists to study the interaction of the smallest particles
- cosmologists to model the way the universe develops
- maritime experts to simulate global ocean currents
- epidemiologists to project the spread of infectious diseases

- aeronautic engineers to simulate the flow of air over aircraft.

According to Project Director Professor Arthur Trew, 'Hector is critical for UK scientists to compete internationally.'

SOURCE: news.bbc.co.uk/1/hi/Scotland/Edinburgh_and_east/6384481.stm, 'Edinburgh site for super-computer'

HECTOR XT4 units at the University of Edinburgh.

PHOTO SOURCE: © P. TUFFY, UNIVERSITY OF EDINBURGH

---

the same effect. This can be done with special software that links the CPUs of servers via a private or public network such as the Internet, all or part of the time. Probably the best worldwide example of such use of computer power is the SETI@home project, aimed at processing radio telescope data to search for evidence of extra-terrestrial intelligence. Anyone with a computer, no matter the size, can become involved by downloading and running a small software package. Redundant time on the individual computer is used to perform the processing in the background and the results are reported back to the University of California, Berkley, USA. There are over 5 million users in more than 200 countries who up to December 2006 had contributed 19 billion hours of processing time. The speed of this virtual supercomputer is only just less than the current world's fastest supercomputer, Blue Gene – and all at virtually no cost!

distributed computing
The connection of several (relatively) small computers to give the processing power of one larger computer.

Mainframe computers

Mainframe computers are less powerful and significantly less expensive than supercomputers costing several thousand to several hundred thousand euros. Businesses that must handle business transactions and store large amounts of data in a central computer often use mainframes, typically banks, insurance companies, large retail chains and universities. While the processing speed of mainframes is

mainframe computer
A computer larger than a midrange computer but smaller than a supercomputer.

often not higher than that of the fastest PCs, they often have multiple processors and their memories are significantly larger, measured in terabytes. They are also capable of handling many input and output channels in parallel. By some estimates, 40–50 per cent of the world's business data reside on mainframes.

Midrange computers

midrange computer
A computer larger than a microcomputer but smaller than a mainframe.

Midrange computers are smaller than mainframes and less powerful. They are usually used as a shared resource, serving hundreds of users that connect to them from personal computers. Therefore, they act as servers, computers used to communicate to other computers, both through the Internet and locally within organizations.

Microcomputers

microcomputer The smallest type of computer; includes desktop, laptop and handheld computers.

workstation A powerful microcomputer providing high-speed processing and high-resolution graphics. Used primarily for scientific and engineering assignments.

Microcomputers is the collective name for all personal computers (PCs), notebook computers and handheld computers. More powerful microcomputers are sometimes called workstations. Workstations are typically used for computer-aided design (CAD), computer-aided manufacturing (CAM), complex simulation and scientific applications. As the performance of PCs steadily improves, computers that in the past were classified as midrange computers are now marketed as PC servers, and the lines between computer categories continue to blur.

The power of microcomputers in terms of speed and memory capacity doubles about every two years. Most PCs now sold to individuals and businesses cost less than 1000 euros.

Computers on the go: notebook, handheld and tablet computers

notebook computer
A computer as small as a book, yet with computing power similar to that of a desktop microcomputer.

personal digital assistant (PDA) A small handheld computer. Many PDAs require the use of a special stylus to click displayed items and to enter handwritten information that is recognized by the computer. An increasing number of PDAs also serve as mobile phones, music players and GPS devices.

stylus A pen-like marking device used to enter commands and data on a computer screen.

tablet computer
A full-power personal computer in the form of a thick writing tablet.

In today's mobile society, computers are increasingly used outside the office. Notebook or handheld computers are used to record and retrieve data for people on the go. The notebook computer (also called a laptop) is a compact, light, personal computer powered by a rechargeable battery. All new notebook computers are constructed with internal circuitry that enables them to connect to networks and the Internet without wires or cables. (Wireless technology is covered in Chapter 5.) So far, notebooks have trailed PCs in terms of speed, memory and hard disk capacity.

One highly popular class of computing machinery is the handheld computer, also known as the personal digital assistant (PDA). Handheld computers appeared on the market in the early 1990s but became popular only towards the end of the decade. These devices are small enough to fit in the palm of your hand, and typically a stylus (a pen-like pointing and drawing device) is used to enter data through a touch screen, although some handhelds also have a small keyboard or can plug into a folding portable keyboard. A growing number of PDAs are merged with mobile phones.

Another recent development in computers is the tablet computer, often called a tablet PC. It is a full-power PC in the form of a thick writing tablet. It looks like a notebook computer without a keyboard, although it can be connected to a keyboard and a mouse. Instead of a mouse, the user uses a stylus. The user can handwrite text, which automatically turns into typed text (as with some of the smaller

Industry **SNAPSHOT**

Web on the move

Mobile browsing of the Internet is set to outstrip PC-based surfing in the next five years according to Ronan Cremin, Director of Development Initiatives for mTLD, the global registry for the .mobi suffix. 'Ten years ago if you wanted to make a call you pretty much had to go to a desk or wall phone. To me it is inconceivable that in five years from now people will go to a PC to get to the Web. It'll be right there in your pocket.'

SOURCE: 'Mobile Internet just coming to life says .mobi', Maggie Holland, http://www.itpro.co.uk/news/91695/mobile-internet-just-coming-to-life-says-mobi.html?searchString=handheld

New services such as Google Mobile and increasingly powerful mobile devices are driving growth in mobile internet usage.

handheld computers). The stylus is also used to click icons and select items from menus. The tablet PC is enthusiastically received among salespeople and hospital staffs. Forms now can be filled out directly on screen, eliminating hours of paperwork for sales representatives and nurses.

Converging technologies

In recent years there has been a trend of technology convergence, building several technologies into a single piece of hardware. This is true especially in handheld units. A unit might be called a mobile phone, or a digital camera, but it is also a computer and several other things. In homes, personal computers can be turned into entertainment centres that transmit sound and television broadcast to other computers or to sound systems and TV sets. Expect to see a growing convergence of digital technologies both in mobile units and in home devices.

technology convergence
The combining of several technologies into a single device, such as mobile phone, digital camera and web browser.

A peek inside the computer

It is not necessary to look under a car's bonnet to drive it, but it is important to know enough about how a car is built to know which car to buy. Similarly, professionals must know enough about the major components of a computer to understand what computing

control unit The circuitry in the CPU that fetches instructions and data from the primary memory, decodes the instructions, passes them to the ALU for execution, and stores the results in the primary memory.

arithmetic logic unit (ALU) The electronic circuitry in the central processing unit of a computer responsible for arithmetic and logic operations.

microprocessor An electronic chip that contains the circuitry of either a CPU or a processor with a dedicated and limited purpose, for example a communications processor.

machine cycle The steps that the CPU follows repeatedly: fetch an instruction, decode the instruction, execute the instruction and store the result.

clock rate The rate of repetitive machine cycles that a computer can perform; also called frequency. Measured in GHz.

data word The number of bits that a CPU retrieves from memory for processing in one machine cycle. When all other conditions are equal, a machine with a larger data word is faster.

power and capabilities they buy or recommend for buying. The following discussion introduces the computer's most common parts and peripheral equipment and describes in some detail how these devices work.

The central processing unit

The CPU is the computer's brain, where all processing takes place. The CPU consists of two units: the control unit and the arithmetic logic unit (ALU). These units store and process data. The CPU is a silicon chip with multiple circuits. It carries signals that execute all processing within a computer. Because the chip is so small, it is often called a microprocessor, or simply a processor.

Current technology enables chip makers to print circuits on silicon that is 0.1 micron thick, one thousand times thinner than a human hair, allowing engineers to increase the processing speed of computers and yet use less energy and give off less heat.

The machine cycle When a program starts running in a computer, the CPU performs a routine sequence comprising four operations.

● Fetch – the first instruction from a program is taken into internal memory.
● Decode – the instruction is interpreted to find out what is to be done.
● Execute – the instruction is carried out.
● Store – usually the operation's result is needed for further operations and so is stored.

Each routine sequence is called a machine cycle. CPUs can perform billions of machine cycles per second. The rate of repetitive cycles is called frequency, or clock rate. One cycle per second is 1 hertz. Computer frequencies are measured in megahertz (MHz, millions of hertz), or gigahertz (GHz, billions of hertz). During the time it takes your eye to blink (about 0.2 second), a computer can execute hundreds of millions of instructions. Therefore, timing of computer operations is measured in very small fractions of a second (see Table 4.2).

The word The data word (or 'word' for short) is the maximum number of bits that the control unit can fetch from primary memory in one machine cycle. The word's size is determined by the size of the CPU circuitry that holds information for processing. Obviously, the larger the word, the more instructions or data can be retrieved per second. Therefore, all other things being equal, the larger the word, the faster the computer. Current microcomputers have words of 32 and 64 bits.

Table 4.2 Computer time

1 millisecond = 1/1,000 (0.001) second
1 microsecond = 1/1,000,000 (0.000001) second
1 nanosecond = 1/1,000,000,000 (0.000000001) second
1 picosecond = 1/1,000,000,000,000 (0.000000000001) second

Why you should...
understand some technical details

Business Studies students and other non-IT professionals often ask: 'Why do I have to study computer hardware?' The answer is threefold. You must know enough about hardware to be able to communicate your needs to IT professionals who can provide you with the devices you need for your work; if you are in a position to choose among various options and make a decision on certain hardware pieces, you must be sufficiently knowledgeable about hardware to make informed decisions; and since you are or will be a professional, you will have to purchase hardware for your personal use. Keeping abreast of development in hardware will make you an informed consumer. You will be able to optimize your purchases.

In addition, knowledge of new technologies might give you ideas about how to develop new products and services to improve your organization's competitive position. Throughout history, necessity has been the mother of invention, but this is not so with information technology. Time and again inventions have been available long before business puts them to use. Professionals who realize that a certain development can give their companies an advantage will be rewarded for their vision.

Computer power

What makes one computer more powerful than another? There are two major factors to consider: processing speed and memory capacity. A computer's speed is determined mainly by (1) the CPU clock rate (measured in MHz or GHz), and (2) the amount of information the CPU can process per cycle (determined by the size of the data word and the capacity of internal communication lines, referred to as *buses*).

All other things being equal, the greater the clock rate, the faster the machine, because it can fetch, decode, execute and store more instructions per second. Also, all other things being equal, the larger the data word, the faster the computer. A larger word means that in each trip to the primary memory, the control unit can retrieve more bits to process. Therefore, the CPU can execute a program faster.

You might have seen advertisements promoting a '64-bit computer'. This means that the data word's capacity is 64 bits. You must be cautious with regard to word size. A larger word does not always mean a faster computer, because the speed at which the bits move between the CPU and other components depends on the capacity of internal communication lines. The system bus – also called simply the **bus** – which is the electronic lines or traces used for communication inside the computer, might have a width of only 32 bits, while the word might contain 64 bits. The number of bits is also referred to as the width of the bus.

Buses have their own clock rate. The bus that computer makers usually mention in ads is the front side bus, which is the bus connecting the CPU to the memory. A typical front side bus clock rate is 800 MHz. The combination of bus width and clock rate determines throughput. **Throughput** is the number of bits per second that the bus can accommodate. Only considering both factors, CPU clock rate (so many GHz) and bus throughput, enables you to compare properly the speeds of different computers.

Computer speed is also measured in **MIPS**, millions of instructions per second, which is an inaccurate measure, because instructions have various levels of complexity. However, computer speed expressed in MIPS is often used to indicate overall processing speed because all factors that determine speed are considered: clock rate, data word size and bus throughput, as well as other speed factors that

bus The set of wires or soldered conductors in the computer through which the different components (such as the CPU and RAM) communicate. It also refers to a data communications topology whereby communicating devices are connected to a single, open-ended medium.

throughput A general measure of the rate of computer output.

MIPS Millions of instructions per second; an inaccurate measure of computer speed.

An ergonomic keyboard.

ergonomics The science of designing and modifying machines to better suit people's health and comfort.

mouse An input device that controls an on-screen pointer to facilitate the point-and-click approach to executing different operations.

trackball A device similar to a mouse, used for clicking, locking and dragging displayed information; in this case, the ball moves within the device rather than over a surface.

trackpad A device used for clicking, locking and dragging displayed information; the cursor is controlled by moving one's finger along a touch-sensitive pad.

we do not discuss here. In recent years, computer makers have also used the term 'transactions per minute' (TPM), referring mainly to database transactions, but this ratio, too, is not an absolute measurement.

Input devices

Computers must receive input to produce desired output. Popular input devices include the keyboard, mouse, trackball, microphone and various types of scanners. The most common input device is the keyboard.

Keyboard

The keyboard contains keys that users press to enter data and instructions into primary memory and instruct programs to run. All keyboards include the basic letters of the alphabet, numbers and punctuation marks, plus several function keys numbered F1, F2, and so on, that can be activated to execute preprogrammed functions. Keyboard manufacturers have also added keys that facilitate web browser commands such as Back and Forward, and music keys such as Volume, and Play/Pause.

Ergonomic keyboards The repetitive motion of typing can cause repetitive-stress injuries (RSIs). In response, ergonomic keyboards are gaining popularity. Ergonomics is the study of the comfort and safety of human beings in their working environment. Ergonomic keyboards are split in the middle, and the two parts are twisted outward to better fit the natural position of the forearms.

Mouse, trackball and trackpad

A mouse is an input device that controls an on-screen pointer to facilitate the point-and-click approach to executing different operations. When the user moves the mouse on the surface of a desk or a pad, the computer detects the movements, translates them into digital coordinates on the screen, and moves the pointer to imitate the mouse's movement. The buttons are used for clicking, locking and dragging displayed information. A trackball is similar to a mouse, but the ball moves within the device, rather than over a surface. With a trackpad, a user controls the cursor by moving his or her finger along a touch-sensitive pad. Many notebook computers have built-in trackpads. Many mice and trackballs have a built-in wheel that scrolls pages displayed on the monitor.

Mice, trackballs and keyboards are also available as wireless units that use infrared or radio technology. These units give users more flexibility, especially for software-based presentations, in which the presenter may move around with the mouse in his or her palm.

Touch screen

Sometimes a single device, such as a touch screen, may serve both as an input and output device. A touch screen lets the computer user choose operations by touching the options on the computer screen. Some common public applications use touch screens to provide advice to tourists, and select items at self-serve supermarket checkouts.

touch screen A computer monitor that serves both as input and output device. The user touches the areas of a certain menu item to select options, and the screen senses the selection at the point of the touch.

Source data input devices

In some businesses, the speed of data entry is a top priority. These businesses use machine reading devices, such as bar-code scanners, known as source data input devices. They copy data directly from the source, such as a bar code or magnetic ink characters, without human intervention. They can also record data directly from other sources, including cheques and credit cards.

source data input device A device that enables data entry directly from a document without need for human keying. Such devices include bar-code readers and optical character readers.

Source data technology Mark-recognition devices are essential to successful source data entry. Special devices use *optical mark recognition (OMR)* to detect the positions of marks on source documents. Millions of people use this method every week to mark their choice of lottery numbers. Another less accurate but much more flexible technology used for source data entry is *optical character recognition (OCR)*. Unlike optical mark recognition, OCR technology is often used to try to interpret handwritten and printed texts not originally designed for source data entry. Postal services around the world have experimented with OCR to replace human eyes and hands in the tedious job of mail sorting.

Banking Since the early 1960s banks all over the world have used a special method of recognizing the bank sort code, account number, cheque number and amount on the millions of cheques that need to be processed every day. The clever aspect of this is that three of the four elements can be preprinted on the cheque before it is written on. If you have a cheque book take a look and you will see that the sort code, account number and cheque number are on every blank cheque. Therefore the processing time is reduced when the written cheque is presented to the bank. A special device called a magnetic-ink reader uses magnetic-ink character recognition (MICR, pronounced MIKE-er) to detect these numbers. A person at the bank enters the amount of the check, also in magnetic ink. The cheque can then be used as the input to systems that update account details.

magnetic-ink character recognition (MICR) A technology that allows a special electronic device to read data printed with magnetic ink. The data are later processed by a computer. MICR is widely used in banking. The bank code, account number and the amount of a cheque are printed in magnetic ink on the bottom of cheques.

Credit cards Credit cards, too, facilitate source data entry. Card number and holder information are coded on the magnetic strip on the card's back or more recently on an embedded microchip which can hold much more information than the magnetic strip. When you make a purchase with your credit card, the card is passed through the reader at the point of sale (POS) to record the account number. The total amount charged is either keyed manually or recorded automatically from the cash register.

Imaging

A growing number of organizations are imaging, or image processing, their documents. Doing so allows not only the storage of enormous amounts of data in less space than paper but also much more efficient retrieval and filing. By scanning and storing images, many companies have already reduced millions of paper

imaging The transformation of text and graphical documents into digitized files. The document can be electronically retrieved and printed to reconstruct a copy of the original. Imaging has saved much space and expense in paper-intensive business areas.

documents to digitized pictures. This technology is particularly useful when documents include signatures and graphics.

Once scanned, the original document can be destroyed because an exact copy can be generated on demand. Since it is in electronic form, it can be indexed. Indexing enables you to search a document by keywords and numbers. This reduces the average time of searching a document from several hours to about five seconds.

Speech recognition

speech recognition
The process of translating human speech into computer-readable data and instructions.

Speech recognition – also called voice recognition – is the process of translating human speech into computer-readable data and instructions. Although speech recognition systems vary in sophistication, all receive voice input from a microphone and process it with software.

Ethical and Societal **ISSUES**

Computers may be hazardous to your health

An increasing number of studies show that working with computers threatens workers with a variety of hazards. These risks include repetitive-stress injuries (RSIs) due to long periods of repeated motions. As work with computers has grown, RSIs have grown, too, to the extent that some scientists call these injuries an epidemic.

The most common computer-related type of RSI is carpal tunnel syndrome. It is the result of repetitive use of a keyboard. The injury causes pain in the forearms due to swelling and pressure on the median nerve passing through the wrist. Carpal tunnel syndrome may cause permanent disability. In some cases workers are unable to return to work due to this injury.

Our eyes, too, are strained from computer work. Studies found that a programmer's eyes make as many as 30,000 movements in a workday. These are movements up, down and to the sides, which strain the eye muscles. However, other studies found that while staring at a computer monitor people blink at one-sixth of the frequency that they blink normally. Blinking is important for moisturizing the eyeball, which helps kill harmful germs and eases eye strain. Short breaks from work with computers that involve keyboards and video displays reduce eye soreness, visual blurring and upper-body discomfort.

The argument has been made that it is an employer's moral obligation to educate employees about such risks and to provide an environment that minimizes them. Both factors, the economic and ethical, have moved many employers to try to reduce the increasing 'injuries of the Information Age'. They do so by purchasing and installing ergonomic equipment, training employees how to use computers in a way that minimizes injuries, and enforcing periodic breaks from repetitive activities such as typing. The breaks help prevent both RSIs and eye strain. There is a wealth of information available from professional bodies including the UK Health and Safety Executive (HSE) which has a database of court judgments in RSI cases. According to the HSE website nearly 375,000 people in Great Britain suffered from a musculoskeletal disorder (MSD) and many working days are lost. The database can benefit people with a need for information about work-related RSI including employers, trade unions, insurers and designers of computer equipment. As a professional it is likely you will spend much of your workday sitting in front of a computer. As a manager it is certain that your staff will do so. You need to know the health implications of working with IT.

Output devices

Output devices include all electronic and electromechanical devices that deliver the results of computer processing. We receive most information in visual form, either on screen or on paper. Therefore, this discussion focuses on the most popular output devices: monitors and printers. Output also includes audio signals, received through speakers and earphones, or downloaded to digital audio players.

Monitors

The most common output device is the computer monitor, which looks like and uses technology similar to a television screen. There are two major types of monitors: cathode-ray tube (CRT) and flat-panel display. Images on a monitor are made up of small dots called pixels (short for 'picture elements').

Flat-panel monitors have gained popularity as monitors for personal computers and handheld computers after years of their use in notebook computers. Their price has decreased tenfold over the past several years. The advantages of flat-panel monitors are their slim profile, their sharper images and their lower consumption of power. The most common types of flat-panel monitor are the *liquid crystal display (LCD)* and *plasma*. Each of these technologies is continually improving and the answer to the question 'Which is better?' depends on when you ask! Any type of high-definition television (HDTV) set can be connected to a computer (if it has the proper socket) and serve as a computer monitor.

The greater the number of pixels per unit area on the screen, the sharper the picture. Picture sharpness is called resolution. It is expressed as the number of pixels that fit the width and height of a complete screen image. Monitors come in several resolutions. The resolution required for clear text is 640 × 350. If you multiply these numbers, you get the total number of pixels on the screen. Common resolutions are 1024 × 768, 1280 × 1024, 1600 × 1200 and 1920 × 1200.

Good colour monitors can display more than 16 million colours and hues. The number of colours and the overall quality of pictures also depend on the quality of the video card used inside the computer. The video card contains memory and circuitry to manipulate and display two- and three-dimensional images.

PHOTO SOURCE: © ARTMANN WHITLE

The dominance of flat-panel monitors means increasing numbers of retailers no longer sell CRT monitors.

Printers

Printers can be classified into two basic types based on the technology they use to create images on paper: non-impact and impact.

Non-impact printers The printer most commonly used today in businesses is the laser printer, which is a *non-impact printer* because it creates images on a page without mechanically impacting the paper. Laser and ink-jet printers produce very high-quality output, including colour. Laser printing technology can create typeset quality equal to what you see in magazines and textbooks. All non-impact

cathode-ray tube (CRT) A display (for a computer or television set) that uses an electronic gun to draw and paint on the screen by bombarding pixels on the internal side of the screen.

pixel The smallest picture element addressable on a monitor, short for 'picture element'. In an LCD monitor, it is a triad of three transistors controlling the colours of red, green and blue that can be switched on and off and kept on with varying amounts of electricity to produce various colours and hues. In a CRT monitor, the triad is made of phosphorous dots that are excited by an electron gun.

resolution The degree to which the image on a computer monitor is sharp. Higher resolution means a sharper image. Resolution depends on the number of pixels on the screen and the dot pitch.

printers have fewer moving parts than impact printers and are, therefore, significantly quieter. They are also much faster. The excellent quality of their output makes laser printers the choice of many individual and corporate users for desktop publishing.

Two qualities to check when purchasing a laser or ink-jet printer are speed, measured in pages per minute (PPM), and density, measured in dots per inch (DPI). The higher the density, the sharper the output. Desktop printers produce output at 300, 600 and 1200 DPI or more. The speed of desktop laser printers is 4 to 25 PPM. Colour laser printing is somewhat slower, because of the time it takes the printer to compose the image. Larger, commercial laser printers reach speeds of more than 400 PPM. The low prices of laser and ink-jet printers might be misleading. Over the life of the printer, the buyer will pay much more money for the cartridges than for the printer.

Impact printers Printers are considered *impact printers* if they reproduce an image on a page using mechanical impact. Of this type, the only printers you might still encounter are dot-matrix printers which have low-quality output but are still in use in many businesses, particularly where multi-part stationary is used, as the impact is needed to make the carbon copy.

Storage media

To maintain programs, data and information for later use, data must be stored on a non-volatile medium, that is, a medium that retains data even when not connected to electric power. Often, we also want to move stored data to a computer that is not part of a network, and we need to back up important programs and data as well. For these purposes, we use external storage media, that is, storage media outside the computer's memory. The terms 'storage media' and 'storage devices' are often used interchangeably.

External storage devices come in different forms and use different materials, each with strengths and weaknesses. Important properties to consider are capacity, access speed and access mode. As always, cost must be considered, too.

Storage devices differ in the technology they use to maintain data (such as magnetic or optical) and in their physical structure (disks, tapes or other forms). Physical structure might limit ways in which data can be organized on the medium. While disks allow any type of

Industry **SNAPSHOT**

Squeezing more bytes

IBM is developing a new storage technology called Millipede, which allows computers to store data at a density of a trillion bytes per square inch, about 20 times denser than the magnetic disks available today. The technology, called nanotechnology, uses 4000 very fine silicon tips that punch holes onto a thin film of plastic. The tiny holes represent bits. The technology is called nanotechnology, because it is at the level of atoms. A storage device the size of a postage stamp will hold more than 1 trillion bits. This is the size of 600,000 digital camera pictures.

IBM headquarters at la Défense, Paris.

organization, tapes allow only sequential organization. This section first discusses modes of access, then looks at specific media and technologies, and then considers the trade-offs that managers must consider when evaluating what type of storage media is best for a particular business.

Modes of access

There are two basic types of access modes in data storage: sequential and direct (random) access (see Figure 4.2). In sequential storage, data are organized one record after another. With sequential storage (the only option for magnetic or optical tapes), to read data from anywhere on the tape, you have to read through all the data before that point on the tape. Retrieving files from sequential devices is slower and less convenient than on devices that utilize direct access. In direct access, records are not organized sequentially, but by the physical address on the device, and can be accessed directly without going through other records.

Because storage and retrieval are slow on sequential storage devices and because they are inexpensive, tapes are suitable for backup purposes. Direct access storage media are the only practical way to organize and query databases.

Magnetic tapes

Magnetic tapes similar to those used in tape recorders and VCRs are also used to store computer data. While some tape drives still use open reel tapes, most now use tape cartridges. Quantum, a storage media manufacturer, offers tape cartridges with a capacity of 3.5 TB (terabytes) that access data at a rate of 250 MB

sequential storage A file organization for sequential record entry and retrieval. The records are organized as a list that follows a logical order, such as ascending order of ID numbers, or descending order of part numbers. To retrieve a record, the application must start the search at the first record and retrieve every record, sequentially, until the desired record is encountered.

direct access The manner in which a record is retrieved from a storage device, without the need to seek it sequentially. The record's address is calculated from the value in its logical key field.

magnetic tape Coated polyester tape used to store computer data; similar to tape recorder or VCR tape.

Figure 4.2 Sequential and direct access

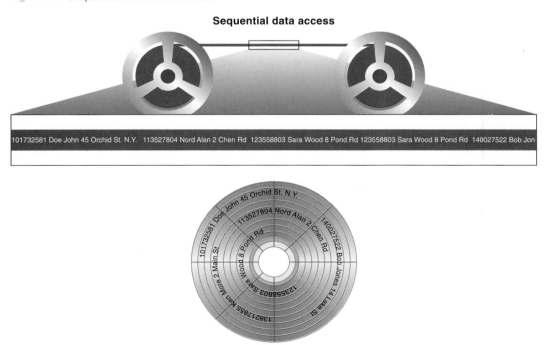

Sequential data access

101732581 Doe John 45 Orchid St. N.Y.   113527804 Nord Alan 2 Chen Rd 123558803 Sara Wood 8 Pond Rd 123558803 Sara Wood 8 Pond Rd 140027522 Bob Jon

Direct data access

per second. The cost of storage is measured in how much money is spent on each byte of storage capacity. In terms of storage capacity, tape storage costs about one-twentieth of magnetic disk storage.

Backing up all or a designated part of data from its original storage medium is often done regularly. AOK, Germany's largest health insurance company with more than 25 million policyholders, uses 128 300-GB tape drives to store 44 TB of data. The amount of data grows at a rate of 6 per cent per year. The company is well prepared for any disaster that might destroy data.

Magnetic disks

magnetic disk A disk or set of disks sharing a spindle, coated with an easily magnetized substance to record data in the form of tiny magnetic fields.

The most widely used storage medium is the magnetic disk. Magnetic disks include hard disks and 'floppy' disks (so called because they consist of flexible material although they have been encased in rigid plastic for years). As with information on magnetic tape, information on magnetic disks is coded in magnetized spots on the disk's surface. The 3.5-inch floppy disks are now being replaced by portable media such as writable CDs and portable flash memory drives that connect to universal serial bus (USB) ports.

universal serial bus (USB) A ubiquitous socket that enables the connection of numerous devices to computers.

PCs always come with at least one hard disk built in. (Hard disks are often mistakenly called hard drives. The disk is the storage medium itself; the drive is the mechanism that stores data to it and retrieves data from it. However 'hard disk' and 'hard drive' are commonly used to mean the combination of the two, because the drive and disk are sold and installed as one unit.) Hard disks are capable of storing up to 500 GB of data.

hard disk A stack of several rigid aluminum platters coated with easily magnetized substance to record data. Usually installed in the same box that holds the CPU and other computer components, but may be portable.

Spending on storage devices accounts for about 30 per cent of all IT expenditure of businesses. In recent years the most important impetus for acquisition of hard disks has been the construction of data warehouses, large databases that maintain mainly consumer purchase records.

Optical disks

optical disk A disk on which data are recorded by treating the disk surface so it reflects light in different ways; includes CD and DVD.

Optical disks are recorded by treating the disk surface so it reflects light in two different ways. A special detecting device detects the two different reflections, which represent ones and zeros of digital coding. The main advantage of optical disks is their storage capacity and portability. CDs are also less expensive than hard disks in terms of cost per bytes. Standard DVDs can store 4.7 GB per side for a total of 9.4 GB. More advanced DVDs, using techniques called blue laser and double storage, can reach capacities of 50 GB. However, the disadvantage of all optical disks is that the speed of storage and retrieval is currently slower than that of hard disks.

You might have noticed CD drive speeds listed in the form of 52X, 60X or another X-number. Years ago, the original data retrieval (transfer) rate of CD drives was 150,000 bits per second. This number represents single speed, or '1X'. Thus, 60X means $60 \times 150,000 = 9,000,000$ bits per second. The greater the data retrieval rate, the more desirable the drive. Note that writable CDs usually have different reading and writing speeds. Reading is often faster than writing. So, you might find that a CD drive reads at 60X but writes at only 24X.

flash memory A memory chip that can be rewritten and can hold its content without electric power. Thumb drives, as well as ROM, are made of flash memory.

Flash memory

Flash memory is becoming popular for both primary memory (memory inside the computer) and external storage. Flash memory is a memory chip that can be rewritten and hold its content without electric power. Flash memory consumes very little power and does not need a constant power supply to retain data when disconnected. It offers fast access times and is relatively immune to shock or vibration. These qualities make flash memory an excellent choice for portable devices such as MP3 players, or as independent portable storage.

As an independent memory device, flash memory takes two main forms: as a memory card (often used in digital cameras and other portable devices), and as a USB drive, sometimes called a thumb drive or USB flash drive. (The name 'drive' is a misnomer; there are no moving parts or disks in flash memory.) This plugs into the computer through a USB port. As USB ports come standard in all microcomputers, it is easy to use a flash drive to save data or transfer data between computers. USB drives come in storage capacities of up to several gigabytes, and their cost is decreasing rapidly.

Transfer rate (speed of storage and retrieval) of flash memory in USB flash drives and memory cards is usually indicated in the same manner as that of optical disks: so many Xs. A memory card of 80X is considered fast. Cards of the same storage capacity are significantly different in price due to transfer rate.

Flash memory is often called solid state memory. In addition to its use in USB flash drives and memory cards, it is used in solid state disks. A solid state disk (SSD) is an alternative to magnetic disks. Again, the word 'disk' is a misnomer, because this type of storage involves no disk. SSDs are used by organizations to store frequently used software to prevent data processing 'bottlenecks.'

USB drive Any storage device that connects to a computer through a USB socket, but especially flash drives.

flash drive A storage device containing flash memory. Flash drives are used in numerous electronic devices and often are designed to connect to a computer through a USB port.

solid state disk (SSD) Flash memory that serves as external storage medium as if it were a hard disk.

Business considerations in evaluating storage media

Before spending money on storage devices, managers must consider several factors: the purpose of data storage, the amount of data to be stored, the required speed of data storage and retrieval, how portable the device needs to be and, as always, cost.

Use of stored data The first consideration before adopting storage media is how the data will be used, mainly, whether they will be used for current operations or as backup. If they are to be used for backup only, and not processing, magnetic tape or CDs would be a proper choice. Magnetic tape is less costly and holds more data per reel or cassette than a single CD; this should be a consideration, too. If the users need to access individual records quickly, then magnetic hard disks are the best choice. Thus, a business that allows customers to retrieve their records online should use fast magnetic disks. If the information is archival, such as encyclopedias or maps used by library patrons, the library should place the information on CDs or DVDs, because the user needs fast, direct retrieval of specific information (records), and might not tolerate sequential search on a tape.

Amount of data stored When storage volume is the most important factor, managers must first consider price per megabit or megabyte, that is, the ratio of money spent to storage capacity. If the medium is to be used solely for backup, their low cost makes magnetic tapes and CDs an ideal choice. If the medium is to be used for fast retrieval, fast magnetic disks would be the best choice. If much data must be stored, especially large files such as pictures, sound and video, but the speed of finding a particular file or record is not so important, a DVD is a good choice.

For some purposes, the absolute capacity of the device, not the density, is important. When a set of very large software applications and/or data must be stored on a single device, a device with a

A USB data storage device.

PHOTO SOURCE: © CALVIO

large capacity must be selected. For example, if a sales rep must be able to demonstrate applications totalling 4 GB, it might be more economical to store the data on five CDs, but this would be impractical because the rep would either have to first copy the content of all the CDs onto every PC where she makes a demonstration (which for security reasons might be prohibited by the hosting party), or she would have to swap the CDs throughout the demonstration. A small portable hard disk or USB flash drive of at least 4 GB would be a more practical option, albeit significantly more expensive.

Speed   The speed of magnetic disks is often measured in rotations per minute (RPM). Current disks come with speeds of 5400, 7200, 10,000 and 15,000 RPM. For disks of the same size, the greater the RPM the shorter the data transfer time and usually the better the performance overall. While the great capacity and low cost of CDs are appealing, the transfer rate of magnetic hard disks is still significantly better than that of CDs and their faster relatives, DVDs. If very high speed is required, SSD is currently the best choice, although its price is significantly higher than that of magnetic disks.

Unit space and portability   Sometimes the cost of a gigabyte stored is not the most important consideration, but the physical size of the storage medium is. A portable hard disk drive might be economical and fast, but it is more practical for a travelling salesperson to carry a CD rather than an external hard disk. And even though a CD is significantly less expensive than a USB flash drive, the salesperson might find it more convenient to carry a 4 GB USB drive than carrying several CDs. CDs do not fit in shirt pockets, while a USB flash drive can be attached to a key chain or clipped to a shirt pocket. Thus, even if storage cost is not as attractive as that of CDs, portability and the fact that USB ports are ubiquitous in PCs might push one towards selecting a USB flash drive.

Cost   Once managers agree on the best type of data storage device for a particular business use, they need to consider cost. The approach is simple: obtain the largest size of storage for the smallest amount of money.

Reliability and life expectancy   Although this is usually not the highest priority, businesses must also consider the storage medium's reliability and life expectancy. For instance, optical disks are more reliable and durable than magnetic disks. Magnetically stored data remain reliable for about 10 years, whereas CDs and DVDs are expected to store data reliably for 50 to 100 years (although they have not been around long enough to prove that).

Trade-offs   As you can see, several factors must be considered when purchasing storage media, and often you must trade one quality of the device for another. For example, while USB drives are convenient and fast, they are also expensive and unacceptable for storing large amounts of transactional data, or even backing up large amounts of data, because of their relatively small capacity. Table 4.3 summarizes characteristics of the most popular storage media. Obviously, terms such as 'moderate cost' and 'high capacity' are relative. Storage capacities and speeds of almost all storage media have increased over the years, and costs have decreased. Thus, the specific capacities, retrieval speeds, and costs change all the time. The table is presented for general comparison and reference, whereby 'high' and 'low' for each medium are relative to the other media.

Considerations in purchasing hardware

Decisions about purchasing computers are usually made by an organization's IS professionals or with the help of a consulting firm. But surveys show a new trend: involving end users in the decision-making process. More and more companies realize that effective use of computers

Table 4.3 Characteristics of storage media for business purposes

Medium	Storage density (bits/ square inch, or physical size)	Recording and retrieval speed	Cost	Ideal for...	Capacity per device	Limitations
Magnetic hard disk	High	Very high	High	Immediate transactions	Very high	Bulky, heavy
Magnetic tape	High	Slow	Very low	Backup	Very high	Not suitable for immediate processing
Optical tape	Very high	High	Low	Backup	Very high	Limited market
Recordable CDs	Very high	Medium	Very low	Backup, distribution of software	Low	Low capacity per device
Flash memory	High	High	High	Backup, portability	Medium	Expensive

depends on whether their employees are satisfied with the computers and other equipment installed in their workplace.

Before deciding what to purchase, consider the following variables:

- The equipment's power: its speed, its memory size and the capacity of its storage devices, such as the hard disk installed in the computer.

- Expansion slots: computers should have enough slots to add circuitry cards for additional purposes, such as graphic cards and wireless cards.

- The number and type of external ports, or sockets used to connect a computer to external devices.

- The monitor type and resolution: higher resolution is more pleasing and less straining to the eyes. Larger monitors allow many software applications to be opened simultaneously and require less scrolling.

- Ergonomics: ergonomic equipment does not strain the back, arms and eyes. For example, working with the keyboard must be comfortable. Traditional keyboards cause muscle pain when used for long sessions. Consider purchasing an ergonomic key-board. Consider a trackball instead of a mouse; it requires only moving fingers rather than the forearm.

- Compatibility: IT managers must ensure that new systems will integrate with existing hardware, software and networks. A new computer might have a different operating system or internal architecture, and if it is to be used to host an important application, care must be taken to ensure that the application will run on the new machine. Managers must consider backward compatibility, in which newer hardware is compatible with older hardware. (The same

port A socket on a computer to which external devices, such as printers, keyboards and scanners, can be connected. Also, software that enables direct communication of certain applications with the Internet.

backward compatibility Compatibility of a device with another device that supports only an older standard. For example, USB 2.0 is backward-compatible with computers that support only USB 1.1 devices.

applies to software.) For example, USB 2.0 devices are backward-compatible with USB 1.1 ports (although the communications speed then deteriorates to the speed of the older port.

- The hardware footprint: if space is scarce, you might want to consider the size of the computer and its peripheral equipment. The footprint is the area that a computer occupies.
- The reliability of the vendor, the warranty policy and the support given after the warranty expires: ask if the vendor provides a website and 24-hour help via telephone.

- Power consumption and noise: computers that consume less power help save money on electricity and usually also give off less heat. Computers use fans to cool down the circuitry. Quiet fans will make the work environment more pleasant.
- Scalability: IT purchasing managers try to extend the life of their hardware purchases by ensuring that any equipment they buy is scalable. The principle of scalability implies that resources – in this case, hardware – can be expanded or upgraded, to provide increased power as demands increase.
- Cost: all of the factors just discussed must be weighed against cost. Careful study might yield hardware with excellent performance for an affordable price. Perusing print and web-based trade journals is extremely helpful. Many periodicals provide tables evaluating comparable hardware, based on laboratory tests by impartial technicians. You do not have to be an IT professional to understand their evaluations.

Software: instructions to the computer

software Sets of instructions that control the operations of a computer.

application software Software developed to meet general or specific business needs.

system software Software that executes routine tasks. System software includes operating systems, language translators and communications software. Also called 'support software'.

programming The process of writing software.

machine language Binary programming language that is specific to a computer. A computer can execute a program only after the program's source code is translated to object code expressed in the computer's machine language.

assembly languages Second-generation programming languages that assemble several bytes into groups of characters that are human-readable to expedite programming tasks.

programming languages Sets of syntax for abbreviated forms of instructions that special programs can translate into machine language so a computer can understand the instructions.

Software is a series of instructions to a computer to execute any and all processes, such as displaying text, mathematically manipulating numbers or copying or deleting documents.

There are two major categories of software: application software and system software. Application software enables users to complete a particular application or task, such as word processing, investment analysis, data manipulation or project management. System software enables application software to run on a computer and manages the interaction between the CPU, memory, storage, input/output devices and other computer components.

Programming languages and software development tools

Programs are needed for absolutely every operation a computer conducts. An operation can be as simple as adding 1 + 2, typing a word or emitting a beep, or as involved as calculating the trajectory of a spacecraft bound for Mars. The process of writing programs is programming.

The only language that computer hardware understands is a series of electrical signals that represent bits and bytes, which together provide computer hardware with instructions to carry out operations. But writing programs in that language – which is called machine language – requires a programmer to literally create long strings of ones and zeroes to represent different characters and symbols. Assembly languages make programming somewhat easier because they aggregate common commands into 'words', although many of those 'words' are not English-like. Higher-level programming languages enable the use of English-like statements to accomplish a goal, and those statements are translated by special software into the machine language. Software development tools are even easier to use because they require practically no knowledge of programming languages to develop software. Programmers have at their disposal literally thousands of different programming languages, such as Visual Basic, Java, and C++. Programmers and nonprogrammers alike can use software tools such as web page development tools, which provide menus, icons and palettes that the developer can select to create intricate web pages, forms and animation. To develop the software development tools themselves, as well as to develop highly specialized software, programmers still have to write code in programming languages.

Figure 4.3 shows how programming languages have evolved dramatically over the years. Their different stages of development are known as generations. First- and second-generation languages were quite inefficient tools for code writing. They required lengthy written code for even the simplest instructions. In third- and fourth-generation languages, shorter, more human-friendly commands replaced lengthy code (see Table 4.4 for a comparison of high- and low-level programming). Ultimately, it would be nice to be able to program using the daily grammar of your native language – English, Spanish, Hebrew or any other language. But even then, the so-called natural language would have to be translated by another program into machine language.

Fourth-generation languages (4GLs) make application development even easier. They are built around database management systems that allow the programmer to create database structures, populate them with data and manipulate the data. Fourth-generation languages are significantly less procedural than 3GLs. With 4GL commands, the programmer often only needs to type what is to be done, but doesn't need to specify how the procedure accomplishes the task.

Figure 4.3 The evolution of programming languages

Human language:
Future
• Use natural
  language
• No need to learn
  new syntax

Fourth generation:
1980s
• More english-like
• Many preprogrammed
  functions
• Includes data management
  features
• Easy to learn and use

1990s–2000s
• Object-oriented programming
• Visual programming tools

Third generation:
1950s
• English-like
• Problem oriented
• Easier to learn
  and use

Second generation:
1950s
(Assembly languages)
• Shorter codes than
  machine language
• Machine dependent

First generation:
1940s
(Machine languages)
• Difficult to learn and use
• Long instructions
• Machine dependent

Table 4.4 Advantages and disadvantages of higher-level programming languages

Advantages of higher-level programming	Disadvantages of higher-level programming
Ease of learning the language	Less control over hardware
Ease of programming	Less efficient memory use
Significantly shorter code	Program runs more slowly
Ease of debugging	
Ease of maintenance (for example, modification of a procedure)	

Visual programming

CD TASK

visual programming language A programming language that provides icons, colours and other visual elements from which the programmer can choose to speed up software development.

To accelerate their work, programmers can use one of several visual programming languages, such as Microsoft Visual Basic or Borland Delphi. These languages let programmers create field windows, scroll-down menus, click buttons and other objects by simply choosing the proper icon from a palette. Seeing exactly and immediately how boxes and menus look on screen reduces the chance of bugs and lets programmers finish their jobs faster than if they had to write code. The appropriate code is written automatically for them when they click on elements. However, the programmer can always go back to the code and add or change statements for operations that cannot easily be accomplished by using the visual aids. Thus, knowledge of the programming language is still required.

Object-oriented programming

In traditional programming, programmers receive specifications of how a program should process data and how it should interact with users, and then they write code. If business changes and the program must be modified, the programmer must change the code. Programmers spend 60–85 per cent of their time maintaining software. Maintenance is mainly modifying programs

Table 4.5 Advantages of object-oriented programming (OOP) over procedural languages

OOP advantages
Requires less code than other languages
Requires less time than programming in other languages
Enhances program modularity and reusability
Makes code maintenance easier
Enhances ability to create user-friendly interface
Is appropriate for graphic- and sound-enhanced applications

Why you should...
be software savvy

As a professional, you should regard software as a tool to further your productivity and education. Software can automate many processes that professionals must accomplish. Even simple software such as electronic spreadsheets can be used to build decision-support applications. Software vendors offer a huge variety of programs. While it is doubtful that any individual can become knowledgeable about all available software, knowledge of the types of software and particular applications lets you make informed comparisons and suggestions for improving your organization's software portfolio and your own library of personal software.

to meet new business needs, but also debugging of errors that were not detected in the testing of the developed code. In object-oriented programming, software developers treat objects as parts, or standardized modules that work together and can be used and reused. Instead of creating large, complex, tightly intertwined programs, programmers create objects. Objects are developed in standard ways and have standard behaviours and interfaces. These modules enable software to be assembled rapidly rather than written laboriously. See Table 4.5 for a list of advantages of OOP. The most popular OOP languages are C++ and Java.

Software tools for the Web

Because an increasing amount of software is developed for websites, special software languages and tools have been developed for these tasks. Programming languages include JavaScript and PHP. Web page development packages include FrontPage and Dreamweaver. The main advantage JavaScript is that the code produced – often called applets – can be executed well regardless of the operating system that the computer uses. Therefore, the same applet will be executed in the same way on a computer running Windows or one running Mac OS X. This is a great benefit especially when the applets are developed to be posted at a website.

Application software

Programs designed to perform specific jobs, such as calculating and executing a company's payroll, are collectively called application-specific software. Programs that serve varied purposes, such as developing decision-making tools or creating documents, are called general-purpose application software. Spreadsheets and word processors are general-purpose applications.

General-purpose applications are available as packaged software. Application-specific software is not always so readily available. Managers must decide whether an off-the-shelf software package fits all needs. If it does, the company can simply purchase it. But if off-the-shelf or other ready-made software cannot address an organization's specified needs, managers must have a program developed, either within the organization or by another organization specializing in that type of software. We discuss alternative ways to acquire ready-made software in Chapter 12, 'Choices in Systems Acquisition'.

object-oriented programming (OOP) language A programming language that combines data and the procedures that process the data into a single unit called an 'object', which can be invoked from different programs.

applet A small software application, usually written in Java or another programming language for the Web.

application-specific software A collective term for all computer programs that are designed specifically to address certain business problems, such as a program written to deal with a company's market research effort.

general-purpose application software Programs that serve varied purposes, such as developing decision-making tools or creating documents; examples include spreadsheets and word processors.

packaged software General-purpose applications that come ready to install from a magnetic disk, CD or file downloaded from a vendor's website.

Office productivity applications

The purpose of *all* software is to make the work of people more productive. However, applications that help employees in their routine office work often are called simply 'productivity tools'. Often, the tools are called desktop productivity tools, because they were developed to support home and office users on their personal computers.

- *Word processors* such as Microsoft Word are used mainly to type letters, articles and other text documents, but they also automate otherwise laborious tasks such as creating tables of contents and indexes.

- *Spreadsheets* such as Microsoft Excel no longer limit users to entering numbers and performing basic arithmetic calculations. They include a long list of complex mathematical, statistical, financial and other functions that users can integrate into analysis models. Executives can build their own decision-support models with this robust tool. Spreadsheets also provide a large array of preformatted charts from which the user can select for presentation purposes.

- *Presentation tools* such as Microsoft PowerPoint enable professionals and salespeople to quickly develop impressive presentations. One does not need to be a graphics expert, because the tools provide wide selections of font types and sizes and allow the users to embed almost any art that they find (with permission!) or have created in graphics programs. Animations, sound and video clips can be integrated into presentations.

- *File management and data management tools* enable the creation and manipulation of local or shared databases. Popular database management systems such as Microsoft Access are relatively easy to learn and create simple databases. They often include features that professional developers can use to create more complex databases.

- *Graphics* programs make it easy to create intricate graphics and manipulate digital photographs. They are often used to create graphics to be placed on web pages. The large selection of these tools includes Adobe's Illustrator and Photoshop, Corel Paint Shop and MGI PhotoSuite.

- *Desktop publishing tools*, such as Microsoft Publisher, enable both expert and novice to easily create professional-looking pamphlets, newsletters, cards, calendars and many other items for publication on paper or as web pages. More professional tools, such as Quark, by a company of the same name, have significantly increased the productivity of the publishing industry.

- *Project management tools* help managers of any type of project – such as building construction, product development and software development – to plan projects and track their progress. Project managers enter information such as tasks and their expected completion dates, milestones and resources required for each task: labour hours, materials and services.

Software developers often create suites of productivity tools. For example, most versions of Microsoft Office suite include a word processor (Word), spreadsheet (Excel), presentation application (PowerPoint), database management system (Access), and an email application (Outlook), and all can be integrated. You can create tables in a spreadsheet, copy them into a word-processed document or a presentation, and ensure that when you modify the tables in the spreadsheet they also change in the document or presentation.

Groupware applications are programs that enable workers to collaborate in real time over the Web. They not only eliminate the need to travel and sit in the same physical room, but also facilitate expression of ideas by demonstrating them through the combination of text, images, drawings, sound, animation and video.

The Zoho Office Suite is an example of groupware that is beginning to challenge the market dominance of Microsoft Office.

System software

System software includes programs that are designed to carry out general routine operations, such as the interface between user and computer, loading a file, copying a file or deleting a file, as well as managing memory resources and operating peripheral equipment such as monitors and printers. The purpose of system software is to manage computer resources and perform routine tasks that are not specific to any application. On one hand, system software is developed to work in partnership with as many applications as possible; on the other, applications can work with system software only if they are developed to be compatible with that software. The following discussion covers major types of system programs.

operating system (OS)
System software that supports the running of applications developed to utilize its features and controls peripheral equipment.

Operating systems

The operating system (OS) is the single most important program that runs on a computer and the

3-D city models, such as this one of Milan, help city planners maintain existing facilities and plan new urban environments.

Figure 4.4 The operating system mediates between applications and the computer, and controls peripheral devices

most important type of system software. As Figure 4.4 illustrates, operating systems perform basic tasks, such as recognizing input from the keyboard and mouse, sending output to the computer display, keeping track of files and directories (groups of files) on disks, and sending documents to the printer. Without an operating system, no application can run on a computer.

From user to OS to CPU Figure 4.5 shows the OS's position in the logical operation of a computer. The user interacts with the user interface using menus, icons and commands the

Figure 4.5 Computers operate on a number of layers, starting from the user interface and moving inward to the hardware

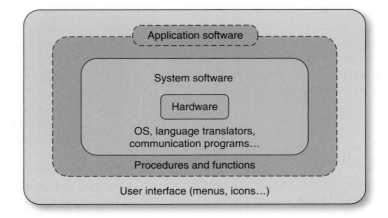

Table 4.6 Popular operating systems

Name	OS Developer	Runs on . . .
Linux	Linus Torvalds and other individuals and companies	Pcs, mainly servers
Mac OS X	Apple Computer	Macintosh PCs
MS-DOS	Microsoft	PCs
NetWare	Novell	Usually network servers
OS/400	IBM	IBM iSeries (the renamed AS/400) midrange computers
OS390 (formerly MVS)	IBM	IBM mainframes
Palm OS	Palm	Handheld computers (PDA)
Sclaris	Sun Microsystems	Sun and other computers
UNIX	AT&T (originally) and other software companies	Various versions for IBM, Macintosh, Sun and other computers
Windows 95, 98, Me, NT, 2000, XP, 2003	Microsoft	PCs
Windows Vista	Microsoft	PCs
Windows CE	Microsoft	Handheld computers (PDAs)

application provides. The application converts some of the user's input into commands the OS understands, and the OS commands the CPU to carry out the operation.

In addition to performing input and output services and controlling the CPU, many OSs perform accounting and statistical jobs, including recording times when a user logs on and logs off, the number of seconds the operator used the CPU in every session, and the number of pages a user printed. Some OSs also perform utilities such as hardware diagnostics and disk checks, as well as security functions such as the ability to set user passwords and restrict access to files and computer resources. Table 4.6 provides a list of popular operating systems.

utilities Programs that provide help in routine user operations.

Other system software

While operating systems are the most prevalent type of system software, there are other types of system programs:

- Compilers and interpreters are used to translate a program written in a higher language code into machine code, which the computer can then process.
- Communications software supports transmission and reception of data across computer networks. We discuss networking and telecommunications in Chapter 5.
- Utilities include programs that enhance the performance of computers, such as Symantec's Norton SystemWorks, which checks PCs for inefficiencies and fixes them. Utilities

also include antivirus programs, firewalls and other programs that detect and remove unwanted files and applications.

Open source software

The great majority of business and individual software is proprietary, that is, software that is developed and sold for profit. The developers of proprietary software do not make the source code (the full set of original program statements) of their software public. The developer retains the rights to the software. In most cases you do not actually own the copies of applications that you purchase; you only purchase licences to use those applications. In contrast to proprietary software, there are programmers who freely contribute to the development of a growing number of computer programs not for profit. The developers of open source software can obtain the source code free of charge, usually on the Web. Anyone who can contribute features is invited to do so. Anyone who wishes to download the latest version can do so free of charge. An open source program can be developed by a random group of programmers, rather than by a single company.

The advantages of open source software over proprietary software are clear: the software has fewer bugs because thousands of independent programmers review the code, and it can offer more innovative features by incorporating ideas from a diverse set of experts from different countries and cultures who collaborate. The motive for developing and improving open source software is not monetary, but rather the satisfaction of solving programming problems and the recognition of one's contribution. Programmers who improve such software do it for fame and recognition by their peers the world over. They collaborate mainly via the Internet. They post patches of code that improve current code, or add extensions and plug-ins to enhance functionality of an application. These extensions are free for all to download and use. The major disadvantage is that development and support depend on the continued effort of an army of volunteers.

There are hundreds of useful open source applications. They include the popular web browser Mozilla Firefox, the email application Thunderbird, the relational database management server MySQL, and the powerful programming language PERL (Practical Extraction and Report Language). OpenOffice.org, which can be freely downloaded at www.openoffice.org, provides a complete alternative to Microsoft's Office suite of productivity applications.

Linux is the best known open source operating system. A Finnish graduate student named Linus Torvalds developed it for his own use, but he has never claimed rights to the software. Hundreds of programmers have contributed code to Linux.

Many governments, both local and national, have decided to move to open source software. They do so mostly to save money, but also to improve operations. Many adopters of Linux, for instance, have reported a tenfold improvement in the speed of their software-based operations when they moved from a commercial OS to Linux. Forty-two per cent of Argentine companies use Linux. The governments of Brazil, Peru and Chile mandated that all public administration agencies use only open source software when available.

Of course there are dangers associated with following the open source route. If you are using propriety software, then the vendor is likely to offer support and at the very least is obliged to deal with problems such as bugs in the software. With open source software, if a bug needs fixing who is going to deal with it? You may have to either rely on skills in your own company or, if that is not possible, hire an outside contractor to solve your problem. Both solutions involve an extra cost. The major players in open source, such as Linux, are well monitored to ensure quality, but the same is not true of most open source code. There are also issues relating to the very open nature of the source code. You may find that you are unwittingly using pirated code from proprietary software that has been stolen by an open source contributor.

Industry **SNAPSHOT**

Free software nation

In an attempt to save millions of dollars, the president of Brazil instructed the government and state-owned companies to switch from proprietary operating systems to free operating systems, such as Linux. The major loser from this move is Microsoft. President Luiz Inacio Lula da Silva also decreed that any company or research institute that receives government funding to develop software must license it as open source, that is, the software's source code must be accessible to all, free of charge. This is part of a general effort to make IT and Internet access more affordable to this large nation of 183 million people. In 2005, only 10 per cent of Brazilians had access to the Internet.

SOURCE: T. Benson, 'Brazil: Free Software's Biggest and Best Friend', *New York Times* (www.nytimes.com), 29 March 2005

Rio de Janeiro, Brazil – getting behind open source software.

PHOTO SOURCE: © NIKO VIJEVIC

Ethical and Societal **ISSUES**

Software piracy

Software piracy, the illegal copying of software, is probably one of the most pervasive crimes. Software piracy has several forms: making copies from a single paid copy of the software; using the Internet to download software from a website without paying for it, or copying software through use of peer-to-peer applications; using one licensed copy to install an application on multiple computers; taking advantage of upgrade offers without having paid for a legal copy of the updated version; using for commercial purposes copies that were acquired with discounts for home or educational use; and using at home a copy that was purchased by an employer under a licence to use only on the employer's premises. The software industry has established organizations to protect software developers from piracy: Business Software Alliance (BSA), the Software and Information Industry Association (SIIA) and the Federation Against Software Theft (FAST). These organizations were established by major software companies and are supported by the majority of the world's software development firms.

As the amount of software sold on the market grows, so grow the estimated losses that the software industry suffers from piracy. In the 1980s and 1990s, the global financial damage was estimated at US$10–12 billion annually. However, a survey conducted jointly by BSA and the IT research company IDC (International Data Corporation) reported that about 36 per cent of the world's installed software was pirated. A spokesperson for BSA explained: piracy deprives local governments of tax revenue, costs jobs in the technology supply chain (developers, distributors, retailers), and cripples local software companies. Eighty-six countries produce software. All are victims of the phenomenon.

Critics say that even if the estimates of pirated software are correct, the conclusions are exaggerated, because not all who pirated software would necessarily acquire it if they had to pay for it. Still, it is reasonable to assume that many pirates actually needed the software, and would pay for it had piracy not existed.

The software piracy 'map' varies in intensity and monetary damages: in the Asia-Pacific region

53 per cent of the software used was pirated, causing US$7.5 billion in losses; in Eastern Europe, 71 per cent and US$2.1 billion; in Western Europe, 36 per cent and US$9.6 billion; in Latin America, 63 per cent and US$1.3 billion; and in the African and Middle-East region, 56 per cent and US$1 billion. The rate in North America was the lowest, 'only' 23 per cent, but due to large absolute numbers of copies, the estimated loss was US$7.2 billion.

A previous joint study by BSA and IDC estimated that a 10 per cent drop in the rate of business software piracy by 2006 could boost Australia's GDP by US$6.8 billion. It also estimated that a similar reduction globally would create an estimated 1.5 million jobs and generate US$400 billion of economic growth. Reducing the piracy rate to 15 per cent could add US$142 billion to the US gross domestic product (GDP), create more than 130,000 high-tech jobs and generate an additional US$23 billion in tax revenues by 2006.

Laws in most countries treat software the same way as they do books, videotapes and other types of intellectual property: copies (except for one copy for archival purposes) may not be made without permission of the copyright or patent holder. Yet, the crime is pervasive because it is easy to commit and is rarely punished. And of course the digital storage of text and pictures means that even the old laws covering intellectual copyright of these are inadequate. Consider how easy it is to download whole sections of text for that assessed essay without referencing – don't do it!

Software licensing

The next time you 'purchase' software read carefully the 'purchase' contract. You might be surprised to see that you do not own the software you have just obtained. Most of the software that organizations and individuals obtain is not purchased; it is licensed. The client receives a limited permission to use the software, either indefinitely or for a set time. When the use is time-limited, the client pays annual licence fees. The only exceptions to this rule occur when an adopter uses its own employees to develop the software, when it hires the work of a software development firm, or when the adopter uses software developed by people who explicitly allow the user to change the software and sell the product.

Considerations for packaged software

When an application is developed specifically for an organization, specific program goals and custom requirements are considered during the development process. Such requirements include business needs, organizational culture needs, the need to interface with other systems and performance issues, such as response time. However, organizations find ways to satisfy many needs with off-the-shelf software as well. Many trade journals, such as *PC World* and *PC Magazine*, maintain labs in which they test competing applications. Experts test different applications on the same computer and report the results.

SUMMARY

More and more professionals outside the IT field find themselves in the decision-making role regarding the purchase and use of computer hardware. Therefore, understanding hardware is important.

For ease of reference, computers are classified into several categories according to their power. The most powerful are supercomputers, used mainly by research institutions for complex scientific calculations. Somewhat less powerful are mainframe computers; many organizations still use them to process large databases and perform other tasks that require speed and large primary memory. Midrange computers are less powerful than mainframe computers and are often used as servers. Microcomputers include PCs and smaller computers, such as notebook, handheld and tablet computers.

Regardless of their size and power, all computers must have several components to function. The 'brain' of every computer is its central processing unit (CPU), which controls four basic operations: (1) it fetches instructions from memory, (2) it decodes them, (3) it executes them, and (4) it stores the results in memory.

The rate at which the CPU does all this is the computer's clock rate.

A computer's word is the number of bits that can move through its CPU in one machine cycle.

Speed and memory size are the main determinants of a computer's power.

The larger part of a computer's memory, RAM (random access memory), is volatile; that is, it keeps data only as long as electrical power is supplied. ROM (read-only memory) is nonvolatile. Unlike data in RAM, data stored in ROM stays in ROM when you turn the computer off. Similarly, all secondary storage media, such as magnetic disks, optical disks and flash cards, are nonvolatile.

Imaging devices help process large amounts of text and graphic data and have made the work of banks and other industries more productive.

When evaluating external storage, factors to consider are the medium's density, its transfer rate, the capacity, portability and the form of data organization that it allows. The latter determines the mode of access (sequential or direct).

On tapes, data can be organized and retrieved only sequentially, therefore tapes are good for backup but not for transactions. Direct access storage devices, such as RAM, magnetic disks and optical disks, allow random organization and retrieval. Direct organization provides faster storage and retrieval of records that must be accessed individually and quickly, such as records in airline reservation systems. Only direct access devices are suitable for processing databases.

When purchasing computers, managers should consider computer power and other factors in addition to cost. Managers should consider expandability of RAM, the availability of sockets (ports) for connecting peripheral equipment, and compatibility with existing hardware and software.

Like many new technologies, information technology may pose health risks to users. The most common problems computer users experience are carpal tunnel syndrome and repetitive-stress injuries caused by the repetitive use of the keyboard over long time periods. Today, manufacturers of computer equipment pay more attention to health hazards and try to design devices ergonomically.

'Software' is the collective term for computer programs, which are sets of instructions to computer hardware.

Software is classified into two general categories. System software manages computer resources, such as CPU time and memory allocation, and carries out routine operations, such as translation and data communication. Application software is a program developed specifically to satisfy some business need, such as payroll or market analysis. Application software can include programs that carry out narrowly focused tasks, or general-purpose applications, such as spreadsheets and word processors.

To develop software, programmers use programming languages and software development tools. Third-generation languages (3GLs) are more English-like than machine language and assembly languages, and allow more productive programming, meaning that they use less time to develop the same code. Fourth-generation languages (4GLs) are even more English-like and provide many preprogrammed functions. Object-oriented programming (OOP) languages facilitate creation of reusable objects, which are data encapsulated along with the procedures that manipulate them. Visual programming languages help programmers develop code by using icons and other graphics while code is developed automatically by manipulating the graphics.

As an increasing amount of software is linked to the Internet, many software tools have been created especially for development of web pages and the software that links web pages with organizational information resources, such as databases. They include programming languages such as Java, JavaScript and PHP, and web page development packages such as FrontPage, Dreamweaver and GoLive. Java and other languages for the Web produce code that runs on various computers and therefore is very useful for the Web.

All code written in a programming language other than machine language must be translated into machine language code by special programs, either compilers or interpreters. The translation creates object code from the source code. Software offered for sale is usually object code.

Some application programs are custom designed, but many are packaged. The majority of packaged applications are purchased off the shelf, although 'off the shelf' might actually mean downloading the application through the Internet.

Office productivity tools help workers accomplish more in less time. The most pervasive of these tools include word processors, spreadsheets, presentation tools, file and database management software, graphics programs, desktop publishing tools, and project management tools. Some of them are offered as suites.

Groupware helps people in separate locations collaborate in their work.

The most important type of system software is operating systems. The newer operating systems carry out an ever-growing number of functions, and now include networking and security features. Other system software includes communications software and utilities.

Open source software is being adopted by a growing number of businesses and governments. The source code and its documentation are open to all to review and improve. Open source applications and system software can be downloaded from the Web.

While some software is purchased, much of it is licensed. The user purchases the right to use the software for a limited time or indefinitely, but does not own the software.

Businesses can follow a systematic evaluation to determine the suitability of off-the-shelf software to their needs. Applications should be tested with real transactions to find out whether they satisfy minimum requirements, such as response time.

Consideration of software includes many factors, among which are fitness for purpose, ease of learning to use, ease of use, reputation of the vendor and expected quality of support from the vendor.

While software prices have decreased over the years, software piracy is still a problem. About a third of the software used around the world has been illegally copied.

TRENT COURIER SERVICES REVISITED

Trent Couriers' business has expanded from a one-person bicycle messenger service to a company with bicycles, cars and trucks, as well as main office staff. As it expanded, the firm upgraded its information systems to streamline its processes and handle its increasing customer load. Let's examine some of the changes it has made.

Trent Couriers has purchased quite a bit of software through the years. As Trent Couriers has grown, it has used software to perform routine business functions, develop new routes and generate employee schedules. It has also begun to use its financial software to analyse route profitability and to motivate healthy competition among its messengers.

What would you do?

1   Trent Couriers has used many different types of input and output devices throughout its history. How many can you find? Create a two-column chart and list them under the headings Input and Output. Can you think of any other devices or technologies they haven't thought of yet that might help them?

2   When Andrew Langston decided he needed a new information system, he started by listing the basic functions that he needed software to perform. Why would he start with software needs first? Would you do the same?

3   Explain the importance to Trent Couriers of keeping up to date on software developments. Where did Andrew get his information on current software? What business systems did this improve? Where else could Trent Couriers look for software news? List some sources for Andrew.

New perspectives

1   Review Andrew and Sarah's decision to buy a server and handheld computers. What advantages does source data technology give to the messengers themselves? To the central office staff?

2   Andrew's cousin works for a seafood company. His company uses a Linux-based system, and he is recommending that Andrew switch from his Windows-based system to Linux. List the pros and cons of this step for Trent Couriers.

Review questions

1   You have decided to buy parts and build your own personal computer. At the minimum, what are the components that you would need for this device to be considered a computer?

2   Most people never get to see a supercomputer, let alone use one. Why? What are the most frequent uses of this type of computer?

3   IT professionals often speak of the merging of technologies. Think of handheld computers and mobile phones. Give an example of such merging.

4   When a computer is offered for sale, one of its advertised characteristics is something such as '4 GHz'. What does that mean, and what does it measure?

5 What is the difference between volatile and nonvolatile memory? Give one example of volatile memory and one example of nonvolatile memory.

6 Among the external storage devices discussed in this chapter, all but one store data on the surface of some material, and one in circuitry. Which one?

7 What does footprint mean in hardware? When is a footprint important in the office?

8 On a continental tour, a travelling salesperson makes software-based presentations at every place he stops. He has ensured that there is a PC and projecting equipment at every site he visits. Every so often, he needs to change the content of his presentation. He wants to carry as little as possible. What data storage device would you recommend he carry?

9 Why would any programmer today use an assembly language rather than a higher-level language?

10 4GLs help nonprogrammers develop useful applications. How are they more suitable for this purpose than 3GLs?

11 There are so many ready-made software packages; why do some companies commission software development projects?

12 Office applications are often called productivity tools. Why?

13 What is the difference between system software and application software?

14 Linux is a free and stable operating system, which is a great advantage. What are the disadvantages of adopting it?

15 What are the main elements to consider when purchasing software for an organization?

16 What is open source software? To what does the word 'source' refer?

Discussion questions

1 Computers fail significantly less frequently than copy machines and printers. Why?

2 The end user's role in making hardware purchasing decisions is growing. Analyse the technological and operational reasons for this trend.

3 Would you replace a PC with a handheld computer for your studies or work? Why or why not?

4 Which storage medium would you use in each of the following situations: (1) airline reservation system, (2) information on employee benefits and professional conduct, and (3) online answers to customers' frequently asked questions (FAQs)? Explain your choices.

5 Comment on the following statement: the useful life of a PC is about two years, therefore, it is not important whether the vendor is still in business in two or three years.

6 Thanks to DVD and other advanced technologies, a PC can combine the functions of a computer, telephone, fax machine and television set. Would you give up your home telephone and television set if you could use your PC to make calls and watch television? Why or why not?

7 You might have heard of the electronic book, a handheld device that allows readers to read a book from a CD. What are the advantages and disadvantages of such devices when compared with traditional books? Think in terms of portability, text clarity, searching for specific words or pages, and so on. What would you prefer: an electronic book or a paper book? Why?

8 Try to count how many hours per week you use a personal computer: at your home, in the PC lab, in the library, or elsewhere. Have you become a 'computer junkie' in the Information Age? Do you, or does society in general, have an alternative to IT dependence?

9 Almost daily a new electronic device, often one that combines several technologies, is offered for sale. People sometimes refer to some of these devices as 'gadgets', hints that they might be nice to have but not really useful. How do *you* delineate the difference between a gadget and helpful device?

10 Think of a standard application such as a payroll system. What might drive an organization to develop its own payroll application rather than purchase one off the shelf?

11 A decision to adopt Linux or another open source operating system is not an easy one for

IS managers. What are their concerns? (*Hint:* Think of the relationships between OSs and applications.)

12 Widespread application software, such as OpenOffice.org, that runs on a variety of OSs threatens the software giant Microsoft. Why?

13 Increasingly accurate voice-recognition software and sophisticated software that can interpret commands in natural language are bringing us closer to the days of operating a computer by speaking to it. Would you rather speak to a computer than use a keyboard, mouse or some other input device? Why or why not?

14 Why is software piracy so pervasive? What are your innovative ideas to reduce this problem?

15 Do you think open source software will proliferate or disappear?

16 In what ways can young people who seek IT careers benefit by participating in improving open source software?

Tutorial activities

1 Recommend one of the three hardware configurations described in the table below for each of the scenarios listed. Assume that all of the hardware configurations cost the same. Explain your choices.

a) The employees of this firm do a lot of graphic design work. Graphics require large programs. Printouts must be high quality.

b) This firm uses the computer mainly for word processing. The biggest application occupies 24 MB.

c) Employees of this firm use scientific programs that run for many hours.

d) It is imperative that employees be able to print reports quickly with reasonable print quality. They almost always print their reports from portable storage devices.

2 Assume you can choose among magnetic tapes, magnetic hard disks, recordable optical disks (CD-R: write once, read many) and flash memory USB drives. Consider each scenario independently of the others. For each of the following purposes, explain which one of the media you would choose and why. Start by saying which medium you have chosen. Then explain why.

a) You need to store thousands of employee records for several years. This is only a backup procedure. The information will never be processed from the backup medium.

b) The storage medium is used as part of an airline reservation system.

c) Your business sells machines that must be maintained well by your clients. You wish to provide them with a digital version of the maintenance manual. The manual includes an index (like one at the end of a book) with links to the proper pages.

d) You are a sales manager who travels often. You must store a large PowerPoint presentation that you show to prospective customers in their office. You do not carry a laptop computer, but there is a PC wherever you go. You do not want to carry CDs,

Features	Computer configuration		
	A	**B**	**C**
RAM	512 MB	1 GB	512 MB
External storage			
Hard disk	200 GB	120 GB	60 GB
Thumb drive (USB 2.0)	256 MB	512 MB	256 MB
Speed (clock rate)	1.7 GHz	3.06 GHz	5 GHz
Printer	Laser	Ink-jet	Laser
	1200 DPI	600 DPI	600 DPI
	20 PPM	12 PPM	16 PPM

because you found that the graphic-rich presentation moves too slowly from CDs.

e) You have a business on the Web. You maintain your own server and site. You provide much textual and graphical information from the site. Customers can search products and make purchases.

f) You want to store all the paintings of Impressionist painters for use by your local library patrons. Patrons can search by artist name, artist nationality, or by the painting's topic. The library would like multiple copies of what you store, and to be able to loan them to patrons for viewing at home.

g) You use the medium for a large database that your employees manipulate frequently.

h) You work for HMRC, and you need to archive the tax records of millions of taxpayers for several years. The archiving is done after all processing of tax filings are complete and after all refunds and payments have been made. HMRC employees must occasionally go back and retrieve specific records from these files, and when they need a record, they want to access it directly.

3 HeadHunter, Inc., is a new personnel recruiting and placement company. The well-established and cash-rich management consulting company that founded HeadHunter is intent on providing adequate financial resources for the new firm to acquire information systems. HeadHunter has opened offices in ten cities worldwide.

Recruiting specialists exchange written correspondence with prospective clients, both managers looking for new positions and companies that might hire them. Records of both recruits and client companies must be kept and updated. All ten branches should be able to exchange information in real time to maximize the potential markets on both continents. HeadHunter professionals will often travel to make presentations before human resource managers and other executives.

The majority of HeadHunter's own personnel are university graduates who lack programming skills. HeadHunter management would like to adopt software that is easy to learn and use.

a) List the types of software the firm needs, both system software and applications.

b) Research trade journals. Suggest specific software packages for the firm.

4 Your company is about to open a new branch. You were selected to equip the new office with 20 personal computers, 10 notebook computers, and 5 laser printers. Management has asked that you purchase all the equipment from a single online vendor. Each PC must be purchased complete with a 19-inch LCD monitor. After interviewing employees about their typical computing needs, you developed the following scale:

PCs: Every 1 MHz of clock rate receives 1 point; every 1 MB of RAM receives 10 points; every 1 GB of hard disk storage receives 1 point. For CD–RW, each 1X of reading speed receives 1 point (writing and rewriting speeds are not essential, but the capabilities are required).

LCD monitors: Every 1:100 of contrast ratio gets 10 points; every 10 cd/m2 of brightness receives 1 point. Other features are not essential.

Laptops: The same scoring as for PCs.

Printers: Every 1 PPM receives 100 points; every 1 DPI receives 1 point.

Research three online vendor sites for this equipment. Prepare a spreadsheet table with three columns, one for each vendor, and enter the information you found about each piece of equipment for each vendor. Enter a formula to add up the total number of points at the bottom of each column. Do not consider any factor that is not mentioned here. Find the vendor who is the best value for money.

5 Try to forget the shapes of PCs, monitors, keyboards and mice. Use a word-processing application to write a two-page description of your own ideas for an ergonomic workstation. Explain what about today's PCs and peripheral equipment does not fit human hands, eyes and ears, and how you would like to change these devices' features and shapes for more comfortable and effective use. Be as revolutionary as your imagination lets you.

6 Log on to www.openoffice.org and prepare a report that covers the following points: (1) Who

established this site, and for what purpose? (2) What type of application is the subject of this site? (3) Who contributed the original source code for this project? (4) Who is invited to participate in this project? (5) Would you recommend a small business with little cash to download and use the applications? (6) Would you recommend a larger and richer organization to do so? Why or why not? In your assessment, address the issues of compatibility with other software, support, ease of training and ease of use.

Companion CD questions

1 Compare similar computers from three different manufacturers. Use a spreadsheet to list each component, its specifications and its price. Which computer is the better value?

2 Do some research and list at least two visual programming languages. Why is visual

programming better than the programming methods that came before?

Video questions

1 A friend has asked you to help him decide what computer to buy. Make a list of questions you would ask to help him decide what computer to buy. Indicate how the answers to each question will help you decide what hardware to recommend.

2 What components are on the computer you use most often? Be specific about sizes and speeds.

3 Would you buy software from one of the kiosks? Why or why not?

4 Other than the two issues mentioned on the clip, can you think of other downsides to this method of delivery?

From ideas to application
REAL CASES

Case study **4.1**

Captivating

The South African insurance industry has been booming in recent years. Metropolitan South Africa is one of South Africa's largest insurance companies and the fourth largest issuer of life insurance. As is typical for insurance companies, the organization needs to store massive amounts of information. It is headquartered in Cape Town and employs more than 6500 people in 224 branches throughout the country. For many years the only way to store policies, contracts, invoices and other documents was in the old familiar way: a microfiche was made from the original paper document and then both were stored. Searching for a desired document meant that a clerk had to know which filing cabinet

contained the document and then had to approach it and physically search for it, or, if it had already been copied on microfiche, search for the particular microfiche and review it under a microfiche lens.

The Metropolitan Building in Cape Town, South Africa.

The huge volumes of data created a growing problem. They were becoming difficult and costly to manage. Metropolitan had 31 million microfiche images, and the documents kept coming in. Every day the company received 80,000 paper documents. Search and retrieval of client documentation held on microfiche was time-consuming and inefficient. It slowed down response to customer applications and enquiries and delayed internal administrative processing. When a client file was requested, a librarian had to search for it in an archive, manually locate the microfiche, make a copy, dispatch that copy to the party that requested it, and then manually refile the original microfiche. The process was labour-intensive and slow.

The double storage – of the paper document and the microfiche – also added to the cost. The double storage was required in order to comply with legal archiving regulations. Employees used paper documents as soon as they were received. Because paper documents were processed before they were filmed, the microfiche documents could not be considered 'legal archives' due to the risk of a 'knowledgeable person' tampering. In case there was suspicion of document tampering, the microfiche would be compared to the original.

The IT professionals of Metropolitan approached Xcel, a British company that specializes in document imaging. Xcel designed and tested a pilot system to capture all client documents less than one year old for customers whose last name started with the letters A, B or C. The test was successful, and Xcel proceeded to implement the imaging system for all documentation. Metropolitan had to image both the entire microfiche library and the daily inflow of 80,000 documents that come in by mail. The policy adopted was to scan all urgent documents immediately and store them as images, regardless of other documents queued for processing.

The new system can scan more than 150,000 documents per day, both from microfiches and paper. It uses indexing to subdivide each client file for identification, classification (by the type of policy or other relationship with the client), and other criteria. The system can also image documents unattended overnight. It is seamlessly interfaced with other information systems that require some information from the scanned documents. The scanner has an image enhancement module that enables it to reduce the file size of scanned documents by 10–40 per cent while increasing the image quality through software processes called despeckling, deskewing and border removal (cropping image margins that contain no useful information). A human operator manually indexes the document policy number. If a microfiche image is unreadable for processing purposes, the operator can request rescans until the image is legible. Incoming paper documents are scanned at a rate of over 35,000 daily.

The imaging system only ensures clean and legible documents. It is not a document management system. All scanned documents are eventually stored by Documentum, which is a large document database and a computer program that enables employees to retrieve indexed imaged documents. Incoming faxes are 'cleaned' by the imaging system and communicated to Documentum as well, which routes them automatically to the proper employee for processing.

Metropolitan reduced the average time of retrieving a document from three hours to less than five seconds. Employees can access any document from their PCs, and can do so simultaneously; that is, several employees can view the same document at the same time. Because paper documents are now imaged before processing, the images are considered legal documents, and the original documents can be destroyed. Eliminating paper storage saved much money. The system affords scalability, the ability to add components and connect more PCs to it. If needed, more scanners can be connected, and more employees can control them through their computers.

Thinking about the case

1 What hardware is used as part of and with the new system?

2 The imaging system only scans and stores scanned documents. Why is it important that it be linked to another system? What is the purpose of that other system?

3 The new system saved costs in several ways. List and explain each of the cost savings. The system also saved cycle time. Explain where and how time was saved.

4 What is the importance of scalability of such systems?

SOURCE: 'Captiva Capture System Cuts Document Storage and Maintenance Costs for South African Insurance Company', Captiva Software UK Ltd., 2005; Business Reports & Independent online (www.busrep.co.za), 18 March 2005

Case study **4.2**

Making the fleet greener

Companies that operate a fleet of cars have always needed to consider the economic aspects to ensure they are getting good value for money. However, they now have to add environmental considerations, and not just for altruistic reasons. CO_2 emission figures play an important part in taxation calculations. CFC Solutions, a fleet software specialist, has carried out research into this area. They found that virtually all companies that use software to monitor CO_2 output and fuel consumption of their fleet also have a 'green' policy in place. Andy Leech, Sales and Marketing Director of CFC Solutions, says 'It's a question of ensuring that the standard CO_2 figure of each car is contained in the software and the actual fuel consumption recorded, ideally by importing the information from a fuel card. This allows you to set up the software so that the total CO_2 figure for each vehicle can be monitored. From there you can identify management action that needs to be taken. You can see, for example, which cars and drivers are not achieving the kind of fuel consumption you would expect and check whether there is a problem mechanically or with the driving style.' As well as this specific targeting of vehicle or driver you can also take a company-wide view to analyse the types of journey being made, opportunities for car sharing, the relative efficiency of car models and so on to help make strategic decisions to both save money and increase the company's green credentials.

Aberdeenshire Council's waste management service is responsible for the collection and disposal from over 100,000 households spread over 2500 square miles, predominantly small, widely dispersed communities. Alex Black, Waste Manager, commented that 'Providing an efficient service is very challenging because of the expansive, rural area in which we operate. This problem was exacerbated by the fact that a number of bins were being missed during rounds, meaning extra journeys.' The council decided that there was a need to track the vehicles so that the routes could be analysed. They chose Fleetstar-Online, an Internet-based solution from Cybit. The waste management fleet was fitted with a small electronic in-vehicle-unit (IVU) which tracks the vehicle using global position systems (GPS) and transmits the data to Cybit's online control centre. The council can then view the data from any Internet browser. According to Alistair Black, 'Fleetstar-Online provides the accurate means of tracking vehicles and analysing performance.' More specifically, 'if there are any complaints, such as missed collections, we can check immediately whether the refuse truck has been in that area by running a vehicle replay report. We also use Fleetstar-Online to schedule our vehicles' routes, including re-routing to improve efficiency and productivity.' As far as the future is concerned, Alistair Black says, 'For us it is about improvements in efficiency and productivity as opposed to keeping a check on our drivers though the system is currently being investigated as a means of monitoring the lone worker which would allow us to ensure the safety of our mobile workforce in remote locations.'

Pertemps Recruitment maintains a fleet of 550 cars and 25 vans. The Fleet Manger, Adrian Harris, was looking for a fully integrated fleet management system that could provide in-depth reporting on fuel consumption. The solution was for it to develop its own software, called Midas. According to Adrian the system can report on drivers' monthly mileages and lead to measures to reduce them, and it can analyse fuel efficiency to help in decision-making in vehicle replacement. Administration savings are significant. Adrian's estimate of the average cost of dealing with a fuel expense claim is £28, but with Midas that is reduced to a matter of pence. The system developed in-house is now available to other fleet operators. A small business with up to 100 vehicles would pay around £5 per user per month for the system. Adrian concludes, 'The system provides lower fuel usage which is a benefit in terms of costs to both businesses and drivers and a benefit in terms of lower emissions to the environment. Basically everyone is a winner!'

Household recycling and waste being collected in Scotland.

Thinking about the case

1   Aberdeenshire Council chose to buy a commercial system whereas Pertemps chose to develop their own in-house. What are the pros and cons of these different decisions?

2   Identify the hardware requirements for Aberdeenshire council in order to implement Cybit's software.

3   There seem to be no disadvantages to the systems described. Why isn't every fleet in the world using such software?

SOURCE: 'Softly, Software', *Fleetworld*, February 2007 and 'Case Study – Aberdeenshire Council dramatically increase productivity', http://www.cybit.co.uk/CaseStudies/Aberdeenshire.aspx

Case study **4.3**

Inside the transformation of Arsenal FC

BY WILL STURGEON

Since 1999 Arsenal Football Club had been planning a move from its home at Highbury in North London.

Not least in these considerations was the role IT now plays in the big-business world of Premiership football, and Highbury had never been built with cabling, computers or server rooms in mind.

Adrian Ford, commercial director at Arsenal, said: 'Highbury was like an antique. It was fabulous to look at but you wouldn't really want to use it.'

The new ground is just 500 metres from the turnstiles of Highbury, built on the site of one of North London's largest rubbish dumps (Tottenham fans insert your own joke here).

The stadium cost £263 million to build and was seven years in the planning. Overall the project will cost £450 million including the building of alternative refuse facilities – a project which cost £63 million alone. The entire project is expected to be finished by 2010.

It includes 150 corporate boxes which go for between £75,000 and £150,000 each per season. Then there are 6700 premium seats going for around £2500 to £4500 each and 160 Diamond club seats. The Diamond club costs £25,000 to join and £25,000 per season for two seats.

It is obvious that football is embracing its big-business status.

Ford said: 'If you're wealthy and you want the best facilities to watch football, you can buy that here.'

Making such a slick – some might say sterile, and certainly corporate – operation run smoothly relies heavily upon IT – something that couldn't be said of the club's previous home.

Ford said: 'IT is absolutely crucial here. It used to be the case that the amount of IT required on a match day was minimal.'

But that is far from the case now, with everything from the turnstiles, accessed using contactless smart card 'Club Cards', to the electronic point-of-sale units at more than 300 catering points all connected to the network.

Arsenal's new Emirates Stadium.

'If all this stuff went down we would have real problems', said Ford.

Paul Farmer is the head of IT at Arsenal and has overseen many of the changes, having been with the club for more than ten years. The move to the new stadium saw Farmer's IT budget upped considerably to around £16 million.

'Everything from buying a pint or a scarf to passing through a turnstile is reliant upon IT', said Farmer, adding that even the digital advertising hoardings around the ground are networked.

The stadium has 80 wireless access points, 500 electronic point of sale (EPOS) tills, more than 100 smart card-enabled turnstiles, also capable of reading bar codes on anything from paper tickets to MMS messages on mobile phones – allowing for scaleable ticketing options in the future.

Of the 60 servers deployed within the stadium, 15 deal solely with hospitality systems, compared to two dedicated to the club's website.

Most of the servers are from Dell. 'I do try to be consistent in terms of who our providers are', said Farmer. 'Ninety per cent are Dell though we have got some HP, unfortunately.'

It's a complex network and one which Farmer admits proved a daunting challenge to set up.

'This was an intimidating scenario for the IT department', Farmer added, especially given that his eight-man IT team didn't increase in size when it moved from the low-tech environs of Highbury to the Emirates Stadium.

But the club wasn't without examples to follow. The club admits it has taken its lead to a degree from US sports stadiums where Arsenal's goal of a cashless environment is already becoming a reality. This move is being driven in part by the US catering company Arsenal employs, who brought experience of cashless EPOS to Emirates Stadium.

The move towards card-only transactions – and preferably club-issued smart cards at that, which can be topped up with cash and spent anywhere in the ground – means the club can capture a great deal more data on its customers than before, enabling it to tailor marketing activities more effectively. Arsenal uses CRM software from Cyber to streamline the processing and analysis of this data.

Farmer's eight-man team manages 1000 devices including those 60 servers, more than 300 PCs and

the 500 EPOS. As such, careful monitoring of the network and systems is essential. The reliance upon IT means potential problems must be spotted before they arise.

'Being reactive may have worked at Highbury but not any more'. said Farmer, who employs CA's management software widely across the network to this end, as well as the US software giant's Mail Manager and XOSoft services for email archiving and retrieval and failover and disaster recovery respectively.

Farmer says the latter service means that 'If there is a catastrophic failure on our email server or ticketing systems we can move over to a failover.'

With a potential 70-plus games per season in all, downtime on any core system would be hugely problematic – on ticketing it could have huge consequences for the business.

In fact, although the IT is hardly pervasive, visitors to the stadium might be forgiven for thinking the only thing it doesn't have an impact on is the performance of the players.

However, one of the 60 servers the stadium houses is given over to running the Pro-Zone application, which processes player data to analyse the work done by every single player on the pitch to help the management team spot weaknesses in everything from formation and tactics to work rate.

But it remains to be seen what trophies all this IT can actually help the club to win.

Thinking about the case

1   The move from Highbury to the Emirates Stadium allowed the IT infrastructure to be developed from new. If the club had not moved to the new stadium, would they have been able to achieve all of the developments described above?

2   There are some examples given in the case of the use of monitoring software to help avoid problems. Can you identify them? Can you think of some other examples that would be useful in this application area?

Chapter 5

Business networks
and telecommunications

LEARNING OBJECTIVES

Modern telecommunications technology allows businesses to send and receive information in seconds. Except when a physical transfer of goods is involved, geographical distances are becoming meaningless in business transactions. When using computers and other digital devices, people can now work together as if they were sitting next to each other, even when they are thousands of miles apart. Financial transactions and information retrieval take seconds, and wireless technology enables us to perform these activities from almost anywhere and while moving. Understanding the technology underlying telecommunications – its strengths, weaknesses and available options – is essential to making informed business decisions.

When you finish this chapter, you will be able to:

Describe business and home applications of digital telecommunications.

Identify the major media and devices used in telecommunications.

Explain the concept of protocols.

Compare and contrast various networking and Internet services.

List networking technologies and trends that are likely to have an impact on businesses and information management in the near future.

Discuss the pros and cons of telecommuting.

Trent Courier Services

COMMUNICATION IS KEY

Mark Johnson, one of Trent Couriers' longtime car messengers, was hopelessly stuck in traffic. A serious accident involving two lorries had snarled traffic on the bypass; it was at a dead stop. He desperately needed to contact his customer – a medical supply firm – to alert it that his delivery would be delayed. So he used his hands-free mobile phone to call the customer. His contact at the supply firm acknowledged his delay and told him that the supplies were a routine delivery to a hospital pharmacy and not to worry – as long as the hospital received the delivery sometime that day, they'd be fine. Mark apologized for the glitch and promised to get off at the next exit as soon as he could move again. Then he used his group email program to warn other messengers to stay off the bypass for the time being. Maybe he could save somebody else a headache.

From beepers to mobile phones

When mobile phone technology hit the UK, Trent Courier Services replaced its collection of beepers. Andrew Langston had seen their competitive advantage almost immediately. The company could contact its messengers instantly; they didn't need to find a phonebox. Also, text message alerts could be sent to the entire delivery fleet. Now messengers could be rerouted around trouble spots. Of course, there was always the occasional delay of one or two messengers, such as Mark Johnson was experiencing, but the problems now could be isolated.

As soon as the media began reporting a link between mobile phone use and car accidents, Andrew decided to purchase hands-free car kits so that messengers could communicate safely with customers and the office. These devices also meant that his messengers didn't miss calls while they were fumbling for their phones.

Increasing efficiency and customer satisfaction

Mary Thomas updated delivery information from the messengers' handheld computers into the database. As the business grew, however, Mary spent more and more of her time uploading data from the handheld computers. A representative from the company's mobile phone service provider told her about a wireless card that messengers could use to upload delivery information to the company's database. The messengers plug the card into a slot on their handheld computers and access the Internet through the mobile phone providers' connection. Not only did this innovation save Mary time, it also meant that messengers could update delivery information immediately upon delivery so that the company could provide this information to their customers right away. Delivery confirmations now could be sent via email directly to the senders as soon as deliveries were made. Mary Thomas in the central office no longer had to confirm special deliveries. Messengers did that immediately and copied her on their transmittals, saving her time and the company money, all while increasing customer service.

PHOTO SOURCE: © PCC/ALAMY

Competitors up the ante

Trent Couriers' competitors hadn't stood still either. One of its major competitors had improved its service by offering a standard one-hour delivery time in nearby communities – half of Trent Couriers' standard delivery time. So, Andrew responded by opening two satellite offices to get messengers to remote destinations more quickly. That allowed Andrew to match his competitor's new time frame and still make a profit on deliveries.

An additional benefit of the three-office configuration was enhanced data security. In 2004, when pipes burst and flooded the main office, Trent Couriers did not have a recovery plan. Now, every time any data is recorded at one of the offices, it is automatically duplicated on disks at the other two offices via the Internet. Andrew felt much more secure knowing that the duplication in computing services was ready, if needed.

Choosing the right network service providers

To link its three offices, Trent Couriers used an Internet service provider (ISP) offering digital subscriber line (DSL) service, and a company that specialized in installation of virtual private networks (VPNs). Andrew found the DSL service to be fast enough for his company's needs and very affordable, but the connection was not reliable enough for Trent Couriers. So Andrew and Sarah Truesdale, the office manager, found themselves looking for an alternative. They considered cable, but the companies that offered those services would have to dig their trenches to the office sites, and they couldn't get to Trent Couriers for six to eight weeks.

Some time earlier, Andrew noticed strange aerials popping up in the neighbourhood. He remembered someone mentioning that a telecom company was establishing fixed wireless service in the area. Perhaps he could use that service. Indeed, the service was available at a fee comparable to the DSL service, and Andrew subscribed Trent Couriers. The company that provided the VPN software made all the necessary arrangements to ensure that communication among the three offices remained private. Now, Trent Couriers' three offices would have high-speed wireless Internet access as well as secure interoffice communications at a reasonable rate.

Intranets and extranets

As the staff became more comfortable with Internet technology, they began to see its usefulness for other business functions. For example, the human resources manager set up an intranet to inform staff of the benefits programme options and general company news. That information could be accessed from all three offices and through the mobile phones that messengers carried. He also set up a short orientation video to introduce new employees to the company.

Sarah and Mary began to consider an extranet to expedite transactions with the firms that maintained their van and bicycle fleets. They also explored the option to use the extranet of a national office supply superstore.

Telecommunications in business

Telecommunications, which is essential to today's smooth business operations, is the transmittal of data and information from one point to another. The Greek word *tele*, which means 'distance', is part of such words as 'telegraph', 'telephone' and other words referring to technologies that allow communications over large distances. Thus, telecommunications is communications over a distance. Telephone, fax, email, the World Wide Web – none of these essential business services would be available without fast, reliable telecommunications. Networking technologies have brought several improvements to business processes:

> **telecommunications**
> Communications over a long distance, as opposed to communication within a computer, or between adjacent hardware pieces.

- *Better business communication.* When no physical objects need to be transferred from one place to another, telecommunications technology can make geographical distance irrelevant. Email, voice mail, instant messaging, faxing, file transfer, mobile telephony and teleconferencing enable detailed and instant communication, within and between organizations. Telecommunications can also be used by one person to monitor another person's performance in real time. The use of email has brought some secondary benefits to business communications by establishing a permanent written record of, and accountability for, ideas. The result is more accurate business communications and less need for manual recording. Web-based instant messaging is used to support online shoppers in real time.

- *Greater efficiency.* Telecommunications has made business processes more efficient. Any information that is recorded electronically can become immediately available to anyone involved in a business process, even when the business units are located far apart. For example, as soon as an order is placed, anyone in the organization who will ever be involved with it can view it: from the marketing people, to purchasing officers, to manufacturing managers, to shipping workers, to billing and collection clerks.

- *Better distribution of data.* Organizations that can transmit vital data quickly from one computer to another no longer need centralized databases. Business units that need certain data frequently might store it locally, while others can access it remotely. Only fast, reliable transfer of data makes this efficient arrangement possible.

- *Instant transactions.* The availability of the Internet to millions of businesses and consumers has shifted a significant volume of business transactions to the Web. Both businesses and consumers can shop, purchase and pay instantly online. Wireless technology has also made possible instant payment and data collection using small radio devices, such as electronic toll collection tags. In addition to commercial activities, people can use telecommunications for online education and entertainment.

- *Flexible and mobile workforce.* Employees do not have to come to the office to carry out their work as long as their jobs only involve the use and creation of information. They can telecommute using Internet connections. Salespeople, support personnel and field workers are more mobile with wireless communication.

- *Alternative channels.* Services that used to be conducted through specialized dedicated channels can be conducted through alternative channels. For example, voice communication used to be conducted only through proprietary telephone networks, but is now also conducted through the Internet, which has decreased its cost. Radio and television broadcasts were conducted through radio frequencies and company-owned cables. Newer technologies enable organizations to broadcast over the Internet and provide telephone services over the Internet as well. Furthermore, Internet technologies allow individuals to broadcast text and sound to subscribers' computers or to web-capable mobile devices. (We discuss these technologies in Chapter 7, 'The Web-Enabled Enterprise'.)

CD TASK

At the same time you enjoy the great opportunities created by telecommunications technology, you must recognize that it poses great risks. Once an organization connects its ISs to a public network, security becomes a challenge. Unauthorized access and data destruction are constant threats. Thus, organizations must establish proper security controls as preventive measures. We discuss the risks and solutions in Chapter 13, 'Risks, Security and Disaster Recovery'.

Telecommunications in daily use

We have grown so used to networks that we no longer think much about them in daily life; however, they are pervasive. Here is an overview of the most widespread telecommunications uses.

Mobile phones

The American term for a mobile phone is a cellular phone, which derives its name from the territories of service providers, which are divided into areas known as cells. Each cell has at its centre a computerized transceiver (transmitter-receiver), which both transmits signals to another receiver and receives signals from another transmitter. When a call is placed on a mobile phone, the signal is first transmitted to the closest transceiver, which sends a signal through landlines that dial the desired phone number. If the receiving phone is also mobile, the call is communicated to the transceiver closest to the destination phone. As the user moves from one area, or cell, to another, other transceivers pick up the transmission and receiving tasks.

CD TASK

Using mobile phone networks, people can transmit and receive calls almost anywhere, freeing them from a fixed office location. They can also be used for email and faxing, and many are web-enabled. Many mobile phones have been merged with digital cameras, PDAs and GPS (global positioning system) circuitry. 'My car is my office' is a reality for many professionals who spend much of their time travelling. As technology advances and more capabilities are squeezed into smaller casings, some professionals can say, 'My pocket is my office.'

The major advantage of mobile phones is that they are attached to people, not offices. This is why, despite the higher cost of mobile phones over landline phones, some companies have decided to discard the latter and adopt the former for some or all of their employees.

Videoconferencing

People sitting in conference rooms thousands of miles apart are brought together by their transmitted images and speech in what is called videoconferencing. Businesses use videoconferencing to save on travel costs and lodging, car fleets and the time of highly salaried employees, whether they work in different organizations or at different sites of the same organization. From national and global perspectives, videoconferencing also reduces traffic congestion and air pollution. The increasing speed of Internet connections makes it easy for anyone with a high-speed link to establish videoconferences either by using a peer-to-peer link or by using the services of a third party, a company that specializes in maintaining videoconferencing hardware and software. In the latter case, businesses pay either a monthly fee for unlimited conferences, or every time they use the service.

> **videoconferencing** A telecommunication system that allows people who are in different locations to meet via transmitted images and speech.

Fax

Facsimile, or *fax*, is the transmission and reception of images over telephone lines. A fax machine digitizes an image and transmits the representative bits to a receiving fax machine. The receiving machine converts the digitized codes back into an image. Fax machines provide an easy means of communicating text and graphical images. Because it is based on digital images, faxing does not have to be executed through traditional telephone lines but can go through the Internet, using special software. Fax functions can also be combined with scanning, printing and copying functions in 'multifunction' machines.

PHOTO SOURCE: © TOM GUFLER

Videoconferencing is becoming an increasingly popular cost-saving option for a range of organizations.

Wireless payments and warehousing

Radio frequency identification (RFID) technology, mentioned in Chapter 3 and covered in more detail later in this chapter, enables us to conclude transactions and to make payments quickly. Stockholm's Congestion Charging system uses a wireless payment method. Drivers are loaned an electronic tag which they carry in their car. This communicates with 'gates' over the road at various points and this will automatically create a direct debit of the driver's account. The system is flexible in that charging can vary throughout the day and even take into account exceptions to payment. For example, the Lindingo district is accessible to the mainland only via the congestion charged area. It would be unfair to charge the residents if they are only 'passing through' when they have no choice. So any vehicle that enters the congestion charge area from Lindingo and leaves within 30 minutes pays no charge. With the electronic tag this exception is dealt with easily.

RFID technology is also used in warehouses where employees can use handheld units to check a central system for availability and location of items to be picked up and stored from and to shelves or bins. When storing, the handhelds are used to update inventory databases. Such systems have made the work of 'untethered employees' more efficient compared with older systems that require physical access to a computer terminal. Wireless communications have many other uses, some of which are discussed in detail later in the chapter.

Peer-to-peer file sharing

One of the most interesting developments in worldwide telecommunications is peer-to-peer (P2P) file sharing through the Internet: anyone with access to the Internet can download one of several free applications that help locate and download files from any online computer. You might have heard of some of these applications: LimeWire, BearShare, Morpheus, KaZaA and others. While the concept has well served scientists who share scientific text files and application developers who exchange code, the greater use has been in downloading artistic files, such as music and video files. Because unauthorized duplication and use of such files violates copyright laws and deprives recording and film companies of revenue, these industries have sued some violators in court. These actions and the proliferation of legal services that sell individual music tracks online for a small charge per track have reduced the use of file sharing for illegal copying, but have not eliminated it.

Since some files, especially movies, could take hours to download even with fast connections, some software divides up the designated file and downloads

peer-to-peer (P2P) file sharing Software applications that enable two Internet users to send and receive to each other. The technology is highly objectionable to organizations that sell copyrighted materials because the software promotes violation of copyrights.

Industry **SNAPSHOT**

Technology and copyright

In a precedent-setting case, a Belgian court appointed an expert to look into ways of automatically identifying copyright material in P2P operations. The expert identified seven ways Scarlet, one of Belgium's largest ISPs, could block such traffic without intrusively monitoring transactions, hence maintaining customers' privacy. Scarlet were given six months to implement the technology to block copyright material or face a daily fine of €2500.

SOURCE: 'Block P2P, Belgian court tells ISP' by Stephen Withers, *IT Wire*, 7 July 2007

each segment from a different online computer. For example, BitTorrent lets you conduct a search for a file. It finds several sources, and then downloads each segment of the file from a different source. It then combines the segments back into a complete file. A movie that would take several hours to download if copied from a single computer could take only several minutes from a large number of sources. If the owner of one computer turns it off, the software automatically tries to download the segment from another computer. The application poses a threat to the film industry. What is further threatening to both the music and movie industries is that these software packages work with each other, and that BitTorrent has been incorporated into some of the other file sharing applications.

> **bandwidth** The capacity of the communications channel, practically its speed; the number of signal streams the channel can support, usually measured as number of bits per second. A greater bandwidth also supports a greater bit rate, i.e., transmission speed.

Web-empowered commerce

Increasingly fast digital communication enables millions of organizations to conduct business and individuals to research, market, educate, train, shop, purchase and pay online. Whole industries, such as online exchanges and auctions, have been created thanks to the Web. Web-based commerce is the subject of an entire chapter (Chapter 7) and is illustrated with many examples throughout the book.

CD TASK

Bandwidth and media

While people can enjoy technologies without understanding how they work, educated professionals often do need to understand some fundamental concepts to be able to participate in decision-making when selecting networking equipment and services. This section introduces bandwidth and networking media.

> **transmission rate** The speed at which data are communicated over a communications channel.

Bandwidth

A communications *medium* is the physical means that transports the signal, such as a telephone line, a television cable or a radio wave. The bandwidth of the medium is the speed at which data are communicated, which is also called the transmission rate, or simply the bit rate. It is measured as bits per second (bps). Table 5.1 shows common bit rate measurements. As is often the case, bandwidth is a limited resource. Usually, the greater the bandwidth the higher the cost of the communications service. Thus, determining the type of communications lines to install or subscribe to is an important business decision.

When a communications medium can carry only one transmission at a time, it is known as baseband. Dial-up connections through regular phone lines and

> **bits per second (bps)** The measurement of the capacity (or transmission rate) of a communications channel.

> **baseband** A communications channel that allows only a very low bit rate in telecommunications, such as unconditioned telephone twisted pair cables.

Table 5.1 Transmission speed measurement units

bps = Bits per second
Kbps = Thousand bps
Mbps = Million bps (mega bps)
Gbps = Billion bps (giga bps)
Tbps = Trillion bps (tera bps)

broadband High-speed digital communication, sometimes defined as at least 200 kbps. T1, cable modem and DSL provide broadband.

Ethernet computer network connections are examples of baseband. When a line is capable of carrying multiple transmissions simultaneously, it is said to be broadband. Cable television, DSL (direct subscriber line), fibre-optic cables and most wireless connections are broadband. In general, broadband offers greater bandwidth and faster throughput than baseband connections, and in common usage the term 'broadband' is associated with a high-speed networking connection, which is required for fast transmission of large files and multimedia material.

Media

There are several types of communications media, that is, means through which bits are transmitted. Media can be tangible, such as cables, or intangible, such as radio waves. The most available tangible media are twisted pair cable, coaxial cable and optical fibre (see Table 5.2). Intangible media include all microwave radio technologies, which support wireless communication. Recently, the electric power grid has also been added as a medium for communications. All can be used to link a business or household to the Internet. Later in the chapter we discuss the various Internet connection services and also refer to typical periodic cost of the services.

Table 5.2 Networking media

Medium	Availability	Bandwidth	Vulnerability to electromagnetic interference
Twisted pair cable	High	Low to medium	High
Radio waves	High	Medium to high	Low (but vulnerable to RFI)
Microwave	Low	High	Low
Coaxial (TV) cable	High	High	Low
Optical fibre	Moderate but growing	Highest	Nonexistent
Electric power lines (BPL)	Very high	High	High

Twisted pair cable Twisted pair cable is used in computer networks and in telephone networks. It consists of pairs of insulated copper wires that are twisted together to reduce *electromagnetic interference (EMI)* and encased in a plastic cover. Twisted pair cable is a popular medium for connecting computers and networking devices because it is relatively flexible, reliable and low cost. Twisted pair cable is also used in telephone networks, but in many countries, twisted copper wires are now used only between the telephone jack and the central office of the company providing the telephone service. The typical distance of this link is 1.5–6 kilometres (about 1–4 miles), and is often referred to as 'the last mile'. The central offices themselves are connected with fibre optic cables, but it is often the 'last mile' media that determine the overall speed of the connection. In recent years many 'last mile' connections have also been converted to optical cables.

> **twisted pair cable** Traditional telephone wires, twisted in pairs to reduce electromagnetic interference.

Coaxial cable Coaxial cable is sometimes called TV cable or simply 'cable' because of its common use for cable television transmission. It is widely used for links to the Internet. Television companies use the same network they employ to transmit television programming to link households and businesses to the Internet.

> **coaxial cable** A transmission medium consisting of thick copper wire insulated and shielded by a special sheath of meshed wires to prevent electromagnetic interference. Supports high-speed telecommunication.

Optical fibre Fibre optic technology uses light instead of electricity to represent bits. Fibre optic lines are made of thin fibreglass filaments. A transmitter sends bursts of light using a laser or a light-emitting diode device. The receiver detects the period of light and no-light to receive the data bits. Optical fibre systems operate in the infrared and visible light frequencies. Because light is not susceptible to EMI (electromagnetic interference) and radio frequency interference (RFI), fibre optic communication is much less prone to error than twisted pair and radio transmission. Optical fibres can also carry signals over relatively longer distances than other media.

> **radio frequency interference (RFI)** The unwanted reception of radio signals that occurs when using metal communication lines. Optical fibres are not susceptible to RFI.

Some optical carriers support bit rates of up to several terabytes per second (Tbps), expected to reach 10 Tbps (10,000,000,000,000 bits per second) in the foreseeable future. This great bandwidth enables multiple streams of both Internet and television transmission. Some telecommunications companies have laid optical fibre lines to offer households both services, directly competing with TV cable companies.

> **microwaves** Short (high frequency) radio waves. Used in telecommunications to carry digital signals.

Radio and satellite transmission Radio frequency (RF) technologies use radio waves to carry bits. There are several wireless technologies that transmit through air or space. Some of the most popular for personal and business networking, such as Wi-Fi and Bluetooth, are discussed later in this chapter. Microwaves are high-frequency radio waves that can carry signals over long distances with high accuracy. You have probably noticed the parabolic dishes on the roofs of some buildings. They are so numerous on rooftops and high towers because microwave communication is effective only if the line of sight between the transmitter and receiver is unobstructed. Clusters of microwave aerials are often installed on high buildings and the tops of mountains to obtain a clear line of sight. Terrestrial microwave communication – so-called because signals are sent from and received by stations on the earth – is good for long-distance telecommunications but can also be

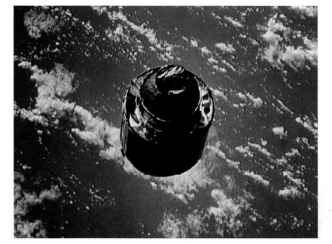

Large companies lease telecommunication satellite frequencies to transmit data coast to coast and across national borders.

used in local networks in and among buildings. It is commonly used for voice and television communications. When radio communication is used outside buildings, it is vulnerable to weather conditions. Thunderstorms, fog and snow might degrade communication quality.

Signals can also be transmitted using microwaves via satellite links. There are two major types of satellites: geostationary, also called GEO, and low earth orbit, also called LEO. Both types serve as radio relay stations in orbit above the earth that receive, amplify and redirect signals. Microwave transceiver dishes are aimed at the satellite, which has antennas, amplifiers and transmitters. The satellite receives a signal, amplifies it and retransmits it to the destination.

GEO satellites are placed in orbit 35,784 kilometres (about 22,282 miles) above the earth. At this distance the satellite is geosynchronized (synchronized with the earth); that is, once it starts orbiting, the satellite stays above the same point on earth at all times, without being propelled. Thus, a GEO satellite is stationary relative to the earth. Because they orbit at such a great distance above the earth, three GEO satellites can provide service for every point on earth by relaying signals among themselves before transmitting them back down to their destinations.

Because of the great distance from the earth to satellites, the communication is fine for transmitting data because delays of a few seconds make no significant difference. However, a delay of even two or three seconds might be disturbing in interactive communication, such as when voice and pictures are communicated in real time. You might have noticed such delays when reporters use devices that communicate to a television station. When the presenter in the studio asks a question, the reporter on location receives the question with a noticeable delay.

LEO satellites minimize this shortcoming. These lower-cost satellites are placed about 800–1000 kilometres (500–600 miles) above the earth. The signals' round-trip is short enough for mobile telephoning and interactive computer applications. Unlike GEOs, LEO satellites revolve around the globe every few hours. Multiple LEOs are required to maintain continuous coverage for uninterrupted communication.

Electrical power lines One communications medium that had been available for years but has only recently been tapped for telecommunications is the electric power grid. The bits in an electric power grid are represented by electric impulses, but they must be distinct from the regular power that flows through the grid. Engineers have succeeded in overcoming this technical challenge. The service is referred to as broadband over power line (BPL) or power line communication (PLC). BPL is covered in more detail later in the chapter.

network A combination of a communications device and a computer or several computers, or two or more computers, so that the various devices can send and receive text or audiovisual information to each other.

From the point of view of organizations, among the important factors in choosing a networking medium are availability, current and potential bandwidth, and vulnerability to electromagnetic interference (EMI) or radio frequency interference (RFI). Your business's current and future needs for data security, as well as compatibility with an already installed network, are also factors. Cost is another important consideration. For example, one of the great qualities of optical fibre is that it is practically immune to EMI. However, it is more expensive than other options.

node A device connected to at least one other device on a network.

Networks

In the context of data communications, a **network** is a combination of devices or **nodes** (computers or communication devices) connected to each other through one of the communication channels just discussed. We will often use the word 'computer' for a device that is networked, but this is only for convenience. Any compatible device that can transmit and receive on a network is part of it.

CD TASK

Types of networks

Computer networks are classified according to their reach and complexity. There are three basic types of networks: LANs (local area networks), which connect computers, printers and other computer equipment for an office, several adjacent offices, an entire building or a campus; MANs (metropolitan area networks), which span a greater distance than LANs and usually have more complicated networking equipment for midrange communications; and WANs (wide area networks), which connect systems in an entire nation, continent or worldwide. Some people also include a fourth category: PANs (personal area networks), which encompass connections between personal digital devices such as PDAs and tablet computers.

LANs A computer network within a building, or a campus of adjacent buildings, is called a local area network, or LAN. LANs are usually established by a single organization with offices within a radius of roughly 5–6 kilometres (3–4 miles). LANs are set up by organizations to enhance communications among employees and to share IT resources. Households might set up LANs to share a broadband link to the Internet and to transmit digital music, pictures and video from one part of a home to another.

In office LANs, one computer is often used as a central repository of programs and files that all connected computers can use; this computer is called a server. Connected computers can store documents on their own disks or on the server, can share hardware such as printers, and can exchange email. When a LAN has a server, the server usually has centralized control of communications among the connected computers and between the computers and the server itself. Another computer or special communications device can also exercise this control, or control can be distributed among several servers. A peer-to-peer LAN is one in which no central device controls communications.

In recent years the cost of wireless devices has decreased significantly, and many offices as well as households now network their computers wirelessly, or create networks in which some of the computers are wired and some are not. Wireless LANs (WLANs) offer significant benefits: installation is easy because you don't have to drill through walls to install wires, and you can move equipment wherever it is needed. Wireless networks offer significant savings in some environments. Wireless LANs are less costly to maintain when the network spans two or more buildings. They are also more scalable. Scalability is the ease of expanding a system. It is easy to add more nodes, or clients, to a WLAN, because all that is needed is wireless circuitry in any device that comes within range of a wireless network.

However, wireless LANs have a significant drawback: they can be less secure than wired LANs. On a wired network, there are several measures that might be taken to guard against unauthorized access. On a wireless network, security measures exist (which are being upgraded all the time), but at present they are limited compared with those for wired networks, are not always easy to set up and can slow down communications. Anyone using a WLAN should keep informed about the latest security measures and take them to ensure that communications are secure. Some of these measures are covered later in the chapter.

local area network (LAN) A computer network confined to a building or a group of adjacent buildings, as opposed to a wide area network.

server A computer connected to several less powerful computers that can utilize its databases and applications.

peer-to-peer LAN A local area network (LAN) in which no central device controls communications.

wireless LAN (WLAN) A local area network that uses electromagnetic waves (radio or infrared light) as the medium of communication. In recent years almost all WLANs have been established using Wi-Fi.

scalability The ability to adapt applications as business needs grow.

In April 2007 The Cloud, Europe's leading wireless broadband network, launched the City of London Network.

PHOTO SOURCE: © GEOGPHOTOS/ALAMY

wide area network (WAN) A network of computers and other communications devices that extends over a large area, possibly comprising national territories. Example: the Internet.

value-added network (VAN) A telecommunications network owned and managed by a vendor that charges clients periodic fees for network management services.

Internet service provider (ISP) An individual or organization that provides Internet connection, and sometimes other related services, to subscribers.

PAN (personal area network) A network of devices typically within a small radius that enables a user to use two or more devices wirelessly, such as wireless keyboard and mouse.

MANs A *metropolitan area network (MAN)* usually links multiple LANs within a large city or metropolitan region and typically spans a distance of up to 50 kilometres (about 30 miles). For example, the LAN in a chemistry lab might be linked to a research hospital's LAN and to a pharmaceutical company's LAN several miles away in the same city to form a MAN. The individual LANs that compose a MAN might belong to the same organization or to several different organizations. The high-speed links between LANs within a MAN typically use fibre optic or wireless broadband connections.

WANs A wide area network (WAN) is a far-reaching system of networks. One WAN is composed of two or more LANs (or MANs) that are connected across a distance of more than approximately 48 kilometres (or 30 miles). Large WANs might have many constituent LANs and MANs on different continents. The simplest WAN is a dial-up connection to a network provider's services over basic telephone lines. A more complex WAN is a satellite linkup between LANs in two different countries. The best-known WAN is the Internet.

WANs can be public or private. The telephone network and the Internet are examples of public WANs. A private WAN might use either dedicated lines or satellite connections. Many organizations cannot afford to maintain a private WAN. They pay to use existing networks, which are provided in two basic formats: common carriers or value-added networks.

A common carrier provides public telephone lines that anyone can access or dial up, and leased lines, which are dedicated to the leasing organization's exclusive use. The user pays for public lines based on time used and distance called. Leased lines are dedicated to the leaseholder and have a lower error rate than dial-up lines, because they are not switched among many different subscribers.

Value-added networks (VANs) provide enhanced network services. VANs fulfill organizational needs for reliable data communications while relieving the organization of the burden of providing its own network management and maintenance. Many businesses use VANs for their electronic data interchange (EDI) with other businesses, suppliers and buyers. However, due to cost considerations, an increasing number of organizations prefer to conduct commerce via the Internet rather than through VANs. VAN services cost much more than those offered by Internet service providers (ISPs). (Many VAN providers also provide Internet links.) This issue is discussed in Chapter 7.

CD TASK

PANs A PAN (personal area network) is a wireless network designed for handheld and portable devices such as PDAs, mobile phones and tablet or laptop computers, and is intended for use by only one or two people. Transmission speed is slow to moderate, and the maximum distance between devices is generally 10 metres (33 feet). For example, Maria and Simon meet at a conference and exchange electronic business cards using their Bluetooth-enabled PDAs. When Maria gets back to her office, the PDA automatically synchronizes with her office notebook computer, updating the address book on the notebook with Simon's information. (Bluetooth and other wireless technologies are covered later in the chapter.)

Networking hardware

network interface card (NIC) Circuitry embedded or installed in a computer to support proper linking of the computer to a network.

hub In networking, a device connecting several computers or other electronic devices.

Networks use a variety of devices to connect computers and peripheral devices (such as printers) to each other, and to connect networks to each other. Each computer or device connected to a network must have a network interface card (NIC), which connects through a cable or a wireless antenna to a hub, switch, bridge or router, which in turn connects to a LAN or WAN. A hub is a common device often used as a central location to connect computers or devices to a local network. A

Industry **SNAPSHOT**

You can take it with you

Slingbox is a piece of hardware that you can connect to your cable box, satellite receiver or digital video recorder. It then can stream your favourite TV programmes to a PC anywhere in the world. It uses wireless connection or mobile phone connection. Thus, you can access your DVR from your PC and select preferred programmes for viewing in your hotel, far from home.

SOURCE: D. Tynan, 'TV on the Run', *PC World,* May 2005, p. 136

PHOTO SOURCE: © SLING MEDIA, INC.

Sling Player Mobile also allows you to 'Slingbox from your phone'.

switch is like a hub, except that it is more 'intelligent'. Communications that go through a hub are broadcast to all devices attached to the hub; communications through a switch go only to designated devices on the network. A bridge is a device that connects two networks, such as a LAN, to the Internet. A router routes data packets to the next node on their way to the final destination. It can connect dissimilar networks and can be programmed to act as a firewall to filter communications. Routers keep tables of network addresses, known as Internet Protocol (IP) addresses, which identify each computer on the network along with the best routes to other network addresses. You are not likely to see a WAN router, but you might have seen a router used to support a LAN in a small office or in a household. A repeater amplifies or regenerates signals so that they do not become weak or distorted.

Another type of networking hardware that might be familiar to home computer users is the modem. A modem – a word contracted from *mod*ulator-*dem*odulator – in traditional usage is a device whose purpose is to translate communications signals from analogue to digital, and vice versa. For many years the only way to link to the Internet was to dial up, meaning connecting over regular telephone lines. These lines were originally designed for analogue – continuous – signals rather than for digital signals, which consist of discrete bursts. A modem turns the digital signal from your computer into an analogue signal that can go out over the phone lines. A modem on the receiving computer transforms the analogue signal back into a digital signal the computer can understand. The former transformation is called modulation and the latter is called demodulation.

A dial-up connection with a modem is very slow (usually no faster than 56 Kbps), so most users and small businesses today are turning to faster connections that use digital signals throughout the connection, such as DSL and cable connections. Even though the medium transfers digital signals, the word 'modem' is now used for the devices that connect computers to the Internet with these technologies. Thus, for example, if you use the service of a cable company to link to the Internet, the device connecting your computer's network card to the cable is called a cable modem. If you use a DSL service, the device used is called a DSL modem, and if you use a power line, the device is called a BPL modem.

switch In networking, a device that is able to direct communications to certain devices on the network. Compare with a hub which broadcasts to all connected devices.

bridge A device connecting two communications networks that use similar hardware.

router A network hub, wired or wireless, that ensures proper routing of messages within a network such as a LAN and between each device on that network and another network, such as the Internet.

repeater A device that strengthens signals and then sends them on their next leg towards their next destination.

modem (modulator/ demodulator) A communications device that transforms digital signals to analogue telephone signals and vice versa, for data communications over voice telephone lines. The term is widely used for all devices that connect a computer to a wide area network, such as the Internet, even if the device does not modulate or demodulate.

Virtual private networks

A LAN is a private network, because it provides access only to members of an organization. Though a firm does not own the lines it leases, the network of leased lines might be considered a private network, because only members authorized by the organization can use it. In the Internet age, many companies that cannot afford a private network can create a virtual private network (VPN). Although the Internet is discussed in Chapter 7, VPNs are important in the context of the current discussion.

A virtual private network (VPN) can be thought of as a 'tunnel' through the Internet or other public network that allows only authorized users to access company resources. The 'virtual' in VPN refers to the illusion that the user is accessing a private network directly, rather than through a public network. VPNs enable the use of intranets and extranets. An intranet is a network that uses web technologies to serve an organization's employees who are located in several sites that might be many miles apart; an extranet serves both the employees and other enterprises that do business with the organization. It is important to understand that once a LAN is linked to a public network, such as the Internet, technically anyone with access to the public network can obtain access to the LAN. Therefore, organizations that link their LANs to the Internet implement sophisticated security measures to control or totally deny public access to their resources.

Switching techniques

Imagine that your telephone could connect to only one other telephone. Of course, this limitation would render the telephone impractical. The same is true of communications when using computers. You want to be able to link your computer to every other computer on a network. Or, imagine that you can link to any other computer, but you have to wait for a specific communications path to open to conduct a conversation; no other path is available to you. So you might wait a long time until no one is using any segment of that path to make your call. Obviously, this wait would be very inconvenient. To avoid such inconveniences, data communications must have mechanisms to allow your messages to be routed through any number of paths: if one is busy, then another can be used. These mechanisms, called switching techniques, facilitate the flow of communications and specify how the messages travel to their destination. There are two major switching techniques – circuit switching and packet switching.

Circuit switching In circuit switching, a dedicated channel (a circuit) is established for the duration of the transmission. The sending node signals the receiving node that it is going to send a message. The receiver must acknowledge the signal. The receiving node then receives the entire message. Only then can the circuit be allocated for use by two other communicating parties. Traditional telephone communication is the most common type of circuit-switching communication. The advantages of circuit switching are that data and voice can use the same line and that no special training or protocols are needed to handle data traffic. One disadvantage is the requirement that the communications devices be compatible at both ends.

Packet switching In packet switching, a message is broken up into packets. A packet is a group of bits transmitted together. In addition to the data bits, each packet includes sender and destination information, as well as error detection bits (see Figure 5.1). Each of the message's packets is passed from the source computer to the destination computer, often through intermediate nodes. At each node, the entire packet is received, stored and then passed on to the next node, until all packets, either kept together or reassembled, reach the destination.

Figure 5.1 A packet

| Destination address | Source address | Data | Error detection bits |

On their way to their final destination, the packets are transmitted independently to intermediate nodes. Different packets of the same message might be routed through different paths to minimize delay and are then reassembled at their destination. This type of switching offers some advantages. Sending and receiving devices do not have to be speed-compatible because buffers in the network might receive data at one rate and retransmit it at another. The lines are used on demand rather than being dedicated to a particular call. With packet switching, a host computer can have simultaneous exchanges with several nodes over a single line. The main disadvantage of packet switching is that it requires complex routing and control software. When the load is high, there are delays. When the network is used for voice communication, a conversation with long delays might sound unnatural. Therefore, voice communication in traditional telephone systems uses circuit switching.

Frame relay is a high-speed packet-switching protocol used in WANs. The frames are variable-sized packets. The service provider's software determines the route for each frame so it can arrive at the destination the fastest. The variable size of packets allows more flexibility than with fixed-sized units; communication lines can be used more efficiently. One reason is the higher ratio of data bits to nondata bits (such as destination and source addresses) in each packet is greater. Larger packets also enable lines to stay idle for less time.

> **frame relay** A high-speed packet switching protocol used on the Internet.

Circuit switching is ideal for real-time communications, when the destination must receive the message without delay. Packet switching is more efficient, but it is suitable only if some delay in reception is acceptable, or if the transmission is so fast that these delays do not adversely affect the communication. The switching rules in a network are part of the communication protocol. These protocols, along with increasingly faster Internet connections, enable the growing use of the Internet for packet-switching telephoning, known as VoIP, which we discuss later.

Multi-protocol label switching (MPLS) is a relatively recent packet-switching technology that enhances services such as VoIP. Messages are broken up into packets, and packets are still transmitted independently, but all are routed through the same path on the network. This minimizes the time gaps between receptions of the packets. Therefore, content that must be communicated in real time – such as voice and video – is received at higher quality than if the packets are routed through different paths.

Protocols

A communications **protocol** is a set of rules that govern communication between computers or between computers and other computer-related devices that exchange data. When these rules govern a network of devices, the rule set is often referred to as a *network protocol*. If a device does not know what the network's agreed-upon protocol is, or cannot comply with it, that device cannot communicate on that network.

> **protocol** A standard set of rules that governs telecommunication between two communications devices or in a network.

In a way, a protocol is like human language and basic understanding. Human beings make certain gestures when they start a conversation, and certain words signal its end. Each element of the language, be it English, Chinese or Hindi, means the same thing to all parties who speak that language. Computers, too, need an agreed-upon set of rules to communicate. Some protocols are designed for WANs, others are designed for LANs, and some are designed specifically for wireless communications. This discussion addresses only some of these protocols. Protocols, often called 'standards', do not necessarily compete with each other. They often work together or serve different purposes. The most important and pervasive set of protocols for telecommunications and networks today is called TCP/IP.

TCP/IP

Communication on the Internet follows mainly TCP/IP (Transmission Control Protocol/Internet Protocol), which is actually a set of related protocols. TCP ensures that the packets arrive accurately and in the proper order, while IP ensures delivery of packets from node to node in the most efficient manner.

A computer connected directly to the Internet backbone – the highest speed communication channel – is called a host. IP controls the delivery from one host to another until the message is received by the host to which it was sent or one that is connected to a device to which it was sent. The host forwards messages to devices connected to it. Often, we call hosts servers. For example, your university or college has at least one email server. That email server forwards to your computer email messages addressed to you.

Every device on the Internet backbone is uniquely identified with a numerical label known as an Internet protocol number, or IP number, a 32-bit numeric address, presented in four parts separated by full stops, such as 146.186.87.220. Each of these parts can be a number between 1 and 254. If you know the IP number (also called the IP address) of a website, you can enter those numbers in the address box of a web browser. However, it is easier to remember names and words, and therefore most organizations associate their IP numbers with names. The process of associating a character-based name such as *course.com* with an IP number is called domain name resolution, and the domain name resolution service is DNS (domain name system). DNS servers are maintained by Internet service providers (ISPs) and other organizations. In large organizations, a server can be dedicated as a DNS server.

If a LAN is linked to the Internet through a router and a modem, the entire network has an IP number unique on the Internet. That number is stored in the router. To uniquely identify devices on the LAN, the router assigns local IP numbers to individual computers and devices. These IP numbers identify the computers only within the LAN. It is the router that is identified uniquely on the Internet.

Servers and many other computers and devices are assigned permanent IP numbers, called a static IP number. A computer connected to the Internet intermittently might be assigned a temporary IP number for the duration of its connection only. Such a number is called a dynamic IP number. It is assigned by the host through which that computer is connecting to the Internet. Dynamic IP numbers give an organization flexibility with its limited number of assigned IP numbers: only modems seeking a connection to the Internet are assigned IP numbers. And the number is disassociated from a device that logs off. The server can then reassign the IP number to another modem that has just logged on. Some broadband providers assign static IP numbers; others assign only dynamic IP numbers.

TCP/IP (transmission control protocol/Internet protocol) A packet-switching protocol that is actually a set of related protocols that can guarantee packets are delivered in the correct order and can handle differences in transmission and reception rates.

backbone The network of copper lines, optical fibres and radio satellites that supports the Internet.

host A computer that contains files and other resources that can be accessed by 'clients', computers linked to it via a network.

Internet Protocol (IP) number A unique number assigned to a server or another device that is connected to the Internet for identification purposes. Consists of 32 bits.

DNS (domain name system) Hardware and software making up a server whose purpose is to resolve domain names (converting them back to IP numbers) and routing messages on the Internet.

static IP number An Internet Protocol number permanently associated with a device.

dynamic IP number The IP number assigned to a computer that is connected to the Internet intermittently for the duration of the computer's connection.

Ethernet

The Institute of Electrical and Electronics Engineers (IEEE) sets standards for communication protocols. IEEE 802.3, known as Ethernet, is a highly popular LAN protocol. Ethernet uses either coaxial cable or twisted pair cable. Different generations of Ethernet support speeds from 10 Mbps (10Base-T) to 100 Mbps (100Base-T or Fast Ethernet) to over 1 Gbps (Gigabit Ethernet and 10 Gigabit Ethernet). Ethernet is known as a contention-based protocol, because devices on the network 'contend' with other devices on the network for transmission time. Each device constantly monitors the network to see if other devices are transmitting. A protocol called CSMA/CD (carrier sense multiple access with collision detection) ensures that there are no collisions in transmission and that each device transmits without interfering with another.

Ethernet The design, introduced and named by Xerox, for the contention-based data communications protocol.

Gigabit Ethernet A network protocol often used in local area networks (LANs) supporting up to 1 Gbps.

Wireless protocols

CD TASK

All wireless devices use radio transceivers (transmitter-receivers). The radio waves carry the digital signal, the bits. Depending on the protocol followed, the devices use different radio frequencies for their work.

IEEE 802.11 Wi-Fi IEEE 802.11 is a family of wireless protocols, collectively known as Wi-Fi (for 'wireless fidelity'). The term originally applied to the IEEE 802.11b standard that supports communication within about 100 metres (300 feet) of a wireless router at a maximum speed of 11 Mbps. The more advanced 802.11g standard supports speeds of up to 54 Mbps for the same range. The g standard is backward-compatible with the b standard, meaning that you can add b or g devices to a g network. However, in a mixed b and g network, throughput for the b devices will likely be at the lower 802.11b speed. Both standards use a radio frequency in the 2.4–2.5 GHz range. This is the same frequency used by microwave ovens and some cordless phones. However, the Wi-Fi transmitting and receiving circuitry constantly looks for the best frequency (such as 2.401 GHz or 2.402 GHz) on which to communicate within that range, so 'collisions' with other devices are minimized. If interference with other devices or nearby wireless networks is a problem, the 802.11a standard is an option. The 802.11a standard operates in the 5 GHz range, and supports speeds of up to 54 Mbps at distances of about 20 metres (60 feet). However, the a standard is incompatible with the other Wi-Fi standards, and therefore is much less popular.

A single Wi-Fi router can be connected to an access point (AP), which in turn is connected to a wired network and usually to the Internet, allowing tens to hundreds of Wi-Fi-equipped devices to share the Internet link. A direct link to a wireless router or AP creates a hotspot. Hotspots allow Internet access to anyone within range who uses a wireless-equipped device, provided logging in is not limited by controlled access codes. Figure 5.2 illustrates a home wireless LAN (WLAN).

As mentioned earlier, security has been a concern for Wi-Fi networks. The earliest 802.11 standards had serious security flaws; 802.11g and 802.11a have improved security by offering the wired equivalent privacy (WEP) protocol and the Wi-Fi protected access (WPA) and WPA2 security protocols. These protocols offer encryption, the ability to scramble and code messages through encryption keys that are shared only between the sender and receiver. Of course, to receive the protection of these protocols, they must be enabled on your wireless computer or device.

Wi-Fi hotspots are appearing everywhere, from airports and restaurant chains to the local library. However, businesses also use wireless LANs for many types of

IEEE 802.11 A standard for wireless communication. Several other IEEE 802.x standards have been approved by the Institute of Electrical and Electronics Engineers.

Wi-Fi A name given to the IEEE 802.11 standards of wireless communication. Wi-Fi technologies are used in hotspots and in home and office networks. Wi-Fi is usually effective for a radius of 300 feet.

access point (AP) An arrangement consisting of a device connected to the Internet on one end and to a router on the other end. All wireless devices link to the Internet through the router.

hotspot An area, usually of 300-feet radius, in which a wireless device can connect to the Internet. The hotspot is created by installing an access point consisting of a device connected to the Internet on one end and to a router on the other end. All wireless devices link to the Internet through the router.

Industry **SNAPSHOT**

Wi-Fi health concerns

A recent BBC *Panorama* programme highlighted the potential risks to school children caused by the proliferation of Wi-Fi networks in UK schools. There are calls for urgent clarification. 'Schools can't afford to delay while the scientists make up their minds', says John Dunford of the Association of School and College Leaders. And it is not only schools which are seeing the rise in such networks. Home use of Wi-Fi is growing and even if you do not have one in your home, you could be affected by your neighbour's. The increase in city-centre Wi-Fi networks is also a concern for some people. However, the Health Protection Agency (HPA) is making reassuring noises, sort of! Current evidence suggests that Wi-Fi does not represent a risk with low power signals of typically 0.1 Watt. However, the HPA does want more research. In the meantime, schools can't wait. 'Unless there is evidence that they are damaging, schools will continue to develop them – because they're finding that they're essential', says Dr Dunford.

SOURCE: 'Schools want urgent WiFi advice', Sean Coughlan,
http://news.bbc.co.uk/1/hi/education/6676205.stm

PHOTO SOURCE: © LISA F. YOUNG

encryption The conversion of plaintext to an unreadable stream of characters, especially to prevent a party that intercepts telecommunicated messages from reading them. Special encryption software is used by the sending party to encrypt messages, and by the receiving party to decipher them.

operations. You will find a WLAN in almost every warehouse. Workers holding PDAs or specialized electronic units communicate with each other and receive information about the location of items by section, shelf and bin. For example, the forklifts in many warehouses are equipped with Wi-Fi transceivers to help their operators locate parts. Conference centres and universities use WLANs to help guests, students and staff to communicate as well as link to the Internet through a hotspot.

All new aeroplanes for long flights are equipped with WLANs. Boeing started equipping its large airplanes with Wi-Fi in 2003. Lufthansa, British Airways, Japan Airlines, Scandinavian Airlines System and other airlines have equipped their long-range jetliners with the technology to allow paying passengers to use a hotspot 12 miles above ground.

Utility companies are converting manually read electric, gas and water meters to wireless meters. Older versions still require a person to read the meter and record the reading, but new meters use networks that relay the signal to the utility company's office and automatically update each customer's account in the company's computers. Wireless meters save millions of labour hours and overcome common problems, such as meters enclosed in locked places, inaccurate reading and, occasionally, an aggressive dog.

Figure 5.2 A wireless home network

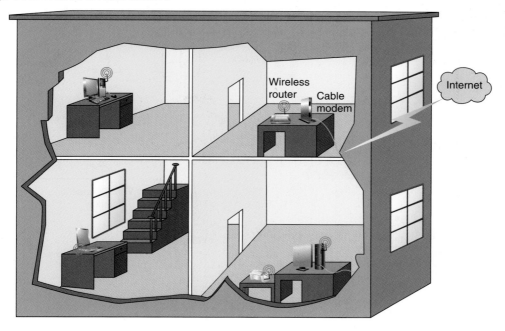

A growing number of electronic devices, such as mobile phones, PDAs, digital cameras and video game consoles, are equipped with wireless circuitry. This rids their owners of the need to physically connect a device to a computer or a router for communication. For example, with a wireless-enabled digital camera you can send digital pictures from your camera to your PC, or directly to a friend via a hotspot over the Internet.

IEEE 802.15 Bluetooth Named after a Scandinavian king who unified many tribes, the Bluetooth standard was developed for devices that communicate with each other within a short range of up to 10 metres (33 feet) in the office, at home and in motor vehicles. It transmits voice and data. Bluetooth was later adopted by IEEE as its 802.15 standard, which is compatible with the early versions of Bluetooth. Typical Bluetooth devices include wireless keyboards and mice, wireless microphones for mobile phones (especially for use in cars while driving), and increasingly, digital entertainment devices. For example, you can purchase a wrist-worn MP3 player that uses Bluetooth to transmit the music to earbuds or headphones, avoiding the wires that typically connect a portable player to headphones. Bluetooth is considered a personal area network (PAN) technology, because it typically supports a network used by only one person. Bluetooth use the 2.4–2.5 GHz radio frequency to transmit bits at a rate of 1 Mbps.

> **Bluetooth** A personal wireless network protocol. It enables wireless communication between input devices and computers and among other devices within 10 metres.

IEEE 802.16 WiMAX IEEE 802.16, worldwide interoperability for microwave access (WiMAX), increases the range and speed of wireless communication. It might potentially reach up to 110 kilometres (about 70 miles) with a speed of 100 Mbps; however, it typically reaches 13–16 kilometres (8–10 miles). This standard can cover whole metropolitan areas and provide Internet access to hundreds of thousands of households that either cannot afford an Internet service or for some reason cannot obtain access. This has created a threat to the business of ISPs, who count on subscriber fees for revenue, because an entire metropolitan area can

> **WiMAX** The IEEE 802.16 standard for wireless networking with a range of up to 50 km (31 miles). (WiMAX stands for the organization that promotes that standard, Worldwide Interoperability for Microwave Access.)

Figure 5.3 How WiMAX works

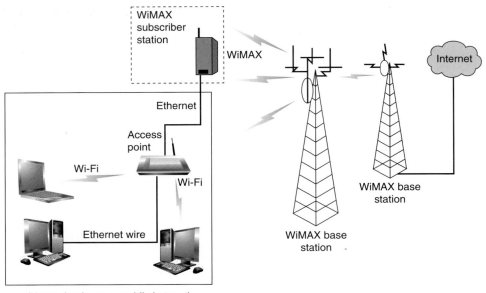

(Home, business or public hotspot)

become one huge hotspot. Milton Keynes has become the UK's first trial metropolitan area for WiMAX. The trial began in 2006 and as of July 2007 there were 154 connected trialists. The feedback from them, following a survey by the company running the trial, Pipex, was generally favourable and the next step is to increase the trialist number to 500. The next area earmarked for the introduction of WiMAX is Warwick. WiMAX is a metropolitan area network (MAN) technology. Figure 5.3 shows how WiMAX works. A household, office or public hotspot can use a router to link multiple devices either by linking directly to a WiMAX base antenna that is linked to the Internet, or by using a relay antenna that receives the signal and retransmits it to the Internet-linked antenna. If a mobile user's equipment included the proper WiMAX communication device, the user could communicate with the Internet moving at speeds of up to 150 Km/H (about 94 MPH), which enables convenient use of the Internet while sitting in a moving vehicle (though the driver should not be going that fast!). An extension of this standard, 802.16e, supports mobile Internet communication. However, a newer, special standard dedicated to mobile communications is 802.20.

mobile broadband wireless access (MBWA) IEEE 801.20 standard to support continuous wireless connection while moving in vehicles.

IEEE 802.20 MBWA Mobile broadband wireless access (MBWA) functions similarly to mobile phone communications, because it controls communication from stationary towers. The purpose of MBWA is to provide mobile communication that is compatible with IP services. This should enable worldwide deployment of affordable, always-on wireless access. The principle is simple: place wireless routers on towers, so that mobile phones can use VoIP and access other Internet resources over wide areas and, eventually, globally. MBWA is expected to work at speeds over 1 Mbps, using licensed radio frequencies below 3.5 GHz. If the standard is successfully implemented globally, it will reduce subscriber fees significantly and pose severe competition to providers of mobile phone services.

The 802.20 standard is designed to be compatible with 802.11 (Wi-Fi) and 802.15 (Bluetooth). It can support Internet communication at a moving speed of up to 250 Km/H (156 MPH). MBWA promises to support practically everything that we now do with

Table 5.3 Wireless networking protocols

Protocol	Max. range	Max. speed	Main use
802.11a	19 metres (60 feet)	54 Mbps	LAN
802.11b	100 metres (300 feet)	11 Mbps	LAN
802.11g	100 metres (300 feet)	54 Mbps	LAN
802.15 Bluetooth	10 metres (33 feet)	1 Mbps	PAN
802.16 WiMax	50 km (31 miles)	100 Mbps	MAN
802.20 MBWA	Global	4 Mbps	Mobile voice, data and Internet communications

telephones and through the Internet: web browsing, file transfer, email, VoIP, video telephony and videoconferencing, audio streaming (such as listening to transmitted music), web-based gaming and file sharing. Table 5.3 summarizes relevant features of the 802.xx wireless protocols discussed here.

Generations in mobile communications

Networking professionals often refer to generations of mobile communication technologies. Each generation refers to a communication protocol or a combination of protocols. The differences among generations are mainly in capabilities (e.g., enabling a mobile phone to access additional resources) and transmission speed. The first generation, 1G, was analogue and used circuit switching. Then 2G protocols became the first to provide digital voice encoding, and they worked at faster transmission rates. They include the GSM (global system for mobile) and CDMA (code division multiple access) protocols, the details of which are outside the scope of this discussion. They lack security measures. Then 2.5G, between 2G and 3G, stepped up the speed of digital mobile communication to 144 Kbps and enabled limited Internet access by mobile phones through packet switching. The 2.5G protocol combines digital mobile telephoning with some IP capabilities. This is the set of protocols used by most mobile phones in the early 2000s.

Industry **SNAPSHOT**

Complementary technologies

In a way, 3G mobile technologies compete with Wi-Fi, but it seems that eventually the technologies will complement each other: we will use 3G outdoors and Wi-Fi indoors. Wi-Fi is significantly less expensive to use than 3G. Fixed-mobile convergence (FMC) is a system whereby a single telephone device will contact an access point using short range wireless communication when in range and general mobile communications methods when outside the range. The user does not need to know which is being used or do anything special – the device does the work.

The 3G protocols support transmission rates of 1 Mbps. The protocols support video, videoconferencing and full Internet access. The 4G protocol devices operate only digitally and with packet switching, transmit at bandwidths of up to 100 Mbps, and include tighter security measures. Some of the protocols that comprise 4G are still under development. The high speed of the technology will enable the holder of a mobile phone handset to watch a DVD-quality video, listen to CD-quality music files, browse the Web and make a telephone call at the same time.

Internet networking services

CD TASK

Both organizations and individuals can choose from a variety of options when subscribing to networking services. The proliferation of high-speed connection services, also called broadband services, is mainly the result of businesses' and individuals' rush to the Internet.

Cable

Cable Internet links are provided by television cable firms. The medium is the same as for television reception, but the firms connect the cable to an Internet server. At the subscriber's residence, the cable is split – one part is connected to the television set, and the other is connected to the computer via a bridge that is often called a cable modem. Both television transmission and data are transmitted through the same line. The cable link is always on, so the computer is constantly connected to the Internet. The subscriber does not have to dial up any telephone number.

digital subscriber line (DSL) Technology that relieves individual subscribers of the need for the conversion of digital signals into analogue signals between the telephone exchange and the subscriber jack. DSL lines are linked to the Internet on a permanent basis and support bit rates significantly greater than a normal telephone line between the subscriber's jack and the telephone exchange.

The major downside of cable is that cable nodes are shared by all the subscribers connected to the node. Therefore, at peak times, such as television prime time (7–11 p.m.), communication speed slows down. The speed also slows down as more subscribers join the service in a given territory.

Digital subscriber line (DSL)

With normal telephone service, the telephone company filters information that arrives in digital form and then transforms it to analogue form; thus, it requires a modem to transform the signal back to digital form. This conversion constrains the capacity of the link between your telephone (or computer) and the telephone company's switching centre to a low speed of 56 Kbps.

With digital subscriber line (DSL), data remain digital throughout the entire transmission; they are never transformed into analogue signals. So, the telephone

Industry SNAPSHOT

Broadband on the rise

In 2005, there were 150 million subscribers to broadband links (cable and DSL) in the world, most of them in the Asia-Pacific region. The number is expected to grow to 400 million by 2009. The gap between the number of DSL subscribers and cable subscribers is growing. The reason is simple: while there are more than 1 billion telephone subscriber lines in the world, there are only 530 million homes with cable service.

SOURCE: IMS Research, 2005

Industry SNAPSHOT

The United States, a broadband laggard

Because of little competition among telecommunications companies, the United States lags behind other countries in the proportion of households that enjoy broadband links to the Internet. Only 42 per cent of American households had broadband in 2005 (mainly through cable and DSL). The proportion was greater in Japan, South Korea, Denmark and Canada, where more broadband companies compete for business, thereby driving down the cost. In South Korea, for instance, 73 per cent of households had broadband links. The speed of broadband in those countries is greater than what Americans experience and the service is less expensive. In Japan, for example, some households reach 100 Mbps. About 20 per cent of US households could not have access to broadband even if they chose to subscribe to the service, because broadband is not offered where they live.

SOURCE: S. Lacy, 'America: Still the High-Speed Laggard', *Business Week*, 6 April 2005

company can transmit to subscribers' computers at significantly higher speeds of up to 8 Mbps. To provide DSL service, the telecommunications company connects your telephone line to a DSL bridge (often called a DSL modem). At the telephone company's regional central office, DSL traffic is aggregated and forwarded to the ISP or data network provider with which the subscriber has a contract. Often, the telephone company is also the ISP.

T1 and T3 lines There are several types of DSL, whose details are beyond the scope of this book, but they can be generally placed in one of two categories: symmetric and asymmetric. Asymmetric DSL (ADSL) allows reception at a much faster rate than transmission, that is, it is faster downstream than upstream. (Often, the respective terms 'download' and 'upload' are used.) The reason for the faster download is that home users and small businesses usually receive significantly more information (from the Web, for example) than they transmit. Symmetric DSL (SDSL) is designed for short-distance connections that require high speed in both directions. Many ADSL technologies are actually RADSL (rate adaptive DSL) technologies; the speed is adjusted based on signal quality. Some ADSL technologies let subscribers use the same telephone lines for both Internet connection and analogue voice telephone service. Symmetric DSL lines cannot share lines with telephones.

The bit rates of DSL lines are closely related to the distance of the subscriber's computer from the regional central office of the telephone company. Telecommunications companies might offer the service to subscribers as far as 6100 metres (20,000 feet) from the central office, but the speed then is usually no faster than 144 Kbps, unless the company has installed a DSL repeater on the line. Some companies do not offer the service if the subscriber's address is not within 4500 metres (15,000 feet) of the central office. Most subscribers have ADSL, so the upstream speed is significantly lower than the downstream speed.

Leased lines

Leased lines are point-to-point dedicated digital circuits provided by telephone companies. They are expensive and, therefore, only businesses that must rely on high speeds are willing to accept the high cost of subscribing to the service. Most universities, as well as large companies, use leased for their backbone and Internet connections.

leased lines Point-to-point dedicated digital circuits provided by telephone companies.

Ethical and Societal **ISSUES**

Telecommuting: pros and cons

Often, when you are introduced to people, you mention your occupation, and then you might be asked, 'Where do you work?' Many employed people now answer, 'At home.' They do not commute; they *telecommute,* or, as some prefer to call it, they *telework.* They have the shortest commute to work: from the bedroom to another room in the home that is equipped with a PC and a broadband Internet link. For an increasing number of workers, IT provides all that's needed to create the goods their employers sell: software, analysis reports, literature, tax returns and many other types of output. If they need data from the office, they can connect to their office intranet using VPN software and retrieve the required information. If they need to talk to supervisors or co-workers, they use their computers to conduct videoconferencing. And when they complete their product, they can simply email it or place it on a remote server.

Telecommuting on the rise According to the UK Office of National Statistics, more than 2.1 million people already work from home, with 8 million more spending at least some of their working week in their home instead of the office. In certain parts of the UK the benefits are obvious. A success story reported on www.itwales.com shows how rural locations can support telecommuting. 'Reynoldston is a small village in Gower (outside of Swansea) and is widely known not only as the home of King Arthur's stone but for its spectacular coastal views. For architectural consultant, David Clarke, Reynoldston was the ultimate retirement destination from his busy Oxford practice. However, his retirement plans hinged on one factor . . . the availability of broadband, so that he could continue work as a specialist architectural consultant. Just like hundreds of other people moving to Wales for the first time, David couldn't fathom that such a remote community could have access to broadband. But it does, thanks to the Reynoldston Community Wireless Network, a village initiative that provides a local wireless network to homes in the village. Now David's consultancy is flourishing as he benefits from a better work/life balance, reduced travel costs and more time to spend with his clients.'

Telecommuting has increased productivity and reduced employee stress. Pitney Bowes, a business communications company with 32,000 employees, noticed increased productivity in employees on their telecommuting days. Managers there believe that telecommuting increases productivity because it accommodates both the 'morning person' and 'night owl' who can work at the time of day that best fits their preferences. From an economic perspective, telecommuting saves travel cost and time. It also decreases pollution. And it might reduce unemployment by allowing people who would otherwise not work because they are not within commuting distance the opportunity to join the workforce.

Employment opportunities Telecommuting enables people who could otherwise not work to join or rejoin the workforce. This includes not only people who live far away from the offices of companies that would like to hire them but also whole groups in the population that otherwise might not be able to join certain businesses. Disabled people and parents of small children can work from home. Older people who would rather retire than commute might stay in the workforce if allowed to work at home. Organizations hungry for labour can tap a larger supply of workers if they offer telecommuting.

Saving time and money Organizations like telecommuting because it saves the cost of office space. Studies have shown that for each teleworker the annual saving on office space is US$5,000–10,000. When Nortel Networks allowed 4000 of its 13,000 employees to telecommute, it saved US$20 million per year on real estate. Studies also have shown that teleworkers are more productive by 15–50 per cent than their office counterparts. Telecommuters like their arrangement because they save the time and money they would spend on commuting. Telecommuting reduces millions of tons of pollutants, saves billions of gallons of petrol, and frees billions of personal hours for leisure time. AT&T, the telecommunications giant, reported in 2000 that its telecommuting programme increased productivity by 45 per cent and saved 50 per cent on office space costs. Another report, by British Telecom and Gartner Group, said that telecommuting reduced office space and other costs equivalent to 17 per cent of annual salary costs.

The downside However, not everyone is so enthusiastic about telecommuting. Sociologists have mixed opinions about the phenomenon. On one hand, telecommuting allows people to work who would otherwise remain outside the workforce, such as older professionals and many disabled people. On the other hand, it has been found that employers tend to pressure telecommuters to work harder than office workers. In the office an employee works a set number of hours, but the home worker has no defined workday; his or her workday is, the employer often assumes, 24 hours per day. In addition, telecommuters are more estranged from their fellow workers. For telecommuters, there is no office in which to foster new social ties and camaraderie.

The AT&T report said that teleworkers typically worked an hour more per day than their office-bound colleagues, which amounted to 250 hours per year. The British Telecom and Gartner Group report said that the average telecommuter works 11 per cent more hours than his or her office-bound brethren. Perhaps this extra time is what companies observe as added productivity. Although this extra work time is good for corporations, it is not so good for workers: when you telecommute, you work more for no additional compensation.

Telecommuting might foster isolation. Teleworkers share fewer experiences with other people. In addition, leaving the workplace behind means leaving behind one more community that gives many people a sense of belonging, even if this belonging amounts only to having a sandwich together at lunchtime and complaining about the boss. At the same time, some managers might prefer to see their employees in the office and keep them in their 'line of sight'.

On a wider level, telecommuting could severely affect some segments of national economies. Imagine the huge drop in revenue of large city restaurants during lunchtime if the number of commuters rushing to grab lunch between 12 and 2 p.m. were to halve. Some cities' dining industries could crumble if the telecommuting trend continues at the current pace. Many people live in cities mainly because of proximity to their offices, thus further movement to suburbs and remote residential areas would gut many other industries in central cities.

Many workers, given the option to work at home, have decided to return to the office. Interestingly, this happens also in the very industries that are so amenable to telecommuting, such as software development. These returning workers claim they missed social interaction with their peers, hallway chats, lunches with friends and direct communication with fellow workers and supervisors. But telecommuting has grown, and will probably continue to grow, especially thanks to greater availability of broadband services and their declining monthly fees. If the trend continues, offices occupied by organizations will be significantly smaller than they are now and will serve as the symbolic rather than physical centres of the organizations' activities.

Satellite

Businesses and households in rural areas and other regions that do not have access to cable or DSL might be able to obtain satellite services, which use microwave radio transmission. In fact, satellite service providers target these households. The service provider installs a dish antenna that is tuned to a communications satellite. Satellite connections might reach a speed of 45 Mbps. Many people use a free satellite service, the global positioning system (GPS). While a proper device is required to enable reception from the satellites (which were launched into orbit by the US government), anyone can communicate free of charge. The satellite transmits back to any GPS device its location on earth by longitude and latitude.

Fixed wireless

Another alternative for households and small businesses that cannot obtain cable or DSL connections to the Internet is fixed wireless. Fixed wireless is point-to-point transmission between two stationary devices, usually between two buildings, as opposed to mobile wireless, in which people carry a mobile device. ISPs

fixed wireless A network of fixed transceivers to facilitate connection to the Internet. Requires line of sight between transceivers.

that specialize in fixed wireless services are often referred to as WISPs, wireless ISPs. They install microwave transceivers on rooftops instead of laying physical wires and cables. Subscribers connect their computers to the rooftop transceiver. They can communicate at speeds up to 2 Mbps. Repeaters are installed close to each other to enhance the signal, which can deteriorate in the presence of buildings and trees, and foul weather. Transmission rates depend on the distance between the receiver and the base station. Up to 14 kilometres (9 miles) from the base station, the speed is 100 Mbps; speeds drop to about 2 Mbps at about 56 kilometres (35 miles) from the base.

Fixed wireless is highly modular – the telecommunications company can add as many transceivers as it needs to serve a growing number of subscribers. Unlike cable service, the company does not need franchise licences. The technology is suitable for both urban and rural areas.

Optical carrier

OC (optical carrier) A family of several very high-speed technologies using optical fibres. Usually, the standard is marked as OC-3, OC-12, OC-48, etc.

Companies willing to pay high fees can enjoy very high connection speeds. The services are denoted with OC, the acronym for optical carrier, because all of these services are provided through optical fibre lines. The number next to OC refers to data speed in multiples of 51.84 Mbps, considered the base rate bandwidth. Thus, when available, the services are denoted as C-1, C-3, C-9, C-12, C-18, C-48, and so on through C-3072. For illustration, OC-768 (40 Gbps) enables you to transmit the content of seven CDs in 1 second. Typical businesses that purchase the services are ISPs, providers of search engines and businesses that wish to support content-rich websites and high-volume traffic. However, media companies have also purchased such services because the high speeds support streaming video. Among companies that use OC-768, for instance, are Deutsche Telecom, NBC, Disney, the US Department of Defense Advanced Research Projects Agency (the agency that developed the Internet), NASA and Nippon TV.

Broadband over power lines (BPL)

As mentioned in the discussion on communications media, electric power lines are capable of carrying digital signals. Subscribers simply plug their BPL modem into standard electrical wall outlets. Usually, utility companies partner with telecommunications companies to provide broadband over power lines (BPL). Interestingly, even if BPL service availability is to lag far behind cable and optical fibre in terms of subscribers and revenue, utility companies are likely to invest in the technology for their own use. They can use BPL to monitor power consumption down to the household, detect power failure in real time, track power outages by region, automate some customer services and remotely control substations. Collecting and analysing such business information might make the utility companies more efficient.

broadband over power lines (BPL) A broadband service provided over electric power lines.

The speed and monthly service for BPL are similar to those of DSL, but the highest current speeds are lower than the highest speeds offered by DSL providers. The hope was that households in rural areas, where neither cable nor DSL service is available, could enjoy BPL. However, the density of households in rural areas is lower than the density of households where the other services are already offered. Utility companies have found that investing in the equipment required to provide BPL to a small number of households does not make business sense, and therefore it is unlikely that many rural areas will be offered BPL.

The future of networking technologies

CD TASK

This section takes a look at networking technologies and trends that are likely to have a great impact on businesses and the management of information in the near future: broadband telephoning, radio frequency identification and the convergence of digital technologies.

Broadband telephoning

While regular long-distance telephone companies charge according to the number of minutes a call lasts, Internet service providers (ISPs) charge customers a flat monthly fee for connection to the Internet. With the proper software and microphones attached to their computers, Internet users can conduct long-distance and international conversations via their Internet connection for a fraction of regular calling costs. The technology is called Internet telephoning, IP telephoning, or VoIP (Voice over Internet Protocol). Organizations can purchase the proper software or use the services of companies that specialize in providing IP telephoning, offering inexpensive use of their VoIP hardware and software for PC-to-PC, PC-to-telephone and telephone-to-telephone voice communication.

VoIP (Voice over Internet Protocol) Technologies that enable voice communication by utilizing the Internet instead of the telephone network.

PC-to-PC calls can be conducted free of charge by using the service of a company such as Skype. Phone-to-phone service requires an additional modem, but it does not require a new phone or phone number, and it does not require routing calls through a home computer.

In 2007, British Telecom announced that the number of UK subscribers to its Broadband Talk and Softphone VoIP services had hit the one million mark.

In addition to sound quality, there are other differences between traditional and VoIP telephone services. Most VoIP services do not include the ability to call an emergency number such as 999. Also, when your link to the Internet is down, so is your VoIP service. Since the phone uses a modem that requires electric power, if power is out, the phone cannot be

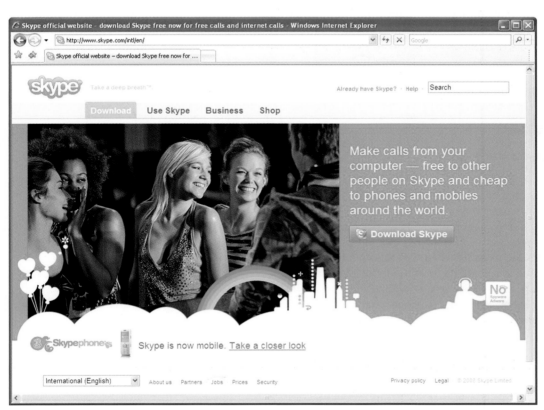

PHOTO SOURCE: © SKYPE LIMITED

Skype was founded in 2003 and generates revenue through its premium services such as VoIP calls to landlines and mobile phones.

used. However, VoIP providers offer some advantages over traditional telephoning. A subscriber receives a special converter into which the telephone number is programmed. The subscriber can take the converter anywhere there is a broadband link to the Internet and use it. This makes the VoIP telephone portable.

Some experts see the future of telephony in a convergence of the mobile phone and VoIP phone: you will use only one mobile phone. When outside the home or office, you will use the mobile phone network; when back home or in the office, the phone will communicate through a VoIP service. This will reduce the higher cost of mobile phone minutes.

Radio frequency identification

In Chapter 3 you learned about the great efficiency and business intelligence that companies, especially in manufacturing and retail, can gain from one particular type of communications technology: radio frequency identification (RFID). This section explains in more detail how RFID works. RFID tags can be very tiny, about the size of a rice grain, or several square inches, depending on the amount of information they need to contain and the environment in which they are used. They are not always flat; they can be cylindrical. The tags need very little power. Passive tags use power from the reader that queries them; active tags have their own tiny batteries, which increase the range of the reading range. These tiny batteries last a long time.

An RFID system works as follows: objects are equipped, often embedded, with a tag. The tag contains a transponder. A transponder is a radio transceiver (transmitter-receiver) that is activated for transmission by a signal that is transmitted to it. The tag is equipped with digital memory that is given a unique electronic product code (EPC). The interrogator, a combination of an aerial, a transceiver and a decoder, emits a signal activating the RFID tag so the interrogator can read data from it and write data to it. (Although the interrogator also writes

Industry **SNAPSHOT**

Getting under your skin

A night club in Barcelona, Spain, offers its regular customers a chance to get 'chipped' instead of bringing their wallets when they visit. A tiny RFID chip called VeriChip after the company that manufactures it is injected painlessly into their arm and resides under the skin. The chip, the size of a rice grain, is housed in a glass capsule. A reader identifies customers when they enter. Another reader charges their drinks and other expenses at the club to the customers' accounts. Removing the chip is done with the same syringe-like device with which it was injected. The same capsule can be used with patients to track diseases and treatments.

SOURCE: 'Barcelona Clubbers Get Chipped', BBC online (http://news.bbc.co.uk), 29 September 2004

An inplantable VeriChip microchip next to a grain of rice.

to the tag, it is often called a reader.) When an RFID tag enters the reader's electromagnetic zone, it detects the reader's activation signal. The reader decodes the data stored in the tag's memory, and the data are passed to a host computer for processing.

In the US, Wal-Mart, Gillette, Procter & Gamble and 84 other companies embarked on a project that might radically change supply chains. The companies use microchips that are embedded in products to replace the ubiquitous bar codes for tracking and checkout at store registers. Each microchip holds a product identification number. The microchips communicate with wireless computers, including handheld and laptop computers, as they are moved in the production line, packed, picked, shipped, unloaded, shelved and paid for by customers. As the product moves, the information about its location is communicated to a network of computers to which all businesses involved in the production and sale have access. This is often a Wi-Fi network. The big benefits are a just-in-time (JIT) system that minimizes inventory throughout the supply chain to almost zero and shelves that are always stocked. JIT, or a situation that is close to JIT, can be accomplished thanks to up-to-the-minute information about available inventory and when the next shipment from a supplier is needed. 'Smart shelves', equipped with tiny wireless transceivers, alert staff whenever the shelf is running out of units, so the staff can put more units on the shelf immediately.

RFID is used for many other purposes as well, as Figure 5.4 shows. For many businesses, the main impediment is the price of an RFID tag. As the unit cost of each tag reduces, it is likely that the uses of the technology, such as thoses as listed in Table 5.4, will increase.

Converging technologies

Recall the discussion of converging hardware technologies in the previous chapter. Convergence occurs also in networking technologies. Mobile phones used to be able to transmit and receive only through a dedicated network of analogue or digital transceivers. Now many are constructed with dual technologies, so that they can serve both as a 'traditional' mobile phone and a wireless web phone. When the circuitry detects that it is within the range of a hotspot, calling switches to VoIP to save cost. As mentioned earlier, a landline phone is no longer just a line phone but can be also a VoIP phone. And eventually, we will be able to use the same phone as a landline phone, a VoIP phone and a mobile phone, depending on availability of service and the cost and quality we are willing to accept.

At home, new television sets are designed to connect to cable, satellites and the Internet, not only alternately, but concurrently. Thus, we will be able to watch a sports game and chat online about it at the same time through the same device, using two different networking technologies. PDAs can already function as television sets and phones. Soon they will be able to do so simultaneously. For individuals, this means they can carry a single device that will connect them to any type of network, erasing the lines between radio, television, telephone and Internet surfing. To businesses this gives an opportunity to provide new information services and manage a more effective and efficient salesforce.

Wireless technologies can be combined in the same device to enhance functionality. For example, a portable digital music and video player can use Wi-Fi to communicate with your PC or another Wi-Fi device (possibly another music/video player) to download files. It can then use Bluetooth to transmit the music to your wireless earphones. When WiMAX is implemented, some local radio stations are likely to use MANs as additional broadcast channels. With proper software you can then select from the songs to which you have just listened and have them downloaded to your portable player or home computer.

Figure 5.4 RFID applications

Use	Example
Access control	Cards used to replace door keys.
People tracking	Keep children within school. Track prisoners on probation and prevent fleeing.
Animal tracking	Track pets.
Livestock management	Track life cycle of farm animals (e.g., feeding and immunization). Equip each cow with a unique ID to track diseases.
Antitheft measures	Transponders integrated into car keys. Only a legal key can start the engine.
Transportation	At airports, safety inspection of tagged luggage.
Retail	Tracking products in pallets and on shelves. Contactless payment.
Pharmaceuticals	Prevent drug counterfeiting.
Health care	Tag people who enter and leave an epidemic zone.

Table 5.4 Future uses of RFID

Use in...	Activity
Shopping	Identify dresses in your size, if you hold or wear a personal tag. Enhanced product information on your PDA/cell phone. Personalized customer service. Passive self-checkout. Dynamic pricing by demand. Return RFID tagged items without receipt.
Product information	Scan an RFID tag of an item and download additional information about it from an Internet site to your mobile phone. Use your mobile phone to check the price of an item while in a competitor's store.
Manufacturer serving customers	Send recall message to customer mobile phone or email address. Send warranty and recall messages to customer.
Appliances	Washing machine automatically sets proper wash cycle based on information on tags attached to clothes. Refrigerator alerts you about expired or recalled foods, notifies you about items consumed and prepares shopping lists. It can also log on to the Internet and search for recipes of dishes you can prepare with refrigerated items.
Agriculture	Tags attached to crops can transmit information about weather and soil conditions and trigger automatic irrigation.
Waste management	Track hazardous materials to ensure proper disposal. Sort recyclable items.

SUMMARY

Telecommunication is communication over distance, primarily communication of bits representing many forms of data and information. In the past decade, telecommunications technology has driven the major developments in the dissemination and use of information.

Telecommunications technology has changed the business environment. Businesspeople are increasingly more mobile; they can use mobile phones for greater availability to their employers and customers, using the phone for both voice and data communications. Videoconferencing brings together people who are thousands of miles apart. Peer-to-peer file sharing enables sharing of research, software code and artistic works.

Different media have different bandwidths, meaning that they are capable of carrying different numbers of bits per second (bps) without garbling messages. Wired media include twisted pair, coaxial and optical fibre cable. Wireless media include light waves (infrared) and radio waves, including terrestrial and satellite microwave.

Networks are classified according to their reach and complexity. When computers are connected locally within an office, a campus, or a home, the arrangement is called a local area network (LAN). A metropolitan area network (MAN) connects LANs within a radius of about 50 kilometres (30 miles). When computers communicate over longer distances, the network is called a wide area network (WAN). Personal area networks (PANs) connect individual devices at short range.

Although it uses the public Internet, a network can be turned into a virtual private network (VPN) by using tight security measures.

There are two ways to switch a communication line. In circuit switching, a message is communicated in its entirety from the transmitting computer to the receiving computer while the communication path is fully devoted to the exchange between the two nodes. In packet switching, data are divided into packets of bits and transmitted via several paths on the network. Internet protocols work with packet switching.

Network protocols are sets of rules to which all devices on a network must adhere. Communications on the Internet adheres to a set of protocols called TCP/IP. Ethernet has long been a popular protocol for wired LANs. Wireless protocols open great opportunities for more people to enjoy Internet links and for mobility while communicating. The most important are the IEEE 802.xx protocols, which include the popular Wi-Fi, Bluetooth and WiMAX standards.

Wireless technologies make it easy and affordable to create wireless LANs (WLANs) and hotspots. They allow workers mobility while retrieving information in warehouses and other work environments. They enable airline and retail customers to link to the Internet with portable computers. They make the reading of utility meters much less labour-intensive and more accurate.

Organizations and individuals have a variety of choices when subscribing to networking services. They can choose among digital subscriber lines (DSL), cable lines, T1 and T3 lines, satellite links, fixed wireless service, optical carriers (OC) and broadband over power lines (BPL). OC is expected to reach the speed of 10 Tbps in the foreseeable future.

As Internet links become faster, Internet telephoning, also know as Voice over Internet Protocol (VoIP), is gaining in popularity. Several companies offer the service, which is significantly less expensive than a land telephone line.

Wireless technologies support the increasingly popular RFID technologies. They support a variety of noncontact identification and payment mechanisms, from quick toll and gas payment to cattle tracking to sophisticated supply chain management, and many future uses are anticipated.

Much like hardware, telecommunications technologies are merging. The same device can now use several different networks simultaneously, such as mobile telephone networks, the Internet and television broadcasts.

Increasing numbers of employees now telecommute. Telecommuting has advantages, but it does not serve some basic human needs, such as socializing, the short hallway chat during lunch break, and the clear separation between work and family obligations.

TRENT COURIER SERVICES REVISITED

Trent Couriers has upgraded its telecommunications systems – from beepers to mobile phones, from handheld computers to handheld computers with a wireless Internet connection, from a single local office to three networked offices, and from DSL Internet access to fixed wireless access. At each point, Andrew Langston has expanded his communications ability.

What would you do?

If Trent Couriers could have connected its offices to the Internet via coaxial cable or T1 line in time, should it have opted for either of those connections over fixed wireless access? Investigate the costs and capabilities of each and give your opinion.

Now that messengers carry mobile phones, Trent Couriers can track their movements for every delivery and know where they are at all times. Consider Trent Couriers' existing 'family' culture. Should it follow its couriers' moves to check for efficiency? Why or why not?

A local marketing company has approached Andrew to see whether he would be willing to sell his customer list to them. Providing the information would be simple for Trent Couriers. Do you think it should do so? Why or why not?

New perspectives

During a conversation with a representative from the mobile phone company, the representative suggested to Mary that Trent Couriers purchase smart phones for their messengers. What would be the advantage of smart phones over the mobile phones that they are now carrying? Would this investment be financially worthwhile?

Andrew has seen customers at Starbucks wirelessly logging on to the Web through Wi-Fi connections. What factors should he consider to determine whether Wi-Fi devices would be a good option for his business?

A traffic-monitoring company has called on Andrew to offer its service. The representative says that his company can provide real-time traffic reports in the Stoke-on-Trent area. Dispatchers would be able to receive periodic or on-demand reports through their handheld web-enabled devices and view traffic conditions as they happen. Should Trent Couriers consider this service? What does it need to know to decide? Draw up a list of questions that Andrew should ask the representative.

Review questions

1 If we could see all the paths of data communications, we might be overwhelmed. Give some examples.

2 Why can't whole bytes be transmitted over a distance?

3 What makes one channel medium capable of greater data communication speed than another?

4 On many communication lines repeaters are used. What for? What does a repeater do?

5 Networking professionals speak of 'the last mile'. What is 'the last mile', and what is its significance?

6 Would an astronomy observatory 20 miles away from a city or town be able to get DSL service?

7 What risks to organizations does the growing use of networks pose?

8 What is a virtual private network? Why is it called 'virtual'?

9 What is a network protocol?

10 What are the technical advantages of optical fibres over other communications media?

11 What is the difference between circuit switching and packet switching?

12 Why does circuit switching accommodate voice communication more effectively than packet switching?

13 What is VoIP? Since VoIP uses packet switching, why is voice quality better now than several years ago?

14 What is ADSL? What does the A stand for, and what does it mean in terms of communicating with the Internet? Why do households receive only ADSL services and not other DSL services?

15 What is BPL? Why is the technology potentially available to almost every home?

16 Explain the notions of WAN, LAN, MAN and PAN.

17 What are hotspots, and how can they help businesspeople?

18 What is the purpose of WiMAX, and why is it in competition with subscriber broadband services?

19 Mobile phones are already wireless. Why should companies be interested in equipping employees with Wi-Fi-enabled mobile phones?

Discussion questions

1 Wi-Fi is all around us. Is there any downside to its pervasiveness?

2 People express themselves differently when they speak (either face to face or via the telephone) versus when they send and receive email. What are the differences? Which do you prefer when communicating with someone you don't know personally? Which do you prefer when you know the person?

3 Every home with access to the Internet can now inexpensively become a hotspot. How so?

Are there any risks in turning a home into a hotspot?

4 What are the implications of telecommunications for group work?

5 As broadband services cover larger and larger regions and become less expensive, the number of small businesses and home businesses grows. What is the relationship?

6 Some organizations stopped allocating offices to their sales representatives. Why, and is this a wise move?

7 List and explain the benefits of video-conferencing to an organization. List and explain the benefits to society.

8 Anything that does not take space can be traded solely via telecommunications networks. Do you agree? Explain your answer.

9 Do you see any undesirable effects of humans communicating more and more via computer networks rather than in person or over the telephone? What don't you like and why? What do you like about it?

10 List several industries in which telecommuting would be infeasible. Explain why.

11 Wi-Fi circuitry is now embedded in consumer electronic devices such as digital cameras and mobile phones. Give an example of what you could do with the Wi-Fi capability of a digital camera.

12 If you were given the opportunity to telecommute, would you? Why or why not?

13 Suppose that you are a middle manager. Would you allow the people who report to you to telecommute? Why or why not?

Tutorial activities

1 Ima Jeenyes completed her book, *How to Become a Millionaire upon Graduation*. She used a word processor to type the manuscript. She saved the book as a file of 5.7 MB. Ima lives in Bristol. The publisher asked that Ima transmit the book via the Internet to the publisher's office in Manchester. Ima can transmit the file at a guaranteed speed of 400 Kbps. Because each packet of data transmitted must also contain some nondata

bits, assume the total number of bits to transmit is equivalent to 6 MB.

How long (in minutes) does it take to transmit the book? Ignore the distance between the cities. Remember how many bytes make up 1 MB. Show your calculations clearly using a spreadsheet. Use measurement units throughout your calculation.

2   Justin Tyme uses a DSL modem to transmit a report from his office to headquarters. The DSL affords an average bit rate transmission (upload) of 250 Kbps. Since the transmission protocol adds additional bits to data bytes, assume that, on average, there is 1 additional bit for each transmitted byte. On average, a page contains 3000 characters, including spaces. Justin is allotted only 3 minutes for the transmission. How many pages can he transmit?

3   Find out which residential telecommunication services are available where you live and how much they cost. You might find several DSL and cable services, and perhaps also satellite and BPL services. Calculate the ratio of maximum downloaded bit rate per euro (or your local currency) to monthly fee for each service. Which service provides the 'biggest bang for the buck', that is, the greatest speed per euro of monthly fee?

4   Broadband services provided in Japan, South Korea and Canada are usually faster and less expensive than in the United States. Use the Web to research why this is so. Write a one-page report discussing the reasons.

5   Search the Web for a site that enables you to check your high-speed (broadband) link: DSL, cable, or (if you connect from university or college) leased line. Follow the instructions. Usually, you simply have to click one button. Do so and wait for the response. Print out the response. Wait a minute, and repeat the process. The speeds are likely to be different. Why?

6   You are a telecommunications guru and love to help individuals and businesses. Assume that dial-up, cable, DSL, T3 line and satellite links to the Internet are available everywhere unless the particular scenario indicates otherwise. Consider the following scenarios and suggest the best overall type of link (consider communication speed, cost and any other factor you believe is relevant). Each scenario is independent of the others. For each scenario, explain why you selected the option.

a) An author works at home writing articles for a magazine. Once per week she must transmit an article to her editor. She rarely uses the link for any other purpose.

b) A large company maintains its own website for online catalogs and purchase transactions by its customers. Hundreds of customers visit the sites daily and make purchases.

c) A small business uses the Internet for daily research. Owners have heard that some links are shared by other subscribers in the same area, which might slow down the connection or even pose security threats. Thus, they would like to avoid such a service. They do need a speed of at least 200 Kbps.

d) A farm in South Africa needs a link of at least 200 Kbps. People on the farm can receive television signals only through a satellite dish. The closest telephone central office is 12 miles away.

e) An Internet service provider specializes in hosting websites of small businesses.

f) A cruise ship wants to provide Internet service to vacationers on the third deck. The ship cruises in the Caribbean. The link's speed must be at least 250 Kbps.

7   Team up with another student from your class. Select a bank branch close to your school. Interview the branch personnel about the telecommunications equipment used between the branch and (a) other branches, (b) headquarters, and (c) other institutions, such as credit information companies, if any. Use the discussion in this chapter to identify the various communications devices that the branch uses. List the devices and state their roles at the bank.

8   Team up with two other students from your class. Each of you should send an email message to one other team member. One of you may use the university's facilities, but the other two should use a subscriber's address, such as an AOL or Hotmail address. When you receive the

messages, try to get the routing information: which servers did the messages pass through on their way to you? How long did it take the messages to get to the server from which your own computer retrieves the messages? Print out the route your computer generated.

Companion CD questions

1 This chapter discusses RFID as an application of wireless networking. Some people have raised privacy concerns about the use of RFID. Do some research and summarize these concerns. Do you agree with them? Why or why not?

2 Do you have a network at home? If so, which type of network is it? What made you decide on this type of network? If not, if you were to set one up, what kind would you choose and why?

Video questions

1 The video segment does not define Wiki. What is a Wiki?

2 Could Trent Couriers use a Wiki? In which ways?

From ideas to application
REAL CASES

Case study 5.1

Mobile phone banking in Africa on the rise

More than 800 million mobile phones were sold in developing countries in the last three years according to FinMark Trust, a research think-tank in South Africa. Twice as many Africans have mobile phones than have land lines according to the International Telecommunications Union. Associated with this significant expansion in mobile phone usage, in Africa particularly, is a lack of physical banking infrastructure. For example, in Ingwavuma, a rural town in the KwaZulu-Ntal province of South Africa, there are just two ATMs and the nearest bank is a 90-minute drive away. These factors mean that in many African countries, including South Africa, Nigeria and the Democratic Republic of Congo, 'the use of cell phone banking is becoming relevant'

according to Jeremy Leach, executive director of FinMark Trust.

A joint report 'Mobile Phone Banking and Low-Income Customers: Evidence from South Africa' from the World Bank's Consultative Group to Assist the Poor (CGAP), the United Nations Foundation and the Vodafone Group Foundation, summarizes a study they carried out of 515 low-income individuals in South Africa, 300 of whom do not yet use mobile banking, with the remaining 215 customers of Wizzit, a mobile-banking subsidiary of the South African Bank of Athens. Wizzit targets the 16 million people in South Africa, that is 46 per cent of the adult population, who are 'unbanked' or have difficulty accessing conventional banking services. Since it was launched in December 2004, Wizzit has acquired over 50,000 customers. For a new customer signing up is easy. They simply key their national identity number into their mobile phone. For existing customers Wizzit provides a call centre 15 hours per day in the 11 official languages of South Africa.

Whilst the survey recognizes its limitations in terms of sample population, the findings, particularly from the existing Wizzit customers, are encouraging. These customers generally found the system to be faster, cheaper and more convenient than traditional banking. Although customers must still visit a branch to make a deposit, most transactions such as checking their account balance, transferring money to friends and family and making payments such as utility bills can all be done without a trip to the bank. For someone living in a major European city that might not be such a big deal, but for someone on a low income in South Africa when the average journey time is 32 minutes at a cost that might represent a significant percentage of their monthly income, the benefits of mobile banking become clear. Of course the service is not free. Customers have to pay a charge to sign up and then pay a per-transaction charge, but this is a fraction of the cost of visiting a remote branch.

A mobile phone user in Soweto, South Africa.

It seems that the early adopters of Wizzit's services are people with relatively higher incomes, more technologically sophisticated and well educated. The challenge now seems to be to target those poor people who either are not aware of the potential of mobile banking for them or who think that they are ineligible for a bank account at all. Traditionally to open a bank account a potential customer would need to supply documentation such as proof of income and address – many are unable to do so. These are specifically the people for whom Wizzit was designed.

If the South African model is successful then there is every possibility that it will be copied in the rest of Africa, which tends to remain a cash economy with its inherent security problems. According to Brian Richardson, Wizzit's CEO, the model is more than technology. 'We have many requests from banks to come and implement the Wizzit model. One challenge is that many IT departments feel threatened by Wizzit and believe they can develop it themselves. We are quite sure that they can but the Wizzit model is much more than technology and this point is often missed. What is of as much if not greater importance is the methodology utilized in opening accounts, educating customers etc.' Wizzit does not use mass media advertising. Instead it markets its services through 2000 'WIZZ Kids' who are typically youngsters from the target low-income population. They educate potential people on the benefits of mobile banking and earn commission for each new customer they sign up.

Thinking about the case

1   Do you think that the South African model of mobile banking will be a success? What about the rest of Africa? What about the rest of the developing world? What telecommunications infrastructure needs to be in place?

2   Are there inherent security problems with banking over a mobile phone network? How can these be resolved?

3   Is there much difference between a South African using Wizzit's mobile banking facilities and a resident of central London using conventional banking in association with Internet banking?

SOURCE: John Yarney, 'African mobile-phone banking poised for growth', IDG News Service, 17 May 2007 and Consultative Group to Assist the Poor (CGAP), the United Nations Foundation and the Vodafone Group Foundation, 'Mobile Phone Banking and Low-Income Customers: Evidence from South Africa', 2006

Case study **5.2**

WiMAX by the sea

The traditional British sea-side resort of Brighton is also a thriving centre for new media. One in five businesses in the city is allied to the creative industries. It has a high percentage of young people involved in these industries and other related IT businesses and many became early adopters of Wi-Fi. The Loose Connections project means that nobody in Brighton is further than ten minutes from a free wireless broadband hotspot. This has proved a boon for mobile workers across the city. However, the city council realized that a more radical approach was needed to service schools and other aspects of local authority connectivity. According to Bill Parslow, Head of ICT and eGovernment, Wi-Fi has its drawbacks. 'Whilst there are clear benefits to its use, perhaps for small community mesh networks, 802.11b or g neither had the range nor the security levels that made us comfortable with sending potentially sensitive information over the airwaves. 2.4 GHz, the frequency used for WiFi, is also particularly sensitive to the odd coastal sea mist that occasionally rumbles in soaking up Wi-Fi strength.' The solution was the creation of the Brighton Metranet (Metropolitan Internet), a WiMax standard broadband infrastructure covering the whole of the city. 'Whereas Wi-Fi might have a range of 50 m in reality, the Brighton's Metranet's longest link at the moment is 7.5 km', explains Bill Parslow.

The initial pilot linked seven schools and three university sites with the main access point 140 m in the air on the rooftop of Brighton's tallest building. Line of sight helps for longer range. However, the advantage of WiMax is that it is also capable of non-line-of-sight (NLOS) connection by using multiple paths and reflections of buildings and so on. This is a principal that can be followed in many similar situations relating to local government. Local councils tend to own enough high ground such as town halls and other housing blocks. Connection to a university then gives access to academic networks, giving European and worldwide high-speed connectivity. The benefits of the Brighton Metranet are many. Obviously the original school and other council offices are connected, but it also allows the wider public low-cost, high-speed connectivity. The general public also have potential access to council IT services such as social services, the local health authority and so on. The social aspects were expressed in a bid put forward in 2006 called 'Digital City Healthy City' which aimed to integrate with the NHS Connecting for Health project by linking up several service agencies that deliver care outside the hospital context using remote patient monitoring. The following example scenario shows how the technology and agencies could be brought together for the greater good of the individual.

The lifestyle of a disabled person living independently in the community would be significantly enhanced. For example, if they have mobility problems, they could be living in a Smart House with monitoring devices, which include a smoke detector which summons emergency services, a fall detector and a bed occupancy sensor all connected to a single Wi-Fi access point. Thanks to support and tutoring from a Digital Champion at their local UK online centre, they could become a confident computer and Internet user. This would increase their ability to interact socially and combat isolation and exclusion, through participation in local blogs, chat rooms and attending online meetings.

Thinking about the case

1 The reservations regarding security of WiFi may be reasonable. Does this mean that anyone using a WiFi connection in a city or airport is subject to security problems?

2 Could the example scenario at the end of the case study work without the Brighton Metranet?

3 Can you think of any other ways that the WiMax network could help the residents of Brighton?

SOURCE: Bill Parslow, 'Brighton Unwired with WiMAX', http://www. egovmonitor.com/node/707

The Brighton Metranet's use of WiMAX's technology allows it to reach most locations within 10 km of its primary access point in central Brighton.

PHOTO SOURCE: © PAUL MCARDLE

Case study **5.3**

VoIP takes hold with small businesses

BY ANTHONY PLEWES

It may be a truism but, nonetheless, voice over IP has the capacity to transform how companies deal with their communications. Large enterprises have been dipping their toe in the water for several years and now it appears that small and medium-sized companies are following suit, says Anthony Plewes.

Investing in Voice over IP has become a priority for SMEs, with some 60 per cent considering investing in it during 2007, according to a survey by silicon.com and The Bathwick Group. In terms of planned investment, it lags behind only laptop and handheld computers.

This trend is significant as VoIP lies at the heart of convergence; it allows voice to be carried over data networks, eliminating the historical divergence between voice and data.

Although VoIP describes a very specific technology, there is often confusion among SMEs about exactly what it means for their business. Put simply, there are two different communications areas where VoIP plays a role. The first of these is what can be called Internet telephony, where phone calls are delivered over the Internet; and the second is IP telephony, which in essence is the replacement of the legacy PBX within a corporation. Both of these areas are relevant to SMEs and confusion between the two has served as a significant barrier to the uptake of the latter.

Internet telephony

To many SMEs, Voice over IP is synonymous with telephony over the Internet. Until recently, the lack of high-bandwidth connections made Internet telephony little more than a curiosity, but nearly all of the small businesses in the silicon.com/Bathwick Group survey now have access to broadband Internet services, and therefore the bandwidth to take Internet telephony seriously. For companies with a substantial amount of international calling or audio conferencing, it can provide massive savings on their telephone bill.

Skype has played a major role in popularizing Internet telephony and remains one of the most important players in the market. However, unlike most telephony services, Skype uses a peer-to-peer network of Skype users to deliver the calls rather than a service provider per se.

What attracts many people to Skype is the perception that it makes calling free. This is only partly true: calls are only free between Skype-enabled computers. Skype can be used to call traditional telephone numbers but this involves 'breakout' – the call must leave the Internet and be terminated on a telephone network. This service, SkypeOut, carries a usage charge which must be prepaid. The savings offered are by rating calls as local rather than national or international.

Vonage is more like a traditional operator than Skype. It offers consumers and businesses a normal telephone number but routes the calls over the Internet. Vonage says the operator has more than two million users worldwide. The number of users in the UK is confidential but Vincent Potier, director of marketing at Vonage UK, says around 20 to 25 per cent

A German businessman using VoIP.

of these are SMEs. 'Our sweet spot is companies with one to 10 employees and we have a large number of self-employed sole traders as customers', he says.

Because the telephony service uses IP, Vonage is able to offer a range of interesting features, such as allowing the user to choose their own dialling code for their business. This is useful to home-based businesses which might be located in rural areas but want to look as if they are based in London, for example. Vonage also allows subscribers to set up a whole range of virtual numbers with area codes in their main trading locations without needing to have a presence in the city. It is also possible to set up international virtual numbers in the countries in which Vonage operates.

However, Vonage and other Internet telephony services rely on customers' broadband connections, most of which do not provide high quality of service (QoS) for voice and the number of simultaneous callers are limited by the upload capacity. Vonage, for example, recommends that in order to conduct a high-quality audio call, each user will need 90 Kbps upstream and down. The problem here is that while ADSL downstream speeds are rapidly improving, the same cannot be said for upstream.

IP telephony

While Internet telephony has attracted techies, consumers and cost-conscious businesses alike, the development of IP PBX technology for SMEs is much more significant.

Guenter Junk, CEO of Sywx, one of the first companies to focus solely on IP telephony for SMEs, says: 'Communications are changing for SMEs. Where the telephone used to be the primary form of communication, it is now just one of many, and IP telephony helps companies knit it all together.'

IP telephony is a fairly major undertaking and is best broken down into three phases. The first phase is IP trunking, where multi-site SMEs can make substantial cost savings by connecting their sites together by effectively eliminating inter-site call costs. Productivity can also be improved through having a unified call plan across the business, allowing colleagues in different sites to work together better.

The next phase is to link remote or home workers into the office network using a VPN over broadband connections. Voice over IP gateways allow the remote worker to access PBX functionality remotely and collaborate with their colleagues.

Trevor Evans, business development manager in Alcatel's SME business, says: 'It is possible to connect a single person to the office network with standard broadband connections. But if the employee needs to speak to external people over the connection, they will probably need a better connection including some elements of quality of service.'

The final phase is to spread IP telephony throughout the organization with IP phones on the employees' desktop. This set-up completely eliminates the requirement to have separate sets of cabling for voice and data networks, and provides for simplified management.

IP phones on the desktop also open up a whole new world of telephony applications, as IP telephony can be very easily integrated into the company's back-end systems. For example, it only requires a simple XML application and the entire company directory can be accessed from the phone.

Steven Frost, SMB market manager at Cisco UK & Ireland, says: 'VoIP is only the starting point, the real benefits come from features such as unified messaging.' Although unified messaging can be done without VoIP, combining all communication on a single IP network makes its deployment and management straightforward. It also offers functionality such as presence and can be integrated directly into business processes. For example, companies could create a click-to-call button in their accounts package to call late payers of invoices. Features such as these are a real boon to company productivity.

Despite the clear advantages, there is still conflicting evidence about exactly how many SMEs have made it all the way to IP telephony. Alcatel, which heralds from a traditional PBX background, says it has now reached the tipping point for IP telephony sales to companies with more than 100 employees. For this market it is now selling more IP than legacy TDM systems. But in the sub-100 employee market, Alcatel is still mainly selling legacy PBXs, with IP telephony making up only a fairly insignificant 5 to 8 per cent of sales.

Alcatel's Evans says: 'Our customers are still finding barriers to deployment, particularly the cost of auditing and upgrading the LAN by putting QoS on it.' Other earlier barriers such as security and scalability have been largely overcome, although companies need to pay close attention to security if combining VoIP with Wi-Fi networks.

Even IP telephony specialists such as Cisco have found that SMEs have been slower to adopt IP telephony than larger companies. Cisco's Frost says: 'It has taken smaller companies a while to adopt VoIP partly because the technology was designed for larger enterprises, but now we have developed the right product set and the right channels to meet the SME requirements. The channel is vitally important for SMEs, because they want to buy from local companies. We've had to train them in both voice and data skills.'

The relatively slow take-up of IP telephony in the SME market is not surprising. Equipment makers have long focused on larger enterprises and it is only relatively recently that fully functional telephony systems have been within reach of the smallest companies. Businesses with more than 20 employees are well placed to benefit from the advantages of premise-based IP telephony, while smaller companies without many internal IT skills are more suited to hosted offerings.

Companies of all sizes, though, are able to benefit from Internet telephony as long as they remember its limitations and mainly use it for internal communications.

Thinking about the case

1 It seems that enterprises with few employees have been slow to take up VoIP. Why is this the case? Will improved Internet connections help to increase the take-up?

2 Are a high volume of international calls the main deciding factor in the introduction of VoIP?

Databases and data warehouses

Data are usually collected in a way that does not make them immediately useful to businesspeople. Imagine building a model palace from a pile of building blocks. You have a good idea of what you want to build, but first you have to organize the blocks so it is easy for you to find and select only the blocks you need. Then you can combine them into substructures that eventually are integrated into your model. Similarly, data collected by organizations must be organized and stored so that useful information can be extracted from the database in a flexible manner.

When you finish this chapter, you will be able to:

Explain the difference between traditional file organization and the database approach to managing digital data.

Explain how relational and object-oriented database management systems are used to construct databases, populate them with data, and manipulate the data to produce information.

Enumerate the most important features and operations of a relational database, the most popular database model.

Understand how data modelling and design create a conceptual blueprint of a database.

Discuss how databases are used on the Web.

List the operations involved in transferring data from transactional databases to data warehouses.

THE VALUE AND USES OF DATABASES

As Trent Couriers grew, so did its reliance on databases. By the time the company had grown to a size of 90 employees, Andrew was using databases to create weekly schedules for part-time and full-time employees, track customer orders, store and access employee and customer information, organize and report financial data and provide crucial information for marketing strategies. As his database needs expanded, he transitioned from one database management system to another.

Moving up: from Microsoft Access to Oracle

In the early days, Andrew had relied on Microsoft Access and Excel for his company's database needs. When he hired his first part-time messengers, he used an Excel spreadsheet to set up weekly schedules. He stored customer and order information in an Access database. As business grew, so did the size of the database. Karen Brown, an IT consultant who worked in an office on the second floor of his building, told him that he should consider using a more powerful database management system (DBMS). When Mary Thomas suggested that Trent Couriers create an intranet so that messengers could upload delivery information through their wireless connections, the need to switch to a more powerful DBMS became urgent. Microsoft Access wouldn't be able to handle the number of concurrent users that Trent Couriers anticipated. Andrew decided to hire Karen to help the office shift to Oracle. An Oracle database would be able to accommodate both the increased size of the database and the need for concurrent access.

Tapping the power of databases

Then Andrew turned his thoughts to using his data to better his service – to maintain his existing customers and strengthen his relationships with them. He also wanted to find out who would be good potential customers. He hired Karen to run SQL queries and create reports. Surely he could find valuable information by exploring customer information and buying patterns.

First Andrew wanted to find out who his preferred customers were – those who used his service most often and provided the most revenue. The consultant used data-mining software to delve into the data and identified a profile. To his surprise, Andrew found that the legal and medical-supply firms were most profitable. He'd always thought the pottery companies were his best clients because of the special handling their objects required. But lawyers and pharmacists needed faster delivery and special services, such as delivery confirmation, which commanded premium rates and generated additional revenue at no further cost per delivery to Trent Couriers. Andrew designated those customers as VIPs and tagged their database files. VIPs would receive priority delivery on the routes from now on.

Also, Andrew was interested in the purchasing patterns of customers. He planned to target those opportunities with a promotion to gain new clients. Again, the consultant came back with interesting news: law firms with branches throughout South Cheshire used Trent Couriers' service most often on weekdays between the hours of 10 a.m. and 1 p.m. So Andrew decided to locate other similar firms and develop a direct-mail promotion to them – discounted deliveries for setting up an account and scheduling 30 orders in a month's time. Andrew also added additional messengers during that time frame to be sure to handle deliveries smoothly.

Managing digital data

Businesses collect and dissect data for a multitude of purposes. Digital data can be stored in a variety of ways on different types of media, as discussed in Chapter 4. They can be stored in what can be called the traditional file format, in which the different pieces of information are not labelled and categorized, but are stored as continuous strings of bytes. The chief advantage of this format is the efficient use of space, but the data are nonetheless difficult to locate and manipulate. By contrast, the database format, in which each piece of data is labelled or categorized, provides a much more powerful information management tool. Data in this format can be easily accessed and manipulated in almost any way desired to create useful information and optimize productivity.

The impact of database technology on business cannot be overstated. Not only has it changed the way almost every industry conducts business, but it has also created an information industry with far-reaching effects on both our business and personal lives. Databases are behind the successful use of automatic teller machines, increased efficiency in retail stores, almost every marketing effort, and the numerous online search engines and electronic storefronts on the Web. Combined with interactive web pages on the Internet, databases have made an immense contribution to commerce. Without them, there would be no online banking, no online consumer catalogues, no online searches for information, no online stock brokerages and no online chat rooms. Their impact on business has allowed fewer people to complete larger tasks, and their power has allowed organizations to learn more about us, as consumers, than we might realize. Imagine: every time you enter the address of a website, a special program performs a search in a huge database and matches your request with one of millions of addresses. Every time you fill out an online form with details such as your address, phone number, National Insurance number or credit-card number, a program feeds the data into a database, where each item is recorded for further use.

In virtually every type of business today, you must understand the power of databases. This chapter reviews approaches to organizing and manipulating data.

The traditional file approach

There are two overall approaches to maintaining data: the *traditional file approach* – which has no mechanism for tagging, retrieving and manipulating data – and the **database approach**, which does have that mechanism. To appreciate the benefits of the database approach, you must keep in mind the inconvenience involved in accessing and manipulating data in the traditional file approach: program-data dependency, high data redundancy and low data integrity.

> **database approach** An approach to maintaining data that contains a mechanism for tagging, retrieving and manipulating data.

Consider Figure 6.1, which is an example of a human resource file in traditional file format. Suppose a programmer wants to retrieve and print out only the last name and department number of each employee from this file. The programmer must clearly instruct the computer to first retrieve the data between position 10 and position 20. Then he must instruct the computer to skip the positions up to position 35 and retrieve the data between positions 36 and 39. He cannot instruct the computer to retrieve a piece of data by its column name, because column names do not exist in this format. To create the reports, the programmer must know which position ranges maintain which types of data and insert the appropriate headings, 'Last Name' and 'Department', so that the reader can understand the information. If the programmer miscounts the positions, the printout might include output like '677Rapap' as a last name instead of 'Rapaport'. This illustrates the *interdependency of programs and data* of the traditional file approach. The programmer must know *how* data are stored to use them. Perhaps most importantly, the very fact that manipulation of the data requires a programmer is probably the greatest disadvantage of the file approach. Much business data is still processed this way. New data resources are rarely built this way, but the existing ones must be maintained with this challenge in mind.

Figure 6.1　The layout of a human resource file in traditional file organization

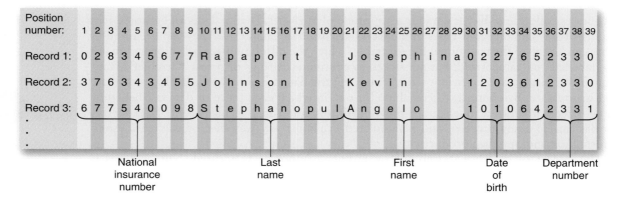

| | National insurance number | Last name | First name | Date of birth | Department number |

Other challenges with traditional file storage are high data redundancy and low data integrity, because in older file systems files were built, and are still maintained, for the use of specific organizational units. If your last and first name, as well as address and other details appear in the files of the department where you work as well as in the payroll file of the Human Resource department, there is duplication of data, or **data redundancy**, which wastes storage space (and consequently money) and is inefficient. When corrections or modifications need to be made, every change has to be made as many times as the number of locations where the data appear, which takes time and might introduce errors. If the same data were entered correctly in one place but incorrectly in another, your record is not only inaccurate, but might appear to represent a different person in each place. Inaccuracies hurt **data integrity**. Often, the traditional file approach to storing data leads to low data integrity.

data redundancy The existence of the same data in more than one place in a computer system. Although some data redundancy is unavoidable, efforts should be made to minimize it.

data integrity Accuracy, timeliness and relevance of data in a context.

 CD TASK

The database approach

In the database approach, data pieces are organized about entities. An **entity** is any object about which an organization chooses to collect data. Entities can be types of people, such as employees, students or members of fan clubs; events, such as sales transactions, sports events or theatre shows; or inanimate objects, such as inventoried or for-sale products, buildings or minerals. In the context of data management, 'entity' refers to all the occurrences sharing the same types of data. Therefore, it does not matter if you maintain a record of one student or many students; the entity is 'student'. To understand how data are organized in a database, you must first understand the data hierarchy, described in Figure 6.2, which shows a compilation of information about students: their first names, last names, years of birth, enrolment numbers, departments and campus phone numbers. The smallest piece of data is a **character** (such as a letter in a first or last name, or a digit in a street address). Multiple characters make up a field. A **field** is one piece of information about an entity, such as the last name or first name of a student, or the student's street address. The fields related to the same entity make up a **record**. A collection of related records, such as all the records of a college's students, is called a **file**. Often, several related files must be kept together. A collection of such files is referred to as a database. However, the features of a database can be present even when a database consists of a single file.

entity Any object about which an organization chooses to collect data.

character The smallest piece of data in the data hierarchy.

field A data element in a record, describing one aspect of an entity or event. Referred to as attribute in relational databases.

record A set of standard field types. All the fields of a record contain data about a certain entity or event.

Figure 6.2 Data hierarchy

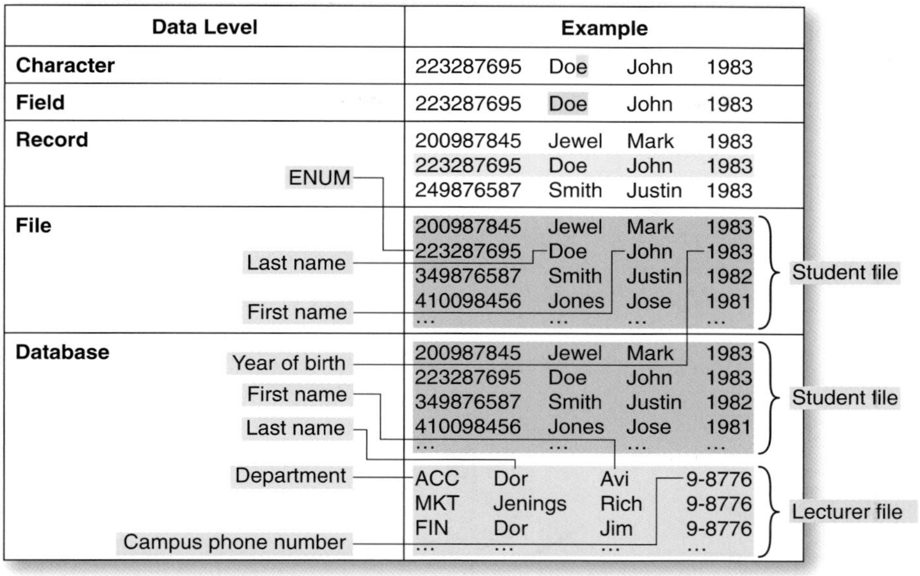

Data Level		Example			
Character		223287695	Doe	John	1983
Field		223287695	Doe	John	1983
Record	ENUM	200987845	Jewel	Mark	1983
		223287695	Doe	John	1983
		249876587	Smith	Justin	1983
File		200987845	Jewel	Mark	1983
	Last name	223287695	Doe	John	1983
		349876587	Smith	Justin	1982
	First name	410098456	Jones	Jose	1981
		...	...	...	...

Student file (covers File rows)

Database	Year of birth	200987845	Jewel	Mark	1983
	First name	223287695	Doe	John	1983
	Last name	349876587	Smith	Justin	1982
		410098456	Jones	Jose	1981
		...	...	...	...

Student file

	Department	ACC	Dor	Avi	9-8776
		MKT	Jenings	Rich	9-8776
	Campus phone number	FIN	Dor	Jim	9-8776
		...	...	...	...

Lecturer file

Once the fields are assigned names, including Last Name, First Name, ENUM and the like, the data in each field carries a tag – a field name – and can be easily accessed by that field name, no matter where the data are physically stored. One of the greatest strengths of databases is their promotion of application-data independence. In other words, if an application is written to process data in a database, the application designer only needs to know the names of the fields, not their physical organization or their length.

Database fields are not limited to holding text and numbers. They can hold pictures, sounds and video clips. Fields can hold any content that can be digitized. For example, when you shop online, you can search for a product by its product name or code, and then retrieve its picture or a video clip about the product.

While a database itself is a collection of several related files, the program used to build databases, populate them with data and manipulate the data is called a **database management system (DBMS)**. The files themselves *are* the database, but DBMSs do all the work – structuring files, storing data and linking records. As you saw previously, if you wanted to access data from files that were stored in a traditional file approach, you would have to know exactly how many characters were designated for each type of data. A DBMS, however, does much of this work (and a lot of other work) for you.

If you are using a database, you want to be able to move rapidly from one record to another, sort by different criteria, create different types of reports and analyse the data in different ways. Because of these demands, databases are stored on and processed from direct access storage devices, such as magnetic disks or CDs. They can be backed up to sequential storage devices such as magnetic or optical tapes, but cannot be efficiently processed off such media because it would take too long to access the records.

Queries Data are accessed in a database by sending messages called 'queries', which request data from specific records and/or fields and direct the computer to display the results. Queries are also entered to manipulate data. Usually, the same software that is used to

file A collection of related records, such as a customer file containing details of all customer names, billing addresses, delivery addresses, credit limits and so on.

database management system (DBMS) A computer program that allows the user to construct a database, populate it with data and manipulate the data.

Figure 6.3 Different database views reveal different combinations of data

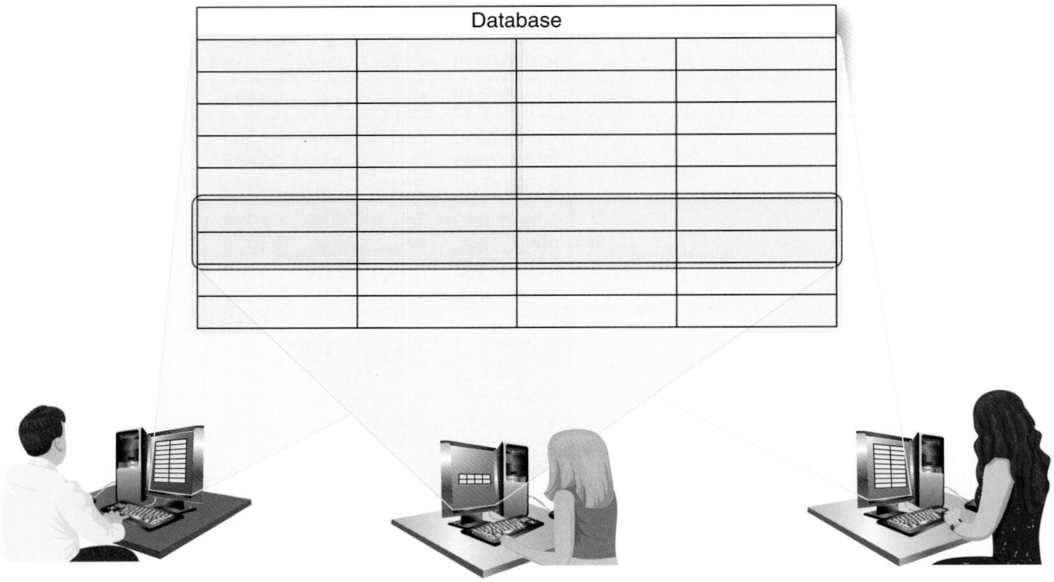

construct and populate the database, that is, the DBMS, is also used to present queries. Modern DBMSs provide fairly user-friendly means of querying a database.

Security The use of databases raises security and privacy issues. The fact that data are stored only once in a database for several different purposes does not mean that everyone with access to that database should have access to *all* the data in it. Restricting access is easily dealt with by customizing menus for different users and requiring users to enter codes that limit access to certain fields or records. As a result, users have different *views* of the database, as abstractly illustrated in Figure 6.3. The ability to limit users' views only to specific columns or records gives the database administrator (DBA) another advantage: the ability to implement security measures. The measures are implemented once for the database, rather than multiple times for different files. For instance, in the database in Figure 6.4, while a human resource manager has access to all fields of the employee file (represented by the top, middle and lower parts of the figure), the payroll personnel have access only to four fields of the employee file (middle part of the figure), and a project manager has access only to the Name and Hours Worked fields. Views can be limited to certain fields in a database, or certain records, or a combination of both.

> **database administrator (DBA)** The individual in charge of building and maintaining organizational databases.

DBMSs are usually bundled with a 4GL (fourth-generation programming language) module. Programmers can use this module to develop applications that facilitate queries and produce predesigned reports.

Database models

A *database model* is the general logical structure in which records are stored within a database and the method used to establish relationships among the records. There are several database models. They differ in the manner in which records are linked to each other. These differences, in turn, dictate the manner in which a user can navigate the database, retrieve

Figure 6.4 Different views from the same database

View of Human Resource Manager				
NIN	Name	D.O.B.	Hire Date	Marital Status

View of Payroll Personnel			
NIN	Hourly Rate	Benefits Code	Hours Worked

View of Project Manager	
Name	Hours Worked

desired records and create reports. The oldest models, the hierarchical and network models, are still used in some databases that were built in the 1970s and 1980s, but are no longer used in newly constructed databases. Virtually all new databases are designed following the relational and object-oriented models.

The relational model

CD TASK

The relational database model consists of tables. Its roots are in relational algebra, although you do not have to know relational algebra to build and use relational databases. However, database experts still use relational algebra terminology: in a relational database, a record is called a *tuple*, a field – often referred to as a column – is called an *attribute*, and a table of records is called a *relation*. This text uses the simpler terms, as do the popular software packages: fields, records and tables.

To design a relational database, you need a clear idea of the different entities and how they relate. For example, in a DVD store database, the entities might be Customer, DVD Rental, DVD and Distributor. A single table is built for each entity (though each table can contain from only a few to potentially millions of records). DVD Rental is an associative entity, and you can see in Figure 6.5 that the DVD Rental table associates data from the Customer and DVD tables.

Maintenance of a relational database is relatively easy because each table is independent of the others, although some tables are related to others. To add a customer record, the user accesses the Customer table. To delete a record of a DVD, the user accesses the DVD table. The advantages of this model makes relational database management systems the most popular in the software market. Virtually all DBMSs that are offered on the market accommodate the relational model. This model is used in supply chain management (SCM) systems and many other enterprise applications and local, individual ISs.

To retrieve records from a relational database, or to sort them, you must use a key. A key is a field whose values identify records either for display or for processing. You can use any

relational database model A general structure of database in which records are organized in tables (relations) and the relationships among tables are maintained through foreign keys.

table A set of related records in a relational database.

key A field in a database table whose values identify records either for display or for processing. Typical keys are part number (in an inventory file) and National Insurance number (in a human resources file).

CD TASK

Figure 6.5 A relational database

Customer Table

CustID	CustName	CustPhone	CustAddr
33091	Jill Bronson	322-4907	203 Oak Dr
35999	John Smith	322-5577	519 Devon St
36002	John Sosik	342-0071	554 Spring Dr
36024	Jane Fedorow	322-7299	101 Grant Ave

Primary key

Composite primary key

DVD Rental Table

CustID	CopyNum	Date Rented	Date Returned
35999	4452-1	1-5-06	3-5-06
36002	4780-3	3-5-06	
36024	5312-2	2-5-06	5-5-06

Copy Table

CopyNum	TitleNum
4452-1	4452
4452-2	4452
5312-1	5312
5312-2	5312
5312-3	5312
7662-1	7662
7662-2	7662
5583-1	5583

Primary key in *Title* and part of a
composite primary key in *Copy-Title*

Title Table

TitleNum	Title	Category	DistribNum	RentPrice
4452	Enter the Dragon	Martial Arts	277	€4.00
5312	The Ring II	Thriller	305	€4.00
7662	Star Wars III	Sci-Fi	372	€5.00
5583	White Noise	Thriller	589	€2.50

Primary key in *Distributor* and foreign key in *Title*

Distributor Table

DistribNum	DistribName	Phone
277	HK Corp	1-877-555-0550
305	Columbia	1-888-222-3654
372	Lucas Films	1-247-233-6996
589	Booh Inc	1-866-222-9999

CD TASK

field as a key. For example, you could ask the database for the record of John Smith from the Customer table by using the CustName field as a key. That is, you enter a query, a condition that instructs the DBMS to retrieve a record with the value of CustName as 'John Smith'. A key is *unique* if the value (content) in that field appears only in one record.

Why you should...

know about data management

A national car rental company knows the precise number of vehicles to hold for late-booking, high-paying travellers. A restaurant chain detects consumer buying patterns that the company then uses to boost its sales of special meals. How do businesses find this information?

Transactions are recorded at the boundaries of a company in its contacts with external entities, such as customers and suppliers. Data captured this way make up the greater part of most organizational databases. They provide the raw material for essential information that helps answer questions such as: What is the total amount of money we owe debtors? What is the backlog of a certain product that we manufacture? What was the average sales volume per employee last quarter? However, to be able to extract useful information, the data must first be organized in well-designed databases. And to know what information you can draw from a database, you must understand how databases are structured and what combinations of data can be created for you on demand.

Imagine a sales clerk who cannot immediately respond to a customer about the availability of an item or an online shopper who cannot display the details of an item that is actually available for sale at the site. Customers experiencing this are not likely to patronize the business again. Imagine a treasurer who cannot figure out in real time how much cash the company has in the bank. The company might miss an important deal. Available and reliable information is the most important resource of any business, in any industry. Thus, professionals must understand at least the fundamentals of data organization and manipulation. You will be a more productive professional if you know how databases and data warehouses are built and queried, and what types of information can be extracted from them.

Sometimes a key is composed of several fields so that their combination provides a unique key.

As you can see, database design requires careful forethought. The designer must include fields for foreign keys from other tables so that join tables can be created in the future. A table might include foreign keys from several tables, so that there is much flexibility in creating reports with related data from several tables. The inclusion of foreign keys might cause considerable data redundancy. This complexity has not diminished the popularity of relational databases, however.

If there is more than one record with 'John Smith' (because several customers happen to have that same name) in the CustName field, you might not retrieve the single record you desired. Depending on the application you use for the query, you might receive the first one that meets the condition, that is, a list of all the records with that value in the field. The only way to be sure you are retrieving the desired record is to use a unique key, such as a National Insurance number, an employee ID, or, in our example, a customer ID (CustID).

A unique key can serve as a **primary key**. A primary key is the field by which records in a table are uniquely identified. If your query specified that you wanted the record whose CustID value is 36002, the system would retrieve the record of John Sosik. It will be the John Sosik you wanted, even if there are more records of people with exactly the same name. Because the purpose of a primary key is to uniquely identify a record, there must be a unique value in that field for each record.

> **primary key** In a file, a field that holds values that are unique to each record. Only a primary key can be used to uniquely identify and retrieve a record.

Usually, a table in a relational database must have a primary key, and most relational DBMSs enforce this rule; if the designer does not designate a field as a key, the DBMS creates its own serial number field as the primary key field for the table. Once the designer of the table determines the primary key when constructing the records' format, the DBMS does not allow a user to enter two records with the same value in that column. Note that there might be situations in which more than one field can be used as a primary key. Such is the case with motor vehicles, because two different fields can uniquely identify the record of a particular vehicle: the vehicle identification number (VIN) and its registration plate number. Thus, a database designer might establish one of these fields as a primary key to retrieve records. In Figure 6.5 in the DVD Rental table both CustID and CopyNum can be used as a primary key.

composite key In a data file, a combination of two fields that can serve as a unique key to locate specific records.

foreign key In a relational database: a field in a table that is a primary key in another table. Foreign keys allow association of data between the two files.

join table In relational database manipulation, a table created by linking – that is, joining – data from multiple tables.

one-to-many relationship In a database, a relationship between two tables such that each record in the one table can be associated with several records in the other table, but each record in the other table can be associated with only one record in the first table.

many-to-many relationship In databases, a relationship between two tables whereby every record in a table can be associated with several records in the other table.

For some business needs you must use a composite key, a combination of two or more fields that together serve as a primary key, because it is impractical to use a single field as a primary key. For example, consider flight records of a commercial airline. Flights of a certain route are the same every week or every day they are offered, so the daily Virgin Atlantic flight from London Heathrow to Johannesburg – VS601 – for instance, cannot serve us well to retrieve a list of all the passengers who took this flight on 3 May 2007. However, we can use the combination of the flight number *and* date as a composite primary key. To check who sat in a particular seat, a composite key consisting of three fields is needed: flight number, date and seat number.

To link records from one table with records of another table, the tables must have at least one field in common (i.e., one column in each table must contain the same type of data), and that field must be a primary key field for one of the tables. This repeated field is a primary key in one table, and a foreign key field in the other table. In the DVD store example, if you ever want to create a report showing the name of every distributor and all the DVD titles from that distributor, the primary key of the Distributor table, DistribNum, must also be included as a foreign key in the Title table. The resultant table (Figure 6.6) is called a join table. Note that although DistribNum was used to create the join table, it does not have to be displayed in the join table, although it could be.

Since the relationships between tables are created as part of manipulating the table, the relational model supports both one-to-many and many-to-many relationships between records of different tables. For example, a one-to-many relationship is created when a group of employees belongs to only one department. All would have the same department number as a foreign key in their records, and none will have more than one department key. There is *one* department, linked to *many* employees. A many-to-many relationship can be maintained, for instance, for lecturers and students in a college database. A lecturer might have many students, and a student might have many lecturers. This can be accomplished by creating a composite key of lecturer ID and student ID. In our example of the DVD store, there is a many-to-many relationship between customers and the DVDs they have rented. The DVD Rental table enables the store manager to create a history report of customers and their rentals. It is clear that more than one customer has rented a certain DVD, and the same customer has rented many different DVDs.

The major vendors of relational DBMSs are IBM, Oracle and Microsoft, at a worldwide market share in licensing revenues of about 34 per cent, 34 per cent and 20 per cent,

Figure 6.6 A join table

Distributor	Telephone	Title
HK Corp	1-877-555-05-50	Enter the Dragon
Columbia	1-888-222-3654	The Ring II
Lucas Films	1-247-233-6996	Star Wars III
Booh Inc	1-866-222-9999	White Noise

respectively. IBM licenses DB2, Oracle licenses DBMSs by the company name, and Microsoft licenses SQL Server and Access. These DBMSs are an essential part of enterprise applications such as SCM and CRM systems.

The object-oriented model

The object-oriented database model uses the object-oriented approach, described in Chapter 4, to maintaining records. In object-oriented technology, an object consists of both data and the procedures that manipulate the data. So, in addition to the attributes of an entity, an object also contains relationships with other entities and procedures to manipulate the data. The combined storage of both data and the procedures that manipulate them is referred to as encapsulation. Through encapsulation, an object can be 'planted' in different data sets. The ability in object-oriented structures to create a new object automatically by replicating all or some of the characteristics of a previously developed object (called the parent object) is called inheritance. Figure 6.7 demonstrates how the same data maintained in a relational database at the DVD rental store would be stored and used

object-oriented database model A database, in which data are part of an object, that is processed using object-oriented programs.

encapsulation In an object oriented data model, the combined storage of both data and the procedures that manipulate them.

Figure 6.7 An object-oriented database

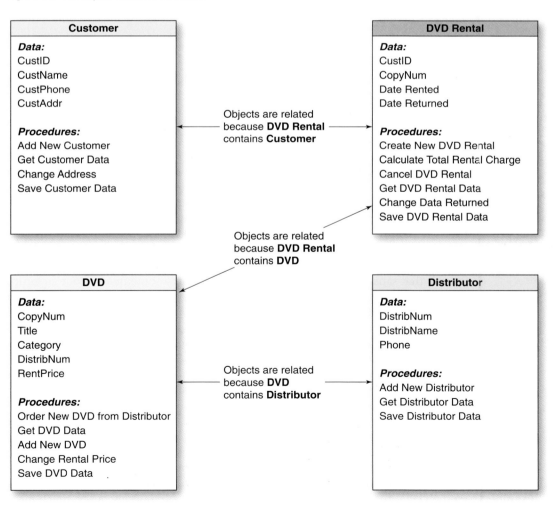

inheritance The ability in object-oriented structures to create a new object automatically by replicating all or some of the characteristics of a previously developed object.

in an object-oriented database. The relationships between data about entities are not kept by way of foreign keys, but through the relationships of one object with another. One advantage of this is the reduction of data redundancy.

Some data and information cannot be organized as fields, but they can be handled as objects, such as drawings, maps and web pages. All these capabilities make object-oriented DBMSs (OODBMSs) handy in computer-aided design (CAD), geographic information systems and applications used to update quickly thousands of web pages daily, because they can handle a wide range of data – such as graphics, voice and text – more easily than the relational model.

Similar to relational DBMSs, OODBMSs provide a graphical user interface (GUI) to manage the DBMS. The user can choose objects from 'classes', which are groups of objects that share similar characteristics. Elements of OODBMSs are often incorporated into relational databases, and such databases are sometimes known as *object-relational databases or hybrid databases*.

Object-oriented databases (OODBs) do not store records, but data objects, which is an advantage for quick updates of data sets and the relationships among them. For instance, in the example of the DVD store, in the OODB the relationship between a DVD and its distributor is not established through a foreign key; it exists because the DVD class contains the Distributor class. However, object-oriented databases also have some disadvantages, compared with relational databases. For example, there is dependence between applications and data; they are simply 'wrapped' together. Changing the structures of tables in a relational database does not require changes in applications that use the data in those tables, while it would require changes in applications in an object-oriented database. This dependence also limits the ability to enter *ad hoc* queries in an OODB, that is, to enter queries at will. While not as popular and as well understood as relational databases, OODBs are gaining adopters.

Several software companies have developed popular object-oriented DBMSs. Among them are Objectivity/DB (Objectivity Inc.), ObjectStore (Progress Software Inc.) and Versant (Versant Corporation).

Relational operations

CD TASK

relational operation An operation that creates a temporary table that is a subset of the original table or tables in a relational database.

As mentioned before, the most popular DBMSs are those that support the relational model. Therefore, it would be beneficial for you to familiarize yourself with a widely used relational database, such as Access, Oracle or SQL Server. To use the database, you should know how relational operations work. A relational operation creates a temporary table that is a subset of the original table or tables. It allows you to create a report containing records that satisfy a condition, create a list with only some fields about an entity, or produce a report from a join table, which combines relevant data from two or more tables. If so desired, the user can save the newly created table. Often, the temporary table is needed only for *ad hoc* reporting and is immediately discarded.

The three most important relational operations are *select*, *project* and *join*. *Select* is the selection of records that meet certain conditions. For example, a human resources manager might need a report showing the entire record of every employee whose salary exceeds € 60,000. *Project* is the selection of certain columns from a table, such as the salaries of all the employees. A query might specify a combination of selection and projection. In the preceding example, the manager might require only the ID number, last name (project) and salary of employees whose salaries are greater than € 60,000 (select).

One of the most useful manipulations of a relational database is the creation of a new table from two or more other tables. As you might recall from our discussion of the relational model, the joining of data from multiple tables is called a *join*. We have already used a simple example from the DVD store database (Figure 6.6). However, join queries can be much more complex. For example, a relational business database might have four tables: SalesRep, Catalogue, Order and Customer. A sales manager might wish to create a report showing, for each sales rep, a list of all of the customers who purchased anything last month, the items each customer purchased and the total amount spent by each customer. The new table is created from a relational operation that draws data from all four tables.

The join operation is a powerful manipulation that can create very useful reports for decision-making. A join table is created 'on the fly' as a result of a query and only for the duration the user wishes to view it or to create a paper report from it. Design features allow the user to change the field headings (although the field names are kept the same in the internal table), place the output in different layouts on the screen or paper and add graphics and text to the report. The new table might be saved as an additional table in the database.

Structured Query Language

Structured Query Language (SQL) has become the query language of choice for many developers of relational DBMSs. SQL is an international standard and is provided with most relational database management programs. Its strength is in its easy-to-remember intuitive commands. For instance, to create a list of all titles of thriller DVDs whose rental price is less than € 5.00, the query would be:

> **Structured Query Language (SQL)** The data definition and manipulation language of choice for many developers of relational database management systems.

> SELECT TITLE, CATEGORY FROM DVD
> WHERE CATEGORY = 'Thriller' AND RENTPRICE < 5;

Statements like this can be used for *ad hoc* queries or integrated in a program that is saved for repeated use. Commands for updating the database are also easy to remember: INSERT, DELETE and UPDATE.

There are several advantages to integrating SQL in a DBMS:

- With a standard language, users do not have to learn different sets of commands to create and manipulate databases in different DBMSs.
- SQL statements can be embedded in widely used third-generation languages such as Visual Basic or C and object-oriented languages such as C++ or Java, in which case these languages are called the 'host language'. The combination of highly tailored and efficient 3GL or object-oriented statements with SQL statements increases the efficiency and effectiveness of applications accessing relational databases.
- Because SQL statements are portable from one operating system to another, the programmer is not forced to rewrite statements.

Some relational DBMSs, such as Microsoft Access, provide GUIs to create SQL queries: SQL queries can be placed by clicking icons and selecting menu items, which are internally converted into SQL queries and executed. This capability allows relatively inexperienced database designers to use SQL.

The schema and metadata

When building a new database, users must first build a schema (from the Greek word for 'plan'). The schema describes the structure of the database being designed: the names and types of fields in each record type and the general relationships among different sets of records or files. It includes a description of the database's structure, the names and sizes of fields, and details such as which field is a primary key. The number of records is never specified because it might change, and the maximum number of records is determined by the capacity of the storage medium.

> **schema** The structure of a database, detailing the names and types of fields in each set of records, and the relationships among sets of records.

Fields can hold different types of data: numeric, alphanumeric, graphic or time-related. Numeric fields hold numbers that can be manipulated by addition,

Figure 6.8 Schema of the Employee table in an Access database

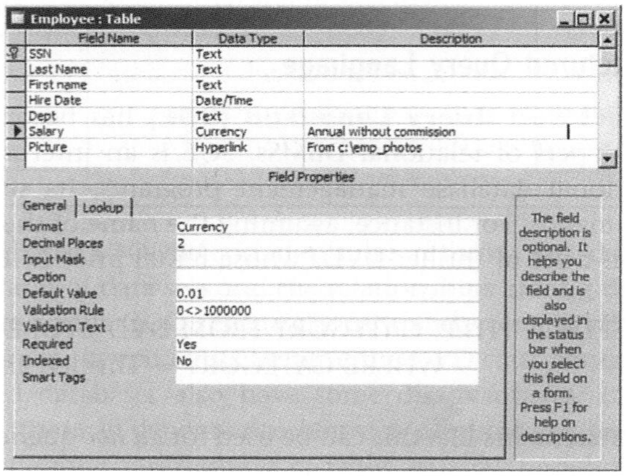

multiplication, averaging and the like. Alphanumeric fields hold textual values: words, numerals and special symbols, which make up names, addresses and identification numbers. Numerals entered in alphanumeric fields, such as National Insurance numbers or post codes, cannot be manipulated mathematically. The builder of a new database must also indicate which fields are to be used as primary keys. Many DBMSs also allow a builder to positively indicate when a field is not unique, meaning that the value in that field might be the same for more than one record.

Figure 6.8 presents the schema of a database table created with the Microsoft Access DBMS. The user is prompted to enter the names and types of fields. Access lets the user name the fields and determine the data types. The Description section allows the designer to describe the nature and function of the fields for people who maintain the database. In the lower part of the window the user is offered many options for each field, such as field size, format and so on. In Access the primary key field is indicated by a little key icon to its left.

data dictionary The part of the database that contains information about the different sets of records and fields, such as their source and who may change them.

The description of each table structure and types of fields become part of a **data dictionary**, which is a repository of information about the data and their organization. Designers usually add more information about each field, such as where the data come from (such as another system, or entered manually); who owns the original data; who is allowed to add, delete or update data in the field; and other details that help DBAs maintain the database and understand the meaning of the fields and their relationships. (Some people prefer to call this **metadata**, meaning 'data about the data'.) Metadata include:

metadata Information about the data in a database, often called data dictionary.

- The source of the data, including contact information.
- Tables that are related to the data.
- Field and index information, such as the size and type of the field (whether it is text or numeric), and the ways the data are sorted.
- Programs and processes that use the data.
- Population rules: what is inserted, or updated, and how often.

data modelling The process of charting existing or planned data stores and flows of an organization or one of its units. It includes charting of entity relationship diagrams.

Data modelling

Databases must be carefully planned and designed to meet business goals. How they are designed enables or limits flexibility in use. Analysing an organization's data and identifying the relationships among the data is called **data modelling**.

Data modelling should first be done to decide which data should be collected and how they should be organized. Thus, data modelling should be proactive. It is a good practice to create data models periodically, so that decision makers have a clear picture of what data are available for reports, and what data the organization might need to start collecting for improved decision-making. Managers can then ask experts to change the relationships and design new reports or applications that generate desired reports with a few keystrokes.

Many business databases consist of multiple tables with relationships among them. For example, a hospital might use a database that has a table holding the records of all its doctors, another one with all its nurses, another one with all the current patients, and so on. The administrative staff must be able to create reports that link data from multiple tables. For example, one report might be about a doctor and all her patients during a certain period. Another might revolve around a patient: details of the patient and a list of all the caregivers who were involved in his rehabilitation, as well as a list of medications. Thus, the database must be carefully planned to allow useful data manipulation and report generation.

Effective data modelling and design of each database involves the creation of a conceptual blueprint of the database. Such a blueprint is called an entity relationship diagram (ERD). An ERD is a graphical representation of all entity relationships, an example of which is shown in Figure 6.9, and they are often consulted to determine a problem with a query or to implement changes. Boxes are used to identify entities. Lines are used to indicate a relationship between entities. When lines shaped like crow's-feet are pointing to an object, there might be many instances of that object. When a link with a crow's-foot also includes a crossbar, then all instances of the object on the side of the crow's-foot are linked with a single instance of the object on the side of the crossbar. A second crossbar would denote 'mandatory', which means that the relationship must occur, such as between a book title and author: a book title must have an author with which it is associated. A circle close to the box denotes 'optional'.

> **entity relationship diagram (ERD)** One of several conventions for graphical rendition of the data elements involved in business processes and the logical relationships among the elements.

● In the figure, the crow's-foot on the Department end of the Department/University relationship indicates that there are several departments in one college, indicating a one-to-many relationship between University and Department. In addition, the crossbar at the University end of the University/Department link indicates that a department belongs to only one college.

● A department has many lecturers, but a lecturer might belong to more than one department; thus, the relationship between Lecturer and Department is many-to-many, represented by the crow's-feet at both ends of the link.

● A course is offered by a single department, indicated by the crossbar at the Department end of the Department/Course link.

● A lecturer might teach more than one student, and a student might have more than one lecturer, thus the crow's-feet at both the Lecturer and Student ends of the many-to-many relationship between Lecturer and Student.

Figure 6.9 An entity relationship diagram (ERD)

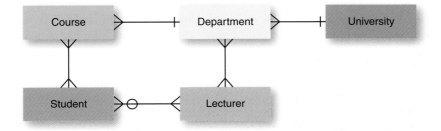

Figure 6.10 Fields of the Lecturer entity

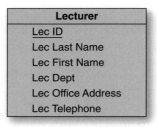

- However, the ring at the Student end indicates that a lecturer does not have to have students at all. The ring means 'optional', and is there for cases of lecturers (or professors) who concentrate on research and therefore do not teach.

Figure 6.9 provides an initial ERD. The designers must also detail the fields of each object, which determines the fields for each record of that object. The attributes are listed in each object box, and the primary key attribute is underlined. Usually, the primary key field appears at the top of the field list in the box. Figure 6.10 is an example of possible attributes of a Lecturer entity. You should be aware that database designers might use different notations. Therefore, before you review an ER diagram, be sure you understand what each symbol means.

The examples given here are quite simple. In reality, the reports that managers need to generate can be quite complex in terms of relationships among different data elements and the number of different tables from which they are assembled. Imagine the relationships among data maintained in libraries: a patron might borrow several titles; the library maintains several copies of each title; a title might be a book, a videotape or a CD; several authors might have published different books with the same title; librarians must be able to see availability and borrowed items by title, by author and by patron; they should also be able to produce a history report of all the borrowing of each patron for a certain period of time; and so on. All of these relationships and the various needs for reports must be taken into account when designing the database.

Databases on the Web

The Internet and its user-friendly Web would be practically useless if people could not access databases online. The premise of the Web is that people can not only browse appealing web pages but also search for and find information. Most often, that information is stored in databases. When a shopper accesses an online store, he or she can look for information about any of thousands, or hundreds of thousands, of items offered for sale. For example, when you access the site of Amazon.co.uk, you can receive online information (such as an image of an electronics item, price, shipping time and consumer evaluations) for thousands of items offered for sale. Wholesalers make their catalogues available online. Applications at auction sites receive enquiries by category, price range, country or origin, colour, date and other attributes and identify records of matching items, which often include pictures and detailed descriptions. Behind each of these sites is a database. The only way for organizations to conduct these web-based businesses is to give people outside the organizations access to their databases. In other words, the organizations must link their databases to the Internet.

From a technical point of view, online databases that are used with web browsers are no different from other databases. However, an interface must be designed to work with the Web. The user must see a form in which to enter queries or keywords to obtain information from the site's database. The interface designers must provide a mechanism to figure out data

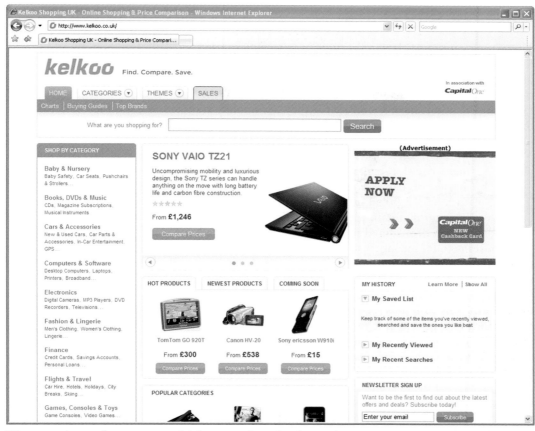

When you shop online you query databases and receive the results on your screen

that users insert in the online forms so that they can be placed in the proper fields in the database. The system also needs a mechanism to pass queries and keywords from the user to the database. There are several such interface programs, including CGI (Common Gateway Interface), Java servlets and active server pages (ASPs), as well as API (application program interface). The technical aspects of these applications are beyond the scope of this book. The process is diagrammed in Figure 6.11.

To ensure that their production databases are not vulnerable to attack via the Internet, organizations avoid linking their transaction databases to the Internet unless these are databases dedicated to online transactions, in which case the organization must apply proper security software. They must also be careful when linking a data warehouse (discussed next) to the Internet.

Figure 6.11   Active server pages and similar software enable data queries and entry via the Web

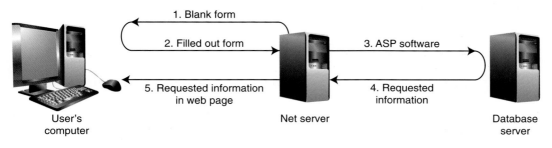

1. Blank form

2. Filled out form

3. ASP software

5. Requested information
in web page

4. Requested
information

User's
computer

Net server

Database
server

Data warehousing

The great majority of data collections in business are used for daily transactions and operations: records of customers and their purchases and information on employees, patients and other parties for monitoring, collection, payment and other business or legal purposes. The transactions do not stay in these databases long; usually only a few days or weeks. However, many organizations have found that if they accumulate transaction data, they can use it for important management decisions, such as researching market trends or tracking down fraud. Organizing and storing data for such purposes is called data warehousing.

data warehouse A huge collection of historical data that can be processed to support management decision-making.

A data warehouse is a large, typically relational, database that supports management decision-making. The database is large because it contains data, or summaries of data, from millions of transactions over many years and/or from national or global transactions rather than from a short period or a single region. It might maintain records of individual transactions or summaries of transactions for predetermined periods, such as hourly, daily or weekly. The purpose of data warehouses is to let managers produce reports or analyse large amounts of archival data and make decisions. Data-warehousing experts must be familiar with the types of business analyses that will be done with the data. They also have to design the data warehouse tables to be flexible enough for modifications in years to come, when business activities change or when different information must be extracted.

Data warehouses do not replace transactional databases, which are updated with daily transactions such as sales, billing, cash receipts and returns. Instead, transactional data are copied into the data warehouse, which is a separate database. This large archive contains valuable information for the organization that might not be evident in the smaller amounts of data typically stored in transactional databases. For example, an insurance company might keep monthly tables of policy sales; it can then see trends in the types of policies customers prefer in general or by age group. Such trends are meaningful only if they are gleaned from data collected over several years. Data from transactional databases are added to the data

data mart A collection of archival data that is part of a data warehouse, usually focusing on one aspect of the organization such as sales of a family of products or daily revenues in a geographic region.

warehouse at the end of each business day, week or month, or might be added automatically as soon as a transaction is recorded in a transactional database. While a transactional database contains current data, which are disposed of after some time, the data in data warehouses are accumulated and might reflect many years of business activities.

Businesses often organize their data warehouse as a collection of data marts, smaller collections of data that focus on a particular subject or department. If data marts need to be used as one large data warehouse, special software tools can unify data marts and make them appear as one large data warehouse.

Industry SNAPSHOT

Data explosion

Albert Einstein said 'We can't solve problems by using the same kind of thinking we used when we created them.' This is also true of the technology that has lead to the vast increase in data held by companies worldwide. Typically a business today stores ten times more data than in 2000 and according to Gartner, one of the world's leading IT research and advisory companies, storage requirements are likely to increase by a factor of 30 by 2012.

SOURCE: 'Dealing with the data explosion', Richard Soundy, ComputerWeekly. com, 4 September 2007

Ethical and Societal ISSUES

Every move you make

The widespread use of database management systems coupled with web technologies allows organizations to collect, maintain and sell vast amounts of private personal data fast and cheaply. Millions of credit-card transactions take place in the world, each carrying private information. Millions of personal data items are routed daily to corporate databases through sales calls and credit checks. Millions of consumer records are collected and updated daily on the Web. For businesses, such data are an important resource; for individuals, such large data pools and the ways they are used threaten a fundamental human right: privacy.

Out of hand – Out of control You have just received a letter from the John Doe Investment Co. In the letter, the president tells you that at your age, with a nice income like yours, the company could provide you with innovative investment services. How did the company know about your existence? About your annual income? Could it be that some time ago you applied for a credit card? The company receiving the information sold part of it, or all of it, to the John Doe Investment Co. You now enjoy your credit card but you paid a hidden cost for it.

The Web: a source of data collection In the preceding example, you were at least aware that you gave somebody information. But many consumers provide information routinely without being aware of it. A huge amount of personal data is now collected through the Web. You might wonder why the home pages of so many websites ask you to register with them. When registering, you often provide your name, address and other details. The site asks you to create a user ID and password. If the pages you are accessing contain private data such as your investment portfolio, a user ID and password protect you, but if you are accessing news or other nonpersonal pages, a user ID and password actually serve the site operator. From the moment you log on to the site, the server can collect data about every move you make: which pages you are watching and for how long, which icons you click and in which order, and which advertising banners you click. In many cases, the organization that collects the data doesn't even own the site. The site owner hires a business such as DoubleClick to collect data. When you click an advertisement, that information is channelled into DoubleClick's huge database. What does the firm do with the database? It sells parts of it to other companies, or it slices and dices the information to help other companies target potential buyers belonging to certain demographic groups. And, no, it does not bother to tell you. While the software of such companies as DoubleClick can only identify the computer or IP number from which you logged on to a site and not you, personally, the information can be matched with you, personally, if you also use your personal ID and password.

Web bugs In addition to Web cookies, companies also use clear GIFs to track our web movements. A 'clear GIF', better known as a 'web beacon' or 'web bug', is a graphic image on a website used to monitor a surfer's activity. The image is usually undetectable because it usually consists of a single pixel. The bug links the web page to the web server of a third party, such as DoubleClick. The third party's server obtains the URL (web address) of the user as well as the URL of the site from which the user views the page. As long as the bug is 'displayed' by the user's computer, the third-party server can request session information from the user's web browser. Session information includes click stream and other activities performed by the user while visiting the site. In DoubleClick's own words: 'Companies use clear GIFs on their websites to learn more about their visitors' use of their websites and may be used to target ads to those visitors on other websites' (www.doubleclick.com/us/about_doubleclick/privacy/clear-gifs.asp).

Our health online Allowing medical staff and pharmacists to share patient medical information might help them help us. Imagine yourself being injured on a trip thousands of miles from your home. If the doctor treating you can immediately receive information about your sensitivities to certain medications, it might save your life. However, any electronic record residing on a database that is connected to a public network is potentially exposed to unauthorized access by people who do not have a legitimate need to know.

The upside In spite of the downside of collection of personal data, there is also a positive side. Database technology enables companies to provide us with better and faster services. It also makes the market more competitive. Small firms often cannot afford the great expense of data collection. For much less money, they can purchase sorted data – the same data that are available to the big, strong industry leader. So, the wide availability of data contributes to a more egalitarian and democratic business environment. The winners are not only vendors but also consumers, who can purchase new and cheaper products.

And while many of us complain that these huge databases add to the glut of junk mail and spam, better information in the hands of marketers might actually save consumers from such annoyances.

After all, those annoying communications are for products and services you don't need. With more specific information, marketers can target only those individuals that might be interested in their offerings. While you shop, special tracking software can tell the online business, at least indirectly, what you do not like about the site. This enables businesses to improve their services. For example, many online retailers discovered that a hefty proportion of shoppers abandoned their virtual shopping carts just before the final purchase. Analysis of collected information discovered that some people wanted to know the handling and shipping charges before they charged their credit cards. Now, most online retailers provide clear shipping information and charges earlier.

From database to data warehouse

Unlike data warehouses, transactional databases are usually not suitable for business analysis because they contain only current, not historical, data. Often, data in transactional databases are also scattered in different systems throughout an organization. The same data can be stored differently and under other names. For example, customer names might be recorded in a column called Name in one table and in two columns – First Name and Last Name – in another table. These discrepancies commonly occur when an organization uses both its own data and data it purchases from other organizations, or if it has developed more than one database that contains the same data under a different label. When management decides to build a data warehouse, the IT staff must carefully consider the hardware, software and data involved in the effort.

The larger the data warehouse, the larger the storage capacity, the greater the memory and the greater the processing power of the computers that are needed. Because of capacity needs, organizations often choose mainframe computers with multiple CPUs to store and manage data warehouses. The computer memory must be large enough to allow processing of huge amounts of data at once. The amount of storage space and the access speed of disks are also important. Processing millions of records might take a long time, and variations in disk speed might mean the difference between hours or minutes in processing time. And since a data warehouse is considered a highly valuable asset, all data must be automatically backed up. Keep in mind that data warehouses grow continually, because their very purpose is to accumulate historical records. Retail chains such as Tesco record millions of sales transactions daily, all of which are channelled into data warehouses. Some have data warehouses that hold tens or hundreds of terabytes of data. However, not only retailers have augmented their hardware for large data warehouses. So have banks, credit-card issuers and health-care organizations, among other industries. Many organizations accumulate not only sales transactions but also purchasing records so they can produce information from which to make better purchasing decisions, such as which suppliers tend to offer lower prices for certain items at certain times of the year.

The data from which data warehouses are built usually come from within an organization, mainly from transactions, but they can also come from outside an organization. The latter

Industry **SNAPSHOT**

The data behemoth

Wal-Mart, the world's largest company, is well known for its appetite for retail data. With 6000 stores worldwide and 100 million people passing through its doors every week, the company is a voracious collector of data. In 2005, the company had 260 terabytes of data in its data warehouses on mainframe computers in Bentonville, Arkansas, USA, where it is headquartered. Experts estimated that this amount of data was twice as large as all the data posted on the world's websites.

ASDA, a major UK supermarket chain, is owned by Wal-Mart.

PHOTO SOURCE: © ASDA.COM

might include national or regional demographic data, data from financial markets and weather data. Similar to metadata in any database, data-warehouse designers create metadata for their large data pools. To uncover the valuable information contained in their data, organizations must use software that can effectively 'mine' data warehouses. Data mining is covered in Chapter 10, 'Business Intelligence and Knowledge Management'.

The designers must keep in mind scalability: the ability of the data warehouse to grow as the amount of the data and the processing needs grow. Future growth needs involve good planning in terms of both hardware and software.

Phases in building a data warehouse

Once an organization has ensured that it has adequate hardware and software, it can begin building the data warehouse. Three phases are involved in building a data warehouse from transactional data: extraction, transforming and loading (ETL). Figure 6.12 describes the process.

In the *extraction* phase the builders create the files from transactional databases and save them on the server that will hold the data warehouse. In the *transformation* phase the builders 'cleanse' the data and modify it into a form that allows insertion into the data warehouse. For example, they ascertain whether the data contain any spelling errors, and if there are any, they fix them. They make sure that all data are consistent. For instance, Warwickshire might be denoted as Warks, Warwicks or Warwickshire. Only one form would be used in a data warehouse. The builders ensure that all addresses follow the same form, using uppercase or lowercase letters consistently and defining fields uniformly (such as one field for the entire street address and a separate field for post codes). All the data that express the same type of quantities are 'cleansed' to use the same measurement units.

In the *loading* phase the builders transfer the transformed files to the data warehouse. They then compare the data in the data warehouses with the original data to ascertain completeness. They document the data for users, so the users know what they can find and analyse in the data warehouse.

Figure 6.12 Phases in preparing and using a data warehouse

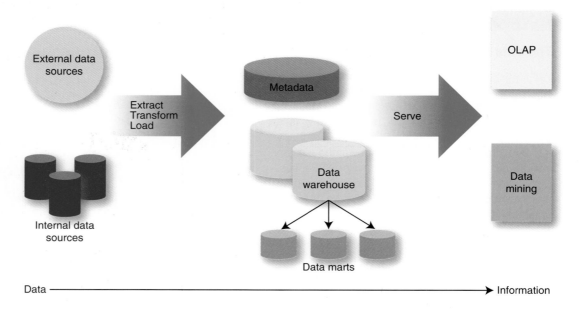

The new warehouse is then ready for use. It is a single source for all the data required for analysis, it is accessible to more users than the transactional databases (whose access is probably limited only to those who record transactions), and it provides a 'one-stop shopping' place for data. In fact, it is not unusual for a data warehouse to have large tables with fifty or more fields (attributes).

Once the data warehouse is in operation, much of the ETL activity can be automated. Depending on the needs of its users, the structure and content of the data warehouse might be changed occasionally. Once the data warehouse is ready, techniques such as data mining and online analytical processing (OLAP) can be used to exploit it. Managers can then extract business intelligence for better decision-making. Data mining, OLAP and business intelligence are discussed in Chapter 10.

SUMMARY

In their daily operations, organizations can collect vast amounts of data. These data are raw material for highly valuable information, but data are useless without tools to organize them, store them in an easily accessible manner, and manipulate them to produce that information. These functions are the great strength of databases: collections of interrelated data that, within an organization and sometimes between organizations, are shared by many units and contribute to productivity and efficiency.

The database approach has several advantages over the more traditional file approach: less data redundancy, application-data independence and greater probability of data integrity.

The smallest piece of data collected about an entity is a character. Multiple characters make up a field. Several fields make up a record. A collection of related records is a file, or in the relational model, a table. Databases usually contain several files, but the database approach can be applied to a single file.

A database management system (DBMS) is a software tool that enables us to construct databases, populate them with data and manipulate the data. Most DBMSs come with 4GLs that can be used to develop applications that facilitate queries and produce reports.

There are several database models, which are general logical structures of records in a database: hierarchical, network, relational and object-oriented. By far, the most popular model is the relational model, which is used to build most new databases, although object-oriented databases are gaining popularity. Some vendors offer DBMSs that accommodate a combination of relational and object-oriented models, called object-relational.

The links among entities in a relational database are maintained by the use of keys. Primary keys are unique identifiers. Composite keys are combinations of two or more fields that are used as a primary key. Foreign keys link one table to another within the database.

In an object-oriented database, data sets along with the procedures that process them are objects. The relationship between one set of data and another is by way of one object containing the other, rather than by foreign keys.

SQL has been adopted as an international standard language for querying relational databases. SQL statements can also be embedded in code that is produced using many programming languages.

To construct a database, a designer first constructs a schema and prepares metadata, which is information about the data to be kept in the database.

To plan databases, designers conduct data modelling. Before they design a database they create entity relationship diagrams, which show the tables required for each data entity and the attributes (fields) it should hold, as well as the relationships between tables. Then they can move on to constructing a schema, which is the structure of all record structures of the entities, and the relationships among them.

Many databases are linked to the Web for remote use. This arrangement requires web server software, such as active server pages and Java servlets, which allow users to enter queries or update databases over the Internet.

Data warehouses are huge collections of historical transactions copied from transactional databases, often along with other data from outside sources. Managers use software tools to glean useful information from data warehouses to support their decision-making. Some data warehouses are made up of several data marts, each focusing on an organizational unit or a subject.

In each addition of data from a transactional database to a data warehouse, the data are extracted, transformed and loaded, a process known by its acronym, ETL.

The low price of efficient and effective database software exacerbates a societal problem of the Information Age: invasion of privacy. Because every transaction of an individual can be easily recorded and later combined with other personal data, it is inexpensive to produce whole dossiers on individual consumers. This poses a threat to privacy. However, commercial organizations insist that they need personal information to improve their products and services and to target their marketing only to interested consumers.

TRENT COURIER SERVICES REVISITED

Trent Couriers gathers and maintains many types of data in its database. It has tried to ensure its security and safe backup while still being accessible to customers and employees. Let's explore some of the issues it faces in managing its database.

What would you do?

1 Trent Couriers' database is vital to its operations. The case at the beginning of the chapter didn't mention its supplier data. Trent Couriers has suppliers for its fleet of cars and vans and for its office supplies. What sorts of data would it likely keep about its suppliers? What controls and limits should it put on its supplier data? Make a recommendation to Andrew Langston on who should be able to review and change that data and where the data should be maintained.

2 Andrew had run into IT consultant Karen Brown many times and began talking to her about his IT concerns. When he realized that he was going to need a database management system, he decided to take her advice and purchase Oracle. What sort of research should Andrew have done to make sure that Oracle was the best solution? What advantages and disadvantages should he have considered when purchasing a new DBMS?

New perspectives

1 Trent Couriers has used SQL queries and reports to identify VIP customers and discover its most profitable clients and services. It also has a website. How could it use website tracking data to enhance its services? What departments would be interested in this information? Discuss and list as many as you can.

2 Andrew has heard that databases can also store digital images. Are there any parts of Trent Couriers' data operations that might use digital images? If so, which?

Review questions

1 It is easier to organize data and retrieve it when there is little or no dependence between programs and data. Why is there more such dependence in a file approach and less in the database approach?

2 Spreadsheets have become quite powerful for data management. What can be done with database management systems that cannot be done with spreadsheet applications? Give several examples.

3 What is the difference between a database and a database management system?

4 DBMSs are usually bundled with powerful 4GL modules. Why?

5 What are the advantages and disadvantages of object-oriented databases?

6 What is the relationship between a website's local search engines and online databases?

7 When constructing a database, the designer must know what types of relationships exist between records in different data sets, such as one-to-many or many-to-many. Give three examples for each of these relationships.

8 Can you think of a one-to-one relationship in a relational database? Give an example.

9 What is SQL? In which database model does it operate? Why is it so popular?

10 What is a data warehouse? How is it different from a transactional database?

11 Why is it not advisable to query data from transactional databases for executive decision-making the same way you do data warehouses?

12 What are the phases of adding data to a data warehouse?

13 What does it mean to cleanse data before they are stored in a data warehouse?

14 What are data marts? How different are they from data warehouses?

Discussion questions

1 Retail chains want to ensure that every time a customer returns to purchase something, the record of that purchase can be matched with previous data of that individual. What objects that consumers often use help the retailers in that regard?

2 Increasingly, corporate databases are updated by their consumers rather than corporate employees. How so?

3 Can you think of an industry that would not benefit from the promise of a data warehouse? Explain.

4 Shouldn't those who build data warehouses trim the data before they load it to data warehouses? Why do they usually not cut any data from transactions?

5 The combination of RFID and database technology will soon enable retailers to record data about consumers even when they have not purchased anything at the store. Can you think of an example and how the data could be used?

6 A retailer of household products maintains a data warehouse. In addition to data from sales transactions, the retailer also purchases and maintains in it daily weather data. What might be the reason?

7 Many organizations have posted privacy policies at their websites. Why do you think this is so?

8 Consider the following opinion shared by some people: database management systems and data-warehousing techniques are the greatest threat to individual privacy in modern times. What is your opinion?

9 The proliferation of organizational databases poses a threat to privacy. After reading the following passage, what would you say to someone in response to these statements: 'I'm a law-abiding citizen and pay my taxes promptly. I don't care if anyone reviews my university grades or my income statements, because I have nothing to hide. I have no reason to worry about violation of my privacy. All these complaints about violation of privacy are not valid. Only individuals who have something to hide need to worry.'

10 Civil rights advocates demand that organizations ask individuals for permission to sell personal information about them. Some also demand that the subjects of the information be paid for their consent. Organizations have argued that they cannot practically comply with these demands and that the demands interfere with the free flow of information. What is your opinion?

11 Organizations whose websites offer visitors some control of how their personal information is collected and used offer one of two options: 'opt out' or 'opt in'. Explain each term.

12 Some people say that as long as the concept of 'informed consent' is applied, individuals should not complain about invasion of their privacy. What is 'informed consent'? Do you agree with the argument?

13 The affordability of sophisticated DBMSs and data warehouses makes the business world more 'democratic' and puts all businesses almost on an equal footing. How so? Explain.

14 Businesses rarely allow customers to scrutinize and correct records that the organizations keep about them. Technologically, does the Web make it less expensive for organizations to allow that?

Tutorial activities

1 Acxiom.co.uk is a data services firm. Browse this company's site and research its activities at its own site and at other websites. Write a two-page summary of the company's activity: What does the company sell? How does it obtain what it sells? Who are its customers, and what

do they do with what they purchase from Acxiom?

2　Research the business of DoubleClick.com. What type of data does the company collect and sell? How does it collect the data? Who are the company's customers, and how do they use the services or data they buy from DoubleClick?

3　Research web resources to write a two- to four-page research paper titled 'Object-Oriented Databases', in which you explain the differences and similarities between relational databases and object-oriented databases, and their comparative advantages and disadvantages.

4　Mid-County Hospital holds data on doctors and patients in two tables in its database (see the tables below): DOCTOR and PATIENT. Use your DBMS to build the appropriate schema, enter the records and create the reports described.

　　a)　A report showing the following details for each doctor in this order: Last Name, First Name and Ward. Arrange the report by ascending alphabetical order of the last names.

　　b)　A report showing the entire record with the original order of columns of all the doctors whose salary is greater than €100,000 who work for either one of the following wards: Internal (INT), Obstetric-Gynecological (OBG), Oncology (ONC).

　　c)　A report showing the following details for all of Dr Anderson's patients. Dr Anderson's first and last name should appear once at the top of the report. In each record, the join report should show Doctor's ID, Last Name and Ward (from the DOCTOR table), and Patient's Last Name, First Name and Date of Admission (from the PATIENT table).

5　Mr Lawrence Husick is an inventor who, with other inventors, obtained several patents. Use the search engine found at http://gb.espacenet.com/ to search the UK Intellectual Property Office to find all the patents that mention Lawrence Husick as an inventor. Type up the patent numbers along with their corresponding patent titles (what the invention is).

6　Your team is to design a relational database for an online pizza service. Customers log on to the site and provide their first and last names, address, telephone number and email address. They order pizza from a menu. Assume that each item on the menu has a unique number, a description and a price. Assume there is one person per shift who receives orders and takes care of them, from giving the order to the kitchen to dispatching a delivery person. The system automatically records the time at which the server picked up the order. The business wants to maintain the details of customers, including their orders of the past six months. The following are reports that management might require: (1) a list of all the orders handled by a server over a period of time; (2) summaries of total sales, by item, for a period; and (3) a report showing all of the past week's deliveries by server, showing each individual order – customer last name and address, items ordered, time of order pickup and last name of delivery person. (You can assume the last names of delivery people are unique, because if there is more than one with the same last name, a number is added to the name.)

　　a)　Chart the table for each entity, including all its fields and the primary key.

　　b)　Draw the entity relationship diagram.

DOCTOR

ID#	LIC#	Last Name	First Name	Ward	Salary
102	8234	Hogg	Yura	INT	187,000
104	4666	Tyme	Justin	INT	91,300
221	2908	Jones	Jane	OBG	189,650
243	7876	Anderson	Ralph	ONC	101,800
256	5676	Jones	Ernest	ORT	123,400
376	1909	Washington	Jaleel	INT	87,000
410	4531	Carrera	Carlos	ORT	97,000

PATIENT

NIN	Last N	First N	Admission Date	Insurance	Doc ID
055675432	Hopkins	Jonathan	01/04/06	BlueCross	221
101234566	Bernstein	Miriam	28/04/07	HAP	243
111654456	McCole	John	31/03/06	Kemper	221
200987898	Meanny	Marc	27/02/07	HAP	221
367887654	Mornay	Rebecca	03/04/06	HAP	410
378626254	Blanchard	George	30/03/07	BlueCross	243
366511122	Rubin	David	01/04/06	Brook	243

7   Your team should contact a large organization, such as a bank, an insurance company or a hospital. Interview the database administrator about the database he or she maintains on customers (or patients). What are the measures that the DBA has taken to protect the privacy of the subjects whose records are kept in the databases? Consider accuracy, timeliness and appropriate access to personal records. Write a report on your findings. If you found loopholes in the procedures, list them and explain why they are loopholes and how they can be remedied. Alternatively, log on to the site of a company that posted a detailed privacy policy and answer the same questions.

Companion CD questions

1   You and a friend would like to catalogue your CD collections. Create a simple database that will hold all of your titles in one table and your friend's titles in another table.

2   Write a query to show you which titles you and your friend both own.

From ideas to application
REAL CASES

Case study 6.1

Coping with growth

TÜV NORD Group is one of Germany's largest technical service providers offering a wide range of consulting, testing and servicing. It is particularly well known throughout Germany for its automobile emissions testing centres and has expertise in most areas of technical safety, environmental protection and the conformity assessment of management systems and products. It has a workforce of nearly 7000 and is represented in 36 countries throughout Europe, Asia and America. It has recently merged with another company, Rheinisch-Westfälisch, leading to a potential doubling in size of its 2 terabyte SAP Business Warehouse (BW). This mission-critical database contains performance data from a vast number of company activities such as safety inspections, security testing and so on.

In addition to the doubling in size of the BW database, the merged companies expected a growth in employment in excess of 35 per cent. In order to cope with this growth the company decided to update its BW software and database management system. This allows more concurrent users without a corresponding degradation of response time.

The figures are quite mind-boggling. The group manages its IT operations with four administrators responsible for the database, operating system, server hardware and storage area network. The BW holds 2.1 terabytes (expected to increase to 4 terabytes) and is stored along with 25 multidimensional analytical data cubes, each with 16 dimensions. In addition, the company manages 24 terabytes of totally raw storage, prior to 'cleansing'. 'Our SAP system has perhaps 35,000 tables, and every table has three or four indexes', according to Sven Otromke, SAP system Manager of TÜV NORD Group. 'As we customize the system we add more indexes, but after several years it

The sign for a TÜV centre in Germany.

is difficult to remember exactly why any given index was added. With Dynamic Management Views you can see how long it has been since an index has been used, and this helps us decide when indexes can be removed. Every time we can remove an extraneous index, it means one less index needs to be maintained, and this in turn improves performance.'

It is not just the physical storage and handling of the large volumes of data that cause problems. The administrator of the Storage Area Network (SAN) needs to be aware of back-up and recovery procedures. Before the merger, the use of local tape streamers was sufficient as the data volume was less than 20 GB. However, the increase in data volume meant that TÜV NORD needed to move to a system of tape libraries located in the data centres in Hanover, Hamburg and Essen, while smaller locations are connected to the large office geographically closest to them. Depending on what they want to access, employees can access data either from a central location or via local servers in the branch offices. Backup is carried out incrementally on a daily basis and once a week TÜV NORD carries out a full backup of the complete storage volume. For legal reasons, the data held by TÜV NORD require long-term archiving. Data are transferred to media which can then be stored in a safe location away from the primary site.

The TÜV NORD Group also makes use of database mirroring. A 'hot-standby' of the live system is maintained by sending a replica of each transaction to the mirror database. Therefore with the live database in Hannover and a mirror in Hamburg the group can provide continuous working. If, for example, the Hannover centre becomes non-operational because of a fire, then the Hamburg centre can fill in immediately.

Thinking about the case

1 Does TÜV Nord need to have a different approach to operational data and archived data? Does it need a different approach to data that it archives for legal reasons and old data that it can use for strategic development?

2 The use of a mirror database seems to solve all the problems of data recovery. Is this true? What are the costs?

SOURCE: 'Germany's TUEV NORD Deploys SQL Server 2005 for 2-Terabyte SAP Business Warehouse', http://www.microsoft.com/casestudies and 'Securing Data with Software Solutions from Symantec. TÜV Nord Gruppe', http://www.symantec.com/enterprise/solutions/successes/detail.jsp?csid=tuv_nord_gruppe

Case study **6.2**

Children at risk . . .

As a result of the Public Inquiry held into the child abuse case involving Victoria Climbié the Children's Bill passed into UK law in November 2004. Victoria died after years of abuse by relatives. Part of the problem was that several agencies (social services, the police, etc.) each had only part of the information about Victoria and there was no way for these pieces of information to be brought together. An important aspect of the Bill proposed the setting up of a central children's database and the UK government announced in 2005 that the database, the Information Sharing Index, would be operational by the end of 2008 with a view to improving the welfare protection of young people. The central register would be accessible to all relevant agencies and organizations with the intention of facilitating effective and speedy response to problems and concerns. This involves the establishment of 150 local authority registers coordinated by an over-arching system that creates a single identification number for all children.

Any professional who comes into contact with a child, such as a doctor or social worker, can add a flag indicating a concern. Nine local authorities were chosen to pilot the scheme and as a result the Department for Education and Science (DfES) told all local authorities that they must have an Integrated Children's System (ICS) in place by January 2007. Some local authorities created systems more advanced than that required by the

The Information Sharing Index was designed to improve communication across organizations but the idea has created significant debate.

PHOTO SOURCE: © ANTHONY TUENI

DfES. According to Carey Sherman, Somerset's business and finance manager for children's social care, 'Limiting ourselves to the government's ICS requirements would confuse staff because some of the processes finished at an odd point and our social workers would have to operate two different systems.'

Whilst no one would argue with the principles behind the initiative, there are various criticisms about the implementation. According to Anna Smallwood of Socitm Consulting, there is confusion in many local authorities about the integration of the ICS with other government child care initiatives as well as with other local authority IT systems. Lack of effective training for child social workers could also be a problem. 'Social workers want better quality systems to help them analyse the information they are taking in, but some of them will need time to understand the new ways of doing things.'

However, the most stinging criticism came in a report published in November 2006 by the Foundation for Information Policy Research (FIPR) which suggested that the database will actually put children at greater risk.

'The proposed surveillance system is contrary to the basic principles of data protection and human rights law', said Professor Douwe Korff of London Metropolitan University, one of the authors of the report.

'It replaces professional discretion (in both meanings of the word) with computerised assessments of human behaviour that are inherently fallible.'

'The system violates private and family life and intrudes on children's rights without justification. The government's aims are laudable, but this is not the way to go about achieving them.'

The report suggests that the £200 million (nearly € 300 million) cost will divert money from more traditional child care. This economic argument is one made against many IT systems and is answered simply by conducting a cost/benefit analysis. Not so easily dealt with is the issue of data protection and privacy. By opening the database to so many agencies that can then draw conclusions from the data, there is a real danger of mistakes being made. The report cites an example whereby a nine-year-old child was taken into care after social workers misinterpreted medical data. In another example, police shared information about a nine-month-old child under the guise of crime prevention. With so many people, over 400,000 civil servants, having access to the database, there is potential for many more such cases. According to Professor Ross Anderson, chair of the FIPR, 'when building systems that process personal information, you can have scale, or functionality or security. You can even have any two of these, but you cannot have all three. If we are to have secure and functional child protection systems, they will have to be local rather than central.'

The most worrying aspect of the database, according to the report, is that of what it calls 'e-discrimination'. To quote part of the executive summary of the report, 'In the past, it has been well documented that children who were black, or from poor neighbourhoods or travelling families, suffered disproportionate police attention because of the expectation that they would be more likely to offend. The expectation could easily turn into a self-fulfilling prophecy. A system that attempts to predict which children will become delinquent, by totting up negative indicators from health, school and other records, runs the serious risk of recreating the same problems – especially as the information, analysis and professional opinions it contains will be made available to many of the public-sector workers who come into contact with the child. A perfectly law-abiding youngster from a difficult home background, who has perhaps struggled to overcome learning and health difficulties, may find at every turn that teachers expect less, and that police attention is more likely. As the causes of this discrimination are online, the youngster cannot mitigate them simply by dressing neatly and being polite. The data and algorithms used as a basis for discrimination might not be accessible to the victim (whether practically or at all) and thus a victim of unjustified discrimination might end up with no recourse. This raises serious data protection concerns relating to the appropriateness of collecting, processing and retaining the data.'

Child abuse is a very emotive subject and anything that can reduce the risks must be a good idea. However, as can be seen from the above arguments, there are other issues that must be taken into account when proposing the bringing together of data from a variety of sources and opening the database up to many people. Similar arguments have been raised in the UK over the introduction of identity cards and the creation of a comprehensive DNA database.

Thinking about the case

1   Professor Anderson suggests that the problem with the national database could be resolved by having 150 local, unconnected databases. Do you think this would solve the problem? Are there any drawbacks with this approach?

2   As stated above, proposals to introduce a database containing DNA data about every UK citizen has resulted in heated debate. What are the advantages? What are the drawbacks?

SOURCE: Iain Thomson, 'Children's database puts kids at risk', http://www.computing.co.uk/vnunet/news/2169272/children-database-puts-kids; Ross Anderson et al., Foundation for Information Policy Research, 'Children's Databases – Safety and Privacy', http://www.fipr.org/childrens_databases.pdf

Case study **6.3**

Tesco

BY SCOTT RAEBURN

Tesco is the UK's grocer, or so many people think. It is, of course, so much more than that. A truly colossal global company, it is the UK's market leading supermarket with over 30 per cent market share. Its leading competitor has less than 20 per cent share. But a look at the 2007 Annual Report paints a much larger picture. This group valued at more than £40 billion had revenue of £42.6 billion in the year ended February 2007. Its annual profits were £2.6 billion, or about £82 per second, 24/7. It employs 413,000 people in 1898 UK stores and 1365 other stores worldwide, including Eastern Europe, Turkey and China. When it opened its first store in the USA in late 2007 it truly had a supermarket empire 'on which the sun never sets' (with apologies to Queen Victoria).

Tesco was founded in 1919 in London's East End by a collaboration between a tea retailer (T. E. Stockwell) and Jack Cohen, who wanted to sell tea and other groceries. From a single market stall to listing on the London Stock Exchange in 1947 to being the UK's second leading supermarket grocery chain by the early 1990s, Jack and his successors proved that they could. So what changed in the mid 1990s that made them world beaters? What makes 12+ million customers use their Clubcard to shop in Tesco at least once per week? The answer is simple – data information and the way Tesco used it.

The pivotal moment was when Tesco brought in the firm of dunnhumby (yes, it is all lowercase!) to help with analysing data from a loyalty card scheme it had tried in three stores. With dunnhumby's help, the trial was extended to run through 1994, generating till data, analysing it the dunnhumby way and sending appropriate rewards to the customers.

The new insight which generated the rewards is now called 'relevance marketing' by dunnhumby. Traditional market segmentation schemes were based on what the customer was – gender, age, educational attainment, job, area lived in and so on. Customers were 'averages' of each type, according to which classification scheme was used. Dunnhumby instead worked on the concept that customers should be classified by what they bought (and didn't buy) in-store. Each individual customer should be identified and their buying patterns remembered, in an updated version of what traditional British corner shops did back in the 1950s and 1960s. Instead of sending a promotional offer to all customers, send an individual reward to each customer based on his/her buying pattern. This can encourage repeat spending for some goods and tempt the customer with offers on others. And it worked. The trial stores in and around Tesco Head Office all showed very positive customer response to the Clubcard scheme. When rolled out across the stores, it led to a step-change in Tesco's performance. About five years after introducing Clubcard, Tesco was the UK market leader. Today it is exporting its approach across the world. And it's all based on analysing data effectively.

Dunnhumby does this by adding in classifications to data as they arrive from tills and stores. Each transaction has 40–50 customer classifications added. It forms part of a time series going back to when the customer joined Clubcard. Each product also has about as many variables attached to it and the

The Tesco Clubcard's success has provided the company with unparalleled information on its customers.

cross-correlation of customer patterns and product attributes provides the base data for Tesco's Clubcard operations.

It is said that the dunnhumby database contains 40+ terabytes of data; that it could drill-down to find everything an individual cardholder had bought in the past ten years! Clive Humby, one of the founders of dunnhumby, saw data-mining as an art as well as a science. Normal database work is based on queries, constructed by a user in a language such as SQL (Structured Query Language), which the database then reports on. Data-mining turns that on its head and uses software to tell the user about relationships within the data; it tells the user which questions to ask! Add to that Zodiac, dunnhumby's software to find external sources of data which can supplement the till purchase data, and interesting patterns emerge. The dunnhumby database takes data from the electoral roll, the Land Registry (England and Wales) and the General Register Office (Scotland), the Office of National Statistics and others.

The UK's three large credit reference companies, Experian, Equifax and Claritas, maintain records on every adult in the UK and their credit worthiness. Dunnhumby collects data from each one, combining it with the other sources to add to the picture of its customers. Commercial companies such as Thomson Intermedia, specialists in advertising media intelligence, have struck agreements with dunnhumby which allows their knowledge of the effectiveness of advertising to be combined with dunnhumby/Tesco's customer insight. This allows dunnhumby to offer Tesco both large-scale information on buying habits for items such as 'organic products' and individual mailings reflecting what Clubcard customers bought in the last quarter.

All this has been brought together as the Crucible database, something about which Tesco and dunnhumby are very protective. All references to Crucible are now missing from the dunnhumby website (there used to be some details). It's not mentioned on the Tesco website. The *Guardian* newspaper in the UK is not impressed by this 'exhaustive – and secret' database. But neither Tesco not dunnhumby are breaking any rules. All the requirements of the Data Protection Act are met. No personal data identifying an individual is ever sold to other companies. But they know an impressive amount about their customers. It is said that during the initial trials with dunnhumby in 1994, when Humby presented three months' worth of results to the Tesco Board, Chairman Lord MacLaurin responded 'you know more about my customers after three months than I know after 30 years'. And that from 14 stores. The rise of Tesco shows the effectiveness on a national scale.

Interestingly, the final trigger for Crucible came from the UK Government. Changes to the law in 2001 allowed voters to restrict the use of their own electoral role (ER) entry. Whereas the ER used to be available to anybody who wanted it for any purpose, after the change many voters restricted their entry to the full version used for election purposes only, with no entry appearing in the version which could be sold to the public. This led to the need for replacement data sources by the credit reference agencies and their customers. Crucible was the Tesco/dunnhumby response.

The operation to mail customers four times a year is very impressive – the combined mailings represent 6 per cent of all the items handled by Royal Mail and other postal companies. It is said that the first of these mailings in 1996 was the largest single direct mailing in UK history at the time addressed to individuals (as opposed to the 'Occupier' or 'The Householder').

Of course, other companies don't want to be left out. With one-third of UK households members of Clubcard, Tesco has available real data on a sample of customers which no market research company could hope to survey. In effect, 12 million respondents are unlikely to be wrong. So dunnhumby sells a 10 per cent sample to Tesco suppliers for up to £50,000 per year, depending on volume sold. It's expensive, but Tesco buyers expect suppliers to talk the same language as themselves and Tesco is the largest buyer of these products in the UK! Companies such as Sky, Gillette and Orange also buy anonymized data based on dunnhumby data – it's the best consumer data available.

In a final, some would say almost Orwellian twist, the credit reference agency Experian has been working for several years with academics to develop Mosaic, a consumer profiling system which uses census surname data to track ethnicity, religion, colour and culture. Earlier versions of this system were used by 190 of the top 200 UK companies and the three UK political parties. The lead researcher has said that he could see no reason why Tesco shouldn't be allowed to analyse which ethnic groups buy their Asian products. This would be readily possible using Crucible data based on the surnames of Clubcard users. This is a potentially very sensitive area for database work. However, two police forces, with all the resources of the Police National Computer and government databases, have used Mosaic rather than official data to understand local policing needs. The NHS is also a customer.

So Tesco and dunnhumby may actually know more about the UK population than any other single organization (now that Tesco owns some 84 per cent of dunnhumby). Does MI5 know?

Case study questions

1 Which sources of data for Tesco come from within the company and which are external to the company?

2 This case is about growth based on effective use of data. Was the collection and analysis of accurate data enough to explain the subsequent growth of Tesco?

3 What insights can the proper use of the contents of a data warehouse give to Tesco executives?

SOURCES: The *Guardian*, 27 September 2005; *Financial Times*, 11 November 2006; *The Times*, 21 April 2007; The *Wall Street Journal*, 6 June 2006; www.tesco.com; www.loyalty.vg; www.dunnhumby.co.uk

Case study **6.4**

Information overload

BY STEWART BAINES

Businesses are drowning in data – but how much good is it doing them? Stewart Baines finds out how to retrieve and understand essential corporate information.

IT professionals are regularly asked to solve the 'information overload' problem but the term may be a misnomer. Almost three in five managers of the 1000 surveyed by Accenture said they miss information valuable to their jobs every day. On average, respondents to the survey of UK and US professionals spend up to two hours per day scrabbling to find data. If we're so replete with information, why can't we find what we need?

As information volumes increase, so do two other things: the number of data sources and the places to put it. Greg Todd, senior executive for Accenture Information Management Services, says: 'It's a consistent theme – there's so much information being thrown up by different technology platforms.'

RSS feeds, email, search engines and corporate intranets are competing with internal reporting systems that may not always have access to all of the data streams that employees need. An increasing

CRM Real Time Dashboards, such as this example from Netsuite, are partly an attempt to address the issue of information overload, providing users with customized data snapshots instantly.

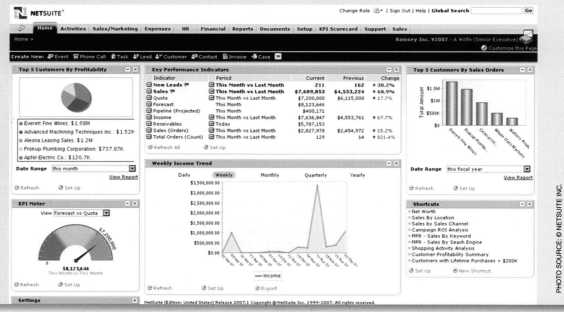

choice of potential storage locations (and therefore places for people to look for it) makes the mess complete.

Employees also store information on their own hard drives, which makes it difficult or impossible for others to find. IT departments compound the problem by duplicating data in different systems or storing too much of it as they frantically try to ward off future compliance problems.

Richard Kellett, head of technology strategy for SAS UK, says: 'It's a bit of a comfort blanket. If you keep everything then you can answer any question from the business, theoretically. But what you end up with is something that costs a lot and delivers little.'

Before tackling the problem, companies need to understand whether they're dealing with structured or unstructured data. Data from a company's logistics, finance or marketing activities can be pulled into a database that can then be fed to executives using a reporting system or dashboard. A collection of dials and gauges providing an at-a-glance analysis of business performance can be a crucial way to keep everyone in the business informed.

For a dashboard to work, though, a reporting system has to integrate data from separate systems, which must themselves be sophisticated enough to export it. The alternative is to move to a single platform with built-in reporting capabilities.

Netsuite, co-founded and funded by Oracle CEO, Larry Ellison, provides a hosted business management for SMEs and is carving out a niche for itself here. The company provides online CRM, shipping, inventory management and financial services, among others.

The idea is that by putting everything into the same underlying databases, managers can get a joined-up view of the business. This means no rushing around to see if you have the inventory to hand when someone calls up with a large order, for example.

Craig Sullivan, VP of International Products at Netsuite, says: 'There's a benefit to see all of your key metrics for the business in one place.'

But moving from piecemeal back-office systems to a unified platform carries its own investment overhead – and once you've moved, you have to persuade the employees to use the new system. Gavin Whatrup, group IT director at Creston, a collection of PR, advertising and direct marketing businesses, knows getting grassroots buy-in for new working practices can be a challenge.

He says: 'We suffer as an industry with unstructured data, particularly email. People use it as primary, sometimes their only, data store. It's completely wrong.

'But in marketing there isn't much top down control. People work independently and use their own processes.' He takes a hands-off approach, leaving employees to manage their own information flow on the basis that as successful businesses they must be doing it right.

Surely there are other ways to handle unstructured data, without negotiating tensions between centralized and individual ways of working? Mapping desktops to network drives and using enterprise search appliances s one way to mitigate the problem.

Another is to bring order to unstructured information in automated ways. Adrian Butcher, strategic ECM consultant at document management vendor Open Text, says: 'An example would be extracting an order number or customer name from an email and using that to directly access information in a CRM or ERP system.'

That still leaves companies with the challenge of collecting the most valuable asset of all: the tacit information that exists in people's heads. How do you get 15 years of unspoken rules and experiences out of the senior support engineer's head and into a digestible format for other people? Depending on the size of the company, wikis, blogs and corporate social networking software could be a way forward.

For now, though, many companies probably have enough of a challenge managing what they already have. And while they continue to grapple with that, more of it keeps piling up.

Thinking about the case

1 Which is more important to an organization, structured or unstructured data?

2 It there a point at which the cost of extracting and processing the vast collection of data outweighs the benefits?

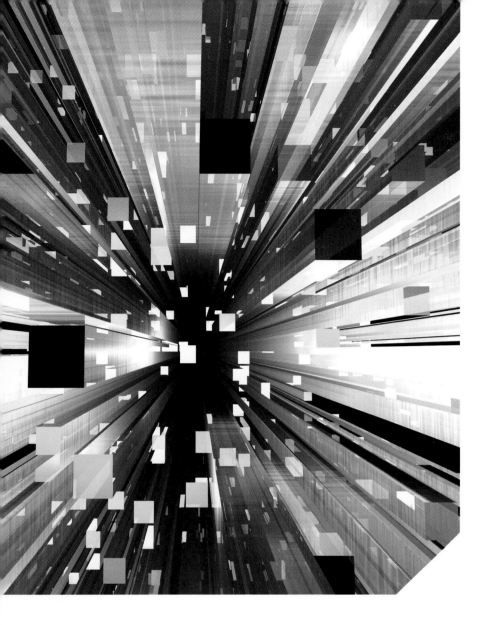

PART THREE

Electronic commerce

SpareBitz.com

Eric Wilson watched with pride as his son, Steve, walked across the stage to shake hands with the Chancellor of the University and formally gain his Business Studies Degree. Eric realized that his dream of his son following in his footsteps in running the home appliance repair shop that had been in the family for two generations was not going to happen; and that was quite right. Steve needed to make use of the skills and knowledge gained in his undergraduate studies. Having said that, Steve had always shown a great interest in the business side of the shop and had enjoyed working there out of term time. But to be honest, the business was not doing too well. The number of repairs had gone down significantly over the past few years although he had noticed that more people were asking him about spare parts so that they could do the repairs themselves.

Expansion into spares

Eric should have had faith in his son. He realized that the spare parts operation of the business had potential. The shop 'Wilson's Appliance Repairs' was rebranded as SpareBitz. Eric had an important job to play in the shop – he was the expert you could trust. Customers were confident in Eric's ability to undertake the repair if necessary, but were also happy to receive his advice on how to perform the repair themselves. Stock was a problem. With so many different appliances, each with potentially hundreds of parts, SpareBitz often did not have what was needed. However, over the years Eric had built up excellent relations with the various suppliers. It was the boast of SpareBitz that if they didn't have the part they would get it within a week. Steve used his business acumen to formalize these relationships to make sure that SpareBitz thrived. In a few years there were branches in the High Streets of more than a dozen towns in the North East. Steve had made sure that each shop was managed by someone who was capable of undertaking the repair if need be so that they could give the best possible advice to the customer who wanted to buy

the spare part and do the work for themselves. SpareBitz had built up a reputation as the place you could trust. In addition the shops conducted a bit of trade in appliance sales when a repair was not possible or uneconomical. Soon Eric felt able to retire, happy in the knowledge that the business was in good hands.

Useful contacts

'I'm not sure I'm a reunions sort of person', Steve told his wife as they got ready for the journey down south. 'Stick in the mud', Helen retorted, with a smirk. 'It's always interesting seeing what people have done with their lives – and you might make a few useful contacts.'

Later that evening Steve had to admit that, as usual, his wife was right. It was fascinating to see the wide range of business and industry that his peers had found themselves in. One of the most interesting was Carl Dobson. He had shared a few modules with Carl in his time at University although they were not on the same course. Carl had studied Internet Business Development and had done well for himself. He ran a company that helped small business to make the most of the Internet. 'So, has SpareBitz got a web presence?' asked Carl. 'Well, I've got a website that I put together myself', replied Steve proudly. 'Nothing flashy, but it at least tells anyone who looks at it where my shops are and how to get in contact.' Carl frowned. 'So really just a not-very-high-tech entry in the yellow pages!' Steve opened his mouth to protest but realized that Carl spoke the truth. As proud as he was of his few Internet pages, built using Dreamweaver learned from a book, it probably didn't bring in much trade. He didn't even know how many people visited his site. 'But surely', insisted Steve, 'my little business isn't suitable for the World Wide Web. All of my customers come from the North East, a matter of miles from my shops.' 'A common misconception, mate', replied Carl. 'Just because a website can be viewed by someone the other side of the world doesn't mean that it's inappropriate for someone just a few miles away. Look at one of the big players in E-commerce for example: Tesco's. They do lots of business on their online store but you can bet most of those customers are only a few miles from their local store. I think it's not possible to be more than a few miles from your nearest Tesco's, unless you live in the Scottish Highlands!' 'Are you suggesting I try to emulate Tesco's?' Carl spluttered his drink. 'Don't be daft. Of course your little enterprise is not in the same league, but it doesn't mean you can't dabble in using the Web to your advantage, more than you have with your little website.'

An idea forms

The next day, as they returned from the Midlands to the North East, Steve had to confess that Helen had been right about the useful contacts. The more he thought about it the more he realized that his business was living in a pre-web age. It was his get-up-and-go that had shaken his father's old-fashioned business into a thriving enterprise, but he was now in danger of missing out on the next big thing – perhaps. Being a level-headed businessman, he realized that decisions like this should not be taken without proper consideration. As they turned into their drive he made his mind up. Fishing out the business card that Carl had given him he pushed the buttons on his mobile. 'Hi Carl. Steve Wilson here . . . Yes it was a great evening. Good to see what people have done with their lives.' Helen suppressed a laugh. 'I've been thinking about some of the things you were saying. How do you feel about conducting a feasibility study for me about turning SpareBitz into a web-enabled enterprise?'

Business challenges

Steve Wilson needs answers to lots of questions before he is willing to commit himself to extending the operations of SpareBitz onto the World Wide Web. These issues are discussed in the next two chapters.

In Chapter 7, 'The Web-enabled Enterprise', you learn how businesses use the Internet to achieve strategic advantage and how SpareBitz can use the Internet to extend service to its existing customers and to increase its customer base.

In Chapter 8, 'Challenges of Global Information Systems', you learn how sharing electronic information and operations across international boundaries can bring tremendous efficiencies – and challenges – to operations such as SpareBitz.

Chapter 7

The web-enabled enterprise

LEARNING OBJECTIVES

The Web has been the most exciting development in the field of information systems and telecommunications in recent years. The combination of advanced telecommunications technology and innovative software is revolutionizing the way people communicate, shop, make contracts and payments, educate, learn and conduct business. Numerous companies throughout the world have been established thanks to the enabling power of the Web, and existing ones have used the Web to extend their operations. Firms conduct business electronically with each other and directly with consumers, using a variety of business models. This chapter focuses on web technologies and businesses on the Web.

When you finish this chapter, you will be able to:

Describe how the Web and high-speed Internet connections are changing business operations.

Explain the functionality of various web technologies.

Compare and contrast options for web servers.

Explain basic business-to-business and business-to-consumer practices on the Web.

Explain the relationship between web technologies and supply chain management.

Give examples of features and services that successful business websites offer.

Learn about online annoyances such as spam and adware, and how to protect against online identity theft.

SpareBitz.com

FIRST STEPS IN E-COMMERCE

Steve Wilson was pleased with how things were going for SpareBitz.com. His numerous meetings with Carl had caused him to think carefully about his business processes. Carl had explained that putting the business on the Web meant a review of the objectives of the current business. They needed to study the competitors, such as Ezee-fix.co.uk, and look at the service offered to customers. The good news was that, although there were competitors, Steve's initial ambitions were not particularly grand and the costs involved could be minimized, hence reducing the risks. These costs included the obvious ones such as website design. Carl persuaded Steve that the simple website needed a major overhaul and that Steve did not have the necessary skills or expertise to turn it from a 'billboard' advertising the company to a fully functional e-commerce site. At least that is how it appeared until Carl introduced Steve to a software package that allowed the building of an e-commerce application by using various templates as 'building blocks'. The user interface of the software was very intuitive and with a bit of guidance from Carl, Steve was able to create a usable e-commerce site for his small enterprise.

Maintaining the catalogue

Of course the website is only one side of the story. For the system to work properly there was a need to maintain a catalogue of products which meant taking the existing suppliers' catalogues and consolidating them into a single Microsoft Access database. The design of this was definitely beyond Steve's competence, so Carl arranged for a colleague to meet with Steve to discuss the requirements and develop a solution.

A home for the site

Another issue, which would not be just a one-off cost but require monthly payments, was the need for the hosting of the site. It did not take long to realize that having their own server was not sensible for a business such as SpareBitz so Carl recommended organizing a contract with an Internet Service Provider (ISP). 'Have you checked your domain name?' Carl asked. 'What do you mean?' Steve had a worried look on his face because he thought he knew what Carl was getting at. 'Obviously there can't be two registered users for the same name so if someone else owns SpareBitz.com then you will need to think of another.' Now Steve really was worried. 'That name has gained a reputation and changing it would cause real problems.' Luckily a quick search of the Internet showed that there was an old domain name SpareBitz.com which had now been deleted and SpareBitz.com was available. 'Let's grab it quick', Carl and Steve both said together.

The contract with the ISP also required some calculations about web traffic, that is how many customers SpareBitz.com could expect per month, the size of the downloads and so on. Steve needed to make a few wild guesses, but fortunately his contract with the ISP was flexible so that

if his online business was more successful than he had estimated he could change his ISP usage to cope.

Who will visit?

'Now what about marketing?' asked Carl. 'I thought we were relying on using our existing customer base', replied Steve. 'Well certainly that is the least costly but I think we can do a bit more for not too much extra. We can rely on conventional advertising such as leaflets in local stores but we can't expect much support from shops selling products that we are encouraging people to repair rather than buy new! There are methods of getting your site noticed by casual web surfers. We can embed keywords into your web pages so that anyone searching for Hoover, for example, will see your site in the search list. For a bit more money we can become a sponsored link that will highlight our site. We can also try some viral marketing by getting the site mentioned in blogs and other social networks.'

Web business: growing and changing

With approximately 8900 company-operated and franchised stores in more than 20 countries, Blockbuster Inc. is the world's largest video rental company. It uses a website to promote its services, but the company's online presence did not amount to more than advertising until 2003, when management decided to allow customers to rent movies through the Internet. What happened to make management change its tune? It was competition. Netflix in the United States and LOVEFiLM in the UK along with other companies throughout Europe began offering an online movie order method: pay a monthly fee, select your movies online, get them in the mail (free shipping!), mail the movies back, and they'll send you more. No need to drive to any store. This business model was popular with renters, and Wal-Mart and Netflix started nibbling into Blockbuster's revenues. Blockbuster management could not allow the company to be left behind. It decided to offer a similar service with the added convenience of the customers being able to return their tapes and DVDs to any Blockbuster store. Blockbuster, like an increasing number of brick-and-mortar businesses, had jumped on the e-commerce bandwagon.

CD TASK

Is this the most efficient way to satisfy the movie-at-home audience? Experts say that shipping a physical object such as a tape or DVD to customers will soon be a thing of the past. Movies are information, and any information can be digitized and whisked to a customer over the Web. As the number of customers with high-speed Internet links grows, enjoying a movie at home will take one of two forms: either a requested movie will be streamed to the customer while the customer is watching, or a copy of the movie will be transferred to the customer. This business model is becoming a reality in the UK with the BBC iPlayer giving viewers the ability to catch up with programmes missed over the last seven days, download and store programmes for 30 days and watch television programmes streamed over the Internet. Competitors for on-demand television include Channel 4OD and Virgin Media. As broadband increases in speed and availability, you will be able to watch films not only on your computer's monitor but also on a regular HDTV set. Just as the film rental industry has changed dramatically within a few years from in-store rental to over-the-web order to over-the-web download, other industries have changed and will continue to change thanks to faster Internet links and new web technologies. Business on the Web is growing and changing form all the time.

Web technologies: a review

Several standards and technologies enable the Web to deliver rich information. The following is a review of some nonproprietary standards and technologies.

HTTP

Hypertext Transfer Protocol (HTTP) Software that allows browsers to log on to websites.

HTTPS The secure version of HTTP.

Uniform Resource Locator (URL) The address of a website. Always starts with *http://* but does not have to contain *www*.

domain name The name assigned to an Internet server or to a part of a server that hosts a website.

In Chapter 5, you learned about protocols. The protocol used to transfer and download web information is Hypertext Transfer Protocol, or HTTP. A secure version of the protocol for confidential transactions is HTTPS (HTTP Secure). Under this protocol, each web server is designated a Uniform Resource Locator (URL), which is a unique address for a website. The address is the IP number (also called IP address) assigned to the site, but in most cases the site also has a domain name made up from letters. The term 'URL' also refers to the domain name. Each web page has its own URL, which contains the IP number or domain name of the site. Because the domain name must be unique, when an owner of a website reserves a domain name to be associated with an IP number, no other site can be associated with that domain name. Note that domain names often start with – but do not have to include – *www*.

The last part of a URL, such as the '.com' in www.thomson.com, is the top-level domain (TLD). In addition to .com, .org, and .edu, many other TLDs can be requested for a domain name, some of which are reserved for certain types of organizations and professions, and some that are not. The only organization that is authorized to approve new TLDs is the Internet Corporation for Assigned Names and Numbers (ICANN), a not-for-profit organization established specifically for this purpose.

Industry **SNAPSHOT**

An island domain

All countries are allocated a specific Internet domain name with the exception of the USA. The theory behind this is that in the same way as the UK invented postage stamps and does not show its name on stamps issued, the US 'invented' the Internet and so has the same privilege.

The tiny Pacific nation of Tuvalu is allocated the Internet name .tv. The government of the island had repeated requests from companies wishing to make use of the obvious appeal of these two letters and in 1998 it auctioned off the .tv domain name to a Canadian entrepreneur. The deal included a guaranteed US$50 million over ten years and a 15 per cent stake in the company selling rights to domain names ending in .tv, which effectively doubled the gross domestic product of the Pacific nation of 10,000 inhabitants. Roads have been laid, outlying islands now have electricity and schools have

been built. The money has also been used to fund Tuvalu's membership of the United Nations, which requires annual fees of US$20,000. On 5 September 2000 Tuvalu became the 189th member of the UN.

SOURCE: Mark Ward, 'Net Gains for Tuvalu', http://news.bbc.co.uk/1/hi/sci/tech/1067065.stm

Citizens of Funafuti, Tuvalu's capital.

While domain names consisting of catchy and meaningful words are considered prized assets, companies such as Amazon.co.uk and Google have demonstrated that the name itself is worthless unless the service provided is excellent. Few people know what these names mean (abundant like the Amazon rainforest; and googol, an impossibly large number), but everybody knows of these sites and the purpose of their business. Therefore, new Internet companies do not spend as much energy seeking an attractive domain name as they did in the past.

HTML and XML

Hypertext Markup Language (HTML) is the most common programming language for creating web pages and other information viewable in a web browser. It determines the look and location of text, pictures, animations and other elements on a web page. Extensible Markup Language (XML) enables the creation of various types of data. It is most often used not for determining the *appearance* of visual elements on a web page but to convey the *meaning* or content of the data. The World Wide Web Consortium (W3C), the organization responsible for web standards, has combined the two markup languages HTML and XML into a standard called Extensible Hypertext Markup Language (XHTML).

Every file displayed on the Web is coded with a markup language such as HTML or XML. Simply put, markup languages provide a system of standardized 'tags' that format elements of a document, including text, graphics and sound. Formatting includes opening and closing tags preceding and following a part of the document, such as <b> at the start of bold text, and </b> at the end of bold text. Other tags are marked to link to another page either at the same site or another site, and others create links to email addresses. Browsers interpret HTML and XML tags and display the text in the fashion defined by the tags, or allow other software to pick up data from the page and process it or copy it into the proper place in a database.

As in HTML, tags are used in XML to mark data elements. However, XML tags define 'what it is', as opposed to 'how it looks'. The following illustrates the difference between HTML tags and XML tags:

HTML
<font size ='2'>Oz & Jones Enterprises, Ltd.</font>
<b>ST4 2DE</b>

XML
<company name>Oz & Jones Enterprises, Ltd.</company name>
<postcode>ST4 2DE</postcode>

XML tags can be used in the same page with HTML tags to indicate both what the data means (which is not visible to the user) and how each element should be displayed.

> **Hypertext Markup Language (HTML)** A programming language for web pages and web browsers.
>
> **XML (Extensible Markup Language)** A programming language that tags data elements in order to indicate what the data mean, especially in web pages.
>
> **XHTML** A standard that combines HTML standards and XML standards.

File transfer

File Transfer Protocol (FTP) is a common way of transmitting whole files from one computer to another. Every time you download a file from a website or attach files to email, you are using an FTP application. The file transmitted can be of any type: text, graphics, animation or sound. FTP is embedded in browsers and therefore is 'transparent' to the users. You can also use a separate FTP utility, many available as shareware, to manage transmitting files.

Businesses use FTP to place files on a server for sharing among professionals. FTP is also useful for placing files on a server that hosts a website. And it's convenient for retrieving large

> **File Transfer Protocol (FTP)** Software that allows the transfer of files over communications lines.

files that might exceed an email box's size limits. For example, authors can place large chapter and figure files in a folder on a server maintained by their publisher. Manufacturers often place whole assembly and maintenance manuals or videos at their website so customers can download them any time.

FTP has already changed the way in which many software firms sell their products. Instead of spending a significant amount of money copying new software on storage media, packaging it and shipping it, developers simply post their software products on their websites and let buyers download them for a fee. Music lovers can use FTP to download music files.

RSS

RSS Really Simple Syndication, a type of application using XML for aggregating updates to blogs and news posted at websites.

Really Simple Syndication (or in a newer version, Rich Site Summary) **(RSS)** is a family of XML file formats. An RSS file is installed at websites to help users check updates to the site. When users subscribe to the RSS service of a site, the software communicates to their computers short descriptions of web content along with the link to the site. Users can instruct the software to automatically transmit new or updated information to their own computers. This software is useful for news websites and sites that host blogs and podcasts (see the next sections). Subscribers to mass media sites such as newspapers and news services such as Reuters can receive the latest news without actively going to the site or receiving email messages. At some websites you might see a button with the letters RSS or XML. If you click them, the site will automatically send your computer updates of designated information, by topic.

Blogs

blog A contraction of 'web log'. A website where participants post their opinions on a topic or set of related topics; these postings are listed in chronological order.

A **blog** (a contraction of 'web log') is a web page that invites surfers to post opinions and artistic work, as well as links to sites of interest. Blog sites focus on a topic or a set of related topics, and provide an easy way to post web pages or update existing ones. Most blogs contain commentaries and humorous content. Users can simply click a button to open a window in which they type text, and click another button to post it. The text is added to the web page either automatically or after a review by the blog's operators. Some blog sites simply let 'bloggers' add comments on a topic, with the most recent comment appearing at the top, similar to the way online newsgroups work. Many companies have established blogs, and invite employees to use them for self-expression. The policy might encourage new ideas from which the company can benefit. Some, however, shun the idea, because management believes blogs are too informal and uncontrolled.

One interesting feature of some blogs is *trackback*. Trackback software notifies bloggers when their posts have been mentioned elsewhere on the Web, so they and their readers can extend the discussion beyond the original blog. Below each post there is a BackTrack button or similar option. When it is clicked, a new window pops up listing the sites mentioning the post.

The commercial potential of blogs has not escaped businesspeople. As traffic grows at some popular blogs, entrepreneurs have started selling advertising space at the sites. The old rule on the Web is still much in force: the greater the number of eyeballs, the greater the commercial potential of the site.

The importance of blogs to commercial organizations is primarily to find out what blog participants think and say about the organizations. Many organizations use special software that combs blogs for postings that mention the organizations' names. PR people then read the content and relay feedback to others in the organization as needed. For example, an anonymous blogger boasted that he could break Kryptonite bicycle locks with a pen. Within a week the posted item was mentioned in various press articles and Kryptonite recalled the locks. Software tools exist that comb blogs, identify company names, and automatically track discussions. Such tools can turn blog data into useful market research information.

Podcasting

While blogging is publishing text and other visual material, podcasting is publishing sound. To podcast is to make a digital audio recording, usually of voice, and post the file on the Web so that people can download it and listen to it. RSS software called an *aggregator* or *feed reader* automatically checks for new content and downloads files from a designated site in the same way as is done for text files from online newspapers. Similarly to subscribing to such newspapers, users can subscribe to a podcast site to receive the latest audio files. The files are usually in MP3 format, which can be played on any portable player, including Apple Computer's iPod, from which the word 'podcast' was born. However, one does not need this specific MP3 player to enjoy podcasts.

> **podcasting** The practice of posting sound files at a website for automating downloading and playing by subscribers.

Podcasting has several potential uses. It already serves as 'time-shifted' broadcast of radio stations that post their programmes for later listening. It is used by some museums for audio tours. Some schools and universities have experimented with the concept to deliver lessons to remote students. Whatever the use, people can listen to their favourite content wherever they can obtain a link to the Internet, without paying radio licence fees.

Podcasting opens business opportunities. For example, garageband.com is a website that invites aspiring musicians to post their music tracks free of charge so they can be podcast. This exposes to the world talented people who could not otherwise afford to broadcast their work. Podcasting does more than post MP3 files for downloading. By allowing computers to automatically check for new music tracks, the method helps create a following for an artist, which might result in a future fan base willing to pay for a CD or downloaded music files.

Instant messaging

Instant messaging (IM) offers users real-time online interactivity. It might be thought of as 'real-time email', because, unlike email, it is synchronous. IM allows a user to detect whether another person who uses the service is currently online,

> **instant messaging (IM)** The capability for several online computer users to share messages in real time; also called chatting online.

and the user can then exchange information with an entire group (referred to as a 'chat room'), or with only one other 'chatter' in privacy. Some IM applications include two-way video, which turns the chat into a video-conference, and most also include FTP to allow sending and receiving files.

Free IM applications are operated through a server, or a group of connected servers, which provides a directory and functions as the hub for all callers. Some IM setups, such as AOL Instant Messenger (AIM), Yahoo! Messenger, MSN Messenger and ICQ, have become the electronic meeting places for millions of people, making them an attractive target for online advertisers. To overcome the need to use multiple IM applications, some software developers produce universal IM applications that allow, for example, an AIM user to chat with an MSN Messenger user. Trillian and Pidgin (formerly know as Gaim) are two of these applications.

While IM sounds as if it is just for fun, it also can serve an important business purpose. Many online retailers post a special button on their web pages that lets shoppers establish real-time communication with a sales representative. This instant access fosters more personal service and saves telephone costs. For example, IKEA, the Swedish furniture giant, has 37 country-specific websites linked from ikea.com and most of these have a chat application that enables customers to talk to a virtual representative by clicking on 'Ask Anna'. This can help to reduce the volume of calls to the traditional call centre operatives. Generally customers will abandon the site when they cannot get answers while shopping. Using the telephone is often a bad option for those who use their telephone line for a dial-up Internet connection, and email is inefficient and time-consuming. IM enables sales agents to handle several enquiring customers at a time. Such applications also enable the company to 'push' answers from a library of answers such as sizes of furniture, instead of typing them.

CD TASK

Cookies

If you have ever surfed the Web, your computer probably contains cookies. A cookie is a small file that a website places on a visitor's hard disk so that the website can remember something about the surfer later. Typically, a cookie records the surfer's ID or some other unique identifier. Combined with data collected from previous visits, the site can figure out the visitor's preferences. The user can opt to allow cookies, and the option is exercised by checking a box in the browser's configuration window. On the user's hard disk, the cookie subdirectory (folder) contains a cookie file for each cookie-using website that the surfer has visited. Cookies might hold server URLs. When you instruct the browser to reach a URL from which you have a cookie, the browser transmits the information from the cookie to the server.

> cookie A small file that a website places on a visitor's hard disk so that the website can remember something about the visitor later, such as an ID number or username.

Cookies have an important function in web-based commerce, especially between businesses and consumers. They provide convenience to consumers. If the cookie contains your username and password for accessing a certain resource at the site, you do not have to reenter the information. For example, when a user logs into their eBay account they can choose to keep signed in for the day even if they switch off their computer. This would obviously not be a good idea if they shared their computer with several other users! Cookies often help ensure that a user does not receive the same unsolicited information multiple times. For example, cookies are commonly used to rotate banner ads that a site sends so that a surfer receives different advertisements in a series of requested pages. They also help sites to customize other elements for customers. For example, when a retailer's site identifies a returning customer, it can build a page showing a list of items and information in which the customer might be interested based on previous purchases.

Some cookies are temporary; they are installed only for one session, and are removed when the user leaves the site. Others are persistent and stay on the hard disk unless the user deletes them. Many cookies are installed to serve only first parties, which are the businesses with which the user interacts directly. Others serve third parties, which are organizations that collect information about the user whenever the user visits a site that subscribes to the service of these organizations. These organizations include DoubleClick and FastClick.

While cookies can make online shopping, investing and reading more convenient, they also open the door for intrusion into a person's privacy. Remember that every piece of information you provide while your browser is configured to permit cookies can be recorded and kept for further use – use over which you have no control. Choices you make when selecting menu items, clicking buttons and moving from one page to another are also recorded. Such activities are often called clickstream tracking. Although some organizations post privacy policies at their websites and tell you what they will or will not do with the information they gather, you cannot see what information they have compiled by using cookies and how they use it. Especially worrisome are third-party cookies, which collect your browsing and shopping habits across many websites. This is akin to a spy who follows you from one store to another. Software designed to trace and report your online behaviour without your knowledge is called spyware. It includes cookies and other, more sophisticated applications that are installed on your computer unbeknownst to you and transmit information about you while you are online.

> **clickstream tracking** The use of software to record the activities of a person at websites. Whenever the person clicks a link, the activity is added to the record.

> **spyware** A small application stored surreptitiously by a website on the hard disk of a visitor's computer. The application tracks activities of the user, including visits to websites, and transmits the information to the operator's server.

Proprietary technologies

In addition to these and other widely used and usually free web technologies, many companies offer proprietary technologies. A proprietary technology is the intellectual property of its developer and is not free for all to use. These software packages include local search engines for finding information about specific items; shopping cart applications for purchase, including selection of items to place in a virtual cart and credit-card charging; wish lists, which allow shoppers to create lists of items they would like others to purchase for them; and a host of software packages that are invisible to visitors but help the site owner to analyse and predict visitor behaviour, especially shopper behaviour. The latter technologies might not be considered web technologies per se, but they analyse data that is collected from visitors accessing websites. For example, Amazon.co.uk uses software that follows the estimated age for those whom a shopper purchases items, and offers new items that fit the progressing age of the shopper's family and friends.

Options in establishing a website

A website is, practically speaking, the web pages that make up the information and links to web technologies that the site provides. To establish a web business, an organization must have access to an Internet server and the ability to control its content. Recall that an Internet server is a computer that is connected to the Internet backbone. Businesses have two options when establishing a website: installing and maintaining their own servers, or contracting with a web hosting service.

Owning and maintaining a server

Installing and maintaining a server at the business's own facility is a costly option, but it gives the business the greatest degree of control. Setting up a server requires expertise, which may

load balancing The transfer of visitor enquiries from a busy server to a less busy server.

mirror An Internet server that holds the same software and data as another server, which may be located thousands of miles away.

pure-play A business operating with clients only via the Web, as opposed to operating via stores or other physical facilities.

bricks-and-mortar A popular term for companies that use physical structure for doing business directly with other businesses and consumers, such as stores. Often used to contrast with businesses that sell only online.

web hosting The business of organizations that host, maintain and often help design websites for clients.

shared hosting An arrangement by which the websites of several clients are maintained by the hosting vendor on the same server.

or may not be available within the business. The business must obtain a high-speed physical link to the Internet backbone. It must also employ specialists to maintain the server or many servers on which the website resides. In large organizations these specialists might be employees of the company; in smaller ones, they might be contract personnel whose services the company hires. The specialists purchase a server (or several servers) for the company, connect it to the Internet through a high-speed dedicated line, register a domain name for the site, and install the proper software for managing the server and creating web pages. The specialists 'scale up' the server system when the business grows and handle issues such as load balancing to ensure quick response and to minimize the probability of site crashing. A site crashes when too many people try to log on and the software stops responding to anyone. Load balancing transfers visitor enquiries from a busy server to a less busy server for identical information and services. Thus, the specialist often must connect mirrors, servers on which the same content and applications are duplicated.

A large company whose entire business is done online, often called a pure-play web company, or a bricks-and-mortar company that owns stores but also offers the same or many of the same items for sale online, usually has its own servers and manages them fully. These companies employ crews that manage Internet networking, the hardware and software of the site, and the people responsible for updating the web pages.

Using a hosting service

A majority of organizations that have a commercial presence online either do not own servers or else they own servers but let someone else manage at least some aspect of the site. These organizations use web hosting services. Web hosting companies specialize in one or several types of web hosting: shared hosting, virtual private server hosting, dedicated hosting, or co-location. Some also offer free service, but this service rarely involves features beyond posting web pages. Therefore, this option is not viable for most businesses.

In shared hosting the client's website is stored on the host's same physical server along with the sites of other clients. The hosting company owns the server and the server management software. It offers space on the servers for hosting websites. This is a relatively inexpensive option. The client can use templates provided by the hosts for building pages, or, for an extra fee, have the host's designer design the website. However, many clients prefer to design and upload their own web pages. The service includes transaction and payment software for use by the subscribing businesses' clients. If the server is shared, the host might not be able to allow a client to maintain its own domain name, such as www.myownco.com, but only a subdomain that contains the host's domain name, such as myownco.myhost.com. However, special software employed by many hosts allows clients to use their own domain names, and although the server has only one IP address, the software directs traffic to the proper site on the server. If an independent domain name is important, this is a factor that a business must consider before selecting a hosting service.

Small businesses with a limited number of products to sell can select a host such as Freezone.co.uk for shared hosting. The company offers 'Home' hosting services but also offers two services aimed at commercial operations, BusinessPlus and Business Advanced. Large search engine and portal companies, such as Yahoo!, offer similar services. Clients have access to easy-to-use web design software tools to create the pages of their new site. This type of option is often a 'turnkey' solution for a small business that wishes to go online almost overnight. In addition to disk space and help with website design, the hosting company typically also provides a number of email addresses and a control 'dashboard', a mechanism for the client business to control remotely content and other aspects of the site. Some hosts also offer to list the new site on frequently used search sites, such as Yahoo! and Google. Many of the hosts also help with domain name registration.

In shared hosting, hundreds of businesses might share the same server and storage space. Therefore, the host often limits the storage space allotted to each client, the number of transactions performed per month, or simply the amount of data, in megabytes, that the site transmits per month. Also, a technical problem in one site could affect the functionality of the other sites residing on the server.

The purpose of a virtual private server is to create the impression that the client maintains its own server. Virtual private server technology enables one server to be virtually split into many addressable servers, each for a different client and with its own domain name. This option is usually less expensive than renting a dedicated server, while enjoying the same benefits, including full control of the content of the virtual server.

Some companies might want to use entire physical servers all for themselves and therefore can opt for dedicated hosting. In dedicated hosting the host dedicates a server to the client,

virtual private server Part of a server that serves as an Internet server for a client of a web hosting company, while other clients share the same physical server.

dedicated hosting An arrangement in which a web hosting organization devotes an entire server to only the website of a single client organization, as opposed to having multiple clients' sites share one server.

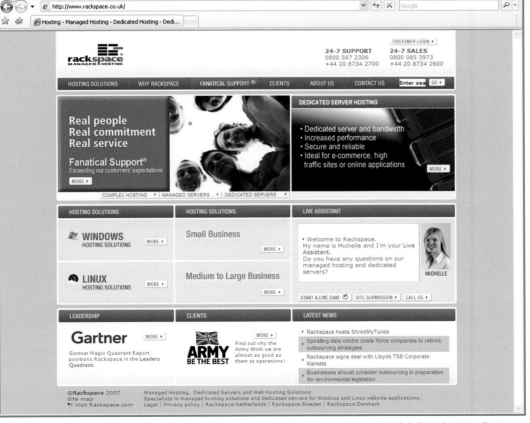

Web host companies accommodate both small and large web-based commercial sites. Large clients often prefer dedicated servers or co-location of their servers at the host's secure site

and the client can fully control the content on the server's disks. The host is responsible for networking management. For example Rackspace.co.uk offers such a service and allows the client to select from several servers. The greater the server's power, the higher the monthly fee. This service is more expensive than shared hosting, but it comes with several advantages. There are fewer restrictions on storage space and transactions, and since only one site resides on the disks, no other site can affect its functionality. Renters of dedicated servers usually have *root access*, which means they act as unrestricted administrators of that computer. The greater control of the dedicated server option comes with a price: this option is more expensive than shared hosting or a virtual private server.

co-location The placement and maintenance of a web server with servers of other subscribers of the service provider. The servers are co-located in the same facility.

In some cases a company might want to fully manage its own web servers but prefers the expertise of a hosting company in managing networking and security. Some hosting services accommodate such demand by offering a co-location service. The client owns the servers and manages their content, but the servers are co-located with the servers of other clients as well as those of the host in a secure (physical) site. This approach has been taken by some online retailers because it affords some advantages: the client does not have to employ hardware and network specialists, spend money on building a special secure location for the server, or ensure power supply. All these concerns are transferred to the hosting company. Co-location is usually the most expensive of hosting options. The client must purchase and run the servers, as well as pay for the co-location.

Considerations in selecting a web host

A majority of businesses do not maintain their own web servers or co-locate them; they use host services. When a decision is made to use such a service, managers must consider several factors. Table 7.1 lists the major factors. Hosts can be compared using points, for example, on a scale of 1 for the best and 5 for the worst. A simple evaluation method is for managers to compare each factor for the prospective host, compare the total scores and then make a decision. The evaluators might wish to assign different weights to the various items based on how important each item is to the business.

dynamic web page A web page whose contents change while the visitor watches it.

The business should be able to use a database management system (DBMS) for cataloguing its products and enable online shoppers to perform searches. Thus, the DBMS offered is important. It also might need to use dynamic web pages, pages that enable communication between the shopper's browser and the database. Such pages can be built with several programming tools: CGI, Java servlets, PHP and ASP (Active Server Pages). Since the functionality of databases and dynamic pages, as well as some features on the pages, depends on the operating system that the hosts use, all this software must be considered. For example, if the client elects to build and maintain the web pages and prefers to use ASP, notice should be taken that such software will run only on a server running Microsoft Windows. Similar restrictions apply to some page features that can be developed with the web developing tool FrontPage. Most hosting companies offer the use of a combination of software popularly called LAMP, which is an acronym: Linux for operating system, Apache for server management software, MySQL for DBMS, and PHP or Python or Perl for developing dynamic web pages. All of these resources are open source software, and therefore do not require licence fees for the host, who can thus make the service more affordable. However, many hosts also offer other software, including Windows, for higher fees. In addition to these issues, the client should ensure satisfactory shopping cart, credit-card processing and other applications at the site.

Storage space limitations might become a serious inhibitor, especially if the business expects to offer a growing number of products and augment the information provided through the site. The client should enquire about options to increase storage space on demand and its cost.

Table 7.1 Factors to consider for each web hosting company

Factor	Points
Type and quality of applications provided (shopping cart, credit-card processing, statistical analysis, etc.)	_____
Storage space	_____
Quality of technical support	_____
Traffic limits	_____
Availability of email accounts and services	_____
Scalability	_____
Support of page design	_____
Security	_____
Uptime ratio	_____
Setup fee	_____
Monthly fee	_____

Most hosts provide technical support 24 hours per day, 7 days per week throughout the year, known as 24/7/365. The client should ensure such service and know exactly what support services are included in the contract.

Technical support involves the quality of the equipment that the hosting company provides, the security measures it maintains, the sophistication of server and load management, and the technical skills of its personnel. Companies should enquire about past downtimes and recovery time frames for the hosting company because they are an important part of technical support. If the client needs help in developing and updating web pages, the evaluators should explore the appearance and functionality of current clients of the hosting company.

Some hosting companies charge extra fees for shared hosting if the site experiences activity above a predetermined amount of data that is transferred (downloaded from the site or uploaded to it) or number of visits from web surfers, known as *hits*. In such arrangements additional fees are charged for over-the-limit data transfer or hits. Web hosting companies price their services this way because the greater the number of hits, the more bandwidth they must allocate. The size of every file that is downloaded or uploaded is recorded, and if the limit – say 200 GB – has been exceeded, there is additional charge. If the client's business grows, the cost might end up much greater than planned.

All hosting firms provide subscribers with several email addresses. Some also provide forwarding to other email addresses. Clients should examine these factors as well as the size of email boxes, autoresponding (automating email reply), and access to mailing lists.

Scalability is the ability of an organization to modify the capabilities of IT to accommodate growing needs. In this context, it is the ability for a website to grow – an important factor for most businesses. It is best to select a hosting company that has the hardware, software and expertise to accommodate varying traffic levels and that can demonstrate its ability to develop a site from a simple, static one (one that does not require interactivity) to a heavily trafficked, interactive one. This applies to disk space, growing sophistication of software used, faster backup mechanisms and other resources.

Smaller businesses often need help with the design of their web pages. They need to discover whether the hosting company maintains experienced and available web design personnel.

The host's physical site must be well secured against physical entry as well as intrusion through the Internet. Clients should ask for information about security measures. Some hosts are so careful as to not even advertise where they keep servers. Yahoo! is one such host.

Businesses want their websites available all the time. Downtime denies them business and damages their reputation. Hosting companies usually advertise their uptime as a percentage. For example, they might say they guarantee 99 per cent uptime. This means that the client should expect the site to be down 1 per cent (87.6 hours) of every year. Companies that need a higher uptime, such as 99.9 or 99.99 per cent, should take notice of this and ensure that the host has the resources to claim such a high number of 'nines'. Such resources often include the availability of power backup and redundancy, the placing of the site on two or more servers.

Setup and monthly fees are self-explanatory. Some hosting companies offer large discounts to clients that sign multiyear contracts.

More than meets the eye

However a business chooses to run its website, there are several elements that must be present to conduct business, which are illustrated in Figure 7.1. While the shopper (a consumer or corporate purchasing officer) sees only web pages, several applications and databases actually support online shopping and purchasing: an application that provides an enquiry interface for the shopper, which is connected to a catalogue that is actually a database consisting of visual and text product descriptions; an application that takes the order, which is connected to an inventory application that is also connected to the product catalogue database; a credit-card application that verifies authenticity of credit-card details and balance; and, in many cases, an order-fulfilment system that displays on monitors located in warehouses which items are to be picked off shelves and where they should be shipped. The latter system might include an automated conveyor system that picks the items with little human labour.

B2B Business-to-business, a term that refers to transactions between businesses, often through an Internet link.

B2C Business-to-consumer, a term that refers to transactions between a business and its customers, often through an Internet link.

Web-enabled business

Web-enabled business is often classified by the parties involved in the interaction: business-to-business (B2B) and business-to-consumer (B2C). Some people also add government-to-consumer and government-to-business. Auction sites, such as eBay.co.uk are sometimes referred to as consumer-to-consumer (C2C) sites, but we consider them B2C, because the business does intervene in several parts of the transaction, as well as charging the parties commissions. Following are descriptions of the business models of the most pervasive types of web-based business.

B2B trading

Business-to-business (B2B) trading takes place only between businesses. Consumers of the final goods and services are not involved. In general, the volume of e-commerce between

Figure 7.1 The components of a web-based retailing operation

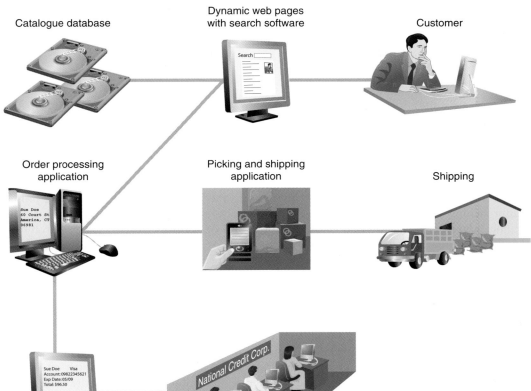

Catalogue database

Dynamic web pages
with search software

Customer

Order processing
application

Picking and shipping
application

Shipping

Credit-card verification
application

Credit card company

Industry **SNAPSHOT**

B2B commerce, the old way . . .

In June 2005, CitiBank, one of the world's largest financial institutions, discovered that some tapes it shipped with UPS were lost. The tapes included the names, Social Security numbers, account numbers and payment history of 3.9 million customers. They were en route to a credit bureau, one of several that use such information to maintain and sell people's credit history and rating. CitiBank management decided that it would start transmitting such information, encrypted, over communication networks. The question arises: why did the company wait so long to use technologies that had been available for years?

A Citibank branch in London.

businesses is about ten times as great as that of business-to-consumer e-commerce. And although not all electronic B2B transactions take place on the Internet, most do. This section discusses the major forms in which businesses communicate with each other and undertake intra-business transactions.

Advertising

Online advertising is done mainly in two ways: through search engines and through banners. Although advertising on the Web is aimed not just at consumers, most of it is directed to them. Regardless of media, advertisers are interested in reaching as many people who might buy their goods or services as possible. On the Web, advertisers are interested in what they call 'traffic volume', that is, the number of people who come across their messages. As the number of people who log on to the Web increases, so does advertiser interest in this medium. According to www.internetworldstats.com, the estimated number of people online is approaching 1.2 billion in 2007, nearly one-fifth of the world population. With this traffic volume, advertisers are willing to spend a lot of money on web advertising. The research firm eMarketer estimated that the world's corporations spent nearly € 4 billion on search advertising in 2005; that is, they paid the owners of search sites, such as Google and Yahoo!, to ensure that their company names either came up at the top of search results or were listed as 'sponsored' sites in the search list that appears. Because in 2005 search engine advertising was estimated at about 45 per cent of all web advertising, we might conclude that total spending on web advertising was about € 8.6 billion – and the trend is upwards.

search advertising
Placing ads at search engine websites.

Search advertising, which is any form of advertising through an online search site, is regarded by businesses as being highly effective. Shoppers have discovered that the fastest way to find a business that can sell them the product or service they need is by looking up the product or service on the Web, and the most effective searches are through the best-known services and those that identify the largest number of web pages: Google, Yahoo!, MSN and AOL (see Figure 7.2).

banners Advertisements that appear on a web page.

Banners are images placed on a website that link to the site of the company selling the product or service. Usually the image is wide horizontally, or elongated

Figure 7.2 Spending on search advertising

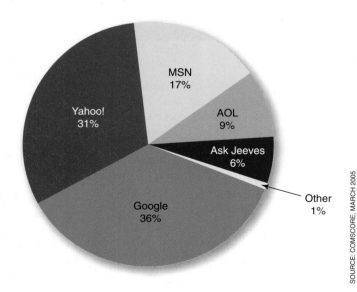

vertically, hence the term 'banner'. However, any image placed for advertising is referred to as a banner. In recent years, a growing number of online newspapers and journals have placed banners in interesting articles. Popular blog sites also attract advertisers.

How does a potential advertiser know how much traffic a site attracts? The most basic metric that can be measured at a site is the number of impressions. An impression occurs whenever a browser downloads the page containing the banner. More useful metrics are provided by several companies that rate website visits similar to rating television viewing. For instance, comScore, an online rating firm, maintains a panel of 1.5 million English-speaking online consumers from around the world whom the firm polls periodically. The companies produce several metrics for subscribing companies. Usually, subscribers of online rating firms are high-traffic sites that generate large revenues from advertising.

> **impression** In web advertising, the event of an ad displayed on a surfer's monitor.

In addition to impressions, rating companies measure other metrics. One is *unique visitors per month*. If the same person visited a site several times during a given month, the person is counted only once. The reason? Advertisers are interested in reaching many people, not the same people with many visits. Another metric is *unique visitor pages*, which are the number of different pages at the site that a single visitor accessed. The reason for this metric is that the same visitor is exposed to different ads at the site. Reach percentage is the percentage of web users who have visited the site in the past month, namely, the ratio of visitors to total web population.

> **reach percentage** The percentage of web users who have visited a site in the past month, or the ratio of visitors to the total web population.

As in print advertising, the site owner charges the advertiser by the ad's size (so many pixels by so many pixels) and by the number of impressions. Using the IP numbers of computers accessing the pages with the banners, the advertiser can easily count impressions.

It is said that word of mouth might be the most effective advertising at no cost. Free advertising on the Web often takes the form of multiple mentions on blogs and other social networking sites. In August 2006 a four-piece band from Sheffield, the Artic Monkey's, achieved the distinction of having Britain's fastest-selling debut album; and yet their fame and success was all built without the usual media-industry hype associated with new, probably manufactured, bands. Neither was it as a result of a reality television show and associated marketing. Their early tunes and gigs were made available to fans for free and were subsequently shared on MySpace and other social networking sites. Their fame snowballed so that by the time their debut album was released its success was assured, all without any conventional marketing.

Exchanges and auctions

In the old days, a meeting place of buyers and sellers had to be tangible such as a marketplace or a shop. Until recently, finding a buyer for scrap metal, used scientific equipment, or any other commodity might have taken a long time. Also, the buyer and seller had to pay high finder's fees to individuals and firms that specialized in such intermediary trade. On the Web, the marketplace can include as many sellers and as many buyers as wish to participate, as long as they have access to the Internet.

An intranet is a network used only by the employees of an organization. An extranet limits site access to the employees of particular organizations, usually business partners. An extranet might be viewed as connecting intranets of business partners.

> **intranet** A network using web browsing software that serves employees within an organization.

> **extranet** A network, part of which is the Internet, whose purpose is to facilitate communication and trade between an organization and its business partners.

An exchange is an extranet for organizations that offer for sale, and bid on, products and services of a particular type. Unlike a public auction site such as eBay or uBid, access is usually limited to subscribers, and the subscribers often pay a periodic fee to the site's operator. Auction sites whose purpose is to serve as a meeting place of buyers and sellers in a particular industry are sometimes operated by an industrial association. Others are established by entrepreneurs for the sole purpose of making profit. When the purpose is only to provide a place where sellers compete for the business of a single buyer, the buyer operates the site.

When the site is established by a private business as a meeting place for multiple buyers and sellers, the operator is impartial and profits from transaction fees paid either by one party or both, the seller and buyer, whenever a sales transaction is signed. One of the largest of these exchange sites is ChemConnect, where sellers can auction off chemicals, plastics and natural gas. ChemConnect has 9000 client members in 150 countries. The president of a petroleum company who makes 15 per cent of his natural gas purchases and sales at the site summarized the advantage of such exchanges to businesspeople. In the past he had to spend a day and use the phone to find buyers or sellers for a single purchase or sale. Now, he posts the information online and 150 interested people see it.

Auction sites sell a great variety of items, including live ones. PEFA.com, in Zeebrugge, Belgium, is a private auction site for fresh fish. More than 500 buyers, usually large companies from all over Europe, purchase 60 different species of fish – fresh, farmed, processed and frozen – worth several hundred million euro through the site from sellers in 18 ports. The site accommodates buyers and sellers in seven languages. It also allows subscribers to use PEFA's database, so they can receive rich information on market conditions and statistics. The database is available in 11 languages.

Some electronic markets are established by a single buyer or by an organization that represents many buyers. For example, ChoiceBuy.com is a site operated by Choice Hotels International, a company that franchises the hotels Comfort Inn, Quality, Clarion, Sleep Inn, Econo Lodge, Rodeway Inn and MainStay Suites. The total number of hotels it franchises is over 5000 worldwide. In 1999, the company established the website so it could concentrate all the purchases for the hotels through a single channel. The site invites sellers to offer their products. For the sellers this is an opportunity to obtain big contracts. For the hotels, this is a way to enjoy great discounts, which ChoiceBuy.com obtains through its buying power. For Choice Hotels it is a way to generate revenue from the transaction fees that the bidders pay, and

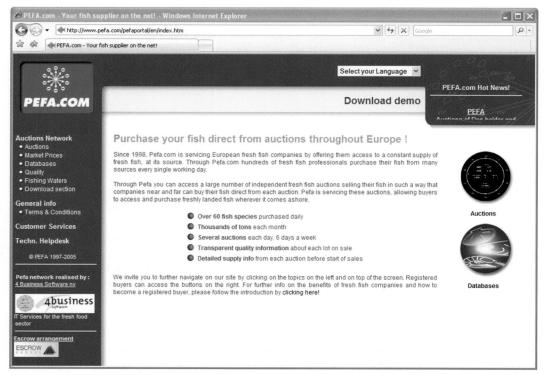

The home page of PEFA.com.

indirectly a way to attract more franchisees that, of course, pay the company franchise fees. Independent hotels are allowed to make their own purchases, and they do buy for € 1 billion annually, but an increasing number of the purchases are made through the site. In 2004, ChoiceBuy.com processed 5236 orders for toilet paper, towels and other supplies for more than 1000 hotels in its franchise. Processing orders through the site not only saves money for the hotel operators but also enriches Choice Hotels. Since all transactions are electronic, they are automatically recorded and provide valuable data from which useful information can be gleaned.

Many exchanges require businesses to register as members and to pay an annual fee. Many guarantee sellers that they will receive payment even if the buyer defaults, an important and attractive consideration for sellers. Electronic marketplaces bring markets closer to what economists call perfect markets. In a perfect market no single buyer or seller can affect the price of a product. On the Internet, all buyers and sellers have access to the same information at the same time. Thus, no single buyer or seller has an information advantage over competitors.

Online business alliances

Companies in the same industry – competitors – often collaborate in establishing a website for one or several purposes. One major purpose might be to create buying power by consolidating purchases. Another might be to create a single place for customers, assuming that a greater choice will benefit the group. The concept is not new. In America estate agents or 'realtors' have collaborated in the multiple listing system (MLS), whereby multiple agencies have access to real estate that is registered for sale with one of them. This system, which was in place way back in the early twentieth century, is now managed on the Web.

In some cases, the purpose of an alliance site is the same as an auction site operated by a single company, but the operator is a business that works for the allied companies. The purpose of such a site is to set the prices of purchased products and services. Big players in an industry, such as airlines or car manufacturers, establish a shared company that operates the site. Suppliers are invited to sell through the site and compete among themselves. The competition drives prices down. The allies enjoy lower costs and greater profit margins.

Star Alliance is one of several airline alliances, such as OneWorld, SkyTeam and Orbitz. Star Alliance established an extranet for two purposes: to concentrate purchases from parts and service providers, and to represent the group to its clients, airline passengers. The alliance includes Air Canada, Air New Zealand, Austrian Airlines, Lufthansa, Scandinavian Airlines, United, Varig and other companies. On the consumer side, the airlines collaborate in frequent flier programmes: you can fly with any of them and accrue miles with the entire alliance rather than with a single airline. The Star Alliance site provides several useful services for travellers of all member airlines. On the B2B side, the alliance solicits bids from suppliers of aircraft parts and maintenance services, food, ground equipment, office supplies and other products and services. The allies use the extranet to share information about inventory levels, facilitate joint planning and forecasting for material requirements and facilitate communication and business transactions between the airlines and suppliers. The hub for joint purchasing has saved the allies millions of euros annually.

Similar alliance sites have been established by firms in the general retail industry, the food industry and the hospitality industry (hotels).

B2C trading

Although business-to-business trading on the Internet is much larger in volume, online business-to-consumer (B2C) trading has caught the headlines in recent years, and that has prompted the establishment of a multitude of Internet companies.

E-tailing

CD TASK

You can shop the Web for virtually any item you want, from collectibles to cars, order these items online and receive them at your door. At various retail sites, shoppers can use sophisticated search applications to find information on desired items, read other shoppers' reviews of items such as books and music CDs, post their own opinions, drop an item in a virtual shopping cart, change their minds and remove the item, or decide to buy the item and pay by providing a credit-card account number or through a debit service such as PayPal. Online retailing – *e-tailing* – continues to grow throughout the world for several reasons: greater availability of faster communication lines to households, growing confidence in online purchases and the increasing ability to find the item one searches and rich information about it.

Buy.co.uk, Amazon.co.uk and the e-tailing arms of bricks-and-mortar retail chains such as Tesco and WH Smith are among thousands of e-tailers. Their sites combine friendly and enticing web pages, database management systems and transaction software to provide shopping and buying convenience. Companies that sell online have smaller expenses than those selling from stores because they do not have to buy or rent shops and use labour to operate cash registers. They do, however, maintain large warehouses and pay for picking, packing and shipping, three activities known as **fulfilment**. In some cases, however, they do not even need to maintain their entire inventory because they can simply route orders directly to manufacturers, who ship the items directly to the customer.

> **fulfilment** Picking, packing and shipping after a customer places an order online.

An important element of online retailing is selection. Compare the variety of products that can be offered at a web storefront with the selection offered by a bricks-and-mortar store: a typical CD store offers about 25,000 different titles, while Amazon offers 500,000 titles, just about every CD title, available for sale. There are also fewer returns because shoppers have more information at hand before they make their purchases. So, shoppers are more satisfied with their buying decisions, and web businesses save the costs of dealing with returns. Another explanation for fewer returns is the creation of what marketers call one-to-one relationships. Using cookies, the website software can track the clickstream of shoppers who browse the site and track their interests. When the same shopper logs on again, the software offers new items that fall within his or her interest area. And with every visit, the software learns more about visitors and their preferences.

As Table 7.2 summarizes, consumers find several advantages to shopping online: convenience, time-saver, search mechanism, comparative shopping and product reviews. E-tailers

Table 7.2 Web-shopping benefits

Benefit	Because shoppers can . . .
Convenience	Shop from anywhere at any time of the day.
Time-saver	Visit numerous online stores in a few minutes; it would take them hours to do so at shopping malls.
Search mechanism	Find who sells a specific item within seconds by using search engines.
Comparative shopping	Quickly compare quality and price across multiple sellers.
Product reviews	Read product reviews by independent experts and other shoppers, often on the same web page that describes the item.

face mounting challenges, however. The competition is just a click away, so it is critical to offer a wide selection and excellent service, in addition to low price. E-tailers provide easy-to-use online tools to track shipments, and many make returns easy. Some bricks-and-mortar retail chains allow returns to physical stores.

The greatest challenge for e-tailers is turning shoppers into buyers and then turning the buyers into repeat buyers. To this end, many e-tailers have linked their customer relationship management (CRM) applications, discussed in Chapter 3, to their websites. Using cookies and other software, they not only collect large amounts of information about individual shoppers, but also constantly update their profiles. The purpose of consumer profiling is to know the consumers better so the business can serve them better while streamlining its marketing and sales operations.

> **consumer profiling** The collection of information about individual shoppers in order to know and serve consumers better.

While consumer profiling might sound benign, many privacy advocates claim that it violates privacy rights. Imagine that every time you log on to a site, this fact is recorded. Then, when you click on an icon, it is recorded, too. The software at the server side also records the time you spent at each specific page, assuming the longer you spent, the more interested you are. Chances are the site will send you promotional emails about the items displayed on that carefully viewed page. Also, the next time you log on to the site, you might find that this particular page appears on your computer monitor faster than before. These subtle changes result from intelligent analysis of the information you provided knowingly or unknowingly to the site – and perhaps other sites that forwarded the information to this retailer. Many retailers also sell the information they collect to data brokers such as Acxiom, who combine personal data and sell the records to other companies. Privacy advocates object to such observation and sales of data without the user's consent.

Affiliate programmes Many e-tailers, as well as other online businesses, offer affiliate programmes to website owners. The affiliate, the website owner, places a link, usually a banner, to the e-tailer at the site. Affiliates are compensated in one of several ways: *pay per sale*, in which only if a visitor ended up purchasing something is the affiliate paid a fee; *pay per click*, in which the affiliate is paid a small fee whenever a visitor clicks the banner; or *pay per lead*, whereby a lead means that the visitor clicked through to the advertiser's site and filled out a registration form to receive periodic information. Retailers usually use the pay per sale model.

Some e-tailers have hundreds or even thousands of affiliates. Amazon.com and other large e-tailers probably have tens of thousands of affiliates. These programmes provide huge, effective advertising for online businesses.

Some companies make money by being affiliate aggregators. LinkShare (www.linkshare.com) and Commission Junction (www.cj.com) let you choose from hundreds of affiliate advertisers, some offering commissions of up to 40 per cent. You can pick the ones you want to mention at your website.

Competition Amazon.co.uk has taken a step beyond affiliate programmes to cooperate with competitors. It includes its competitors on its own site. When you use the search engine at the company's site for a certain item, it brings up the product description and price from Amazon.co.uk's database and also the same type of information from other companies' databases. Although these companies are direct competitors, Amazon benefits from this cooperation in two ways: it attracts more shoppers to visit its site first, because they know there is a high probability that they will find the item they want at the site, even if they end up buying from another company; and it receives a fee from these affiliated companies whenever they sell through Amazon's site.

conversion rate In marketing, the proportion of shoppers who end up buying from the organization. The term also applies to online shopping.

Conversion One measure of online retail success is conversion rate, the proportion of site visitors who make a purchase to the total number of visitors in a period of time, usually one year. This proportion has steadily increased over the years from a mere fraction of a per cent in the late 1990s to several percentage points now. Interestingly there is a geographical skew in conversion rates. The Internet media and market research organization Nielsen//NetRatings found in a survey that Internet shoppers in the UK and Australia show a high conversion rate, probably because the English-speaking population have an easy access to US eCommerce suppliers. Hong Kong, on the other hand, has one of the lowest conversion rates despite having an Internet environment that is based on high-speed connections. The low conversion rate is probably because the urban environment of Hong Kong is suitable for traditional physical shopping and therefore most potential e-shoppers use the Internet to make price comparisons and learn about products but then purchase in person. In general, pure-play e-tailers, companies that sell solely over the Web, enjoy higher conversion rates than bricks-and-mortar retailers who also sell online.

Auctions and reverse auctions

Similar to auctions among companies, some websites serve as auction hubs for individuals. The most prominent of the sites is eBay, but there are others, such as eBid and CQOut. The business model is simple: sellers list information about the items or services they offer for sale, and if a sale is executed, the site owner collects a fee. Because the sites provide only a platform for a transaction that eventually takes place between two consumers, some people like to call online auctions consumer-to-consumer e-business. To participate in auctions one needs to register as a member. To help bidders know better to what extent they can count on the integrity of the seller, eBay publishes the number of feedback comments it receives on a member, and the number and percentage of positive feedbacks.

reverse auction (name-your-own-price auction) An online auction in which participants post the price they want to pay for a good or service, and retailers compete to make the sale; also called a name-your-price auction.

The ability of websites to serve as prompt exchanges of information has supported another popular business model, the reverse auction or name-your-own-price auction. Priceline.com invites consumers to post requests for services and prices they are willing to pay. Although they also deal in home mortgages, the services are mostly for travel, such as flights, cruises, lodging and car rentals. Customers can post the destination, day and time of a flight, as well as the maximum price they are willing to pay. Then, airlines are invited to consider the requests. The first airline to accept the terms wins the offer. Shoppers are required to transmit a credit-card account number. The account is charged as soon as an airline accepts the deal. Priceline.co.uk's revenue comes from the fees that airlines and other businesses pay to use the service.

Content providers

On the Web, content means information, such as news, research results, statistics and other useful information, as well as artistic works such as music, pictures and video clips. The definition of content could also be extended to include job postings and online dating services. Over the years, individuals and organizations have spent increasing amounts of money on content. Although most news can be obtained free of charge, many articles cannot. Some audiences welcome for-fee content, especially if it is highly specialized. Given a choice, many people prefer to read the same information online rather than on paper because they can use search operations to quickly find specific articles. This might be one reason why many prefer to subscribe to the electronic version of a newspaper. Content revenues also have grown since companies such as Apple started selling individual song files online.

Industry SNAPSHOT

Auction tools

The success of on-line auctions has spawned another industry – that of software specifically designed to make the most of these sites. For example, Auctionlotwatch.co.uk offers tools for alerting buyers about lots that are soon due to finish without any bids, hence representing a potential bargain bid. Another piece of software looks for common misspellings. An item that has been listed for, say, a CD by the Beetles will not be found by most sellers looking for a Beatles CD – potentially another bargain for someone using the wrong spelling as a search word. There are also tools for sellers. Auction Harvest looks at the final selling price of similar items to give the seller an idea of the selling price for their item.

PHOTO SOURCE: © AUCTION LOTWATCH

Bill presentment and payment

Because it is so easy to transfer funds online from one bank account to another, and it is so easy to send information, including bills, by email, many utility companies try to convince customers to accept electronic bills and pay them online. Some customers accept the option of electronic bill presentment but refuse to sign an agreement that would enable the company to automatically charge their bank account. Obviously, banks are always a participant in electronic payment if the charge is to a bank account (which is how most utility and mortgage companies want to be paid), but some banks, for their own reasons, refuse to join such trilateral initiatives.

Electronic bill presentment and payment (EBPP) saves utility companies and financial institutions that bill customers regularly a significant amount of money. The bills are presented automatically, directly from the companies' information systems to payers' email addresses, and therefore save labour, paper and postage. Direct charge to a bank account saves the labour involved in receiving and depositing cheques. Yet, EBPP is spreading slowly. Most people still prefer to pay their bills by cheque and through the mail, partly because fraud on the Internet has increased in recent years, especially through a practice called phishing, discussed in the Ethical and Societal Issues feature. Figure 7.3 illustrates the practice. Note that the fictitious site is not secure. The legitimate one is secure; note the 's' in https://. Also note the bank warnings to customers. This particular email was sent to a person who does not even have an account with the bank.

> **phishing** The criminal practice of luring Internet users to provide their personal information via email or the Web. Phishing almost always results in fraud or identity theft.

Figure 7.3   Phishing plagues web commerce. An email arrives that prompts the recipient to update personal information at a fictitious but legitimate-looking website (bottom left). Note how similar the features in the fictitious (left) and legitimate website (right) are.

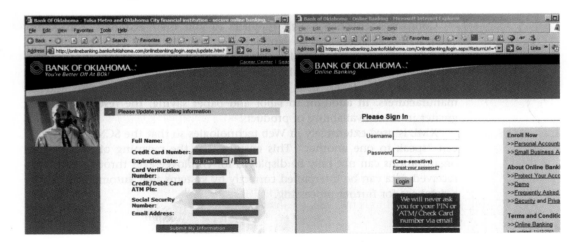

Industry **SNAPSHOT**

Anti-phish tool

When you receive an email message that sends you to your bank's website to reenter your personal details, you should ensure that the site is indeed your bank's. SpoofStick is a free add-on to your browser, which you can download from www.spoofstick.com and install on your computer. Whenever you direct your browser to a site, a line underneath the URL box will tell you the correct site, such as: 'You're on Barclays.co.uk.com' or 'You're on 218.97.169.53.' The former is the legitimate site. The latter is the site for the link the phishers sent you.

Dispersed workforce

The Web enables companies to purchase labour from many more people than their own employees. For example, companies can augment their intellectual pool by using the Web to employ talent beyond their own employees'. They can enjoy more labour for less money by offering cash for research and development (R&D) solutions provided by researchers outside their organizations.

InnoCentive Inc. is a subsidiary of the pharmaceuticals company Eli Lilly and Company. It operates InnoCentive.com, a website connecting scientists with companies. Companies whose R&D staffs cannot find a solution to a biological or chemical problem can post the challenge at the site and offer a cash reward for a practical solution. Scientists and researchers from around the world can register with the site and work on solutions. The site is operated in seven languages to accommodate scientists and organizations from all over the world. So far, Eli Lilly and 30 other companies, including Dow Chemical Co. and the giant consumer product company Procter & Gamble, have awarded sums of US$4,000 to US$100,000. The site has more than 150,000 registered scientists located in 150 countries.

When a company employs a staff of researchers it must pay them regardless of how fruitful their efforts are. When offering cash for solutions, many more scientists might work for the company, but the company pays only the scientist who solves the problem. The cost savings can be huge.

M-commerce

In Chapter 5 you learned about the many wireless technologies that enable people to access the Web while away from the office or home. Wireless technologies enable what some people call mobile commerce, or m-commerce. Mobile devices already let users log on to the Internet, but they can also provide an additional benefit to businesses: a device can be located with an accuracy of several feet, much like locating a mobile phone. As soon as you come within a few blocks of a store, your handheld computer or phone could beep and display a promotional message on its monitor.

m-commerce Mobile commerce, enabled by advances in technology for mobile communications devices.

M-commerce allows people to use their mobile devices to experience an event and react immediately. For example, they might view a horse race and place bets from their seat. Or, they can see a demonstration of a product at a public place and order it online. Impulse shopping will no longer be limited to shopping malls. Recall our discussion in Chapter 5 of future uses of RFID. Mobile devices might be equipped with RFID readers so their owners can use a product's electronic product code (EPC) to download information about it from the Web.

Smart mobile devices might be helpful in sales force automation. Travelling salespeople are able to access data through the mobile device almost anywhere. They are able to access corporate databases through their company's intranet. Both travelling salespeople and consumers already practice m-commerce whenever they transact while using a hotspot or a web-capable mobile phone.

Experts believe that the most attractive mobile application might not be online buying, but the delivery of highly relevant information, custom-tailored to the user's current location and activity. Location services include downloading coupons at the store in which the consumer has just entered, finding out about nearby restaurants, or reading product reviews while shopping at an appliance store.

In the United States, mobile phones manufactured as of 2006 must, by law, include global positioning system (GPS) capability, so that people can be located in case of emergency. As telephoning and other technologies are merged into a single device that can also link to the Web, the potential for marketing and pushing information might be too tempting for businesses.

So far, however, predictions about the growth of m-commerce in North America and Europe have not materialized. The only countries where m-commerce has become popular are Japan and South Korea. In Japan, subscribers to the DoCoMo's i-mode service use their smart mobile phones to purchase drinks from vending machines, buy food at fast-food

Industry **SNAPSHOT**

Surfing the Web 30,000 feet up

For several years airlines have looked at the possible use of mobile telephones on aeroplanes and with the increased functionality of mobile devices to allow web browsing there is a potential for passengers to work (or play!) rather than rely on the in-flight entertainment. However, there is an interesting contrast between the attitudes in the United States and Europe. Recent movements in the US have been away from airborne Internet access, with the Federal Communications Committee voicing concerns that mobile telephone signals have a potential to disrupt other radio communications. This negative attitude has lead Boeing to drop its plans for an in-flight web browsing service at a reported cost of US$1 billion. The opposite is the case in Europe, with regulatory bodies working towards approval. 'It's going through the approval process right now' according to Charlie Pryor, spokesman for OnAir, a potential mobile phone service provider sponsored by Airbus. 'We expect some decisions within a month'.

SOURCE: W David Gardner, 'FCC Say "No" to Cell Phones on Airplanes, But Europe Says "Yes"', *Information Week*, 23 March 2007

restaurants, and shop at Web sites of online retailers. Purchases are charged to the mobile phone service provider, NTT. It is expected that the United States and Europe will catch up to Japan and South Korea. In September 2007 the UK's five largest mobile telephone firms introduced a payment system designed to make handsets into digital wallets. Called PayForIt, the new scheme is designed for paying for goods and services that have low individual value, up to £10. Such sales could be ringtones, train tickets and parking fees.

Privacy proponents have already voiced concerns about m-commerce. Apparently, not many people are happy to find out that commercial organizations can track them down any-time when their mobile device is on. These devices not only allow consumer profiling, as already practised by many online retailers, but can also tell retailers and other organizations your exact location at any given time. The result might be 'We know who you are, what you have done on the Web, and where you are now.'

Supply chains on the Web

Supply chains extend from commercial organizations to both suppliers and buyers. Organizations connect their supply chain management (SCM) systems to their suppliers at one end, and to their buyers at the other end. Thus, an organization might be a participant among other buyers in an extranet managed by one of its suppliers, and a participant among several sellers in an extranet of a buyer. Large retailers manage extranets through which their suppliers' SCM systems can provide useful information to their own, so they can track orders and ship-ments, as well as collect useful information for decision-making on which supplier to select for which order. In this regard, a large retailer's extranet becomes a marketplace for many sellers and a single buyer.

In the years before the opening of the Internet to commercial activities, many companies invested in Electronic Data Interchange (EDI) systems to exchange documents electronically with business partners. EDI consists of certain standards for formatting documents such as orders and invoices, software that translates the data properly, and the networks through which the information flows between subscribing organizations. The networks are owned and managed by value-added network (VAN) companies, telecommunications companies that manage the traffic of EDI between the business partners. Subscribers pay for this service. Although EDI provides some advantages, such as a high degree of data security and nonrepu-diation (inability to deny sent messages), companies that want to connect to establish similar data exchange with business partners can use the web technologies on the Internet. XML, in particular, enables business partners to set standards for data formats in web pages. Dynamic page technologies, the software that links web pages with databases, automate much of the business activity with business partners. Orders can automatically trigger notices to ware-house personnel on their stationary or handheld computers to pick and pack items for shipping. The information automatically flows into the accounting ISs as well as SCM sys-tems of both the buyer and seller. Figure 7.4 illustrates how information flows between organizations.

Companies encourage their suppliers to join their extranets. For example, Tesco, the UK's leading supermarket, allows its suppliers to access the same databases that are used by Tesco's staff. These suppliers can gain information about stock levels at different stores, delivery requirements and so on. Similarly Cisco, the worldwide leader in networking for the Inter-net, allows their suppliers to connect to their internal systems using a password. This security feature means that suppliers are not able to view company confidential information or details about competitive suppliers. However, they are able to identify market trends and provide a better service to Cisco.

XML is used extensively in web technologies so that the SCM systems of two organizations can 'speak to one another'. This ensures that the meaning of data exchanged between the

Figure 7.4   Online supply chain management

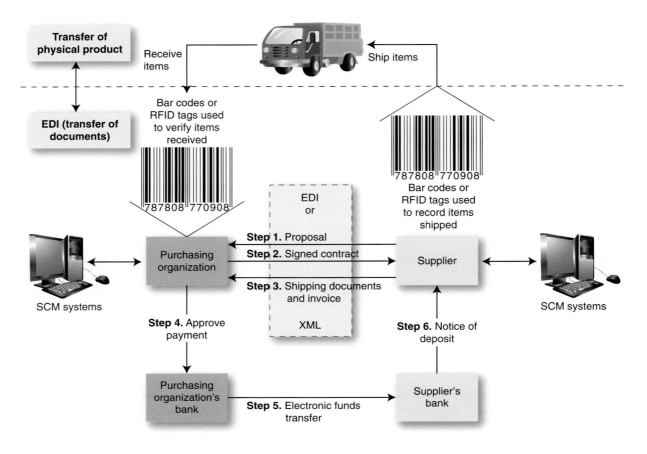

organizations can not only be displayed for employee eyes through web browsers but that the received data can be interpreted correctly by systems that automatically capture and store it in a database for further processing.

Rules for successful web-based business

Most organizations that operate a website do so to sell either products or services. Web software and the ability to connect web servers to organizational information systems open great opportunities. Often, whether online business succeeds depends not only on availability of the proper software but on how it is used. There are several elements to consider, especially if the site is to support B2C commerce.

Target the right customers

Targeting the people or organizations that are most likely to need the products and services you offer has always been the most important effort in marketing, with or without the Web. On the Web, targeting includes identifying the sites your audience frequently visits. For

Ethical and Societal **ISSUES**

Online annoyances and worse

The Web provides excellent opportunities, but its wide availability combined with ingenuity have created some practices that range from mildly annoying to criminally dangerous.

Spam Spam is the term for unsolicited commercial email. Spam does not have to be camouflaged to be so. The mere fact that it is not invited makes it spam. The reason for spam is simple: it is the most cost-effective marketing method. Even if a fraction of a per cent of the recipients end up purchasing the product or service touted, the spammer profits. Both individuals and organizations dislike spam. Individuals have to wade through a long list of unsolicited emails to get to useful emails. Organizations face an increasingly costly burden. Consider: if spam makes up half of the email the organization receives, the organization must employ twice the bandwidth it really needs for communications and twice the space on email servers. Obviously, it pays twice as much as it could for operating an email system. Screening software, known as antispam software, has helped to some extent, but spam is still on the rise and still causes waste of resources. By some estimates, spam constitutes about three-quarters of all email flowing on the Internet.

The Direct Marketing Association (DMA) defends the right of businesses to send unsolicited commercial email as a legitimate and cost-effective way of doing business. Indeed, the method gives small, entrepreneurial businesses a chance to compete. The DMA sees no difference between junk 'snail' mail, which most of us reluctantly tolerate, and spam.

On the other hand, the European Coalition Against Unsolicited Commercial Email (EuroCAUCE) calculated the amount of spam we might soon receive unless new laws stop the phenomenon. Their calculations are as follows. 'EUROSTAT's Yearbook for 2000 included figures for the number of businesses in various territories in 1996. There were 18.444 million businesses in the 15 countries comprising the European Union, ranging from "No Salaried Staff" (i.e. smaller even than "very small") to "Large". So take 1 per cent of that, and we get 184 440 possible senders, each of whom, for the purposes of this thought experiment, sends one message' per year 'complete with instructions for "opting out"'.

'Let's take a working year: 52 weeks less 4 weeks annual leave less an additional 5 days for legal holidays gives us 47 weeks. At 35 hours per week (this is Europe, after all) we get 47*35 = 1645 hours over a working year to deal with these 184 440 messages. That works out to 184 440/1645 = just a little over 112 messages per hour, or a bit less than two messages per minute. Not every sender makes it easy or convenient to "opt-out": some require using a different reply address, others require a visit to a website, and so on, which means that some time must be allowed to parse the message for the relevant information. This calculation does not take excessive downloading time into account, but assumes that the messages appear in time to be dealt with.'

Opting out, then, is not a realistic option but EuroCAUCE does not believe that opting in – avoiding receiving email unless you specifically ask for it – would solve the problem either. Antispam legislation in many countries has not reduced spam. According to most laws, spam is a crime only if the sending party hides its true identity.

Is unsolicited commercial email a legitimate marketing tool, or is it a nuisance that should be eradicated by strictly enforced laws? Would it be fair to outlaw an efficient way for businesses, especially entrepreneurial businesses, to approach potential customers?

Pop-up windows You browse the Web, stop to read an interesting article, and a few seconds later a window pops up, partially covering the text you were reading. The pop-up contains an advertisement. You look for the little X to close the window. It is not in the normal top-right corner. You finally manage to close the window, but as soon as you do, another one pops up. And so on, and so forth, more and more windows. When you finally close the main site's window, you discover that several other windows popped up *behind* the window. The site owner is paid by advertisers to run these pesky windows, which is legitimate. However, many people are quite annoyed by the practice. Some employ special applications or turn on a browser option that prevents pop-up windows. Is this a good solution? Not always. Many sites have links that open a little window, such as a help screen or an explanation of a term. If you block all pop-up windows, such windows do not open. If you use a selective pop-up 'killer', you have to program it to allow pop-up windows for individual sites. Thus, even with a solution, pop-up windows waste surfers' time. Web surfers might not like pop-up windows, but advertisers love them, because they are an effective marketing tool.

Adware A growing number of organizations use adware, software that delivers ad banners or pop-up advertising windows on the Web. Often, the banners hide large parts of the information on the page. Adware is often tailored to users, based on their profiles, such as previous interests. Some companies use adware that pops up deliberately to cover banners of competing companies that paid to advertise at the site a user visits. The visitor might not even know that the ad is not originating from the website, but from another one.

Spyware A more disturbing 'ware' is spyware. As discussed in this chapter, spyware is software that uses the Internet connection of a computer to transmit information about the user without the user's knowledge or permission. Usually, the software transmits information about users' activities with their computers, including their every move on the Internet. It sits on the computer's hard disk, secretly collects information, and transmits it to the computer of a company, usually for marketing purposes, but also for industrial espionage. Some surreptitious software is also designed to pop up windows. Some countries have criminalized adware and spyware,

but in much of the world the software does not violate any law.

Phishing A growing number of web users receive a special kind of spam that intends not to sway them to buy something but to defraud them. The practice is called phishing, a play on 'fishing'. Criminals send thousands of messages that look as if they were sent from a bank, a credit-card company, or any other financial institution or an organization where the recipient has authority to withdraw funds. The email provides a web link where the recipient is urged to go and supply personal information, including codes that are used to withdraw or transfer funds. One of many 'reasons' is 'explained' in the message: your account must be renewed, the bank lost your details, you need to verify your personal information or the account will be revoked, and many others. Thousands of people have fallen prey to the con artists, who use the information to withdraw funds. The most obvious sign that an email message tries to phish is a message from an institution with which you have never transacted, such as a bank where you do not have an account. A more subtle sign is the URL that appears in the browser once you click the link: the domain name is not the one of the legitimate organization. Suspect every email message that asks you to update your personal information online. Call the organization using the legitimate number you have on file and ask if the message is genuine. Banks and other institutions rarely use email to ask for an 'account information update'. Phishing continues to grow. Industry statistics suggest that 5 per cent of recipients of a phishing email subsequently visit an associated website and hand over personal data.

---

instance, a business that sells sporting goods should create clickable links at sites that cover sporting events and provide sports statistics. Banks that offer mortgage loans should create links at estate agents' sites. And any business that targets its products to young people should do so at popular music sites. This principle should also apply to blogs and popular podcasts. Podcasting can include visual advertisements displayed by the player software.

CD TASK

Capture the customer's total experience

By using cookies and recording shoppers' movements, CRM software can create electronic consumer profiles for each shopper and buyer. The shopper's experience with the site then becomes an asset of the business. Such marketing research fine-tunes the portfolio of products that the business offers and tailors web pages for individual customers. It also can be used to 'market to one' by emailing the shopper about special deals on items in which he or she has shown an interest.

Personalize the service

CRM software and web page customization software can be combined to enable customers to personalize the pages and the service they receive when they log on to the site. Letting shoppers and readers select the type of email content they want is welcome, but sites should respect privacy by letting customers opt in rather than opt out. Opting in means that the customer can actively check options to receive email and other promotions, while opting out requires the customer to select *not* to receive such information – an annoyance to many customers.

The Web also enables companies to let consumers tailor products. IKEA, the Swedish furniture retailer, offers a kitchen design service online allowing customers to plan their room, selecting from IKEA products. The finished design is then linked to an order making a seamless link between requirements and fulfilment.

Shorten the business cycle

One reason people like to do business on the Web is that it saves them time. Businesses should keep looking for opportunities to shorten the business cycle for their customers, from shopping to paying to receiving the items they ordered. Fulfilment, the activities taking place after customers place orders online, is one of the greatest challenges for online businesses.

Those who can ship the ordered products fastest are likely to sustain or increase their market shares. Some have decided to outsource the entire fulfilment task to organizations that specialize in fulfilment, such as UPS's e-Logistics and FedEx's Supply Chain Services. E-Logistics, for example, offers to receive and store the business's merchandise in its warehouses, receive orders online, and then pick, pack and ship them to the online business's customers. It also offers a product return service. A shorter business cycle is not only important for customer satisfaction but also enables the company to collect faster because credit cards are usually charged upon shipping.

Let customers help themselves

Customers often need information from a web-enabled organization. Such information includes the status of an order, the status of a shipped item and after-sale information such as installation of add-on components and troubleshooting. Placing useful information and downloadable software at the site not only encourages customer loyalty but also saves labour.

Practically every online business now sends email messages with the status of the order, a tracking number and a link to the shipping company for checking the shipping status. Hardware companies can post online assembly instructions for their 'assembly required' products. In addition to including Frequently Asked Questions (FAQs) information, some companies have used knowledge management software (discussed in Chapter 10) that can answer open-ended questions.

Be proactive and de-commoditize

Expecting customers to visit your website every time they need your service might not be enough in today's competitive marketplace. Customers now demand not only prompt email replies to their queries but also proactive alerts. For example, the travel websites Orbitz and Travelocity email airline customers gate and time information if a customer's flight is delayed or if gates change. Some manufacturers email customers about product recalls or to schedule periodic service appointments.

These initiatives, as well as many others, are efforts to *de-commoditize* what companies sell. A commodity is any product that is sold for about the same price by a multitude of vendors in a highly competitive market, usually with a thin margin of profit. By adding a special service or additional information, the company keeps the products it sells from becoming a commodity. Adding an original service or information to the product differentiates the 'package' that online shoppers purchase from the 'package' sold by competitors.

E-commerce is every commerce

You might have noticed that the title of this chapter does not contain the term 'e-commerce'. You might have also noticed that this is not the only chapter in which web-enabled business activities are discussed. In fact, every chapter in this book gives examples of what is popularly referred to as e-commerce. Web technologies have been integrated into the business world to a degree that makes it difficult at times to realize which activities take place inside the organization and which involve information flowing from other places through the Internet. We have become so used to the integration of the Web into our daily activities, especially the commercial ones, that the lines between commerce and e-commerce have been blurred. We will eventually stop using the term 'e-commerce' and simply consider the Web another means of supporting business, much the way we consider technologies like the telephone and fax.

SUMMARY

Some industries have changed dramatically and continue to change thanks to web technologies. Any product whose sole purpose is to deliver information or any other product that can be digitized will eventually be delivered over the Web.

HTTP is an Internet standard that enables addressing of web servers with domain names. HTTPS is a secure version of the protocol for confidential transactions. HTML is a markup language for presentation of web pages. XML is a markup language for delivery of information about data communicated through web pages. XHTML combines features of HTML and XML. FTP is a protocol for uploading and downloading files. RSS is software that uses XML to automatically update text and audio from the website that posts it to subscriber online devices. It is the main enabler of podcasting. Blogs enable people to conveniently create discussion web pages by posting comments and responding to them. Instant messaging online chat services enable people to correspond in real time and help businesses serve online customers. Cookies help websites to personalize the experience of visitors. Along with other software that spies on unwitting web surfers, they might provide detailed information about web users.

In addition to a large number of nonproprietary web technologies, many more are developed and licensed to organizations by software vendors.

An organization has two options when deciding to do commerce online: own and maintain its own web servers at its own facilities, or contract with a web hosting company. When contracting with a web host, there are several degrees of service: shared hosting, virtual private servers, dedicated hosting and co-location.

When selecting a web hosting company, organizations should consider several factors: type and quality of application provided, storage space, quality of technical support, traffic limits, availability of email accounts and services, scalability, support of page design, security, uptime ratio, setup fee and monthly fee.

Web-enabled commerce can generally be classified as business-to-business (B2B) or business-to-consumer (B2C). In the former, businesses use networks to trade with other businesses, possibly through an extranet. In the latter, businesses advertise and sell goods and services to consumers via the Web. The greater volume of e-commerce is conducted between businesses.

Business-to-business trading often relies on electronic data interchange (EDI), which is conducted over value-added networks. XML facilitates interorganizational online trading similar to EDI. When linked to internal ISs, web technologies enhance supply chain management. Online interorganizational commerce often takes place through an extranet.

With the proliferation of wireless handheld computers and smart mobile phones, the next wave in B2C might be mobile commerce, popularly called m-commerce. It is already popular in Japan, but to a much smaller degree in Europe and the United States.

To be successful, an online business must target the right customers, capture the customer's total experience, personalize the service, shorten the business cycle, let customers help themselves and be proactive.

Spam, and to a lesser degree spyware, adware and pop-up windows, have become online annoyances. Society is trying to strike a balance between allowing these phenomena to continue as a form of commercial promotion and free speech, and curbing them to reduce the public's waste of resources. Phishing has become a pervasive crime, defrauding people and stealing their identities.

SpareBitz.com

SPAREBITZ REVISITED

The SpareBitz website included a customer feedback form and Steve noticed that there were several negative comments about the late delivery of items. Some of these were down to Steve and staff not being able to fulfil orders quickly enough, but most were because of delays in deliveries from suppliers and delays by the Royal Mail.

What would you do?

1　What changes to his own order fulfilling system can Steve take to minimize the customer complaints?

2　What can be done about the external problems in the process (Steve's supplier's and Royal Mail)?

New perspectives

1　Steve wants to find out more about who is visiting his site, what they are looking at and whether the visit turns into an order. What methods can Steve use to help him in this analysis?

Review questions

1　What is streaming video and on what does the success of companies that stream video rather than rent DVDs depend?

2　What is HTML, and why is it needed to use the Web?

3　What is XML? How is it different from HTML, and what purpose does it fulfil in web commerce?

4　What is the relationship between a domain name and an IP number?

5　When you visit a website and click a Download button, you activate software that adheres to a certain protocol. What protocol is that?

6　What is instant messaging (IM), and how can it support business operations? How does IM reduce telephone costs?

7　What is RSS, and for which industry is it especially useful?

8　What is blogging, and what potential does it have for businesses?

9　What is podcasting, and how is it different from radio broadcasting?

10　In the context of the Web, what is a cookie? What is the benefit of cookies for online shoppers? What is the risk?

11　What is the difference between first-party cookies and third-party cookies? Which is usually disliked more by consumers, and why?

12　What is an intranet, and what purposes does it serve?

13　What is an extranet, and what purposes does it serve?

14　When contracting with a web hosting company, what is the difference between a shared server and a dedicated server?

15　What is co-location? What are its benefits?

16　When selecting a web hosting company, one of the important factors to consider is uptime ratio. What is it, and why is it important?

17　What does 'unique monthly visitors' mean in online lingo? Who uses this metric and for what purpose?

18 What is a reverse auction? Would it be practical without the Web? Why or why not?

19 What is phishing? How do people get 'phished'?

Discussion questions

1 Streaming movies to subscribers' homes over the Web has already replaced video stores in some parts of the world. What other services do you think will change business models when large parts of the population have high-speed broadband connections?

2 Sun Microsystems Corp. coined the slogan 'The network *is* the computer.' What does that mean?

3 Some top-level domains (TLDs) are reserved for certain organizations. Why is this important? Would you prefer that anyone could register a TLD of his or her choice?

4 Podcasting is said to allow subscribers to 'time-shift'. What does that mean, and does this give listeners a benefit they do not have with radio programmes?

5 E-tailers can use their software to charge different shoppers different prices. This is called price discrimination, and it is legal. Some observers say that shoppers discriminate based on price when they decide from whom to buy, and therefore it is ethical for e-tailers to price-discriminate. Do you agree?

6 Do you see blogging and podcasting as a threat to the written and broadcast media? Explain.

7 One of the most frustrating types of events to an e-tailer is shopping cart abandonment. From your own online shopping experience, what are the things that would cause you to abandon an online shopping cart?

8 M-commerce will give organizations the opportunity to send location-related advertising, that is, they will send to our handheld devices advertising based on where we are. What is your feeling about this?

9 Some parts of the world have legislated voting through the Internet. There are thoughts of a wider 'teledemocracy'. At present online voting is restricted to 'big issues', such as the selection of State Representatives in some states in America. But the technology could easily be used for voting on wider issues such as new taxes, budget cuts and so on. Do you favour this teledemocracy? Why or why not?

10 Gambling on the Web is growing fast. Do you see a danger in this phenomenon more than in gambling in traditional ways? Does web gambling have more or less social impact than casino gambling?

11 You have a new home business. You sell a consumer product for which you have a patent. You believe there will be much demand for it. To promote it, you decide to purchase a list of 2,000,000 email addresses of people who fit into the demographic groups that are likely to purchase the product. The seller told you that these were addresses only of people who did not opt out from receiving messages from businesses. After you emailed the promotional message, you received hundreds of angry email messages, including one from the European Coalition Against Unsolicited Commercial Email (EuroCAUCE). Was there anything wrong in what you did? Why or why not?

12 The owners of a small business tell you that they would not be able to reach enough customers to survive if they couldn't use mass, unsolicited email. You strongly object to spamming. How do you respond to them?

13 Scott McNealy, CEO of Sun Microsystems, said: 'You already have zero privacy. Get over it!' Some observers say that expecting privacy when using the Internet is ridiculous; the Internet is a public network, and no one should expect privacy in a public network. Do you agree? Why or why not?

14 A student established a website that serves as an exchange of coursework. Students are invited to contribute their marked work and to search for assignments that other students contributed. When criticized, the student claims that this, too, is a way to do research. He argues that the moral responsibility rests with those who access his site, not with him. Do you agree? Why or why not?

15 There have been international efforts to harmonize laws addressing free speech on the Web. Do you think such efforts can succeed? Why or why not?

Tutorial activities

1 Find three commercial sites that operate in three different markets and offer affiliate programmes. Write up a summary: What do they sell? What do their affiliate programmes promise, and in return for what? Classify each programme as pay per sale, pay per click, pay per lead or another type, and explain why you classified the way you did.

2 Choose a topic in which you are interested. Select three different search engines (e.g., Google, Yahoo!, and MSN) and use them to look for information about the subject. Rank the performance of each site. A long list of sites that provide too broad a range of information is bad; a shorter list of sites that provide more narrowly defined information is good. Explain your ranking.

3 You have been hired by a pizza delivery service to design a website. The site should be attractive to families and young professionals and should allow them to order home delivery. Use a web page development application to build the home page of the business. Submit your page to your instructor.

4 The following table contains some of the elements offered by a web hosting firm. Assume that all other elements are satisfactory. Explain in writing to a person who has never learned about the subject what each of the shown elements means, including restrictions. Your 'student' is a small-business owner who sells 500 unique dolls and is interested in also selling online. Will this be a good option for her in the short run? Explain. If you need to make some reasonable assumptions that are not mentioned here, do so.

Feature	Description
Storage	5 GB
Your own domain name	Yes
Monthly data transfer	110 GB
MySQL database	Available
Shopping cart	Available
Email accounts	30
Website templates	Available
Setup fee	None
Monthly fee	€29.95

5 Prepare your curriculum vitae as an HTML document. If you wish, include your scanned photograph. Submit your work by email, or post it to your website and email the website link to your professor.

6 Consider the following options for a business that wishes to use a website: maintaining their own server at their facility, using a host for a shared server, using a host for a virtual private server, using a host for a dedicated server. You are a consultant. Consider each of the following scenarios independently of the others, and recommend the best hosting option to the business. Consider all the relevant factors, such as purpose and cost.

a) A family store at a shopping centre. The owners want to make the public aware of what the store offers. They want to pay as little as possible for this web presence.

b) A large retail company. Management wants to be able to execute purchases from suppliers through the new website, and to allow their own customers to shop and buy through the site. It is willing to employ its own team and facility for the servers.

c) A small business. The owners insist on having their own domain name. They wish visitors to have every sense that the site is run and controlled by the owners.

d) A small business. Management does not want to register and pay for its own domain name.

e) A large pure-play (Internet-only) e-tailer. It needs to change the list of products daily. Its web design team might want to change the DBMS, shopping cart application and other applications when the need arises. It already owns the servers but no longer wants to manage networking, backup, redundancy and security.

f) A bricks-and-mortar retailer that wants to extend its sales operations to the Web. It has a web design crew that is capable of changing content and is expert at using and modifying web applications such as dynamic pages and shopping cart applications. However, management does not want to purchase servers or manage their networking and security.

7 Team up with another student to analyse the privacy policies of three companies that specialize in collecting consumer information on the Web. All must be companies that install third-party cookies. There are at least ten such companies. List the common factors of the three companies. Then list the factors in which they differ. For each of the differing elements, which company treats consumers better, in terms of less invasion of privacy and more disclosure of its activities? Among other factors, see if the companies offer opt-in or opt-out options.

8 With two other team members, prepare a rationale for an original business idea that could generate revenue on the Web. Prepare the rationale in a way that would convince a venture capitalist to invest money in this new business.

Companion CD questions

1 Have you paid for a product or service using e-cash? If so, describe your experience. Would you do it again? If not, would you consider using e-cash? Why or why not?

2 Visit three sites that use e-commerce. Compare the look and feel of each site. Is it easy to make a transaction on the site? Does the site have any features that make doing business extremely easy or difficult? What are they?

Video questions

1 Have you downloaded music from an online site? If so, describe your experience. Would you do it again? If not, would you consider doing it? Why or why not?

2 Do you think pay-as-you-go music services are a good alternative to illegal music file sharing? Why or why not?

From ideas to application
REAL CASES

Case study **7.1**

Ocado: an Internet supermarket

BY MARTIN RICH

Ocado is an Internet supermarket based in Hatfield, twenty miles north of central London. When it started in 2001 it delivered to customers only in a distinct area close to its base, but from 2003 onwards it also delivered in a number of urban areas of the United Kingdom outside London. Though Ocado carries goods which are also sold by the established Waitrose chain of supermarkets, it has been set up as an autonomous

An Ocado delivery van delivering Waitrose shopping in Cheam, Surrey, England.

PHOTO SOURCE: © HELENE ROGERS/ALAMY

company in which the John Lewis Partnership (which owns Waitrose) has a 25 per cent stake. The company was started by three former bond traders who had worked at Goldman Sachs, and was originally named 'Last Mile Solutions' because of its emphasis on reengineering the final stage of the delivery process to customers' homes.

Although long-established – it has been in existence for around 100 years and has been owned by John Lewis since the 1930s – Waitrose covers a relatively small geographical area, up to around 150 miles from London. Also, while Waitrose has expanded the number of stores that it operates in recent years, these stores are typically medium-sized supermarkets; they have few very large outlets and they have not, on the whole, developed small outlets in the same way that some of the large national chains have. Where they have opened new large outlets recently, they have branded these as 'food and home' and have sold household goods, similar to those stocked in John Lewis department stores, alongside groceries.

Ocado started operations in 2002, in conjunction with the logistics firm GIST, whose depot they initially used, and using computers from Sun Microsystems and an established suite of e-commerce software from Intershop. The John Lewis Partnership already had some experience of using Intershop software as a platform for its online department store.

Ocado is carefully branded as being 'in association with Waitrose' so that it benefits from the established brand and from Waitrose's existing supply chain, and carries Waitrose's own-brand products, but is nevertheless perceived by customers as being a distinct service.

Superficially, Waitrose, as a regional player in the traditional supermarket business, would appear a good candidate to introduce an Internet supermarket with greater geographic coverage. In practice, however, Ocado started with a very limited geographic range and took two years to begin significant expansion outside London. Ocado does now service some major cities where there are few, if any, Waitrose outlets. Conversely Ocado does not, on the whole, operate in rural areas where drops are likely to be further apart and the logistics more difficult. In these areas Waitrose offers a simple store-based home delivery service. Within urban areas it makes sense for an Internet supermarket to be very focused on specific areas, partly because this makes it possible to deliver to many customers in a short time, partly because the supermarket's vans themselves are an effective form of advertising, and partly because the supermarket can build up very detailed information about buying patterns among customers in a particular area.

Ocado's advertising has been carefully targeted at relatively cash-rich time-poor customers, notably at affluent families with young children and two working parents.

By late 2006 Ocado considered the possibility of opening further distribution centres, but their business model continues to be based on serving a large area from a single centre. Ocado's delivery vans use 'demountable pods' to carry the food, so six of these can be loaded onto one lorry for the first part of their journey to customers, and each pod can then be transferred to a different van for the last mile. This is in contrast with Tesco, which is both the largest supermarket chain in Britain and the largest online food retailer, which fulfils most of its Internet orders from local supermarkets. Ocado's approach needs economies of scale to work (compared to Tesco's which could be introduced on a small scale with relatively limited investment), but if implemented well, can offer accurate time-slots and few substitutions, where customers are asked to accept different goods from those that they originally ordered.

For many years the trend in grocery retailing (and many other forms of retailing) has been towards customers picking items off shelves for themselves. This has been driven partly by a will to give customers choice (for example, by choosing loose fruit and vegetables) but mostly to save cost. Internet retailing reverses this trend, and its emergence raises the issue of how the cost of paying staff to pick items off shelves can be justified.

Ocado's core target market is firmly middle-class and pressed for time. Waitrose is already differentiated, in London at least, by presenting itself as a slightly more exclusive supermarket than its rivals. A lot of early advertising was directed to consumers who were thought to be open to Internet shopping, and who already had Waitrose or John Lewis store cards – to the extent of sending aprons and other free gifts to their target customers before the service started.

Ocado does aim to have an edge over their competitors in terms of logistics. Purchasers are offered a 'green van' option, where they can choose a slot when a van is already scheduled to be in their area. This is promoted as something that would appeal to environmentally conscious customers, but it also means that customers help Ocado to cluster deliveries in one area close together, which simplifies their logistics. Because the business model is based on customers choosing their delivery slots early, and on monitoring stocks in the central warehouse closely, the aim is to keep substitutions down to 2 per cent of all goods delivered. Complex routing software and satellite navigation in the vans are used to ensure that they can offer one-hour delivery slots: an ambitious service given the amount and unpredictability of traffic in London. Ocado waives their delivery fee on most orders over £75 (they have recently introduced a complex structure for delivery charges), so they rely on the efficiency and scale of their central warehouse to keep costs down.

Despite the business model, it is impossible to avoid substitutions completely, because there will always be occasions when a supplier is unable to fulfil, or predictions about demand are inaccurate.

In 2003 it was reported that Ocado had already lost £76.8 million, and although Ocado's directors expressed a wish to move into profit 'soon', the real objective was to expand the business by 5 per cent a week. In practice, the business has expanded by 50 per cent in each year of operation so far, and showed an operating profit (though it still had a lot of debts) for the first time in early 2007.

Case study questions

1 How easy would the Ocado idea be to replicate? Is there the possibility that another player could take Ocado's ideas and implement them more effectively?

2 Despite the attractiveness of the distribution centre approach, in practice cheap and simple approaches such as Tesco's have a better record of being profitable. What is necessary to achieve the economies of scale needed for Ocado's approach to be more profitable?

3 What concerns can you see if Ocado continues to expand into broader geographical areas? What would be a realistic aim in terms of expanding their coverage?

4 What sort of synergy exists with the John Lewis Partnership as part-owners? What do they get out of putting investment into Ocado?

5 What alternative strategies can you see for Ocado in the future?

6 What possible further applications can you see for the business model adopted by Ocado?

SOURCES: K. Boyer and M. Frohlich, 'Ocado – An Alternative Way to Bridge the Last Mile in Home Delivery?', Michigan State University, 2002; G. Clapperton, 'Supermarket Switch', *Guardian*, 17 November 2003; M. Feisst, 'Ocado on road to profits and site expansion', *Daily Telegraph*, 7 September 2006

silicon.com

Case study **7.2**

Amazon reaches out beyond its border

BY ELIZABETH BIDDLECOMBE

Businesses are learning to use technology to collaborate not only within their organizations but outside them too. Amazon.com is one example. Elizabeth Biddlecombe explains how they've done it.

From the outset Amazon.com has epitomized the e-commerce era. This is not just because of its use of the Web as its window to the customer, but also because of the systems it has used to connect with retail partners.

The company has exposed its technology platform and product data to third-party developers who have found all manner of ways to link words in text documents and weblogs – and even data from MP3 files – to goods for sale on Amazon.com.

Craig Berman, director of platform and technology communications at the Seattle-based company, says this diverse group includes developers creating applications that enhance associate sites. Others have commercial applications 'that help marketplace sellers manage business on Amazon.com', he says.

They are lured by the commission they make on each sale, while at a very basic level, Amazon reaps the reward of increased traffic through its virtual checkout.

'The great thing about enabling third parties to sell on the site is that it does provide low prices and great selection to customers', Berman explains. 'The flip side is that it allows developers to build their own profitable businesses.'

This open approach has spawned its own industry, with people writing books on how to make money through the Amazon e-machine. Two years after its launch in July 2002, some 65,000 developers had signed up to the web services platform.

One such developer is UK-based consultancy Inside C, which has developed an alternative method for customers to shop at Amazon. Its Inside Messenger application is based on the MSN Messenger instant messaging client and allows shoppers to query Amazon's database for particular products. Users keep a dedicated address in their contact list, which they click to search for an item on Amazon, though they never leave the IM client to do so.

Such applications are based on the company's E-Commerce Services (ECS) platform – itself using XML and Linux – which allows access to detailed product and pricing information.

When Amazon released version 4.0 of the platform, it incorporated new features such as the ability to link to images of products, the retrieval of all the customer reviews for a particular product or, if they prefer, particular reviews written by a specific reviewer. More sophisticated searches can be incorporated and developers can add the shopping cart functionality to their website.

At the end of January 2005 Amazon announced that ECS 4.0 was also available on its French and

Amazon is increasingly 'personalizing' its website for each of its customers.

Canadian sites, rounding out the capabilities to all six of its localized websites.

This is one part of Amazon Web Services (AWS) with another component being the web-crawling Alexa Web Information Service.

Suppliers themselves benefit from being able to plug into these systems. They can download the latest product information, manage their inventory, submit refunds and work out pricing for their goods.

Oregon-based consultancy Monsoon LLC is set up to help retailers, particularly smaller outfits with limited technological resources, plug into Amazon Web Services.

One sector that has benefited from this interfacing of systems is second-hand thrift shops that can now sell their books via Amazon. For instance, one US thrift store chain called Savers has been able to log into the system, price books competitively and then sell them. The company found itself making $8000 in book sales per week while before using AWS it would have been recycling them.

But obviously another key reason for Amazon's e-commerce prowess is its customer-facing technologies.

Berman says the company focuses on providing three things to seed the customer experience: low prices, a vast selection of products and a convenient, enjoyable experience online.

Part of that experience is driven by Amazon's use of personalization – the way it recognizes repeat customers, logs their past purchases and tries to prompt further spending.

Berman notes a collection of ways that Amazon tries to achieve the latter – in customer reviews, product ratings, the uploading of images and wish lists. Its recent investment in a weblog called 43 Things might signify that it is planning to tap into blogs as the latest way to create a community and motivate sales.

However, Berman will not provide comment on the rationale behind the investment. Nor, he says, does Amazon comment on speculation as to how the company might incorporate blogging, social networking or any other technology into its strategy.

Yet if history is any indication, Amazon will no doubt continue to find ways to use technology to reach out to partners, suppliers and customers.

Thinking about the case

1 Amazon seem to be 'giving away' access to its e-commerce applications to third-party developers. Does this seem like good business sense?

2 Can you think of ways that Amazon might use technology in the future to 'reach out to partners, suppliers and customers'?

PART ONE
The information age

1 Business information systems: an overview
2 Strategic uses of information systems
3 Business functions and supply chains

PART TWO
Information technology

4 Business hardware and software
5 Business networks and telecommunications
6 Databases and data warehouses

PART THREE
Electronic commerce

7 The web-enabled enterprise
8 Challenges of global information systems

PART FOUR
Managers and
information systems

9 Managers and their information needs
10 Business intelligence and knowledge
management

PART FIVE
Planning, acquisition
and controls

11 Systems planning and development
12 Choices in systems acquisition
13 Risks, security and disaster recovery

Chapter 8

Challenges of global information systems

LEARNING OBJECTIVES

A growing number of organizations operate globally or, at least, in more than one geographic market. These organizations face some challenges that have a considerable impact on their information systems. The organizations have to meet the challenge of operating globally by providing international information systems to accommodate the free flow of information both within a single company's divisions and between multinational corporations. These issues have always been important to multinational companies but are of increasing relevance because so many companies operate a website, and websites are accessible globally.

When you finish this chapter, you will be able to:

Explain why multinational corporations must use global information systems.

Provide elementary advice for designing websites for an international audience.

Cite the cultural, legal and other challenges to implementing international information systems.

SpareBitz.com

EXPANDING GLOBALLY

It came as a bit of a surprise to Steve Wilson when SpareBitz received its first order from Canada. It seemed that the customer had drawn a blank on finding the right spare part for a lawnmower he had shipped out there when he emigrated. He didn't want to throw it away and buy what he considered to be an inferior local mower. When he happened onto the SpareBitz website he was delighted to see the promise that the part would be found and delivered within a week. Steve put all his efforts into meeting this special order and had to overcome several new hurdles, not least sorting out customs clearance. When he sat down and analysed this sale he realized that he hadn't made any profit on it if you costed in all his time and the extra postage. So should he change his website so that it was only possible to order parts for delivery within the UK? His business brain kicked in. Could this be a profitable income stream? How much potential was there for overseas sales? With a few tweaks to his e-commerce operation, Steve was able to be prepared for requests for spares from virtually any part of the globe. He really was 'World Wide' now! Some of the considerations were to do with currency. A link to a currency converter was made available to website visitors, although the site automatically allowed potential customers to view their order in UK pounds, US dollars or euro at the touch of a button. At this stage Steve decided that language was not an issue. The volume of sales did not make it worthwhile to offer multilingual versions of the website.

Backwards and forwards

'There's something very odd here.' Charlie Evans, the Warehouse Manager, had just walked into Steve's office. 'It seems that this washing machine part that we have shipped in from Poland is just about to be sent out to a customer – in Poland!' Further investigation showed that many of the overseas orders were going a very roundabout route from supplier to customer. 'What we need is a set of agreements with our overseas suppliers, similar to those we have with UK suppliers that will ship the items directly to the customers.' When the company's accountant, Debbie Long, heard about this plan she realized that she needed to be involved. 'At the moment we pay import duty on the spares and the customer then pays import duty to receive the part from us. Do UK trading rules apply even if the object of the sale has never reached our shores? After all, the website is UK-based.'

Personal data

SpareBitz maintains a database of customer details. Many of its sales came from repeat customers.

While deliveries are being instigated either from the company itself or from UK-based suppliers, Steve is happy that they are fulfilling the requirements of the UK Data Protection Act. However, if they were to give overseas suppliers customer information such as an address for delivery then there is a concern that, unwittingly, SpareBitz could be falling foul of the law. Steve called to his secretary. 'Sally. Can you get me the company lawyers on the telephone please. We may have a problem.'

Multinational organizations

An increasing number of the world's corporations have branched into countries all over the globe, becoming true multinationals. While they might have headquarters in a single country, they operate divisions and subsidiaries in different countries to take advantage of local benefits. For instance, a company might establish engineering facilities in countries that offer large pools of qualified engineers, build production lines in countries that can supply inexpensive labour, and open sales offices in countries that are strategically situated for effective marketing.

Because of this spread of operations, a company's nationality is not always obvious. For example, consider IBM and Philips. While IBM is known as an 'American' corporation because its headquarters and most of its research activities are in the United States, the company has numerous subsidiaries in other countries. These subsidiaries are registered and operate under the laws of the respective countries, and they employ local workers. Likewise, Philips' headquarters is in the Netherlands and yet it owns one of the largest US sellers of electric razors, Norelco. Similarly, Intel, an American company, has major research and development facilities in Israel, where some of its latest microprocessors have been developed.

One hundred of the 500 largest Canadian companies have majority US ownership, and 90 per cent of US multinational companies have Canadian offices. Japanese companies own whole US subsidiaries in every imaginable industry. British companies have the largest foreign investment in the United States. Thanks to the North American Free Trade Agreement (NAFTA) and agreements between the United States and the European Union, we might witness the internationalization of many more American, Canadian, Mexican and European corporations.

Multinational corporations must use global information systems, which are systems that serve organizations and individuals in multiple countries. These companies might have unified policies throughout their organizations, but they still have to abide by the laws of the countries in which each unit operates, and be sensitive to other local aspects of their interaction with other businesses as well as consumers. Therefore, unlike organizations that operate in a single country, multinational companies have the burden of ensuring that their information systems and the information flowing through the systems conform to laws, cultures, standards and other elements that are specific to countries or regions.

> **global information system** Any information system that crosses national borders.

The Web and international commerce

The emergence of the Web as a global medium for information exchange has made it an important vehicle for both business-to-business (B2B) and business-to-consumer (B2C) commerce. In 2004, more than 888 million people regularly logged on to the Internet across the globe. About two-thirds of them come from non-English-speaking countries, as Figure 8.1 shows, and more than half of all e-commerce revenues come from these countries. The ratio of non-English speakers to English speakers has steadily grown over the years.

CD TASK

Figure 8.1 Two-thirds of Internet users come from non-English-speaking countries

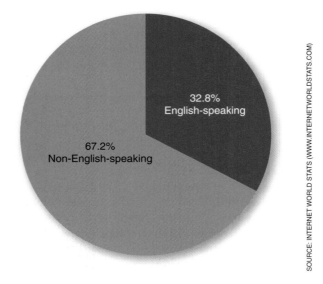

SOURCE: INTERNET WORLD STATS (WWW.INTERNETWORLDSTATS.COM)

The spread of Internet use opens enormous opportunities for businesses the world over. Some of the countries with current low participation rates have the greatest potential, such as China. About 87 million Chinese logged on in 2005, but the growth in Internet usage in Asia from 2000 to 2007 is over 250 per cent compared to the rest of the world's growth in the same period of just under 200 per cent. The Chinese market is expected one day to be the world's largest in terms of consumer spending.

The Web offers opportunities not only to increase revenue but also to save on costs. Consider, for example, how much money is saved when, instead of printing product and service manuals on paper and shipping them to customers, companies publish them on the Web, ready to be downloaded at a user's convenience. Furthermore, imagine the convenience if the manuals were prepared using not only text and graphics but also animation for easier and more informative use. Some companies place video clips to instruct buyers how to assemble the products they purchased. Many companies have stopped enclosing manuals with their retail products. They invite you to log on to their website and peruse the product's manual in your own language. This saves not only paper and printing, but also much of the labour involved in customer service. By placing maintenance manuals in multiple languages on their websites, some companies cut as much as 50 per cent of their customer service costs.

Industry **SNAPSHOT**

Low penetration but room for growth

In 2007, the world population was estimated at 6.6 billion people. About 18 per cent of the population used the Internet on a regular basis. Africa is second only to Asia in population size, with 933 million people. Yet, only 33.5 million of Africa's inhabitants (3.6 per cent) used the Internet regularly. In contrast, 69.5 per cent of the inhabitants of North America used the Internet regularly. However in the period 2000–2007, the growth in Internet usage in Africa was a staggering 643 per cent. The growth in the Middle East over the same period approached 500 per cent.

SOURCE: www.internetworldstats.com

Table 8.1 Imperatives to heed when designing websites for an international audience

Plan	Plan the site before you develop it. A site for an international audience requires more planning than a national one.
Learn the preferences	Learn the cultural preferences, convention differences and legal issues, or use experts who know these preferences. Tailor each local site (or the local section of your site) to the way in which the local people prefer to shop, buy and pay.
Translate properly	Use local interpreters to translate content for local audiences. Do not use software or other automated methods, unless humans review the translated material. Experienced translators are attentive to contemporary nuances and connotations.
Be egalitarian	Do not let any audience feel as if it is less important than other audiences. Keep all local sections of your site updated and with the same level of information and services.
Avoid cultural imperialism	If the local language or culture has a word or picture for communicating an idea, use it; do not use those of your own country. Give the local audience a homey experience.

Organizations that wish to do business globally through their websites must be sensitive to local audiences. Thus websites should be tailored to the audiences they are meant to reach. A majority of web users prefer to access the Web using a language other than English, so organizations must provide their online information and services in other languages, as well as English. As Table 8.1 shows, organizations must plan and carefully design their global sites so that they also cater to local needs and preferences, a process sometimes called glocalization.

glocalization The planning and designing of global websites so that they also cater to local needs and preferences.

Glocalization is a combination of universal business models and management philosophy with some adaptations for local audiences. One example of an organization that glocalizes is McDonald's. While the restaurant chain's logo and many other features are the same throughout the world, it makes some menu changes to appeal to local palates. Sometimes, other elements are changed. For example, in France, the restaurant chain replaced its familiar Ronald McDonald mascot with Asterix the Gaul, a popular French comic book character. Much like the presence of a global restaurant chain, websites are present everywhere someone can link to the Web. Therefore, website designers must keep glocalization in mind.

Think globally, act locally

Marketing experts often advise companies that operate internationally to 'think globally, act locally'. Acting locally means being sensitive to regional customs and language nuances. When interest in the company's business increases, especially from consumers, it is advisable to open a local office and let a local team handle both the website and fulfilment operations. Recall that fulfilment in online business includes picking, packing and shipping. When most of the business comes from one country or region, the business, its website and its information systems are managed centrally, but when a growing proportion of transactions take place in other regions, businesses find that they must decentralize control.

Thinking globally and acting locally might sound like contradictory ideas, but they are not. Recall our discussion of strategies in Chapter 2. Thinking globally has to do with the company's strategic planning. It involves decisions such as product lines and business alliances. However, the same strategy can be followed with a local flavour. For example, the same product, in whose

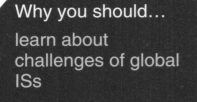

Why you should…

learn about challenges of global ISs

By default, every business that establishes a website in some way uses a global information system. Multinational corporations have used global information systems many years before the advent of the Web. They used private international banking systems and other EDI systems. All businesses can benefit from the use of global ISs, but they also face challenges. Neglecting to pay attention to such issues as different cultures, language nuances, conflicting national laws and different standards can hurt the

Businesses that cater to international audiences must 'glocalize' their websites as shown below. Emirates has succeeded in meeting this challenge, providing a sophisticated online presence that caters for a diverse range of cultural requirements on a global level.

business's reputation and cause loss of revenue. Professionals who work for companies that conduct international business or for organizations that might do so in the future must be aware of the challenges involved in designing websites and using ISs for international trade.

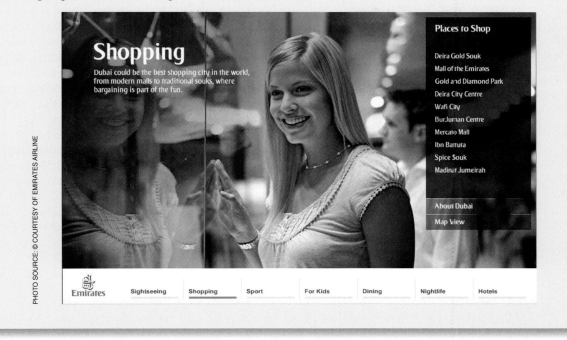

PHOTO SOURCE: © COURTESY OF EMIRATES AIRLINE

design and production the company holds a competitive advantage, can be packaged and advertised with local motifs. The local branch of the company might still recruit the engineers with the same excellent qualifications as those of their peers in other countries, but apply different interview tactics and social benefits, which fit the customs and holidays of that country.

Challenges of global information systems

While the Web offers great opportunities for establishing international ISs, global ISs are not without their challenges, both for B2B and B2C commerce. Some of the challenges that businesses must address are technological barriers, regulations and tariffs, electronic payment mechanisms, different languages and cultures of the audiences, economic and political considerations, different measurement and notation standards, legal barriers and different time zones. These challenges are discussed in the following sections.

Technological challenges

Not all countries have adequate information technology infrastructures to allow resident companies to build international ISs. International ISs, especially those using the Web, often incorporate graphics to convey technical or business information, and those applications, as well as interactive software, require increasingly fast (broadband) communication lines. The bandwidth available in some parts of the world, for example many African countries, is too narrow for high-volume transmission of graphically and animation-rich web pages. Thus, companies might have to offer two versions of their sites, one for wide bandwidth and another for narrow bandwidth. Often, companies use one site, but provide the same content in both graphically rich and text-only pages, or the same video for download at different speeds.

Another technological challenge has to do with language. You might recall the earlier discussion of how characters are represented by bytes in computers. This setup is fine for languages with up to 256 (2^8) characters, such as English and other languages whose alphabetic root is Latin. But eight-bit bytes are not sufficient for languages with larger numbers of characters, such as Chinese. The solution for this obstacle is to ensure that computers can use Unicode, with double-byte characters – allowing for up to 65,536 (2^{16}) characters. However, if only the servers are programmed to accommodate Unicode, while the other systems (such as databases and applications on computers interacting with the servers) work with single-byte characters, then these back-end systems will record and display gibberish. Thus, entire systems must be reprogrammed or use special conversion software. As computers convert to operating systems that support Unicode, displaying different character sets should be less of a problem.

Unicode An international standard to enable the storage and display of characters of a large variety of languages – such as Asian, Arabic and Hebrew – on computers.

Other points that might sound trivial can also wreak havoc in international ISs or prevent individuals and companies in some world regions from transacting with companies that did not make their websites and applications flexible. For example, fields such as telephone numbers should be set for variable length, because the number of digits in telephone numbers varies by country. Similarly virtually every country uses some form of postal code but the structural rules of, for example, a UK post code are very different from a US zip code. Web forms must be able to accept various formats, hence sacrificing error-checking that might be carried out if the form was only to be used in one country.

Regulations and tariffs

Countries have different regulations on what may or may not be imported and which tariff applies to which imported product. While many executives know they might be missing out on great deals with overseas businesses, they are afraid that exploring international opportunities would entail too many hassles. They are also afraid that even with the proper research, employees might not know how to comply with the laws of destination countries, let alone calculate how much the organization would have to pay in taxes, tariffs, custom duties and other levies on exported or imported goods.

Companies such as NextLinx help exporters and importers who use the Web for commerce. The NextLinx software is integrated with a company's ERP systems and website. When a business from another country places an order, the information – such as type of item and destination country – is captured by the software, and an export manager can see how much the company will have to pay in tariffs, receive an estimate of how long the goods will stay in the seaport or airport before they are released from customs and, if the manager wishes, also receive information on regulations, licence required, shipping companies in the destination country and other useful information. Since the software is linked to the Web, it is continuously updated and provides useful information immediately. The software also calculates, on the fly, the total cost of delivering the goods to the buyer's door. It also provides more than 100 forms that exporters can fill out and save electronically. The logistics component of the application offers shipping options with land, sea and air carriers; books shipping space; and tracks shipping status. Several studies have shown that US companies have turned away about 80 per cent of online orders that come from other countries because they are not familiar with export regulations. This service can expedite the process.

Differences in payment mechanisms

One of the greatest expectations of e-commerce is easy payment for what we buy online. Credit cards are very common in North America and are the way businesses prefer to be paid online. However, this practice is not widespread in other regions of the world. The high rate of stolen credit cards, especially in Eastern Europe, attaches risk to such payments and deters potential online customers. The *Economic Times* reported in May 2007 that in India a mere 1 per cent of total spending (not just online purchases) is made using credit cards with only 28 per cent of the 'affluent' population owning a credit card, compared to 90 per cent in Hong Kong. And it is not just the developing world where lack of credit card ownership can have an effect on potential e-commerce sales. In Austria only 32 per cent of the population own a credit card according to the Lafferty Group. Americans are more willing to give credit-card details via the Web than people from other nations. Until citizens of other countries become willing to do so, payment through the Web, and therefore B2C trade, will not reach its full potential.

Americans pay with credit cards in 20 per cent of all transactions and in almost all online transactions. In Japan, on the other hand, only 8 per cent of transactions involve credit cards, and most Japanese are reluctant to use credit cards for online purchases. This calls for a different mechanism of payment. In Japan, many people who order merchandise online prefer to pick it up at convenience stores called '*konbini*', and pay there for what they purchased. Since shipping companies are reluctant to leave parcels unattended when the recipient is not home, the alliance of e-tailers and *konbini* affords not only payment confidence but also convenience. E-tailers from other countries who want to operate in Japan must be aware of these preferences.

Language differences

To communicate internationally, parties must agree on a common language, and that can create problems. For instance, data might not be transmittable internationally in real time because the information must first be translated (usually by human beings). Although some computer applications can translate 'on the fly', they are far from perfect. Another hurdle is that national laws usually forbid businesses to run accounting and other systems in a foreign language, leading to an awkward and expensive solution: running these systems in two languages, the local one and English, which is the *de facto* international language.

Companies that are in the forefront of web-based e-commerce have translated their original websites into local languages. They localize their sites by creating a dedicated site for each national audience. But translation can be tricky. For instance, the Taiwanese use the traditional set of Chinese characters, but people in the People's Republic of China prefer the simplified character set. Spanish terms in Spain might be different from those in Latin America. In addition, mere linguistic translation might not capture cultural sensitivities. Therefore, some companies prefer to leave web design and translation to their local overseas offices.

Several companies, such as TRADOS Inc., offer translation software and services to companies involved in global commerce. TRADOS' software package by the same name translates web pages into many languages, including those requiring special characters such as Hindi, Chinese, Greek and Hebrew, but also ensures consistency of terms and sentence structure in different languages. When web pages are translated, the software ensures that the XML tags and statements are retained from the original languages, so that the company maintaining the website can continue to use the same XML code for online transactions with companies and shoppers in its new markets. Other tools translate MS Word documents into multiple languages. One such tool is Wordfast.

Cultural differences

Cultural differences refer in general to the many ways in which people from different countries vary in their tastes, gestures, preferred colours, treatment of people of certain gender or age, attitudes about work, opinions about different ethical issues and the like. ISs might challenge cultural traditions by imposing the culture of one nation upon another (cultural imperialism). Conservative groups in some countries have complained about the 'Americanization' of their young generations. Governments might be inclined to forbid the reception of some information for reasons of undesirable cultural influence. An example of such fear is the French directive against use of foreign words in government-supported mass media and official communications. A similar example is the ban by the Canadian province of Quebec on the use of non-French words in business signs. These fears have intensified with the growth of the Internet and use of the Web. Because the Internet was invented and first developed in the United States and is still used by a greater percentage of Americans compared with any other single nation, its predominant culture is American.

As mentioned previously, companies that use the Web for business must learn cultural differences and design their sites accordingly. Web designers need to be sensitive to cultural differences. People might be offended by the use of certain images, colours and words. For example, black has sinister connotations in Europe, Asia and Latin America; the index-finger-to-thumb sign of approval is a rude gesture meaning 'jackass' in Brazil; the thumbs-up sign is a rude gesture in Latin America, as is the waving hand in Arab countries; and pictures of women with exposed arms or legs are offensive in many Muslim countries.

Conflicting economic, scientific and security interests

The goal of corporate management is to seize a large market share and maximize its organization's profits. The goal of a national government is to protect the economic, scientific and security interests of its people. Scientific information is both an important national resource and a great source of income for foreign corporations, so occasionally those interests conflict.

For instance, companies that design and manufacture weapons have technical drawings and specifications that are financially valuable to the company, but also valuable to the security of their country. Hence, many governments do not allow the exchange of weapon designs. Often, products whose purpose has nothing to do with the military are included in the list of prohibited trade items, because of the fear that they could be converted for use against the country of origin. In recent years, the list has included some software packages. The result is that, although home divisions of a company can use such software, their sister divisions in other countries cannot.

Consider some of the encryption applications offered by software developers. When Phil Zimmermann, developer of PGP (Pretty Good Privacy), offered this encryption application for free downloading, he was faced with federal criminal charges and severe penalties. His purpose was to allow individuals and companies to scramble their communications via computer networks. Companies use such software to protect corporate information. However, strong encryption methods are on the US federal government's list of restricted exports because, like weapons, they could compromise America's national security. Under public pressure, the government dropped the charges. In 2001, when it was found that the 9/11 terrorists used the software to encrypt their communication, Zimmermann expressed regret.

Another problem that arises with international information interchange is that countries treat trade secrets, patents and copyrights differently. Sometimes business partners are reluctant to transfer documents when one partner is in a country that restricts intellectual property rights, while another is in a country that has laws to protect intellectual property. On the other hand, the employees of a

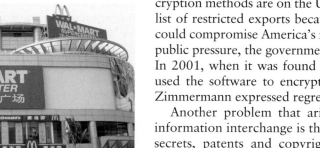

Some nations are afraid that cross-border information flow promotes cultural imperialism.

division of a multinational corporation might be able to divulge information locally with impunity. Intellectual property is tightly protected in the United States and Western Europe, and American trade negotiators and diplomats have put pressure on some countries to pass and enforce similar laws. Reportedly, the legislatures of several Asian nations have passed such laws or have revised existing laws in response to this pressure from the West.

Political challenges

Information is power. Some countries fear that a policy of free access to information could threaten their sovereignty. For instance, a nation's government might believe that access to certain data, such as the location and quantity of natural resources, might give other nations an opportunity to control an indigenous resource, thereby gaining a business advantage that would adversely affect the resource-rich country's political interests.

Governments are also increasingly recognizing software as an important economic resource, leading some countries to dictate that companies operating within their borders must purchase software from within their borders. For example, until 1997, Brazil's authorities

Industry SNAPSHOT

Collaborating with the censors

Companies that wish to do business in a large market where political interests limit freedom of speech often yield to government pressure. Microsoft Corp. cooperates with China's government in censoring the company's Chinese-language web portal. The company's policy of cooperation affects blogs. It works with the authorities to omit certain forbidden language. Bloggers are not allowed to post words such as 'democracy', 'human rights', and 'Taiwan independence'. Attempts to enter such words generate a message notifying the blogger that such language is forbidden. Several groups have tried to pressure executives at Microsoft, Yahoo!, Google, Cisco Systems and other companies to urge the Chinese government for reforms on free expression, but free speech is no match for the economic interest of these companies. China's estimated online population is 87 million, second only to the United States.

SOURCE: C. Woodward, 'Microsoft Censors Blogs at Chinese Portal', Associated Press, 13 June 2005

Google's corporate headquarters in Beijing, China.

allowed local businesses to purchase software from other countries only after demonstrating that the software was not available domestically. The rule was enforced even if the business was owned by a foreign company. These policies can hinder standardization and compatibility of international ISs by preventing use of the same software throughout a multinational corporation.

As mentioned in Chapter 4, however, the recent trend in less rich countries is to adopt free open source software to avoid high costs. National governments in South America as well as local governments in Asia and Europe have adopted policies of using only open source software whenever it is available. Global corporations must ensure compatibility with the software adopted by governments and corporations in such locales.

Companies must also be aware of limits that some governments impose on Internet use. China, Singapore and many Arab countries impose restrictions on what their citizens can download, view and read. Free speech is not a universal principle. In practical terms, this means that executives might want to rephrase or cut out some content from their websites or risk their sites being blocked by some governments. This is an especially sensitive issue if a company enables employees or customers to use blogs at its website, in which they express their personal opinions.

Ethical and Societal ISSUES

Legal jurisdictions in cyberspace

Imagine: you surf the Web and come across a virulent site that preaches hatred and violence. You file a complaint in court, but the court cannot do anything because the site is maintained in another country that does not uphold your country's law. Or, you shop on the Web and purchase an item from a site that is physically maintained on a server in another country. When you receive the item, you discover that it is of a lower quality than promised. When you contact the site, the owners are rude and unresponsive. You decide to sue, but under which country's laws? These problems are two examples of the legal challenges in today's electronic global markets.

Global free speech In the spring of 2000, the International League against Racism and Anti-Semitism (LICRA), the Movement against Racism (MRAP), and the Union of French Jewish Students (UEFJ) filed a lawsuit against the American Internet company Yahoo! in a French court. The organizations complained that Yahoo!'s auctioning of more than 1200 Nazi-related items amounted to 'banalization of Nazism', which violates French law. The Nazi items offered for sale on the site included everything from Nazi flags and uniforms to belt

buckles and medals. In November 2000, Judge Gomez ruled that a French court had jurisdiction over Yahoo! for violations that occur within France. He ordered Yahoo! to block French citizens' access to auctions of Nazi items within three months or face a fine of 15,000 euro per day.

Like many global e-commerce sites, Yahoo! did not require its webmasters to maintain a dedicated site for each language. French users merely saw a customized overlay using the main Yahoo! pages that are viewed by all visitors. This technique has enabled Yahoo! to offer country-specific and language-specific versions of its site at relatively low cost. Yahoo! screened out the items from its French site, but this did not satisfy the court because French citizens could still view the items via the general site.

To countries that have been subjected to a ruthless occupation, free speech is less important than preventing offences such as 'banalization of Nazism'. In the United States, however, free speech is legally protected even when someone's opinion or trade of objects is offensive. Yahoo! decided to remove such items from all its servers, but also took up the case in the US courts, arguing that foreign courts should not be able to negate the First Amendment of the US Constitution which concerns freedom of speech. After the original ruling and several appeals, the only thing that is clear is that the situation is unclear!

Consider this example: a ruling against a company registered in India by a court in Germany, and an appeal in a court in India of a court decision made under the laws of Germany. This legal tangle is the result of doing business globally. More than one law might govern a business practice or communication of ideas. The legal environment used to be confined to national boundaries, and jurisdiction used to refer to a territory. No longer so. Now the 'territory' is cyberspace. It is difficult to define jurisdictions in cyberspace. The lingering question is, 'Whose law applies?'

Consumer protection by whom? Where can consumers sue for e-commerce transactions gone wrong? Suppose you purchased an item from a site located in another country, and the item has a defect or arrived after the time promised. Because your request for compensation or another remedy has not been answered satisfactorily, you decide to sue the e-tailer. Where do you file the lawsuit? Your own country? The e-tailer's country? The venue of e-commerce lawsuits is still undecided in many parts of the world.

In November 2000, the European Union (EU) passed a law that lets consumers file lawsuits against an online business in any of the member countries composing the EU. Before the amendment to the 1968 Brussels Convention (which regulates commercial-legal issues in the Union), consumers could sue an online business only in courts in the country of the online business. Now, if a website has directed its business at consumers in a certain country, the consumers can sue the website's owner in their own national courts. Businesses vehemently opposed the move, but consumer advocates said people would be more confident about online shopping if they knew they could get redress in their local courts.

Two approaches to jurisdiction As you have seen, the issue of e-commerce jurisdiction is broad. The US Federal Trade Commission and European government organizations have examined the issue in an attempt to reach an international agreement such as the one reached within the EU.

There are two approaches to such agreement. One approach is the *country-of-origin* principle, whereby all legal matters are confined to the country from which the site operates. Under this principle, the laws of that country apply to the operations and conduct of the site and whoever interacts with the site, regardless of their own location. Therefore, a lawsuit could be brought only in the country of the website and would be adjudicated according to that country's laws. Under this principle it is likely that many firms would opt to establish websites in countries with lax consumer protection laws.

The other approach is the *country-of-destination* principle, whereby the laws of the country to which the site caters apply regarding dealings with the site, regardless of the site's country. The EU adopted this approach within its territory. It might take several years until there is international agreement on e-commerce jurisdiction.

Different standards

Differences in standards must be considered when integrating ISs internationally, even within the same company. Because nations use different standards and rules in their daily business operations, sometimes records within one company are incompatible. For instance, the bookkeeping records of one division of a multinational company might be incompatible with the records of other divisions and headquarters. As another example, the United States still uses the English system of weights and measures (inches, feet, miles, quarts, pounds and so on), while most of the rest of the world (including England) officially uses the metric system (centimetres, metres, litres, kilograms and the like). There are also different standards for communicating dates, times, temperatures and addresses. The United States uses the format of month, day, year, while the rest of the world records dates in the format of day, month, year. A date recorded as 10/12/08 might be misinterpreted. The United States uses a 12-hour time notation with the addition of a.m. or p.m., while other parts of the world use a 24-hour notation (called 'military time' in the United States because the US military uses this notation). The United States uses Fahrenheit temperatures, while other countries use Celsius temperatures. Americans communicate addresses in the format of street number, street name and city name. Citizens of some other countries communicate addresses in the format of street name, street number and city name.

Using different standards can be extremely costly. In 1999, NASA lost track of a spacecraft that it sent to Mars. Reportedly, an investigation found that an error in a transfer of information between the Mars Climate Orbiter team in Colorado and the mission navigation team in California led to the spacecraft's loss. Apparently, one team used English units, and the other used metric units for a key spacecraft operation. The information was critical to the manoeuvres required to place the spacecraft in the proper Mars orbit. The cost to US taxpayers was US$125 million.

Companies that want to operate globally must adapt their ISs to changing formal or *de facto* standards. In recent years the growing number of countries joining the European Union (EU) imparted significant power to this bloc. Corporations in non-EU countries have grown

European Article Number (EAN) A European standard of product code, similar to UPC but containing more information.

accustomed to adapting their systems to those of the EU. For example, in 1976, Europeans adopted the 13-digit European Article Number (EAN), while American companies used the 12-digit Universal Product Code (UPC). The additional bar in the EAN barcode identifies the product's country of origin. For seven years the American Uniform Code Council (UCC) promoted the use of the European standard. In 2004, the organization officially adopted it. Retailers embarked on a hectic effort to modify information systems to recognize, record and process UPCs of 13 bars instead of 12 bars so they could meet the January 2005 deadline. Most barcode readers could already read the extra bar, but the software in back-office systems – such as sales, shipping, receiving and accounting systems – had to be modified. Best Buy, the large electronics and appliance retailer, spent 25,000 hours of staff and hired consultant time to ensure that cash registers, several software applications and databases could process and store the extra digit.

Universal Product Code (UPC) A code usually expressed as a number and series of variable width bars that uniquely identifies the product by scanning.

Global Trade Item Number (GTIN) A number that uniquely identifies products and services. The GTIN is a global standard succeeding the EAN and UPC.

The UCC is trying to expand product codes to 14-digit Global Trade Item Numbers (GTINs). This code is large enough to identify more than 100 times the number of products and manufacturers that the 12-digit UPCs could. GTINs are designed to support global supply chains. Eventually, manufacturers and retailers might have to use either GTINs or another standard of larger codes embedded in RFID tags. The major push for using RFID tags is taking place in the United States, and American standards could expand to Europe and the rest of the world.

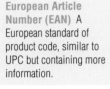

CD TASK

Legal barriers

The fact that countries have different laws has a great impact on global business in general, and on e-commerce in particular. The differing laws can pose serious challenges to international transfer of data, free speech and the location of legal proceedings when disputes arise between buyer and seller.

Privacy laws Although many of the challenges involved in cross-border data transfer have been resolved through international agreements, one remains unresolved: respect for individual privacy in the conduct of international business. Interestingly, despite the importance attached to privacy, that value is not even mentioned in the constitutions of the United States and many other countries. Nonetheless, a majority of the democratic nations try to protect individual privacy. An EU working party concerned with privacy recently wrote to Google regarding the latter's policy of retaining log data for two years on queries that identified the search term, the Internet server and other information derived from cookies. The response

Industry **SNAPSHOT**

International Hall of Shame

Privacy International (PI) is an international organization that monitors governments and commercial organizations around the world for violations of privacy. Each year, the members and affiliated organizations of PI present the 'Big Brother' awards to the government and private sector organizations in their countries that have done the most to threaten personal privacy in their countries. Since 1998 more than 40 ceremonies have been held in 16 countries and hundreds of awards have been given out to some of the most powerful government agencies, individuals and corporations in those countries. A 'lifetime menace' award is also presented. To counterbalance the shameful awards, PI also gives awards to individuals and organizations that have made an outstanding contribution to the protection of privacy. You can read more about it at www. privacyinternational.org/bba.

from Google was to reduce this period to 18 months. Whether this is satisfactory to the EU and where other search engines such as Yahoo! fit in this dispute remain to be resolved.

Countries differ in their approaches to the issue of privacy, as reflected in their laws. Some are willing to forgo some privacy for the sake of a freer flow of information and better marketing. Others restrict any collection of personal data without the consent of the individual.

Data protection laws from various countries can be generally described by three different criteria:

- Whether the laws apply to the collection and treatment of data by the private sector (companies), the public sector (governments) or by both.
- Whether the laws apply to manual data, to automated data or to both.
- Whether data protected under the law are only those concerning human beings or those concerning both human and 'legal' entities (that is, organizations).

Except for the US and Canadian privacy acts, privacy laws apply to both the public and private sectors; that is, government and private organizations are subject to the same regulation of collection, maintenance and disclosure of personal data. More than half the laws (including US federal statutes) encompass manual and computerized record-keeping systems. Denmark, Austria and Luxembourg are among the countries that protect the privacy of some types of corporations.

Countries that support protection of corporate data argue that it is difficult to separate data about individuals from data on business activities involving or performed by individuals, especially with small businesses. For example, the financial information of a small business also reveals financial information about the people involved with and/or running the business. Furthermore, a large corporation might unfairly compete against a smaller firm if it has access to the smaller firm's data.

The European Union (EU) enforces a privacy law called the Directive on Data Privacy. The EU defines personal data as 'any information relating to an identified or identifiable natural person; an identifiable person is one who can be identified, directly or indirectly, in particular by reference to an identification number or to one or more factors specific to his physical, physiological, mental, economic, cultural, or social identity.' Some of the principles of the directive are in stark contrast to the practices of US businesses and therefore limit the free flow of personal data between the United States and the EU. For example, consider the following provisions and how they conflict with US practices:

- Personal data can be collected only for specified, explicit and legitimate purposes and not further processed in a way incompatible with those purposes. However, in the United States, businesses often collect data from people without having to tell them how the data will be used. Many US corporations use personal data for purposes other than the original one, and many organizations purchase personal data from other organizations, so subjects do not even know that the data is used, let alone for what purpose. Obviously, these activities would not be allowed under the EU directive.

- Personal data can be processed only if the subject has given unambiguous consent or under other specific circumstances that the directive provides. Such circumstances are not required by American laws. In the United States, private organizations are allowed to process personal data without the subject's consent, and for practically any purpose.

- Individuals or organizations that receive personal data (the directive calls them 'controllers') not directly from the subject must identify themselves to the subject. In the United States, many organizations purchase personal data from third parties and never notify the subject.

- People have the right to obtain from controllers 'without constraint at reasonable intervals and without excessive delay or expense' confirmation that data about them are processed, to whom the data are disclosed, and the source that provided the data. They are also entitled to receive information on the 'logic involved in any automatic processing of data concerning' them at least in the case of automated decision-making. Decision-making, practically speaking, means using decision-support systems and expert systems to make decisions on hiring, credit extension, admittance to educational institutions, and so forth. None of these rights is mandated by any US law.

- People have the right to object, 'on request and free of charge', to the processing of personal data for the purpose of direct marketing, or to be informed before personal data are disclosed for the first time to third parties or used for direct marketing. Furthermore, controllers must expressly offer the right to object free of charge to disclosure of personal data to others. American companies use personal data *especially* for direct marketing, never tell subjects that they obtain data about them from third parties, and rarely offer subjects the right to object to disclosure of such data to other parties.

American companies are very busy collecting, buying and selling personal data for decision-making and marketing purposes. The American view is that such practices are essential to efficient business operations, especially in marketing and extension of credit. Thus, this huge discrepancy between the European and American approaches does not allow unrestricted flow of information.

The EU directive is only a framework within which member states may maintain their own, more restrictive, laws. Consider, for example, the French law, which states, 'An individual shall not be subject to an administrative or private decision involving an assessment of conduct which has, as its sole basis, the automatic processing of personal data defining his profile or personality.' This provision limits the use of a computer as a decision aid in certain circumstances. For instance, this law forbids automatic decisions for credit applications or admittance to a college. While the latter decision is often accompanied by human intervention, the former is often automated in the United States and other countries.

The EU directive recognizes that countries outside the EU use personal data that are transferred from the EU. It therefore provides that when a 'third country does not ensure an adequate level of protection within the meaning of [the directive], member states shall take the measures necessary to prevent any transfer of data of the same type to the third country'. This provision has created an interesting situation: agents of the European Data Protection Authorities (DPAs) arrive at least monthly in the United States to monitor American companies that process personal data of European citizens to ensure that the EU Directive on Data Protection is obeyed regarding these citizens. These representatives monitor the ISs of companies such as Visa, MasterCard, American Express and other credit-card issuers. Companies that want to do business in EU member states must accept the restrictions of the directive on their practices. Business leaders on both continents hope that a way can be found to bridge the gap between the two approaches to data privacy, but it seems that a legal solution will not come before a change in culture.

In the meantime, a practical solution has been sponsored by the US federal government. The EU agreed that the US Department of Commerce could establish a Safe Harbor, an arrangement for US companies that have agreed to comply with the EU directive regarding EU citizens so that European companies can trade with these US companies without fear of violating the directive. By June 2005, 739 US companies had joined the list. You can view information about the Safe Harbor arrangement and the list of companies that have joined at www.export.gov/safeharbor.

> **Safe Harbor** A list of US corporations that have agreed to conform to European Union data protection laws with regard to EU citizens. The arrangement enables the corporations to continue to do business with European companies.

Since privacy laws regarding employees – not just consumers – are also different in the United States and the European Union, American companies employing European citizens must comply with EU laws regarding transfer of employment information. They must comply with the DPAs. Under the Safe Harbor arrangement, claims of European citizens against US companies regarding privacy are heard (with some exceptions) in the United States. To be sure they are not breaking the law, European companies that wish to transfer personal data to US companies can simply check at the above-mentioned website to see if those US companies are listed.

Applicable law As discussed in the Ethical and Societal Issues box in this chapter, countries have differing laws regarding free speech, which can have a grave impact on what a company may or may not display from its servers. Some of the other laws that can affect online business address gambling, auctioning and sales of alcoholic beverages and drugs. After establishing online business in some countries, some companies discovered that their practice was not in compliance with a local law. For example, eBay discovered that Dutch and Italian laws required that a certified auctioneer be present at any auction. This made its online auctions illegal in these countries. Some countries have changed their laws to accommodate online business, but others have not. Such legal discrepancy among jurisdictions should not come as a surprise to executives; they must research the legal environment in every jurisdiction where they intend to do business. The lessons of Yahoo!, eBay, and other online pioneers prompted many companies to employ legal research experts before they started business in a new jurisdiction. Often, this effort is part of a larger effort to research the local culture and practices. Some companies have hired local experts to help them in assessing local considerations and in some cases executives decided to avoid doing online business in certain countries altogether.

Different time zones

Companies that operate in many global regions, especially multinational corporations, must craft policies for the work of both their employees and information systems. Teleconferencing systems must be available much of the day, and in many cases, 24 hours per day, so that employees in many time zones apart can communicate to discuss problems that need immediate resolution. Teams in support centres might have to work in shifts to accommodate clients worldwide. For example, when arranging for a teleconference between offices in New York,

Different time zones must be considered by all organizations that do business in multiple countries.

London and Sydney it is very difficult to find the time that is least inconvenient. There is an interesting website, http://www.timeanddate.com/worldclock/meeting.html which tries to help by showing when participants are liable to be in the office, at home or asleep!

In their global supply chain management systems, managers must be aware of what might seem to be incorrect time stamping in shipments and payment records. For example, consider interaction between a corporation's German manufacturing plant and its South Korean assembly plant. Because South Korea is seven hours ahead of Germany, shipping records could show that subassemblies were shipped from Germany a day before they were ordered in South Korea. To eliminate confusion, the systems at both locations can be designed to record the local times of both locations, or only that of a single location, such as the company headquarters' time.

SUMMARY

As more and more companies use the Web for business, both B2C and B2B, they realize that they must accommodate non-English-speaking audiences and tailor their sites to local preferences. They also must be carefully attuned to the cultural differences and payment preferences of different world regions, as well as be aware of legal and tariff issues.

Organizations that engage in international trade, especially through the Web, must also be aware of the linguistic, cultural, economic and political challenges involved in such trade.

One important unresolved issue is the discrepancy between the laws governing the collection and manipulation of personal data in two economic powers, the United States and the European Union, which have incompatible data privacy laws. This difference restricts the flow of personal data between the United States and the EU. The Safe Harbor arrangement enables EU companies to do business with US businesses that comply with EU policies on handling personal data of its citizens.

Several cases have demonstrated that the old legal approach of territorial jurisdiction is inadequate when so much information is communicated and so much business is conducted on the Internet. Issues such as free speech and consumer litigation of e-tailers have brought to light the need for an international legal reform for cyberspace.

SPAREBITZ REVISITED

SpareBitz.com came from very humble origins. However, it has continued to expand not just nationally but internationally. It does not just deal with spare parts for household appliances but also the appliances themselves, mostly manufactured in Eastern Europe.

What would you do?

1 Contracting with manufacturers in another country involves communicating with the company, understanding the laws of the country and uncovering political, economic and technological issues that might affect trade. Describe the obstacles you think SpareBitz might face if it chose to expand to manufacturing in other countries such as China.

2 Sales to overseas customers are rising rapidly, with customers from the European Union, North America and even some from Africa. How should SpareBitz deal with payment and currency issues with regard to these sales?

New perspectives

It is becoming apparent that the original website, designed for UK customers, needs to have a multinational flavour. How should the company go about this? Should there be just one site that suits all nationalities and cultures? Is language the only problem?

Review questions

1 What is meant by the term 'global information systems'?

2 Executives of multinational corporations are advised to think globally and act locally. What does this mean?

3 Manufacturers and retailers have used product bar codes for many years. What information does the 13-digit European Article Number (EAN) contain that the 12-digit Universal Product Code (UPC) did not, and why is this information important?

4 Is every website a form of global IS? Why or why not?

5 Using software for automatic translation of web pages into other languages for local audiences saves much labour cost and time. If you were an executive for a company that maintains a multilingual website, would you settle for software-based translation only? Why or why not?

6 Many organizations, especially multinational corporations, must consolidate reports to ensure smooth operations. These reports include currency, measurements and dates. How would you help them receive reports 'on the fly' that are in the desired currency and format?

7 Many European countries have stricter privacy laws than the United States. What is the impact of this discrepancy on multinational corporations with offices on both continents? In terms of business functions, which activities, in particular, are affected?

8 Give three examples of cultural imperialism. Why do you think your examples reflect cultural imperialism?

9 Some countries have laws restricting collection and maintenance of data on small companies. Do such laws make sense to you? How can they protect the privacy of individuals? Give an example.

10 What are the implications of different time zones for global supply chain management systems?

11 Countries can adopt either a country-of-origin law or a country-of-destination law. What is the difference between the two approaches? Which is more helpful to consumers and which is more helpful to e-tailers? Explain.

Discussion questions

1 Test yourself: What are the 'nationalities' of the following corporations? Consider nationality to be the country where the corporation is registered: Total (petroleum), Bull (computers), Olivetti (office appliances), BP (petroleum), CheckPoint (security software), LG (electronics), Corona (beer), Heineken (beer), Thomson (electronics), Goodyear (tyres), JVC (electronics), Braun (small appliances), Siemens (electronics), Nokia (mobile telephones).

2 Some observers said that modifying applications and databases to move from 12- to 13-digit product bar codes was similar to the efforts to address the Y2K problem in the years leading to 2000. Search the Web to learn about the Y2K issue. In what way are the two issues similar?

3 The US Department of Commerce has relaxed restrictions on the export of encryption (scrambling) software for communications, but it still bans the export of many such applications. Do you agree with this policy? Why or why not?

4 Thirteen of the European Union countries use the euro as their common currency. Does this help or hinder international ISs? Explain.

5 Do you agree with the rule of the French court in the Yahoo! Nazi item auctions case? Why or why not?

6 Consider sensitivity to privacy in Europe. Are Europeans more sensitive to *government* handling of private information or to *business* handling of private information? Now answer the question regarding the USA.

7 Apparently, the EU has stricter privacy laws than the United States, and not many US companies are willing to comply with the EU Directive on Data Protection. The Safe Harbor arrangement is one way to resolve the issue, but only several hundred companies have subscribed. How would *you* resolve the conflict?

8 If a non-English-speaking country had established the Internet, do you think that country would impose its own 'cultural imperialism' on the Web? Why or why not?

9 Which legal approach do you prefer for e-commerce: country of origin or country of destination? Answer the question as a business person, then answer it as a consumer.

10 If some countries clearly adopt the country-of-origin approach for legal issues of e-commerce, online retailers might move to operate from those countries. Why?

11 An American company employs engineers in California and in several Asian and European countries. The engineers exchange emails and communicate via VoIP, teleconferencing and collaborative project management tools. The Americans often use phrases such as 'Let's touch base in a week', 'Right off the bat' and 'all the way to the end zone'. An executive instructs them to avoid such phrases in communication with colleagues from other countries and perhaps even with any colleague. Why?

Tutorial activities

1 You are an executive for Bidway.com, an auction site that has successfully competed with eBay and Yahoo! in the UK. Management decided to open use of the site to residents of all countries. You were given an important assignment: collect intelligence that will ensure that the company's move from a national business to an international business is smooth. If you envisage that there might be too many difficulties in certain countries, management will accept your recommendation to block bidding by residents of those countries, but you must be careful not to miss potentially profitable markets. Prepare an outline of all the aspects about which you will collect intelligence for each country and explain why this item is important.

2 The United States is the only country that still uses English measurement units rather than metric ones. Even the English officially moved to the metric system many years ago. The US Congress has unsuccessfully attempted to make the official move. Research on the Web and summarize your findings in two pages: Why does the United States still use the English system? When was the last attempt to officially move to the metric system? Does the use of English measurement units put US companies

at a disadvantage when competing on international contracts? How has software solved the challenge? Give examples of engineering software that resolves this challenge.

3   You are the international sales manager for Aladdin Rugs Ltd, a multinational company headquartered in the UK. At the end of every month, you receive reports from the national sales managers of your company's operations in South Africa, Germany and Japan. The products are sold by area. The managers report the units sold and income from sales in their national currencies: Rand (R), euro (€), yen (¥) and pounds sterling (£). Use your spreadsheet program to consolidate the sales reports you received, as follows.

   a) Under 'Totals', enter formulas to convert square yards to square metres and enter another formula to total the area in square metres for all four countries.

   b) In a financial newspaper such as the *Financial Times* or on the Web, find the rates of exchange for the three currencies against the pound on the last business day of last month. Enter a formula that will convert all non-sterling currency to pounds. (Extra challenge: program a macro to do the calculations.)

   c) Test all formulas with actual numbers.

4   Google and other sites offer web-based translation services. Test the quality of such tools. Write a message of 50 words in English. Use the tool to translate it into German or another language with which you might be familiar. Copy the translated text, paste it to be translated, and translate it into English. Compare the original and translated English messages. How good is the translation tool? About how much of the text in the translated version came out identical to the original? Did you find anything funny in the back-translated text?

5   Team up with three other students. Decide on three keywords with which the team will conduct a web search. All of you should use the same search engine. One team member should record the number of sites found in the United States, another in Germany, another in France and another in the Netherlands. Also, record the sites the team found whose domain name is non-US but that used English rather than, or in addition to, the local language.

   Prepare a brief report detailing what you recorded. Write your own conclusion: how dominant is English on the Web? Do you think the Web is 'Americanized'? Do you consider what you found to be cultural imperialism?

6   'Electronic immigrants' are residents of one country who are employed by a company in another country. They are the result of what some people call 'off shoring' of jobs. They deliver the results of their work through the Internet or private communications networks. Your team should conduct research with four companies in four different industries, one of which is in software development. The title of your research is 'The Electronic Immigrant: Economic and Political Implications'. Contact the human resource managers of the four companies, present the issue and ask for the managers' opinion: can the company use 'electronic immigrants'? Can it be hurt if competitors use them? Do the HR managers think the national economy can gain or lose from the phenomenon? Do they foresee any political ramifications? Your team should use a word processor to prepare a neat report starting with half a page of background on each company.

Companion CD questions

1   The version of MS Office you own probably has been manufactured for use only in the country in which you live. Why would software manufacturers limit sales of software versions to various countries?

2   Assume you have built a website for SpareBitz. The company now wants to sell its products overseas. Other than modifying the site to accept other currencies, what other changes have to be made to the site?

From ideas to application
REAL CASES

Case study **8.1**

Export with confidence

The products of Fairchild Semiconductor are installed in a large array of items, from satellites and motor vehicles to mobile phones, medical devices and home appliances. The company is a world leader in design and manufacturing of microprocessors that control power. It calls itself The Power Franchise. The company has manufacturing facilities in the United States, South Korea, China, Malaysia, Singapore and the Philippines, and 36 offices in 17 countries. It sees the entire world as its market. Fairchild ships more than 17 billion units of products annually. Some products are shipped to as few as 6 countries, while others are shipped to as many as 45 countries.

The microchips are designed in the United States and South Korea. Manufacturing starts in the United States. Then, the chips are sent to plants in Asia for assembly and testing. The products are then shipped to customers around the globe. Customers can order products online at the company's website. Over the

The Petronas Towers in Kuala Lumpur, Malaysia, where Fairchild has one of several assembly and test plants that play a central role in the global development of their products.

PHOTO SOURCE: © ROBERT CHURCHILL

past decade Fairchild established additional design and manufacturing facilities in Korea and China. With facilities as well as customers in a growing number of countries, complying with both US and other countries' export and import laws became complex. Work-in-progress is often shipped from one country to another, and then to another or back to the original country for further processing. Logistics managers decided to use the services of a company that specializes in software that helps manage such complex operations. Fairchild approached NextLinx, a company with expertise in software that supports online logistics.

Together, the companies configured and implemented NextLinx software called Trade Export Solution, which automates Fairchild's global logistics. The software provides information on laws and regulations of each country where Fairchild transacts, as well as customs duties. For each shipment it figures out the fastest and least costly carriers as well as the minimum duties to be paid. The application provides digital forms that enable employees to enter details on content, value and destination of a shipment. The various costs are calculated automatically for the country and particular seaport or airport. The system ensures full compliance with each country's regulations. In recent years, many new regulations have had to do not with economics but with homeland security. They may forbid the export of certain types of microchips to some countries, or the export of certain items from some countries. All this information is closely monitored by NextLinx and added to the documentation and automated forms.

The software has been implemented in every facility of the company in the world. It is integrated into Fairchild's enterprise resource planning (ERP) systems as well as into the shipment application of its major shipping carrier. Shipping clerks can check easily retrievable trade documentation and be sure that all shipping complies with the destination country's regulations. This saves the typical labour-intensive search for trade compliance documentation. This helps the company to clear 90 per cent of its shipments with the proper authorities before the shipment reaches the destination country. The system also shortened shipping durations and reduced shipping delays. As a result, Fairchild could reduce the amount of raw materials inventory it carries.

The use of the new system reduced the number of employees involved in shipping processes, but it also had another positive effect. It standardized shipping procedures and records worldwide. The same shipping procedures and records are maintained at every facility of the company, anywhere in the world. This enables the company to easily implement the procedures and documentation in new facilities it might establish in the future.

Thinking about the case

1 The software Fairchild integrated into its ERP system reduces risk. What risk?

2 The software saves costs. What costs?

3 Why is it important to integrate an application such as NextLinx's to the ERP system of the adopting global company?

4 Why is standardization of processes so important to a company such as Fairchild?

SOURCES: www.nextlinx.com/news/casestudies/case_fairchildsemi.shtml, 2005; www.fairchildsemi.com, 2005

Case study **8.2**

Frontier TV

For several years the European Commission have been considering revising and extending the 'TV without Frontiers' directive of 1989, last amended in 1997. This was prompted by changes in market trends and the introduction of new technology. The old directive was effectively becoming obsolete as it was drafted when video services were available only through traditional TV channels. The switch from analogue to digital technology suggests that the number of digital pay-TV subscribers will increase significantly, with a corresponding rise in the number of channels available. Similarly so-called non-linear video services make the application of the old EU law inappropriate. Non-linear technology provides on-demand services which are very difficult to regulate prior to transmission, as the viewer can choose to view the content at any time. For content from established providers such as the BBC, regulation of on-demand services is difficult, and for providers that rely on content provided by the general public, such as YouTube, regulation is virtually impossible without stringent censorship. In

May 2006 organizations and companies from seven European countries objected to the initial proposals of the EU. These companies included Yahoo!, Vodaphone, NTL and Cisco. The organizations included the UK Confederation of British Industries (CBI), the Federation of German Industries and the Confederation of Netherlands Industry and Employers. Their main complaint was that regulators would be unable to find and track the multitude of online publishers of video content, including bloggers offering video and other online interactive services.

In October 2006 a UK Parliamentary Committee heard evidence from, amongst others, Jeremy Beale, the head of the CBI's e-business group, who told them that putting restrictions on the European online market place would push consumers to services outside the EU, stunting development of Internet TV in the UK and Europe. The same committee also heard concerns about attempts to weaken the 'country of origin' principle which allows broadcasters to offer pan-European services, while complying with laws of the country of their home-base.

Probably as a consequence of these and similar objections throughout the EU, the final directive has taken a pragmatic view. A press release from Brussels in March 2007 states that 'At the heart of the new

The introduction of digital television is presenting European regulators with new challenges.

Directive is the country of origin principle, which was already the cornerstone of the original 'Television without Frontiers' Directive of 1989. This principle has played a pivotal role in boosting cross-border satellite TV and the progressive establishment of pan-European TV channels since the end of the 1980s. It will in future also ensure that audiovisual media service providers other than broadcasters (such as providers of video-on-demand, news-on-demand, sport-on-demand or providers of downloadable audiovisual content for mobiles) will have to comply only with the legislation of the country where they are established, and not with 27 different national legal systems.'

However, in addition to this flexibility there is also a requirement that member states take measures to protect minors and prohibit content that would incite religious or racial hatred. There are also indications that the EU supports the concept of national regulatory authorities that are independent from national governments to encourage democracy and media pluralism.

On a more commercial note, the 'TV Without Frontiers' allows more advertising and 'product placement' – putting a sponsor's product in a TV show.

Member countries may add to theses regulations by setting stricter national rules that will apply to all companies based in their country.

Thinking about the case

1   Is it right that the EU should produce overarching regulations that apply to all member countries?

2   How does this affect non-EU countries? For example, Yahoo! has sites based in many countries of the world. Is it acceptable to post a video that promotes racial hatred if the site is based in the USA but not if it is based in the UK?

3   What would be the economic consequence for European TV companies if the regulations are over restrictive?

SOURCES: 'Can Internet TV have frontiers', Rand Corporation, www.rand.org; 'Boosting the Diversity of European TV and On-Demand Services', Press Release, 9 March 2007, Europa.eu/rapid/pressReleasesAction.do; 'EU sets new digital media rules', news.bbc.co.uk, 25 May 2007

Case study **8.3**

China's Internet revolution

BY DAN ILETT

China is a booming Internet society, but how are its many constituent parts embracing the medium? Dan Ilett found a mix of priorities and a few surprises.

They say a wise man learns from others' mistakes. In China's case that appears to be true.

As development rumbles on at incredible speed (8 per cent GDP growth last year), China's people are harnessing the power of the Internet to trade, talk and learn.

Beijing hotel manager Jason Shan says: 'I use the computer for talking to friends and meeting new people. I sometimes download songs and pictures and upload them to my mobile phone. I also play some games and my wife keeps some documents for her study. People at our level use computers for this sort of thing but we're not technicians.'

There is nothing special about people using computers to do any of these things, except when you consider that huge communities on the Internet are forming and changing the way people live and learn in China.

According to research by Ipsos Insight, the mean number of hours spent online in China (17.9 in one month) surpasses all other countries.

Porter Erisman, VP for Chinese trading website Alibaba says: 'The Internet is at the core of community. If you look at online communities in the West . . . in China it's like that but on steroids. The culture is incredibly social and people always want to be connected to friends and family.

'People absorb new technologies so quickly. In China a few years ago not only did you not have *Auto Trader* magazine, you didn't have autos [but now China has both]. So everything in China leaps to the next level very quickly.'

There are currently 110 million Internet users in China – a figure estimated to rise to 184 million by 2010 according to data from eMarketer.

Chat rooms, bulletin board systems (BBS) and blogs have become extremely popular in Chinese culture. So much so that people base their buying decisions largely on recommendations – just as in other countries. But in China some would argue that traditional media are not as trustworthy as advice from a neighbour.

T.R. Harrington, MD of Shanghai-based Darwin Marketing, says: 'The BBS forums have a tremendous influence. If you look at media in China, the government controls it, so it's not always what the people believe. They feel like they get the best opinions from their fellow men from the bulletin boards.'

Community posts are becoming so popular that advertisers such as Harrington have teams of people posting information on them.

He adds: 'It's labour-intensive but labour is cheap here. If someone can provide value then I'm willing to listen. It makes sense not to push a product but to try and contribute something.'

Sage Brennan, MD of analyst house Pacific Epoch, believes it is waves of young people who are creating these online communities.

He says: 'BBS really reflects what young people are interested in. Chinese people are looking around at what things to buy, what to consume. I'm

An upmarket internet cafe in Guilin, China.

sure that a lot of the recent growth in China's consumer economy is being driven by this new communication. The buying focus is still ultimately made by recommendations from friends and family.'

Computer games are fuelling a society that almost lives in a virtual world. According to Chinese government figures, around four million PCs are bought every year in China as the popularity of computer games fuels the demand for Internet cafés.

Alibaba's Erisman says: 'I went on a two-month bike ride in rural China and in every town I couldn't get a seat in the Internet café. The villages are just beginning to get them.

'But if you're a young woman with some disposable income, you could be up at 1:00 a.m. chatting online comparing products. Just as guys are crazy about online games, women are crazy about buying things online.'

China is riding a wave of consumerism, part of which is undoubtedly fuelled by the Internet. One website helping people to trade online is called Taobao – a China-specific consumer marketplace owned by Alibaba, which competes with eBay.

Erisman says: 'It's all about friends getting together and shopping. China went from no consumer e-commerce to being crazy about it in about two years. We launched [Taobao] three years ago. The market wasn't there then so we had to build it.

'eBay came here first. They had a four-year head start. The problem was that they never created a local product. Our team built something totally unique for China and surpassed eBay very quickly.'

One word that seems synonymous with the Internet in China in the Western media is censorship. Yahoo! China, which is also operated by Alibaba, is one US media company that has come under heavy criticism for agreeing to cooperate with government rules on what it can publish.

Erisman says: 'I don't spend any time worrying about censorship. I would only work in a job where I was making a positive impact. There's no question that Internet companies foreign and local have had an overwhelmingly positive impact on the lives of most Chinese.

'Our model on censorship is no different to foreign media in China. Then you have to ask whether we can do more good than harm by following the laws. Of course the answer is yes.

'People have blogs in China where they can chat and say just about anything they want. The international critics are focused on the one per cent of things you can't do. But when you look at the 99 per cent of things you can do it's not even an ethical dilemma. You can pursue profit and do the right thing at the same time. They're not mutually exclusive.'

Thinking about the case

1   The debate about censorship on the Internet in the West focuses on issues such as pornography and libel. Is there any difference between these arguments and those concerning government-approved content on Yahoo! China?

2   It seems that chat rooms, BBS and blogs are increasing their influence on buying patterns in China. Could the same be said of potential customers in other parts of the world?

PART FOUR

Managers and information systems

'OK, are we all here? I see Martin for information systems, Jean for finance, Tony for marketing, Stephanie for buying, David for operations, and you all know Suzanne and James, our new regional store managers, right? That's everyone. Let's get this meeting under way.'

Lucy Slade, the chief executive of Urban Scene, was calling to order the quarterly strategic planning meeting of her top managers. Lucy was a young executive who had studied Fashion and Textile Management at Nottingham Trent University. She started in the business by designing her own clothing line and selling it on commission to other chains. But she wasn't satisfied with that small niche and needed to accomplish more. No stores in which her fashions were sold had the image that she wanted her clothes to convey – they were too boring and not edgy enough for today's teens. So, she took the next step and opened her own store, making sure it fit her clothing's image. The response from teens had been gratifying. They considered it their first choice for cutting-edge designs. From her first store, she'd gradually built a small chain of 40 shops and expanded from selling her designs to including other manufacturers' compatible lines.

'First, let me tell you some exciting news about our own Lucy's Signature and Streetwear lines. I've been working with Martin and his IS staff on speeding the design-to-manufacture time frame. We've also pulled in operations – thanks, David – to help set up a new supply chain system with our Asian manufacturers. I'll save the details for later, but essentially, we're setting up a digital design system to speed the manufacturing cycle. It's critical that our signature clothing move from inspiration to manufacture in weeks – not the months that it has taken before. Once the new system is operating, we should be able to get new fashions into our stores in six to seven weeks. That's a new

record, considering the physical logistics of getting the clothes to the UK in the first place. But we absolutely have to keep our designs fresh for our customers.'

Lucy turned to Martin Tate, the firm's chief information officer. 'Martin, let's hear from you on the new information systems implementation. How is the integration of the sites going?'

Uniting the chain's information systems

'We're bringing each site on board the new enterprise resource-planning system starting this summer.

Right now we're concentrating on one region at a time. We're meeting some resistance from the local store staff. They've used their existing systems for such a long time that they're hesitant to change. But I'm sending my four IS professionals out to visit each site in their regions with the timetable for implementation and the information packs. The store managers need to be assured that we'll be training them – and their staffs – before we make the switch. Once they see how the new system will streamline their processes, I think it'll help. But since Outer London is first in line, it will be the test for the rest of the system. I'll keep you informed weekly as we move ahead.'

'Let me know if you encounter stiff resistance, okay? I'm planning to visit the stores myself and can speak with the store managers to bring them all on board. Most have been with us from the start, so I think a word from me will help, if you need it.'

Finalizing budget numbers for store redesign

'Jean, have we wrapped up the budget for the store redesign now? Did we hit our numbers for the new spotlighting and sound systems?'

'When I checked the numbers for total costs, we were under budget for the lighting, but retrofitting the sound systems into some of our older shops was challenging. Luckily, our industrial design allowed us to hide some of our wiring in exposed pipes. So, overall, we were over budget by about £2500, which was within our margin for error. I'll bring the numbers by after our meeting so you can check them.'

'Thanks, Jean. Glad that effort is wrapping up. It's critical that the store atmosphere be right. We want our customers – both guys and girls – to enjoy their shopping experience.'

Supplying information and systems for marketing

Lucy turned to Tony Martin, her vice president of marketing, next. 'Tony, two things: how are we doing on clearing out the spring inventory? We need to keep new merchandise flowing into the shops. And how are the sales promotions and planning for the summer coming?'

Tony responded, 'We're changing the rack displays every other week to keep fresh styles in front of customers. And I'm checking with the district sales managers and each shop's sales staff to go over their receipts to see what is hot in each area. The sales associates have been a big help to me to fine-tune for local tastes. They're a real gold mine of trends and ideas. From their verbal feedback we gathered yesterday, superbaggy guys' jeans are going over great in the northeast, and the low rider cargo skirts and logo tees are a hit with women in the southeast. The women's platform shoes and flip-flops are moving well across the board. And accessories will be big for summer sales. We'll need more stock in the next week or so.'

'Great. Work with buying and operations on re-stocking, okay? Let's take advantage of the automated order system. And let's also look into some summer sales – last year's sales really boosted our numbers.'

Lucy shifted her focus to Stephanie and David. 'OK, buying and operations, can you briefly highlight our international goals and operations?'

Going global for buying and operations

Stephanie Viner, the head buyer, started first. 'As you know, I'm working a season ahead of the rest of you. I just returned from the winter fashion shows in Milan. In a couple of weeks, I'll head to New York – a new frontier for us. Lucy wants us to start thinking globally, and we need to learn more about the US fashion scene. I'll be looking to develop relationships with local firms, and Lucy is joining me for the trip. If we can buy from and sell to America, it's an exciting opportunity for the company. But we have to do it right. Farther down the road a couple of years, we're also looking into the Asian market – Japan as a foothold to start. But more expansion in that region will be contingent on our success in America. You'll be hearing more from us as we firm up additional plans.'

David Moore, head of operations, spoke next. 'Lucy already told you about the upcoming system for speeding design-to-manufacture time frames. With most of our manufacturing in Asia, we needed a way to get the designs to the various shops faster. So that system will cut our time frames substantially.

Building an e-commerce effort

Suzanne and James, the new district shop managers, were the last to report. Suzanne spoke up. 'James and I want to propose that Urban Scene move into e-commerce. We've been talking with shop personnel, and they want to build a website to expand sales. Several of the sales associates are pretty handy with computerized design already. Many of the large chains have established websites to provide additional service for their customers. Since our customer base is teens, who are generally web savvy, it makes sense to try to capture the online market, too. Besides, our high-tech, cutting-edge image fits well with an online presence. If we don't satisfy that market, someone else might. So, we're formally bringing the request here to consider that project.'

Lucy nodded. 'Okay, we can explore that. But I don't want our site to compete with our current shops. Other companies have had problems with websites cutting into shop sales. We don't want to cannibalize existing sales. So let's think of a way to link the two. Also, I'd want the website to mirror our new store image. We've just spent a lot of time and company money upgrading the design of our shops, so let's capitalize on those efforts. We have to have a coherent look and feel to all Urban Scene products and sites. Would you and James get a formal proposal and costs together? You'll need to speak with both Martin and Jean for technology and costs, and then we need to consider David's supply and warehousing end to support the site. Shipping products directly to customers and allowing for their returns would affect our warehouse operations drastically. We aren't currently set up to handle that. Tying everything together is critical, but at least we don't need to start from scratch for operations. Anyway, see what you can come up with in the next few weeks, and when I get back from the States, I'd like to see the plan.'

'Sounds fine.'

Lucy scanned the room and her managers' faces. 'I think that about does it for now. Thanks, all of you, for your dedication. Keep the new ideas coming – we need fresh thoughts all the time. Anything you can come up with to cut costs, boost sales, and streamline operations contributes in a very real way to our bottom line. We have a great team, starting with all of you here and extending out to our shop personnel. Retailing is always a highly competitive industry, and these are tough times, as you know. But let's keep moving ahead. Now let's eat lunch!'

Business challenges

Urban Scene is facing some potential opportunities and problems. Most of its design and retail functions are directly tied to its information systems. So, the success of its information systems is central to its continued survival. Some of those issues are explored in the following chapters:

- In Chapter 9, 'Managers and Their Information Needs', you learn what type of information different levels of an organization need and how Urban Scene can use that knowledge to upgrade and organize its information systems to better serve the business.

- In Chapter 10, 'Business Intelligence and Knowledge Management', you learn how Urban Scene can use knowledge management systems to support its business process and how data mining can be used to establish strategic advantage over its competitors.

Chapter 9

Managers and their information needs

LEARNING OBJECTIVES

Information is needed for decision-making and operations at all levels of management, but managers at different levels of an organization's hierarchy need different types of information. By making information available to virtually every level of an organization, ISs are changing the way organizations operate.

When you finish this chapter, you will be able to:

Explain the link between an organization's structure and information flow.

List the main functions and information needs at different managerial levels.

Identify the characteristics of information needed by different managerial levels.

Recognize the influence of politics on the design of, and accessibility to, information systems.

Describe the ways in which information technology personnel are deployed in organizations.

List and explain the advantages and disadvantages of various personnel deployments.

Explain the importance of collaboration between IS managers and business managers and describe the relationships between the two groups.

SLICING AND DICING
THE INFORMATION

Martin Tate, Urban Scene's chief information officer, was meeting with Mike Roberts, the Croydon operational shop manager, and Anita Belleville, one of his four regional IS managers. The company's new enterprise resource-planning system was installed in the southeast regional shops and had been running for two months now. Martin was following up to ensure that the system was generating needed information for individual managers. He was stunned to find that Mike had avoided using the system's new capabilities. Mike was accustomed to printing out his weekly sales reports and he'd continued with his old ways, despite the system's new capabilities.

Overcoming resistance to the new system

'Mike, you know that with our new system you can view data in several ways, right? I know you've always looked at total weekly sales for the women's and men's clothing lines. Did you know you can view them on screen whenever you want? Not only that, but you can drill down to see which size of jeans, in which colour and style, are selling best. You can also change the view to see which shop floor staff are selling more items – and what they're selling.'

Mike raised his eyebrows. 'Really? I always check informally with the staff on the floor to get their read on daily sales. But I didn't know the system could track actual sales down to the specific inventory item.'

'Sure, we track the items through their bar codes entered in the transaction-processing system so we know when a particular item was sold and by whom. That data is stored in the database, so you can look at real-time data or historical sales for trends – I call

it 'slicing and dicing' the information. That flexibility is why Shirley wanted to implement the new system. She can pull up sales data in her headquarters office and view sales across the business as a whole, regionally, or down to individual shop sales to get a big picture of how we're doing to make long-range plans. James, your regional manager, looks at the same data for the southeast region. He's most interested in ensuring that overall sales are doing well and that your inventory system is supplying you with new stock when you need it. But you can look at more detailed information for your own shop to keep

your finger on the pulse of day-to-day operations. Anita will walk you through the steps to use the system.'

A convert is born

A half-hour later, Mike was pulling up data into tables, bar graphs and line graphs. 'I see that our signature lines sold well after our new advertising promotion. The sales jumped a few days after the newspaper ads came out. I'll tell Tony Martin that his marketing department's advert worked.'

Martin nodded. 'I'm sure he'll appreciate hearing from you. But he accesses the system himself to check whether his print, radio and TV spots are boosting sales. And if sales are lagging in certain regions, then he plans different campaigns or changes their frequency. But if you or your staff have any ideas for your particular shop, just send him an email. You work directly with your customers and can convey any of their concerns or needs.'

'Okay, will do. Thanks for checking in with me.'

'Sure. Work with the system awhile and let Anita and me know if you have any problems. Once you're proficient, I'd like to have you speak to the managers from the north-east region. Could you make time in your schedule? They're next in the ERP implementation and I think you can help troubleshoot some issues for them. They'll appreciate hearing your perspective and can learn from you.'

Reorganizing systems and staff

Urban Scene's growing pains were showing. The company had expanded to 40 stores and was considering expansion to Europe. In addition, it was planning to develop an e-commerce website. With these changes, it was obvious that the company was outgrowing its old ways of operating – and its information systems. Martin Tate, the chain's CIO, was increasingly involved in more aspects of the store's operations and strategic planning.

Creating order from chaos

As Urban Scene grew, it inherited each store's information system (IS). With each addition, the IS staff had to learn the details of more systems, and it became difficult to maintain them all. A few years back, Martin's staff had reached the breaking point – systems were failing and managers had no uniform

method of communicating important information to each other and headquarters staff. So, under Martin's direction, Urban Scene implemented its new enterprise resource planning (ERP) system. The new system allowed a centralized IS organization. In contrast, the stores' system only collected data from transactions and immediately transmitted the data to a database at headquarters. The company had chosen to overhaul its systems to simplify its hardware and software systems, streamline collection and reporting of data and make planning for the future easier. Since many problems could be addressed by IS staff through the Internet, the new centralized system was easing the daily troubleshooting and assistance his staff had to provide for other staff to do their work.

Revamping the IS organization

Since ISs were so central to Urban Scene's business processes – and to its overall success – Martin believed he needed to change his IS staff organization, too. He reviewed the existing practice of local store control over the IS function and decided that it was inefficient. IS staff had little support or direction from top management. So, he devised a system that centralized the organization's network and ERP planning and services, but still provided technical support for each store. He hired or promoted four regional IS managers. Those managers oversaw ten stores each and served as an information centre. Each manager supervised two systems administrators, who were responsible for five stores each and made routine visits. All IS staff reported to the central IS unit and attended periodic training sessions that Martin organized. Martin also set up an agreement with his ERP consultant to provide additional technical backup when needed. The consultants worked closely with his staff to ensure that Urban Scene's system functioned reliably. The on-site IS presence in stores was essential to ensure that sales staff needs were met.

Establishing an e-commerce website

Following a recent strategic planning meeting, Suzanne Granger and James Block, Urban Scene's north and south district store managers, had been working on a plan to develop an e-commerce site. Their mandates from CEO Shirley Steiner had been to be sure that e-commerce sales did not hurt local stores and that the website carry the same brand image as the recently completed store redesign. James had worked out a plan so that any sales on the company's website would be fulfilled by the store closest to the customer. That way, the site would improve store sales and tap into existing transaction-processing and warehousing systems.

Fulfilling the second mandate was proving more challenging. A group of local sales associates were so excited about setting up a site for their friends to buy Urban Scene clothes that they had begun designing a site on their own, without oversight or approval. Suzanne met with them to explain that the site needed to be controlled from headquarters and be a seamless part of Urban Scene's sales effort. She stressed that they needed to work with Martin's staff to coordinate their efforts and tie the site into the existing sales system. The sales associates were disappointed that the website design they'd done so far might not be used, but Suzanne assured them that they would have a chance to meet with Martin and his staff and present what they had developed so far. She told them that whatever path the site development took, they would certainly be able to provide feedback.

Managers and information

Generally speaking, managers at different levels of an organizational hierarchy make different types of decisions, control different types of processes and therefore have different information needs. While companies have many different organizational structures, this chapter will discuss the most common: a generic pyramid-shaped hierarchy with a few leaders at the top and an increasing number of workers at each subsequent managerial and operational level (see Figure 9.1). There has long been a fairly close correlation between the level of work a person does in an organization and the type of IS he or she uses. But today, with computers on every desk, that relationship is no longer as clear. The availability of increasingly flexible and powerful information systems throughout all organizational levels has had a profound effect on organizational structure. For instance, in the past, companies had specialized staff whose main task was to process data and generate information to meet managers' requests. Now, the ability to generate information has been placed directly in managers' hands, all the way up to the chief executive officer, which has contributed to the downsizing of middle management.

Figure 9.1 The management pyramid

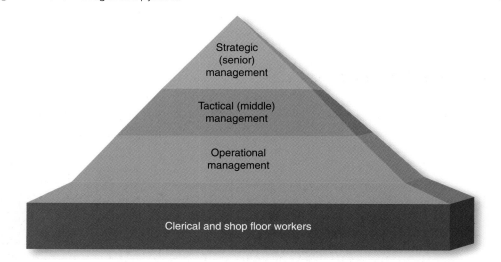

Strategic (senior) management

Tactical (middle) management

Operational management

Clerical and shop floor workers

Most organizations will recognize the importance of information systems and technology and that there are often competing or conflicting requirements from different parts of the business. There is therefore a need for management of the IT function to ensure that resources are used sensibly and fairly throughout the business processes, typically headed by the chief information officer as discussed in Chapter 1. This post is concerned with the strategic use of IT in the business but also the management and control of IT projects and operational IT systems. Technology aside, the politics of information within an organization can undermine optimal business decision-making. Trying to retain power in their hands, and realizing that information is power, managers sometimes oppose the trend of making both data and processing tools available throughout a company. Problems often arise when the potential politics are not considered when developing systems and deciding how people will support those systems.

The traditional organizational pyramid

Every organization needs leadership. The top-level leaders of an organization are a small group of people responsible for running the organization and reporting to one person in the group, who usually bears the title *chief executive officer (CEO)*. Some small, knowledge-intensive companies use a *matrix* organizational structure. A matrix structure distributes leadership among several people, varying by project, product or discipline. However, the management of most organizations still follows a *pyramid model*: the CEO at the top, a small group of senior managers one level down who report to the CEO, a larger number of middle managers who report to the senior managers, many more lower-level managers who report to the middle managers, and so on down the line (see Figure 9.1).

In general, at the bottom of the organizational pyramid are clerical and shop floor workers; in the next layer up are operational managers, who are responsible for overseeing the day-to-day operation of a company; next up is a much narrower layer of middle managers; and at the top are a few senior managers. Due to the nature of their decisions, managers in the top two layers are often referred to as tactical (middle) and strategic (senior) management. Strategic managers are expected to establish corporate strategies with a long-term view, and tactical managers are expected to figure out how to achieve the strategies. Variation in this structure exists among organizations; not every organization has exactly three layers, and there are often sub-layers in the management levels. Also, the distinction between operational and middle managers is not always clear, nor is it necessarily important. Remember that this rough categorization is just for the purpose of discussing information needs. It is best to think of managerial levels as a continuum between two ends, the lowest level being operational managers, and the highest level being top management. It is very likely that your first managerial position will be as an operational manager.

Clerical and shop floor workers

In many organizations, *clerical and shop floor workers* make up the largest group of employees. Included in this group are all types of service workers, such as cashiers in banks, receptionists in hospitals and sales staff in retail stores, as well as traditional production employees in manufacturing organizations. The main characteristic common to workers at this level is that they are not managers. Although they may have high levels of expertise in a particular technology, equipment or process, the scope of their decisions is typically narrower and focused on the work at hand. However, they are not required – and are not expected – to make management-level judgements. Many of these workers operate at their organizations' boundaries, where they interact with other organizations or individuals, including customers. Many take orders for products and services, provide customer service, record sales, issue invoices, record shipments of raw material received and services performed, provide

The central warehouse of Amazon Germany.

maintenance services for equipment leased or sold by their company, and perform any other non-managerial work.

Operational management

Operational managers are in charge of small groups of frontline workers. Examples include the foreperson on a shop floor, a department manager in a department store, and a manager in a bank or insurance company who is in charge of a small unit and authorized to obligate the company for small amounts of money. The people in these positions typically follow general policies handed down by their superiors. Within these policies, they make decisions that affect their units in the short term, that is, within days. For instance, if a subordinate calls in sick, an operational manager in a manufacturing setting is empowered to decide whether to call another employee in from home, in which case the person will probably report late, or to ask another worker to stay for another shift, in which case the company must pay time and a half. In a service industry such as an airline, an operational manager might help ticket agents solve a problem that has cropped up with a passenger's luggage.

Tactical management

Tactical managers, also called middle managers, receive general directions and goals from their superiors and, within those guidelines, make decisions for their subordinates, affecting the near and somewhat more distant future. Usually, they are in charge of several operational managers. Tactical managers are so called because they are responsible for finding the best means (tactics) to accomplish their superiors' strategic decisions. As you remember from Chapter 2, 'Strategic Uses of Information Systems', a strategic decision focuses on *what* to do, while a tactical decision concentrates on *how* to do it.

For example, corporate management may make the strategic decision to provide more of a bank's services electronically: over the telephone and online via personal computers. This broad goal leaves the tactical managers to determine *how* to provide those services. Should the bank develop the necessary computer software in-house? Should it hire a consulting firm? Which services should be offered first? How should the bank educate staff and customers about the new offerings? Tactical managers are expected to provide the best solutions to these problems and refer issues to the strategic level only if their decisions may affect the general strategy outlined.

Strategic management

It is easier to determine which managers make up the strategic level than it is to discern who belongs to the other two levels. The reason is simple: these people are the highest-ranking officers of the organization. In many companies, the president and vice presidents make up the strategic management. When members of the board of directors play an active role in the company's business, they, too, contribute their share to strategic decision-making. However, do not be misled by titles. Some corporations, such as banks, grant vice presidential titles to thousands of their managers. Title alone does not place those people in the strategic level of their organizations.

Strategic managers make decisions that affect the entire organization, or large parts of it, and leave an impact in the long run. For example, such decisions may include merging with and acquiring other companies, opening branches overseas, developing a completely new product or service, moving operations to the Internet, or recommending a major restructuring of an organization.

Characteristics of information at different managerial levels

People in different management levels have different information needs. As shown in Figure 9.2, the information needed by different managerial and operational levels varies in the time span covered, level of detail, source and other characteristics over a broad spectrum. For instance, clerical workers need data that allow them to fulfil daily operations

Amazon's president, Jeff Bezos, inside his company's huge Seattle warehouse.

but not necessarily make decisions. To serve customers and other workers, they must have access to information such as how many units of a certain item are available for sale, how much a certain customer service costs, and how much overtime a certain employee worked last week. Usually, these people make *ad hoc* enquiries to satisfy immediate information needs.

On the other hand, most of the information that managers require is used to make decisions. Operational managers need information based on data that are generally narrow in scope, gathered over a short period of time and useful for decisions that have an impact in the short run, that is, hours, days and weeks. The decisions middle managers make affect a greater number of organizational units for longer periods of time, and they require information extracted from data that are broader in scope and time, and that information may come from outside their departments.

The decision-making process of middle managers and above is less structured than that of operational managers; despite the broader scope of the data – and sometimes *because* of it – there are no proven methods for selecting a course of action that guarantees a predicted outcome.

The decisions that senior managers make affect whole divisions or the entire organization and have long-standing impact. Their decision-making is very unstructured. Senior managers need information gleaned from vast amounts of raw data that have been collected over long periods of time from many or all of an organization's units. The original data for the information come from internal organizational sources as well as external sources, such as the mass media, the Web, national and international trade bulletins and consulting firms.

Data scope

Data scope refers to the amount of data from which information is extracted, in terms of the number of organizational units supplying data or the length of time the data cover. For example, data gathered from just one department have a narrower scope than data from every department of the organization. In addition, one department's data from several months have a broader scope than the same department's data from one week.

Figure 9.2 Characteristics of data and information for different levels of management

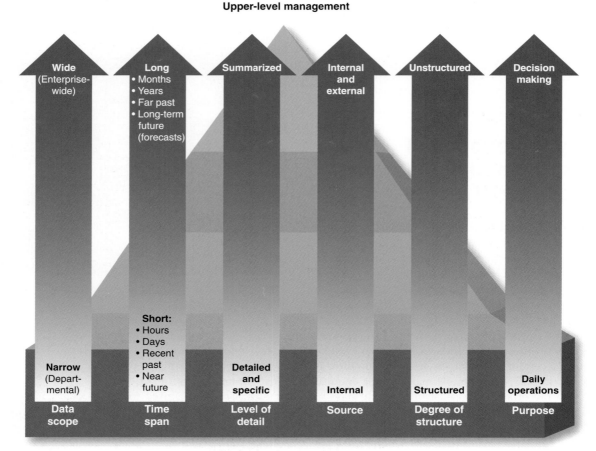

Upper-level management

| Wide (Enterprise-wide) | Long • Months • Years • Far past • Long-term future (forecasts) | Summarized | Internal and external | Unstructured | Decision making |

| Narrow (Depart-mental) | Short: • Hours • Days • Recent past • Near future | Detailed and specific | Internal | Structured | Daily operations |
| Data scope | Time span | Level of detail | Source | Degree of structure | Purpose |

Lower-level management

Data scope is different from level of detail. When a lot of data is summarized into a few figures, such as totals and averages, the level of detail is low; however, the data scope may be high if the data are about numerous people, departments or events. Data scope refers to the number of individuals, departments or events about which data were collected.

To make a strategic decision, top management may need a single figure that is calculated from a wide range of data, such as the average monthly expenditure on television advertising of sports shoes. The data are collected on as many sport shoe manufacturers as possible to produce information that reflects the entire industry, not a single company or a small number of companies. Although the information provided is a single figure, it is derived from vast amounts of data spanning a long time and many corporations. Therefore, the data scope is wide. At the other extreme, the manager of a shop in a manufacturing plant may need only information that is extracted from data collected within that organizational unit. The data scope is then narrow.

Time span

The *time span* of data refers to how long a period of time the data cover. Data that cover hours or days (the time span usually needed by lower-level managers) are said to have a short time span relative to data that cover months, years or decades, which are said to have a long time span. Senior managers typically use data that reach far into the past. They also make extrapolations based on the patterns of performance in the past to forecast what might happen in the future. Data warehouses, which accumulate historical data, are an excellent source for data collected over a long time span. Data mining may produce a pattern that can help make strategic decisions such as a radical way in which a certain item is marketed, or a fundamental change in the disbursement policy of an insurance company because it discovered patterns of fraud in insurance claims. Such decisions might not come about without collecting data over a long time span.

Level of detail

The *level of detail* is the degree to which the information generated is specific. When a department manager looks at the number of shoes sold every day of the week broken down by style, the information is, obviously, very detailed. Operational managers usually consider highly detailed information. Senior managers, in contrast, typically consider information that is highly summarized. This type of information includes totals and averages for categories of products (rather than individual products) over long periods of time. These different levels of detail serve the different operational purposes. Operational managers typically examine actual facts relating to present events so they can control immediate situations, while senior managers are often interested in trends to formulate strategies. The difference can be compared to looking at only several pieces of a puzzle or looking at the entire picture the puzzle forms.

Usually, the more detailed the information, the closer it is to the data from which it is derived, and thus proportionately less processing is involved in generating it. Daily totals of sales in the shoe department are more detailed than an annual total for the entire chain of stores. The latter requires significantly more processing because it combines data from many sources.

Source: internal vs. external

Internal data are collected within the organization, usually by transaction-processing systems, but also through employee and customer surveys. External data are collected from a wide array of sources outside the organization, including mass communications media such as television, radio and newspapers; specialized newsletters published by private organizations; government agencies; and the vast sources of news and statistics on the Web. For instance, to plan the expansion or contraction of a national supermarket chain, top managers cannot rely only on their organization's internal data. They must track national trends. Thus, they need information on national annual demographic changes. Without it, they may spend resources on increasing the number of shops, only to find, a few years later, that their customer base has shrunk. Multinational corporations rely on even more external data; the data they use come from many different parts of the world, from many different sources and often in many different formats. For example, they must rely on demographic and economic statistics of several nations rather than one.

In some industries, almost all the information comes from external sources. For example, managers of mutual funds and pension funds must track changes in the prices of stocks and other securities daily (sometimes even hourly) to be able to optimize the capital gains of the funds. The data they analyse come mainly from stock exchanges. Firms that operate websites that generate advertising revenues rely on data from companies that rate web traffic.

internal data Data collected within an organization, typically by transaction-processing systems, for example the number of sales per month, the value of outstanding credit owed to the organization.

external data Data that are collected from a wide array of sources outside the organization, including mass communications media, specialized newsletters, government agencies and the Web.

Structured and unstructured data

Structured data are numbers and facts that can be conveniently stored and retrieved in an orderly manner for operations and decision-making. The sources of such data are primarily

Why you should...

be information conscious

Imagine you are in charge of eight sales offices, each covering a different part of the world. You want to find out which offices sell well and which do not, which products sell better than others overall, and which products sell better in each region. But you cannot – you have neither the data nor the applications to help you. You know you are missing an opportunity to make better decisions for your company.

Managers are rarely physically involved in the production of their organizations' products and services. Rather, managerial work involves facilitating the generation of products and services. The 'material' managers use in their daily activities is information. They either extract information by themselves or have someone else extract it for them; they exchange information with other managers and with subordinates, and they communicate instructions to their subordinates to attain objectives.

To do all that, managers must know the best sources and applications for producing useful information and the best ways to communicate information. The flow of information is closely linked to the organizational structure. In fact, we often enquire about an organization's structure by asking, 'To whom do you report?' – a question referring to the direction of information flow.

As a manager, you must know which type of information, derived from which type of data, serves your needs best. But more information is not necessarily better; too much information may be confusing and time-consuming to analyse. Understanding what data to rely on, and how to best extract information from it, helps managers optimize their efforts.

internal files and databases that capture transactions. Drawing from transactional databases, data warehouses, too, hold highly structured data. Unstructured data are drawn from meeting discussions, private conversations, email messages, instant messaging records, textual documents, graphical representations and other 'non-uniform' sources.

Structured data are used for daily operations and decisions that are relatively easy to make with the help of proven models. The higher a managerial position, the less structured decisions a manager faces; therefore, unstructured data are extremely valuable in managerial decision-making, especially at the higher levels of an organization.

The nature of managerial work

Managers are paid to plan and control (see Figure 9.3). They plan to minimize uncertainty and reduce risks; they exercise control to ensure adherence to plans. Both responsibilities involve decision-making and leadership. Information systems are a great support throughout the management process.

Planning

In an ideal world, managers would have some way of knowing what the future portends. Then, they could make their decisions accordingly. Unfortunately, managers do not have a crystal ball. But through both short- and long-term planning, they can have something better: a hand in *shaping* the future, not just living through it. As illustrated in Figure 9.4, planning starts with a long-term mission and includes establishing goals and objectives, as well as resource-planning and budgeting for both the short and long term. Most of all, good planning requires good information. The better the information, the clearer the picture managers have of the present and the past and the more prepared they are to plan for the future. By

Figure 9.3 Managers plan and control

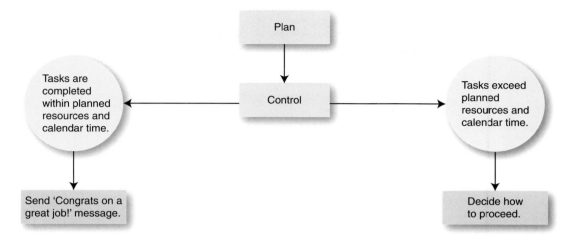

Figure 9.4 An example of a mission statement, strategic goals and tactical objectives for an in-line skate manufacturer

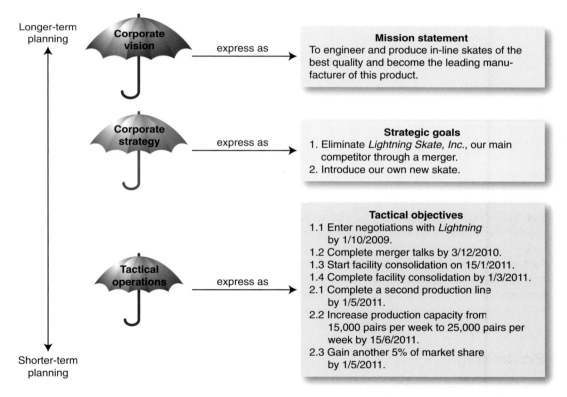

extracting only the most useful facts from raw data, ISs can provide the most salient information. Examples of the most important planning activities are shown in Figure 9.5: scheduling, budgeting and resource allocation.

As any entrepreneur will tell you, the first step in planning is to create a mission statement. How do you envisage the organization in one year, five years and ten years? Within the

Figure 9.5 The main ingredients of planning

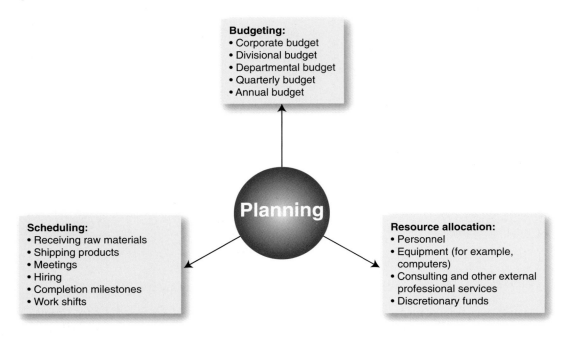

framework of the mission statement, top management sets goals. Goals are a wish list without specific quantities or dates. Goals roughly correspond to strategy. Within the framework of each goal, top managers and middle managers set objectives. Unlike goals, objectives are specific in monetary terms, such as revenues and profits; percentages, such as market share and inventory turnover; dates, such as completion dates for tasks and other results that can be measured. Whereas the mission statement is the basis for long-term planning, objectives are the basis for medium- and short-term planning.

After objectives are outlined, planning includes steps such as the calculation of person-hours required to complete a project and, thus, the size of staff needed; the detailing of a master production schedule; and the specification of quantities of raw materials and their supply lead times. Probably the most important part of any business plan is the budget. The organization's budget is the aggregate of the budgets of all its units.

A growing number of organizations have implemented enterprise-wide ISs, some of which are popularly called enterprise resource-planning (ERP) systems. The reason that ERP systems are so called is that while they support daily operations, they also collect vast amounts of data that can be processed into useful planning information.

Controlling

Any plan, in itself, is useless unless used as a basis for control. *Controlling* consists of monitoring and taking action. *Monitoring* is knowing what is happening. Once plans are in place, managers use them to control ongoing activities by comparing the planned outcome with the actual results, as shown in Table 9.1. Thus, plans are the control tools of an organization. When discrepancies between planned and actual performance are found, managers determine the reason for the variance. If the performance is better than planned, then the plan may be modified. If the performance is worse than planned, then the cause of the discrepancy is investigated and corrected, if possible, or the remaining plan is revised to be more realistic.

Table 9.1 Examples of processes used to control projects

Reviewing project resources and updating milestones
Tracking receiving times of raw materials
Tracking shipping dates
Periodically comparing actual expenditures wih budgetary figures
Periodically examining exception reports
Discussing project progress
Periodically examining project progress reports
Periodically examining performance ratios (for example, revenue per employee, inventory turnover)

Different levels of management use different parts of plans to control operations for which they are responsible. For instance, strategic and tactical managers are concerned with allocating resources to projects, while operational managers are usually concerned with allocating resources among the tasks of a project. So, once a budget for hiring temporary workers to complete a project is approved, department managers decide how to use these workers' time. In controlling, too, ERP systems play a major role by providing daily or even up-to-the-minute facts and figures. So do online analytical processing (OLAP) applications, which are discussed later in this chapter.

Decision-making

Both planning and control activities involve decision-making. Decision-making is covered in Chapter 10, 'Business Intelligence and Knowledge Management', but you may remember from previous chapters that a decision is a commitment to act. A decision is made when a person has to select a course of action from several possible courses. For the time being, let it be said that the higher the level of management, the less routine the manager's activities are, the more open the options are, and the more decision-making is involved. For instance, operational managers usually make relatively simple decisions, such as resolving problems with individual customers, scheduling work shifts and evaluating employee performance. Many of their other activities require fulfilment of tactical managers' directives. At the very top of the organizational pyramid, on the other hand, virtually all of an executive's workday is devoted to meetings to reach decisions. All along the managerial hierarchy, information systems are used to provide information to support decision-making activities.

Managing by exception

Some people think that more information is always better than less. However, there is a limit to the amount of information that managers can handle. A better goal would be to provide managers with information that communicates the most important facts. Too much information creates *information overload*, a situation in which a person is confused and cannot make optimal decisions.

Figure 9.6 An example of a budgetary exception report

10 Percent Exception Report			
Plant: 3706 Cockpit Wiring			
Period: 1/1/2008–31/3/2008			
Item	*Budget Amount*	*Actual Amount*	*Deviation*
Wages	€12,236,000	€10,236,876.34	(−16.4%)
Telephone	€4,700	€5,202.87	10.7%
Office Supplies	€2,500	€3,002.00	12.8%

management by exception A method of management whereby managers review only exceptions from expected results that are of a certain size or type, assuming that smaller deviations are immaterial.

One method of reducing the amount of information managers must consume is management by exception. With this approach, managers review only exceptions from expected results that are of a certain size or type, assuming that smaller deviations are immaterial (see Figure 9.6). For example, a department manager may ask for a periodic report that compares actual and budgeted expenditures and highlights only those line items that are greater than 110 per cent or less than 90 per cent of the budgeted figures. (In this example, the 10 per cent deviation is referred to as the *tolerance*, because it is the limit of deviation that is tolerated.) Or a periodic report on a project schedule may include only activities that have not been completed within seven days of scheduled dates. These exception reports require a manager to determine the cause and make a decision about how to deal with the situation. If 95 per cent of the deviations of time, money and other resources fall within the tolerances, the manager saves much time that would otherwise be devoted to detailed investigation of what caused the deviations.

ISs now can be flexible enough to let managers set their own preferences in reports. Usually, they will want to get reports that show actual expenditures against forecast expenditures, but focus on the exceptions. They can simply set the report software application to boldface, italicize or colour the exceptions to highlight them. Increasingly, reports are not paper reports, but on-demand, on-screen reports.

Leading

Reviewing exception reports focuses on adhering to an organization's agreed-upon plan, which is only a small part of a manager's job. Managers must also lead, which requires having a vision and creating confidence in others to follow that vision. Leadership requires a manager to make work more efficient and effective, create new techniques to achieve corporate goals, inspire subordinates, present a role model for desired behaviour, take responsibility for undesired consequences of decisions made under his or her direction and delegate authority.

Grace Hopper, the late rear admiral in the US Navy who was a pioneer in the field of programming in the middle of the last century, once said that the problem with many companies is that they have enough people with MBA degrees but too few leaders. A person may technically be a good manager and still not be regarded as a leader. Many experts hold that true leadership is an innate trait that may be honed but cannot be learned. Therefore, leadership 'skills' are really techniques that hone existing traits. Although some aspects of leadership may depend on personal qualities – inspiring confidence and communicating well – information systems can help managers become better leaders. ISs can provide an overall picture of an organization's operation that supports brainstorming and generation of new ideas – another important element in leadership. They may inspire innovation and the pursuit of new goals as well.

For instance, two important aspects of good leadership are motivating employees and delegating authority. Employees are motivated when they know that their superiors rely on them. One way to motivate subordinates is by granting them access to more resources such as data, information, knowledge and applications. By so doing, leaders communicate that they trust their subordinates. The subordinates, in turn, appreciate the trust and feel involved and responsible for the organization's well-being.

Trends in organizational structure

Information technology (IT) is the most powerful tool available for increasing efficiency, solving problems and making decisions in businesses today. Its impact contributed to vast organizational restructuring in the 1980s and 1990s, with a trend towards downsizing and 'flattening', which often eliminated levels of management. In the early 2000s, the Internet helped make many companies even leaner, because so many activities could be automated and immediately communicated with little need for human labour.

IT flattens the organization

Before the introduction of computers into business, lower-level managers spent much of their time processing data to produce useful information for their supervisors. Over the past two decades, many companies have used ISs to automate these activities, eliminating the need for several layers of middle managers, leading to increased unemployment amongst managers and other professionals, highly skilled people whose services were no longer needed. Rising productivity thanks to IT means that one professional can now do the work of several professionals, and that fewer managers are needed to monitor and control resources. This shift has led to flatter organizational structures (as shown in Figure 9.7) and has been a major force behind the enormous downsizing in both the manufacturing and service sectors. Studies have been conducted showing that as IT proliferates, organizational staffing in general becomes leaner.

Strategic and operational managers have been affected much less by this trend. Strategic managers are still needed because of their responsibilities for setting the organizational course, and operational managers run the daily operations of the organization. Today, easy-to-use graphical user interfaces and affordable data communications allow senior managers

Figure 9.7 Information systems flatten managerial layers.

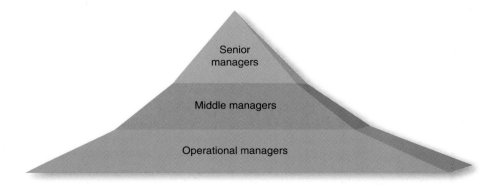

to produce their own information and communicate directly with lower-level managers, who used to be at least two or three layers away. In many small organizations there are simply *no* middle managers between strategic managers and operational managers.

In some companies that make heavy use of the Internet for business, not only is the middle management layer 'lean and mean', but the operational management and office worker layers are as well. For instance, when more and more consumers use corporate websites to purchase products and obtain customer service, there is less need for staff workers to help with these activities. Many organizations also claim that email has flattened their structure because every employee can communicate with any other employee – including top executives. That ability does not necessarily flatten an organization, however. In many organizations the policy is that top executives, including the president, respond to all email messages, which they can receive from any employee at any level. But this electronic correspondence does not affect the actual management of the company. If you take a look at the organizational structure of these companies, you will see that most of them have a clear pyramid with several layers of management. They are not flat organizations.

The matrix structure

The increasing power of information systems in organizations led to an organizational experiment: matrix management. *Matrix management* replaces a strict hierarchical structure with a flexible reporting structure, whereby people report to different supervisors, depending on the project, product or location of the work. While this structure has been successful in some small entrepreneurial organizations that consist predominantly of knowledge workers (such as young high-tech companies), it was less successful in larger, low-tech organizations.

Figure 9.8 shows how a matrix organization might work, with the personnel of each unit reporting to both a divisional and a functional manager. The manager of the personnel in cell 1 reports to both the vice president of marketing and sales and the general manager of Division A. The vice president of marketing is responsible for the marketing of all the company's products and services. The general manager of Division A is responsible for all the activities related to Division A products and services, including engineering, manufacturing *and* marketing. Technologically, IT supports a matrix structure, because both divisional and functional managers can have access to cross-sectional information. Following the example in

Figure 9.8 An example of a matrix organization

	Divisions		
	General manager of product A division	General manager of product B division	General manager of product C division
V.P. of marketing and sales (M&S)	1 M&S personnel assigned to Div. A	2 M&S personnel assigned to Div. B	3 M&S personnel assigned to Div. C
V.P. of manufacturing (Mfg.)	4 Mfg. personnel assigned to Div. A	5 Mfg. personnel assigned to Div. B	6 Mfg. personnel assigned to Div. C
V.P. of engineering (Eng.)	7 Eng. personnel assigned to Div. A	8 Eng. personnel assigned to Div. B	9 Eng. personnel assigned to Div. C

Functions

Figure 9.8, the same database can provide executive information to the vice president of engineering for all three divisions and product information to a division general manager for marketing, manufacturing and engineering activities related to the product.

The matrix structure came about because sometimes divisional supervision (by geography or product, for instance) and functional supervision are equally important. If so, then top management has to be composed of both divisional executives (such as general managers of the divisions and corporate vice presidents) and functional executives (such as vice presidents of finance, marketing, engineering and the like).

Unfortunately, human nature sometimes stands in the way of ideas that look good on paper. Many problems arise when people report to more than one authority, especially when business is not going well or when an individual's performance is in question. Also, power plays may interfere with and undermine rational decision-making. As a result, most of the organizations that tried matrix management abandoned it for the traditional pyramid, in which each manager reports to a single supervisor.

Still, a matrix structure facilitates flow of information because all employees have easier access to their managers. They do not need approval to pass information outside an organizational unit because the lines of reporting are more flexible than in a hierarchical structure. With more vertical and lateral lines of communication, there is less of a tendency to block access to information. The freer communication does have an impact on information needs, and thus on the design of ISs. To serve a matrix organization well, ISs must be integrated, and they must provide easy access to, and incorporation of, different databases and applications.

Managers and their information systems

Employees at different levels in an organization must make decisions that vary in scope and type, as mentioned earlier in this chapter. Figure 9.9 shows the traditional view of the types of information systems needed for an organization's different operational and managerial levels. While these relationships generally hold true, information needs vary widely in practice. With ISs making information available throughout organizational hierarchies, these traditional correlations can become blurred.

Figure 9.9 Types of information systems typically used at different levels of an organization's hierarchy

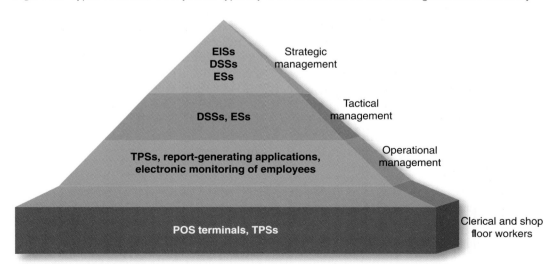

Transaction processing systems

As you may remember from Chapter 1, 'Business Information Systems: An Overview', workers at the bottom of the organizational hierarchy use point-of-sale (POS) terminals, order entry systems, and other transaction-processing systems (TPSs) to enter data at its source at the time transactions take place. These data are the raw materials for producing useful information. TPSs are linked to applications that provide clerical workers and operational managers with up-to-date information, such as the quantity on hand of a certain inventory item, the latest deposit in a customer's bank account, the shipping date and contents of a customer's order, or the latest prescription filled for a customer in a chemist. Clerical workers use the systems to perform their routine responsibilities: serving customers, placing purchase orders with suppliers, and providing information to other employees. TPSs are also used by operational managers, mainly to generate *ad hoc* reports, usually on-screen.

Decision support systems and expert systems

Middle managers must solve problems that are typically more complex and non-routine than those faced by operational managers. Their decision-making tasks require significantly more data. Therefore, they use computer-based decision aids, including decision support systems (DSSs) and expert systems (ESs), to assist them.

Senior managers, too, use DSSs and ESs, although historically they have been more reluctant to use computers in their decision-making. Until several years ago, it was rare to find a PC on the desk of a corporate president or vice president. This reluctance was partly because they perceived desktop computers to be more appropriate for lower-level managers and clerical staff. The sophistication and ease of use of such systems nowadays has probably contributed to the adoption of the systems by many high-ranking executives.

Executive information systems

In addition to the more traditional DSSs and ESs, executive information systems (EISs) provide managers with timely and concise information about the performance of their organization. EIS are often an easy-to-use interface that is linked to online analytical processing (OLAP), data mining, and business intelligence software, which retrieve the data for their analysis from data warehouses. EISs deliver summarized and concise information that helps managers quickly grasp business conditions. For instance, summary information (such as revenue per employee in a specific region) may attract the attention of a manager. Then, the manager can use an EIS to 'drill down' and isolate the data that are related to the cause of a problem.

Many executives also have their PCs connected to external commercial services that provide business and general news, including economic indices, stock and commodity prices and summaries of information sorted by industry on a regional, national and international basis.

While there is a general correlation between managerial level and type of IS, it is important to note that nothing prevents any member of an organization from using any type of IS. Of course, management may not put an EIS at the routine discretion of a clerk, but clerks may use DSSs, ESs and sometimes even EISs for their work. Also, while we discuss different types of ISs, many applications are actually combinations of several types of such ISs. For example, some decision support systems are combined with expert systems techniques and OLAP capabilities to serve as sophisticated EISs.

Information, politics and power

We assume that employees make all their work-related decisions based on what is best for the company and its goals. However, human nature being what it is, employees – including

Industry **SNAPSHOT**

Not necessarily counter-productive

While many employers are concerned about the increasing time employees spend on the Web, one study found an interesting correlation. The National Technology Readiness of the University of Maryland and Rockbridge Associates, Inc. found that employees spent an average of 3.7 hours per week surfing the net, on the job, for personal purposes. However, the same employees also spend an average of 5.9 hours per week online, *at home*, for work-related purposes.

SOURCE: 'Did You Know?', *PC World*, April 2003, p. 23

Evidence suggests that employees surfing casually at work also tend to work more at home online.

managers – often consider their personal interests and their close peers' interests, even when they are making work-related decisions. Politics and power influence daily interactions in organizations. They are doubly important in the context of information systems, because information is often perceived to be a source of power.

Politics

Unfortunately, the process of developing and controlling ISs often involves problematic politics. Politics arise when an individual's or group's interests are put ahead of the organization's as a whole. In contrast, rational decisions are made to achieve organizational goals. Politics can affect ISs adversely in a number of different ways – for instance, when managers are motivated to control systems rather than to make them responsive to the corporation's needs or when managers refuse to use systems that are not designed specially for their organizational unit.

When the interests of individual managers are aligned with those of the organization, both benefit. This alignment of goals is often the case, but not always. For example, a manager may resent other departments' access and use of information that his department creates and maintains because he believes it subjects him to scrutiny. Because of his fears, a manager may oppose expanded access to the information even though it would be in the best interests of the organization as a whole.

Politics also take the form of personal alliances among managers. The unspoken agreement between managers that they will help each other out is common in organizations, but can sometimes undermine their success. For instance, if a senior manager in the IS department has an alliance with a manager in one of the other units, the IS manager may work on the information needs of his friend rather than the more urgent needs of other managers.

The negative impact of politics is also at play when a manager decides not to pull the plug on a development project to save face, even though he knows the project cannot be completed successfully. Organizations invest large amounts of money in the development of new ISs, and about a third of these systems are never completed (for various reasons). However, money could be saved if managers stopped them before the financial loss (and often loss

Ethical and Societal ISSUES

Electronic monitoring of employees

It seems that electronic monitoring of employees is a growing trend for employers who wish to manage productivity and also to provide evidence to be used in law suits brought by employees, customers or the general public. However, the monitoring itself may land the company in the law courts. A landmark case in the European Court of Human Rights ruled in favour of an employee of Carmarthenshire College, South Wales. Lynette Copland took the UK government to court after her personal Internet usage and telephone calls were monitored by her boss. The favourable ruling of €3000 in damages and €6000 costs is obviously significant for her, but more importantly it means that private use of company telecommunications, including Internet access, may be protected by European Human Rights legislation.

There is an interesting conflict here in that in the UK the Regulation of Investigatory Powers Act (RIPA) 2000 has clear guidance regarding the monitoring of work communication, but personal communication at work may be subject to more stringent legislation. Article 8 of the Convention on Human Rights states that 'everyone has the right to privacy and family life, his home and his correspondence'. In this particular case the college had no policy in place informing employees that their communications might be monitored even though Lynette Copland, personal assistant to the College Principal, had her private communications intercepted by the deputy principal. In its ruling, the court stated that 'according to the court's case-law, telephone calls from business premises are prima facie covered by the notions of "private life" and "correspondence" for the purposes of Article 8. It follows logically that emails sent from work should be similarly protected under Article 8, as should information derived from the monitoring of personal Internet usage. The applicant in the present case had been given no warning that her calls would be liable to monitoring, therefore she had a reasonable expectation as to the privacy of calls made from her work telephone. The same expectation should apply in relation to the applicant's email and Internet usage.'

The most important part of the ruling seems to be that the employee did not know that her communication would be monitored. However, there is a wider issue as to what is reasonable monitoring. After all, is it not reasonable to try to prevent employees from accessing inappropriate (pornographic) websites whilst at work? But then who defines 'inappropriate'? What about monitoring performance? A survey in 2005 by the American Management Association involving 526 US companies found that computer monitoring exists in many forms including tracking keystrokes and time logged in as well as use of global positioning systems to monitor mobile phones. According to the survey, 80 per cent of the companies inform employees that they are monitoring content, keystrokes and time logged in. So if they tell the employees, does that make it acceptable?

of morale) grew. People do not like to admit failure because they fear it will tarnish their image. So, often managers decide to continue projects to save their own reputation, resulting in a decision that is out of sync with the good of the organization.

This happened in the United Kingdom with the Pathway project, aimed to develop electronic smart cards for executing and tracking benefits payments. The project was cancelled only after the British government spent (and lost) £698 million on it. In all, the British government is said to have lost more than £1.5 billion on failed IT projects during the period between 1996 and 2002. The US federal government is reported to have lost close to US$10 billion over the past decade and a half because of cancelled information systems development projects. While some losses are unavoidable in any development project, observers say that significant portions of these losses could be prevented if high-ranking decision makers did not try to 'save face'.

Power

Anyone who has worked for an organization recognizes that having access to information is often the road to acquiring power. And power is something that people do not give away willingly. When management decides a new IS should be implemented, department managers usually concur on several issues. But often questions arise for senior executives. For instance:

- *Who owns the system?* Unfortunately, many managers make decisions based on wanting to look powerful, regardless of the consequences. They follow the rule that the more resources they control (people, machinery, funds and so on), the more power they have. Building information system 'empires' is just another way to look – and sometimes to be – powerful. Usually, the department that owns an information system also controls it. That department may have the final say in determining its features and in modifying it. When a system serves more than one department, managers often struggle for control, leading to a system that is not used properly or at all by those who have been denied ownership. Management is often forced to announce which unit owns the system and what rights other units have to it. To resolve disputes when a system serves more than one department equally, top managers sometimes say that they are the owners of the system. Making the proper decision and educating employees about sharing systems is especially important when enterprise applications such as ERP systems are being implemented.

- *Who pays for developing the system?* Everyone wants something for nothing, and managers are no different. So, when several units are going to share a new system, their managers often try to offload the cost of development and operation on each other. Top management's challenge is to allocate the development and operating costs fairly among departments, preferably based on the benefits each group will receive.

- *Who accesses what information?* As noted previously, many managers make decisions to gain power. Since information is power, these managers often try to gain access to as much of it as they can while denying access to as many other people as possible. Many managers don't like their information accessed by people from outside their departments. They dislike scrutiny and don't want to give outsiders an opportunity to judge and question their decisions. Also, many managers feel more powerful when others who need information turn to them first.

- *Who has update privileges?* Update privilege is the authority to modify information in files and databases. Some managers make some decisions based on data collected by departments they do not control. So, if you control the data, you can influence their decisions. Management should give 'view access' on a 'need-to-know' basis. Update access should be given only to users who must update data or applications as part of their jobs. Often, these employees are the database administrator or another high-ranking MIS officer and some of his or her staff. These decisions must be made carefully in order not to alienate other managers. The decisions must be explained satisfactorily to those who may not be given privileges they think they deserve.

Political struggles are especially harmful when several organizational units share systems. Some managers use subversive tactics to undermine the successful implementation of a system. Some managers insist on adding features for the sole purpose of giving themselves more control. Other managers may try to derail the implementation effort by not cooperating with the developers or consultants or by promoting an alternate system. As an increasing number of businesses adopt enterprise-wide applications such as supply chain management systems, these issues become extremely important, because such systems consist of modules that are often implemented one at a time. The implementers must have the cooperation of all business functions that are to be supported by the system. Managers of the various functions must collaborate to ensure success, and they must understand that one of the major purposes of such systems is the sharing of information, and therefore sharing what they may perceive as power.

The not-invented-here phenomenon

Sometimes, managers do whatever they can to *not* use an IS. The reason is known as the not-invented-here (NIH) phenomenon: managers and their subordinates often believe that if the new system is the fruit of an outsider's idea, it will not serve them well. They may know this is not true, but they may still deny others credit for something they feel *they* should have invented. Again, managers may use a variety of tactics to undermine a new system in their department. They may try to convince top management that the system is not needed, or that it does not satisfy their 'unique' business needs.

Top management must be aware of these issues and distinguish valid arguments from political ones. For instance, a manager may ask for IS systems or services that serve both his own interests and the organization's. Such requests are legitimate. But he could damage the organization if the request serves only his own goals, or the goals of his unit. Since an increasing number of ISs are not developed or implemented for individual departments, but for the entire organization, managers must be vigilant to the motives of staff members.

Management of information technology resources

Organizations have their own distinct managerial styles, most of which fall somewhere between two extremes on a spectrum. One extreme is centralized management, which designates staff positions and departments in a strict vertical hierarchy and places control of the organization in a few hands. The other is decentralized management, which delegates authority to lower-level managers. In most organizations, the management and structure of information systems follow the same pattern as the organization's overall management: centralized management tends to want centralized control over ISs; decentralized management is more likely to be comfortable with decentralized management of ISs.

As a growing amount of commerce is carried out online, organizations have faced new challenges of managing their websites, including linking internal applications and databases to those sites. Large organizations, especially, have more than one server linked to the Internet. So, they must question whether individual organizational units should manage their own websites or whether the company should manage all web activities through a single home page – essentially a central website. Different business functions can use the Web for different purposes. For instance, marketing and sales can promote products and services. Human resources can recruit employees, and finance can make electronic payments. Should the design and implementation of these various functions be the responsibilities of individual departments, or should they be cleared through a central department or manager?

The question becomes even more important in multinational organizations, with regional headquarters in different countries. Because many workers today can easily design and create web pages for their departments, managers are often tempted to establish their own unit's website, independent of the central IS organization's priorities. Also, senior executives of some organizations have actually left the IS unit out of the loop when deciding on web design and operational issues, not realizing that problems can arise later – when the website evolves from a mere presence to an important e-commerce vehicle involving many internal resources such as transactional databases and data warehouses. Thus, in many companies the issue of management of IS resources has become more complicated as technology advances.

Centralized vs. decentralized management

How management of any type of resource is conducted depends on the general philosophy of corporate executives. Some organizations emphasize central management of resources, especially resources of expensive types of equipment or investments in assets that may have an impact on the entire organization or large parts of it. Other organizations leave much of the decision-making about acquisition and control of resources to local organizational units and lower-level managers. 'Local' may be actually local in geographic terms, when the organization has multiple locations, or a business unit within a single-site organization. Preferences for managing human and other IT resources are similar. Some organizations concentrate all, or almost all, decisions on hiring IT workers and acquiring IT assets – hardware, software and networks – at corporate headquarters, and some delegate such decisions to the managers of business units. Each approach often impacts the deployment of IT professionals: a centralized approach often results in a relatively large IT unit that is responsible for almost all IT-related issues (Figure 9.10), while a decentralized approach results in a smaller corporate IT group and IT professionals deployed at the business units (Figure 9.11), with significant authority to make decisions on the local unit's information resources.

Figure 9.10 Centralized management of ISs

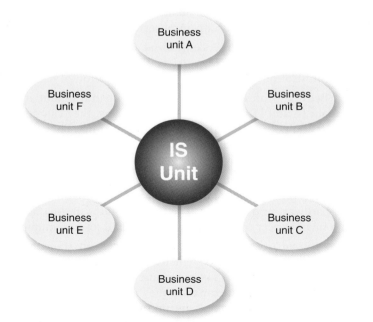

Figure 9.11 Decentralized management of ISs (in fully decentralized management, the central IS unit would not exist)

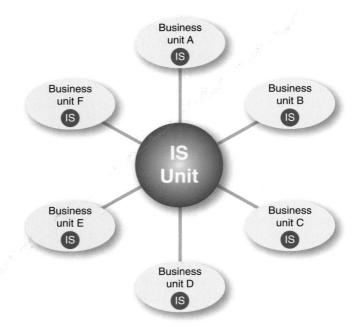

Advantages of centralized IS management

Centralized IS management, as illustrated in Figure 9.12, has several major advantages:

- *Standardized hardware and software*: Centralized ISs can establish corporate software and hardware standards, which saves time and money in purchasing and installation and simplifies interdepartmental sharing of data and information. Standardizing software is particularly important for facilitating data exchange and the sharing of applications. This benefit is especially enhanced by the ability of multi-site organizations to share applications and data by using them off central servers.

- *Efficient administration of resources*: A centralized administration of contracts, licences, and inventories of hardware and software assets is more efficient, and often effective, than dispersed administration. It also supports standardization of hardware and software.

- *Effective staffing*: Because professionals at a corporate central IS unit are usually more knowledgeable about IT and IT skills than other managers, they can do a better job in identifying the most competent individuals to fill IT positions. They speak the same professional lingo as the interviewed candidates, and therefore the communication in the recruiting process is fast and effective.

- *Easier training*: Training employees to use information technology, often a major expense in a company's budget, is much more efficient and less expensive when an organization uses standardized hardware and software. The training staff can do a better job when they can specialize in a small variety of hardware, software and telecommunications standards.

- *Common reporting systems*: Central IS management can easily standardize reporting systems and formats across departments, which many companies and some laws and regulations require for accounting or tax reporting. With standardized reporting, managers do not have to 're-map' the information they receive from one unit to a report with a different format used by another unit. This uniformity saves time and increases clarity. When reports need to be merged, it is easier to merge them (using spreadsheets, for instance) when they share the same format.

Figure 9.12 Centralized vs. decentralized IS trade-offs

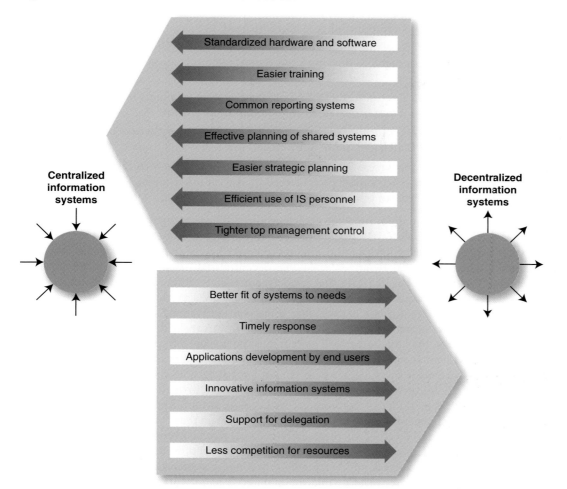

- *Effective planning of shared systems*: Large and complex systems that are shared by several organizational units can best be developed by a central IS department that knows the 'big picture'.

- *Easier strategic planning*: Strategic IS planning considers an organization's entire IS resources. It is easier to link an IS strategic plan to an organization's overall strategic plan when IS management is centralized.

- *Efficient use of IS personnel*: With a centralized IS department, an organization is more likely to employ highly specialized IS professionals who are better qualified to develop information systems, especially the larger and more complex ones, than are IS professionals who are dispersed in non-IS organizational units.

- *Tighter control by top management*: A centralized IS management allows top management to maintain control over the often vast resources spent on ISs.

Advantages of decentralized IS management

Historically, most organizations have moved from a centralized IS management to a decentralized management. Decentralized IS management has several advantages, illustrated in Figure 9.12:

- *Better fit of ISs to business needs*: The individual IS units can use their familiarity with their departments' information needs to develop systems that fit those needs more closely.

- *Timely response of IS units to business demands*: Individual IS units can arrange IS development and maintenance to fit their business units' priorities. They can be more responsive because their responsibility is more focused.

- *Encouragement of end-user development of applications*: In a decentralized setting, end users are usually encouraged to develop their own small applications to increase their productivity.

- *Innovative use of ISs*: Since a business unit's IS team knows its clients better than a centralized one, it has a better chance of implementing innovative ISs.

- *Support for delegation of authority*: Decentralized IS management works best if top management wishes to delegate more authority to lower-level managers.

- *Less competition for resources*: When a business unit manages its own ISs and IS budget, it usually does not have to compete for IT resources with other units. This saves the organization efforts wasted in struggles among managers.

Although you will find many companies with centralized IS management, fully decentralized IS management is rare. Because telecommunications technology is so pervasive and there are so many advantages of sharing information, systems that may have started as separate ISs years ago are usually networked now. Relatively speaking, decentralized management is more advantageous if an organization has divisions that produce completely different products and services. That way, each unit's information needs can be more closely served. Then, the decentralized units can share resources through networking. Some types of systems are usually managed centrally even if they span many different business units, however. With enterprise applications, such as ERP systems, the large integrated system must be managed by a single team.

The main disadvantage of decentralized IS management is that in most cases, important decisions about IT are made by managers who are not knowledgeable enough to make such decisions. Consider the following case. The manager of a unit that provides service to clients asked his two-person group, skilled programmers, to develop an application that field engineers could log into to manage projects. He requested an application that would enable the engineers to create bills-of-materials (BOMs) of assemblies, and access inventory databases, resource availability files, timelines and due date charts. The manager and his programmers struggled to understand the issues involved, and eventually developed a system that failed miserably. The results were: (1) much time wasted while the manager's team worked on understanding the project issues and deciding what approach to use, (2) wasted effort of the IT professionals, and (3) a bad decision on implementation, which resulted in redoing the project almost from scratch. The project was taken over by the corporate IT director and completed successfully.

On the other hand, the main disadvantage of centralizing IS management is that the individual business units that need to use the resource may feel that they do not have enough control. This can cause much friction within the business, particularly if the IS unit is being funded by top-slicing departmental budgets. An alternative funding strategy of the departments buying in IS services from the central unit may help, but still has potential for problems as the departmental manager will see only the service that they are receiving rather than a whole-company picture.

Organizing the IS staff

Now that you have seen the advantages and disadvantages of centralized and decentralized IS management, let's turn to the organization of the IS unit itself. There are various ways to deploy IS staff, even if an organization operates from a single site. This section discusses the two extremes of organizing IS professionals: central IS organization and dispersed IS organization. Not surprisingly, decentralized IS management often calls for dispersed organization of the IS staff.

In *central IS organization* there is a corporate IS team to whom all units turn with their IS needs. In *dispersed IS organization* there is a separate IS team for each business unit. Some arrangements combine elements of both. The approach selected has a direct effect on how IS professionals are positioned in the organizational structure of the business. But regardless of the structure, the goal of any IS organization is to optimize IS services to fit the organization's goals and culture.

Central IS organization

As seen in Figure 9.13, the most common central IS unit organization has the IS director overseeing several departments. One department implements and maintains current systems. Another department runs the information centre, whose function is to provide *ad hoc* advice about hardware, software and telecommunications to business units. The communications department develops and manages local area networks and access to wide area networks. And the data administration department develops and maintains corporate databases, data warehouses and data management and analysis applications. In large organizations there may also be a research and development department, which keeps the IS unit abreast of technological advances and develops ideas for the strategic uses of ISs.

A central IS unit is usually involved in virtually every aspect of IT in an organization. It determines which computers and peripheral equipment are approved for purchase; in some cases it is the only unit that is authorized to purchase hardware. It approves or rejects software purchases, is in charge of training new users and (except for small and simple programs) is the only body that is authorized to develop ISs for business units.

The advantages and disadvantages of a centrally organized IS unit are essentially the same as those for centralized IS management. When centrally managed, the IS unit ensures compatibility of hardware and software and provides the interface between different systems that must work together, such as purchasing and cost accounting; payroll, accounts payable and cost accounting; and sales and accounts receivable. This approach helps all top managers share an organizational vision of how information technology can serve the corporation in the future. It also supports planning of enterprise applications such as supply chain management systems, which are shared by several business functions, and often by many or all of the organization's sites.

Figure 9.13 An example of central IS organization

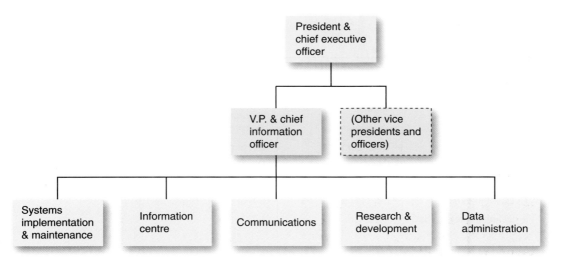

Central IS management often includes a *steering committee* with representatives from a variety of key business units. It establishes priorities for systems development and implementation of communications networks, it considers and prioritizes requests for new systems and it commits funds to projects. It is the organizational institution in charge of the budgets for all or most of the IS services.

In recent years the great majority of organizations have adopted ready-made software such as ERP systems. Others have outsourced some or all of their IS functions. Some now use the services of application service providers (ASPs). But the central IS unit still oversees the implementation of ready-made software, outsourcing and relationships with ASPs.

It is often easier to integrate an IS plan into an organization's overall strategic plan with centralized IS management than with decentralized IS services. On the other hand, when only a central department is available, business units often find themselves overly dependent on – and at times resentful of – the department. The resentment often springs from the lack of control over the services the IS department renders, as other units depend on it for their success. Under a centralized IS organization, business units must receive approval for almost anything they do with computers, software and networks – a situation that can discourage the development of applications by end users, even if they are technologically knowledgeable enough to do so.

Dispersed IS organization

At the other end of the IS staffing spectrum is the approach whereby each unit fulfils its IS needs independently, deciding for itself which systems it needs and how to develop them (see Figure 9.14). There is usually still an IS unit at corporate headquarters, but it is relatively small and serves to coordinate IS needs for departments that cannot handle their own needs. Only large and complex systems, especially those that affect several departments or sites, are implemented under the auspices of this unit.

Each business unit has one or several IS professionals who report to the unit's manager. These workers know their non-IS colleagues' daily operations well and understand their information needs better than central IS personnel do.

In a dispersed IS organization, funds for the development and maintenance of the unit's ISs always come from the unit's own budget, which is intended to optimize the use of resources.

Figure 9.14 An example of dispersed IS organization

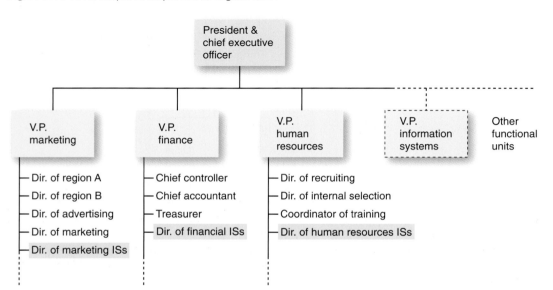

While the unit's IS professionals may seek input from their central IS colleagues, decisions are made by the units fairly independently. In this environment, IS professionals are often involved in many aspects of operations that do not necessarily involve IT, and they may be promoted from an IT position into another type of position within the business. Such a system enhances their chances of advancing up the organizational ladder to general managerial positions.

As Figure 9.14 indicates, an organization that chooses the dispersed IS staffing approach may still have a corporate IS director, possibly a vice president, who oversees a small central IS unit, consults with dispersed IS units and concentrates on larger, more complex enterprise wide IS projects. However, the IS personnel of the various units do not report to the central IS unit.

A hybrid approach

Small companies typically use the central approach to IS personnel because their IT staff levels are small. Among midsize and large companies, a purely central or dispersed IS organization is rare. Most of them use elements of both central and dispersed organization of IS personnel. For instance, a large corporate IS unit may have liaisons in the units who report to the corporate IS unit. Gillette, the world's largest supplier of shaving blades and other toiletry products, has established such an arrangement and found it very beneficial. A relatively large corporate IS unit coordinates intraorganizational systems, while the different sites (including international divisions) develop and maintain their own local systems. This approach helped the company remain on the leading edge of IT while maintaining a strong sense of ownership at the local sites.

In many organizations you will also find employees of other companies serving alongside the IS personnel. These professionals handle services that have been outsourced by the company to an IS service firm. These people may work in a central IS unit or anywhere else in the organization, depending on the contact signed with the service firm. Outsourcing is discussed in detail in Chapter 12, 'Choices in Systems Acquisition'. Many organizations also hire consultants for several weeks or months to help find and implement IT solutions to *ad hoc* problems or to seize opportunities. Again, these consultants work alongside the organization's employees as if they, too, were its employees. Senior consultants often take part in top management meetings.

Regardless of the approach to managing IS personnel and other resources, surveys show that IS implementation is handled differently according to the position of the highest IS officer in the organizational structure. If this person reports to the vice president of finance or another vice president, it is a sign that top management has decided that IT can help automate processes, but cannot change the company's strategic position significantly; the IS personnel then tend to provide primarily technical solutions to business problems. However, if the highest-ranking IS executive reports to the CEO, it is a sign that management considers IT as holding the potential to change significantly the organization's future; the IS professionals are then significantly more involved in strategic planning, and they also search for opportunities rather than just solve problems. The trend has been to upgrade the position from reporting to a vice president to reporting to the chief executive officer because of the importance of ISs to companies' survival.

Challenges for IS managers and business managers

For ISs to be developed and maintained successfully, IS managers and business managers must understand what each party expects from the other and must find the best ways to respond to those expectations. By 'business managers', we mean all managers in charge of areas other than ISs. A growing number of IS managers refer to their non-IT colleagues as customers, and treat them as such. Business managers, for their part, expect to be treated as customers, especially when the cost of the IS services rendered are covered from their unit's budget. What are the expectations?

Why you should...

be interested in the deployment of information systems

You are a marketing manager for Gadgets4Fun. Several months ago you sent a request to your IS department for the development of a website. The site would provide information about the different products Gadgets4Fun sells and allow shoppers to purchase them via the site. You and your staff are still waiting for the site to be established. Calls to the company's central IS department keep yielding the same answer: 'We have a priority list. We will get to it shortly.' Several of your subordinates have told you that they could easily develop the catalogue themselves, including scanned pictures, so that shoppers could at least see what the company offers. Later, IS professionals could add the transactional components. You are not sure your organization would allow your unit to begin. What is the policy? Can your department establish and maintain its own website? Will heads roll if you take the initiative? And if you are allowed to take the initiative, who will later help your personnel upgrade the site?

Knowing how information technology and personnel are deployed in an organization helps managers know how to enquire about, and obtain, useful information. Thus, all managers – both IS and business managers – must be involved in the organization of IS resources in a business. To ensure convenient access to data, managers must not rely on IS professionals to dictate deployment, responsibilities and charges; they should be proactive and participate in the decisions leading to organizing and managing IS resources and adopting policies.

In today's businesses, managers are expected to be knowledgeable consumers of information services. Thus, they should have a clear picture of the organization of ISs and the responsibilities of different IS professionals, whose job it is to satisfy the information needs of business managers.

Business managers' expectations of an IS unit

The first thing that business managers must remember is that they should have a continual dialogue with the company's IS managers, to explore new ways to help their operations. Although business managers are not expected to be well-versed in IT's cutting edge, they should collaborate with the IS manager to explore new technologies to support the work of their subordinates. Business managers need the following from the IS unit:

- *A broad understanding of the business activities*: IS professionals are expected to understand the nature of the activities of the business unit they support: whom does the business unit serve? Where do its raw data come from? What information does it use? What systems do the business unit's systems interface with? Understanding the business helps IS professionals put themselves in the users' shoes and develop systems from the users' point of view.

- *Flexibility and adaptability*: IS professionals are expected to serve their clients under uncertain and changing circumstances. They need to accept changing requirements for systems and services, and accept imprecise requirements for acquisition of new systems. They need to help their clients define requirements.

- *Prompt response to the information needs of the business unit*: Business managers are often disappointed with the long time it takes IS units to react to business needs. A business unit that cannot elicit a prompt response from the IS staff may resort to finding haphazard – and ultimately problematic – solutions to its information needs.

- *A clear, jargon-free explanation of what the technology can and cannot do for the business unit*: To show off their expertise, IS professionals sometimes use technical jargon to communicate ideas. While use of technical terms facilitates communication among same-field professionals, it may cause problems for lay users and professionals of other fields. Business managers and their employees may be reluctant to admit that they do not under- stand certain terms, so communication can break down, resulting in costly misunder- standings. If technical terms must be used, IS professionals should explain them.

● *Candid explanations of what information systems can and cannot do*: Business managers and their employees count on IS professionals to tell them not only what marvels a planned information system will accomplish, but also what the system's limitations are. Outlining the limitations of a system can eliminate disappointment and ensure proper usage of the system. In particular, business managers expect IS managers not to use their budgets for the sake of experimenting with new technology to satisfy professional curiosity.

● *Honest budgeting*: If any of the services rendered to a business unit are carried out at the expense of that unit, business managers depend on IS managers for an honest, detailed assessment of the resources needed to develop a new IS and maintain an existing one. Time and budget overruns often occur in systems development projects. IS managers must detail the work that will be done, how much it will cost in terms of person hours and other resources and how much time each project phase will take.

● *Single point of contact*: To serve the business units after an IS is installed or modified, IS managers should assign one contact person to respond to the business units' questions and problems.

In general, IS managers should treat business managers as clients, although they all work for the same organization. This approach has been adopted in an increasing number of compa- nies. Some have taken the client/vendor model to such an extreme that business managers are allowed to use outside IS vendors if the internal IS unit cannot offer comparable services at comparable prices.

IS managers' expectations of business managers

IS managers are expected to keep themselves abreast of developments in the IT field, suggest adoption of new technologies and make recommendations to improve business operations. To do this job well, IS managers also need clear communication from business managers in three basic areas: basic business planning, general systems planning and specific systems development.

● *Business planning*: To plan ahead, IS managers need to know their own business, but they also need to know their clients' (the business units') plans and needs. For instance, if a business department is planning to hire ten new people to introduce a new product, the IS manager must be informed to budget for purchasing and installing new equipment, installing new software and training the new employees to use it. Business plans for, say, three years into the future will become a part of the organization's overall IS plan, which in turn is a part of the organization's overall strategic plan.

● *Systems planning*: Once an IS unit is called on to develop a new system, it needs a clear explanation of business processes that need support. An IS manager can develop an effec- tive IS only if business managers and their employees clearly communicate the exact processes they want automated.

● *Systems selection or development*: Once the general automation plan is agreed on, the IS manager needs to know what features the business manager wants in the new system. Although IS professionals are more familiar with IT than many users, they still need to know how a new system will be used in daily operations to design or install it correctly. The business manager is responsible for communicating what features are needed in a new system.

● *Participation and partnership*: Much as business units want the IT staff to be partners in meeting their needs, IT managers want the business units to help the IT staff. Business managers are expected to be involved in development and modification of ISs, participate in testing of new systems and provide frequent feedback. They are expected to provide feedback before, during and after development of the systems. This has both technical and psychological benefits: the effort may result in technically better systems, and the morale of the IT staff will be kept high.

This information helps IS professionals include all input, processing and output mechanisms, as well as user interfaces that are intuitive, easy to learn and easy to use.

SUMMARY

Organizations are run by managers. The majority of organizations are structured in a pyramid model with several layers of management. Managers can be roughly classified into these levels: strategic (at the top of the organizational hierarchy), tactical (below top managers) and operational managers (below tactical). Managers at the three levels have different information needs, and typically use different types of information systems to satisfy these needs.

Senior managers make decisions that affect the entire organization, or large parts of it, in the long run. They use highly summarized information that is based on a wide data scope, both in terms of the number of organizational units that the data cover, and the time span: long historic periods, and periods well into the future. The lower the managerial level, the greater the information's level of detail. Most data for decision-making come from internal sources, but some come from external sources. Senior managers operate in highly unstructured environments. The typical information systems they use are executive information systems (EISs), decision support systems (DSSs) and, to a smaller extent, expert systems (ESs).

Middle managers receive strategic decisions as general directives within which they develop tactics to achieve specific objectives. The information they use is processed from data that cover narrower organizational units and shorter time spans. Their typical information systems consist of DSSs and ESs. Like top managers, they must make unstructured decisions.

Operational managers are responsible for daily operations. They make relatively simple decisions that affect only their departments in the short run. The information they need reflects transactions of their own small units and very narrow time spans. However, the information is very detailed and usually comes from more structured data, such as numbers and other data that can be tabulated. Too much information can result in information overload, or the inability to comprehend the meaning of facts and figures. One way to avoid overload is to examine cases that fall outside certain parameters, called management by exception.

Operational managers use transaction processing systems to generate reports. Much of their work involves monitoring, sometimes including electronic monitoring of employees, which may infringe on the employees' right to privacy.

Clerical and other workers typically carry out their supervisors' orders. They use transaction-processing systems to record transactions and satisfy queries from other employees, customers and suppliers.

A major task of middle managers in the past was to screen information and pass it on to higher-level managers. Since information technology allows top managers to extract their information directly and conveniently, many organizations have reduced whole layers of middle management, resulting in a flatter organizational structure.

Information systems help managers to monitor, control and make decisions. They can also help managers be better leaders.

Effective information conveys a message with minimum necessity for interpretation. Many applications allow users to present information in the form that best suits their individual preferences: tabular or graphical, or as dynamic representation of real-time events.

Online analytical processing (OLAP) applications link managers to data warehouses and enable them to produce useful information such as purchasing trends and fraud patterns.

Because information is power, occasionally managers try to obtain power by controlling ISs beyond their real business need. Sometimes, they reject new ISs because the systems were 'not invented here'. Politics harm the effort to deliver and share information for the benefit of the organization as a whole.

Information technology provides very effective and inexpensive means for monitoring employees on the job. As the use of email and the Web becomes pervasive in the workplace, most workers' use of the resources is monitored. Employers say it is their legitimate right to do so, but privacy advocates argue that some practices infringe on workers' right to privacy.

There are many ways to organize the IS staff. At one extreme is a centralized IS organization whereby all of the IS professionals report to the CIO or another person who is the highest IS authority. At the other extreme is dispersed IS organization, which places IS staff within an organization's business units.

Central IS management usually includes a steering committee, whose members are drawn from key business units. Regardless of organization approaches, IS staff are responsible for systems implementation and maintenance, communications networks, research and development, data administration and the information centre.

The advantages of centralized IS management are: standardized hardware, common software, easier training, common reporting systems, effective planning of shared systems, efficient use of personnel and the ability of management to maintain tight control of the company's ISs.

The advantages of decentralization of IS management are: a better fit of systems to particular needs of business units, timely response to requests by business units, encouragement of end-user computing, encouragement of innovation and accommodation of decentralized management style.

Successful use of IS technology depends on understanding and collaboration between managers of business units and IS managers. IS managers must have a broad understanding of business activities. They are expected to respond promptly to the information needs of business units, use jargon-free language when dealing with their non-IS clients, explain what is and what is not possible with ISs, detail the resources that would be needed to implement and maintain a new IS and designate personnel who will be responsible for resolving problems reported by the users.

IS managers expect business managers to project their future information needs, clearly explain the business processes that ISs should support and thoroughly detail the features they desire in a new IS.

URBAN SCENE REVISITED

Urban Scene has implemented a new enterprise-wide information system to standardize its hardware and software and enable increased communication. The new system also has enhanced capabilities, providing quicker, more accurate information to staff. Several levels of managers use the system for their specific needs, but there has been resistance also. The new enterprise resource planning system spurred a reorganization of the IS staff. The company is also setting up an e-commerce site. Examine some of these changes at Urban Scene more closely.

What would you do?

1   Shirley Steiner, Urban Scene's chief executive officer, is concerned that her retail chain stay lean and mean – with the fewest levels in its organization chart to avoid unnecessary costs. She has asked you to categorize the levels in her organization's management pyramid. From the information provided in the Part 3 case and this chapter's opening case, draw a chart and categorize the employees according to strategic, tactical and operational management and clerical and shop floor workers. Do you think that Urban Scene is a relatively flat organization? Why or why not?

2   Now that you have identified different levels within Urban Scene, take another look at this chapter's opening case. What types of data are they interested in at each level? Would you allow managers at all levels access to all the information, or would you 'tie' the level of aggregation to the managerial level? Why?

3   The chapter discussed three ways of organizing an IS staff: central IS organization, dispersed IS organization and a hybrid approach. Which type of organization do you think Urban Scene has? Support your answer with details from the opening case.

New perspectives

1   When he visits the Croydon shop, Martin is shocked to find that Mike Roberts, the shop manager, isn't using the new system to its full capabilities. Why do you think Mike continued to use the new system in his old ways despite the fact that the new capabilities have been announced? Is there anything Martin can do to help ensure other managers begin tapping the power of the new system? Give Martin some suggestions.

2   Urban Scene is using internal sales information in a variety of ways. What types of external information might the company's managers want to know for better decision-making? Where could they get that information?

3   In planning for the company's new website, Suzanne Granger had to explain to some sales staff why they couldn't head up the website development – that the IS staff needed to lead that effort. Take Suzanne's role and write a list of arguments she would have used to explain the reasons to the staff. Be prepared to present your list to the class.

Review questions

1 What are the major tasks of managers in the three levels of management?

2 There is a class of workers whose jobs are information-intensive, although they may not be in managerial positions. Give several examples of these workers.

3 What does the term 'flat organization' mean? Why is information technology said to have flattened some organizations?

4 Operational managers usually do not use DSSs. Why?

5 The amount of information used by senior managers (in terms of number of figures or lines of text considered) is often smaller than the amount of information used by operational managers. Why? Explain and give an example.

6 Give five examples of external information sources and how they are important in decision-making.

7 Why do senior managers rely on external information? Give three examples of external data and the organizations from which they can be obtained. How would an executive use the information for decision-making?

8 'Detailed information must come from a wide range of data in terms of time and number of organizational units.' Do you agree with the statement? Explain.

9 Senior executives often use information that they have recorded on small notes. How would you describe this type of information in terms of how structured it is? Why don't these executives use spreadsheets to record the information?

10 What is the connection between access to information and politics?

11 What methods do managers use to dodge corporate management's attempts to implement a new IS for their departments?

12 What are the main reasons why companies monitor their employees' email and web surfing?

13 We refer to 'management of IS resources'. What do these resources include?

14 A corporation that is a conglomerate of businesses in different industries is likely to have decentralized management of ISs. Why?

15 Some types of IS resources can be well developed and controlled only under centralized management. Give two examples.

16 What are the advantages of centralized and decentralized IS management?

17 Why should IS managers understand business processes, even though their expertise is IT?

18 What is professional jargon? In what circumstance is it appropriate to use professional jargon, and in what circumstances should it not be used?

19 What types of businesses are most likely to adopt a centrally managed IS organization?

20 What types of businesses are most likely to adopt a dispersed IS organization?

Discussion questions

1 Why are the majority of organizations structured like pyramids?

2 Often, it is difficult to distinguish between middle managers and operational managers. Why?

3 Explain the generally accepted adage, 'The higher you are in the organizational hierarchy, the more decisions you have to make.'

4 Executives are sometimes impatient and say, 'Give me the bottom line.' Explain why, in terms of data and information.

5 'A picture is worth a thousand words.' Is this always true? Why or why not? Give an example of a situation in which you would prefer information in tabular rather than graphical form.

6 Managers often strive to put resources under their control. Would you expect fiercer control for information resources than for other resources? Why or why not?

7 When an IS is shared by several departments, a power struggle over ownership may occur. One solution to this may be to pronounce that the system is owned by corporate management. What is the downside of this approach?

8 One benefit of centralized IS management is economies of scale. What does this mean, and how can it be implemented in the context of hardware and software?

9 Why is standardization of hardware and software so important in organizations?

10 One advantage of decentralized management of IS resources is a better fit of ISs to business needs. Why?

Tutorial activities

1 You are the marketing manager of the irrigation products of Voda, Inc. The following are your budgeted and actual figures.

Voda, Ltd.

Irrigation Products Department Budget, Quarter 1

Item	Forecast	Actual	5 per cent exception
Income			
Model P12 Sales	1,250,000	1,452,375	
Model P15 Sales	13,500,000	12,788,992	
Drip Valve V2			
Sales	450,000	452,344	
Expenditures			
Sales Reps'			
Commission	750,000	763,000	
Advertising	500,000	425,000	
Packaging			
Materials	270,000	298,000	
Telephone	5,200	5,790	

Using a spreadsheet, create an exception report to aid in making decisions as to which items to investigate. Add the '5 per cent exception'. Have an asterisk (*) appear in every column for which the actual expense of an item deviated by at least 5 per cent from the budget. (*Hint*: Try the absolute value function.)

Use the appropriate fonts and styles, as used here. Turn in (1) a printout showing the reports and (2) a printout showing the formulas, where applicable.

2 The Web offers much external information that is not available in the more traditional external sources, such as newspapers, printed bulletins, trade journals and newsletters. Assume that you are a human resource manager looking to hire qualified chemical engineers for your petrochemical company. Explore the Web for three sites offering candidates. Prepare a short report answering the following questions: What are the advantages or disadvantages of using the Web, compared with advertising in newspaper help-wanted ads? What are the advantages or disadvantages compared with using a 'headhunting' firm? Include your impression of the sites and the quality of information and service they provide.

3 Team up with another student from your class. Interview managers from administrative units of your college or university. On the basis of the information you collected, write a brief report in which you conclude and explain which type of IS management the institution has: centralized or decentralized.

From ideas to application
REAL CASES

Case study **9.1**

Companies' increasing use of online technology for business meetings

BY ALAN HOGARTH

Business meetings generally get a bad press, as normally very little gets accomplished during them. The majority of meetings are unstructured, uninspiring and unproductive. But they don't have to be that way. Although meetings are part and parcel of any business, the traditional approach to meetings could soon be a thing of the past and it appears that few employees will regret this demise. There is a prevalent view that they have spent too much of their working lives in boring and unnecessary meetings in their organizations generally being lectured at by managers pushing their own agenda. Now, information and communication technology (ICT) is dramatically altering the way in which business meetings take place. We live in a global economy, and people in far-flung locations still need to meet. Increasingly they are doing so via web conferencing services, which let both small and large groups of people share presentations and documents in real time over the Web. The services also deliver handy tools for collaboration such as chat rooms, whiteboards, document annotation, application sharing, web polls and web tours. With most of the services, the audio portion of the conference is handled via the standard phone conferencing.

European organizations are now aware that meetings such as these are a substantial drain on their resources. This tends to be borne out by a number of research projects. For example, a recent survey by Bibby Financial Services indicated that up to 2 million hours a year were wasted by small to medium enterprises (SMEs) in meetings that were seen at best as pointless and at worse as fractious. Many people who attended the meetings were either unprepared, did not

stick to the agenda or they were continually interrupted by mobile phone calls. Further, this cost the sector around £25 million annually. David Scott, Communications Manager of PC World Business, states that, 'Businesses often fall into a routine, having a sales meeting every Friday, say, when there may be nothing new to discuss.'

In order to eliminate some of the problems highlighted, companies can now use technology to facilitate their business meetings. For example, replacing face-to-face meetings with phone or video conferencing using a broadband connection, webcam and conference software such as Skype can replicate a business meeting online. Jerry Roest of PC World Business maintains that, 'In a world where travel is seen as increasingly high-cost, a waste of time and with ecological implications, and where IT costs such as video conferencing are coming down, It's a no-brainer!' Peter Scargill of the Federation of Small Businesses agrees when he argues that 'for routine business meetings, an electronic solution is the answer. Teams can use technology to avoid the necessity of having (face-to-face) meetings.'

Some companies are even questioning the need for meetings at all. It is suggested that one way of avoiding meetings is to put all relevant company reports and documents on the organizations' intranet so that they are accessible to all who want to review them. Alternatively a simpler and more secure approach could be just to email the documents to the relevant parties.

Dedicated videoconference rooms are an increasingly common sight in the offices of major European companies.

At Difference Corporation, a communications company, meetings are rarely held. Essentially business planning meetings are held only twice a year in quiet periods such as January. Difference handles all aspects of communication such as email, phone, text and fax for clients that include Yu!Sushi and the National Trust for Scotland. Their services are technology-focused and include giving customers online access to their reports so they are always kept up to date. The company cuts travel costs and time by using video conferencing and phone conferencing and on one-to-one chats rather than holding group meetings. The company does not like meetings, as they take up too much time. No time is spent discussing past sales figures as 'People will already have seen online information about sales and product approaches and billing', says Serge Cren the managing director. 'There is no need to go over what happened in the past in planning meetings.' Clients are met only at the start of a contractual agreement and then, if contact has to be made, it is done via email, online and phone where other parties can be patched in. With 12 locations in the UK, internal conference calls are essential. Cren says, 'And it's better for the business. There's better interaction within the company and with the clients, people are not forced to sit through meetings that don't concern them.'

However, there can be problems with ICT for meetings. For example, many organizations are concerned about the increasing email burden in the workplace. Research conducted by Loughborough University has identified that 'email communication within the workplace costs UK businesses millions of pounds in lost productivity'. The cost per year was placed at £9.8 million. Another report by NTL: Telewest Business showed that on average office staff spent 42 minutes a day chasing response to 'urgent' emails and 27 minutes responding to voicemails. Stephen Benyon, managing director, states that 'Communication tools that once contributed significantly to productivity have started to become a drain on it. This means that employees can be faced with working longer hours unnecessarily.'

However, despite these cases, there is no doubt that technology can be effective in dealing with internal and external communication, but it must be properly implemented. Roest says, 'There is no point in sending out lots of emails if your company makes a few high-value products for a very select market. It is more appropriate if you want to sell 100,000 items with a £1.00 profit margin and have a potential market of 20 million people.'

Another new development adapted for business is blogging or online diaries. These are useful for keeping staff informed of organizational developments. Scott says, 'The beauty of blogs is that everybody can add comments and ideas. It can be more productive because you are not forcing people to go to meetings and you can see the train of thought in the dialogue. But it is only really for companies that are quite comfortable with IT.'

Case study questions

1 What are the typical problems associated with a traditional business meeting?

2 In what ways can information and communications technology (ICT) alleviate the problems associated with traditional business meetings?

3 What might be the pitfalls of using ICT alone for conducting meetings?

4 Suggest how the problem of excessive emails and voicemails identified in the NTL: Telewest survey might be alleviated?

5 As a client of a business that uses ICT for meetings and reporting, what benefits would you expect to accrue from such an approach?

SOURCE: Sarah Bridge, 'Time Mangers Set the Agenda', article, *Sunday Times*, 4 February 2007

Case study **9.2**

Varied approach to Vista adoption

The introduction of any new software or hardware is a significant consideration for an IT manager, but deploying Microsoft's Windows Vista operating system in every PC in the organization is potentially a major headache. Early indications are that IT managers are moving slowly, worried that there will be compatibility problems with existing software, hardware and networks. Bucking this conservative approach, Papa Gino's Inc. and D'Angelo Sandwich Shops wanted to move quickly, as it saw it as an improvement in the protection of customer credit card data. It consequently applied for membership of Microsoft's Vista Technology Adoption Program (TAP). Chris Cahalin, network manager at Papa Gino's says, 'We already have a district manager with Vista on his laptop and through TAP we have a direct line to Microsoft in case of trouble. The best way to find the kinks is to use it and these resources have really made things happen for us.'

PHOTO SOURCE: © MICROSOFT CORPORATION

The desktop of Windows Vista.

However, as an early adopter Papa Gino's has found some major 'kinks', such as an incompatibility problem between Vista and the company's Cisco network. Cahalin blames Cisco Systems for a lack of preparedness in making sure that Vista could communicate properly with its Secure Socket Layer (SSL) Virtual Private Network (VPN). However, there is a 'Catch 22' situation in that it is likely that Cisco are slow to undertake the necessary work on compatibility because so few of its customers are deploying Vista! For example, Quintiles Transnational is a health care provider with 20,000 employees in over 50 countries including China, India, Africa and Australia. Steven Dietz, Network Manger for Quintiles, is very concerned with security. 'Because we are a pharmaceutical testing company, we do business with all the large pharmaceutical companies and we have to keep data separate and independent from client A and client B. There can't be any confusion and we need to make sure data from client A isn't accidentally sent to client B.' Microsoft boasts that Vista is the most secure operating system yet, which would suggest that adoption should happen as soon as possible. However, Dietz is worried that security features in Vista could conflict with existing built-in security measures, leading to unintended data leakage. Consequently Dietz, like many other computing professionals, is taking a much slower route that Papa Gino's, putting Vista through extensive testing to ensure there are no surprises. Significant deployment will be delayed for at least a year.

However, it might prove difficult to delay for some organizations. StillSecure creates and sells a variety of third-party network software and is struggling to make its products Vista compatible. But as Alan Shimel, chief strategy officer, says 'Every time someone buys a new PC or laptop it comes out of the box with Vista. The world is being forced into the Vista universe kicking and screaming', he said, 'so vendors can't afford to move as slowly as IT shops can. Vista will find its way into corporate IT a lot sooner than most people would like. The more new machines are purchased with Vista pre-installed, the faster we all have to move.'

Thinking about the case

1 Would the problems indicated above have been as significant if the issue had been concerned with new hardware (such as new PC technology) rather than new software (an operating system in this case)?

2 Is it better to be an early adopter (like Papa Gino's) and get the help from Microsoft rather than delay (like Quintiles)? Will Quintiles be forced to deploy before they are ready?

3 Do you think that Microsoft have any moral obligation to the third-party vendors such as Cisco and StillSecure?

SOURCE: Bill Brenner, 'When Microsoft Vista and VPNs don't mix', 25 May 2007 and 'Big Microsoft Vista concerns Big Pharma', 19 June 2007, Computer Weekly.com

silicon.com

Case study 9.3

CEO and CIO still don't see eye to eye

BY GEORGE COLONY

A lot has changed in big business's relationship to technology in the last couple of decades. But, Forrester Research's George Colony argues, there still isn't enough trust between the CEO and the CIO.

Throughout my career, I have watched the 'odd couple' of the chief information officer and the chief executive officer try to live together.

In the 1980s and for most of the 1990s, their paths rarely crossed – the CEO didn't think much about technology, and the CIO rarely interacted with executives beyond his boss, the chief financial officer. With the exception of some techie leaders like Ned Johnson at Fidelity, Fred Smith at FedEx or David Glass at Wal-Mart, chief executives perceived IT/BT (I now refer to information technology as business technology, or BT) as an important underpinning of company operations, but not as a critical strategic tool.

Added to this general ambivalence were the high-profile cases of chief executives having their reputations and budgets scorched by IT/BT projects gone awry: perpetual IRS systems overhauls, Citibank's futile effort to create a 'single customer view' in the mid-1980s, and SAP R/3 'kitchen sink' leaps of faith in the early-1990s come to mind.

Then the dot-com collective insanity hit and CEO panic set in (Amazoning, etc., etc.). In those days, I ran a tech session at the Harvard Business School for CEOs. To prepare for the session, I surveyed chief executives at 25 large companies. When I asked them how much time they spent on technology issues, the response was '25 per cent'. They were

lying: CEOs – even the techies – could not afford to devote a quarter of their time to systems.

But they were certainly spending more time on tech than they had five years earlier – even Jack 'I've never used email' Welch, on his way out the door at General Electric, got religion and started to preach about the digitization of business. Michael Porter, every CEO's favourite academic, got into the act with a naive *Harvard Business Review* piece on the Internet in early 2001, just as the curtain came crashing down on The Web, Act 1.

Fast-forward to 2007. How's the odd couple today? Forrester just surveyed 75 global CEOs, and here's the punch line: 60 per cent of CEOs are satisfied with the overall performance of IT/BT, but only 28 per cent see IT/BT as a proactive leader in innovation. And only 30 per cent see IT/BT as a proactive leader in process improvement.

Now, you can analyse this data simply and conclude that CIOs are in pretty good standing with CEOs, but they have not stepped up to the plate as innovation and process mavens. I interpret the results quite differently.

The fact that 60 per cent of chief executives believe that CIOs are doing a satisfactory job is bad news, not good. Think comparatively: If only 60 per cent of your top executives were satisfied with the performance of the CFO, that would signal meaningful distrust in the financial operations of your company. Chief executives' satisfaction in IT/BT has

Influential Harvard academic, Michael Porter, whose much-discussed 2001 paper, 'Strategy and the Internet', urged business planners to recognize the internet as an 'enabling technology'.

Michael E. Porter

PHOTO SOURCE: © HUW JONES/ALAMY

certainly risen through this decade, but 60 per cent is still too low.

And the fact that CEOs are not looking to the CIO to be a proactive leader in innovation and process is not bad news. Rather, it is a frank assessment by the chief executive that the CIO should not be, indeed cannot be, the driving force in these two areas.

Why? In most companies, the CIO is too busy keeping the ship's engines running smoothly to come up onto the command deck and make suggestions to the captain on course changes. Leading business innovation and process change is not in the skill set of most CIOs – nor should it be.

Does the CIO have a role in process change? Absolutely. IT/BT typically supports and manages the process backbone – think enterprise resource planning – of most companies. When technology is injected into a company, the effort will fail unless it incorporates process change (the way you do work) and organizational change (the way you are organized to do work). I call this the critical triad – technology/process/organization – and the three must always be viewed collectively and as acting in concert. While the CIO brings technology to the table, business executives (especially the CEO) must spend political capital to change process and organization. This is a collaborative effort, with the CIO working with the business people to get the right mix.

How about innovation? Obviously the CIO is always working on systems innovation – that's part of keeping the engines running smoothly. But when it comes to business innovation, he is again not the proactive driver, but rather the steady partner with business executives who are chartered to lead business innovation.

Here's the key: For business executives to effectively drive process change and innovation, they must have a solid understanding of technology. They must be, to coin a term, technology-knowledgeable businesspeople (TKBPs) able to adeptly bring the potential of technology to bear on business change. The goal is to field vice presidents of marketing, executive VPs of strategy, and presidents of divisions who know how to apply technology to get the company to achieve its goals. The CIO must be in the business of educating and teaching the businesspeople so that they can make the leap. IQ (intelligence quotient) and EQ (emotional quotient), must be joined by TQ (technology quotient). And teaching TQ is the province of the chief information officer.

If that happens, chief executives' satisfaction with CIOs will head into the 70 per cent and 80 per cent range – where it belongs. And boards of directors will come to praise the chief information officer if that person can work to develop a TKCEO – a technology-knowledgeable CEO. And that's when the odd couple will see eye to eye – to the benefit of the organization and shareholders.

George Colony is chairman and chief executive officer of Forrester Research.

Thinking about the case

1 The suggestion is that CIOs should be less concerned with 'blue skies thinking' but more concerned with the education of CEOs in how technology can be used. Do you agree with this demarcation?

2 Is there room in today's business world for a true hybrid, a CEO who not only understands what can be done with IT but also how?

Business intelligence and knowledge management

LEARNING OBJECTIVES

As more and more business operations are managed using information from information systems and some-times automatically *by* information systems, large amounts of data are collected and stored electronically. With proper software tools, data stored in databases and data warehouses enable executives to glean busi-ness intelligence, information that helps them know more about customers and suppliers, and therefore helps them make better decisions. Information technology also enables organizations to organize stored knowledge and garner knowledge from vast amounts of unstructured data.

When you finish this chapter, you will be able to:

Explain the concepts of data mining and online analytical processing.

Explain the notion of business intelligence and its benefits to organizations.

Identify needs for knowledge storage and management in organizations.

Explain the challenges in knowledge management and its benefits to organizations.

LOOKING FOR CLUES

Things were going well for Lucy Slade and her chain of shops selling clothes to teens. She had confidence in her management team and they had embraced the new technology aimed at streamlining her business. But there was a nagging worry at the back of her mind. As the empire grew from 40 to nearly 100 shops the impression was that some were performing better than others, but she didn't have the facts to back up her reservations.

She had visited many of the stores as they had implemented the new enterprise resource-planning system and found the staff to be generally in favour of the changes, and yet there seemed to be a lack of consistency in the day-to-day operations of the stores. With her business experience this did not surprise Lucy. She realized that some styles and designs were better sellers in certain areas than others. However, there was a need for someone to see the whole picture to see if there was a chance to bring 'best practice' to all the stores.

When she next had a meeting with Martin Tate, the CIO, she asked him about the possibility of using the knowledge of the best store managers and analysing sales data across all of the stores. 'Sounds to me like you're talking about data mining', replied Martin. 'Leave it to me.'

Analysing the sales

It wasn't long before Martin got back to Lucy with some very interesting proposals. What he wanted was a system that would analyse data about sales, the layout of the stores, special offers in place, what was sold with what, time of day of sale, and so on. Most of these details were readily available and all that was needed was a database to store all of this historical data and then the appropriate software to allow analysis in a variety of dimensions. Lucy, being

the dynamic CEO that she was, gave him the go-ahead (with an appropriate budget!).

It wasn't long before the system was bearing very useful fruit. Analysis of the data showed that certain accessories, such as belts and hats, sold better when displayed next to fashion items that they naturally complemented. That in itself wasn't rocket science, but it was interesting to note which branches were doing better in this respect. The good practice was passed on to those branches which were missing this point.

Returns

An interesting by-product of the system was an analysis of returns. Whenever an item of clothing was returned as being unsuitable, it was customary to take details of the customer. The system could take an overview of this and produce a report showing the branches where there seemed to be an unusually high level of returns. Better than that, it could identify specific customers who regularly returned items a few days after purchase. Whilst there could be perfectly legitimate reasons for this, it was more likely that the customer was 'borrowing' the dress for a night out and then getting their money back. The new system could indicate to the

PHOTO SOURCE: © TONY TREMBLAY

branch manager that the customer had demonstrated such a profile so that some searching questions could be asked, the item of clothing inspected to ensure that there were no marks on it and so on.

Loyalty

'I think we should also investigate the idea of a loyalty card', Martin told Lucy at their next meeting. 'That way we can store details of every sale, who made it and when, what they bought with what and so on. This gives us massive potential for more analysis of our sales.' Lucy held up her hand. 'Hold on. I think an in-depth study of that is needed before we invest a great deal of money in such a scheme. Of course everyone knows Tesco's have benefited greatly from their Clubcard scheme but Sainsbury's abandoned theirs because it was costing more than alternative methods of business intelligence. I will not say "No" but let's do our homework first.'

Data mining and online analysis

Recall from our discussion in Chapter 6 that data warehouses are large databases containing historical transactions and other data. However, data warehouses in themselves are useless. To make data warehouses useful, organizations must use software tools to process data from these huge databases into meaningful information. Because executives can obtain significantly more information about their customers, suppliers and their own organizations, they like to call information gleaned with such tools business intelligence (BI). There are two main uses of these databases: data mining and online analytical processing.

Data mining

Data warehouses could be regarded as a type of mine, where the data are the ore, and new useful information is the precious find. Data mining is the process of selecting, exploring and modelling large amounts of data to discover previously unknown relationships that can support decision-making. Data-mining software searches through large amounts of data for meaningful patterns of information.

While some tools help find predefined relationships and ratios, they do not answer the question that more powerful data-mining tools can answer: 'What are the relationships we do not yet know?' This is because the investigator must determine which relationship the software should look for in the first place.

> **business intelligence (BI)** Information gleaned from large amounts of data, usually a data warehouse or online databases; a BI system discovers not-yet-known patterns, trends and other useful information that can help improve the organization's performance.

> **data mining** Using a special application that scours large databases for relationships among business events, such as items typically purchased together on a certain day of the week, or machinery failures that occur along with a specific use mode of the machine. Instead of the user querying the databases, the application dynamically looks for such relationships.

Industry **SNAPSHOT**

Growing demand for intelligence

Market surveys show that corporations intend to increase their spending on BI software and the rise is even more significant in Europe. According to IDC, a global intelligence and advisory firm spending on BI software and tools in Central and Eastern Europe (CEE) is set to rise to over 100 million euro by the end of 2007. Worldwide, spending on business analytic software alone will grow annually by more than 10 per cent over the next five years, whereas in CEE the growth will be 20 per cent, nearly double the worldwide trend.

SOURCE: IDC Press Release, June 2007, http://www.idc-cema.com/?showproduct=31083

To answer this question, other techniques are used in data mining, including artificial intelligence techniques.

To illustrate the difference between traditional queries and data-mining queries, consider the following examples. A typical traditional query would be: 'What is the relationship between the amount of product X and the amount of product Y that we sold over the past quarter?' A typical data-mining query would be: 'Discover two products most likely to sell well together on a weekend.' The latter query lets the software find patterns that would otherwise not be detected through observation. While data have traditionally been used to see whether this or that pattern exists, data mining allows you to ask *what* patterns exist. Thus, some experts say that in data mining you let the computer answer questions that you do not know to ask. The combination of data-warehousing techniques and data-mining software makes it easier to predict future outcomes based on patterns discovered within historical data.

Data mining has four main objectives:

- *Sequence* or *path analysis*: Finding patterns where one event leads to another, later event.
- *Classification*: Finding whether certain facts fall into predefined groups.
- *Clustering*: Finding groups of related facts not previously known.
- *Forecasting*: Discovering patterns in data that can lead to reasonable predictions.

These techniques can be used in marketing, fraud detection and other areas (see Table 10.1). Data mining is most often used by marketing managers, who are constantly analysing purchasing patterns so that potential buyers can be targeted more efficiently through special sales, product displays, or direct mail and email campaigns. Data mining is an especially powerful tool in an environment in which businesses are shifting from mass-marketing a product to targeting the individual consumer with a variety of products that are likely to satisfy that person. Some observers call this approach 'marketing to one'.

Table 10.1 Potential applications of data mining

Data-mining application	Description
Consumer clustering	Identify the common characteristics of customers who tend to buy the same products and services from your company.
Customer churn	Identify the reason customers switch to competitors; predict which customers are likely to do so.
Fraud detection	Identify characteristics of transactions that are most likely to be fraudulent.
Direct marketing	Identify which prospective clients should be included in a mailing or email list to obtain the highest response rate.
Interactive marketing	Predict what each individual accessing a website is most likely to be interested in seeing.
Market basket analysis	Understand what products or services are commonly purchased together, and on what days of the week.
Trend analysis	Reveal the difference between a typical customer this month and a typical customer last month.

Industry **SNAPSHOT**

Dealing with the devil

Large retailers are investing in a system to get rid of customers! These are the so-called 'devil customers' with behaviours ranging from the legal (but loss-making and inconvenient to the retailer) to fraudulent. Many retailers will accept a returned item even if you cannot show a receipt. Some people take advantage of this and 'return' stolen goods for cash. On a less fraudulent level, many customers are guilty of 'wardrobing', the practice of buying an expensive item of clothing, wearing it for one night with the labels tucked in and then returning it the next day. To minimize theses phenomena, most retailers collect customer details when they return goods, which can then be used to investigate that customer's previous return history. John Lewis uses software from London-based IntelliQ to sift through transactions carried out at all of its shops. 'We have business protection teams who identify the sorts of bad things that criminals do, and the software allows us to look at millions of transactions and identify suspicious ones that match the modus operandi of these criminals', says Peter Kaye, John Lewis's head of business protection. 'An experienced investigator can see what's happening and say "Yes, that transaction is a fraud", or "this one is suspicious".'

The Californian-based company, The Return Exchange, has several retailers using their software, giving them the ability to share information from a larger customer transaction data warehouse. The company uses statistical models to determine if certain 'customers' engage in fraud. If the software determines that a person has defrauded retailers, the stores will stop accepting the person's returns.

However, neither the retail chains nor the company disclose the criteria used to make the decision. Return Exchange does not allow retailers to share customer information.

SOURCE: 'How to get rid of "devil customers",' FT.com, 13 June 2007

A John Lewis department store on Oxford Street, London.

PHOTO SOURCE: © KEVIN FOY/ALAMY

Predicting customer behaviour Data mining is also used in banking, where it is employed to find profitable customers and patterns of fraud. It is also used to predict bankruptcies and loan payment defaults. Various behaviour patterns can be finely tuned into customer profiles. The data are then clustered into smaller groups of individuals who are using banking services that do not best support their activities. Bank employees can then contact these customers and offer advice on services that would serve them better. The result can be greater customer loyalty (measured in fewer accounts closed and fewer moves to other banks). The people who are contacted will hopefully think that the bank is trying to take good care of their money.

Companies selling mobile phone services face a growing challenge of *customer churn* (switching to a competitor). Some surveys show that more than 50 per cent of mobile phone users consider switching to a competitor at any given time, and 15 per cent plan to switch to a competitor as soon as their contract expires. Mobilcom GmbH, a German company with 4.56 million customers and 1100 employees, uses data mining to identify such customers and approach them with inducements to continue or renew their contract before they switch. The company uses an application called DB Intelligent Miner from IBM. The software periodically looks for patterns of customer churns, and assigns each customer a score representing the likelihood of cancelling the contract. The software considers many variables, among which are the number of days to expiration and complaint history. Customer loyalty is extremely important because the cost of obtaining a new customer far exceeds the cost of retaining an existing one, especially in a highly competitive market such as mobile telephones.

To ensure a steady flow of customer data into their data warehouses, companies in almost every industry – from airlines to hotels, dining and gambling – operate customer loyalty programmes similar to the original frequent flier programmes. Membership is often free, and customers leave a record every time they make a purchase even if they do not use a credit card to pay. In many cases mining such data provides business intelligence to target individual customers.

Utilizing loyalty programmes Loyalty programmes such as frequent flier and consumer clubs help organizations amass huge amounts of data about their customers. Some supermarket chains, for example, issue special offers only to the most loyal customers. Harrah's Entertainment Inc., the gambling and hotel chain, uses its data warehouse to target individual customers, rather than groups. The techniques – whose specifics the company refuses to disclose for obvious reasons – enables Harrah's to tailor hotel, dining and gambling packages that are attractive to its customers. It helps discern the small spender from the big spender and decide how to price those services by individual spending patterns at the company's facilities. Harrah's relies heavily on its software applications to price-discriminate. It gives sales agents instructions to charge people who have a history of little spending on gambling higher per-night rates than they charge big gamblers.

Inferring demographics Some companies use data-mining techniques to try to predict what customers are likely to purchase in the future. As mentioned in previous chapters, Amazon.com is a leader in exploiting customer data. The company registered US Patent Number 6,865,546, titled 'Methods and systems of assisting users in purchasing items'. The software developed by Amazon determines the age of the recipient of an item purchased by a customer. The age range is estimated based at least in part on a customer order history of gifts purchased for the recipient. The first gift is associated with the first 'age appropriateness designation'. The second gift is associated with a second age appropriateness designation. An age range associated with the recipient is estimated. The recipient's age progression is calculated, and the company uses it to offer the customer gifts for that person when the customer logs on to the site. So, if you purchase gifts from Amazon.com for your baby niece, do not be surprised if Amazon entices you to purchase items for a young girl, a young woman, and an older woman over the next few decades. Here is another example of what this data-mining tool can do: if you purchased perfume a week before Valentine's Day, it will infer that you bought the item as a Valentine's gift for a woman and offer certain colours for the wrapping paper.

Online analytical processing

Another type of application to exploit data warehouses might not be as sophisticated in terms of the analysis conducted, but is extremely fast in response and enables executives to make timely decisions: online analytical processing (OLAP). Tables, even if joining data from several sources, limit the review of information. Often, executives need to view information in multiple combinations of two dimensions. For example, an executive might want to see a summary of the quantity of each product sold in each region. Then, she might want to view the total quantities of each product sold within each city of a region. And she might also want to view quantities sold of a specific product in all cities of all regions. OLAP is specially designed to answer queries such as these. OLAP applications let a user rotate virtual 'cubes' of information, whereby each side of the cube provides another two dimensions of relevant information.

The power of OLAP OLAP applications either operate on data that are organized especially for such use or process data from relational databases. A dynamic OLAP application responds to commands by composing tables 'on the fly'. To speed up response, databases can be organized in the first place as dimensional. In dimensional databases – also called multidimensional databases – the raw data are organized in tables that show information in summaries and ratios so that the enquirer does not have to wait for processing raw data. However, it is then possible for the user to drill down to more specific data about the source of those summaries. Many firms organize data in relational databases and data warehouses but also employ applications that automatically summarize that data and organize the information in dimensional databases for OLAP. Oracle, Cognos, Hyperion and many other companies sell multidimensional database packages and OLAP tools to use them.

OLAP applications can easily answer questions such as, 'What products are selling well?' or 'Where are my weakest-performing sales offices?' Note that although the word 'cube' is used to illustrate the multidimensionality of OLAP tables, the number of tables is not limited to six, which is the number of sides of a real cube. It is possible to produce tables showing relationships of any two related variables contained in the database, as long as the data exist in the database. OLAP enables managers to see summaries and ratios of the intersection of any two dimensions. As mentioned in Chapter 6, the data used by OLAP applications usually come from a data warehouse.

OLAP applications are powerful tools for executives. For example, consider Figure 10.1. Executives of a manufacturing company want to know how the three models of their product have sold over the past quarter in three world regions. They can see sales in dollar terms (top table) and then in unit terms (second table). They can then drill down into summaries of a particular region, in this case North America, and see the number of units sold not only by model but by model and colour, because each model is sold in three colours. This information might lead them to recommend to the dealer to stop selling Model 3 in blue in North America, because sales of blue units of this model are quite low in this region. While still investigating last quarter's sales in North America, the executives might want to examine the sales performance of each dealer in this region. It seems that Dealer 3 enjoyed brisk sales of Model 1, but not of Models 2 and 3. If the sales picture is the same for another quarter or two, they might decide to stop sales of these models through Dealer 3 and increase the number of units of Model 1 they provide to that dealer.

In a similar manner, Ruby Tuesday is a US based restaurant chain that has an expanding franchise operation in Europe. A problem was identified at one of its restaurants. Managers who examined performance by location discovered that some restaurants were performing well below the chain's average in terms of sales and profit. Analysing the information revealed that customers were waiting longer than normally for tables, and for their food after they were seated. There could be many reasons for this: an inexperienced cook, understaffing or slow waiters, to name a few.

---

online analytical processing (OLAP) A type of application that operates on data stored in databases and data warehouses to produce summary tables with multiple combinations of dimensions. An OLAP server is connected to the database or data warehouse server at one end and to the user's computer at the other.

CD TASK

dimensional database A database of tables, each of which contains aggregations and other manipulated information gleaned from the data to speed up the presentation by online processing applications. Also called multidimensional database.

multidimensional database *See* dimensional database.

drill down The process of finding the most relevant information for executive decision-making within a database or data warehouse by moving from more general information to more specific details, such as from performance of a division to performance of a department within the division.

Figure 10.1 Using OLAP tables

Sales (US$ 000)			
	Model 1	Model 2	Model 3
North America	115800	136941	53550
South America	72550	63021	25236
Asia	65875	53781	17136
Total	**254225**	**253743**	**95922**

Sales (Units)			
	Model 1	Model 2	Model 3
North America	4632	6521	2975
South America	2902	3001	1402
Asia	2635	2561	952
Total	**10169**	**12083**	**5329**

North America (Units)			
	Model 1	Model 2	Model 3
Red	2401	1785	2512
Blue	1766	527	52
White	465	4209	411
Total	**4632**	**6521**	**2975**

North America Dealerships (Units)			
	Model 1	Model 2	Model 3
Dealer 1	102	556	2011
Dealer 2	1578	2450	108
Dealer 3	2358	0	10
Dealer 4	20	520	57
Dealer 5	574	2995	789
Total	**4632**	**6521**	**2975**

Managers at headquarters decided to take a look at the average time between when a customer's bill was opened at the cash register and the time the customer paid. In the restaurant industry this is an indication of an important factor: how long it takes to move from one party to another at a given table. The shorter the time, the better. The average time 'to close a bill' at Ruby Tuesday's restaurants is 45 minutes. At some locations it was 55–60 minutes. Examining additional information, management concluded that the reason for the longer wait was increased demand thanks to an economic boom in the region. The company sent people to change the layout of the kitchen, positions of the cooks and the placement of food. Cooking took less time, serving was faster and the wait time decreased by 10 per cent. More customers could be served, and revenue went up.

OLAP applications are usually installed on a special server located between the user's computer and the server or servers that contain a data warehouse or dimensional databases (although OLAP might also process data from a transactional database). Since OLAP applications are designed to process large amounts of records and produce summaries, they are usually significantly faster than relational applications such as those using SQL (Structured Query Language) queries. OLAP applications can process 20,000 records per second. As mentioned before, when using pre-organized dimensional tables, the only processing involved is finding the table that corresponds to the dimensions and mode of presentation (such as values or percentages) that the user specified.

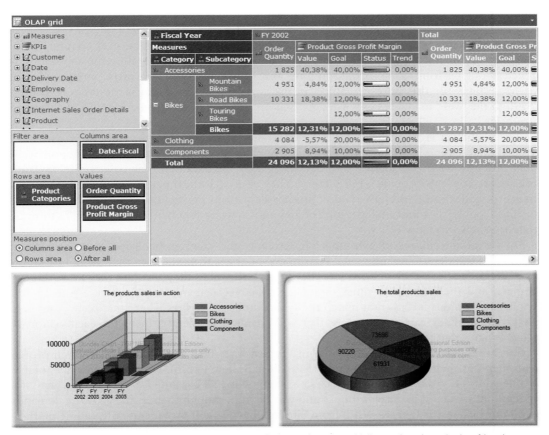

OLAP software, such as this example from Radar-Soft, performs multidimensional analysis of business data, allowing sophisticated trend analysis and data modelling.

OLAP in action OLAP and similar techniques help managers and other users to analyse quickly what is happening in the business. Managers in some companies now track information about their products from the purchasing of raw materials to the receipt of payment not only for operations but so that they can learn more about their clients and their own business. For example, Ben & Jerry's, one of the world's best-known ice cream makers, collects data about every container of ice cream it sells, starting with the ingredients. Each container is stamped with a tracking number, which is stored in a relational database. Using OLAP software, salespeople can track how fast new types of ice cream gain popularity, and which remain stagnant, on an hourly basis. Matching such information with about 200 telephone calls and email messages the company receives weekly, managers can figure out which supplier's ingredients might have caused dissatisfaction with a certain product.

Employees who know very little about programming and report design are discovering that BI software is becoming easier and easier to use. Intelligent interfaces allow them to enter questions in free form or close to free form. A part of the application that is called the semantic layer parses the question, which has been written as if you were speaking to a person, translates it into instructions to the computer to access the appropriate data mart or the proper columns of a data warehouse, and produces the answer, which is a number of charts showing trends. In a few seconds a manager at Tesco's Lands' End store can find out which type of yoghurt was the company's bestseller across the country over the past six months. BI software has become so popular in large companies that Microsoft decided to integrate such software into its popular database management system, SQL Server.

More customer intelligence

CD TASK

Customer relationship management (CRM) has been discussed in several chapters. The major effort of most businesses, especially retail businesses, is to collect business intelligence about customers. Both data-mining and OLAP software are often integrated into CRM systems for this purpose. Since an increasing number of transactions are executed through the Web, managers can use data that are already in electronic form to analyse and strategize.

The challenge is to address the right customer, at the right time, with the right offer, instead of spending large amounts of money in mass marketing or covering numerous websites with ads. Many companies find that using only the data that they collect directly from consumers does not provide a full picture. They approach third parties, companies that specialize in collection and analysis of consumer data from multiple sources. The companies, such as DoubleClick and Engage, use cookies and spyware (explained in Chapter 7) to track web users' clickstreams.

By compiling billions of consumer clickstreams and creating behavioural models, these companies can determine individual consumers' interests from the sites they visited (what do they like?), the frequency of visits (are they loyal?), the times they surf (are they at work or at home?), and the number of times they click on advertisements or complete a transaction. Then, sites can display ads that match the typical interests at sites where the likely customers tend to visit. They can use software that will change the advertisement for each visitor by using cookies that identify the user.

Site Intelligence is a company based in Oxfordshire, UK. They have several high-profile customers for their Visitor Behaviour Information System (VBIS), with Tesco being a notable recent addition. Stuart Gregory, Tesco.com comments: 'We wanted a robust web analytics system that we could manage in-house and was flexible enough to meet the growing demands of all our business managers. VBIS from Site Intelligence will provide us with online marketing intelligence ensuring all our marketing campaigns are measured, evaluated and consistently improved.' VBIS will run on Tesco's own system, analysing customer data from Tesco.net, Tesco Personal Finance and Tesco.com and producing integrated reports which will hopefully lead to improved website design and hence increased customer conversion and retention.

Executive dashboards

dashboard A graphic presentation of organizational performance. Dashboards display in an easy-to-grasp visual manner metrics, trends and other helpful information that is the result of processing of business intelligence applications.

To make the use of BI tools convenient for executives, companies that develop BI tools create interfaces that help the executives to quickly grasp business situations. The popular name of such an interface is dashboard, because it looks something like a car dashboard. Car dashboards provide information in the form of clock-like indicators and scales. BI dashboards use similar visual images. They include speedometer-like indicators for periodic revenues, profits and other financial information; plus bar charts, line graphs and other graphical presentations whenever the information can be presented graphically. Dashboards are available from Business Objects and XeoMatrix, providers of BI software. Similar dashboards are parts of BI tools offered by other vendors, including Siebel, Cognos and SAS. ERP vendors, such as SAP and Oracle, also include dashboards in their applications. Dashboards are often designed to quickly present predefined business metrics such as occupancy ratios in hotels and hospitals, or inventory turns in retail.

At TruServ, a member-owned hardware cooperative of 7000 retailers in 54 countries, executives use dashboards to monitor revenue and sales of individual items. Using the dashboard to conduct analyses, managers can pinpoint trends and changes over time and

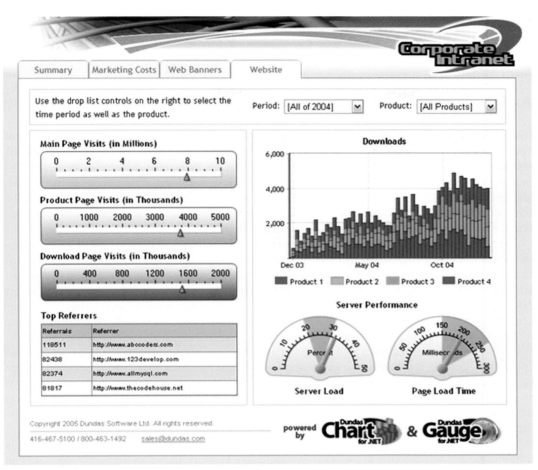

An example of an executive dashboard from Dundas.

receive alerts to help monitor, interpret and make decisions. They can better track inventory. In the past, 20 per cent of the cooperative's inventory was in the 'red zone'. Red zone inventory is either liquidated or sold for a loss after a promotion is ended. The executive dashboard was instrumental in helping TruServ reduce this loss inventory to 5 per cent.

Why you should...
learn about BL and KM tools

Information technology has advanced from fast calculation machines to systems that produce useful information from structured data to software that turns unstructured information into knowledge. Knowing how to use BI tools will help you to independently produce highly useful information from data warehouses and other large data sources. In your work you will also need to use other peoples' knowledge. Much of this knowledge exists in the recorded work and in the minds of colleagues and experts outside your organization. Knowing how to use these tools will help you as well as others perform better. As a knowledge worker you will be able not only to use your own, limited knowledge but also augment it with the experiences of other people.

Knowledge management

Imagine you work for a consulting firm. Your supervisor assigns you to a new client. As a smart professional, the first thing you want to check is whether your firm has had previous experience with this client and what knowledge has been accumulated about the experience. You heard that two ex-employees had contact with this client several years ago. It would be great to discuss it with them, but they are gone. Their knowledge was available to the firm, but it no longer is, because it is not recorded anywhere. The data recorded about the financial transactions with this client cannot provide the knowledge you are seeking: How easy or difficult was the interaction with the client's executives? What are the strengths and weaknesses of that organization? In engineering companies, engineers might want to see if colleagues have already encountered a problem they are trying to solve, and what the solution to that problem was then. IT professionals might want to know if their colleagues have encountered a similar repeating failure with a network management system.

An organization can learn much about its customers, sellers and itself by mining data warehouses and using OLAP software, but such techniques still do not satisfy another important challenge: how to manage knowledge, expertise that is created within and outside the organization. As discussed in Chapter 9, expertise in narrow domains can be programmed in expert systems. However, there is much more knowledge that organizations would like to garner and manage. Effective management of knowledge can help both employees and customers.

knowledge management The combination of activities involved in gathering, sharing, analysing and disseminating knowledge to improve an organization's performance.

Samuel Johnson, the author of an early English dictionary, said that one type of knowledge is what we know about a subject, and the other type is knowing where to find information about the subject. The purpose of knowledge management is mainly to gain the second type of knowledge. Knowledge management is the combination of activities involved in gathering, organizing, sharing, analysing and disseminating knowledge to improve an organization's performance.

Information that can be gleaned from stored data is knowledge, but there is much more knowledge that organizations would like to store that they currently do not. The knowledge that is not maintained in information systems is typically of the type that cannot be extracted from readily captured data at websites or other electronic means of transactions. It is accumulated through experience. Much of it is kept in people's minds, on paper notes, on discussion transcripts and in other places that are not readily accessible to a company's employees. Therefore, knowledge management is a great challenge. Knowledge management is the attempt by organizations to put procedures and technologies in place to do the following:

CD TASK

- Transfer individual knowledge into databases.
- Filter and separate the most relevant knowledge.

Industry **SNAPSHOT**

Chemical mining

By some estimates, 85 per cent of recorded corporate knowledge is in text files. Using a software tool called ClearResearch from Clear Forest Corp., the research staff at Dow Chemical Co. has extracted useful information from various unstructured sources: abstracts of chemical patents registered over the past century, published research articles and the company's own files. The software has reduced the time it takes Dow's researchers to decide what they need to read.

SOURCE: D. Robb, 'Text Mining Tools Take on Unstructured Data', Computerworld (www.computerworld.com), 21 June 2004

- Organize that knowledge in databases that allow employees easy access to it or that 'push' specific knowledge to employees based on prespecified needs.

Knowledge management (KM) software facilitates these activities. As the cost of storage media continues to decrease and database management packages are increasingly more sophisticated and affordable, storage and organization of unstructured information have become less of a challenge. The more difficult issue is development of tools that address the third challenge: quickly finding the most relevant information for solving problems.

Capturing and sorting organizational knowledge

The research company IDC argues that almost half of the work that *knowledge workers* do in organizations has already been done, at least partially. This work includes researching a certain subject, preparing a report and providing information as part of a consulting contract. It estimated that labour worth 2000–3600 euro per knowledge worker is wasted annually because workers try to solve the same problem that other workers have already solved. Organizations could save this duplication, or replication, by collecting and organizing knowledge that is gained by members of the organization.

To transfer knowledge into manageable online resources, some companies require workers to create reports of their findings. Others, especially consulting firms, require their employees to create reports about sessions with clients. However organizations collect information, the results might be several terabytes of potential knowledge, but the challenge for employees is to know how to find answers to specific questions. Some software tools have been developed to help.

Electronic Data Systems Corp. (EDS), an IT consulting firm, requires all of its 130,000 employees to fill out an online questionnaire about their activities once per year. With 20,000 of these employees EDS conducts surveys three times per year. Some of the questions provide multiple-choice answers, which make the input structured and easy to sort and analyse, but some of the most valuable input is in the form of free text. In the past, this part was forwarded to managers who learned and drew conclusions from it. Now, the company uses an automated system, PolyAnalyst from Megaputer Intelligence, Inc., to sort the text information and create links between topics.

Motorola, the giant manufacturer of communications equipment, has 4 terabytes of data managed by a knowledge management application. The application enabled engineers to query this huge resource. Still, unless a worker knew exactly where the proper data was or the names of people who were on a team that had solved the problem at hand, the worker could not find a proper answer. Motorola decided to implement Watson, an application developed by Intellext. Watson is installed on employees' PCs. It is embedded in Microsoft Word, PowerPoint and Outlook. It analyses an employee's document as it is being written, creates an automatic query about the subject, reaches out into the KM program, and pulls information that might be applicable to the task at hand.

Employee knowledge networks

While some tools build knowledge bases and help employees access them, others put the emphasis on directing employees to other employees who have a certain expertise. The advantage of this approach is that an expert can provide expertise that has not been captured in information systems (see Figure 10.2). Large companies, especially multisite ones, often waste money because employees in one organizational unit are not aware of the experience of employees in another unit. For example, one energy company spent € 1 million on a product designed to work on oil rigs to prevent sediment from falling into wells. When the equipment was installed, it failed. The executives of another unit decided to purchase the same

Figure 10.2 Employee knowledge network

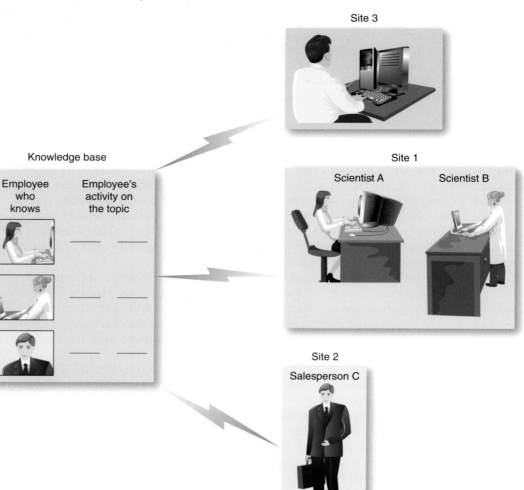

equipment, which, not surprisingly, failed in the other location. Then a third unit, elsewhere, purchased the equipment, which also failed. While one can justify the loss of the first € 1 million as legitimate business expense in the course of trying a product, the other € 2 million was lost because decision-makers did not know that the equipment had already been tried and failed. To alleviate similar problems, some software companies, such as Tacit Systems Inc., AskMe Corporation, Participate Systems Inc. and Entopia Inc., have developed employee knowledge networks, tools that facilitate knowledge-sharing through intranets. Recall that an intranet uses web technologies to link employees of the same organization.

Tacit Systems' ActiveNet tool continuously processes email, documents and other business communications and automatically 'discovers' each employee's work focus, expertise and business relationships. The tool 'mines' this unstructured data to build a profile of each employee in terms of topics and interests. The goal is to ensure that two people who might benefit from creating a connection in a workplace

employee knowledge network Software that facilitates search of relevant knowledge within an organization. The software points an employee with a need for certain information or expertise to co-workers who might have such information or expertise.

Ethical and Societal ISSUES

Knowledge and globalization

In the Middle Ages, Venice considered its expertise in making glassware not only a business trade secret but also a state secret. Divulging glassmaking knowledge to anyone outside the republic of Venice was punishable by death, because much of the state's economy depended on excluding other states and countries from such knowledge. Venice, like other states in that era, would never 'offshore' any of the work to another country. Nowadays, matters are completely different. What was expertise a year ago has become routine work this year and will become automated next year. At that point, the expertise value in the product will have diminished, and to make a profit the organization that used to have a comparative advantage in producing the product will have to use the least expensive labour available. It will offshore manufacturing to a factory in a country were labour is cheaper. The industry in the original country will lose jobs.

Information technology helps create knowledge but also expedites the turning of knowledge into routine, automated processes that can be carried out elsewhere. IT also expedites the transfer of knowledge from countries that created it to countries that can quickly use it. Software used to be developed almost exclusively in the United States and Europe. A growing amount of the software is now developed in India and China. The programmers' expertise is similar, but the wages earned by programmers in those two countries are a fraction of what US or European programmers would be paid for the same work. This is a pivotal element in what is called *globalization* – moving from national economies to a global economy. Is this bad for the US and Europe and good only for countries such as India and China?

BI and KM software is developed mainly in the West, that is the United States, Germany and the United Kingdom. However, these systems are sold anywhere and can help companies in other countries compete with companies in those 'developed' countries. This puts developing countries in a position to gain knowledge much faster than before and compete better. Now, the competition is not only in the manufacturing and service areas but also in research and development.

In the West, some observers view the issue in the following light: 'We used to be a world leader in manufacturing, but other countries now have a comparative advantage in manufacturing, and their workers have taken the jobs that our labourers used to perform. For some time we have had an advantage in providing services, but many of these services are now provided over the Internet and telephone lines by workers in other countries, so the service sector's advantage has diminished. We are still great in innovation and creation of know-how, but we are starting to see this advantage slipping away, too. And when other countries beat us in creation of knowledge, what's left with which to compete?'

Should governments take measures – legal or otherwise – that protect their economic advantages? Should they penalize companies that offshore manufacturing jobs? Should they forbid the sale of know-how to other countries? Should they adopt the Venetian model? Or, should we look at the world as one large economy where each worker and each organization should compete for a piece of the pie regardless of national borders, so that consumers everywhere can enjoy products of the highest quality for the lowest price possible?

do so, so that one can learn from the experience of another about a specific issue. By analysing email and documents, the tool extracts the employee's interests and solutions to problems, and that information is added to the employee's profile. Other employees who seek advice can access the profile, but they cannot see the original email or document created by the employee. This ensures uninhibited brainstorming and communication.

AskMe's software also detects and captures keywords from email and documents created by employees. It creates a knowledge base that holds the names of employees and their interests. An employee can access a web page at which the employee enters a free-form question. The software responds by listing the names of other employees who have created email, text documents or presentations on the subject, and the topics of their work. The employee can view the activity profiles of these people, and then contact them, via the website, by email, instant messages or paging. The responder can use the same website to respond and attach documents that might help the enquirer. AskMe's tool captures the communication, including attached documents, and adds them to the knowledge base. (Note that in this context the knowledge base is not organized as the knowledge bases in expert systems are.)

Of course this automatic capture of details on employees' expertise and knowledge raises ethical issues. Staff may not wish to share their information with other employees. It may be that they are not as involved in the area as they once were and have moved on to other things. Should it be up to the individuals to declare themselves as 'an expert'? More fundamentally, any system that trawls through the emails of employees is in danger of falling foul of privacy laws. If workers are to be allowed to send personal emails, during or outside working hours, will these emails be part of the analysis?

Knowledge from the Web

Consumers keep posting their opinions on products and services on the Web. Some do so at the site of the seller, others at general product evaluation sites such as epinions.com, and some on blogs. By some estimates consumer opinions are expressed in more than 550 billion web pages. This information is difficult to locate and highly unstructured. If organizations could distil knowledge from it they could learn much more than they do from conducting market research studies, such as focus groups, both about their own products and those sold by competitors.

Some companies have developed software tools that search for such information and derive valuable business knowledge from it. For example, Accenture Technology Labs, the

Consumer reviews of a coffee machine on Amazon UK.

Factiva's aggregation of material on the same coffee machine reviewed by consumers on Amazon UK.

technology research and development unit of the consulting firm Accenture, developed Online Audience Analysis. The tool searches thousands of websites daily and retrieves predetermined information about specific products and services. It then uses data-mining techniques to help organizations understand what consumers are saying about corporate brands and products.

Factiva, a subsidiary of Dow Jones & Reuters, promotes a software tool by the same name. Factiva, accessible through a website, gathers information online from over 9000 sources – newspapers, journals, market data and newswires – information that amounts to millions of documents. About 60 per cent of the information is not accessible to the general public. It screens every piece of new information that is posted at any of these websites for information specified by a subscribing organization. The search can be more tailored and specific than searches performed through free search engines such as Google or Yahoo! The software helps organizations add to their knowledge base, especially in terms of what others say about their products and services. The tool takes into account factors such as the industry and context in which an enquirer works to select and deliver the proper information. For example, a key word such as 'apple' means one thing to an employee of a hardware or software organization and something completely different to an employee in agriculture or a supermarket chain.

SUMMARY

Business intelligence (BI) is any information about the organization, its customers and its suppliers that can help firms make decisions. In recent years organizations have implemented a growing number of increasingly sophisticated BI software tools.

Data mining is the process of selecting, exploring and modelling large amounts of data to discover previously unknown relationships that can support decision-making. Data mining helps sequence analysis, classification, clustering and forecasting.

Data mining is useful in such activities as predicting customer behaviour and detecting fraud.

Online analytical processing (OLAP) helps users peruse two-dimensional tables created from data that are usually stored in data warehouses. OLAP applications are said to provide a virtual cube that the user can rotate from one table to another.

OLAP either uses dimensional databases or calculates desired tables on the fly.

OLAP facilitates drilling down, moving from a broad view of information to increasingly detailed information about a narrow aspect of the business.

Executive dashboards interface with BI software tools to help users quickly receive information such as business metrics.

Knowledge management involves gathering, organizing, sharing, analysing and disseminating knowledge that can improve an organization's performance.

The main challenge in knowledge management is identifying and classifying useful information to be gleaned from unstructured sources.

Most unstructured knowledge is textual, both inside an organization and in files available to the public on the Web.

Employee knowledge networks are software tools that help employees find other employees who have expertise in certain areas of enquiry.

One important element of knowledge management is auto-categorization, the automatic classification of information. Auto-categorization has been used in online customer support web pages to reduce the labour involved in helping customers solve problems.

URBAN SCENE REVISITED

Lucy Slade sees great potential in the use of information systems in the gathering of business intelligence

What would you do?

Lucy has asked for a report on how the existing information systems can be used to supply meaningful business intelligence and what needs to be in place to improve on this situation. What might be included in such a report?

New perspectives

Knowledge management systems are being implemented in the retail industry for a variety of tasks. Search the Web for current and potential uses of knowledge management in retail. How prevalent do you think they will become? Prepare to discuss your findings in class.

Review questions

1 What is business intelligence?

2 What is OLAP, and why is it often associated with visual cubes?

3 What is the advantage of using a dimensional database rather than on-the-fly processing in OLAP?

4 Why is online analytical processing usually conducted on warehoused data or dimensional databases rather than on data in transactional databases?

5 What is 'drilling down'?

6 What are data-mining techniques expected to find in the huge data warehouses that they scour?

7 What is knowledge, and how does it differ from other information?

8 In general, what is the purpose of knowledge management in organizations?

9 What is the purpose of employee knowledge networks?

10 What is the benefit of tools that direct employees to experts rather than to stored knowledge?

11 Context is a major factor when using tools to glean knowledge from web sources. How so?

12 Data mining helps mainly in four ways: sequence analysis, classification, clustering and forecasting. Data mining helps determine whether a person has committed fraud. Which of the four types of analysis help do that? Explain why.

13 The Web is a huge resource from which almost any organization could derive knowledge, yet very few do. What is the major challenge?

Discussion questions

1 What does intelligence mean? Do you accept the use of the word in 'business intelligence software tools', or do you think the use of this word is exaggerated compared with what these tools provide?

2 You are an executive for a large retail chain. Your IT professionals use data-mining software. They tell you of the following relationship the software found: middle-aged single men tend to purchase personal grooming products and light bulbs together. Should you assign employees to research the reason for this? What should you do?

3 Employee knowledge network software keeps tabs of much of what employees create on their computers and all the email they send. As an employee, would you be comfortable with such software? Why or why not?

4 The term 'business intelligence' has been used by IT professionals to mean many different things. What might be the reason for this?

5 Can businesses use free search engines such as Google and Yahoo! to efficiently gather useful knowledge for better decision-making?

6 Recall the discussion of expert systems in Chapter 9. In what sense are employee knowledge networks similar to expert systems and in what sense are they different?

7 Consider Amazon.com's data-mining software, which infers demographic information about the recipients of gifts. Is letting software infer demographics less of an invasion of privacy than questionnaires or other forms of direct questioning? Is such inference more effective in obtaining customer information? Why or why not?

8 Some consumer advocates argue that using services such as Return Exchange (see the Industry Snapshot 'Dealing with the Devil') violate privacy, because legitimate customers who make multiple returns might be denied a legitimate right to return merchandise. The sore point is over disclosing the criteria used to determine who is probably engaged in fraud. Do you agree with this resentment, or do you think it is legitimate to use such a practice? What could be the motivation not to disclose the criteria?

9 Companies would like to have systems that would allow them to store all the knowledge that their employees have accumulated. Do you expect that such systems will exist in your lifetime? Why or why not?

10 Suppose a company found a way to debrief you at the end of each working day and store all that you have learned and experienced during the day in an information system. Would you be comfortable with this? Why or why not?

Tutorial activities

1 Search the Web for a story on an organization that successfully used data-mining techniques. Type a four- to five-page paper in which you describe what the software was able to do for the organization and how the results benefited the organization. Emphasize what information the organization now has that could not be obtained without data-mining techniques.

2 Write a one-page report explaining what one can do with an OLAP application that cannot be done with the same data in a spreadsheet or a relational database. Give at least two examples.

3 Go to www.fedscope.opm.gov. Produce the following tables for the latest year for which data is available:

a) Number of US federal employees by category size (large, medium, small) by country of service.

b) Number of US federal employees by category size, only for employees working in Australia.

c) Number of US federal employees by department within the *large* agency category, only for employees working in Australia.

Is the sequence in which you produced the three tables considered drilling down? Explain why or why not.

4 Team up with another student. Select a specific company and write a report about its knowledge management needs. Start with a description of the activities that take place. List the types of employees who could benefit from access to documented expertise. Say which expertise you would take from internal sources and which from external sources. Give examples of knowledge that the company could use.

5 Team up with two other students. The team is to prepare a plan for The Researcher Connection, an employee knowledge network, to help the staff at your institution to develop research ideas and conduct their research. List the elements of your proposed system and convine potential users how it will help them (1) find relevant literature on a research subject, (2) learn who in the institution has done a similar study, (3) learn who in the institution would be interested in collaborating in the research, and (4) perform any other activity that is involved in conducting research and publishing the resultant article. Explain which of the resources to be used in the system already exist and will only need to be tapped (and how).

Companion CD questions

1 Think of a situation in your company or industry in which data mining could be useful. Create a

database and include fields that can be used for knowledge management.

2 Assume you are setting up a website to sell products. What would you consider when setting up the website so that you can effectively mine the data you get through it?

Video questions

1 What data do you think are collected during e-voting?

2 Do some research on the current state of electronic voting. Can the data collected during electronic voting be mined?

From ideas to application
REAL CASES

Case study 10.1

Targeting the Center Parcs market

Center Parcs is a well known brand of European holiday villages that attract visitors to its basic but comfortable bungalows set in woodland, surrounded by various sport and leisure activities and centred around a domed swimming pool that negates any problems with the uncertain weather.

Center Parcs is jointly owned by Center Parcs UK and Center Parcs Europe. The UK villages are owned and operated by Center Parcs UK whilst all other villages in the Netherlands, Belgium, Germany and France are owned and operated by Center Parcs Europe. The European operation attracts more than 3 million visitors per year and generates about 450 million euro. Part of this success comes from the excellent average occupancy of 90 per cent for its bungalows. However, traditionally this came at a significant cost. Twice a year the company would cover the continent

with 5 million brochures. As technology and e-business director for the company, Richard Verhoff commented, 'We were hurt badly by mailing and printing costs.'

The technology-based solution was to reduce the number of mailings while at the same time make them better targeted. Potential customers needed to receive the right brochure at the right time. For example,

PHOTO SOURCE: © CENTER PARCS

customers are more likely to book into a village nearer to home to avoid excessive driving time. Families prefer villages with plenty of activities for their children whereas older clients prefer quieter surroundings. Timing is vitally important. The company need the brochure to drop through the letter box just as the customer is thinking about sorting out the next holiday. All of these points are fairly fundamental. The problem is identifying the customer with the criteria so that the right brochure could be sent to the right person at the right time. A software solution was needed and Center Parcs found it in PredictiveMarketing, which uses the company's customer database to rank prospects by the likelihood that they will respond to a particular campaign. Basically the package is predicting the future. It is using its algorithms to produce a score and the same principle can be used in other spheres of business – will a customer make a repeat purchase, how effective is a particular product in meeting customer needs?

As far as Center Parcs is concerned, the results speak for themselves. For example, in Germany occupancy has increased by 10 per cent even though the number of mailings has dropped from 2 million to 450,000.

Historical data are a massive resource for Center Parcs and yet at the same time a potential headache.

Over the 20 European villages and 38 years of historical data there are vast numbers of business decisions that can be made based on this mass of data, but this is only possible with significant investment in hardware to store and process the data as well as software to extract and transform the data and then supply managers with timely, focused reports. The latest village being built in Reims, France, uses RFID technology to recognize the location of visitors across the whole of the park, adding to the storage headache but also increasing the potential for analysis.

Thinking about the case

1 The predictive analysis software referred to above deals only with mailings about mainland European resorts. Could the operation be extended to include Center Parcs UK? Could it be extended to cover other predictions of customer behaviour?

2 Is there a point at which a company can have too much data?

SOURCE: Linda More, 'Holiday resort speeds data processing', *Computing*, 29 March 2007 and Larry Stevens, 'Predictive Analytics Lets Companies See into the Future', *PC Magazine*, 23 August 2006, http://www.cioinsight.com/print_article2/0,1217,a=186926,00.asp

Case study 10.2

UpMyStreet.com

BY MARTIN RICH

How do you find out about an area that you are thinking about moving to? You can discover all manner of practical information, but on its own that doesn't convey the true character of an area. For that, you really need what is termed *tacit* knowledge – a concept that was identified many years ago by Michael Polanyi, who coined the aphorism 'We know more than we can say.' This has acquired a new relevance in recent years because of the availability of technology that can store and disseminate vast amounts of information.

UpMyStreet.com is one source of information about particular areas in the UK. It was set up in 1998, by Aztec Internet (a specialist Internet advertising consultancy) to provide information about local areas in the UK. Users can type in a postcode, or the name of a town, and see a range of background information

about the location. Postcodes are particularly useful here, because in residential areas they typically refer to a group of about 50 addresses, and it is possible to build a detailed picture of the area covered by an specific postcode. For each area, the site provides a range of information: average house prices, local schools, elected representatives for local and national government. Also available is a 'neighbourhood profile', which is a brief summary of the typical demographics (age, number of people in a household and so on) and buying preferences (such as what sort of food people buy and where they buy it, how likely they are to spend money on cars and holidays, what newspapers they read and what television channels they watch), associated with the area. Such a range of information recognizes the complexity necessary to build a clear picture of an area.

These neighbourhood profiles are known as *ACORN* (a classification of residential neighbourhoods) profiles. The underlying data for these is gathered by CACI – a market research company – and updated annually: they have been available to marketing professionals for many years, but until the launch of UpMyStreet.com were not available to the general

The home page of UpMyStreet.com

public. This effect, that resources that were once expensive, and only available to specialists, are now accessible to anybody with a web browser, can be referred to as *universal access*. However, a corollary of universal access is that specialists typically have access to much more detailed and comprehensive information than is available to the public.

In practice, the ACORN classifications can be inaccurate: there are only about 50 profiles to choose from, and areas can change more rapidly than the classifications can be updated. In an area where a lot of new building, or refurbishment, is taking place, very expensive new properties might be built very close to older and cheaper housing. Small as they are, individual postcode areas often include a mix of demographics. For instance, a suburban residential area might include both families with young children and older, retired people. An area with low housing costs might include a mixture of people in low-paid occupations,

students and those in potentially high-earning jobs but at the start of their career. The site includes a warning not to read too much into the neighbourhood profiles. In practice, professional market researchers with access to huge amounts of data can still build a much more accurate picture of a particular consumer's preferences than could be inferred from the data available through UpMyStreet.com.

From a strategic viewpoint, UpMyStreet.com's purpose has changed over the years. Initially it was created by Aztec Internet, as much as a showpiece for their abilities to create a database as for anything else. By 2003, its financial viability appeared to be in doubt: it was clearly a good idea and had caught the public's imagination but, as with many Internet business ideas, it was unclear how the site could generate any income. It was then acquired by uSwitch.com – a price comparison site specializing in the energy sector, where customers were offered a choice of suppliers as a result of deregulation during the 1990s. Price comparison websites can be regarded as another example of universal access, since in the past it would have been a painstaking task to check and compare prices from many different suppliers. Such sites have become particularly important in the areas of consumer goods, and personal finance where it is often difficult to evaluate different products effectively. uSwitch.com makes money by taking commission payments from some energy suppliers. While originally privately owned, uSwitch.com was acquired by E. W. Scripps, a large American media company, in 2006.

Since acquisition by uSwitch.com, the scope of the UpMyStreet.com website has expanded. One noteworthy feature has been the growth of the discussion groups, known on this site as 'conversations'. These conversations provide more tacit knowledge about an area – because knowing what local people are talking about is one source of knowledge – and they also add *user-generated content* to the site. Another is that actual sold house prices are available, as well as the average prices for an area that have always been shown on the site. To view sold house prices, or to contribute to conversations, users have to register. In this way UpMyStreet.com offers one range of information to anybody browsing the site, and another, broader range of information and services to anybody who wishes to register. Further services which have been added recently also depend on users who register. In particular, the site includes a 'FindMyNearest' service which tells users details of businesses and services, such as plumbers and restaurants, close to a particular address. This has recently been extended to allow registered users to rate these businesses – another example of user-generated content.

How does UpMyStreet.com make money? Two aspects to the business have distinct revenue streams. One is advertising; because the site attracts users who are interested in a particular geographical location, it can carry advertising that is accurately targeted at people in that location. Moreover, the business has developed a sophisticated range of models for advertising, notably through sponsorship of parts of the site. Not all of these are popular with users: for instance some advertisers use pop-up windows which can be irritating, and are often suppressed by pop-up blockers in web browsers. Another revenue stream arises from the fact that UpMyStreet.com provides paid services for businesses, in parallel with offering free services to individuals. For example, they can provide content which can be included in another website, or they can provide specialist reports on an area tailored to a business's particular interests.

Case study questions

1 There are now many discussion areas on the Internet where people can carry out the sort of 'conversations' offered by UpMyStreet.com. How might UpMyStreet.com conversations be differentiated from other discussion areas?

2 Registration for UpMyStreet.com is free. Why might the site wish to persuade people to register, even if they don't directly generate an income for the site?

3 What sort of knowledge might UpMyStreet.com be able to gather about the people who register to use the site, and how might this be useful to the business?

4 What other tacit knowledge might be useful to people thinking of moving to an area, or setting up business in an area, and how could a site such as this help them to acquire this knowledge?

5 What other examples of universal access to knowledge through the Web can you think of, and how do they help with the acquisition and distribution of knowledge?

SOURCES: E-business briefing (2003), http://www.e-consultancy.com/news-blog/newsletter/view.asp?id=640; *New media age:* 'UpMyStreet relaunches with major brands in new ad deals'; W. Pavia, 'Property website reveals what you're really worth,' *The Times,* 4 February 2006

Case study **10.3**

Compliance made easy

BY DANNY BRADBURY

Business intelligence isn't just about enhancing performance, says Danny Bradbury – it can help your company keep the regulators happy, too.

Business intelligence (BI) – sophisticated analysis of corporate data – is often seen as a way to improve performance and increase revenue. But with industry regulators clamping down on companies, some are starting to use the technology to prove their compliance – and in some cases, to hone it.

Alison Whitby, business intelligence practice head at Diagonal Consulting, says: 'Regulations like Sarbanes-Oxley have companies realizing that they're managing their businesses on very suggestive data. So the general push for those companies has been to demonstrate that they have more rigour in terms of their budgeting process and forecasting system.' Many compliance experts are seeing BI as a way to hone that.

Take Richard Price, for example. The head of risk at the Chelsea Building Society used BI software to help tackle his Basel II banking requirements. The regulations place strict requirements on the mitigation of financial risk through judicious planning. He found himself having to marry concise business data with less tangible information for forward-planning purposes. The evidence of such planning can run into reports of up to a hundred pages for a moderately sized financial institution like his, he says.

Much of the focus with Basel II reporting has been on managing credit risk, explains Price. His company has had to think about issues such as feeding credit risk data into solvency calculations, which measure how much capital you have against how much capital you should have to cover your lending.

He explains: 'From an institution's point of view, that high-level understanding – how much capital you're supposed to have – is where business intelligence comes in.' That kind of planning requires extensive what-if analysis, he says: 'An important consideration is how you'll manage under conditions of stress. If we had another severe recession, how would we manage our capital?'

The Chelsea Building Society already had a business intelligence system in place from vendor Infor, which it had used to build a financial model of the business over roughly 15 years. The system includes its own programming language which makes it easier to handle complex analyses, Price says.

Financial data are extracted from a mainframe-based data warehouse, and married with other inputs. He says: 'The most important things that go in are the assumptions from heads of management about things like volumes or severity of house price falls. It's easy to produce actual information but it's harder to produce a coherent forecast.'

One of the most significant implementation problems from a compliance perspective is retaining all the documentation surrounding the report, Price explains. The report, published in a format called the Internal Capital Adequacy Assessment Process, has to be retained for six years.

Price says: 'It's hundreds of megabytes of data and you have to do it annually or as business

A UK branch of the Chelsea Building Society.

conditions dictate. Most businesses are updating their business plans as they go through the year.' Consequently many finance institutions will present two or three of these reports per year at least.

Conducting analytics for forward-looking statements is one way to meet compliance requirements, but regulators also need companies to look backwards.

BI can help with auditing too. Diagonal's Whitby explains: 'Normally compliance is ensuring that you have the right security around your data. BI systems now can not only set up different security levels but can even personalize them.' Pieces of information can be associated with specific individuals, for example, which enables you to more easily build an audit trail of events and transactions leading to a particular business event.

However, Todd Paoletti, director of client self-service solutions at BI vendor Actuate, argues that for companies to build effective audit trails using business intelligence, a clear path must be defined between the report, the business application and the source data.

Paoletti says: 'You must avoid data being "cleansed" into a different or inconsistent format with the original source, or being out of date.' One way to avoid this is to create a middleware layer between the reporting application and the disparate underlying data sources.

Ideally you will use existing performance management tools to help satisfy your compliance reporting requirements, argues Cate Zavod, who works in solutions marketing at Actuate. Reusing parts of existing BI systems enables you to guarantee that the same performance management information will be used for compliance purposes but it will also prepare you for future regulatory impact.

Zavod explains: 'There are thousands of regulatory issues pummelling the financial services industry across the world today. So the more object-oriented your approach in developing these reports and applications, obviously the more reusable they will be, "future proofing" you for the next one that comes down the pipe.'

While some companies use business intelligence tools for reporting to the regulators, others use them operationally to help meet compliance requirements on a day-to-day basis.

Diagonal's Whitby suggests that companies could use alerting systems that can be triggered when certain thresholds are met, as a way of policing internal controls. In a financial services setting, alerts could be set to prevent traders over-extending their position, for example.

Whitby says: 'Rather than having to read through the data every week, the systems push information a lot more. So you can set it up to say that you have typical traffic-light-type coding that says this is a trend we don't like, take action.' The next stage is to trigger workflow that will escalate the problem and stop it becoming a regulatory issue, she adds.

Business intelligence software is already used in many organizations to monitor effectiveness, so it seems like a no-brainer to extend that to keeping a regulatory eye on your operation – and reporting on it after the event.

Thinking about the case

1 The idea of 'future proofing' applications is put forward to deal with legal compliance issues. Can the same principle be applied to business intelligence needs for strategic decisions?

2 It is easy to see the advantage of using sophisticated BI software for compliance issues in a large enterprise. Is the same true for a small to medium enterprise?

PART FIVE

Planning, acquisition
and controls

WORLDWIDE HOST

'Your home away from home.' That motto captures the mission of Worldwide Host, a global hotel chain with premium properties in many European, Asian, and North and South American countries. The up-scale chain has always prided itself on providing personalized service and making its guests feel welcome, wherever they travel. No detail is over-looked for guests' comfort – from a friendly morning wake-up call and freshly squeezed orange juice with breakfast, to on-site gym and spa service, to fluffy towels and bathrobes, to the mints on the down pillows in the evening. But Worldwide Host employees' travel experiences haven't always run as smoothly as its guests'. In fact, the chain's travel division needed upgrading, as its chief information officer, Michael Lloyd, knew all too well.

Outdated travel division, new ideas

As Worldwide Host's CIO, Michael Lloyd often trav-elled to the hotel chain's properties throughout the globe, overseeing its reservations and other infor-mation systems. When he needed to make travel arrangements, Michael used the corporate travel division, composed of approximately 90 full-time employees. Those staff members worked with air-lines and rental-car companies – as well as World-wide's individual hotel staff – to arrange the business travel for all of Worldwide Host's employ-ees. When Michael needed to travel to New York, Tokyo, Johannesburg or anywhere in the world, he would call or email the travel division with details of his trip. Travel staff would arrange the flights, stays at hotel properties and rental cars, and then send him the information. But despite everyone's best efforts, he'd had miscommunications on dates, re-peated calls and emails for clarification and, on more than one occasion, a missed airline connec-tion because of a change in the airline schedule that didn't get passed along to him. If he was just one of the company's business travellers, what was hap-pening with his co-workers? There were hundreds of them scattered across the globe. The travel sys-tem always frustrated Michael because it was ineffi-cient. It had been around for decades and was no longer meeting Worldwide's needs.

One day while travelling, Michael had an idea: what if Worldwide Host moved its travel services exclusively to the Web? Allowing employees to enter their travel needs directly into a web-based system would streamline the reservation process and elimi-nate errors. Such a system could save the company a great deal of time, and hence money. Michael took his idea a step further. Other hotel chains were creat-ing alliances and opening their services to the public via the Web. As a leading hotel chain, Worldwide Host could do the same to remain competitive – revamping its corporate travel division into a fully fledged, e-commerce site, which employees and the general public could use. To accomplish that goal, the company would need to tie its existing travel reservation system into a web-based interface – that much was certain. But it would also need to ensure any new system was compatible with its airline and rental-car partners' systems. That would be a monu-mental effort because of the size of the companies. Each one logged thousands of reservations a day.

Still, the idea had many positive points. The higher public profile could generate additional revenues for Worldwide Host, the airlines and rental-car companies. Currently, any unoccupied rooms, unsold plane seats or unrented cars at the end of the day were lost revenue that couldn't be recouped. All companies needed to run their opera-tions as close to full capacity as possible. So, offering the public access to those unfilled rooms, seats and cars in a combined website could boost reserva-tions, generating additional, much-needed revenue.

He also knew the amount of time it took to arrange his own business travel, with many calls and emails to the travel division. Scheduling vacations through a travel agent meant additional time for the public, too. With today's fast-paced lifestyles, streamlining the process and putting control in the traveller's hands made sense.

Under the current system, Worldwide Host maintained a travel division used only by its own employees. Michael reasoned that with an e-commerce site, the travel division's employees could now serve the general public, spreading the cost of the division over a broader revenue base. Maybe Worldwide Host could move them into a separate subsidiary. The revenues from the subsidiary could also help offset the cost of developing the new system. Michael took stock of the pros and cons of the website in his notebook. The prospect excited him. As soon as he reached his hotel room, he called the chief executive officer, Nathan Plummer, to discuss his idea. The new system would need top executive backing to become a reality.

High-level negotiations

Nathan Plummer was no newcomer to the hospitality field. His grandfather had started Worldwide Host in the 1930s, and Nathan had grown up in the business, along with his sister and brother. He and Michael met several times to map out a strategy for the proposed website. After lengthy internal discussions with Worldwide Host's management staff, Nathan decided to proceed with the e-commerce effort.

To gather initial support for the e-commerce site, Nathan and Michael began negotiating with Worldwide's current airline and rental-car business partners. All of the companies had a depth of experience in reservations systems, but they had never linked them into one all-encompassing system. Despite the difficulties that establishing a unified system could entail, the promise of increased bookings was very tempting. The partners were willing to listen. Nathan and Michael presented additional arguments: the companies could trim the transaction fees they now paid to travel agents for each reservation, saving out-of-pocket expenses. Customers could go online at their convenience to arrange their travel plans. The final point that persuaded the companies to participate was the advantage of partnering to develop the site. Each of the companies had been considering developing its own e-commerce site, but the cost to a single company was a major hurdle. A new combined site would allow each company to share the cost of setup with its partners, plus draw more web traffic than single sites. Also, down the road, other travel organizations could join the alliance.

Meetings were long and involved, but eventually the partners struck a deal – the new website development effort, TripExpert.com, was born. To gather even more support for TripExpert, Nathan assured his partners that he planned to meet with other travel companies, such as additional airlines and hotel chains, cruise lines and theme parks, to enlist their participation in the site once it was up and running.

Information systems: a critical link

With the agreement of the travel companies to participate, Michael now turned to the big issue of the website itself. Key to TripExpert's development was the underlying information technologies. He jotted down some notes from his earlier meetings and brainstorming sessions and set up a meeting with General Data Systems (GDS), Worldwide Host's IS consulting firm. The firm had developed Worldwide Host's computerized reservation system and regularly assisted the hotel chain with upgrades and maintenance. Over the years, Worldwide Host had established a strong relationship with GDS and relied on its staff's expertise in system development, network administration and troubleshooting. Investigating development of the new website would require even closer collaboration between Worldwide and GDS.

GDS's director of new business assigned Judith Keene, his most experienced systems analyst, to the TripExpert project. She had worked on Worldwide Host's systems many times and knew their capabilities well. Also, Michael respected her abilities, and the two had worked well together in the past.

Michael explained his vision of the new system to Judith. 'So what we're talking about is a system based on Internet technology that would handle not only our internal travel needs but extend the reservations capabilities to the general public. Nathan, our CEO, and I spoke with the heads of North Trans and Blue Sky airlines, as well as A-1 and Bargain Rent-a-Car companies. It took some persuading initially, but they realized the advantage of offering a full-service travel site. We'll need GDS's help, Judith, to explore the various options we have. Is a system currently available that we could buy and modify to fit our needs? We need to tie all our companies' systems together someway. Or do we need to start from scratch and build a customized system?'

Judith replied, 'Off the top of my head, I know of pieces that exist – some web-based reservation systems and databases, and there is a mainframe-based system an airline has used for decades. But I'd need to investigate each of your partners' systems to see what their capabilities are. A speedy search engine is critical – customers don't like to wait more than a few seconds for responses when they shop on the Web. Delays were a problem with early e-commerce sites, but technology has come a long way since then. We'll see whether we can purchase a search engine component. Availability of the system will be key, too. Web traffic can spike unexpectedly, so we need to plan for peak demand.'

'I'm also concerned about security. We need to assure the public that their financial information is absolutely safe with us or they won't use the site. Trust in our security will be crucial', said Michael.

Forming a development team

'Since we're on the subject of the needs for the new system, have you discussed setting up a development team to investigate the possibilities?' asked Judith. 'We need members from your travel division, hotel management and reservations staff, and in-house IS staff, to start with. User input is important to make sure we address all the business functions, and your IS staff can help with technical issues. Anyone else?'

Michael responded, 'I think we need to interview staff from the airlines and car companies to get their perspective as users of the system, too, and we'll need you and some of GDS's best systems analysts on the team.'

'Of course – I'll look into our staffing immediately. What about oversight and approval?'

'Nathan will head the executive steering committee, which will also include the chairman of our board, the chief financial officer, VP of hotel management, your director of new business, your CEO, and me. Our top execs need to know how we're proceeding and what plans we are making. This is such a large undertaking that we need management's oversight of our progress.'

'Sure,' Judith said. 'We can work essentially the way we did when developing your new reservations system a few years ago. That system was critical to your business, and this new one will be just as important.'

'So to start with, we'll need to explore the feasibility of each of the options we have. Can you begin looking at the technical aspects – investigate in detail any existing systems? In the meantime, I'll look into scheduling and staffing. Then we'll need to tackle the big issue – economics. Nathan will need a realistic budget for every option.'

'When do you want to meet next?' asked Judith.

'How does your schedule look two weeks from now? Say, on Tuesday morning?'

'Sounds fine. I'll talk with my supervisor to get four of our best analysts lined up for the team. I'll email to let you know.'

'Great. We have a lot of work to do to get TripExpert off the ground.'

Business challenges

After studying the next three chapters, you will know the basics of systems development efforts. You'll explore the issues of planning, systems development, alternatives for acquiring systems, and security and disaster recovery.

In Chapter 11, 'Systems Planning and Development', you learn the steps to creating a plan for a new system, such as the e-commerce travel website for Worldwide Host, and what steps to follow to develop an e-commerce website, including feasibility studies and defining the essential functions of the new system.

In Chapter 12, 'Choices in Systems Acquisition', you learn how Worldwide Host can evaluate the benefits and risks of alternative methods of acquiring an information system, including purchasing or leasing a program to create an integrated system.

In Chapter 13, 'Risks, Security and Disaster Recovery', you learn about the risks threatening information systems, especially those dealing with financial transactions on the Web, and ways to protect systems against attack.

PART ONE
The information age

1 Business information systems: an overview
2 Strategic uses of information systems
3 Business functions and supply chains

PART TWO
Information technology

4 Business hardware and software
5 Business networks and telecommunications
6 Databases and data warehouses

PART THREE
Electronic commerce

7 The web-enabled enterprise
8 Challenges of global information systems

PART FOUR
Managers and
information systems

9 Managers and their information needs
10 Business intelligence and knowledge
management

PART FIVE
Planning, acquisition
and controls

11 Systems planning and development
12 Choices in systems acquisition
13 Risks, security and disaster recovery

Chapter 11

Systems planning and development

Planning and developing new information systems is often complex. Systems planning often requires creating or adjusting strategic plans because of the great impact of IT on business models and operations. Those involved in development have to translate a business opportunity, a solution to a problem, or a directive into a working set of hardware, software and telecommunications components. Once a development project is under way, many people from different disciplines are involved in the effort. Communications skills are extremely important for successful results.

When you finish this chapter, you will able to:

Explain the importance of and steps in IT planning.

Describe the systems development life cycle, which is the traditional approach to systems development.

Explain the challenges involved in systems development.

List the advantages and disadvantages of different system conversion strategies.

Enumerate and explain the principles of agile systems development methods.

Explain the concept of systems integration.

Discuss whether IS professionals should be certified.

A VISION FOR THE FUTURE

Michael Lloyd, Worldwide Host's CIO, was convening a meeting with his TripExpert.com project staff. A few months had passed since he had been given the go-ahead to investigate development of the company's new travel website. He pointed to Worldwide's mission statement, which was posted on the boardroom wall:

Satisfying our guests' and employees' needs is the key to maintaining Worldwide Host's leading position in the global hospitality industry. We are dedicated to superior customer service and continued employee growth.

Michael spoke to the assembled team, composed of Worldwide Host and General Data Systems (GDS) employees. 'As I've mentioned before, this statement

With millions of registered users, Travelocity is a leading provider of consumer-direct travel services and represents the level of success a travel company can achieve with an online presence.

is our guiding principle. Worldwide Host recognizes that information systems are central to its continued success. That's why we're here. We talked earlier about our need to look beyond our day-to-day IS issues, and I urged you all to rethink processes as we move ahead. We have an opportunity to reshape this company and its future – to look beyond our immediate technology needs to new technologies and processes that will allow future expansion and efficiency.' With those initial words of encouragement, the team began to review the information they had gathered since their last meeting.

Investigating existing systems: capabilities and needs

Judith Keene, GDS's top systems analyst, and her co-workers had been looking into the compatibility of Worldwide Host's existing reservations system with their airline and car-rental partners' systems. She noted that capabilities and systems differed: the airlines' reservation software needed to update flight information continually due to weather changes and equipment malfunctions, and airlines and car-rental companies both needed to track the whereabouts of their planes and cars to be sure that they were available where needed. In contrast, hotel systems are more static; properties themselves don't move, and cancellations occur much less frequently than in the airline industry. But the hotel systems needed information on each property that was more detailed – location of room, general appearance, types of beds, availability of meeting rooms, exercise facilities and other details. In short, Worldwide Host's existing system didn't serve quite the same functions, or run on the same platform, as the other two systems. That made the prospect of tying the existing systems into a single system dubious.

Searching for system alternatives

Colin Johnson, another team member from GDS, had been investigating online reservations systems such as Expedia and Travelocity. The best ones were not available for sale or were too expensive. One developed by an airline had been used by travel agents for decades. But it couldn't easily be linked to the Web, and its use was not intuitive – the average web surfer would have trouble with its user interface. Also, the system ran on an old, outdated mainframe system.

Finally, Colin located one new web-based global reservations system whose owners, Reservations Technologies, licensed their product. Since it didn't have all the components TripExpert.com would need, GDS explored the possibility of tying it to part of Worldwide Host's existing reservations systems and working with the owners to develop additional functionalities. In the meantime, GDS hired Alexis Pritchard, who had the expertise to migrate the data from their existing system into this new one.

Stalling out on database development

Alexis Pritchard had been heading up the database team. She and her two co-workers had been talking with Worldwide Host employees to gather information about their existing reservations system and to develop lists of new business needs for the TripExpert.com site. They thought they had covered every new function that the database needed to handle for website connections: aside from increased capacity, they noted that they'd need to display picture files to show web shoppers sample rooms. The travel staff hadn't previously worried about graphics capabilities. They had also listed a requirement for the system to track TripExpert site reservations so that a small web service fee would be added to the room rate. But what they and the Worldwide Host staff completely forgot about were the discounted room rates that were to be offered to last-minute web shoppers. Within three weeks of a reservation date, the system needed to release a block of rooms to the website – rooms that were not already reserved by traditional means. Those rooms were to be made available at a discount to web shoppers, enticing them to book last-minute stays. Worldwide Host hoped to fill more of its hotels by offering the web discount and thus boosting profits.

The database team members were already making preliminary design plans when their omission came to light. They reported the slipup to Michael Lloyd with trepidation. They believed that incorporating the new features into the system's design could mean a delay of about 6 weeks, throwing the whole project behind schedule.

Getting back on track

Michael called in Judith Keene, GDS's lead analyst, to find a solution – and quickly. Delays in the TripExpert system would mean that Worldwide Host would lose competitive ground since other sites were coming online. Judith had worked on Worldwide Host's existing reservations system and knew its capabilities well. She also knew GDS's analysts' skills.

'Michael, let me check Colin Johnson's schedule. He's been working on licensing the web airline-reservation system for us. I think he is ahead of schedule in his investigation of the system's capabilities and his negotiations, so maybe we can borrow him for a while. Is that what your schedule shows? Good. Colin has worked under deadline pressure before and is an experienced analyst. If he and I put our heads together on this problem, I think we can straighten it out.'

'Thanks, Judith. Let me know how it's looking as soon as you can. The database is critical to the site's functioning. If we don't get that component in place, we'll jeopardize the whole system. What good is the front end without the back?'

'Not much,' she answered. 'I'll call Colin right now to see whether he can meet with Alexis's team and me tomorrow. In the meantime, try not to worry. We've hit bad stretches before but come out OK in the end.'

Planning information systems

In recent years a growing number of companies have implemented enterprise ISs such as ERP systems or their major components, SCM and CRM, or other sophisticated systems that serve the entire organization or many of its units. The investment of resources in such systems, both in financial and other terms, is great. The risk in implementing such large systems is also great. If the implementation is successful, the new system can significantly change the manner in which the organization conducts business and even the products or services it sells. For all these reasons it is necessary to plan the implementation of information systems, whether they are developed in-house, made to order by another company, or purchased and adapted for the organization. When planning, it is important to align IS strategies with the overall strategies of the organization. (Some organizations prefer to use the term 'IT planning' rather than 'IS planning'. In this discussion the terms are used interchangeably.)

Steps in planning information systems

IS planning includes a few key steps that are a part of any successful planning process:

- Creating a corporate and IS mission statement.
- Articulating the vision for IS within the organization.
- Creating IS strategic and tactical plans.
- Creating a plan for operations to achieve the mission and vision.
- Creating a budget to ensure that resources are available to achieve the mission and vision (see Figure 11.1).

A *mission statement* is a paragraph that communicates the most important overarching goal of the organization for the next few years. Although the ultimate mission of any organization is to survive and – if it is a for-profit organization – to produce profit for its owners, mission statements rarely say just this. Rather, they say how the organization intends to survive and thrive. For example, in Amazon.com's early years, its mission was to brand itself as the most recognized retailer on the Web and to create the largest possible market share. Management pursued this mission, though it resulted in years of financial loss.

An important part of an organization's overall mission statement is an IS mission statement that is compatible with the larger mission. It is usually a paragraph, or several paragraphs, describing the role of IS in the organization. Often, the IS mission and IS vision are combined into one statement. The IS vision includes the ideal combination of hardware, software and

Figure 11.1 The steps of information systems planning

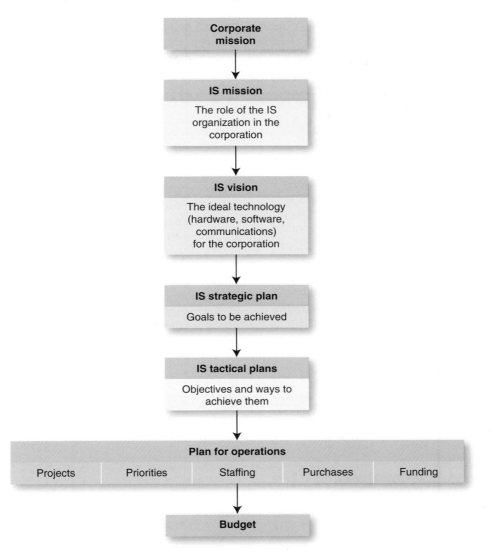

networking to support the overarching mission. For example, Amazon.com's management continues to recognize that innovative IT, especially web and fulfilment technologies, is the most important resource for the organization's success.

The CIO, with cooperation of senior management as well as managers in the IT unit, devises a strategic plan for implementation of IT in the organization. The plan addresses what technology will be used and how employees, customers and suppliers will use it over the next several years. Since IT advances so quickly, strategic IT plans are typically prepared for no longer than five years.

The goals laid out in the strategic plan are subdivided into objectives, which are concrete details of how to accomplish those goals. The objectives typically include resources to be purchased or developed; timetables for purchasing, developing, adapting and implementing those resources; training of employees to use the new resources; and other details to ensure timely implementation and transition.

The objectives are further subdivided into specific operational details. For each project, management assigns a project manager and a team; vendors are selected from whom available components of hardware, software and services will be purchased; and funding is requested. When the financial requests are approved, the corporate budget includes the money to be spent over several months or years on these projects.

Industry **SNAPSHOT**

Planning ahead with AXA Winterthur

Managing an enterprise-wide IT resource is best approached as part of an integrated strategic plan for the company as a whole, according to Christoph Gall, Head of IT strategy and architecture at AXA Winterthur, Switzerland. 'Enterprise Architecture Management (EAM) isn't suitable as a management tool until it has been embedded in an integrated planning process.' Historically, Winterthur had grown from a decentralized organization of independent subsidiaries throughout Europe, each with its own IT department leading to 32 different database products, 15 operating systems and over 30 programming languages. This made analysis of the company's current use and future needs of IT very difficult. With the help of planningIT, a software product from the Berlin-based company Alfabet, they are now able to analyse IT project proposals to judge how well they support the business strategy. Christoph Gall observes that 'EAM is an effective instrument for aligning IT with the requirements of the business strategy.'

SOURCE: 'Optimized IT Planning brings greater Efficiency to AXA's Winterthur', *Computerworld Switzerland online,* 15 March 2007

The home page of AXA Winterthur.

IT planning is not much different from the planning of any other acquisition of resources, starting with a vision of how the resources will be used to accomplish goals and breaking those ideas down into projects and the resources to be allocated to carry the projects to successful completion. In recent years, a growing proportion of IT funds have been spent on software, with most of the funds going to purchase and adapt software, rather than developing it in-house or assigning its development to another company.

The benefits of standardization in planning

One major goal – and advantage – of planning is standardization. When management decides to adopt a certain IT resource for all its units, regardless of function or location, it standardizes its IT. Standardization results in several benefits:

- *Cost savings*. When the organization decides to purchase the same hardware or software for all its units, it has better bargaining power and therefore can obtain lower prices from vendors. This applies to purchasing or leasing computers of all classes – mainframe, midrange and personal computers – as well as licensing software.

- *Efficient training*. It is easier to train employees how to use a small variety of software than to train them how to use a large variety. Less trainer time is required, and – more importantly – employees spend less time on training and more time on their regular assignments. This also saves cost in the form of fewer labour hours spent on training. Even if each employee uses only a single application, but the organization maintains several applications for the same purpose, training time is extended.

- *Efficient support*. Standardizing on a small number of computer models and software applications enables the IT staff to specialize in the hardware and software they have to support. The more focused skills make it easier for the organization to recruit support personnel, and results in more satisfactory service to users.

From planning to development

After planning a new IS or a set of ISs, management decides how to obtain the systems. In a great majority of cases, 'systems' means software. For example, CRM and SCM systems rarely require specialized hardware. An increasing number of new systems are purchased and adapted for an organization's needs rather than developed in-house, although in-house development still takes place in many organizations. The approaches to systems development are the same regardless of who develops the system, the organization or its vendor.

There are generally two approaches to systems development: the systems development life cycle (SDLC) and nontraditional methods, among which are many grouped under the umbrella of agile methods. SDLC is the more traditional approach and has been used for several decades. There are circumstances under which it should still be used. Agile methods developed out of prototyping, an application development approach that emerged in the 1980s aimed at cutting costs and time. Prototyping involves fast development of an application based on initial user requirements and several cycles of user input and developer improvements. Using the philosophy of prototyping – that coding should start as soon as possible and that users should be involved throughout the process – led to several methods of software development called agile methods. The following sections discuss both approaches.

prototyping An approach to the development of information systems in which several analysis steps are skipped, to accelerate the development process. A 'quick and dirty' model is developed and continually improved until the prospective users are satisfied. Prototyping has evolved into agile development methods.

Why you should...

understand the principles of systems development

By and large, organizations have recognized the need to let non-IT managers play major roles in systems development. You might be called on to participate in this process, not just to provide input here and there but as a member of a development team. The IT professionals on the team need your insight into the business activities you run. They need your advice on ways to improve these activities through the use of new or improved ISs. One approach to development, agile methods, actually views the users as sharing at least half of the responsibility for the effort.

Software developers count on you and your co-workers to provide them with proper requirements and feedback. You had better be knowledgeable, active and assertive in software development projects, because you will have to live with the products of these efforts. Also, when your organization decides to discard one IS and adopt a new one, your understanding of the conversion process and proper cooperation will be highly valuable.

The systems development life cycle

systems development life cycle (SDLC) The oldest method of developing an information system, consisting of several phases of analysis and design, which must be followed sequentially.

Large ISs that address structured problems, such as accounting and payroll systems and enterprise software applications, are usually conceived, planned, developed and maintained within a framework called the systems development life cycle (SDLC). The approach is also called 'waterfall' development, because it consists of several distinct phases that are followed methodically, and the developers complete the phases sequentially. The developers do not deliver pieces of the systems before the entire system is fully completed. Although different textbooks might refer to the different phases and sub-phases of the SDLC by different names, or organize them slightly differently, in general, the process follows the same steps. While the SDLC is a powerful methodology for systems development, organizations are sometimes forced to take shortcuts, skipping a step here or there. Sometimes, time pressures, funding constraints, or other factors lead developers to use different approaches to systems development.

The SDLC approach assumes that the life of an IS starts with a need, followed by an assessment of the functions that a system must have to fulfil that need, and ends when the benefits of the system no longer outweigh its maintenance costs, at which point the life of a new system begins. Hence, the process is called a *life cycle*. After the planning phase, the SDLC includes four major phases: analysis, design, implementation and support. Figure 11.2 depicts the cycle and the conditions that can trigger a return to a previous phase. The analysis and design phases are divided into several steps, as described in the following discussion.

systems analysis The early steps in the systems development process, to define the requirements of the proposed system and determine its feasibility.

Analysis

The systems analysis phase is a five-step process (summarized in Figure 11.3) that is designed to answer these questions:

Investigation

- What is the business process that the system is to support?
- What business opportunity do you want the system to seize, what problems do you want it to solve, or what directive must you fulfil?

Figure 11.2 The systems development life cycle

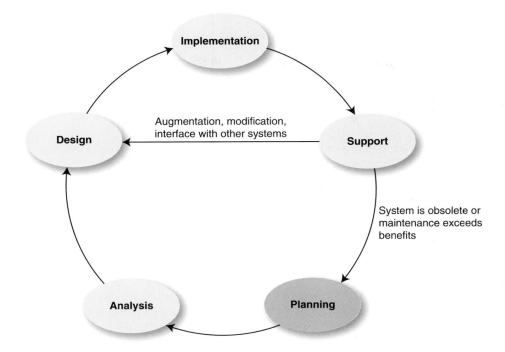

Figure 11.3 Phases in systems analysis

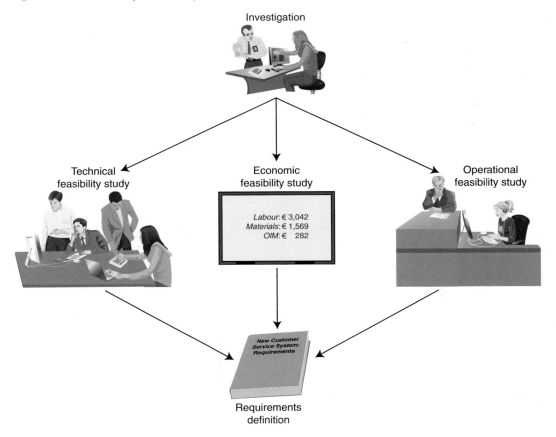

Technical feasibility study

- Is there technology to create the system you want?

Economic feasibility study

- What resources do you need to implement the system?
- Will the system's benefits outweigh its costs?

Operational feasibility study

- Will the system be used appropriately by its intended users (employees, customers, suppliers)?
- Will the system be used to its full capacity?

Requirements definition

- What features do you want the system to have?
- What interfaces will the system have with other systems?

Investigation The first step in systems analysis is investigation, which determines whether there is a real need for a system and whether the system as conceived is feasible. Usually, a small *ad hoc* team – consisting of a representative of the sponsoring executive, one or two systems analysts and representatives of business units would use the new system or be affected by it – is put together to perform a quick preliminary investigation.

The team spends time with employees at their workstations to learn firsthand about the way they currently carry out their duties, and interviews the workers about problems with the current system. This direct contact with users gives workers the opportunity to express their ideas about the way they would like a new IS to function to improve their work. The investigative team prepares a written report summarizing the information gathered. The team members also forward their own opinions on the need for a new system. They will not necessarily agree that a new system is justified.

feasibility studies A series of studies conducted to determine if a proposed information system can be built, and whether or not it will benefit the business; the series includes technical, economic and operational feasibility

If the preliminary report concludes that the business situation warrants investment in a new IS, a more comprehensive investigation might be authorized. The sponsoring executive selects members for a larger analysis team. Usually, members of the original team are included in this augmented group to conduct feasibility studies. The objective of the larger investigation team is to determine whether the proposed system is feasible technically, economically and operationally.

The technical feasibility study A new IS is technically feasible if its components exist or can be developed with available tools. The team must also consider the organization's existing commitments to hardware, software and telecommunications equipment. For example, if the company recently purchased hundreds of units of a certain computer, it is unlikely that management will approve the purchase of computers of another model for a single new application. Thus, the investigators must find out whether the proposed system can run properly on existing hardware.

cost/benefit analysis An evaluation of the costs incurred by an information system and the benefits gained by the system.

The economic feasibility study Like any project, the development of a new IS must be economically justified, so organizations conduct an economic feasibility study. That is, over the life of the system, the benefits must outweigh the costs. To this end, the analysts prepare a cost/benefit analysis, which can be a spreadsheet showing all the costs incurred by the system and all the benefits that are expected from its operation.

Table 11.1 Estimated benefits and costs of an IS (€ 000)

Year	2007	2008	2009	2010	2011	2012
Benefits						
Increase in sales			56,000	45,000	30,000	10,000
Reduction in staff			20,000	20,000	20,000	20,000
Total Benefits	0	0	76,000	65,000	50,000	30,000
Costs						
Analysis	15,000					
Design	37,500					
Implementation	0	56,000				
Hardware	0	20,000				
Operation and maintenance	0	0	5,000	5,000	5,000	5,000
Total Costs	52,000	76,000	5,000	5,000	5,000	5,000
Difference	(−52,000)	(−76,000)	71,000	60,000	45,000	25,000
Discount at 5 per cent	(−49,524)	(−68,934)	61,332	49,362	32,259	18,657
Net present value for six years	43,152					

The most accurate method of economic analysis is the fully quantitative **return on investment (ROI)**, which is a calculation of the difference between the stream of benefits and the stream of costs over the life of the system, discounted by the applicable interest rate, as shown in Table 11.1. To find the ROI, the net present value of the system is calculated by combining the net present value of the costs of the system with the net present value of the benefits of the system, using calculations based on annual costs and benefits and using the appropriate interest rate. If the ROI is positive, the system is economically feasible, or cost-justified. Remember that during the time the system is developed, which might be several years, there are no benefits, only development costs. Operational costs during the system's life include software licence fees, maintenance personnel, telecommunications, power and computer-related supplies (such as hardware replacement, software upgrades and paper and toner purchases). If the system involves a website, the cost of revising and enhancing the site by webmasters and other professionals must also be included.

return on investment (ROI) A financial calculation of the difference between the stream of benefits and the stream of costs over the life of an information system; often used as a general term to indicate that an investment in an information system is recouped or smaller than the cost the system saves or the increase in revenue it brings about.

Table 11.1 presents a simplified example of a cost/benefit spreadsheet and analysis for a small system. Since the net present value of the system is positive (43,152,000 euro), and therefore the benefits exceed the investment, the development effort is economically justified. In the figure, in the year 2012, the net present value starts to diminish. As this value continues to diminish, the organization should consider creating a new system. If the system is not replaced or significantly upgraded, the existing system will become a drain on the organization over time.

Often, it is difficult to justify the cost of a new IS because too many of the benefits are *intangible*, that is, they cannot be quantified in monetary terms. Improved customer service, better decision-making, and a more enjoyable workplace are all benefits that might eventually increase profit but are very difficult to estimate in financial terms. This inability to measure benefits is especially true when the new IS is intended not merely to automate a manual process but to support a new business initiative or improve intellectual activities such as decision-making. For example, it is difficult to quantify the benefits of business intelligence (BI) and knowledge management (KM) systems. Software vendors often promote fast ROI as a selling point, and express it in terms of the short period of time over which the adopting organization can recoup the investment. Still, such claims are difficult, if not impossible, to demonstrate. Therefore, the economic incentive for investing in a new IS is often 'we must use it because our competitors use it' and a general expectation that the new IS will benefit the organization in at least one way.

The operational feasibility study   The purpose of the operational feasibility study is to determine whether the new system will be used as intended. More specifically, this analysis answers the following questions:

● Will the system fit into the culture of this organization?
● Will all the intended users use the system to its full capacity?
● Will the system interfere with company policies or statutory laws?

organizational culture
An umbrella term referring to the general tone of a corporate environment.

Organizational culture is an umbrella term referring to the general tone of the corporate environment. This includes issues such as tendency to share or not to share information among units and people, willingness to team-play and the proclivity of employees to experiment with new ideas and technologies. The development team must consider culture to ensure that the new system will fit the organization. For example, if the system will be used by telecommuters, the organization must be open to telecommunications via the Internet. The analysts must find out whether this need would compromise information security and confidentiality.

Another point the team considers is compliance with statutory regulations and company policy. For example, the record-keeping system the staff wants to use might violate customer privacy or risk the confidentiality of government contracts with the company. If these issues cannot be overcome at the outset, then the proposed system is not operationally feasible.

Requirements definition   When the analysts determine that the proposed system is feasible, the project team is installed. Management or the consulting firm nominates a project leader who puts together a project team to develop the system until it is ready for delivery. The team includes systems analysts, programmers and, often, representatives from the prospective group of users.

system requirements
The functions that an information system is expected to fulfil and the features through which it will perform its tasks.

One of the first pieces of information the analysts need to know is the system requirements. System requirements are the functions that the system is expected to fulfil and the features through which it will perform its tasks. In other words, system requirements are what the system should be able to do and the means by which it will fulfil its stated goal. This can be done through interviews, questionnaires, examination of documents and on-the-job observations.

Once facts are gathered, they are organized into a document detailing the system requirements, and the managers of the business unit, or business units, for which the system is to be developed often sign the document as a contract between them and the developers. This formal sign-off is a crucial milestone in the analysis process; if the requirements are not well defined, resources will be wasted or not budgeted for properly, and the completion of the project will be delayed.

Design

With a comprehensive list of requirements, the project team can begin the next step in systems development, designing the new system. The purpose of this phase is to devise the means to meet all the business requirements detailed in the requirements report. As indicated

Figure 11.4 Phases in systems design

Description of components

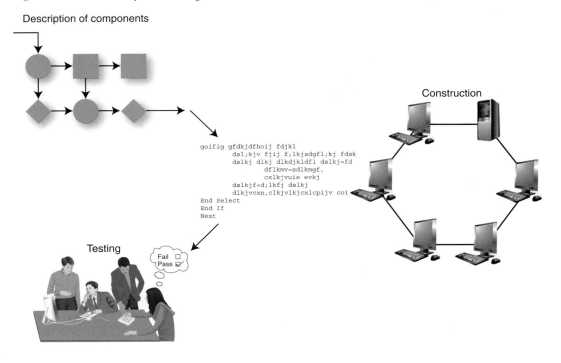

goifig gfdkjdfhoij fdjkl
    dsl;kjv fjij f;lkjsdgfl;kj fdsk
    dslkj dlkj dlkdjkldfl dslkj=fd
        dflkmv=sdlkmgf,
            cxlkjvuie evkj
    dslkjf=d;lkfj dslkj
    dlkjvcxn,clkjvlkjcxlcpijv coi
End Select
End If
Next

Construction

Testing

Fail ☐
Pass ☑

in Figure 11.4, **systems design** comprises three steps: a description of the components and how they will work, construction and testing. If the decision is to purchase ready-made software, the description of components becomes a description of how certain components will be adapted for the particular needs of the purchasing organization, and construction is the actual changes in programming code.

To communicate ideas about data, processes and information gleaned from data, systems analysts and programmers use conventions of symbols. The advantage of such conventions is that visual information can be grasped much faster and more accurately than text, much as a blueprint for a building conveys specifications more efficiently than the equivalent text. One such convention is the data flow diagram.

systems design The evaluation of alternative solutions to a business problem and the specification of hardware, software and communications technology for the selection solution.

Data flow diagrams A **data flow diagram (DFD)** is used to describe the flow of data in a business operation, using only four symbols for these elements: external entities, processes, data stores and the direction in which data flows (see Figure 11.5). *External entities* include individuals and groups of people who are external to the system, such as customers, employees, other departments in the organization or other organizations. A *process* is any event or sequence of events in which data are either changed or acted on, such as the processing of data into information or the application of data to decision-making. A *data store* is any form of data at rest, such as a filing cabinet or a database. Data flows from an external entity to a process, from a process to a data store, from a data store to a process, and so on. Thus, a carefully drawn DFD can provide a useful representation of a system, whether existing or planned.

The use of only four symbols and the simplicity of DFDs are their great advantage. Often, systems analysts produce several levels of DFDs for a system. The highest level contains the

data flow diagram (DFD) A graphical method to communicate the data flow in a business unit. Usually serves as a blueprint for a new information system in the development process. The DFD uses four symbols for entity, process, data store and data flow.

Figure 11.5 Data flow diagram symbols

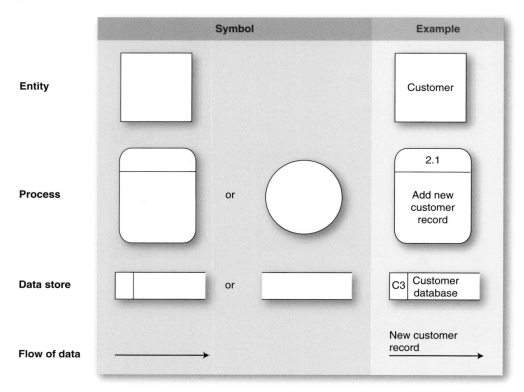

least number of symbols and is the least detailed. A lower level is more detailed; what might be represented only as a general process in the higher level is exploded into several sub-processes. The lowest-level diagram explodes some processes further and is the most de-tailed; it shows every possible process, data store and entity involved. Usually, the first- and second-level diagrams are presented to non-IS executives, and the lowest-level DFD is consid-ered by the IS professionals while they analyse or develop the system.

The DFD in Figure 11.6 shows a process of calculating a sales bonus. A salesclerk is an en-tity entering data (in this case, salespeople's ID numbers), which flows into a process, namely, the bonus calculation, which also receives data from the salespeople database (in this case, the amount each salesperson sold over the past year). The result of the process, the bonus amount for each salesperson, is information that flows into a bonus file. Later, the company's con-troller will use the information to generate bonus payments.

DFD symbols are suitable for describing any IS, even if it is not computer-based. A DFD of the existing system helps pinpoint its weaknesses by describing the flow of data graphically and allowing analysts to pinpoint which processes and databases can be automated, shared by different processes, or otherwise changed to strengthen the IS. If a new IS is needed, a DFD of the conceptualized new system is drawn to provide the logical blueprint for its construction.

While DFDs are easy to learn and use, they have shortcomings – like any diagramming method – and cannot describe a system completely. For example, they do not specify computa-tions within a process or timing relationships among data flows. A payroll DFD, for instance, cannot specify whether employee timesheets are checked as they are submitted or at the end of the week. Such details usually accompany DFDs as textual process descriptions often in struc-tured English to avoid ambiguity.

Figure 11.6 A DFD of a sales bonus system

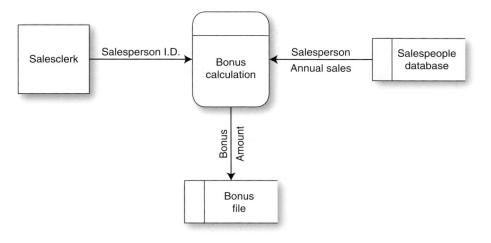

Unified Modelling Language (UML) As an increasing number of developed applications became object-oriented, a new way to describe desired software was needed. Several diagramming sets were developed by the 1970s, but in the late-1990s a *de facto* standard emerged: UML. Unified Modelling Language (UML) is a graphical standard for visualizing, specifying and documenting software. It helps developers to communicate and logically validate desired features in the design phases of software development projects. It is independent of particular programming languages, but it does provide standard visual symbols and notations for specifying object-oriented elements, such as classes and procedures. It also provides symbols to communicate software that is used for constructing websites and web-based activities, such as selecting items from an online catalogue and executing online payments.

UML consists of diagrams that describe the following types of software: use case, class, interaction, state, activity and physical components. A use case is an activity that the system executes in response to a user. A user is referred to as an 'actor'. Use case diagrams communicate the relationships between actors and use cases. Class diagrams describe class structure and contents and use the three-part symbol for class: name, attributes and methods. Interaction diagrams describe interactions of objects and the sequence of their activities. State charts communicate the states through which objects pass, as well as the objects' responses to signals (called stimuli) they receive. Activity diagrams represent highly active states that are triggered by completion of the actions of other states; therefore, they focus on internal processing. Physical diagrams are high-level descriptions of software modules. They consist of components diagrams, which describe the software, including source code, compilation and execution; and deployment diagrams, which describe the configuration of software components when they are executed. Figure 11.7 shows an example of modelling in UML.

Unified Modelling Language (UML) An extensive standard for graphically representing elements of programming, specifically accommodating programming in object-oriented languages and web technologies.

Construction Once the software development tools are chosen, the construction of the system begins. System construction is predominantly programming. Professional programmers translate input, output and processes, as described in data flow diagrams, into programs. The effort often takes months or even years (in which case the users might not be served well due to changes in business needs). When a program module is completed, it is tested. Testing is performed by way of walk-through and simulation.

In a walk-through, the systems analysts and programmers follow the logic of the program, conduct processes that the system is programmed to execute when running, produce output and compare output with what they know the results should be. In simulation, the team

Figure 11.7 A sample UML model and its explanation

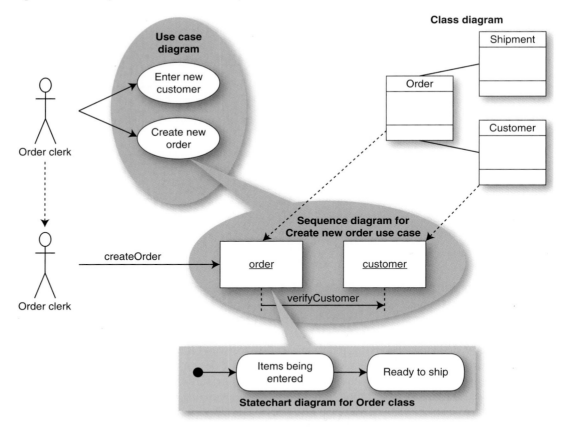

actually runs the program with these data. When all the modules of the application are completed and successfully tested, the modules are integrated into one coherent program.

System testing Although simulation with each module provides some testing, it is important to test the entire integrated system. The system is checked against the system requirements originally defined in the analysis phase by running typical data through the system. The quality of the output is examined, and processing times are measured to ensure that the original requirements are met.

Testing should include attempts to get the system to fail, by violating processing and security controls. The testers should try to 'outsmart' the system, entering unreasonable data and trying to access files that should not be accessed directly by some users or – under certain circumstances – by any user. This violation of typical operating rules is a crucial step in the development effort, because many unforeseen snags can be discovered and fixed before the system is introduced for daily use. If the new system passes the tests, it is ready for implementation in the business units that will use it.

Testing tends to be the least respected phase in systems development. Too often project managers who are under time pressure to deliver a new IS either hasten testing or forgo it altogether. Because it is the last phase before delivery of the new system, it is the natural 'victim' when time and budget have run out. This rush has caused many failures and, eventually, longer delays than if the system had undergone comprehensive testing. A thorough testing phase might delay delivery, but it drastically reduces the probability that flaws will be discovered only after the new system is delivered.

Implementation

The *implementation* of a new IS, also called delivery, consists of two steps: conversion and training. Although training might precede conversion, if training is done on the job it can occur after conversion. Conversion takes place when an operation switches from using an old system to using a new system. Conversion can be a difficult time for an organization. Operators need to get used to new systems, and even though the system might have been thoroughly tested, conversion can hold some unpleasant surprises if certain bugs or problems have not been discovered earlier. Services to other departments and to customers might be delayed, and data might be lost. There are four basic conversion strategies to manage the transition (see Figure 11.8).

conversion The process of abandoning an old information system and implementing a new one.

Parallel conversion In parallel conversion, the old system is used along with the new system for a predetermined period of time. This duplication minimizes risk because if the new system fails, operations are not stopped and no damage is caused to the organization. However, parallel conversion is costly because of the expenses, especially labour costs, associated with running two systems.

parallel conversion Using an old information system along with a new system for a predetermined period of time before relying only on the new one.

Figure 11.8 Strategies used to convert from one IS to another

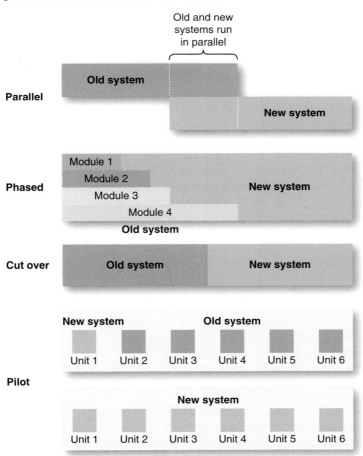

Industry **SNAPSHOT**

Image is everything

The Moscow Narodny Bank (MNB) is the UK's only Russian-owned bank and was established in the City of London in 1919. With offices in London, Moscow, Singapore and Beijing, it handles finance for the import and export of a wide range of products. The business involves the handling of complex and large documents (up to 150 pages each), often with diagrams and charts. There was a need for software that could scan, store and search these documents. MNB turned to Hitec Laboratories who specialize in electronic document management systems, including DataStore®32 which enables the electronic archiving and subsequent retrieval of documents, integrating these with other textual information such as email and word-processed documents.

Implementation first involved the transfer of several thousand existing documents. This was undertaken outside normal working hours in order to minimize disruption. Both of the old and new systems were run in parallel while the project team completed integrity testing on the newly converted files.

At the same time MNB staff were able to become accustomed to working with electronic documents.

The DataStore system is now in regular use by over fifty MNB staff. The original paperwork is stored off site and retrieved only when it is needed for legal reasons.

SOURCE: www.hiteclabs.com

A London branch of the Moscow Narodny Bank.

Phased conversion ISs, especially large ones, can often be divided into functional modules and phased into operation one at a time, a process called phased conversion. For example, conversion of an accounting IS can be phased, with the accounts receivable module converted first, then the accounts payable, then the general ledger and so on. A supply chain management system might be implemented one module at a time: first, the customer order module, then the shipment module, then the inventory control module and so on, up to the collection module. This phased approach also reduces risk, although the benefits of using the entire integrated system are delayed. Also, users can learn how to use one module at a time, which is easier than learning the entire system at once. However, when parts of both systems are used, there might be data inconsistencies between the two.

> **phased conversion**
> Implementing a new information system one module at a time.

Cut-over conversion In a cut-over conversion, also called *direct changeover*, the old system is discarded and the new one takes over the entire business operation for which it was developed. This strategy is highly risky, but it can be inexpensive, if successful, because no resources are spent on running two systems in parallel, and the benefits of the entire new system are immediately realized.

> **cut-over conversion (direct changeover)** A swift switch from an old information system to the new.

Pilot conversion If the new system is to be used in more than one business unit, it might first be introduced for a period of time in a single unit, where problems can be addressed and the system can be polished before implementing it in the other business units. This trial conversion is also possible for systems shared by many departments and disparate sites, as is increasingly the case due to the growing popularity of intranets and extranets. Obviously,

Industry **SNAPSHOT**

Late delivery

A survey carried out by the Economist Intelligence Unit (EIU) has revealed that there is a strong link between late delivery of IT projects and the lowering of business profitability. Over 1000 IT professionals in the Americas, Europe, the Middle East and Asia Pacific were surveyed and it seems that more than 25 per cent of IT projects are delivered late. Denis McCauley, director Global Technology Research for EIU, reflects that 'In business, speed is increasingly of the essence. It is cause for alarm then that so many of those surveyed deliver projects late.'

SOURCE: Miya Knights, 'Few IT projects run to time', http://www.cio.co.uk/news/index.cfm?articleid=1434

piloting reduces risks because it confines any problems to fewer units. It is especially useful for determining how comfortable staff members and other users, such as suppliers and customers, are with a new system, a lesson that can be applied to the later units. As with the parallel strategy, the pilot strategy means that benefits of the full implementation of the system are delayed.

When a system is developed by a software vendor for a wide market rather than for a specific client, conversion often takes place at beta sites. A beta site is an organization whose management agrees to test the new system for several months and provide feedback.

> **piloting** A trial conversion in which a new information system is introduced in one business unit before introducing it in others.

> **beta site** An organization that agrees to use a new application for a specific period and report errors and unsatisfactory features to the developer in return for free use and support.

Support

The role of IT professionals does not end with the delivery of the new system. They must support it and ensure that users can operate it satisfactorily. Support includes two main responsibilities: maintenance and user help. Maintenance consists of post-implementation debugging and updating (making changes and additions), including adding features that were originally desired but later postponed so budget and time limits could be met. Usually, updating is the greater effort.

> **support** The maintenance and provision for user help on an information system.

Debugging is the correction of bugs or problems in programs that were not discovered during tests. Updating is revising the system to comply with changing business needs that occur after the implementation phase. For example, if a company collects personal data for market analysis, managers might want to use the new IS to collect more data, which might require new fields in the databases.

Although maintenance is viewed by IS professionals as lacking in glamour, it should not be taken lightly or left to less-experienced professionals. Company surveys show that up to 80 per cent of IS budgets is spent on maintenance, the cost of which varies widely from system to system. The major reason for this huge proportion is that support is the longest phase in a system's life cycle. While development takes several months to about three years, the system is expected to yield benefits over many years.

Efficient and effective system maintenance is possible only if good documentation is written while the system is being developed, and if the code is written in a structured, easy-to-follow manner. Documentation consists of three main types: paper books, electronic documents and in-program documentation. The latter covers non-executable comments in the code, seen only when reviewing the application's source code. You can see this type of documentation when you retrieve the source code of many web pages. In-program documentation briefly describes what each module of the program does and sometimes who developed it. Printed and electronic documentation are prepared both for programmers, who can better understand how to revise code, and for users who want to learn about the various features of the application.

Agile methods

While the full approach of the SDLC or similar waterfall methods are used to develop ISs, it is widely recognized that these methods are lengthy, expensive and inflexible. Systems developed on the SDLC model are often unable to adapt to vague or rapidly changing user requirements. To overcome these challenges, alternative methods have emerged that are collectively called agile methods. As Figure 11.9 illustrates, agile methods treat software development as a series of contacts with users, with the goal of fast development of software to satisfy user requirements, and improving the software shortly after users request modifications. Agile methods make extensive use of iterative programming, involving users often and keeping programmers open to modifications while the development is still under way. The better known methods are Extreme Programming (XP), Adaptive Software Development (ASD), Lean Development (LD), Rational Unified Process (RUP), Feature Driven Development (FDD), Dynamic Systems Development Method (DSDM), Scrum and Crystal. XP is by far the most documented and best known of these methods.

agile methods Software development methods that emphasize constant communication with clients (end users) and fast development of code, as well as modifications as soon as they are needed.

The differences among the methods are outside the scope of this discussion. However, the major advantage of all agile methods is that they result in fast development of applications so that users can have them within weeks rather than months or years. Users do not have to wait long for modifications of the systems, whether the modifications are required because of programmer errors or because users have second thoughts about some features.

However, the benefits of agile methods do not come without risks. First, the analysis phase is minimal or is sometimes eliminated completely. Reducing or skipping a thorough formal analysis increases the risk of incompatibilities and other unforeseen mishaps. Also, the developers devote most of their time to construction and little time to documentation, so modification at a later date can be extremely time-consuming, if not impossible. Because of the

Figure 11.9 Agile methods emphasize continuous improvement based on user requests

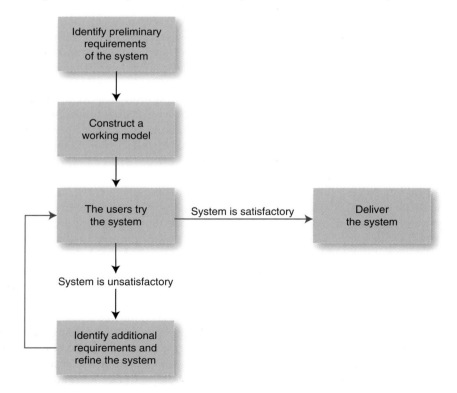

inherent risks, there are times when agile methods are appropriate and others when they are not (see the discussion later in this section).

Software developers who espouse the approach usually subscribe to the *Manifesto for Agile Software Development*, which expresses priorities: individuals and interactions over processes and tools; working software over comprehensive documentation; customer collaboration over contract negotiation; and responding to change over following a plan. You can find the full Manifesto at http://agilemanifesto.org/principles.html. The software developed should primarily satisfy users, not business processes, because users must be satisfied with the applications they use even if that means changing processes. While program documentation is important, it should not come at the expense of well-working software, especially when time is limited and the programmers must decide how to allot their time, on better software or on better documentation. The customers of software development, the users, are not an adverse party and should not be negotiated with but regarded as co-developers and co-owners of the software. Plans are good but might stand in the way of necessary changes. Responding to changing user requirements is more important than following a plan. If there is a development plan at all, it is fine to change it often.

All agile methods aim to have 'light but sufficient' development processes. Therefore, project teams avoid use of formal project management plans, financial spreadsheets for budgeting, task lists, or any other activity that does not directly contribute to development of a functioning application.

While the SDLC or any other waterfall approach requires users to sign off on their requirements and then wait for the system to be completed, agile methods encourage users' involvement throughout the process and encourage developers to change requirements in response to user input if needed. The purpose of agile methods is not to conform to a static contract with the users but to ensure that the users receive an application with which they are happy. To avoid costly redesign, agile methods encourage developers to test each module as soon as it is complete.

For example, Extreme Programming (XP) includes the following principles: produce the initial software within weeks (rather than months) to receive rapid feedback from users; invent simple solutions so there is less to change and necessary changes are easy to make; improve design quality continually, so that the next 'story' is less costly to implement; and test constantly to accomplish earlier, less expensive defect detection. (A *story* is a requirement or set of requirements delivered by the users.) Instead of formal requirements, the developers encourage the users to give examples of how they would like to use the application in a certain business situation. Communication with users is highly informal and takes place on a daily basis.

Unlike more traditional methods, agile methods encourage two programmers to work on the same module of code on the same computer. This fosters constructive criticism and feedback. This is a major feature in XP. The constant communication between the two coders is meant to ensure cross-fertilization of ideas and high-quality software. The idea is that two minds working on the same code create synergy, and that two pairs of eyes are more likely to spot bugs than a single pair.

When to use agile methods

Agile methods are an efficient approach to development when a system is small, when it deals with unstructured problems and when the users cannot specify all the requirements at the start of the project. They are also useful when developing a user interface: the developers can save time by quickly developing the screens, icons and menus for users to evaluate instead of forcing the users to provide specifications.

When a system to be developed is small in scale, the risk involved in the lack of thorough analysis is minimal, partly because the investment of resources is small. (A small system is one that serves one person or a small group of employees. A large system is one that serves many employees, who might be accessing the system via a network from different sites.) If the small-system development takes longer than planned, the overall cost is still likely to be smaller than if a full SDLC were performed.

When users cannot communicate their requirements, either because they are not familiar with technological developments or because they find it hard to conceptualize the system's input and output files, processes and user interface, developers have no choice but to use agile methods. In this case the users are often able to communicate their requirements as the development proceeds. For example, it is easier for marketing personnel to evaluate web pages designed for a new electronic catalogue and promotion site than to describe in detail what they want before seeing anything. Without being shown actual examples, users often can offer little guidance beyond 'I will know it when I see it.' It is easier for future users to respond to screens, menus, procedures and other features developed by IT professionals than to provide a list of requirements for them.

When not to use agile methods

Agile methods might not be appropriate for all systems development. If a system is large or complex, or if it is designed to interface with other systems, using agile methods might pose too great a risk because the methods skip feasibility studies. Some experts do not recommend the use of agile methods for large systems because such systems require a significant investment of resources; therefore, system failure could entail great financial loss. The systematic approach of the SDLC is recommended if the system is complex and consists of many modules, because extra care must be applied in documenting requirements and the manner in which components will be integrated, to ensure smooth and successful development.

For the same reasons, use of agile methods should be avoided when a system is to be interfaced with other systems. The system requirements and integration must be analysed carefully, documented and carried out according to a plan agreed on by the users and developers before the design and construction phases start. This early consensus reduces the risk of incompatibility and damage to other, existing systems. Therefore, accounting ISs, large order-entry systems and payroll systems as whole systems are rarely developed under agile methods. Other factors that should encourage use of waterfall methods are the size of the development team, how often the application is expected to be modified, how critical it is in terms of affecting people's lives and critical organizational goals and how tight the development budget is.

Table 11.2 summarizes factors in deciding when and when not to use agile methods.

Table 11.2 When and when not to use agile methods

When to use agile methods	When not to use agile methods
Small-scale system	Large-scale system
System solving unstructured problems	Complex system
When it's difficult for users to specify system requirements	System with interfaces to other systems
When the development team is small and co-located	When the team is large or distributed in multiple sites
System requirements are dynamic	System requirements are fairly static
System will not put people and critical organization goals at risk	System will significantly affect people's well-being and critical organizational goals
Development project budget is tight	Development is well-funded

Ethical and Societal ISSUES

Should IS professionals be certified?

When organizations commit large amounts of money to developing systems, they count on IT professionals to provide high-quality systems that will fulfil their intended purposes without harming their businesses, their employees or their consumers. But the products of IT professionals often fail and cause serious damage. Some people argue that because of the high investment and high risk usually associated with systems development and operation, IT professionals, like other professionals, should be certified. These people argue that certification would minimize problems caused by ISs. Others argue that certification might stifle free competition and innovation, or even create a profession whose members will make it difficult to pass certification examinations so that current members can continue to enjoy high income.

Certification is meant to guarantee that the experts have passed tests that ensure their skills. The government or other authorized bodies are expected to license experts, thereby certifying which people have knowledge and skills in a particular discipline that are significantly greater than those of a layperson. Proponents of the measure argue that certification could reduce the malfunctioning of ISs.

Certification pros Some experts say certification could minimize the number and severity of IS malfunctions. Civil engineers must be certified to plan buildings and bridges. Doctors pass rigorous exams before they receive their licences and begin to practise without supervision. Public accountants must be licensed to perform audits. Lawyers must pass the bar exams to practise. Why, these people ask, should IS professionals be allowed to practise without licensing?

Software experts do possess all the characteristics of professionals. They work in a field that requires expertise, and the public and their clients usually are not qualified to evaluate their skills. Certification could help the following groups in their relationships with IT specialists:

- *Employers* often hire software professionals without knowing what they are getting. They count on the information included in the candidate's c.v. and, sometimes, on letters of recommendation. Mandatory certification might protect potential employers against charlatans. Also, certification would provide potential employers with information on a candidate's suitability for different levels of performance. For example, a professional might be qualified to participate in a systems development team but not to head the project team.

- *Clients* could benefit from mandatory certification even more. While employers can learn, in time, of the real capabilities of their personnel, businesses that hire consultants have no previous employment experience on which to rely.

- *Society* might enjoy fewer software-related failures. Only those who are qualified would be allowed to engage in development and maintenance of information systems, thereby improving the overall integrity of ISs. Certification is especially needed for those holding key development positions for systems whose impact on society is significant, such as medical ISs and software embedded in weapons systems.

Certification cons Two arguments are raised against mandatory certification:

- It is difficult, if not impossible, to devise a way to measure software development competence. For instance, there are many different methods for developing applications, and there is no proven advantage of one. A computer professional might be very experienced in one method but not in others. It would be unfair to disqualify that individual merely on this basis.

- Some argue that mandatory certification might create a 'closed shop' by using a single entry exam designed to admit very few people. In such a scenario, the status and income of those admitted would be enhanced at the expense of those excluded. With little fear of competition within the closed group, there is often little incentive to improve skills.

Where we operate now Currently, there is no mandatory certification of IT professionals. In fact, there isn't even agreement about who should be considered an IT professional. Some organizations, such as the British Computer Society (BCS), test and certify people who voluntarily take their tests. (About 60,000 people are members of the BCS, out of millions who consider themselves IT professionals.)

Some software companies certify analysts and programmers to install their companies' tools. However, there are no certification regulations for the world's IT professionals that are similar to those for many other professions.

Systems integration

Firms often must wrestle with highly distributed, heterogeneous environments populated with applications for special tasks, which cannot be accessed by systems used for other tasks. Often, the disparate systems cannot 'talk to each other' because they run on different operating systems (or, as IS professionals say, on different platforms).

systems integration
Interfacing several information systems.

Much of what IT professionals do is systems integration, rather than analysis and development of a stand-alone IS. Systems integration looks at the information needs of an entire organization, or at least of a major division of it. The analysts consider the existing, but often disparate, ISs and then produce a plan to integrate them so that data can flow more easily among different units of the organization and users can access different types of data via a single interface. Consequently, many IS service companies call themselves systems integrators. Systems integration has become increasingly important mainly because more and more ISs are linked to websites, because more legacy databases are integrated into new enterprise applications such as SCM and ERP systems and because of the growing linking of ISs between organizations (see Table 11.3). *Legacy systems* are old systems that organizations decide to continue to use because the investment in a new system would not justify the improved features or because the old systems have some advantage that cannot be obtained from newer systems.

Systems integration is often more challenging than systems development. In fact, some IT professionals regard systems development as a subspecialty of systems integration because the integrator must develop systems with an understanding of how data maintained in disparate systems can be efficiently retrieved and used for effective business processes, and because legacy systems must often be interfaced with recently acquired systems.

For example, marketing managers can have richer information for decision-making if they have easy access to accounting and financial data through their own marketing IS. The better the integration, the better they can incorporate this information into their marketing information.

Systems integrators must also be well versed in hardware and software issues, because different ISs often use incompatible hardware and software. Often, overcoming incompatibility issues is one of the most difficult aspects of integration. Consider business intelligence

Table 11.3 Situations calling for systems integration

Linking existing ISs to websites
Linking databases to websites
Interfacing legacy systems with new systems
Linking legacy databases with enterprise applications
Sharing information systems among organizations

Industry **SNAPSHOT**

Going for gold

The BCS is undertaking a promotional campaign to encourage IT professionals to not just become members of the organization but to 'go for gold' by working towards Chartered Information Technology Professional (CITP) status. The BCS chief executive, David Clarke, is quoted as saying, 'In common with other similar standards for professions such as accountants or surveyors, there is an increasing need for top-flight IT professionals to be measured against the industry "gold standard". True IT professionals with CITP status are seen as having high levels of technical skills coupled with business acumen and an ethical and accountable approach to the way they work. Chartered status, especially in an increasingly global market, helps IT professionals secure top jobs and gain more responsibility and rewards. It also helps both them and their organization to stay ahead of the competition.' Of the 60,000 BCS members worldwide, about a third of them have already attained CITP status.

SOURCE: 'BCS campaign encourages IT professionals to go for "Gold Standard" of chartered status', 6 June 2007, www.bcs.org

The home page of the BCS Chartered IT Professional Qualification.

systems, which were discussed in Chapter 10. The concept of extracting business intelligence from large data warehouses involves integration of several ISs. The challenges are great, and by some estimates more than half of all BI projects are never completed or fail to deliver all the expected features and benefits.

Systems integration has become increasingly complex because it now involves the ISs not only of a single organization but of several organizations. In the era of extranets, the challenge is many times more difficult because IT professionals must integrate systems of several different companies so that they can communicate and work well using telecommunications. Imagine how difficult it is to integrate disparate legacy systems of several companies. For this reason, companies often contract with highly experienced experts for such projects.

SUMMARY

IT planning is important especially because investing in IT is typically great and because of the high risk in implementing enterprise applications.

Standardization is often an important part of IT planning. Standardization helps save costs, provides efficient training and results in efficient support.

The systems development life cycle (SDLC) and other waterfall methods consist of well defined and carefully followed phases: analysis, design, implementation and support.

The purpose of systems analysis is to determine what needs the system will satisfy.

Feasibility studies determine whether developing the system is possible and desirable from a number of viewpoints. The technical feasibility study examines the technical state of the art to ensure that the hardware and software exist to build the system. The economic feasibility study weighs the benefits of the system against its cost. The operational feasibility study determines whether the system will fit the organizational culture and be used to full capacity.

System requirements detail the features the users need in the new system.

In systems design, developers outline the systems components graphically and construct the software. Tools such as data flow diagrams and the Unified Modelling Language (UML) are used to create a model of the desired system.

Individual modules are tested during construction but it is also important to test the entire integrated system.

When the system is completed, it is implemented. Implementation includes training and conversion from the old system to the new system. Conversion can take place by one of several strategies: parallel, phased, cut-over or piloting.

The systems life cycle continues in the form of support. The system is maintained to ensure operability without fault and satisfaction of changing business needs.

Agile methods are a popular alternative to the traditional systems development life cycle. Agile methods place great emphasis on flexible requirements and frequent interaction with users. These methods skip detailed systems analysis and aim at delivering a new application in the shortest possible time.

Systems integration is often much more complicated than systems development because it requires the IT professionals to make different applications communicate with each other seamlessly. The complexity is multiplied when integrating ISs of several organizations that must work together over the Web.

Because of the great responsibility of IS professionals, the question of whether certification is needed has come up. If doctors, civil engineers, lawyers and public accountants are subject to mandatory certification, many people argue that IS professionals should be, too.

WORLDWIDE HOST REVISITED

Worldwide Host's TripExpert.com project team has been busy investigating opportunities for development of the new website. They are keeping strategic planning issues in mind as they learn more about options for the site.

What would you do?

The case at the beginning of the chapter lists Worldwide Host's corporate mission statement. From that statement, information given in the opening case, and the examples in the chapter, write a possible IS mission statement for Worldwide Host. Be sure to include information on IS's place in the organization and its chief contributions.

In what ways has the TripExpert.com team been dealing with systems integration, instead of systems development? Cite examples of systems that Worldwide Host is trying to integrate.

New perspectives

The TripExpert.com site is facing a time crunch. The chapter discussed agile methods as ways to speed development of information systems. Would these techniques work for the TripExpert.com project? Why or why not?

The database team overlooked a key new requirement for the database system. Could this mistake have been prevented? If so, how and at what stage of the systems development life cycle?

Review questions

1 Why is IT planning so important?

2 As part of their IT planning many organizations decide to standardize. What does standardization mean in this context, and what are its potential benefits?

3 Why is traditional systems development referred to as a 'cycle'? What determines the cycle's end?

4 Systems developers often use the term 'application development' rather than 'systems development'. Why?

5 What are the benefits using data flow diagrams?

6 SDLC is usually recommended for developing an IS that will be interfaced to other ISs. Give two examples of an IS that is interfaced with at least two other ISs.

7 Recall the discussion of IT professionals in Chapter 1. Of the following professionals, who does the majority of the systems construction job: the CIO, systems analyst, the database administrator (DBA) or the programmer? Why?

8 What are the advantages of agile methods over waterfall development methods, such as the traditional SDLC? What are the risks?

9 Why are agile methods so helpful when users cannot define system requirements?

10 An increasing number of IS professionals prefer to call the end users of their creations 'customers', even if the developers and users are employees of the same organization. Why?

11 What is systems integration?

12 Why is systems integration more complicated in the web era than before?

13 The emergence of the Web as a vehicle for business increased the need for systems integration. How so?

Discussion questions

1 The modern view of systems development is that it should be a continuation of IS planning. Why?

2 Consider a new chain of shoe stores. The marketing department of the company would like

to know the customers and their preferences. What questions would you ask before developing an IS for data collection and analysis?

3 The analysis phase of systems development includes fact-finding. Suggest ways to find facts, other than the ways mentioned in this chapter.

4 In data flow diagrams, a process is always labelled with an action, while entities and data stores are labelled with nouns. Why? Give two examples for each of these elements.

5 You are asked to recommend a conversion strategy for a new accounts receivable system. The system will be used only by the controller's office. Which strategy will you recommend, and why?

6 You are asked to recommend a conversion strategy for a new ERP system that includes accounting, sales, purchasing and payroll modules. Which strategy will you recommend, and why?

7 What are the elements that make the responsibilities of IT professionals similar to those of other professionals?

8 Do you support mandatory certification of IT professionals? Why or why not? If you do, which IT professionals (analysts, programmers, DBAs) would you require to pass tests? Why?

9 Many IT professionals say that trying to certify all specialists in this profession is impractical. Why?

10 Many software companies (such as Microsoft, Oracle and SAP) certify people as consultants for their products. For instance, you might become a certified SAP R/3 Technical Consultant. Is this type of certification the same, in principle, as the certification of a doctor, lawyer or accountant? Explain.

11 Suppose you are the IT director for a hospital. You have a small team that helps the medical and administrative staffs with their computers and applications, but when a new system must be developed, you must hire IT professionals. How would you conduct your search for reliable IS developers? Whom would you contact, and what questions would you ask?

12 You are the CIO for a large university hospital. The medical staff of the oncology ward would like to build an expert system for diagnosis. Your preliminary review shows that the financial investment would be great. What questions do you ask (of both the doctors and your staff) to decide whether to use a thorough SDLC or agile methods to develop the system? List and explain your questions.

13 You are trying to explain to your supervisor the general details of a proposed IS. The IS involves a server connecting many PCs. Your supervisor is not an IS professional and has no idea what a DFD is. How would you prefer to communicate your ideas: verbally; in writing, but without diagrams; with a DFD; or with a combination of some or all of these means? Explain your choice.

14 During development of a new IS, professional jargon might facilitate communication among IS professionals, but it might be detrimental when used to communicate with users. Explain.

Tutorial activities

1 Prepare a ten-minute software-based presentation (use PowerPoint or another application) to make a presentation on the topic: 'Factors that have made IS planning difficult over the past five years.' Include in your presentation developments in hardware, software and telecommunications; globalization; the Internet; the IT labour force; and any other area that has had an impact on IT planning.

2 You were hired as an IS consultant by a small chain of stores that rents domestic appliances. Partly because operations are run with paper records, one store does not know what is going on in the other stores. The owner of this small company thinks that the chain doesn't utilize its inventory efficiently. For example, if a customer needs a lawnmower and the appliance is not available in store A, the salespeople cannot tell the customer if the mower is available at another outlet or offer to bring it for the customer from another outlet. The owner would like an IS that would allow the chain to serve the customers better and that would help with tracking and billing, too. She would like to take advantage of the Web to help both employees and customers. Both should know what is available for rent and at which store at any given time. List the questions you would ask in your fact-finding effort and indicate who in the organization would be asked each question.

3 Assume you are the leader of a team that has just completed construction of a website that

provides information but also allows online purchasing of your company's products. Enumerate and explain the steps you would take to test the system. Prepare a software-based presentation (using PowerPoint or a similar application) to explain all the testing steps and why each must be taken. (*Hint*: Keep in mind different operating systems, web browsers, screen sizes and so forth.)

4   Prepare a DFD that describes the following application:

Gadgets, Inc., sells its items through travelling salespeople. When a salesperson receives a signed contract from a client, he or she enters the details into a notebook computer. The salesperson later transmits the record to the company's mainframe computer at its headquarters. The program records the details in four files: sales, shipping, accounts receivable and commissions. If the buyer is a new customer (one who is not yet in the customer database), the program enters the customer's record into the customer database and generates a thank-you letter. The program also calculates the 5 per cent commission, which is recorded in the commission file with the salesperson's code.

At the end of the month, the program produces a paper report with the records of all the new customers. In addition, if the total monthly sales of the salesperson exceed 100,000 euro, the program generates a congratulatory letter showing that total. If the total is less than 5,000 euro, the program produces a letter showing the total and the sentence: 'Try harder next month.'

5   Prepare a DFD that communicates the following business walk-up car rental scenario:

When a customer approaches the counter at Buggy Car Rental, a counter clerk asks the customer for the details of the desired car. He or she then checks in a computerized database to see whether a car with these features is available. If a car is available, the counter clerk collects pertinent information from the customer (including an imprint of the customer's credit card), fills out a contract and has the customer sign the contract. The customer is then given a key and is told where to find the car in the parking lot. The counter clerk indicates in the database that the car is no longer available. If a car with the desired specifications is not available, the counter clerk offers a car of a higher category at no extra charge. If such a car is not available either, the service person offers an available car of a lower category. The customer either rents it or refuses to rent it.

When the car is returned, the customer pays by cheque or by charging the credit card and returns the keys. The counter clerk gives the customer a copy of the signed contract, indicates in the database that the car is now available, and records its new mileage.

6   Team up with another student. Each of you should select a different agile method from the list appearing in this chapter. Each should write a one-page summary of the principles, benefits and shortcomings of the method. Then, sit together and write a one-page summary of the differences between the two methods along the three points.

7   Team up with another student to search the Web for tools that facilitate software development and choose three tools. List the features provided in each of the tools. Assume that the vendors' claims are true. Which phases and activities of the systems development life cycle does each tool support? Which would you prefer to use in systems development? Why? Prepare a five-minute software-based presentation (using PowerPoint or a similar application) to present your findings and explain your recommendations.

Companion CD questions

1   Use presentation software to create a presentation outlining the steps in IT project management.

2   Use spreadsheet software to re-create the table shown in Table 11.1, but change the amounts shown. Be sure your spreadsheet uses formulas where applicable.

Video questions

1   Visit Basecamp (http://www.basecamphq.com/). Give an example of a project for which you could use this tool.

2   How does this online project management tool compete with stand-alone project management software? Create a table comparing the features of Basecamp with at least two stand-alone project management programs.

From ideas to application
REAL CASES

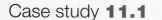

Case study 11.1

The NHS modernization project: another IT casualty?

BY PATRICIA BRITTEN

The United Kingdom's National Health Service (NHS) IT modernization project was the subject of a recent satirical sketch on a Channel 4 television programme that highlighted government mismanagement of computer projects. Problems with the project had also come to the notice of MPs. Questions were asked during a House of Commons debate on NHS finances about the progress of the NHS IT project by Liberal democrat MP Sandra Gidley who commented that the project 'seems to be dragging on somewhat, so far with little apparent benefit for patients'. Shadow Health Minister Stephen O'Brien has also said 'the NHS IT program was conceived in haste by a Prime Minister in need of a headline'. Critics have stated that those in charge of the NHS IT project 'made every mistake in the book'.

The first public signs of trouble came when leaked emails, written by officials leading plans for a technology-based modernization of the NHS, exposed one of the major flaws in the scheme, which was a separation between the IT and business sides of the project. On the IT side was Connecting for Health, an agency of the Department of Health, which had responsibility for delivering new national systems as part of a program costing between £2.3bn and £31bn. The agency's Chief Executive was Richard Granger, the senior responsible owner (SRO) of program delivery and systems within the national program for IT in the NHS.

It is not the content of the emails that is as important as the background to them, which highlights the very

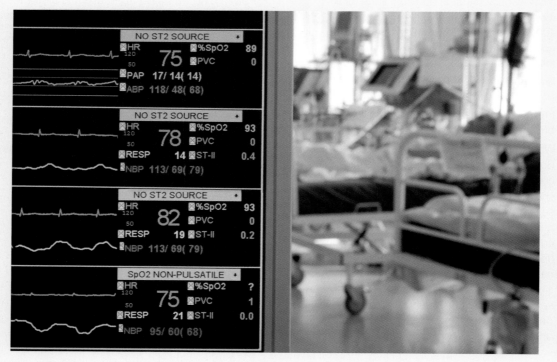

PHOTO SOURCE: © ANDREI MALOV

important human and political side of systems development projects. The email documents are mainly about 'Choose and Book' software but emphasize the implication of late changes on the IT program as a whole.

'Choose and Book' program

The 'Choose and Book' program is one of the principal components of the IT modernization project and aims to give patients a choice of which hospitals to attend for appointments. In his leaked email Granger defended the program's systems and expressed concern over late changes to the 'Choose and Book' program.

On the business side is the Department of Health, as represented by Margaret Edwards, Director of access and patient choice, whose duties include helping to give patients a choice of hospitals to attend for appointments through the so called 'Choose and Book' scheme, which is one of the government's top-10 priorities for the NHS.

The scheme is due to be complemented by a computer system that allows GPs and patients to book appointments online. This is due to replace the laborious process for arranging appointments in which a GP sends a 'referral' letter to the hospital, which later posts an appointment letter to the patient. The e-booking part of 'Choose and Book' is considered by the government to be critical to the scheme and so the software is a key component of the NHS IT program. In January 2005, the then Health Secretary, John Reid, said e-booking would be fully implemented by 2006, but the scheme was not now due to be fully rolled out until 2007 at the earliest, partly because hospitals and GPs do not have integrated systems that can talk to each other.

Late delivery of the system

Edwards' internal email in September 2005 expressed concern that the delivery of version 3.1 of 'Choose and Book' software might be late. Version 3.1 aims to extend patients' choice of hospitals they can attend. She said the Department of Health was committed to delivering extended choice from April 2006, but added that version 3.1 may not be ready in time. This version, she said, allows independent hospitals and Foundation Trusts to be added to the choice for patients. 'I have now been advised that 3.1 will not be available until "summer" 2006 and that this date is not yet guaranteed. "It might be later", said Edwards. At worst, she said, extended choice would have to be delayed. This would "clearly cause major problems both in terms of our political masters" commitments, the reaction of FTs (Foundation Trusts) and I assume the IS (independent sector)'.

In his response, Granger said changes with 'Choose and Book' could affect the wider national program. 'We have already delivered major software upgrades, after they were belatedly requested, on schedule', he said. Connecting for Health will of course do their best to accommodate additional requirements but this will have implications. Granger stated that; 'Strategic reprioritization will need to be undertaken across the program as a whole, for example deferral of electronic transmission of prescriptions, to focus on Choose and Book. Adverse media coverage is unavoidable.' Granger said there was no contract in place for version 3.1. He added, 'Unfortunately, your consistently late requests will not enable us to rescue the missed opportunities and targets. Choose and Book's £20 million IT build contract is now in grave danger of derailing, not just destabilizing, a £6.2 billion program.'

Troubled program

At one level the emails simply highlight a lack of harmony between the IT and business sides of the Choose and Book part of the NHS IT programme. At another level the emails are a possible symptom of something more profound, which is a project in deep trouble. The emails draw attention to the lack of any one person or organization that is responsible for the success or failure of the world's largest civil IT program.

Connecting for Health does not have full responsibility for ensuring that clinicians, for the benefit of patients, use the new systems that it commissions widely. John Bacon, overall SRO of the IT program, suggested to the House of Commons Public Accounts Committee on 31 October 2005 that Granger had never had full responsibility for the engagement of the wider community of clinicians. The scheme was configured, long before Granger was appointed in September 2002, for the IT professionals to achieve success in the delivery of systems, even if many clinicians remained sceptical and distrustful of the new technology and few used it to good effect.

On the business side, the government had given responsibility for ensuring the support of clinicians to the Modernization Agency of the Department of Health. The agency was disbanded in July 2005.

To make matters worse for the project, the people appointed by the government to run the business side have not stayed in the post long enough to see the project through. A project's SRO should remain in post from conception to delivery of benefits, according to the Office of Government Commerce, which advises departments on how to manage IT projects.

On the business side of the national project, the government first appointed John Pattison, an experienced Whitehall research specialist. After helping to set up the national IT program he retired. Pattison was replaced by Aiden Halligan as SRO responsible for engaging clinicians. Halligan announced in September 2004 his intention to leave. In March 2005, Bacon was appointed overall SRO.

'Choose and Book' software: risk factors and time delays

Changes in the requirements demanded by the Department of Health were seen as a major risk to the success of the 'Choose and Book' software in the scheme's business case drawn up in September 2003.

To mitigate the risks, the department simply noted that there existed as part of the contract 'strict change control mechanisms'. The business case added, 'The cost of changes will be borne by the national application service provider up to a maximum limit.'

Whitehall planned to have 205,000 appointments booked online by the end of 2004 but only 63 electronic bookings had been achieved by this date. By 26 October 2005, use of the 'Choose and Book' service had increased to only 20,287 bookings against a potential of 10 million appointments each year. Many of these 20,287 bookings were made by patients over the phone, with the 'Choose and Book' software performing only a limited role.

In October 2006 shadow Health Minister Stephen O'Brien called on the National Audit Office (NAO) to launch a full-scale probe into the project. An earlier report by the National Audit Office contained criticisms of the 'Choose and Book' scheme, and the e-booking support program. This additional inquiry had been scheduled for sometime in 2007 but so far no date has been set or the scope defined.

O'Brien also said that the government had failed to ensure that those in charge of the project had consulted widely enough and fully engaged users in the design and implementation of the new systems. Organizations such as the British Medical Association (BMA) have also complained about the lack of consultation with hospital doctors and GPs. This has led to serious disillusionment among NHS professionals and this will make the management of change very difficult since it depends on the goodwill of the end-users to succeed.

There is also much evidence to suggest that the original contracts were awarded on a least-cost basis, since IT contactors were encouraged to deliberately submit low cost bids to secure the business.

In October 2006, Accenture who were one of the major IT suppliers, withdrew from the project for its own financial health. This was due to expected future losses from continuing the work. This is a bad prognosis for the long-term health of the NHS project.

O'Brien expressed his opinion that Accenture's exit was a mark of the questionable procurement policy undertaken by the Department of Health, where suppliers were encouraged to bid for contracts at far lower prices than they could afford, in the name of saving money.

This is all too depressingly familiar and follows a similar pattern to a previous project undertaken by the London Ambulance Service to computerize its ambulance dispatch service in late 1992. This project was both technically and organizationally flawed, failed to consult end-users, was badly planned, involved unrealistically tight deadlines and awarded contracts to third-party suppliers on a least-cost basis. The project was finally cancelled, having cost in excess of £7.5 million. The NHS and the LAS appeared to have learned from their mistakes and developed a structured approach to the acquisition of IT called POISE (Procurement of Information Systems Effectively) that subsequently became widely used in the NHS. The project management methodology PRINCE 2 was also originally developed for use in large-scale government IT projects and this has now become widely adopted in many industries.

This makes the failure of the current NHS IT project even more surprising. What it does show is that adoption of a methodology does not in itself guarantee success and requires that the procedures and processes be adhered to. Clearly, they were not in this troubled NHS project and it is difficult to predict any remission for this latest IT casualty.

Case study questions

Critics said that those in charge of the NHS IT modernization project 'made every mistake in the book':

1 List those mistakes.

2 Allocate the mistakes to the appropriate stage of the systems development life cycle (SDLC).

3 Summarize what you would have done differently, if you had been in charge of the project. What would you advise Connecting for Health (in charge of the project) to do next?

SOURCE: Articles in *Computer Weekly* in November 2005, *MIS UK* in October 2006 and the *Guardian* newspaper in April 1994

Case study **11.2**

Choice's choices

In Chapter 7 you learned about Choice Hotels International B2B website as a successful enterprise. The company owns and franchises about 5000 hotels worldwide with almost 500 in Europe including the Comfort Inn, Quality and Clarion chains. In 1999 the company established ChoiceBuys.com, a website through which the independent hotel operators can purchase supplies. The combined purchasing power of all of these individual operators reduces costs for each hotel and adds a commission to Choice Hotels' coffers.

Things look bright now, but the road to success was paved with difficulties. Choice had to purchase, develop and redesign the website's software several times. Custom software development and customization of an existing application proved to be quite a challenge.

ChoiceBuys.com was based on software developed by a startup, and that software used to crash often. In 2000, a team of developers was formed to redevelop much of the software. The team used Macromedia ColdFusion, a software tool for developing web applications. The team experienced problems when the web application could not properly access the SQL server database. The system was unstable, performed slowly and was inflexible. The developers

The home page of Choice Hotels International's EMEA website.

then switched to a set of development tools from Rational Software Corp. (Rational Software was later purchased by IBM.) The Java application was to run on a UNIX server.

At this point the development team consisted of 15 contract programmers. Brad Douglas, Choice's vice president of emerging businesses, knew that to maintain the systems, more programmers would be required. He also recognized that his company was not a software development house but a hotel chain and franchiser. Therefore, he elected to find a software package that was ready to meet Choice's business needs. The team's leader, Nikole Smith, used the system requirements that the team had developed as the platform for a request for quotation from software vendors. Of the 24 vendors considered, one, Comergent, had a software package that met 85 per cent of Choice's requirements.

Even so, the software was not geared towards the type of relationship Choice had with its franchisees. It was developed to serve manufacturers who needed to support resellers of their products. The website functions more like an internal purchasing mechanism than a site to attract independent hotels that might choose to make their purchases through it. Choice's chief technology officer now admits that the website should have been better tailored to the needs of the clients rather than those of Choice.

In 2002, when the new software was launched at the website, Choice's revenue from it dropped slightly, from $12 million in 2001 to $11.8 million. The company hired Catalyst Design Group, a consulting firm, to investigate what was wrong with the site. The consulting firm sent representatives to five franchisees. They interviewed the owners and staff of five hotels, and watched purchasing officers as they were using the site. The consultants recorded their difficulties. The officers often got lost when looking for certain options.

Because the site's software generates a separate order for each supplier, the website software was designed to accommodate this mode of operations. To the hotels' purchasing staffs it seemed as if they were using a separate shopping cart for each item they wanted to order. They had grown used to the standard implemented by Amazon.com and other retailers: select and drop as many items as you want into the same shopping cart. Upon the consultants' recommendation, users now see a single shopping cart. The ordered items are then split internally into different orders for different suppliers.

There were other features to fix. The search mechanism did not filter enquiries well enough. Entering 'shampoo' resulted in a long list that included both hair shampoos and carpet shampoos. The site needed software that could help users better define and find the items they were seeking. There was no straightforward mechanism for comparing prices of products of different manufacturers. Comergent and Choice placed an emphasis on helping the hotels create lists of frequently ordered items to shorten the selection process, but the emphasis on this feature overshadowed other features and actually distracted users when they wanted to browse and search.

Redesigning the site's software yielded positive results. The number of hotels using the site rose 13 per cent from 2003 to 2004, and the number of orders increased by 14 per cent. Despite the challenges with the software, the idea of establishing a website for the Partner Services Division proved itself. In 1998, before the site was established, the division's revenue from commissions was $6.4 million. In 2004 it was $14 million.

Counting on the successful website, management decided to start selling its e-commerce expertise. To this end management established PrimarySource.com, a subsidiary that offers hotels outside its franchise chain access to the same purchasing system. Partner Services Technology is the division that operates the site. The first client outside Choice's chain was VGM Club, an organization that makes purchases for 3000 golf and country clubs. This would almost double the buying power of the enterprise, which already serves 3800 hotels.

Thinking about the case

1 Did Choice follow the SDLC method of software development? Did it use an agile method? Explain.

2 Knowing now what has happened during the period 1999–2004, what would you do differently in designing the implementation of the website?

3 If you were Choice's CIO, would you decide to purchase software (as the company did twice), or would you have it custom-developed? Why?

4 Do you think Choice could have done what Catalyst did with the same effectiveness?

5 Should Choice have hired a company such as Catalyst at an earlier time (say, 1999, before the website was launched)? Why or why not?

SOURCES: D. F. Carr, 'Choice Hotels: Supplies and Demand', *Baseline* (www.baselinemag.com), 23 May 2005; www.primarysource.com, 2005; www.comergent.com/customers/customer2/choice_hotels.cfm, 2005

Case study **11.3**

Short-term planning drives IT purchases for SMEs

BY DANNY BRADBURY

Small businesses are constrained by cash flow considerations and the need to purchase IT equipment on an ad hoc basis to meet volatile conditions, says Danny Bradbury.

Small and mid-sized enterprises (SMEs) have their own particular ways of buying IT – which are quite different from the large enterprises that dedicate entire departments to procurement.

According to a survey of 567 small businesses conducted recently by silicon.com and the Bathwick Group, roughly half of all small businesses buy their technology from a reseller, with another 31 per cent buying directly online from the vendor.

One such reseller is WStore, which sells servers, networking equipment and software to its client base. Stewart Hayward, commercial director for the company, says: 'They always want the product quickly. A lot of them don't believe in forward planning, so an SME might buy new PCs but then forget about the networking and probably the cables too.'

The home page of wstore.co.uk.

As small businesses struggle to manage rapid growth and cash flow, long-term IT planning is often not an option. Consequently, resellers such as WStore have to work around them. When buying equipment that is seen as complex (such as networking, which is still seen as something of a black art even today), Hayward finds that small businesses tend to be very loyal and purchase what they know and trust.

'We won't sell Hewlett-Packard into an installed base of Cisco', he explains. On the other hand small businesses are less loyal about their PCs. For such commodity items which are well understood they will often buy on price and convenience, rather than brand name.

This resonates with the results of the survey, which suggest that roughly half of small businesses consider the suitability of a system for a particular purpose to be the most important buying criteria, with 27 per cent believing that cost is the most important factor in such decisions.

It is not surprising that price ranks so highly in small business purchase criteria. Smaller companies often find cash flow to be a particular issue. Responsewave, a small marketing company operating internationally, is a case in point. Managing director Henrik Mandal says: 'Cash flow can be a big problem. One machine with its software on it can be several thousand pounds. If you need 50 machines that's a lot of money you have to put up.'

Consequently Mandal has learned to innovate in his IT procurement. He makes use of leasing agreements when buying his equipment directly from Dell. This allows him to make monthly payments and amortize his investment in IT over a number of years. Because he has no dedicated IT person, this also makes it easier to him to manage technology, which represents only a small portion of his responsibility in the company.

In keeping with this approach, he also uses hosted services for tasks like customer relationship management (CRM), instead of software applications loaded on his own servers. This helps him to keep his IT payments regulated and his management headaches down. The same goes for the server hardware, which he gets on a leased basis from his ISP. It makes it easy to plan his IT budget ahead, he says.

When small businesses do purchase PCs outright, they tend to work them into the ground, getting every last bit of value out of them before replacing the equipment, says WStore's Hayward. They will upgrade PC components repeatedly rather than throw them out and buy new ones every three years, as some larger companies do.

This is certainly the case with Chris Harman, director of IT and operations at magazine publisher Newhall Publications. Harman uses Citrix to centralize his applications, which means he can use older PCs as dumb clients. He is still using desktop PCs from 1997 and is only now upgrading them with flat screens. For both servers and new PCs, he buys any new thin client or flat screen equipment directly online.

Harman uses XDA mobile phones from O2 to hook his salespeople into a hosted third-party web-based application that manages subscription details. He purchased all of the XDAs directly from O2, something which doesn't surprise the mobile operator's head of business acquisition Peter Rampling. For basic voice telephony products, 70 per cent of businesses with fewer than 200 users purchase from small, independent retailers, he points out. 'The interesting thing is that it's a different story when you look at more complex products providing data services', he adds. 'When it comes to Blackberrys and XDAs, the majority of businesses buy from us as a network.'

Companies seem to draw a line between low-value, commodity equipment and high-value items such as latest-generation data phones and value-added services. When dealing with software suppliers who are adding value, Harman has noticed the suppliers tend to avoid selling commodity products such as servers because they make no margin on it and it is simply an inconvenience for them. 'Two or three people that we've had quotes from tell us to source the PC and they'll come in and configure it and install their solution', he says.

As for where SMEs buy IT, a lack of planning, a focus on cost and the need to adapt quickly to volatile conditions push many small-business purchases through commodity outlets such as the Internet or through commodity resellers or retail outlets.

Higher-end value-added resellers that provide support and service contracts will step in when small businesses need independent expertise to help them set up their systems and networks.

Meanwhile subscription-based software-as-a-service models and leasing agreements are a good way for SMEs to regulate cash flow, while third-party hosted software, although still suffering from the damage to its image inflicted by the dot-com crash, is nevertheless proving more attractive to small businesses that want to outsource the management headaches of IT, while planning their IT budget more effectively.

Thinking about the case

1 Why is there such a marked difference between IT purchasing policy for SMEs and that for large enterprises?

2 The passage suggests that SMEs tend to replace/upgrade components of a PC rather than get rid of it and replace it with a newer model. Is this a sensible approach?

Choices in systems acquisition

Developing systems in-house or commissioning a software development firm is the most expensive way to acquire ISs. Other alternatives might be less expensive and offer different benefits. Some of the alternatives have been mentioned in previous chapters, but they are discussed in more depth here and will provide a deeper understanding of systems acquisition.

When you finish this chapter, you will able to:

Explain the differences among the alternatives to tailored system development: outsourcing, licensing ready-made software, contracting with an application service provider and encouraging users to develop their own applications.

List the business trade-offs inherent in the various methods of acquiring systems.

Describe which systems acquisition approach is appropriate for a particular set of circumstances.

Discuss organizational policies on employee computer use.

WORLDWIDE HOST

TAPPING OTHERS' EXPERTISE

Worldwide Host is a leader in the hotel industry, not in software development. CIO Michael Lloyd had convinced his executive team long ago that it made better financial sense for the hotel chain to contract with a software firm to develop or upgrade its information systems while he and his staff concentrated on hardware and day-to-day support. It took time, many interviews and the review of several proposals to find a firm that fit well with Worldwide's unique needs, but General Data Systems (GDS) fit the bill. That firm was a top-notch software developer with a long track record in the industry, and it provided the technical expertise that Worldwide needed to keep abreast of ever-changing technology. The partnership between the two firms allowed Worldwide to keep its IT staffing low and use GDS for help with new business needs and problems. The TripExpert.com website project was just the latest in the two firms' collaboration.

Adding another firm to the mix

Michael was meeting with GDS analysts Judith Keene and Colin Johnson to go over some decisions for the TripExpert.com website. Colin began reporting on his latest information concerning their plans to purchase a licence from Reservations Technologies for an existing reservation system developed for the Web.

'We ran benchmark tests on the system's performance, and it did provide the transaction response time we need on the Web. Its scalability is also good – it can handle projected peak customer demand. We repeated the tests several times with different sets of data, and it performed well. So, that system seems to be a good option for us', he said.

Michael interrupted. 'How long has this company been in business, and who else has used their system? I want to be sure they're reliable since we're staking a big part of Worldwide's future on the TripExpert site.'

'They've been around for about nine years – not long for a software company overall – but pretty old for a web software firm. I checked the background of some of their technical staff, and they received advanced degrees in computer science, artificial intelligence and electrical engineering from Manchester, Edinburgh and Durham Universities. Plus, they gained practical experience at other companies before launching their firm. They are well respected in the field', reported Colin.

'What about their clients?' Michael persisted.

'They've worked with quite a few airlines – GlobalAir, Svenska, Universal Airlines. North Trans, one of your airline partners, recommended them to me. We could set up a time to review some of their operations on-site, if that would make you feel more comfortable.'

'Great. I'd like to hear firsthand from their customers. Let's set that up in the next couple of weeks. I have some travel coming up over the next few months, so the sooner, the better.'

Fitting it all together

Judith asked, 'What about the additional functionalities that we need for TripExpert? Will GDS have to hire programmers for that purpose or will Reservations Technologies take care of it?'

'Their system was designed flexibly to allow easy modifications. They'll create the additional functionalities. The company also offers technical assistance as part of a licensing agreement, if we

need their help in modifying the system to tie into our existing reservations system', Colin responded.

'Speaking of the hotel reservation component, Judith, how are we coming on Worldwide's new system? Are we back on track after the database glitch?' Michael asked.

'We lost five weeks overall after we pulled additional staff in to work on the room rate discounting component. We'll keep trying to gain back a day or two wherever we can. But we need to maintain our quality standards. Also, we need to begin planning our training sessions for your travel division. I've been putting some materials together as we go.'

Michael laughed. 'Another task to add to my list – can't wait.'

Options and priorities

In Chapter 11 you learned about software development and that few companies develop their own ISs in-house. Recall, also, that 'systems' almost always means 'applications', and therefore the terms will be used interchangeably in this chapter, as in Chapter 11. There are generally four alternatives to in-house development, as illustrated in Figure 12.1: outsourcing, licensing, using the service of an application service provider (ASP) and having users develop the system. If an application of the desired features and quality can be obtained from more than one of these sources, then the major factor left to be considered is usually cost. The preference then would be to license, because of immediate availability and low cost. If the application cannot be licensed, the next choice would usually be to obtain use of the system from an ASP because the system is immediately available for use and the organization

Figure 12.1 Alternatives to in-house development of ISs

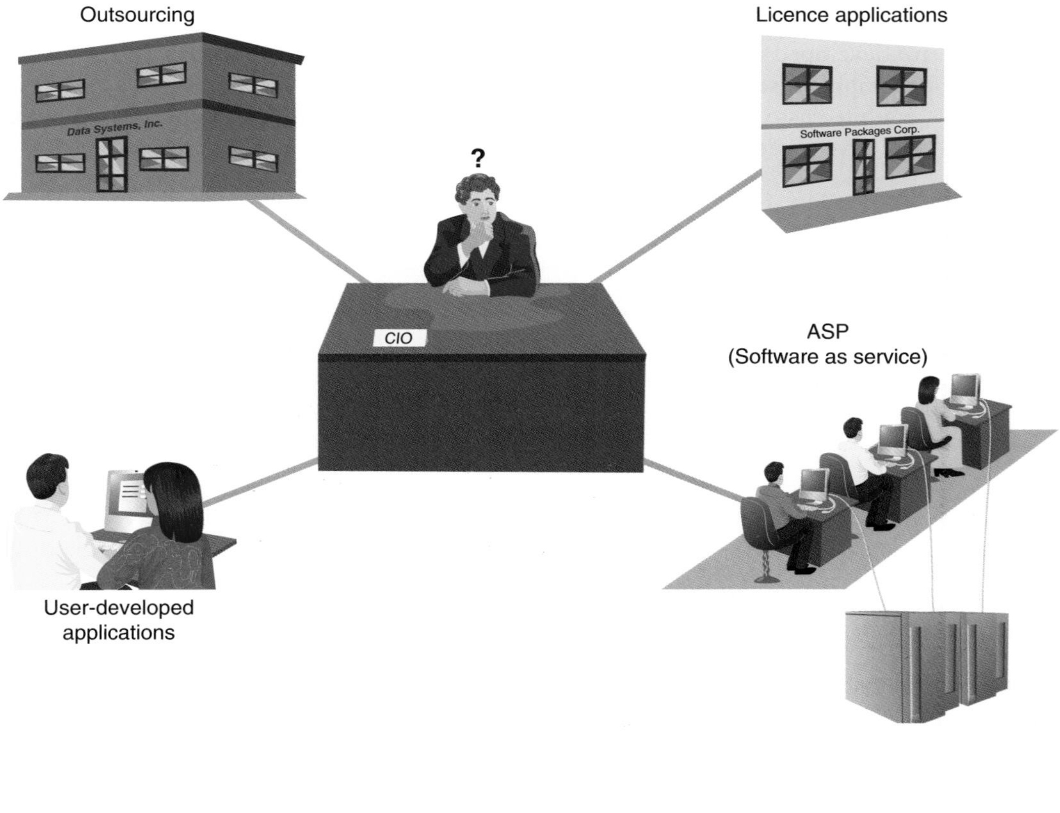

does not have to lay out a large sum up front for such use. If ASPs do not offer the desired IS and non-IT employees can develop it, then this would usually be the chosen alternative. If non-IT employees cannot develop the IS, the choice might then be to outsource the development of the IS. However, as you will see, outsourcing is a concept that might encompass more than just commissioning the development of an application.

There are many factors to be considered in addition to quality and cost. Therefore, these alternatives are not fully comparable, and often cannot be prioritized as simply as they have been here. The purpose of this discussion is to clarify the advantages and disadvantages of these options. As you will see, there are many factors that drive organizations to decide how they acquire ISs and the service that supports the maintenance and use of the systems.

Outsourcing

Outsourcing in general means hiring the services of another organization or individual to perform some of the work that otherwise would be performed by you or your employees. In the IT arena outsourcing has two meanings. One is to commission the development of an application to another organization, usually a company that specializes in the development of this type of application. The other is to hire the services of another company to manage all or parts of the services that otherwise would be rendered by an IT unit of the organization. The latter concept might not include development of new applications.

outsourcing Buying the services of an information service firm that undertakes some or all of the organization's IS operations.

Outsourcing custom-designed applications

Often, an organization has a need that no existing software can satisfy. For example, if the cost-accounting procedures of a particular company are so specific that no commercially available software can perform them, the company must develop custom-designed, or tailored, software. In recent years fewer and fewer companies have developed applications in-house. The majority of custom-designed applications are developed by companies that specialize in providing consulting and software development services to other businesses.

custom-designed (tailored) software Software designed to meet the specific needs of a particular organization or department; also called tailored software.

While custom-designed applications are more expensive than purchased ones, they have several advantages (see Table 12.1).

Table 12.1 Advantages and disadvantages of custom-designed applications

Advantages	Disadvantages
Good fit of features to business needs	High cost
Good fit of features to organizational culture	Long wait for development if IS personnel are busy with other projects
Personnel available for maintenance	Application may be too organization-specific to interface with systems of other organizations
Smooth interfaces with other information systems	
Availability of special security measures	
Potential for a strategic advantage	

- *Good fit to need*: The organization enjoys an application that meets its needs exactly, rather than settling for the near fit of a ready-made program.

- *Good fit to culture*: When custom-developing a system, developers are more sensitive to the organizational culture. Employees enjoy an application that fits their work. When licensing a packaged application, employees sometimes must change their work to accommodate the software.

- *Dedicated maintenance*: Because the programmers are easily accessible to the company, they are familiar with the programs and can provide customized software maintenance. Maintenance includes modification for business changes (including mergers with and acquisition of other organizations) and upgrading of the software when new technologies become available.

- *Smooth interface*: When a system is custom-made for an organization, special care can be taken to ensure that it has proper interfaces with other systems. The new system can communicate smoothly with those systems.

- *Specialized security*: Special security measures can be integrated into the application. Because the program is custom-designed, security measures are known only to the organization.

- *Potential for strategic advantage*: Recall from the discussion in Chapter 2, 'Strategic Uses of Information Systems', that companies gain a strategic advantage when they can employ an IS that their competitors do not have. A unique application might give a business a strategic advantage because it is the only business that can enjoy the application. For example, no CRM application can do for a business what an enterprise application that was developed specifically to serve its customers in a unique way can do.

The greatest disadvantage of tailored applications is their high cost. Tailored software development requires an organization to fund all development costs; in contrast, costs of developing off-the-shelf and other ready applications are distributed over a larger number of expected purchasers. Another disadvantage of custom-designed development is that the production schedule can be delayed because IS personnel might not be available for long periods. Another important downside is that custom-designed software is less likely to be compatible with other organizations' systems. If organizations with different tailor-made systems decide to link their systems, they might incur significant cost to modify one or both of the systems.

Clients of outsourced software development should also be aware of an inherent conflict of this option. On one hand they want the developing firm to conform to a contract that includes specific requirements of the software. On the other hand, specific requirements make the development effort inflexible and potentially costly: if the client company needs to change requirements as the development goes on, the developers might either refuse to deviate from the original requirements or might agree to make the changes for hefty additional charges. Contracts for outsourced software development might also be incompatible with some development methods, such as agile methods, discussed in Chapter 11. The essence of such methods is the clients' ability to request modified or new features as the development goes on, which might stand in stark contrast to the contract.

Many European and North American countries have outsourced development of well defined applications to professionals in other countries, an act often referred to as offshoring. Programmers in India, China and the Philippines earn a fraction of their colleagues in Western countries while often mastering the same level of skills. This might reduce the cost of development significantly. Offshoring has caused layoffs of programmers in clients' countries and created much bitterness among those professionals and supporters of local labour. However, this is part of the growing scope of economic globalization.

offshoring Outsourcing work to employees in other countries.

Industry **SNAPSHOT**

Global competition

India enjoys 44 per cent of the global market of out-sourced software development and back-office services (such as taking orders and tax prepara-tion). India's income from these activities was € 12.2 billion in the fiscal year ended in March 2005. It is not surprising that so many North American and West European countries outsource software develop-ment to India: the hourly rate of a software developer in India is about € 18 while the hourly rate in Europe and the United States and Europe is about € 45.

SOURCES: Associated Press, June 2005; neoIT (www.neoit.com), June 2005

PHOTO SOURCE: © MEDIACOLOR'S/ALAMY

CD TASK

Outsourcing IT services

A large number of businesses have turned to IT companies for long-term services: purchasing and maintaining hardware; developing, licensing and maintaining software; installing and maintaining communications networks; developing, maintaining and operating websites; staffing help desks, running IT daily operations, managing customer and supplier relations, and so on. An organization might use a combination of in-house and outsourced services. It might outsource the development of an IS, but then put its own employees in charge of its operation, or it might outsource both the development and operation of the system. When a business outsources only routine business processes, such as customer order entry or human resource transactions, the practice is sometimes called *business process outsourcing*. Note, however, that this term includes outsourcing many activities, whereas this discussion is lim-ited to only IT services.

In considering whether to outsource IT services, management should ask the following questions:

● What are our core business competencies? Of the business we conduct, what specialties should we continue to practise ourselves?

● What do we do outside our specialties that could be done better for us by organizations that specialize in that area?

● Which of our activities could be improved if we created an alliance with IT organizations?

● Which of our activities should we work to improve internally?

Many companies have come to realize that IT is not their core competency and should not be a focus of their efforts. In addition, the pace of developments in IT might require more expertise than is available within many organizations.

A growing portion of corporate IS budgets is allocated for purchased (outsourced) serv-ices. IT companies that made their reputation by providing hardware and software, such as IBM and Unisys, have seen the revenue from the outsourcing service portion of their business grow faster than the revenue from hardware and software sales. Among the largest IT service providers are IBM, EDS, Accenture, Computer Sciences Corp. (CSC), Unisys, First Data, AT&T, Capgemini and Hewlett-Packard. For the sake of simplicity and clarity here, such companies are called vendors, and the organizations to which they outsource are called

Table 12.2 Typical outsourced IT services

Application development and software maintenance

Hardware purchasing and hardware maintenance

Telecommunications installation and maintenance

Help desk services

Website design and maintenance

Staff training

clients. (Note that some trade journals prefer to refer to vendors as outsourcers.) Outsourcing is typically a long-term contractual relationship in which the vendor takes over some or all of the client's IT functions. Typical outsourced functions are listed in Table 12.2.

IT outsourcing contracts are typically signed for long periods of time, usually for seven to ten years. The sums of money involved are very large. For example, in March 2003 Motorola signed a ten-year, €1.14 billion contract with CSC to handle its IT infrastructure. Until 1 May 2003, when the contract became effective, Motorola handled all of its IT needs in-house. CSC now handles Motorola's worldwide midrange computers, desktop computers, telecommunications and data centres. IBM signed a ten-year, € 1.77 billion outsourcing contract with Deutsche Bank to take care of the bank's IT needs in eight European countries.

There is a peculiar – and paradoxical – aspect to IT outsourcing: while contracts are signed for long periods of time, they typically involve rapidly changing technologies. Vendors often agree to sign outsourcing contracts only if the period is at least five years because of the human resource commitment they have to make, but strategic IT plans – as discussed in Chapter 11 – are for only three to five years. As a result, clients sometimes find themselves bound by contracts that no longer satisfy their needs. They then try to renegotiate the contract. For example, in 2002 Boots the High Street chemist negotiated a ten-year outsourcing contract with IBM worth about € 1 billion. However in 2006, less than halfway through the contract, Boots renegotiated with IBM as they had found that the overhaul of their IT infrastructure, including chip and PIN and a new pharmacy system, had been completed early. Hence Boots wanted to reverse the outsourcing and transfer 100 of the IT jobs back in-house.

Why you should...

understand alternative avenues for the acquisition of information systems

As an increasing number of business activities are supported and enhanced by ISs, it is extremely important for organizations to acquire systems that best fit their needs and are available as soon as possible, and to minimize the cost of systems acquisition and maintenance of the systems. As explained in Chapter 11, employees should involve themselves in the process of deciding which ISs will be introduced into their business units and what features they will have. Since there are several ways to obtain ISs, professionals like you must understand the advantages and disadvantages of each. If you have a concern with a certain approach to acquire the system you need, you should voice it and be able to propose other options.

Advantages of outsourcing IT services

Clients contract for IT services to offload in-house responsibility and to better manage risks. When a client outsources, management knows how much the outsourced services will cost; thus, the risk of miscalculation is eliminated. But there are additional advantages that make the option attractive:

- *Improved financial planning*: Outsourcing allows a client to know exactly what the cost of its IS functions will be over the period of the contract, which is usually several years. This allows for better financial planning.

- *Reduced licence and maintenance fees*: Professional IS firms often pay discounted prices for CASE (computer-aided software engineering) tools and other resources, based on volume purchases; they can pass these savings on to their clients.

- *Increased attention to core business*: Letting outside experts manage IT frees executives from managing it. They can thus concentrate on the company's core business – including developing and marketing new products.

- *Shorter implementation cycles*: IT vendors can usually complete a new application project in less time than an in-house development team can, thanks to their experience with development projects of similar systems for other clients. (However, they are not likely to use less time if they lack experience with such systems).

Industry **SNAPSHOT**

Internet journalism

In 2002 Reuters, the worlds biggest news agency, established a corporate presence in Bangalore, India. Two years later it moved its IT database operations to the sub-continent. It now employs 1500 people to ensure the smooth running of the operation based on secure high-speed telecommunications.

Much of Reuters news reporting is financially oriented with significant numbers of news reports on the state of the US economy direct from Wall Street. However, most US companies put out their press releases and profit statements on the Internet. It seemed a logical step for Reuters to offshore some of their journalism to Bangalore. The local, highly trained journalist can access the information directly and in an appropriate time frame, by working shifts.

Quality assurance is obviously a big issue for a company like Reuters with a strong brand image. Training and education in cultural differences are paramount. They employed Kavita Chandran, a former Bloomberg employee. With her background of ten years in New York, together with Reuters experience in Hong Kong, she was able to spot difficulties in language and communication between New York and Bangalore.

'We have a bright, enthusiastic young staff, who are eager to learn about US markets. I encourage them to read the *New York Times* and *Wall Street Journal* online every day.'

The biggest problem faced by Reuters Bangalore is keeping staff. With the economic boom in India and deregulation of television, there has been a marked increase in financial journalism, both in print and on cable TV. Many are deserting Bangalore for India's financial capital, Mumbai.

SOURCE: Steve Schiffres, 'Here is the news from Bangalore', 2 February 2007, http://news.bbc.co.uk/1/hi/business/6289521.stm

Mumbai, India.

- *Reduction of personnel and fixed costs*: In-house IS salaries and benefits and expensive capital expenditures for items such as CASE tools are paid whether or not the IS staff is productive. IS firms, on the other hand, spread their fixed and overhead costs (office space, furnishings, systems development software and the like) over many projects and many clients, thereby decreasing the expense absorbed by any single client.

- *Increased access to highly qualified know-how*: Outsourcing allows clients to tap into one of the greatest assets of an IT vendor: experience gained through work with many clients in different environments.

- *Availability of ongoing consulting as part of standard support*: Most outsourcing contracts allow client companies to consult the vendor for all types of IT advice, which would otherwise be unavailable (or available only from a highly paid consultant). Such advice might include guidance on how to use a feature of a recently purchased application or on how to move data from one application to another.

As you can see, cost savings is only one reason to outsource IS functions. In fact, studies show that saving money is not the most common reason for outsourcing. Surveys have shown that executives expected several benefits from an outsourcing relationship. Figure 12.2 shows the most cited expectations, such as access to technological skills and industry expertise. To many executives, these expected benefits are more important than cost savings, especially in light of reports that in many cases outsourcing did not save the client money.

Figure 12.2 Expected benefits from IT outsourcing

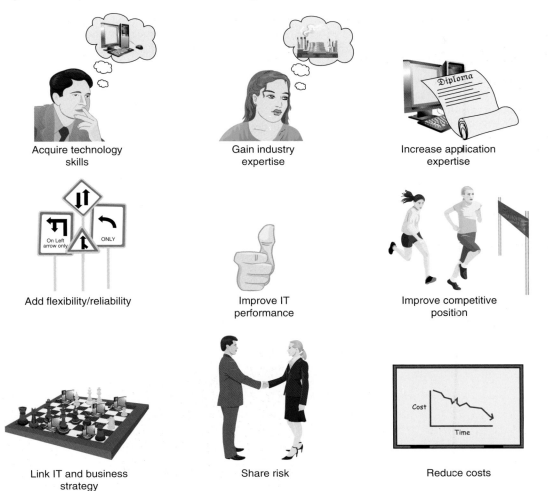

Acquire technology skills   Gain industry expertise   Increase application expertise

Add flexibility/reliability   Improve IT performance   Improve competitive position

Link IT and business strategy   Share risk   Reduce costs

Risks of outsourcing IT services

Despite its popularity, outsourcing is not a panacea and should be considered carefully before it is adopted. There are conditions under which organizations should avoid outsourcing. The major risks are as follows:

Loss of control A company that outsources a major part of its IS operations will probably be unable to regain control for a long time. The organization must evaluate the nature of the industry in which it operates. While outsourcing can be a good option in a relatively stable industry, it is highly risky in one that is quickly changing. Although the personnel of an IS service company might have the necessary IS technical skills, they might jeopardize the client's core business in the long run if they cannot adapt to constantly changing business realities in the client's industry. Sometimes when this problem becomes clear, the client might have disposed of all personnel who could react properly to such developments. Moreover, even if the client organization still employs qualified IT professionals, the vendor might object to their involvement in activities that, according to the outsourcing contract, are outside their jurisdiction.

Loss of experienced employees Outsourcing often involves transferring hundreds, or even thousands, of the organization's employees to the IS vendor. The organization that absorbs the workers can usually employ them with lower overhead expenses than their former employer and use their skills more productively. The client gets rid of this overhead cost, but it also gives up well trained personnel. In addition, if most of the vendor's personnel serving the client are the same employees that the client maintained until the outsourcing contract was signed, the company's ability to gain new expertise from outsourcing could be compromised.

Risks of losing a competitive advantage Innovative ISs, especially those intended to give their owners a competitive advantage, should not be outsourced. Outsourcing the development of strategic systems is a way of disclosing trade secrets. Confidentiality agreements can reduce, but never completely eliminate, the risk. A competitor might hire the same vendor to build an IS for the same purpose, thereby potentially eliminating the first client's advantage. In addition, assuming that these systems incorporate new business or technical concepts, vendors will bring less than their usual level of experience – and therefore fewer benefits – to the project. Outsourcing strategic or core business ISs incurs more risk than outsourcing the routine tasks of operational ISs (see Figure 12.3).

Figure 12.3 Risks of outsourcing are higher at higher levels of decision-making

Industry **SNAPSHOT**

Outsourcing SOX

After several corporate scandals, the United States Congress passed the Sarbanes-Oxley Corporate Governance Act in 2005. Corporations were given ample time to take the necessary steps to comply, some of which involve software that helps to prevent fraud and ensure accurate financial filings. The law, named after its authors, is popularly known as SOX. US corporations spent US$5.5 billion in 2004, and were likely to spend another US$5.8 billion in 2005, to comply with the new law. About a quarter of this sum was spent on software development and modification. Indian software companies have benefited tremendously. Apparently, much of the software engineering work is outsourced to companies in this country, which specialize in SOX-related software.

SOURCE: E. Bellman, 'A Cost of Sarbanes-Oxley: Outsourcing to India', *Wall Street Journal*, 14 July 2005

High price Despite careful pre-contract calculations, some companies find out that outsourcing costs them significantly more than they would have spent had they taken care of their own ISs or related services. Several clients have pressured vendors to renegotiate their outsourcing contracts or have found a way to terminate the contract because executives believed they could enjoy the same level of service, or higher-quality service, by maintaining a corporate IT staff. To minimize such unpleasant discoveries, the negotiating team must clearly define every service to be included in the arrangement, including the quality of personnel, service hours and the scope and quality of services rendered when new hardware and software are adopted or when the client company decides to embark on new ventures, such as e-commerce initiatives or establishment of an intranet.

The most important element of an outsourcing agreement for both parties, but mostly for the client, is what professionals call the service-level agreement. The negotiators for the client must carefully list all the types of services expected of the vendor as well as the metrics to be used to measure the degree to which the vendor has met the level of promised services. Clients should not expect vendors to list the service level and metrics; the *clients* must do it. It is in the client's interest to have as specific a contract as possible, because any service that is not included in the contract, or is mentioned only in general terms, leaves the door open for the vendor not to render it, or not to render it to a level expected by the client.

> **service-level agreement** A document that lists all the types of services expected of an outsourcing vendor as well as the metrics that will be used to measure the degree to which the vendor has met the level of promised services. Usually, the client makes the list.

Licensing applications

CD TASK

Businesses can select from a growing list of high-quality packaged software, from office applications that fit on a CD to large enterprise applications. Therefore, purchasing prepackaged software should be the first alternative considered when a company needs to acquire a new system. Recall that 'purchased' software is almost always *licensed* software. The purchaser actually purchases a licence to use the software, not the software itself. Thus, here the term 'licensing' means purchasing a licence to use. Unless an IS must be tailored to uncommon needs in an organization, licensing a prepackaged system might well be the best option.

Ready-made software can be classified into two groups: one is the relatively inexpensive software that helps in the office, such as Microsoft Office and similar suites, including software that supports more specific tasks such as project management and tax preparation. Such software usually costs tens of dollars to several hundred euros for a single user or thousands of euros for a company with many employees. The other group includes large software applications that support whole organizational functions, such as human resource management and financial management, or enterprise applications that span the entire organization. Such packages include ERP, SCM and CRM applications and typically cost millions of euros.

Software licensing benefits

When licensing a software package, the buyer gains several benefits: immediate system availability, high quality, low price (licence fee) and available support. Immediate availability helps shorten the time from the decision to implement a new system and the actual implementation. If the company maintains an IT staff that develops applications, purchasing software frees the staff to develop the systems that must be specifically tailored to its business needs.

High-quality software is guaranteed through purchase partly because the software company specializes in developing its products and partly because its products would not survive on the market if they were not of high quality. Large developers often distribute pre-release versions, called beta versions, or simply betas, of software to be tested by companies (called beta sites) that agree to use the application with actual data for several months. The beta sites then report problems and propose improvements in return for receiving the fully developed software free or for a reduced licence fee. By the time the software is released to the general market, it has been well tested.

beta version A pre-release version of a software applciation that is given to a company for extensive testing prior to the full release.

Because software companies spread product development costs over many units, the price to a single customer is a fraction of what it would cost to develop a similar application in-house or to hire an outside company to develop it. Also, instead of tying up its own personnel to maintain the software, the buyer can usually contract for long-term service and be notified of new, advanced versions of the application. All software development companies provide after-the-sale support. Often, buyers enjoy a period of three months to one year of free service.

Even large companies that could afford to develop ISs on their own often elect to purchase when they can find suitable software. For example, ING, the financial services firm with 18 million customers worldwide and over 100,000 employees, announced a six-year contract in 2006 for the outsourcing of application development, maintenance and system testing to LogicaCMG at a cost of € 200 million. It is expected that the contract will achieve an annual cost-saving for ING of € 190 million.

You might be more familiar with off-the-shelf applications than with larger, more complex packaged applications. However, in recent years, enterprise applications have constituted a far larger part of IT expenditures on packaged software. As mentioned earlier, enterprise applications are complex applications that serve many parts of an organization, often several departments. They consist of several modules, each of which can be interfaced with another module from the same vendor.

Organizations cannot simply purchase such large applications and install them; they must employ professionals who specialize in the installation of the software, which might take months. Within limits, the providers of these large applications agree to customize part of the applications to the specific needs of a client. However, such customization is very expensive and is often risky; in some cases, customization has taken significantly longer than planned and was not completed to the full satisfaction of the client.

Software licensing risks

Although licensing a ready-made application is attractive, it has its risks:

- *Loose fit between needs and features*: Ready-made software is developed for the widest common denominator of potential user organizations. It might be useful to many, but it will be optimal for few. Companies must take extra care to ensure that ready-made software truly complies with company needs, including organizational culture. Obtaining input from many potential users in the selection process reduces this risk.

- *Difficulties in modifications*: Many companies find that they must have packaged software such as ERP and SCM applications modified to meet their specific needs, and too many of them find that the vendor does a poor job.

- *Bankruptcy of the vendor*: If the vendor goes out of business, the purchaser is left without support, maintenance service or the opportunity to purchase upgrades to an application to which it is committed. Except for checking the financial strength of potential vendors, there is not much the purchaser can do to reduce this risk.

- *High turnover of vendor personnel*: Turnover among IS professionals is significantly higher than in other occupations. If a substantial number of employees involved in application development and upgrading leave a vendor, support is likely to deteriorate, and upgrades will be of poor quality. Purchasers can do little to reduce this risk.

Steps in licensing ready-made software

When selecting a particular software package, companies invest a lot of money and make a long-term commitment to conducting their business in a particular manner. Factors such as the complexity of installation, cost of training, and quality and cost of after-sale service must be considered in addition to the demonstrable quality of the software. Once a company decides that it will purchase a ready-made application, a project management team is formed to oversee system implementation and handle all vendor contact. The project management team has the following responsibilities (see Figure 12.4):

- *Identifying the problem or opportunity*: This step is similar to the initial enquiry and fact-finding step in the systems development life cycle (SDLC), discussed in Chapter 11. The enquiry results in the identification of gross functional requirements and key integration points with other systems. The report generated often serves as a basis for a request for information from potential vendors.

- *Identifying potential vendors*: On the basis of information in trade journals (printed and on the Web) and previously received promotional material, as well as client references, vendors who offer applications in the domain at hand are identified. In addition to these sources, IS people might gather information at trade shows, from other organizations that have used similar technology and from colleagues.

- *Soliciting vendor information*: The project manager sends a request for information (RFI) to the vendors identified, requesting general, somewhat informal information about the product.

- *Defining system requirements*: The project manager lists a set of functional and technical requirements and identifies the functional and technical capabilities of all vendors, highlighting the items that are common to both lists, as well as those that are not. The project management team involves the users in defining system requirements to ensure that the chosen application will integrate well with existing and planned systems.

- *Requesting vendor proposals*: The team prepares a request for proposal (RFP), a document specifying all the system requirements and soliciting a proposal

request for information (RFI) A request to vendors for general, somewhat informal, information about their products.

request for proposal (RFP) A document specifying all the system requirements and soliciting a proposal from vendors who might want to bid on a project or service.

Figure 12.4 Steps in licensing software

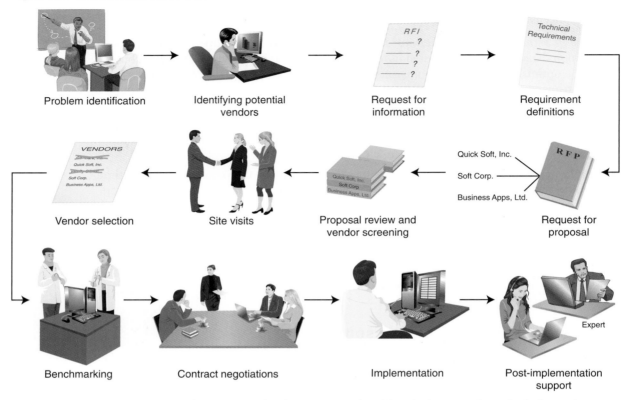

Problem identification → Identifying potential vendors → Request for information → Requirement definitions

Vendor selection ← Site visits ← Proposal review and vendor screening ← Request for proposal

Benchmarking → Contract negotiations → Implementation → Post-implementation support

from each vendor contacted. The response should include not only technical requirements but also a detailed description of the implementation process as well as a timetable and budget that can be easily transformed into a contractual agreement. The team should strive to provide enough detail and vision to limit the amount of pre-contract clarification and negotiation.

- *Reviewing proposals and screening vendors*: The team reviews the proposals and identifies the most qualified vendors. Vendor selection criteria include functionality, architectural fit, price, services and support.

- *Visiting sites*: The complexity of the RFP responses might make evaluation impossible without a visit to a client site where a copy of the application is in use. The team should discuss with other clients the pros and cons of the application.

- *Selecting the vendor*: The team ranks the remaining vendors. The selection factors are weighted, and the vendor with the highest total points is chosen for contract negotiation. Sometimes make-or-break factors are identified early in the process to eliminate vendors that cannot provide the essential service. By now, the team has gathered enough information on the functionality of the various systems.

- *Benchmarking*: Before finalizing the purchasing decision, the system should be tested using benchmarking, which is comparing actual performance against specific quantifiable criteria. If all other conditions are the same for all the bidders, the vendor whose application best meets or exceeds the benchmarks is selected.

- *Negotiating a contract*: The contract should clearly define performance expectations and include penalties if requirements are not met. Special attention should be given to the schedule, budget, responsibility for system support and support response times. Some clients include a clause on keeping the source code in escrow, that is depositing the source code with a trusted third party

benchmarking The measurement of time intervals and other important characteristics of hardware and software, usually when testing them before a decision to purchase or reject.

Table 12.3 How IT managers rank the importance of product purchase factors

Factor	Rating
Quality and reliability	_____
Product performance	_____
Quality of after-sale service and support	_____
Trustworthiness of vendor	_____
Price/performance ratio	_____
Ease of doing business with vendor	_____
Vendor's support for industry standards	_____
Openness of future strategies and plans	_____
Vendor financial stability	_____

(the escrow agent). If the vendor goes out of business, the client will receive the source code, without which the system cannot be maintained. The client should tie all payments to completion of milestones by the vendor and acceptance of deliverables.

● *Implementing the new system*: The new system is introduced in the business units it will serve. Training takes place.

● *Managing post-implementation support*: Vendors expect buyers of their large applications to request extensive on-site post-implementation support. Unexpected lapses or unfamiliarity with the system might require fine-tuning, additional training or modification of the software. It is best to develop an ongoing relationship with the vendor because a solid relationship will foster timely service and support.

When choosing a vendor, organizations look for the quality and reliability of the product, but there are additional factors, such as quality of service and support, vendor's support for industry standards and vendor financial soundness, that are extremely important. In surveys, IS managers have almost invariably revealed the importance of factors considered in selecting a vendor as shown in Table 12.3 (in descending order). Product quality and reliability stand well ahead of the price/performance ratio.

Software as a service

The option to use software applications through the Web was introduced in 1998. An organization that offers the use of software through communication lines is called an application service provider (ASP). The concept is called software as a service (SaaS) or *software by subscription*. CSC, IBM Global Services, Oracle Corp. and Salesforce.com are among the better-known players in this industry, but many other companies offer such services.

An ASP does not install any software on a client's computers. Rather, the application is installed at the ASP's location, along with the databases and other files that the application processes for the client. However, clients can choose to save all the files produced by the application on their own local storage devices. The clients' employees access the application through the Web. They call up the application,

application service provider (ASP) A firm that hires the use of software applications through an Internet link.

software as a service (SaaS) An alternative to developing or licensing software, which enables the client to hire the software through communication lines, usually over the Internet, from an application service provider (ASP).

Table 12.4 Benefits and risks of ASP services

Benefits	Risks
No need to learn to maintain the application	Possible long transaction response time on the Internet
No need to maintain the application	Security risks, such as interception by competitors
No need to allocate hardware for the installation	
No need to hire experts for installation and maintenance	
Timely availability	

enter data, process the data, produce reports online and on paper, and in general use the application the same way they would had it been installed at their location.

As Table 12.4 shows, there are several benefits to renting and using software through the Web, as well as risks. As in any time-limited rental, the client does not have to commit large sums of money up front. No employees have to devote time to learning how to maintain the software, nor to maintaining it once it is installed. No storage hardware is required for the applications and associated data, because the vendor uses its own hardware. And the

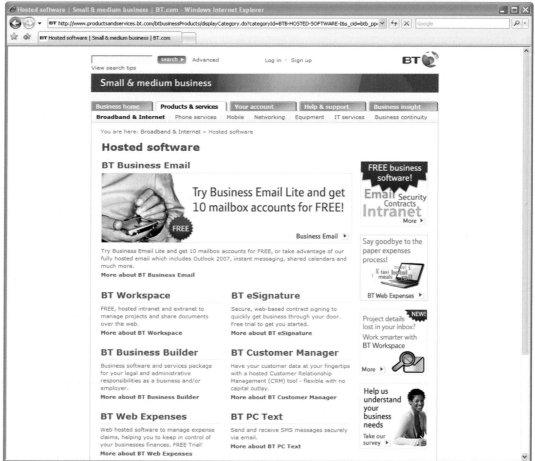

BT now offers a variety of SaaS products, including a CRM tool designed for small and medium businesses.

software is usually available significantly sooner than if installed at the client's location; while it might take years to install and test enterprise applications on-site, an online renter can use the same application three to six weeks after signing a contract. And even if an organization is willing to pay for the software, it might not find skilled personnel to install and maintain the software. For many small companies this option is clearly the best.

The 'software on demand' approach seems to attract a growing clientele. Clients are mainly small and medium corporations, but some large ones also prefer this option. Salesforce.com, which specializes in CRM software, has grown very fast. The company was established in 2000, and by 2005 had 308,000 subscribers.

The obvious risk is that the client cedes control of the systems, the application and possibly its related data, to another party. Although some vendors are willing to make minor changes to suit the client's needs, they will not make all that are requested. Some experts argue that by hiring, clients have less control over their systems, and that it is better to retain the ability to modify applications in-house. Response time might become a problem as well, because neither the ASP nor the client has full control over traffic on the Internet. Also, as with all activities through a public network, there are security risks, such as interception of information by a competitor. For this reason, some clients prefer to use a leased line rather than the Internet to connect to the ASP. When considering using a leased line, IS managers should consider the cost, as leased lines are much more expensive than DSL or cable connections. Organizations should also consider the type of application and data their company is about to use.

Caveat emptor

In recent years faster links to the Internet and a more stable ASP industry have made SaaS an attractive option. However, even with reputable providers, some subscribers were disappointed because the scope of services and level of reliability were not what they had expected when they signed the contract. Managers in organizations considering ASPs should heed the following 'commandments':

1 *Check the ASP's history.* Ask the provider for a list of references, and contact these customers to ask about their experience. Ask how soon the provider switched to a new version of the application they hired.

2 *Check the ASP's financial strength.* Request copies of the ASP's financial reports. Ensure that it has enough funds or secured funding to stay in business for the duration of your planned contract.

3 *Ensure you understand the price scheme.* Ask whether the price changes when you decide to switch to using another application. Ask whether the price includes help-desk services.

4 *Get a list of the provider's infrastructure.* Ask to see a list of the ASP's hardware, software and telecommunications facilities. Ask who the ASP's business partners are that provide hardware, software and telecommunications services. Ask how data, including sensitive data such as credit-card account numbers, are stored and protected. Ask about security measures.

5 *Craft the service contract carefully.* Ensure that the contract includes penalties the ASP will pay if services are not rendered fully. Ensure that your organization will not have to pay penalties for early termination.

One important point to check when examining the list of facilities is uptime. Uptime is the proportion of time that the ASP's systems and communications links are up. Since no provider can guarantee 100 per cent uptime, ASPs often promise 99.9 per cent ('three nines', in professional lingo) uptime, which sounds satisfactory, but it might not be. Three nines mean that downtime might reach 500 minutes per year. This is usually acceptable for customer relationship management systems. Human resource managers or sales representatives, who typically use ISs less than 50 hours per week, might settle even for two nines (99 per cent guaranteed uptime). However, experts recommend that organizations look for ASPs that can guarantee five

uptime The percentage of time (so much time per year) that an information system is in full operation.

nines – 99.999 per cent uptime – for critical applications. This high percentage of uptime ensures downtime of no more than five minutes per year. There are firms that specialize in monitoring the uptime of ASPs. One such company is Towers Perrin, a management consulting firm that monitors the uptime of 200 web-based applications.

Who hires the services of ASPs? Although you will find a variety of companies among ASP clients, the majority of the clients can be classed into four categories:

- Companies that are growing fast and rely on software for deployment of their operations.
- Small companies that do not have the cash to pay up front, but who must use office, telecommunications and basic business operations applications.
- Medium-sized companies that need expensive software, such as enterprise applications, for their operations but cannot afford the immediate payment of large sums (examples are ERP applications from companies such as SAP and PeopleSoft).
- Organizational units at geographical sites where it is difficult to obtain desired software or personnel to install and maintain the software. These sites are typically located far away from a regional headquarters in a less-developed country. The office at that site can then use applications from a more developed country.

storage service provider (SSP) A firm that rents storage space for software through an Internet link.

In 2001, a new type of service provider, similar to an ASP, started to catch the attention of businesses in need of IT services: the storage service provider (SSP). An SSP does not hire software applications, but hires storage space. Instead of spending

Ethical and Societal ISSUES

Computer use policies for employees

The increasing numbers of PCs and the pervasive use of email and the Web in businesses have exposed more and more people to ISs. This enables workers to be more productive, but computers are often used for unproductive, or even destructive, activities. If an employee uses a company car without permission, the act is obviously wrong. But if an employee uses a company computer to store private files, is that wrong? Accessing a company's intranet is legitimate and encouraged. Accessing another employee's file might be wrong. However, some employees might not be aware of the differences. What are the appropriate personal uses of company computers? Is the answer to this question already covered in existing laws? Should companies have policies that define the appropriate uses of their IT resources? Do we need new laws to ensure a law-abiding workforce? The answers to these questions vary.

When there is no corporate policy Although unauthorized use of computers might be considered theft, authorities usually do not deal with it as such. Perhaps this is why most laws do not specifically address unauthorized use of computers. There is, however, one exception: California law states that an employee might use an employer's computer services for his or her own purpose without permission if no damage is caused and if the value of supplies and computer services does not exceed US$100.

If someone from outside a company accessed the company's computer without authorization and used it for any purpose whatsoever, the act would clearly be criminal under the laws of many countries. However, if an *employee* uses the same company computer after hours to prepare a homework assignment for a university class, the act might not be considered unethical, let alone criminal, unless the organization has a clear policy against such activity. What about creating a résumé or writing a letter as part of a job search? Without a company policy, the answer to this question is not clear.

Widespread access to the Web makes the issues even more complicated. Employees have been fired for surfing the Web for their own personal purposes during work time. Some have been fired for surfing the Web during lunch breaks or after work hours; while they did not waste company-paid time, management objected to the specific sites they accessed, mostly those displaying pornographic images.

Company policies work To avoid misunderstanding, employers should provide clear guidelines, stating that any computer use not for the company's direct benefit, without the prior approval of the company, is forbidden. One simple measure that some organizations have taken is to have a written policy that is conspicuously posted, signed by employees upon hiring, or both. The notice could read as follows:

'Company policy forbids any employee, without prior authorization of the employee's supervisor, to (a) access or use any equipment or data unless such access is work-related and required to fulfil that employee's duties, or (b) alter, damage, or destroy any company computer resource or property, including any computer equipment, system, terminal, network, software, data, or documentation, including individual employee computer files. Any such act by an employee might result in civil and criminal liability.'

Many companies do not object to recreational or educational use of their computers by employees outside of company time. If this is the case, the policy should say so. Without a policy, companies should not be surprised when their employees' interpretation of reasonable personal use differs from their employers'. However, if there is no clear policy, employees should always remember that a PC is a work tool that their employer put at their disposal for responsible use as part of their job. It is not there to help their own business or entertain them either during or outside of paid time. Thus, for example, they should not use email or instant messaging to chat with their friends or browse the Web for their enjoyment. Yet, is sending a personal email message during lunch break really much different from using a company pen to write a personal note during lunch break? Perhaps the best way to avoid misunderstanding is to simply ask your employer if what you intend to do is objectionable.

money on the purchase of magnetic disks, a company can contract with an SSP and have all or some of its files stored remotely on the SSP's storage devices. The storage and retrieval are executed through communication lines, in most cases the Internet.

User application development

If an adequate application is not available on the market, or if an organization does not wish to take the risks discussed earlier with purchasing or renting, and if the application is not too complex, there is another alternative to software development: user application development, in which non-programmer users write their own business applications. Typically, user-developed software is fairly simple and limited in scope; it is unlikely that users could develop complex applications such as ERP systems. If end users do have the necessary skills, they should be allowed to develop small applications for immediate needs, and when they do, such applications can be maintained by the end users (see Table 12.5). They should be encouraged to develop applications that will be used for a brief time and then discarded. End users should not develop large or complex applications, applications that interface with other systems, or applications that are vital for the survival of the organization. They should also be discouraged from developing applications that might survive their own tenure in the organization.

> **user application development**
> Development of corporate applications by employees rather than IT professionals.

Managing user-developed applications

The proliferation of user-developed applications poses challenges to managers, both in IT units and other business units. In addition to the rules outlined in Table 12.5, management must cope with the following challenges:

● *Managing the reaction of IT professionals*: IT professionals often react negatively to user development because they perceive it as undermining their own duties and authority. To

Table 12.5 Guidelines for end-user development of applications

End users should develop if . . .	End users should not develop if . . .
End users have the necessary skills	The application is large or complex
The application is small	The application interfaces with other systems
The application is needed immediately	The application is vital for the organization's survival
The application can be maintained by the users	The application will survive the user's tenure
The application will be used briefly and discarded	

solve this problem, management must set clear guidelines delineating what types of applications end users may and may not develop.

- *Providing support*: To encourage users to develop applications, IS managers must designate a single technical contact for users. It is difficult to provide IT support for user-developed applications, because the IT staff members are usually unfamiliar with an application developed without their involvement. Yet, IT staff should help solve problems or enhance such applications when end users think their own skills are not adequate.

- *Compatibility*: To ensure compatibility with other applications within an organization, the organization's IT professionals should adopt and supply standard development tools to interested users. Users should not be allowed to use nonstandard tools. Note that compatibility in this context is for the purpose of transferring data among end users; interfacing user-developed applications with other organizational systems should be discouraged.

- *Managing access*: Sometimes, users need to copy data from organizational databases to their own developed spreadsheets or databases. If access to organizational databases is granted at all for such a purpose, access should be tightly controlled by the IT staff to maintain data integrity and security. Users should be forewarned not to rely on such access when developing their own applications if this is against the organization's policy.

Advantages and risks

There are several important advantages to user development of applications:

- *Shortened lead times*: Users almost always develop applications more quickly than IS personnel, because they are highly motivated (they will benefit from the new system); their systems are usually simpler in design; and they have a head start by being totally familiar with the business domain for which they are developing the application.

- *Good fit to needs*: Nobody knows the users' specific business needs better than the users themselves. Thus, they are apt to develop an application that will satisfy all their needs.

- *Compliance with culture*: User-developed software closely conforms to an individual unit's subculture, which makes the transition to a new system easier for employees.

- *Efficient utilization of resources*: Developing software on computers that are already being used for many other purposes is an efficient use of IT resources.

- *Acquisition of skills*: The more employees there are who know how to develop applications, the greater an organization's skills inventory.

- *Freeing up IS staff time*: User-developers free IS staff to develop and maintain an organization's more complex and sophisticated systems.

However, with all the pros, there are also cons to application development by users. They must be considered seriously. The risks are as follows:

- *Poorly developed applications*: User-developers are not as skilled as IS personnel. On average, the applications they develop are of lower quality than systems developed by professionals. Users are often tempted to develop applications that are too complex for their skills and tools, resulting in systems that are difficult to use and maintain.

- *Islands of information*: An organization that relies on user development runs the risk of creating islands of information and 'private' databases not under the control of the organization's IS managers. This lack of control might make it difficult to achieve the benefits of integrated ISs.

- *Duplication*: User-developers often waste resources developing applications that are identical or similar to systems that already exist elsewhere within the organization.

- *Security problems*: Giving end users access to organizational databases for the purpose of creating systems might result in violations of security policies. This risk is especially true in client/server environments. The creation of 'private databases' known only to the individual user is risky. The user might not be aware that the information he or she produces from the data is 'classified' under an organization's policy.

- *Poor documentation*: Practically speaking, 'poor documentation' might be a misnomer. Usually, users do not create any documentation at all because (1) they do not know how to write documentation, and (2) they develop the application on their own to have it ready as soon as possible, and they don't want to take the time to document it. Lack of documentation makes system maintenance difficult at best and impossible at worst. Often, applications are patched together by new users, and pretty soon nobody knows how to iron out bugs or modify programs.

SUMMARY

There are several alternatives to having applications developed in-house: outsourcing, licensing ready-made software, using the services of an ASP and user application development.

Outsourcing has two meanings in IT: commissioning the development of a tailored application to an IT company, and assigning all or some of the IT services of the organization to a vendor of IT services.

Outsourcing custom-designed applications might afford the organization good fit of the software to need, good fit to culture, dedicated maintenance, smooth interface, specialized security and potential for strategic advantage.

The potential advantages of outsourcing IT services include improving cost clarity and reducing license and maintenance fees, freeing the client to concentrate on its core businesses, shortening the time needed to implement new technologies, reducing personnel and fixed costs, gaining access to highly qualified know-how and receiving ongoing consulting as part of standard support. However, outsourcing IT services has some potential risks: loss of control, loss of experienced employees, loss of competitive advantage and high price. To ensure that the client enjoys all the expected services and their quality, a detailed service-level agreement must be signed with the IT service vendor.

When an organization purchases a licence to use ready-made software, it enjoys high-quality software that is immediately available at low price (licence fee). However, licensed ready-made software has some potential risks: loose fit between needs and the software features, difficulties in modifications, bankruptcy of the vendor and high turnover of the vendor's employees.

Using the services of an ASP has become popular. The concept is also known as software by subscription or software as a service (SaaS). The client pays monthly fees based on the type of application used and the number of users, and its employees use the applications via a network, mostly through the Internet. ASP clients enjoy availability of applications, avoid the costs of storage hardware and large IT staffs, and do not have to make a long-term commitment of capital to software that might become obsolete in two or three years. The downsides of using an ASP are the loss of control over applications, the potentially low speed of interaction and the security risks associated with using an IS via a public network.

There are several advantages to user application development: a short lead time, good fit of application capabilities to business needs, good compliance with organizational culture, efficient utilization of computing resources, acquisition of skills by users and the freeing of IS staff to deal with the more complex challenges of the systems. Disadvantages of user-developed applications include the risk of poorly developed applications, undesirable islands of information and private databases, duplications of effort, security problems and poor documentation. Thus, user development of applications needs to be managed. IS managers need to determine the applications that users should and should not develop and dictate the tools that should be used.

Often, employees do not know which activities are welcomed and which are not. If an organization lacks a clear policy, employees are not discouraged from abusing computers. This abuse is especially true when employees access websites that are objectionable to their employer or when employees use email for purposes not intended by the employer. If no policy has been established, the simple rule is that employees should not use their computers for anything but work.

WORLDWIDE HOST

WORLDWIDE HOST REVISITED

Worldwide Host has developed a solid partnership with General Data Systems, using the software firm to develop new systems or upgrade existing systems. Take a closer look at some of the relationships firms establish in today's marketplace – the ways they are established and their advantages and disadvantages.

What would you do?

1 Worldwide Host has outsourced its software development to General Data Systems. What are some advantages that the hotel chain receives from this arrangement? Make a list of those advantages. What are some possible risks?

2 In the opening case, Michael Lloyd seems concerned about the qualifications of Reservations Technologies, the firm from which Worldwide

plans to license the reservation system. He's asked you to help him develop a list of questions. Prepare a set of questions for him to ask both the company and its clients.

New perspectives

1 The chapter mentions application service providers as an option to acquire software. Do some research about ASPs to see whether any of them offer systems such as the ones Worldwide Host needs to use. Could Worldwide Host use an ASP for any of its needs? If so, which specific needs could be satisfied?

2 Several years in the future Worldwide Host replaces its reservation system with one customized for it by a software development firm. A competitor approaches Worldwide's management and offers to pay an attractive annual fee for a licence to use the system. Should management agree? Why or why not?

Review questions

1 List and explain all the various options now available for an organization to enjoy the services of an IS. What does the organization own and for how long? What doesn't it own but can use?

2 Few organizations would develop an application in-house or pay another company to develop it if a similar application can be licensed. Why?

3 What are the benefits and risks of outsourcing IT services?

4 The major hardware and software makers, such as IBM and Hewlett-Packard, derive an increasing portion of their revenue from outsourcing contracts. Try to analyse why they direct more of their efforts in this direction.

5 What might cause a client to ask for renegotiating a long-term outsourcing contract?

6 You are the CIO of a large manufacturing company. A software vendor approaches you with an offer to have your company serve as a beta site for a new human resource application. What would you do before making a decision?

7 What is an RFI? What is the difference between an RFI and an RFP? The ideal response to an RFP is one that can be easily transformed into a contract. Why?

8 What is the purpose of benchmarking? Often, benchmarking involves visiting other organizations that have applied the system under consideration. Why?

9 What would you benchmark in a system whose purpose is to enter customer orders and accept customer credit-card account numbers for payment?

10 When purchasing an off-the-shelf application, to which phase of SDLC is the post-implementation support and service equivalent?

11 Some organizations charge the purchase price of an application that serves only a particular organizational unit back to the unit. Why does the existence of a charge-back system create an incentive to have users develop their own applications?

12 Why don't users usually document the applications they develop? Why is poor documentation a problem?

13 List and explain the benefits and risks of using the services of an ASP.

14 Some companies use ASPs because they want to concentrate on core competencies. What is a core competency?

15 What is a storage service provider (SSP)? How is it different from an ASP?

Discussion questions

1 Some outsourcing clients have devised contracts with vendors that give the vendors an incentive to develop new, innovative ISs for the client. What elements would you include in a contract like this if you were a manager for an outsourcing (client) company?

2 Vendors like to market themselves as 'partners' with their outsourcing clients. Why?

3 Do you think that development of ISs by end users should be encouraged? Do the benefits of the practice outweigh its risks?

4 Will ready-made software applications ever meet all the needs of all businesses? Explain.

5 The volume of business in the ASP industry was predicted to reach about ten times what it is now. What do you think are the reasons for the much less brisk business of ASPs?

6 If you were in a position to make the decision to hire an enterprise financial software package through an ASP or to hire and install it at your organization's location, would you use an ASP? What elements would you consider (about the vendor and your own organization) before you made the decision?

7 A CIO said that while he would not use a public network such as the Internet with an ASP for some types of ISs, he would use the Web for other types. He said that he would let employees use an accounting application through the Web. Give three examples of applications that you would recommend not to use through the Web and three that you would recommend to use through the Web. Explain your choices.

8 Do you think using applications through ASP services on the Web will increase in popularity or fizzle as an option for acquiring applications? Explain.

9 Explain why you agree or disagree with the following statement: 'Employees are smart enough to know what they should and should not do with their computers. A conduct policy will not prevent wrongdoing.'

10 Should employees be allowed to use their employers' email for private communication at all? Outside of paid time?

11 When using the services of an ASP, the client gains an important element that is often overlooked: support service. Considering only support service, would you prefer to have the hired software installed on your own company's hardware or leave it installed at the vendor's site? Explain.

12 What are the risks of hiring through the Web that you foresee that are not mentioned in the chapter?

13 Recall the discussions of telecommunications and the Internet in Chapters 5 and 7. What developments might encourage more organizations to use the services of ASPs?

14 Assume that you are the CEO of a company that provides computers and access to email and the Web to almost all of its employees. You are about to circulate a new IT use policy in the company. List and explain your rules for employees' use of software, email and the Web.

Tutorial activities

1 You are a manager for a new company that is about to start selling textbooks to university bookstores via the Web. Several firms specialize in software that supports transactions and data collection on the Web. Prepare an RFI for an application to support your new company's effort on the Web, including posted catalogues, orders, shipment tracking, payment and data collection for future marketing. Submit the list of questions you want prospective bidders to answer, and be ready to give your tutor an explanation for including each of the questions.

2 Find an organization that purchased a software application three to six months ago. The application might be in any business area: accounting, payroll, inventory control, financial management, manufacturing, human resources or an integrative enterprise application. Interview the person who recommended the purchase, and summarize the reasoning behind his or her decision. Then interview one or two daily users and summarize the pros and cons they discuss. What, if anything, would you do differently before deciding to purchase this application?

3 In recent years several companies experienced either a total failure or major mishaps when trying to have vendors implement enterprise applications. Consider 'failure' as inability to complete the project or a project that ended up costing the client significantly more than expected, including lost revenue. Find at least three sources about the case. Synthesize, list, and explain what happened and why. Conclude with your own recommendations of what could be done to avoid or minimize the damage. The recommendations should be written so that potential clients of such projects could take proper precautions. Your report should be about 2500 words long.

4 In recent years a growing amount of software has been outsourced by European and US companies to other countries, such as India and China. Research the Web and write a two-page paper that lists and explains the benefits and the disadvantages of offshoring application development.

5 Every online retailer (e-tailer) uses a virtual shopping cart application. Team up with another student, research the Web for companies that sell such applications, and write a 2000-word report that summarizes the following points: (a) Who are the major companies that sell these applications? (b) What are the prices of these packages? (c) How long does it take to install the applications? (d) How is the relationship with the bank processing the credit-card payments established? (e) Are there ASPs that rent the use of such systems over the Internet (namely, the e-tailer uses a shopping cart application installed at the ASP's location)? (f) If there are ASPs that rent such systems, what are the payment schemes?

6 Throughout this book, many organizations that provide information and advice on IT have been mentioned. Explore the websites of these organizations and the websites of IT-related magazines to find the latest statistics on the different alternatives for obtaining ISs. Use PowerPoint to answer the following questions and express your answers in pie charts:

a) What was the amount spent on IT in your country in each of the past three years, and what percentage of this amount was spent on software acquisition?

b) How was the amount spent on software distributed among in-house development, purchased ready-made software, and outsourced development?

Companion CD questions

1 Research database software applications. Under what circumstances should a company (a) purchase an off-the-shelf package, (b) develop its own package, or (c) use an application service provider?

2 Use a spreadsheet package to create a table containing the information you found for Question 1.

Video questions

1 Have you downloaded or traded or shared software illegally? Why did you do it? After watching the clip, would you do it again?

2 What methods are software manufacturers using to prevent software piracy?

From ideas to application
REAL CASES

Case study 12.1

Volvo cars

BY SCOTT RAEBURN

Volvo is a global brand with an image of Swedish solidity, quality and safety. Covering cars, trucks and engineering, it is known worldwide in a range of sectors. However, ownership of the brand is complex. Since 1999 the Volvo Car Corporation (VCC) has been part of the US-based Ford Motor Company (a wholly owned subsidiary in business jargon). The rest of the Volvo brand is owned by AB Volvo of Sweden. Both VCC and AB Volvo have headquarters Göteborg in Sweden. Belgium plays a significant role in Volvo car production, hosting a large manufacturing plant in Ghent which produces around 200,000 cars per year, nearly 50 per cent of VCC global output.

The VCC philosophy of customer service is based on life cycle tracking of vehicles and on customer management. From its initial order through delivery, service and maintenance in use and final disposal, each vehicle

Volvo Group Headquarters, Gottenburg, Sweden.

is to be tracked via its VIN, the internationally agreed Vehicle Identification Number system. Whichever country it is in, however it is licensed or plated by the authorities in each country, the VIN remains the same. Tracking Volvos is a significant task for VCC and its dealers, with many of the cars being used for 20 years or more. With global production currently in the order of 400–450,000 cars per year, that means that the database has to record details for more than eight million vehicles over that period.

This case concerns the Belgian subsidiary of VCC which runs the dealerships there, known as Volvo Cars Belgium (VCB) and based in Brussels. Although a relatively small country, Belgium does figure in the top ten countries for sales of Volvo cars, with 12,600 cars sold in 2005 through its network of 65 dealers. VCB's mission is to sell more cars and IT plays a significant role in this. Michelangelo Adamo, IT supervisor of VCB and its dealer network, is based in Brussels. He has said, 'I am a person who wants to sell more Volvos to customers. We are in the business of selling cars, not IT.' He is concerned with how information and communication technologies (ICTs) can help to sell more cars. To reinforce this approach, Adamo reports to the Customer Service manager rather than an IT boss.

The Customer Service Manager, Christoph Cordier, is the man who used to do Adamo's job, thus giving continuity to the importance of ICTs in achieving sales and performance targets. Together they have developed a service-oriented architecture (SOA) approach to improving customer service at VCB which allows VCC HQ to see the performance of individual dealers, offering help or rewards as appropriate. This dealer management system removed many processes which were still paper-based, replacing them with a web-based system which linked every dealership together and to VCC.

The measure of success for the system was to be an increase in customer approval rating (this had been collected for several years) and measures of the number of parts which arrived overnight from Göteborg to ensure maintenance and repair was done when customers expected.

Cordier remembered a previous attempt at improving customer service measures. This was a paper-based system developed in the mid–late 1990s to map the entire customer experience. Whilst it 'worked', it didn't do what the dealer managers wanted so they didn't use it. What the dealers wanted was access to the Volvo Car Configurator (an online specification and ordering system) and to VIDA (vehicle information and diagnostic system for after-sales) to help with solving problems for customers at any stage of a vehicle's life cycle. With the paper system too cumbersome and time-consuming, going digital seemed to be the obvious solution.

Starting in 2001, the entire process was looked at afresh. All users in dealerships – receptionists, mechanics and sales people, as well as managers – were involved in the work. More than two years were taken in analysing requirements and attempting to find a software package to do everything identified as essential to the system, including the link to VCC in Goteburg. Such a package didn't exist, so a different approach was investigated.

VCB decided to link the dealers in Belgium with a dealer management application (XDMS®) from a local provider, XPower Automotive Software. This created some eight months of work to upgrade hardware across 65 dealerships and to convert dealer and VCB data into the format used by XDMS. But the big advantage of XPower was that it was a partner of Progress Software Corporation of Massachusetts, whose OpenEdge® platform was service-oriented and flexible enough to allow linkage to other systems, including VCC's systems in Göteburg. The technical differences between the VCB and VCC systems were significant. As noted above, the computer systems at VCC have a very large vehicle database to manage and are mainframe legacy systems holding data from many years of production. The much more 'state-of-the-art' systems just introduced at VCB were very different.

Most people involved thought that connecting the two systems would be a major task – except Progress Software. Their Sonic Enterprise Software Bus® is based on the concept of managing messages between disparate systems, a common occurrence on the Web. By brokering or translating transactions between the systems, Sonic removes the need for extensive and difficult system integration projects. And so it proved. Having taken some three years to get the dealership system operating, the link to the mainframe that Adamo thought would be 'difficult, very difficult' actually took only two weeks. Cordier is reported as being 'slightly embarrassed' at the ease of connecting to the two critical systems at VCC.

The two-phase approach with a service-oriented philosophy and modular software running independent processes providing each service has worked very well. Adamo reports that it was possible to combine two different worlds without changing a single line of code.

So was this €1.8 million (some £1.2 million) project a success? One measure was to be customer satisfaction surveys. These surveys are based on a simple scoring system with the poorest performance rated 1 and the best rated 5. Averaged over thousands of customers, the rating is quoted to two decimal places. In 2005, before the system was in place, the average customer service rating was 4.02. In 2006, it was 4.09. Although this doesn't sound much, it's actually an increase of some 2 per cent – quite good for a single transition year. And the system does allow 'drill-down', identifying individual dealers who are performing well and those who need assistance to reach targets. The performance metrics are standard across all dealerships, making comparisons straightforward.

The other measure was to ensure that most parts needed for service and repair tasks arrived in the appropriate Belgian dealership overnight. The new XDMS system automatically orders parts from VCC when service and repair tasks are booked by customers, using the VIN and recommended maintenance procedures. These are shipped overnight, ensuring that 98 per cent arrive where needed the next day and reducing the likelihood that cars are returned to customers later than planned.

This increase in customer service had another benefit. A change in European Union rules controlling the car parts market, going by the unlikely title of the Block Exemption Regulation 2003, meant that the obligation on dealers to order certified Volvo parts from the local subsidiary of VCC was no longer enforceable. Dealers could order certified parts from any source. This meant that VCB faced new competition for parts supply; they no longer had a captive market. However, the new parts service meant that, in spite of the competition, VCB revenues from parts increased by some 33 per cent

to €40 million (approximately £27 million) between 2002 (before the new rules) and 2006.

So what does VCC in Göteburg think of all this? Well, they have noticed the improved performance of VCB in customer service terms. Other parts of the VCC empire in Europe did not have the same improvements as VCB. But other subsidiaries have not moved to adopt the VCB solution. Whilst VCB have clearly 'done the right thing' in getting a reasonably priced, effective solution based on outsourced software systems, others may suffer from the 'NIH syndrome' – not invented here!

The final point is political. But the problems of the US car market may have an influence. At the time of writing, the Ford Motor Corporation have indicated that some of its marques, including Volvo, are for sale. VCC is likely to have a new owner before the end of 2007. Perhaps they might recognize the benefits of outsourced, service-oriented systems in a very competitive car market.

Case study questions

1 How would you describe the IT philosophy of Volvo cars (Brussels)? Give reasons why you agree (or disagree) with it.

2 What are the risks in the use of web services to 'outsource' IT services?

3 What alternative approaches to providing an IT service could Adamo have considered? Which would you have chosen and why?

SOURCES: www.cioinsight.com (7 March 2007); www.volvocars.com (17 August 2007); Progress Software at www.progress.com (17 August 2007)

Case study **12.2**

Acquiring IT systems: the increase in outsourcing to Eastern Europe

BY ALAN HOGARTH

Over recent years the tendency has been for organizations to outsource their IT and systems development activities to the Indian subcontinent, China and the Far East. However, recent studies have indicated that many organizations are now choosing Eastern European

Krakow, Poland.

PHOTO SOURCE: © HAUHU

countries for their outsourcing needs. Essentially this region is viewed as the next potential outsourcing hotspot. A study by Mckinsey in 2006 highlighted that this region holds less than 1 per cent of the global IT outsourcing market, but that by the end of 2008 outsourcing to Eastern Europe could triple to around 130,000 jobs. Further, wages in this region are equivalent to those paid in India and China today and are not likely to rise in the near future whereas India's are liable to rise. Other advantages of the area include its low-risk profile and its proximity to Western Europe as well as a less expensive work force.

It is also suggested that companies should consider recruiting IT specialists from smaller cities in Eastern Europe rather than larger locations like Budapest, Prague and Krakow. There are many smaller cities that have universities where employers can head-hunt skilled graduates. The Mckinsey report notes that there is little evidence of IT outsourcing in the middle-sized cities of Bulgaria, Russia and Romania. Therefore 'labour cost advantage is more likely to remain attractive for the next decade. One example is a city in Poland, Katowice, where there are 7400 university graduates who have suitable talent.'

Russia is another country that offers massive potential for cost-effective IT outsourcing. Daniel Marovitz, Chief Technology Officer for Global Banking at Deutsche Bank's investment banking unit in London when considering outsourcing partners stated that 'We talked about Canada, Ireland and low-cost locations in the United Kingdom. But it really came down to India and Russia.' Marovitz preferred the approaches adopted by companies in Russia and felt that a Russian outsourcer would best suit the requirements of Deutsche Bank in maintaining and enhancing its 5000-user 'client-first' Customer Relationship Management (CRM) system for investment bankers.

However, the problem for many companies used to outsourcing to India is that Russia does things differently. Marovitz explains that 'In India, people want to say "yes" to please and to follow instructions. That can create problems sometimes. In Russia, people aren't afraid to tell you that you have a silly idea that makes no sense whatsoever. But that's what you need. Sometimes you have to stand up and explain why you want something done a certain way. It's easier to have a relationship where the line between employee and vendor gets blurry because the people are active members of the team and not just following orders.' Despite this, according to Forrester Research, the Russian software outsourcing industry at $1 billion is still well below India's, which currently stands at around $24 billion per annum.

For example, IBM claims it will be spending twice as much in India as the whole of the Russian market in 2007, investing overall $6 billion in India over the next three years. Russian providers, although essentially a decade behind the Indians in maturity, do have some advantages. In the Deutsche Bank case referred to earlier, the cost of maintaining a relationship between London and India was potentially much higher than one with Russia in terms of travel, time differences and management costs. To this end Marovitz signed a deal with the software outsourcing firm Luxoft to handle maintenance and enhancement of the applications. Initially 24 programmers were involved, but now Luxoft has about 2000 working on the CRM applications. As Marovitz says, 'In India, there is a high infrastructure cost to make things work. Even a small team can cost a lot of money to work with. With Russia, it's just three and a half hours from London and a three-hour time change. It's easy to do a two-day trip. For those reasons, it seemed like a good fit for us.'

Another company keen to employ Russian IT outsourcers was British Telecom Global Services (BTGS). Again the proximity to Western Europe was a major factor in their decision. They signed a deal with software developer Fathom of Budapest two years ago to upgrade BTGS's web portal for corporate customers. Andy Pennington, portal product manager for BTGS states that 'They are three to four hours away. It's easier to communicate between onshore and offshore people. There wasn't a big cultural divide.'

The creativity of Russian providers has prompted some US companies to recruit them for software development. For example, SirsiDynix, a $100 million company specializing in library management systems signed a deal with Starsoft of St Petersburg to develop a web-portal-based library management system. The work was carried out by two teams, one from each company, who developed the new system in one year. Jack Blount, a SirsiDynix Board Member, says, 'It was extremely successful, and we're very happy with it.'

However, not all projects with Russian outsourcers are so successful. Computer Sciences Corp. (SCS) in Denmark hired StarSoft for a project termed Labka II. However, this was subject to communication problems that caused delays in the project. CSC Program manger Alan Guthrie blamed cultural differences for the problems. He says, 'Russian and European cultures are different. The Russian Team will work longer hours without complaining. There is a shorter workday in Denmark. The Russian style is closer to the US style. They want to overachieve.

Nothing's guaranteed. They want to debate, they want to understand why, they might be more compatible with an American client.'

Despite this, the benefits of IT outsourcing to Eastern Europe may not be as profitable for US companies as for European ones. Companies in Western Europe can benefit most from outsourcing to this region because they are more likely to find communication capabilities better between such countries as Hungary and the Czech Republic than they would in the Far East. Furthermore, in any offshoring location, in Eastern Europe, India or the Far East, the reliability of the infrastructure and political stability has to be of paramount consideration for any company planning to outsource their IT work.

Case study questions

1 Why are companies deciding to outsource their IT work to Eastern Europe?

2 In what ways are Indian and Far Eastern countries' approaches to IT outsourcing work different from those in Eastern Europe?

3 What effect does this have on the decision of companies wishing to outsource their IT development?

4 Why might US companies, compared to Western European ones, find it easier to work with Russian IT outsourcers?

5 What major issues must a company consider prior to any outsourcing strategy in any location?

SOURCES: Margaret Locher, 'Eastern Eurcpe New Outsourcing Hot Spot', *CIO Magazine*, 1 February 2007; Stan Gibson, 'Outsourcing: The Russian Revelation', Silicon Taiga, National Software Development Alliance, online at http://www.silicantaiga.org/home

Case study **12.3**

Moodle and the Open University

BY MARTIN RICH

In the autumn of 2005 the Open University announced that it would develop a new virtual learning environment (VLE) based on a software package known as Moodle. This VLE would support the delivery of learning materials to 200,000 distance-learning students registered with the university, and would also form the basis of a new initiative, known as 'OpenLearn', which would make some learning materials from the Open University freely available to everybody with access to the Internet.

Moodle was originally designed as a course management system and virtual learning environment, created by Martin Dougiamas (a programmer and educator living in Australia) and developed according to open-source principles, where the software itself was offered free, and users were encouraged to develop their own enhancements and share them with one another.

One apparent paradox is that, while the Moodle software itself is free, the Open University's own announcement cited a figure of nearly £5 million as the value of its own investment. Cost is often cited as a reason for choosing open-source software, but this was an example where open-source and a large investment went together.

The Open University chose Moodle because it could become the basis of a whole range of databases and services. As a very experienced and established provider of distance education, the Open University had the resources to develop specialized functions based on Moodle, and their staff had development expertise that would allow them to make a significant contribution to the Moodle community. In turn this would drive the expansion of Moodle; with open-source software there is usually a correlation between the size of the user base and the range of features available. As a specialized distance-learning university, with an international presence, the Open University has very specific requirements for its systems, and the open-source model offered the flexibility to adapt software to work with these.

A further attraction of Moodle was the ability to incorporate tools based on Web 2.0 ideas, such as blogs and wikis, within the system. These encourage both students and educators to contribute material, and to build up a collaborative body of knowledge – in contrast to more traditional approaches to distance education, which depends on giving students access to a static body of learning material. This approach fits well with the OpenLearn project, because the value added to the course material, for Open University students, is the opportunity to participate actively in courses, and to have assistance from tutors. The Open University uses the term 'supported open learning' to describe its own approach: supported because a dialogue between tutors and students is an essential part of the process, and open because students are nevertheless able to use course materials in their own time and at their own pace. Moodle is designed around a 'constructionist' approach, which mirrors the open-source philosophy used to develop it, and encourages all the participants in a course to contribute collaboratively.

Two of the longest-established and most widely used commercial products, used in universities, were WebCT, originally developed by the University of British Columbia and later marketed commercially by a spin-out company, and Blackboard. In 2005 Blackboard Systems and WebCT merged, with the combined business taking the Blackboard name. Although there are a number of smaller players, the merger made Blackboard into the dominant commercial business in the sector.

During 2006 Blackboard took out a 'broad patent' in America covering various features of its VLE products. Depending on the interpretation of this patent, it could have been used to give Blackboard exclusive rights to features that were in fact shared by many packages of educational software, including Moodle. This patent claim was rapidly followed by a legal battle, launched by Blackboard against a much smaller commercial VLE provider (a Canadian company called Desire2Learn). In July 2007 a judge ruled that certain important parts of the patent were 'indefinite', in other words that they did not represent distinctive features that could be protected by a patent. In the immediate term, this ruling represents an important victory for Desire2Learn, but it is likely that this patent battle, and others like it, will continue to run.

Martin Dougiamas, as the creator of Moodle, has taken on a prominent role in the campaign against Blackboard's patent. Not only would Moodle be one product open to accusations of patent infringement, but there are concerns that this sort of patent could stifle innovation, and that it would make further development of Moodle, or any other open-source VLE systems, difficult.

The most prominent example of open-source software is the Linux operating system, based on the long-established Unix system and developed by the Finnish programmer Linus Torvalds. The Linux community started as an amorphous group of technical experts, spread around the world, communicating electronically, and creating enhancements and additions to the operating system. Now many participants in the Linux community are employed, either by specialized companies such as Red Hat, which distributes and supports its

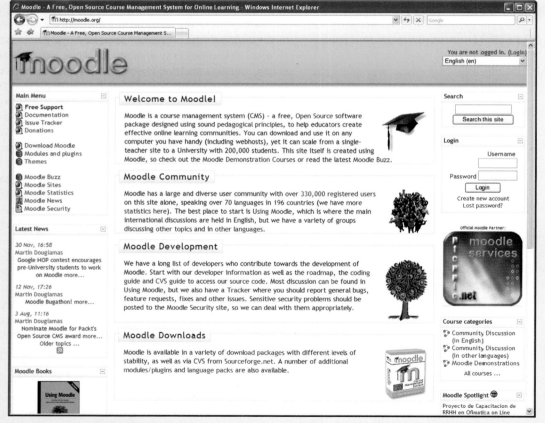

The home page of Moodle.

own version of Linux for end-users, or established players in the IT industry such as IBM, for whom offering Linux-based products is an essential part of their strategy. Although the community remains coordinated by Linus Torvalds, and relies on emails and electronic discussion groups to share ideas, it has become more professional as its product has become more widely used. It will be interesting to see whether something similar happens with Moodle, with increasing numbers of people paid to participate in the Moodle community, and whether the Open University's participation in the community will encourage this process.

Case study questions

1 Although open-source software is available freely, it is not necessarily the lowest-cost approach. What

costs would an organization incur as part of the implementation of a system based on open source?

2 In what sort of conditions would you expect open-source software to be a good choice?

3 Given that the Open University is making a lot of course material available through OpenLearn, it could be argued that there is no point in students enrolling for Open University courses. How can the university ensure that sufficient value is added for students to enrol and to participate actively?

SOURCES: M. Geist (2006), 'Patent battle over teaching tools', BBC news, http://news.bbc.co.uk/1/hi/technology/4790485.stm; S. Hamm, Linux Inc., *Business Week*, 31 January 2005; S. Hoare, 'Universities adapt to a shrinking world', *Guardian*, 7 March 2006; C. Jones and G. Conole, 'Who will own the new VLE?' *Proceedings of the 23rd Ascilite conference*, 2006

Case study **12.4**

To outsource or not to outsource?

BY ANTHONY PLEWES

As IT departments struggle to deal with new networking technologies and increasing demands from the business, many are looking at network outsourcing. Anthony Plewes weighs the pros and cons.

Network outsourcing is one of the highest growth areas in managed services, according to a new report from the Butler Group. The analyst house estimates almost 40 per cent of organizations are likely to outsource part of their infrastructure in the next two years. The market, the analyst believes, is being driven by the enterprise requirement to roll out next-generation network technology.

The simple fact is that companies are trying to do more with their networks. Typical projects IT departments would like to undertake include hardware virtualization or IP telephony, and many companies do not have the internal skills to successfully transition their network to be able to support these new environments.

This was the position in which supermarket retailer Somerfield found itself back in 2000. David Heyes, head of supplier and IT services management at Somerfield, said: 'We had a number of high-profile failures and the board recognized we were trying to do too much with our resources. We believed outsourcing would give us better capacity to meet any new demands to the business.'

Smaller companies can find it difficult to attract specialized networking staff. Outsourcing gives them the flexibility to scale up or down as the business changes and introduce new technology without having to hire new people.

Outsourcing risks

However, while companies can benefit from the technology resources at their outsourcer, not having any internal network skills can be risky. Companies might find it difficult to assess whether they are getting the best value for money and that services are fit for purpose, for instance.

In Somerfield's case, when the time came to review the service at the end of its outsourcing contract, it discovered it was paying 20 per cent over the odds. Heyes also felt the company would have liked to have moved to an IP-based network solution earlier than it had done but he wasn't able to drive this initiative internally.

Of course, lacking the skills to deploy new technology does not necessarily mean companies should outsource all ownership and management. The majority of networking kit is sold through the channel, which means companies can call on the implementation skills of third parties if they want to deploy new technology. They will, however, need to train or acquire staff that can manage the new network.

Is it cheaper?

Outsourcing has long been a popular choice for enterprises looking to save money. Outsourcers are able to offer the benefit of scale because they can centralize the key IT and network functions and service multiple accounts at the same time. This allows them to offer the same service as the internal team but at a lower cost of delivery.

The experience outsourcers have with network management also means they should also have more effective processes based on established best practices to deal with the most common networking issues.

Network outsourcers can make the total cost of ownership (TCO) equation look even more attractive as they are able to source equipment from suppliers at a substantially cheaper rate. Adrian Lau, IT services manager at St Mary's NHS Trust, says: 'We buy our network equipment through Damovo. We use open-book costing where Damovo puts 5 per cent on the list price. This is cheaper than buying through a traditional distributor.'

Open-book costing is becoming more common throughout the network outsourcing industry. Richard Mahony, principal analyst at Ovum, says: 'Contract pricing is becoming more transparent. However, companies that do sign up to open-book pricing, need to be aware of exactly what it covers, as outsourcers will always try and hide some margin somewhere.'

Barriers

Smaller businesses are likely to benefit most from network outsourcing, but are often the most reluctant to take the plunge. At the most basic level, they typically find it difficult to calculate the cost of managing their IT, and often lump it together with general administration costs. This makes it hard for them to understand the savings they could make from outsourcing.

But perhaps the principal barrier for enterprises thinking about network outsourcing is nervousness over security. Enterprises now need to be compliant with multiple regulations and laws, nearly all of which mandate a high level of data security. Any company choosing an outsourcer will need to be doubly sure that it will actually improve on the existing security processes.

Outsourcing for many companies has traditionally meant job losses, which made it an extremely hard sell to employees. However, far from making IT staff redundant, outsourcing the network and support infrastructure should free up IT staff to work on the company's strategic business applications.

Another commonly encountered barrier to outsourcing is that the internal team knows the business best and can react most effectively to its needs. 'Companies need to consider how quickly the outsourcer can react to changing business', says Neil Walker, head of network systems at Cisco. 'The LAN may need quick changes, which they can do quickly in-house.'

St Mary's NHS Trust's Lau agrees. 'We want to have some control over the network and manage the LAN through our internal network manager,' he says. 'We find the LAN is much more straightforward to manage and we get much better response times if we do the simple management internally.' If the Trust has a more complex task that needs the help of external consultants, then it calls on the resources of its outsourcer.

Making the choice

The choice between self-management and outsourcing very much depends on the business's specific situation. While some businesses will choose to outsource just the WAN but keep the LAN in-house, others will outsource them both together in order to get end-to-end service levels from their outsourcer. 'Companies need to make their own decision on the cost/benefit analysis of outsourcing', says Ovum's Mahoney. 'They need to look out for getting the right contract which gives them improved productivity and cost improvements.'

If a company decides its business would be best served by outsourcing the network, there are a number of lessons they should follow. First is not to rely entirely on the outsourcer for technical expertise – the company should have an internal resource that is able to understand and work strategically with the outsourcer.

Second, the company needs to have proper governance of the outsourcer and not relinquish control of the strategic direction of their network.

Third, companies should find an outsourcer with the right cultural match and skills for their industry. This is particularly important in specialized areas such as the NHS because of its unique needs.

Fourth, the outsourcing contract needs to be flexible, so any changes to the customer's business are supported by the outsourcer.

And finally, the company needs to have a clear business case as to why it is outsourcing and communicate this clearly to the outsourcer who can back it up with appropriate service levels.

Thinking about the case

1 According to the passage, Somerfield were paying over the odds for their networking needs. How could they calculate this? How could they have avoided this situation?

2 What unique networking requirements would an NHS client have? Can you think of any other application areas that would have special requirements?

Risks, security and disaster recovery

As the use of computer-based information systems has spread, so has the threat to the integrity of data and the reliability of information. Organizations must deal seriously with the risks of both natural and manmade menaces. A computer expert once noted: 'The only truly secure system is powered off, cast in a block of concrete, and sealed in a lead room with armed guards. And even then I have my doubts.' Indeed, there is no way to fully secure an information system against every potential mishap, but there are ways to significantly reduce risks and recover losses.

When you finish this chapter, you will be able to:

Describe the primary goals of information security.

Enumerate the main types of risks to information systems.

List the various types of attacks on networked systems.

Describe the types of controls required to ensure the integrity of data entry and processing and uninterrupted e-commerce.

Describe the various kinds of security measures that can be taken to protect data and ISs.

Outline the principles of developing a recovery plan.

Explain the economic aspects of information security.

BATTLING BACK FROM ATTACKS

Worldwide Host's TripExpert.com site was fulfilling its promise. The site had been up for ten months now. CIO Michael Lloyd thought back to the end of the website's development project, when he had congratulated the General Data Systems staff for their hard work in getting the site up and running. At the time he did not pay much attention to the fact that the system was linked to a public network. Soon, he realized that such a link requires special consideration. The first event to draw his attention was a prank.

Website defaced

Michael's Webmaster, Susan O'Donnell, rushed into his office one day to report that someone had defaced the TripExpert home page. Since the site was so important to Worldwide, she checked it daily to ensure that it was running smoothly. She was shocked at what she saw on the site when she logged on in the morning. Someone had placed offensive images and language on the page, so she immediately took the site offline.

'It'll probably take us until early afternoon to get the site up again', she said. 'Fixing the home page takes only a few minutes, but ensuring that this doesn't happen again will take longer. We're working on it right now as our top priority.'

Michael responded, 'I'm coming down now to see for myself. We get transactions of about $90,000 an hour from that site. We've got to get it back online as soon as possible.'

Michael and Susan hurried down to the information centre, waved their badges in front of the radio ID scanner, entered their codes and opened the door. Inside, two IS staff members were working to clear the web page of the intruder's messages. All four worked furiously to find the hole that allowed the intruder to deface the home page. They quickly replaced the page with a backup copy. After several hours of hard work, they patched the server software with code that they believed would eliminate the security hole and brought the site back online.

Attacks continue

Five weeks after the defacement incident, Worldwide Host received a second blow: its site was among several that were hit with a denial-of-service attack. Requests were swamping Worldwide's servers. Michael and his IS security chief decided to disconnect the servers from the Net. Michael knew this meant a massive loss of profit, but there was nothing else he could do.

They turned the site on after an hour. Apparently, the attack had subsided, but Michael was worried that the attacker had also tried to damage databases or steal information.

'What is the extent of the problem, Jason? Did they breach any of our internal systems?'

'Doesn't look like it, but they were trying to get into our database. The secure servers that we use for transactions withstood the attempt to penetrate the customer database.'

Michael sighed with relief. 'Our security firm said that secure servers were critical to keeping our transactions private. Our system depends on the safety of our customers' information.'

'Well, the security people were right. I'll keep running my diagnostics on the damaged software', said Jason.

Irish online betting site PaddyPower.com suffered an extortive denial-of-service attack in early 2004.

'Susan is preparing a statement to post on the website to reassure our customers. We need to get that up fast. What else can we do to prevent denial-of-service attacks?'

'Since traffic load is the critical issue, we could add more servers to handle both the attacks and legitimate transactions. But the cost of those extra servers might be high.'

'Let's look into it. We need to keep our site online.'

Goals of information security

In June 2005, hackers invaded the databases of CardSystems Solutions, a company that processes credit-card transactions. Data from about 200,000 subscribers of MasterCard, Visa and other credit-card issuers were stolen. Had the hackers wanted, they could have used the same security breach to steal data from another 40 million accounts. Apparently, CardSystems Solutions did not comply with the data security policies that its clients required. The company paid a heavy toll: in July 2005 Visa and American Express stopped using the organization for their transaction processing. Visa and American Express gave merchants who used CardSystems' services ample time to switch to one of another several hundred companies that provide similar service.

As you have already seen, the development, implementation and maintenance of ISs constitute a large and growing part of the cost of doing business; protecting these resources is a primary concern. The increasing reliance on ISs, combined with their connection to the outside world through a public network, the Internet, makes securing corporate ISs increasingly challenging. The role of computer controls and security is to protect systems against accidental mishaps and intentional theft and corruption of data and application, as well as to help organizations ensure that their IT operations comply with the law and with expectations of employees and customers for privacy. The major goals of information security are to:

- Reduce the risk of systems and organizations ceasing operations.
- Maintain information confidentiality.
- Ensure the integrity and reliability of data resources.
- Ensure the uninterrupted availability of data resources and online operations.
- Ensure compliance with policies and laws regarding security and privacy.

To plan measures to support these goals, organizations must first be aware of the possible risks to their information resources, which include hardware, applications, data and networks; then, they must execute security measures to defend against those risks.

In recent years the European Union has introduced various directives and countries have passed several laws that set standards for the protection of patient and customer privacy and compliance with corporate internal controls. These laws have an important effect on securing information and, therefore, on securing information systems. However, corporate concern should not be focused only on complying with the law. It should ensure that information resources are secure to minimize situations that might practically take them out of business.

Risks to information systems

In recent years, especially because of the growth of online business, corporations have considered protection of their IS resources an increasingly important issue, for good reasons. Downtime, the time during which ISs or data are not available

downtime The unplanned period of time during which a system does not function.

in the course of conducting business, has become a dreaded situation for almost every business worldwide. The estimates by type of application for all industries are mind-boggling. According to a pan-European survey by Global Switch, a data centre provider, IT downtime costs businesses over €400,000 per hour.

Risks to hardware

While stories about damage to ISs by malicious Internet attacks grab headlines, the truth about risks to ISs is simply this: the number-one cause of systems downtime is hardware failure. Risks to hardware involve physical damage to computers, peripheral equipment and communications media. The major causes of such damage are natural disasters, blackouts and brownouts, and vandalism.

blackouts and brownouts Periods of power loss or a significant fall in power. Such events may cause computers to stop working, or even damage them. Computers can be protected against these events by using proper equipment, such as UPS (uninterruptible power supply) systems.

Natural disasters Natural disasters that pose a risk to ISs include fires, floods, earthquakes, hurricanes, tornadoes and lightning, which can destroy hardware, software or both, causing total or partial paralysis of systems or communications lines. Floodwater can ruin storage media and cause short circuits that burn delicate components such as microchips. Lightning and voltage surges cause tiny wires to melt and destroy circuitry. In addition, wildlife and human error occasionally destroy communication lines; animals gnaw cables, and farmers occasionally cut wires inadvertently while tending their crops.

Blackouts and brownouts Computers run on electricity. If power is disrupted, the computer and its peripheral devices cannot function, and the change in power supply can be very damaging to computer processes and storage. **Blackouts** are

PHOTO SOURCE: © COURTESY OF AMERICAN POWER CONVERSION CORP.

UPS units are a solution to extreme changes in voltage and can provide several minutes to several hours of back-up battery power.

total losses of electrical power. In brownouts, the voltage of the power decreases, or there are very short interruptions in the flow of power. Power failure might not only disrupt operations, but it can also cause irreparable damage to hardware. Occasional surges in voltage are equally harmful, because their impact on equipment is similar to that of lightning.

The popular way of handling brownouts is to connect a voltage regulator between computers and the electric network. A voltage regulator boosts or decreases voltage to smooth out drops or surges and maintains voltage within an acceptable tolerance.

To ensure against interruptions in power supply, organizations use uninterruptible power supply (UPS) systems, which provide an alternative power supply for a short time, as soon as a power network fails. The only practical measure against prolonged blackouts in a public electrical network is to maintain an alternative source of power, such as a generator that uses diesel or another fuel. Once the general power stops, the generator can kick in and produce the power needed for the computer system.

> **uninterruptible power supply (UPS)** A device that provides an alternative power supply as soon as a power network fails.

Vandalism Vandalism occurs when human beings deliberately destroy computer systems. Bitter customers might damage ATMs, or disgruntled employees might destroy computer equipment out of fear that it will eliminate their jobs or simply to get even with their superiors. It is difficult to defend computers against vandalism. ATMs and other equipment that are accessible to the public are often encased in metal boxes, but someone with persistence can still cause severe damage. In the workplace, the best measure against vandalism is to allow access only to those who have a real need for the system. Sensitive equipment, such as servers, should be locked in a special room. Such rooms usually are well equipped with fire suppression systems and are air-conditioned, and thus protected also against environmental risks.

Risks to data and applications

The primary concern of any organization should be its data, because these are often a unique resource. Data collected over time can almost never be recollected the same way, and even when they can, the process would be too expensive and too time-consuming to recover the business from its loss. The concern for applications, especially if the applications are not tailor-made, should come second. All data and applications are susceptible to disruption, damage and theft. While the culprit in the destruction of hardware is often a natural disaster or power spike, the culprit in damage to software is almost always human.

Theft of information and identity theft

Sometimes the negligence of corporations and the careless use of technology, especially on public links to the Internet, create security 'holes' or vulnerabilities. In one case, a young man named Juju Jiang installed a program called Invisible KeyLogger Stealth on public-use computers such as those in use at airports or Internet cafes. Keystroke logging software records individual keystrokes. For one year, his software secretly recorded more than 450 usernames and passwords, which he used to access existing bank accounts and create new ones. Jiang was caught when he used an application called GoToMyPC. Subscribers to the GoToMyPC service can use an application by the same name to link to a PC from another PC and fully control the remote one as if they were sitting in front of it. Using the application, he remotely accessed and used one of his victims' PCs. Using the PC at home, this person noticed that the cursor was moving 'by itself'. The cursor opened files and subscribed to an online payment transfer service. Jiang pleaded guilty in court.

> **keystroke logging** Automatically recording the keystrokes of a computer user. The logging is done by special software, usually surreptitiously with the intention of later using secret access codes.

In 2005 keystroke logging was put to work online on a massive scale by a criminal ring. As discussed in Chapter 7, spyware software is used for several purposes. This time spyware was used to install a keystroke logging application that recorded communication with the victim's bank, insurance company or other financial institutions. The collected data included credit-card details, usernames, passwords, instant messaging chat sessions and search terms. Some of the data were then saved in a file hosted on a server in the United States that had an offshore-registered domain name. Sunbelt, a company that develops and sells antispam and security software, managed to obtain access to a victim's computer and track what the spyware did.

The company reported that the online thieves obtained confidential financial details of customers of 50 international banks. The keystroke logging software was small (26 KB), and took advantage of Internet Explorer browsers. For example, it accessed the browser's Protected Storage area, in which users often save their usernames and passwords for convenient automatic logins. Sunbelt recommended disabling this feature.

In some cases employees unwittingly give away important information such as access codes. Con artists use tricks known as social engineering. They telephone or email an employee who has a password to access an application or a database, introduce themselves as service people from a telephone company, or the organization's own IT unit, and say they must have the employee's password to fix a problem. Employees are often tempted to provide their password. The 'social engineers' then steal valuable information.

Once criminals have a person's identifying details, such as a National Insurance Number, date of birth or credit-card number, they can pretend to be this person. This crime is called identity theft. The imposter can easily withdraw money from the victim's bank accounts, put charges on the victim's credit card, and apply for new credit cards. Since an increasing number of applications for such instruments as well as financial transactions are executed online, identity theft has become a serious problem. According to the UK Home Office, in 2006 identity theft cost the country over £1.7 billion in various sectors of the economy, from fraudulent

social engineering
Deceptive methods that hackers use to entice people to release confidential information such as access codes and passwords. Often, the crooks misrepresent themselves as technicians who need one's password for fixing a problem in a network.

identity theft The criminal practice of obtaining enough personal information to pretend to be the victim, usually resulting in running up that person's credit cards or issuing new credit cards under that person's name.

Industry **SNAPSHOT**

Losing your identity

A investigation by *Which?* magazine found that one in every four adults had either been a victim of identity theft or knew someone who had. As shocking as this statistic is, it has lead to a more useful side-effect. Two-thirds of all individuals are concerned about the problem, with many taking measures to counteract it. However, according *Which?* 33 per cent of adults do not take any precautions such as shredding personal documents, using a variety of passwords for online banking and checking personal credit files. This maybe time well spent. According to Equifax, a credit checking agency, a victim of identity theft could take up to 300 hours to clear their name. They also warn about sites such as Facebook and Friends Reunited. Putting personal

information such as dates of birth on these benign websites can open the door to fraudsters wishing to steal your identity.

SOURCE: 'Identity theft affecting one in four UK adults', Silicon.com

Why you should...

understand risks, security and disaster recovery planning

As explained and demonstrated throughout this book, information is the lifeblood of any modern organization. Practically every aspect of business depends on the currency of processed data and the timely provision of information. This fluent process can be achieved only if information systems are protected against threats. As a professional, you must be aware of what might happen to the ISs upon which you and your colleagues or subordinates depend. You must protect the systems against events that threaten their operation and make it impossible to carry out critical business activities. When a new system is developed, you should ask the developers to provide a system that not only supports the functions of your business unit but also incorporates controls that will minimize any compromise of the system. And to be prepared for a disaster, you should know how to implement your part of the business recovery plan to help restore operations as soon as possible.

As you can see from the snapshots and case studies in this chapter, computer disasters come in many forms but they can be summarized thus:

- They can affect hardware, software or data.
- They can be as a result of human intervention or physical problems (such as fire or flood).
- If people are involved then the problem can be because of an accident or it can be from some sort of malicious act, including terrorism.

tax and benefit claims to unpaid court fines because of a false identity being given at the time of the offence, to extra costs for ensuring the proper person turns up for a driving test and so on.

Both social engineering and breaking access codes to steal data from online databases have caused huge damage to corporations. Connecting databases to the Internet is necessary for proper operation of multisite organizations and organizations that must share data remotely with business partners. The only way to minimize hacking into such systems is to improve security measures.

In recent years identity theft has been more prevalent as part of *phishing*, a crime discussed in Chapter 9. Crooks spam millions of recipients with bogus messages, supposedly from legitimate companies, directing them to a site where they are requested to 'update' their personal data including passwords. The sites are ones constructed by the criminals who steal the personal data and use it to charge the victim's credit account, apply for new credit cards, or – in the worst situations – also apply for other documents or for loans online.

Data alteration, data destruction and web defacement

Alteration or destruction of data is often an act of mischief. Data alteration is not a new phenomenon. In 1983, a group of American teenagers accessed a computer system at Sloan-Kettering Cancer Center in New York via a modem and altered patients' records just for 'fun'. An alert nurse noticed a double – and lethal – dose of a medication in a patient's record and called a doctor. She saved the patient's life.

As mentioned before, an organization's data are often the most important asset it owns, even more important than its hardware and applications. Even if data are altered or destroyed as a prank, the damage to the organization is great. The effort to reinstate missing or altered records from a backup copy might entail expensive labour. Even if the actual damage is not great, IT staff must spend a lot of time scanning the data pools to ascertain the integrity of the entire resource, and they must also figure out how the perpetrator managed to circumvent security controls. This activity itself wastes the time of high-salaried employees.

Often, the target of online vandals is not data but the organization's website. Each day, some organizations find that their websites have been defaced. Defacement causes several types of damage: first-time visitors are not likely to stay around long enough or revisit to learn about the true nature of the site, and they might associate the offensive material with the organization; frequent visitors might never come back; and shoppers who have had a good experience with the site might leave it forever because they no longer trust its security measures.

CD TASK

To deface a website, an intruder needs to know the site's access code or codes that enable the Webmaster and other authorized people to work on the site's server and update its pages. The intruder might either obtain the codes from someone who knows them or use special 'brute force' software that tries different codes until it succeeds in accessing the pages.

Website defacing is done to embarrass an organization or as an act of protest. In June 2005 Microsoft's United Kingdom website was defaced with a banner 'FREE RAFA – HACK IS NOT A CRIME'. The banner referred to Rafael Nunez-Aponte, who had been arrested in the United States for attacks on US government websites. Zohn-h, an Estonian security firm that tracks website attacks, recorded 392,545 attacks on websites, of which 322,188 were for the mere purpose of defacement, in 2004. The firm estimated that 2500 web servers are successfully attacked daily.

The best measure against defacement, of course, is software that protects against unauthorized access, or as it is more commonly known, hacking. However, since such software might fail, the public damage can be minimized by ensuring that members of the organization monitor the home page and other essential pages frequently. When the defacement is detected shortly after it occurs, the defaced pages can be replaced with backups before too many visitors have seen the rogue pages. An increasing number of websites are restored within hours or even minutes from the defacement.

The cure to any unauthorized entry to an IS is for the organization to find the hole in its security software and fix it with the appropriate software. Such software is often called a 'patch'. Software companies that sell server management applications often produce patches and invite clients to download and install them.

honeytoken A bogus record in a database on a honeypot or productive server that is likely to draw an intruder's attention. If the intruder changes the record, the security officers know that the server has been attacked and can fix vulnerabilities.

honeypot A duplicate database on a server connected to the Internet to trace an intruder. The server is dedicated specifically for detection of intrusions and is not productive. The honeypot is there to be attacked in lieu of a productive server. The traces can be used to improve security measures and possibly catch the intruder.

To combat hackers, organizations use honeytokens. A honeytoken is a bogus record in a networked database that neither employees nor business partners would ever access for legitimate purposes. When the intruder copies the database or the part of the database that contains that record, a simple program alerts security personnel, who can start an investigation. The program that detects the incident might also reside on a router or another communications device that is programmed to send an alert as soon as it detects the honeytoken. To entice the intruder to retrieve the honeytoken when only searching for individual records, the honeytoken might be a bogus record of a famous person, such as a medical record of a celebrity in a medical database or the salary of the CEO in a payroll database.

To learn of security holes and methods of unauthorized access, organizations can establish honeypots. A honeypot is a server that contains a mirrored copy of a production database (a database that is used for business operations), or one with invalid records. It is set up to make intruders think they have accessed a production database. The traces they leave educate information security officers about vulnerable points in the configuration of servers that perform valid work. In some cases security people can follow an intruder's 'roaming' in the honeypot in real time. Note, however, that different sources have different definitions of the terms honeypot and honeytoken. For example, some define honeypot as any trap set for abusers, including a physical computer, and a honeytoken as a special case where the trap is only data.

Computer viruses, worms and logic bombs

Computer viruses are so named because they act on programs and data in a fashion similar to the way viruses act on living tissue: computer viruses easily spread from computer to computer. Because so many computers are now connected to one another and many people share files, people unknowingly transmit to other computers viruses that have infected their own files. Once a virus reaches a computer, it damages applications and data files. In addition to destroying legitimate applications and data files, viruses might disrupt data communications: the presence of viruses causes data communications applications to process huge numbers of messages and files for no useful purpose, which detracts from the efficiency of transmitting and receiving legitimate messages and files. The only difference between a computer virus and a worm is that a worm spreads in a network without human intervention. A worm attacks computers without the need to send email or open any received files. Most people refer to both types of rogue code as viruses, as does this book.

Almost as soon as email became widespread, criminal minds used it to launch viruses. The Melissa virus of 1999 was an early demonstration of why you should be suspicious of email messages even when they seem to come from people or organizations you know. In the Melissa case, an innocent-looking email message contained an attached Microsoft Word document that, when opened, activated a macro that sent an infected message to the first 50 entries in the victim's Microsoft Outlook address book. Many other viruses spread in a similar way: the recipient is tempted to open – and thereby activate – a file that is attached to a message. The program in that file then destroys files, slows down operations or does both, and uses vulnerabilities in the operating system and other applications to launch copies of itself to other computers linked to the Internet. Since Melissa, there have been thousands of virus and worm attacks, and millions of computers continue to be infected.

Some viruses do not affect any files, but the speed at which they spread and their repeated attacks slow down network traffic to an intolerable crawl. In January 2003 the Slammer worm struck more than 75,000 computers in just ten minutes. The number of infected computers doubled every 8.5 seconds. According to MessageLabs Inc., which scans email for viruses, in August 2003 its software detected more than 1 million copies of the 'F' variant of the Sobig virus within 24 hours of its first detection. Many organizations had to shut down their email services because of the Sobig virus.

There are many more viruses waiting for victims. CERT/CC (Computer Emergency Response Team/Coordination Centre), operated by Carnegie Mellon University, works for the US government and is one of the major distributors of information to the whole of the world on new viruses, worms and other threats to computer security. It estimated that there are at least 30,000 computer viruses somewhere on public networks at any given time; other sources estimate the number at 40,000. CERT says that about 300 new ones are created each month.

One way to protect against viruses is to use antivirus software, which is readily available on the market from companies that specialize in developing this kind of software, such as Symantec and McAfee. Subscribers can regularly update the software with code that identifies and deletes or quarantines new viruses, or choose automatic updates, in which virus definitions are updated automatically when the computer is connected to the Internet. However, if a new virus is designed to operate in a way not yet known, the software is unlikely to detect it. Most virus-detection applications allow the user to automatically or selectively destroy suspect programs. Another way to minimize virus threats is to program network software, especially email server software, to reject any messages that come with executable files that might be or contain viruses. Some email applications, such as Microsoft Outlook, are programmed to reject such files.

Some viruses are called Trojan horses, analogous to the destructive gift given to the ancient Trojans. In their war against Troy, the Greeks pretended they were

virus Destructive software that propagates and is activated by unwary users; a virus usually damages applications and data files or disrupts communications.

worm A rogue program that spreads in a computer network.

CD TASK

antivirus software Software designed to detect and intercept computer viruses.

Trojan horse A malicious piece of software hidden with a benign and legitimate software that one downloads or agrees to otherwise accept and install on one's computer. The Trojan horse then causes damage.

Industry SNAPSHOT

Government advice

The website for the UK Department for Business, Industry and Regulatory Reform (formerly the Department of Trade and Industry) has plenty of advice about virus protection. Its suggestions for avoiding the downloading of viruses from email include:

- Make sure people are wary of strange emails, especially if they do not recognize the sender, or if the message is unusual.

- Never rely on email to alert users to a virus infection that is carried by email. If you can, use the telephone, or have written warnings placed at entrances to workplaces or even on potentially infected machines. Users are more likely to open the virus email before the warning.

- Install antivirus software and keep it up to date. Remember that this will not only protect you and your company but may also protect your clients and other contacts. The company involved in this case study received news of its own infection from the worst possible source, a client that it had infected.

- If you outsource IT services, make sure that you provide defined procedures and requirements to your outsource agent before the contract is signed. Make security (including virus management) part of the contract, and ensure you retain the right to monitor activities.

SOURCE: www.berr.gov.uk

PHOTO SOURCE: © CROWN COPYRIGHT

abandoning the city's outskirts and left behind a big wooden horse as a present. The Trojans pulled the horse into the city. When night fell, Greek soldiers hidden within the horse jumped out and opened the gates for thousands of their comrades, who conquered the city. In computer terms, a Trojan horse is any virus disguised as legitimate software or useful software that contains a virus. Many people also refer to spyware that comes with useful software as Trojan horse software.

A growing number of viruses and worms take advantage of vulnerable features of operating systems, most notably Microsoft Windows. Most attack this company's operating systems because the large majority of organizations worldwide use Microsoft operating systems to run their servers and computers. In the same way software vendors provide patches against direct intrusion into computer systems, they also distribute security patches against viruses and worms. However, it is up to security professionals and network administrators to implement those patches as soon as they become available. Six months before the SQL Slammer worm attack, Microsoft distributed patches to fix the vulnerability that the worm exploited. Unfortunately, many companies did not apply the patch. On 25 January 2003, the worm attacked 300,000 servers worldwide. Within 14 minutes, servers with the popular database software SQL Server started to crash on five continents. The South Korean Internet service was totally shut down for several hours, some airlines were forced to cancel flights because of problems with electronic check-in and many ATMs owned by Bank of America were disabled.

Some rogue computer programs do not spread immediately like a virus but are often significantly more damaging to the individual organization that is victimized. A logic bomb is software that is programmed to cause damage at a specified time to specific applications and data files. It lies dormant until a certain event takes place in the computer or until the computer's inner clock reaches the specified time; the event or time triggers the virus to start causing damage. Logic bombs are usually planted by insiders, that is, employees of the victimized organization. In one case, a man named Timothy Lloyd was convicted of planting a logic bomb on Omega Engineering's computer system after he found out he was about to be fired. Lloyd, who had worked for the company for 11 years, planted six destructive lines of code on a company network server. He had tested the bomb and then reconstructed all the files. Twenty days after he left the company, the bomb erased all of the company's contracts, designs and production programs, as well as proprietary software used by the company's manufacturing machines. The 31-year-old man's act cost the company an estimated $12 million, led to laying off 80 employees and diminished its competitive position in the electronic manufacturing market. A plant manager for the company who testified at Lloyd's trial said the company would never recover from this sabotage. Lloyd was sentenced to 41 months in prison.

> **logic bomb** A destructive computer program that is inactive until it is triggered by an event taking place in the computer, such as the deletion of a certain record from a file. When the event is a particular time, the logic bomb is referred to as a time bomb.

Non-malicious mishaps

Unintentional damage to software occurs because of poor training, lack of adherence to simple backup procedures, or simple human error. Although unintentional damage rarely occurs in robust applications, poor training might result in inappropriate use of an application so that it ruins data, unbeknownst to the user. For instance, when faced with an instruction that might change or delete data, a robust application will pose a question such as: 'Are you sure you want to delete the record?' or issue a warning such as 'This might destroy the file.' More common damage is caused by the failure to save all work and create a backup copy. Destruction of data often happens when using a word-processing program to create text files and when updating databases.

Unauthorized downloading and installation of software that might cause damage can be controlled by limiting administration rights to employees. Many organizations instruct operating systems to deny such rights to most employees. They program ISs to accept new software installation only when the proper access codes are entered.

Risks to online operations

The massive movement of operations to the Internet has attracted hackers who try to interrupt such operations daily. In addition to unauthorized access, data theft and defacing of web pages, there has been a surge in denial-of-service attacks and hijacking of computers.

Denial of service

In February 2005, people who tried to access the websites of the Japanese prime minister and cabinet office could not do so because the sites were victims of a denial-of-service attack. Denial of service (DoS) occurs when someone launches a frequent and unusually large number of information requests to a website. The mere logging in to a site is such a request. The intention of such log-in requests is to slow down legitimate traffic on the site's server; business can slow to a halt. The server's or servers' frantic efforts to handle the massive amount of traffic denies legitimate visitors and business partners access to the site.

denial of service (DoS) The inability of legitimate visitors to log on to a website when too many malicious requests are launched by an attacker. Most DoS attacks are distributed (DDoS).

Such attacks are usually perpetrated from multiple computers, in which case they are called distributed denial-of-service (DDoS) attacks. In most such attacks, the perpetrator launches software that uses other people's computers for the attack – unbeknownst to them. Professionals call the computers used in these attacks 'zombies.' Zombie computers not only exacerbate the volume of calls but also make it impossible to track down the generator of the DDoS. Practically all DoS attacks now are of the DDoS type.

distributed denial of service (DDoS) Multiple log-in requests from many computers to the same website, so that the website is jammed with requests and cannot accept enquiries of legitimate visitors.

Because it is impossible to stop anyone from trying to log on to a website, there is no full cure for a DDoS attack, but equipment is available that can filter most of the illegitimate traffic targeting a site. The equipment detects repeated requests that come from the same IP numbers at an abnormal frequency and blocks them, and it can be programmed to block all incoming communication from suspected servers. The equipment can filter about 99 per cent, but using the equipment slows down communication, so the site's response is slowed. In addition, blocking requests might also deny access to legitimate visitors from suspected servers, especially if the server is used by an ISP who provides Internet access to thousands of people and organizations. One way to mitigate DoS attacks is for an organization to use multiple servers, which is a good idea anyway to handle times of legitimate traffic increases.

No organization is immune to DDoS. Some of the most visible websites have been attacked, including those of eBay, Amazon, CNN and the US White House. All had to shut down their sites for several hours. Amazon, eBay and other sites have lost revenue as a result. Even CERT has been forced to shut down its site. A DDoS attack sent information into its website at rates several hundred times higher than normal. One report from the University of California at San Diego estimated that there are 4000 DDoS attacks somewhere in the world each week.

Computer hijacking

You might not be aware of it, but there is a good chance your networked computer has been hijacked. No, nobody would remove it from your desk, but if it is connected to the Internet, it is used by other people. Hijacking a computer means using some or all of the resources of a computer linked to a public network without the consent of its owner. As you have seen, this has been done for DDoS, but it is also done for other purposes.

hijacking In the context of networks, when computers are remotely taken advantage of by people who are not authorized to do so by the lawful owner. The computer is 'hijacked' after a controlling application is surreptitiously installed on the computer's hard disk. Hijacked computers are exploited to participate in spamming or DDoS attacks.

Hijacking is carried out by surreptitiously installing a small program called a *bot* on a computer. Like many viruses, these programs are downloaded unwittingly by people who use chat rooms and file-sharing networks. When your computer is hijacked, your Internet connection might slow to a crawl. The damage to corporations in the form of reduced productivity can be great. The main purpose of hijacking computers is spamming: using hijacked computers to send unsolicited commercial email to large numbers of people, often millions of addresses. Spammers do so for two reasons: they hide the real source of the email so that they cannot be identified and pursued, and they take advantage of the hijacked machines'

Industry **SNAPSHOT**

Big rewards and a light sentence

Because so many viruses attack operating systems developed by Microsoft, in 2003 the company started offering monetary rewards of $250,000 each for informants who help arrest and convict criminals who launch such viruses. Two informants helped to arrest and convict Sven Jaschan, a German teenager who launched the Sasser worm in May 2004. Sasser exploited a flaw in Windows 2000 and Windows XP and caused hundreds of thousands of PCs to crash and reboot. The two informants shared the $250,000 reward. The 19-year old Jaschan was sentenced to 21 months of suspended arrest for a probation period of three years. While on probation, he had to provide 30 hours of community service either at a hospital or a retirement home – later he found a job as a programmer.

In an even more astounding case of 'poacher turned gamekeeper', a Chinese virus writer, Li Jun, received a four-year sentence along with several job offers, according to the *Changjiang Times*. One of the companies hit by his virus offered Li the position of technology director with a salary of a million Yuan, over € 90,000, which contrasts with the amount of money Li made from the sale of his program to online thieves at 145,000 Yuan!

SOURCES: J. Evers, 'Sasser Author Gets Suspended Sentence', CNET News.com (http://news.com.com/), 8 July 2005; http://www.securityfocus.com/brief/595?ref=rss, 25 October 2007

computer resources – CPU time, memory and communications link – to expedite the distribution of spam.

Antivirus software vendor McAfee estimated that from April to June 2005, 13,000 additional computers were hijacked, an increase of 63 per cent over the same period in the previous year. In all, Symantec – another antivirus vendor – estimated that hundreds of thousands of computers were infected with bots. Other experts estimate the number in the millions. The main targets are corporate and household computers with fast Internet connections shared by two or more computers.

To hijack computers, spammers exploit security holes in operating systems and communications software, and then surreptitiously install email forwarding software, much as one would install a virus. Most users do not notice the extra work their computers do. One precaution is to check why a computer continues activity (such as hard disk work) when the owner does not use it. Computer owners can also install special software that detects email forwarding applications.

Computer hijacking is also done to turn computers into zombies to help a DDoS. Instead of exploiting the computers to send email, they are used to send repeated service requests to web servers. The MSBlast worm was programmed to launch a DDoS attach against the Microsoft Windows Update site on the 16th of each month starting in August 2003. Microsoft posted a patch against the bot and later reported that by April 2004 its update system had removed the virus from 9.5 million computers.

Table 13.1 Common controls to protect systems from risks

Program robustness and data entry controls
Backup
Access controls
Atomic transactions
Audit trail

Controls

controls Constraints applied to a system to ensure proper use and security standards.

Controls are constraints and other restrictions imposed on a user or a system, and they can be used to secure systems against the risks just discussed or to reduce damage caused to systems, applications and data. Table 13.1 lists the most common controls. Controls are implemented not only for access but also to implement policies and ensure that nonsensical data are not entered into corporate databases.

Program robustness and data entry controls

A computer program is said to be 'robust' if it is free of bugs and can handle unforeseen situations well. Robust applications can resist inappropriate usage, such as incorrect data entry or processing. The most robust programs consider every possible misuse or abuse. A highly robust program includes code that promptly produces a clear message if a user either errs or tries to circumvent a process. For example, a website invites users to select a username and password, and the operators want passwords that are not easy to guess. The application should be programmed to reject any password that has fewer than a certain number of characters or does not include numerals. A clear message then must be presented, inviting the user to follow the guidelines.

Controls also translate business policies into system features. For example, Blockbuster Video uses its IS to implement a policy limiting debt for each customer to a certain level. When a customer reaches the debt limit and tries to hire another DVD, a message appears on the cash register screen: 'Do not rent!' Thus, the policy is implemented by using a control at the point of sale. Similar systems do not allow any expenditures to be committed unless a certain budgetary item is first checked to ensure sufficient allocation. A spending policy has been implemented through the proper software.

backup Periodic duplication of data in order to guard against loss.

RAID (Redundant Array of Independent Disks) A set of magnetic disk packs maintained for backup purposes. Sometimes RAIDs are used for storing large databases.

Backup

Probably the easiest way to protect against loss of data is to automatically duplicate all data periodically, a process referred to as data backup. Storage media suitable for routine backup were discussed in Chapter 4. Many systems have built-in automatic backup programs. The data might be duplicated on inexpensive storage devices such as magnetic tapes. Manufacturers of storage devices also offer Redundant Arrays of Independent Disks (RAID) for this purpose. RAID is a set of disks that is programmed to replicate stored data to provide a higher degree of reliability.

Of course, backing up data is not enough. The disks or tapes with backed up data must be routinely transported off-site, so that if a business site is damaged by a disaster, the remote storage can be used since it is likely to be spared. In the past, many companies had a truck haul backup disks and tapes to the storage location at the end of every business day, and some might still do so. However, due to the great developments in telecommunications in recent years, most corporations prefer to back up data at a remote site through communications lines. Often, the backup disks or tapes reside thousands of miles away from the organization's business offices. For additional protection, backup disks or tapes are locked in safes that can withstand fire and floods.

Redundant arrays of independent disks (RAID) automatically back up transactions onto disks that can be removed and stored in a safe place.

Companies can also use the services of firms that specialize in providing backup facilities. The vendor maintains a site with huge amounts of disk space linked to the Internet. The online data backup service typically provides client organizations with an application that copies designated files from the client's systems to the remote disks. For obvious reasons, some professionals call this type of service 'e-vaulting'. One company that provides the service is Iron Mountain (www.ironmountain.co.uk).

Access controls

Unauthorized access to information systems, usually via public networks such as the Internet, does not always damage IT resources. However, it is regarded as one of the most serious threats to security because it is often the prelude to the destruction of websites, databases, and other resources, or theft of valuable information.

Access controls are measures taken to ensure that only those who are authorized have access to a computer or network or to certain applications or data. One way to block access to a computer is by physically locking it in a facility to which only authorized users have a key or by locking the computer itself with a physical key. However, in the age of networked computers, this solution is practical only for a limited number of servers and other computers. Therefore, these organizations must use other access controls, most of which rely on software.

access controls
Hardware and software measures, such as user IDs and passwords, used to control access to information systems.

Experts like to classify access controls into three groups: what you know, what you have and who you are. 'What you know' includes access codes such as user IDs, account numbers and passwords. 'What you have' is some kind of a device, such as a security card, which you use directly or which continuously changes coordinated access codes and displays them for you. 'Who you are' includes your unique physical characteristics.

The most common way to control access is through the combination of a user ID and a password. While user IDs are usually not secret, passwords are. IS managers encourage users to change their passwords frequently, which most systems easily allow, so that others do not have time to figure them out. Some organizations have systems that force users to change their passwords at preset intervals, such as once a month or once every three months. Some systems also prevent users from selecting a password that they have used in the past, to minimize the chance that someone else might guess it, and many require a minimum length and mix of characters and numerals. Access codes and their related passwords are maintained either in a special list that becomes part of the operating system or in a database that the system searches to determine whether a user is authorized to access the requested resource.

A more secure measure than passwords is security cards, such as RSA's SecureID. The device is distributed to employees who need access to confidential databases, usually remotely.

PHOTO SOURCE: © COURTESY OF AMERICAN POWER CONVERSION CORP.

Fingerprint readers have been adopted by an increasing number of organizations as biometric controls. This mouse verifies a thumbprint in less than a second.

Employees receive a small device that displays a six-digit number. Special circuitry changes the number both at the server and the device to the same new number every minute. To gain access, employees enter at least one access code and the current number. The device is small enough to be carried on a key chain or in a wallet. This two-factor access control increases the probability that only authorized people gain access. This is an example of using both what you know and what you have.

In recent years, some companies have adopted physical access controls called biometrics. A **biometric** characteristic is a unique physical, measurable characteristic of a human being that is used to identify a person. Characteristics such as fingerprints, retinal pictures, or voiceprints can be used in biometrics. They are in the class of 'who you are'. When a fingerprint is used, the user presses a finger on a scanner or puts it before a digital camera. The fingerprint is compared against a database of digitized fingerprints of people with authorized access. A growing number of laptop computers have a built-in fingerprint scanner for the same purpose. The procedure is similar when the image of a person's retina is scanned. With voice recognition, the user is instructed to utter a word or several words. The intonation and accent are digitized and compared with a list of digitized voice samples.

> **biometric** A unique, measurable characteristic or trait of a human being used for automatically authenticating a person's identity. Biometric technologies include digitized fingerprints, retinal pictures and voice. Used with special hardware to uniquely identify a person who tries to access a facility or an IS, instead of a password.

Several manufacturers of computer equipment offer individual keyboard-embedded and mouse-embedded fingerprint devices. For example, SecuGen Corporation offers EyeD Mouse, a mouse that includes a fingerprint reader on the thumb side of the device. It verifies a fingerprint in less than a second. Using biometric access devices is the best way not only to prevent unauthorized access to computers but also to reduce the workload of Help desk personnel. Up to 50 per cent of the calls Help desk personnel receive come from employees who have forgotten their passwords.

Atomic transactions

As you know, in an efficient IS, a user enters data only once, and the data are recorded in different files for different purposes, according to the system's programmed instructions. For instance, in a typical order system, a sale is recorded in several files: the shipping file (so that the warehouse knows what to pack and ship), the invoice file (to produce an invoice and keep a copy in the system), the accounts receivable file (for accounting purposes) and the commission file (so that the salesperson can be compensated with the appropriate commission fee at the end of the month). As indicated in Figure 13.1, a system supports atomic transactions when its code allows the recording of data only if they successfully reach all their many destinations. An **atomic transaction** (from the Greek *atomos*, indivisible) is a set of indivisible transactions that are either all executed or none are – never only some. Using atomic transactions ensures that only full entry occurs in all the appropriate files.

> **atomic transaction** A transaction whose entry is not complete until all entries into the appropriate files have been successfully completed. It is an important data entry control. (Atom = Indivisible)

For instance, suppose the different files just mentioned reside on more than one disk, one of which is malfunctioning. When the clerk enters the sale transaction, the system tries to automatically record the appropriate data from the entry into

Figure 13.1 Atomic transactions ensure updating of all appropriate files. Either all files are updated, or none are updated and the control produces an error message

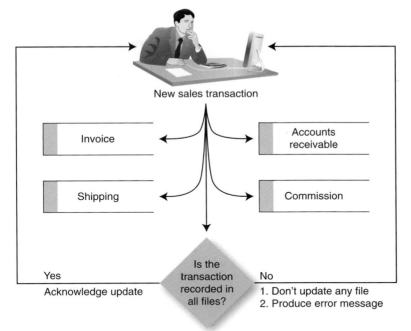

each of the files. The shipping, accounts receivable and invoice files are updated, but the malfunctioning commission file cannot accept the data. Without controls, the sale would be recorded, but unknown to anyone, the commission would not be updated and the salesperson would be deprived of the commission on this deal. However, an atomic transaction control mechanism detects that not all four files have been updated with the transaction, and it doesn't update any of the files. The system might try to update again later, but if the update does not go through, the application produces an appropriate error message for the clerk, and remedial action can be taken.

Note that this is a control not only against a malfunction but also against fraud. Suppose the salesperson collaborates with the clerk to enter the sale only in the commission file, so he or she can be rewarded for a sale that has never taken place – and then plans to split the fee with the clerk. The atomic transactions control would not let this happen.

Audit trail

In spite of the many steps taken to prevent system abuse, it nonetheless occurs. Consequently, further steps are needed to track transactions so that (1) when abuses are found, they can be traced, and (2) fear of detection indirectly discourages abuse. One popular tracking tool is the audit trail: a series of documented facts that help detect who recorded which transactions, at what time and under whose approval. Whenever an employee records a transaction, such a system prompts the employee to provide certain information: an invoice number, account number, salesperson ID number and the like. Sometimes an audit trail is automatically created using data, such as the date and time of a transaction or the name or password of the user updating the file. Such data are recorded directly from the computer – often unbeknownst to the user – and attached to the record of the transaction.

audit trail Names, dates and other references in computer files that can help an auditor track down the person who used an IS for a transaction, legal or illegal.

Industry **SNAPSHOT**

Big on biometrics

Interest in biometric technologies has steadily increased worldwide. In the United States and Europe, companies such as Alcatel, Nuance Communications and SAFLINK Corp. have developed security methods that dispense with passwords and personal identification numbers and instead use face recognition, fingerprints and vein recognition. The global biometric market was $719 million but is expected to grow to $4.6 billion by 2008. Japanese corporations are especially interested in such technologies since the Personal Information Protection Law was passed in April 2005. Japan's second largest bank, Mitsubishi Tokyo Financial Group, receives 2000 applications daily for a credit card that identifies users by the veins in their palms.

SOURCE: 'Japan's Biometric Security Firms See Demand Booming', Reuters, 16 August 2005

A UK police officer scans the fingerprint of a motorist using a mobile scanner.

PHOTO SOURCE: © 67PHOTO/ALAMY

The laws and regulations of many countries require certain policy and audit trail controls, and since so many operations are performed using ISs, the controls must be programmed into software. In the United States, the Sarbanes-Oxley Act of 2002 requires corporations to implement audit trails and other measures in their systems.

Audit trail information helps uncover undesirable acts, from innocent mistakes to premeditated fraud. The information helps determine who authorized and who made the entries, the date and time of the transactions and other identifying data that are essential in correcting mistakes or recovering losses. The audit trail is the most important tool of the *information systems auditor* (formerly known as the electronic data processing auditor), the professional whose job it is to find erroneous or fraudulent cases and investigate them.

Security measures

As you've seen so far in this chapter, the great increase in the number of people and organizations using the Internet has provided fertile ground for unauthorized and destructive activity. This section describes several ways that organizations can protect themselves against such attacks, including using firewalls, authentication and encryption, digital signatures and digital certificates.

Firewalls and proxy servers

The best defence against unauthorized access to systems over the Internet is a firewall, which is hardware and software that blocks access to computing resources. Firewalls are routinely integrated into the circuitry of routers, as discussed in Chapter 5. Firewall software screens the activities of a person who logs on to a website; it allows retrieval and viewing of certain material, but blocks attempts to change the information or to access other resources that reside on the same computer or computers connected to it.

> **firewall** Hardware and software designed to control access by Internet surfers to an information system, and access to Internet sites by organizational users.

It is important to note that while firewalls are used to keep unauthorized users out, they are also used to keep unauthorized software or instructions away, such as computer viruses and other rogue software. When an employee uses a company computer to access external websites, the firewall screens for viruses and active attempts to invade company resources through the open communications line. It might also be programmed to block employee access to sites that are suspected of launching rogue programs, or to sites that provide no useful resources. The firewall then prohibits the user from logging on to those sites.

As Figure 13.2 illustrates, a firewall controls communication between a trusted network and the 'untrusted' Internet. The firewall can be installed on a server or on a router. Network professionals use firewall software to check which applications can access the Internet and which servers might be accessed from the organization's network.

To increase security, some companies implement the DMZ (demilitarized zone) approach. The DMZ is a network of computers that are connected to the company's trusted network (such as an intranet) at one end and the untrusted network – the public Internet – at the other end. The DMZ includes resources to which the organization allows direct access from the Internet. It might include a website and computers from which people can download files. A DMZ provides a barrier between the Internet and a company's organizational network, which is usually an intranet. The connection between the DMZ and the organization's trusted network is established by using a proxy server.

> **DMZ** Demilitarized zone, a network of computers and other devices connected to the Internet where visitors are not allowed direct access to other resources connected to the DMZ. DMZs are used to serve visitors while minimizing risk of unauthorized access.

A proxy server 'represents' another server for all information requests from resources inside the trusted network. However, a proxy server can also be placed between the Internet and the organization's trusted network when there is no DMZ. For example, this might be the arrangement when the organization establishes its website as part of its trusted network. The proxy server then retrieves web pages for computers, requesting them remotely through the Internet. Thus, external computers requesting web pages never come in direct touch with the computer hosting the web pages. When a business hires the services of an ISP, the proxy server is often the one operated by the ISP.

> **proxy server** A computer that serves as an intermediary between two servers on the Internet, often for the purpose of security or filtering out certain information.

Both the organizational network server and proxy server employ firewalls. In Figure 13.2, the firewalls would be installed on the server of the organizational network and the router. The router is often called a 'boundary router'. The double firewall architecture adds an extra measure of security for an intranet.

Authentication and encryption

With so much web-based commerce and other communication on the Internet, both businesses and individuals must be able to authenticate messages. That is, they must be able to tell whether certain information, plain or encrypted, was sent to them by the party that was

Figure 13.2 Firewalls

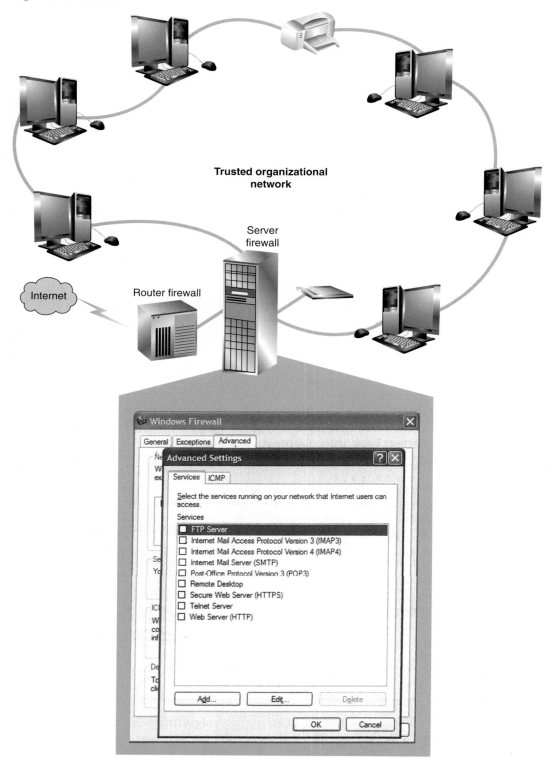

supposed to send it. Note that the word 'message' is used here for any type of information, not only text. It might be images, sounds or any other information in digital form.

Authentication is the process of ensuring that the person who sends a message to or receives a message from you is indeed that person. Authentication can be accomplished by senders and receivers exchanging codes known only to them. Once authentication is established, keeping a message secret can be accomplished by transforming it into a form that cannot be read by anyone who intercepts it. Coding a message into a form unreadable to an interceptor is called encryption. Authentication often occurs also when an encrypted message is received, because the recipient needs to ensure that the message was indeed encrypted and sent by a certain party.

Both authentication and secrecy are important when communicating confidential information such as financial and medical records. Authentication and secrecy are also essential when transacting business through a public network. For example, millions of people now buy and sell shares of stock and other financial products on the Web, businesses and individuals make purchases through the Web and use credit-card account numbers for payment and medical clinics use the Web to transmit patient records to insurance companies. All must authenticate the recipient and keep the entire communication confidential.

To authenticate the users and maintain secrecy, the parties can use encryption programs. Encryption programs scramble information transmitted over the network so that an interceptor receives only unintelligible data. The original message is called plaintext; the coded message is called ciphertext. Encryption uses a mathematical algorithm, which is a formula, and a key. The key is a unique combination of bits that must be used in the formula to decipher the ciphertext. As indicated in Figure 13.3, the receiving computer uses the key to decipher the ciphertext back into plaintext.

Public-key encryption

As Figure 13.4 indicates, when both the sender and recipient use the same secret key (which is the case in the earlier example), the technique is called symmetric encryption. However, symmetric encryption requires that the recipient have the key before the encrypted text is received. Therefore, the key is referred to simply as a *secret key* or *private key*. While it is fairly simple to keep the secrecy of a message when the sender and

authentication The process of ensuring that the person who sends a message to or receives a message from another party is indeed that person.

encryption The conversion of plaintext to an unreadable stream of characters, especially to prevent a party that intercepts telecommunicated messages from reading them. Special encryption software is used by the sending party to encrypt messages, and by the receiving party to decipher them.

plaintext An original message, before encryption.

ciphertext A coded message designed to authenticate users and maintain secrecy.

symmetric (secret or private key) encryption Encryption technology in which both the sender and recipient of a message use the same key for encryption and decryption.

Figure 13.3 Encrypting communications increases security

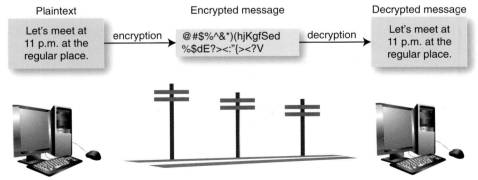

Plaintext		Encrypted message		Decrypted message
Let's meet at 11 p.m. at the regular place.	encryption →	@#$%^&*)(hjKgfSed %$dE?><:"{><?V	decryption →	Let's meet at 11 p.m. at the regular place.

Figure 13.4 Symmetric (secret key) and asymmetric (public key) encryption

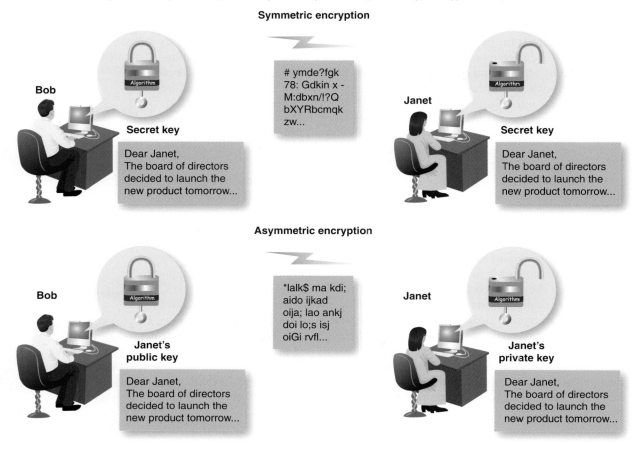

recipient have the same key beforehand, it is impractical in daily transactions on the Internet. For example, a retail website would not be able to function if every time a new buyer registered it required a secret key to ensure confidentiality. Therefore, in such communication, there must be a way for the sender to communicate the key to the recipient before the message is sent. To this end, the parties use an asymmetric encryption comprising two keys: one is public, and the other is private. It is clear why this type of encryption is also called public-key encryption.

A public key is distributed widely and might be known to everyone; a private key is secret and known only to the recipient of the message. When the sender wants to send a secure message to the recipient, he uses the recipient's public key to encrypt the message. The recipient then uses her own private key to decrypt it. There is a mathematical relationship between the public and private keys. The public and private keys are related in such a way that only the public key can be used to encrypt messages, and only the corresponding private key can be used to decrypt them. It is virtually impossible to deduce the private key from the public key. All applications that use public keys and private keys use the same principles. What differentiates them from one another is the different encryption algorithm each uses.

Online businesses often switch site visitors to a secure server when visitors are asked to provide secret information such as credit-card account numbers or other personal information. The secure server provides the visitor's web browser with the site's public key. The browser uses it to encrypt the credit-card number and any other personal information. The secure server uses the private key to decrypt the information. Once an encrypted exchange is established, the server can send the visitor's browser a secret key that both can use. Moreover, the server can change that key often during the session to make decryption more difficult.

Transport Layer Security

A protocol called Transport Layer Security (TLS) is used for transactions on the Web. TLS is the successor of Secure Socket Layer (SSL) and works following the same principles as SSL, with some improvements that are outside the scope of this discussion. It is part of virtually all current web browsers. Current versions of browsers use TSL with a 128-bit key. TLS uses a combination of public key and symmetric key encryption. It works as follows:

> **Transport Layer Security (TLS)** The successor of Secure Sockets Layer (SSL), the software in the web browser responsible for secure communication.

1 When a visitor connects to an online site, the site's server sends the visitor's browser its public key.

2 The visitor's browser creates a temporary symmetric (secret) key of 128 bits. The key is transmitted to the site's server encrypted by using the site's public key. Now both the visitor's browser and the site's server know the same secret key and can use it for encryption.

3 The visitor can now safely transmit confidential information.

How safe is a 128-bit key? It would take 250 PCs working simultaneously around the clock an estimated 9 trillion times the age of the universe just to decrypt a single message. This is the reason why practically all financial institutions use 128-bit encryption, and if you want to bank online, you must use a browser that supports this key length. However, how long it takes an interceptor to decipher depends on current speed of hardware and sophistication of code-breaking software. As hardware becomes faster and software becomes more sophisticated, standard keys usually are set longer.

When you log on to secure servers you might notice that the 'HTTP://' in the URL box at the top of the browser turns into an 'HTTPS://' and a little closed padlock appears on the bottom of the browser. It is advisable not to transfer any confidential information through the Web when these two indications do not appear. HTTPS is the secure version of HTTP, discussed in Chapter 7. HTTPS encrypts communication using SSL or TSL. Luckily, all this encryption and decryption is done by the browser. When you access a secure area of a website, the communication between the site's server and your web browser is encrypted. The information you view on your screen was encrypted by the software installed on the site's server and then decrypted by your browser.

> **HTTPS** The secure version of HTTP.

Digital signatures

A digital signature is a way to authenticate online messages, analogous to a physical signature on a piece of paper, but implemented with public-key cryptography. The digital signature authenticates the identity of the sender of a message and also guarantees that no one has altered the sent document; it is as if the message were carried in an electronically sealed envelope.

> **digital signature** An encrypted digest of the text that is sent along with a message that authenticates the identity of the sender and guarantees that no one has altered the sent document.

When you send an encrypted message, two phases are involved in creating a digital signature. First, the encryption software uses a hashing algorithm (a mathematical formula) to create a message digest from the file you wish to transmit. A *message digest* is akin to the unique fingerprint of a file. Then, the software uses your private (secret) key to encrypt the message digest. The result is a digital signature for that specific file.

How does it work? Follow the flowchart in Figure 13.5. Suppose you want to send the draft of a detailed price proposal to your business partner. You want to be certain that the

Figure 13.5 Using digital signatures

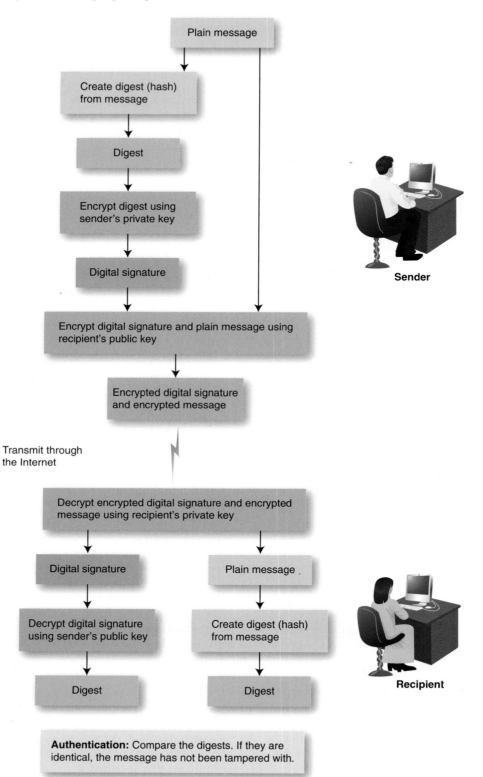

Authentication: Compare the digests. If they are identical, the message has not been tampered with.

document you intend to send is indeed the one she receives. She wants the assurance that the document she receives is really from you.

1 You attach the price proposal file to an email message. The entire communication is essentially one message, indicated as 'Plain message' in Figure 13.5.

2 Using the hashing software, your computer creates a message hash, the message digest, which is a mathematically manipulated file of the message and is not readily readable by a human.

3 You then use a private key that you have previously obtained from the public-key issuer, such as a certificate authority, to encrypt the message digest. Your computer uses your private key to turn the message digest into a digital signature.

4 The computer also uses your private key to encrypt the message in its plain (unhashed) form. Your computer sends off both files.

5 Your business partner receives the encrypted files: the digital signature (which is an encrypted message digest) and the encrypted message, which usually come as one file.

6 Your business partner's computer uses her private key (which is mathematically related to her public key, which you used) to decrypt both your digital signature and your encrypted unhashed message.

7 The decrypted digital signature becomes the message digest. Hashing the decrypted unhashed message turns this message into a digest, too.

8 If the two message digests are identical, the message received is, apparently, the one you sent, unchanged.

Since the message digest is different for every message, your digital signature is different each time you send a message. As described here, senders of encrypted messages obtain the public key of the recipient from an issuer of such keys. In most cases, the issuer is a certificate authority, and the recipient's public key is included in the recipient's digital certificate, which is discussed next.

Digital certificates

To authenticate a digital signature, both buyers and sellers must use digital certificates (also known as digital IDs). Digital certificates are computer files that serve as the equivalent of ID cards by associating one's identity with one's public key. An issuer of digital certificates is called a certificate authority (CA), an organization that serves as a trusted third party. A CA certifies the identity of anyone who enquires about a party communicating on the Internet. Some CAs are subsidiaries of banks and credit-card companies and others are independent. American Express CA, Digital Signature Trust Co., VeriSign Inc. and GlobalSign NV are just a few of the numerous companies that sell digital certificates. To view a long list of CAs you can go to www.pki-page.org. A CA issues the public (and private) keys associated with a certificate.

digital certificates Computer files that serve as the equivalent of ID cards.

certificate authority (CA) An organization that issues digital certificates, which authenticate the holder in electronic business transactions.

A digital certificate contains its holder's name, a serial number, expiration dates and a copy of the certificate holder's public key (used to encrypt messages and digital signatures). It also contains the digital signature of the certificate authority so that a recipient can verify that the certificate is real. To view the digital certificate of a secure online business, click the padlock icon in your browser (located at the end of the URL address in Windows Internet Explorer 7). The images at the bottom of page 500 show the certificate window that you would open. Clicking the Details tab brings up the version, serial number, signature encryption method, issuer name and other details of the certificate.

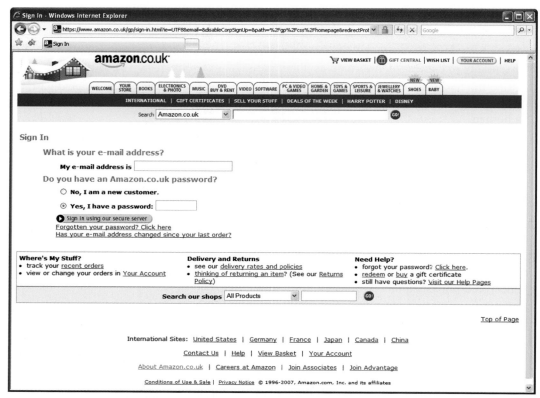

The https:// in the Address Field and the padlock icon at the end of the Address Bar indicate that you are communicating with a secure server.

Digital certificates are the equivalent of tamperproof photo identification cards. They are based on public-key encryption techniques that verify the identities of the buyer and seller in electronic transactions and prevent documents from being altered after the transaction is completed. Consumers have their own digital certificates stored on their home computers'

A digital certificate.

hard disks. In a transaction, a consumer uses one digital key attached to the certificate that he or she sends to the seller. The seller sends the certificate and his own digital key to a certificate authority, which then can determine the authenticity of the digital signature. Completed transaction documents are stored on a secure hard disk maintained by a trusted third party.

The recipient of an encrypted message uses the certificate authority's public key to decode the digital certificate attached to the message, verifies it as issued by the certificate authority, and then obtains the sender's public key and identification information held within the certificate. With this information, the recipient can send an encrypted reply.

When using the Web, encryption and authentication take place automatically and are transparent to the users. However, there is an indication in the browser's window if the communication is secure. In Microsoft Internet Explorer and Firefox, a small padlock appears in the lower-right corner. In Netscape, an open padlock appears in the lower-right corner if the site you reached is not secure, and a closed padlock appears if it is secure. You might see these signs as soon as the page requiring your password appears in your browser. If you double-click the padlock, a window opens with details on the digital certificate that the site uses, such as the certificate issuer's name, the date it was issued and the date it expires.

The downside of security measures

Security measures – especially passwords, encryption applications and firewalls – have a price that relates to more than money: they slow down data communications, and they require user discipline, which is not always easy to maintain. Employees tend to forget their passwords, especially if they must replace them every 30 or 90 days.

Employees are especially annoyed when they have to remember a different password for every system they use; in some companies, there might be four or five different systems, each with its own access control. A simpler solution is an approach called SSO (single sign-on). With SSO, users are required to identify themselves only once before accessing several different systems. However, SSO requires special software that interacts with all the systems in an organization, and the systems must be linked through a network. Not many organizations have installed such software.

> **SSO (single sign-on)**
> Enabling employees to access several information systems by using a single password.

CIOs often cite SSO as an effective way to bring down the amount of work their subordinates must do. Such was certainly the case at Welwyn Hatfield Council. The English council authority uses over 20 different IT systems to provide local government management. Much of the data on these systems are of a sensitive nature and each has its own protocols for access. A significant amount of time was being spent by the help-desk function in resetting forgotten passwords. The introduction of IBM's Tivoli Access Manager meant that users had to remember only one log-in action. Even better is that if new IT systems are introduced the SSO will 'learn' the new access protocols. The SSO has lead to a much easier log-in for users and much more efficient use of the help-desk personnel. Encryption slows down communication because the software must encrypt and decrypt every message. Remember that when you use a secure website, much of the information you view on your screen is encrypted by the software installed on the site's server and then decrypted by your browser. All this activity takes time, and the delay only exacerbates the Internet's low download speed during periods of heavy traffic. Firewalls have the same slowing effect; screening every download takes time, which affects anyone trying to access information, including employees, business partners and consumers.

IT specialists must clearly explain to managers the implications of applying security measures, especially on systems connected to the Internet. The IT specialists and other managers must first determine which resource should be accessed only with passwords and which also require other screening methods, such as firewalls. They must tell employees what impact a new security measure will have on their daily work, and if the measure will adversely affect their work, the specialists must convince the employees that the inconvenience is the price for protecting data. The IT specialists should also continue to work on methods that minimize inconvenience and delays.

Recall the discussion of virtual private networks (VPNs), which enable employees to access ISs using special security software involving passwords and encryption. This approach allows employees to access an intranet only from computers equipped with the proper VPN software and only if they remember passwords. However, it is possible to use a token (such as a keyfob) that receives a password, such as RSA's SecurID®. The password changes frequently and the user does not have to remember it, because it appears automatically on the keyfob. There is no need to use VPN software. If someone steals a password, the thief cannot use it for more than a few seconds because it then changes. This enables Wawa employees to access the intranet from any computer in the world.

Recovery measures

Security measures might reduce undesirable mishaps, but nobody can control all disasters. To be prepared for disasters when they do occur, organizations must have recovery measures in place. Organizations that depend heavily on ISs for their daily business often use redundancy; that is, they run all systems and transactions on two computers in parallel to protect against loss of data and business. If one computer is down, the work can continue on the other computer. Redundancy makes the system fault tolerant. However, in distributed systems, doubling every computing resource is extremely expensive, so other measures must be taken.

The business recovery plan

business recovery plan
Organizational plan that prepares for disruption in information systems, detailing what should be done and by whom, if critical information systems fail or become untrustworthy; also called business recovery plan and disaster recovery plan. Also known as business continuity plan.

To prepare for mishaps, either natural or malicious, many organizations have well planned programmes in place, called business recovery plans (also called *disaster recovery plans*, *business resumption plans* or *business continuity plans*). The plans detail what should be done and by whom if critical systems go down. In principle, the systems do not have to be ISs. However, most of the attention and resources in recovery plans are devoted to measures that should be taken when ISs go down or if IS operations become untrustworthy.

The 2005 Hurricane Katrina on the US Gulf Coast was a wake-up call for many executives, reminding them in terrible terms of the need for recovery planning. Concern about disaster recovery has spread beyond banks, insurance companies and data centres, the traditional disaster recovery fanatics. Many customer service and retail firms realize that they can easily lose customers if they don't deliver services and products in a timely manner, which is why the terms 'business recovery', 'business resumption' and 'business continuity' have caught on in some circles. In interactive computing environments, when business systems are idle, so are the people who bring in revenue. Employees cannot do their work, customers cannot purchase and suppliers cannot accept requests for raw materials and services. In addition, companies' reputations can be harmed, and competitive advantage and market share lost.

Experts propose nine steps to develop a business recovery plan:

1 *Obtain management's commitment to the plan.* Development of a recovery plan requires substantial resources. Top management must be convinced of the potential damages that paralysis of information systems might cause. Once management is committed, it should appoint a business recovery coordinator to develop the plan and execute it if disaster occurs.

2 *Establish a planning committee.* The coordinator establishes a planning committee comprising representatives from all business units that are dependent on computer-based ISs.

The members serve as liaisons between the coordinator and their unit managers. The managers are authorized to establish emergency procedures for their own departments.

3 *Perform risk assessment and impact analysis.* The committee assesses which operations would be hurt by disasters, and how long the organization could continue to operate without the damaged resources. This analysis is carried out through interviews with managers of functional business areas. The committee compiles information regarding maximum allowable downtime, required backup information, and the financial, operational and legal consequences of extended downtime.

4 *Prioritize recovery needs.* The disaster recovery coordinator ranks each IS application according to its effect on an organization's ability to achieve its mission. Mission-critical applications, those without which the business cannot conduct its operations, are given the highest priority. The largest or most widely used system might not be the most critical. Applications might be categorized into several classes, such as:

mission-critical applications Applications without which a business cannot conduct its operations.

- *Critical*: Applications that cannot be replaced with manual systems under any circumstances.
- *Vital*: Applications that can be replaced with manual systems for a brief period, such as several days.
- *Sensitive*: Applications that can be replaced with acceptable manual systems for an extended period of time, though at great cost.
- *Noncritical*: Applications that can be interrupted for an extended period of time at little or no cost to the organization.

5 *Select a recovery plan.* Recovery plan alternatives are evaluated by considering advantages and disadvantages in terms of risk reduction, cost and the speed at which employees can adjust to the alternative system.

6 *Select vendors.* If it is determined that an external vendor can better respond to a disaster than in-house staff and provide a better alternative system, then the most cost-effective external vendor should be selected. Factors considered should include the vendor's ability to provide telecommunications alternatives, experience and capacity to support current applications.

7 *Develop and implement the plan.* The plan includes organizational and vendor responsibilities and the sequence of events that will take place. Each business unit is informed of its responsibilities, who the key contacts are in each department, and the training programmes available for personnel.

8 *Test the plan.* Testing includes a walk-through with each business unit, simulations as if a real disaster had occurred, and (if no damage will be caused) a deliberate interruption of the system and implementation of the plan. In mock disasters, the coordinator measures the time it takes to implement the plan and its effectiveness.

9 *Continually test and evaluate.* The staff must be aware of the plan at all times. Therefore, the plan must be tested periodically. It should be evaluated in light of new business practices and the addition of new applications. If necessary, the plan should be modified to accommodate these changes.

The plan should include the key personnel and their responsibilities, as well as a procedure to reinstitute interactions with outside business partners and suppliers. Because an organization's priorities and environment change over time, the plan must be examined periodically and updated if necessary. There will be new business processes or changes in the relative importance of existing processes or tasks, new or different application software, changes in hardware and new or different IS and end users. The plan must be modified to reflect the new environment, and the changes must be thoroughly tested. A copy of the plan should be kept

Industry **SNAPSHOT**

Why they invest in recovery measures

A survey carried out by SunGard Availability Services found that nearly half of the responding companies considered that they were failing to address the requirements of the new British standard for business continuity management (BCM) BS 25999. Regarding the results of the survey, Julian Thrussell, product manager BS 25999, BSi Management Systems, said, 'Clearly there remains a significant amount of work to be done but the fact that these businesses are thinking about the new Standard now is a positive sign. Organizations need to recognize the value of BS 25999 certification in terms of delivering competitive advantage and demonstrating resilience and responsible governance.'

SOURCE: http://www.sungard.com/news/default.aspx?announceID=899 #Continuity

off-site, because if a disaster occurs, an on-site copy might not be available. Many companies keep an electronic copy posted at a server many miles away, so that they can retrieve it from wherever their officer can have Internet access.

Although the threat of terrorism has increased awareness for the need of recovery plans, CIOs often find the tasks of earmarking funds for disaster recovery programmes difficult because they cannot show the return on investment (ROI) of such an 'investment'. Most companies institute recovery programmes only after a disaster or near disaster occurs. Usually, the larger companies have such programmes. Even at companies that do have recovery plans, experts estimate that most of those plans are never tested. Worse, some experts observed that one out of five recovery plans did not work well when tested.

Recovery planning and hot site providers

Companies that choose not to fully develop their own recovery plan can outsource it to companies that specialize in either disaster recovery planning or provision of alternative sites. Strohl Systems, EverGreen Data Continuity and other companies provide both planning and software for disaster recovery. The software helps create and update records of key people and procedures. Fewer companies provide alternative sites – hot sites – chief among them is SunGard Availability Services. They provide backup and operation facilities to which a client's employees can move and continue operations in case of a disaster. These back-up centres are usually equipped with desks, computer systems and Internet links. Customers can use the duplicate databases and applications maintained for them. The company also provides hotel rooms and air mattresses for people who need to work long hours. Worldwide, the company maintains redundant facilities totalling 279,000 square meters (3 million square feet), equipped with software and networking facilities to enable a client organization to resume business within hours.

> **hot site** A location where a client organization hit by a disaster can continue its vital operations. The structure – often underground – is equipped with hardware and software to support the client's employees.

The economics of information security

Security measures should be dealt with in a manner similar to purchasing insurance. The spending on measures should be proportional to the potential damage. Organizations also need to assess the minimum rate of system downtime and ensure that they can financially sustain the downtime.

Ethical and Societal ISSUES

Terrorism and PATRIOTism

Information technology can help track down criminals and terrorists, but it also helps criminals and terrorists in their efforts. The technology can help protect privacy and other civil rights, but it can also help violate such rights. The growing danger of terrorism and the continued effort of governments to reduce drug-related and other crimes led to controversial use, or abuse, of IT. In the UK the controversial Regulation of Investigatory Powers Act (RIPA) and the much less snappily titled Uniting and Strengthening America by Providing Appropriate Tools Required to Intercept and Obstruct Terrorism Act of 2001, the PATRIOT Act, for the USA give law enforcement agencies extra surveillance and wiretapping rights. Similar legislation has been passed in countries throughout the world. They generally permit the reading of private files and personal Internet records without informing the suspected citizen and without need for a law enforcement agency to present to the court a probable cause. 'Our constitutional freedoms are in jeopardy. Now is the time to restore real checks and balances to the worst sections of the Patriot Act' called a web posting of the American Civil Liberties Union (ACLU) in 2005, when the law was reconsidered by the US Congress. On the contrary, said many members of Congress, the law should be enhanced to give the FBI even freer hand.

The Electronic Privacy Information Centre (EPIC) explains the major concerns with the Act, which made changes to 15 existing laws. The Act gives more power than before to law enforcement agencies in installing pen registers and trap and trace devices. A pen register is any device that records outgoing phone numbers. A trap and track device – a caller ID device, for instance – captures and records incoming telephone numbers. Similarly, the Act extends the government's authority to gain access to personal financial information and student information, even if the subject of the investigation is not suspected of wrongdoing. Agents only have to certify that the information likely to be obtained is relevant to an ongoing criminal investigation. In the past, the government had to show to a judge probable cause – a reasonable suspicion that the subject of an investigation is committing or is about to commit a crime. If a government attorney 'certifies' that the information collected is likely to be relevant, the judge must grant permission to install the device and collect the information.

Previous laws generally referred only to telephones, but the new Acts expand communication tapping to the Internet. This practically allows law enforcement agencies to record, without probable cause, email addresses and URLs. Some jurists opine that this actually allows the agencies to record not only email sender and recipient addresses and web addresses but also the content of email messages and web pages.

Even before adoption of theses various Acts, security agencies used 'packet sniffing' devices connected to the servers operated by Internet service providers (ISPs). The devices are supposed to monitor the email traffic of suspects. However, millions of other subscribers use the same servers and therefore are subject to the same surveillance.

When tapping communications, law enforcement agencies need the cooperation of a third party, such as a telephone company or an ISP. In the past, the law limited the definition of such third parties. Now in the USA under the PATRIOT Act, there is no limitation. Therefore, if a university, public library, municipality, or an airport provides access to the Internet – such as through a hotspot – all users of these services are subject to surveillance. Furthermore, that third party is prohibited from notifying anyone, including unsuspected users, of the surveillance.

Proponents of the Act want to leave all its provisions in place beyond 2005 and add two provisions. They would like to allow the FBI to demand records without first obtaining an approval from a prosecutor or a judge. Some would also amend the law to require the US Postal Service to let FBI agents copy information from the outside of envelopes in the mail.

Again, we are faced with an old dilemma: How far should we allow our governments to go in their efforts to protect us against crime and terrorism? At what point do we start to pay too much in terms of privacy and civil rights for such protection? And when terrorists strike or threaten to strike, should we give up our liberties for more security?

How much security is enough security?

From a pure cost point of view, how much should an organization spend on data security measures? There are two types of costs that must be considered to answer this question: the cost of the potential damage, and the cost of implementing a preventive measure. The cost of the damage is the aggregate of all the potential damages multiplied by their respective probabilities, as follows:

$$Cost\ of\ potential\ damage = \sum_{i=1}^{n} Cost\ of\ disruption\ i \times Probability\ of\ disruption\ i$$

where i is a probable event and n is the number of events.

Experts are usually employed to estimate the cost and probabilities of damages, as well as the cost of security measures. Obviously, the more extensive the preventive measures, the smaller the damage potential. So, as the cost of security measures goes up, the cost of potential damage goes down. Ideally, the enterprise places itself at the optimum point, which is the point at which the total of the two costs is minimized, as Figure 13.6 illustrates.

When budgeting for IT security, managers need to define what they want to protect. They should focus on the asset they must protect, which in most cases is information, not applications. Copies of applications are usually kept in a safe place to replace those that get damaged. They should also estimate the loss of revenue from downtime. Then, they should budget sums that do not exceed the value of what the measures protect – information and potential revenues. Even the most ardent IT security advocates agree that there is no point spending €100,000 to protect information that is worth €10,000.

Calculating downtime

All other factors being equal, businesses should try to install ISs whose downtime is the lowest possible, but if obtaining a system with a higher uptime adds to the cost, they should consider the benefit of greater uptime against the added cost. Mission-critical systems must be connected to an alternative source of power, duplicated with a redundant system or both. Often, such systems must be up 24 hours per day, 7 days per week.

When the service that the business provides depends on uninterrupted power, the systems are often connected to an alternative off-grid power source, such as a generator.

Figure 13.6 Optimal spending on IT security

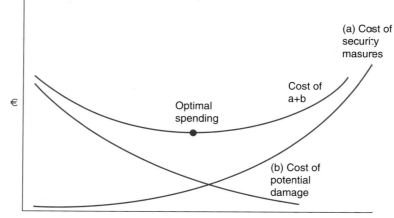

Security level

Recall the discussion of system uptime in Chapter 7. Experts can provide good estimates of the probability that systems will fail, both in terms of power failure in a certain region and for particular applications. Experience in operating certain systems, such as ERP and SCM systems, can teach the IT staff for how many minutes or seconds per year the system is likely to fail. For example, if the uptime of a system is 99 per cent ('two nines'), it should be expected to be down 1 per cent of the time, and if 'time' means 24×7, downtime expectancy is 87.6 hours per year (365 days $\times$ 24 hours $\times$ 0.01). This might be sufficient for a system supporting some human resources operations, but not an airline reservation system or an SCM system of a global company. For these systems, the number of nines must be greater, such as 99.999 per cent, in which case there would be only 5.256 minutes of downtime expected per year ($365 \times 24 \times 60 \times 0.00001$).

More and more ISs are now interfaced with other systems, which makes them a chain or cluster of several interdependent systems. For example, if system A is connected to system B, B depends on A, and the uptime of the systems are 99 per cent and 99.5 per cent, respectively; the probability of uptime for B is the multiplication of these probabilities, or 98.505 per cent. Therefore, you could expect the systems to be down 0.01495 of the time, about 131 hours per year. This is a greater downtime than if system B operated independently. The greater the number of interdependent systems, the greater the expected downtime.

Redundancies, on the other hand, reduce expected downtime. For example, if two airline reservation systems operate in parallel, each can serve all the transactions, and the probabilities of their failures are 2 per cent and 3 per cent, the probability that the reservation service will be down is 0.06 per cent (0.03×0.02), just 0.0006 of the time. This downtime is significantly smaller than the downtime of a service based on either system individually. This is why so many companies rely on redundant power sources and systems, such as duplicate databases, mirrored servers and duplicate applications, especially when many of their operations are executed online, and even more so when the operations depend on constant online interaction with customers.

There might be no point in spending much money to increase the 'nines' of uptime for every system. For example, if the only purpose of an IS is to help access a data warehouse to glean business intelligence (recall the discussions in Chapters 6 and 10), spending a huge amount of money to increase its number of nines from 99 to 99.999 is probably not a wise choice. For a data warehouse, if an analysis cannot be performed immediately, it can usually be performed later without serious ramifications.

SUMMARY

The purpose of controls and security measures is to maintain the functionality of ISs, the confidentiality of information, the integrity and availability of data and computing resources, the uninterruptible availability of data resources and online operations, and compliance with security and privacy laws.

Risks to ISs include risks to hardware, risks to data and applications and risks to networks.

Risks to hardware include natural disasters, such as earthquakes, fires, floods and power failures, as well as vandalism. Protective measures run the gamut from surge protectors to the maintenance of duplicate systems, which make ISs fault-tolerant.

Risks to data and applications include theft of information, identify theft, data alteration, data destruction, defacement of websites, computer viruses, worms, and logic bombs, as well as nonmalicious mishaps such as unauthorized downloading and installation of software.

Risks to online operations include denial of service and computer hijacking.

To minimize disruption, organizations use controls. Controls include program robustness and constraints on data entry, periodic backup of software and data files, access controls, atomic transactions and audit trails.

Access controls also include information that must be entered before information resources can be used: passwords, synchronized numbers and biometrics. Biometric technologies are growing in popularity because they do not require memorization of passwords, which employees tend to forget.

Atomic transactions are an important control that ensures information integrity: either all files involved in a transaction are updated, or none is.

To protect resources that are linked to the Internet, organizations use firewalls, which are special hardware and software to control access to servers and their contents.

Encryption schemes scramble messages at the sending end and descramble them at the receiving end. Encryption is also used to authenticate the sender or recipient of a message, verifying that the user is indeed the party he or she claims to be and to keep messages secret.

To encrypt and decrypt messages the communicating parties must use a key. The larger the number of bits in the key, the longer it takes to break the encryption. In symmetric encryption, both users use a private, secret key. In asymmetric key encryption, the parties use a public and a private key.

The public–private key method does not require both parties to have a common secret key before the communication starts. To encrypt, the sender needs the recipient's public key; to decrypt, the recipient uses his or her private key. This system is a useful feature that lets consumers and organizations transact business confidentially on the Web.

TLS and HTTPS are encryption standards specially designed for the Web. They are embedded in web browsers.

Organizations can purchase public and private keys along with an associated digital certificate from a certificate authority. Digital certificates contain the certificate holder's public key and other information, such as the issue and expiration date of the certificate.

Many organizations have business recovery plans that are developed and periodically tested by a special committee. The plans identify mission-critical applications and prescribe steps that various employees should take in a disaster.

A growing number of companies also use the services of organizations that specialize in providing alternative sites, hot sites, to continue operations in case of a disaster, such as a massive terror attack, natural disaster or power outage.

When considering how much to invest in security measures, organizations should evaluate the cost of the potential damage on one hand, and the cost of security on the other hand. The more that is spent on security, the smaller the potential loss. Organizations should spend the amount that brings the combined costs to a minimum.

A system that depends on other systems for input has a greater downtime probability than if it is used independently of other systems. Redundant systems significantly reduce downtime probability.

Governments are obliged to protect citizens against crime and terrorism and therefore must be able to tap electronic communication of suspects. Such practices often collide with individuals' right to privacy.

WORLDWIDE HOST

WORLDWIDE HOST REVISITED

Worldwide Host's website has been up and running for several months now. In that time, the TripExpert site has been defaced, experienced a denial-of-service attack and has been hit with an attempt to invade the customer database. Putting its system on the World Wide Web has certainly introduced challenges to Worldwide's IS staff. Let us look at some computer security issues in more depth.

What would you do?

1   Jason Theodore, Worldwide Host's IS security chief, informs Michael Lloyd that there have been a growing number of Trojan horse attacks that target specific businesses. The perpetrators send emails to specific employees who have access to important financial information. The senders disguise themselves as a colleague and ask the employee to go to a website or open an attachment that installs a virus that is able to send sensitive financial information back to the perpetrator. Develop a list of recommendations for Michael Lloyd to distribute to employees to help safeguard Worldwide Host.

2   Severe weather is always a concern for IS personnel. If a flood or power outage hits Worldwide Host's offices, it could take down its entire operations. Michael Lloyd has asked you to help him develop a disaster recovery plan. What measures would you recommend Worldwide Host take to prepare for and recover from a disaster?

3   The chapter discussed controls on information systems to help secure them. From the description in the opening case, you know that Worldwide Host uses secure servers and physical access controls for its information systems. What other types of controls should it be using to safeguard its systems? Develop a list for Michael Lloyd and his security chief.

New perspectives

1   Worldwide Host handles thousands of transactions involving customers' credit cards. The TripExpert.com employees are complaining that the response time for the new system is much slower than their old reservations system. Michael Lloyd knows that this is the result of security measures – use of passwords, encryption and decryption, and screening of transactions. He is meeting with the travel staff to explain the security–response trade-off. Prepare an outline of his speech for him, which discusses the pros and cons of the security measures.

2   Michael Lloyd has been approached by a vendor that provides disaster recovery services at an alternative site. Should Worldwide Host consider use of such a service? If so, for what systems and business functions?

Review questions

1   What are the goals of security measures for ISs? Explain.

2   All the data of your company are concentrated in two databases. All employees use PCs or laptop computers. All use a corporate network. You are to prioritize protection of the following elements of your company: PCs and laptops, the databases, the corporate network. Which is the element about which you are most concerned, and why?

3   Data alteration and destruction are dreaded by many IS managers more than any other

mishap. Why? Is the threat of website defacement as severe as data destruction or alteration? Why or why not?

4 Some companies still make a duplicate copy of disks or tapes and transport them to a remote site as a precaution against loss of data on the original storage media. What is the preferred way of keeping secured copies of data nowadays? Give at least two benefits and one possible drawback of the new way.

5 Comment on the following statement: If your computer is connected to an external communication line, anyone with a similar link can potentially access your systems.

6 What is a honeytoken and how is it used by companies?

7 What is a honeypot and how is it used by businesses?

8 What is the difference between a virus and a worm? Which is potentially more dangerous and why?

9 Why is encryption that uses the public-key method so important in electronic commerce?

10 What is an audit trail? What audit trail information would you have for a shipping record?

11 This chapter gives an example of an atomic transaction. Give another example from any business area.

12 What is the difference between authentication and confidentiality?

13 What are biometric access controls? How are they better than passwords?

14 What is a firewall, and how does it work?

15 What is a DDoS? How is it executed, and what is the purpose of zombies in a DDoS? What can organizations do to prevent a DDoS attack?

16 What is the purpose of business recovery plans?

17 A growing number of companies have implemented business recovery plans, but there are still many without such plans. Why?

Discussion questions

1 Companies that process credit-card transactions for merchants have their computers vaulted behind concrete walls, iron bars and heavy steel doors. Employees must enter a code into a keypad to enter the vaults. Yet, every so often information on millions of credit-card accounts is stolen without any physical break-in. How so?

2 In the Blockbuster example of system controls, the cash register displays the message 'Do not rent!' when a patron reaches the maximum debt allowed. However, the customer service representative might still hire a DVD to the customer. What would you do to better enforce the chain's policy?

3 A NATO military officer in Vienna, Austria orders an item whose part number is 7954. The clerk at the supply centre in Stafford, England receives the order through his computer and ships the item: a ship's anchor, not realizing that Vienna is located hundreds of miles from any ocean. Apparently, the officer wanted to order item number 7945, a fuel tank for a fighter aircraft, but he erred when entering the item's number. What controls would you implement both at the entry system and at the systems employed at the supply centre to prevent such mistakes?

4 The average loss in a bank robbery is several thousand euro, and the culprit has an 85 per cent chance of being caught. The average damage in a 'usual' white-collar fraud is several tens of thousands of euro. The average amount stolen in computer fraud is several hundreds of thousands of euro, and it is extremely hard to find the culprit. Why is the amount involved in computer fraud so high, and why is it difficult to find the culprits?

5 To prevent unauthorized people from copying data from a database, some companies forbid their employees to come to work with USB flash memory devices and subject them to body searches. Is this an effective measure? Why or why not?

6 The majority of criminals who commit computer fraud are insiders, that is, employees. What measures would you take to minimize insider fraud through ISs?

7 Would you prefer that your identity be verified with a biometric (such as your palm or fingerprint, or your cornea picture), or with a password? Why?

8 Explain in an intuitive way why the downtime probability of a system that depends on another system is greater than if it were operating independently.

9 Employees often complain about the hurdles they have to pass whenever they need to access data and the slow response of ISs because of firewalls and encryption measures. As a CIO, how would you explain the need for such measures to employees? Would you give them any say in the decision of how to balance convenience and protection of data and applications?

10 Organizations often use firewalls to block employee access to certain websites. Do you agree with this practice, or do you think it violates employee privacy?

11 Firewalls might keep track of web pages that employees download to their PCs. Do you think this practice violates employee privacy?

12 When financial institutions discover that their ISs (especially databases) have been broken into, they often do not report the event to law enforcement officers. Even if they know who the hacker is, they do what they can to avoid publicity. Why? Should they be forced to report such events?

13 When hackers are caught, they often argue that they actually did a service to the organization whose system they accessed without permission; now, they say, the organization knows its system has a weak point, and it can take the proper steps to improve security. Do you agree with this claim? Why or why not?

14 A CIO tells you, 'We regularly review all of the potential vulnerabilities of our information systems and networks. We implement hardware, software and procedures against any potential event, no matter the cost.' What do you say to this executive?

15 Is the potential for identity theft growing? Explain.

16 Encryption helps individuals and organizations to maintain privacy and confidentiality, thereby helping protect civil liberties. However, encryption also helps terrorists and criminals hide their intentions. Some governments have laws that forbid non-government agencies to use strong encryption software. The idea is to allow people to encrypt their communication, but not enough to prevent the government from decrypting the communication in surveillance of suspected criminals and terrorists. Do you favour such laws, or do you advocate that everybody have access to the strongest encryption software possible? Explain.

Tutorial activities

1 Research the impact of the Sarbanes-Oxley Act on ISs. Write a two-page report explaining the major controls that EU corporations must incorporate in their ISs to satisfy the Act if wishing to do business in the US.

2 Log on to a secure website. Figure out which icon you have to click to receive information on the security measures used in the session. Send your professor an email message detailing the site's URL and all the information you obtained: the length of the key that is used for encryption, the type of digital certificate used, the issuer of the digital certificate, the date it was issued and its expiration date, and so forth. Explain each item.

3 Use Excel or another spreadsheet application to show your work when solving the following problems:

   a A company uses three information systems that are linked sequentially: System A feeds System B, and System B feeds System C. Consider the following average uptimes: System A, 98 per cent; System B, 97 per cent; System C, 95 per cent. What is the average expected downtime (as a percentage) of System C?

   b A CIO states, 'Our online transaction system has availability of five nines. However, we hired the services of an ASP for using our human resources information systems. Our HR system has availability of only three nines.'

      i Calculate the minutes of downtime per week for each of these systems.

      ii Explain why the company must have such a high number of nines for one system but can settle for a significantly lower number of nines for the other system.

4 Team up with another student. Research the Web for recovery planning expenditures in

your country or worldwide over the past five years. Prepare a table showing the expenditure amounts. Add an analysis that explains the reasons for changes in the expenditures.

5 Your team should evaluate the business recovery plan of your college or university. If there is none, write a business recovery plan for the institution. If there is one in place, evaluate its weaknesses and make suggestions for improvement. Prepare a ten-minute, software-based presentation of your findings and suggestions.

CD questions

1 Do you run antivirus software on your home computer? Is it up to date? If not, why not?

2 What security measures have you implemented to protect your home computer? Will you do anything differently after reading this chapter?

Video questions

1 Under what circumstances would you use system restore?

2 Have you used system restore? If not, would you?

From ideas to application
REAL CASES

Case study **13.1**

The tester

The case studies in this book usually revolve around organizations. This story is about a person, a 'soldier' in the war against cybercriminals. Meet Mark Seiden, security tester extraordinaire. 'Tell me which information your bank keeps most secret', he challenged a top bank executive two years ago, 'and I'll get it anyway.' The executive complied. He told Seiden he wanted the identities of clients who were negotiating secret deals, so secret that many people inside the bank referred to them by code names. He also wanted the financial details of some mergers and acquisitions in which his bank was involved. The executive knew that those two types of information were kept under strict electronic locks by the bank.

A week later Seiden visited the executive again in his office. He gave him a printout of the secret information. He also gave the man photocopies of the floor plans of each bank office and a suitcase filled with backup tapes from which Seiden could reconstruct all

the files maintained on the bank's computers. Seiden spent two weekend nights to obtain the information.

Seiden, with 35 years of experience in computer programming, is one of a small group of professional intruders, experts who are paid by corporations to find security loopholes, both in physical facilities and software. Companies hire Seiden to help improve security

Even the most sophisticated IT security systems can be compromised if the wider business environment in which they are implemented is not secure.

PHOTO SOURCE: © FRANZISTA RICHTER

systems and procedures to protect their ISs and other sensitive corporate assets.

Business is booming for Seiden and his colleagues. As hackers increase their invasion of corporate databases and steal information from a growing number of organizations, executives are learning fast why it pays to hire the services of such people. Experts say that in the early days of the Internet, breaking into corporate ISs was mainly a matter of showing off one's prowess. Now, it has become a crime of greed. The main targets are personal information and credit-card account numbers. In a survey conducted by the FBI in 2005, 87 per cent of the polled corporations said they had routine security audits, an increase from 82 per cent in 2004. An analyst for the Gartner Group said that North American corporations spent more than $2 billion on security consultants in 2004, an increase of 14 per cent from 2003.

Much of the work such consultants do has nothing to do with hacking. Seiden has a wardrobe of uniforms and other corporate garbs. They include a uniform the FedEx drivers wear, and a windbreaker that Iron Mountain workers wear when they drive their vans to pick up backup files for credit card-processing firms. He also holds a set of tools that help him pick locks, at which he is adept. If you ask, he will tell you that the easiest way to enter a locked room is through the plenum space between the hard ceiling and the tiles underneath, space used for wiring and ventilation. Remove a tile, and you are in a safe room that is no longer so safe.

So how did Seiden get that precious information about the bank? The bank maintains some of the best security software, so Seiden did not even try to crack it. He obtained a badge that the bank often handed out to outside consultants. Wearing the badge he could enter the room where the bank's computers were housed at headquarters. He noticed that the master keys to the building as well as the building's floor plans were stored in a file cabinet that took him only two minutes to pick. Roaming freely in 'safe' rooms, he also found the backup tapes.

He then used social engineering to obtain information. Pretending he was a bank employee, he telephoned the accounting department and asked whom he should contact for assigning a code name to a project. Equipped with the name of the clerk who assigned code names, he went to her office and noticed that she placed sheets with code names in a folder and locked the folder in a file cabinet. Since the office was in a locked area, she had no reason to lock the file cabinet (which Seiden could pick anyway, if he needed to). He later explored the folder and obtained the code names of secret clients and information about confidential mergers and acquisitions that the bank was negotiating.

Seiden agrees that corporations cannot defend themselves against every intrusion, physical or otherwise. He agrees with the analogous construction of a house without windows: it can be built, but nobody would want to live in it. What corporations should do, he says, is ensure that when an intrusion occurs they know about it and take measures to ascertain that this type of intrusion does not happen again.

Thinking about the case

1 The case mentions three different ways of obtaining information illegally. What are they?

2 Why do you think corporations are spending increasing amounts of money on the services of security testers? Can you cite some recent mishaps that would prompt a corporation to do so?

3 Refer to the analogy of 'a house without windows.' You are the CEO of a large corporation. Give an example of a measure you would never take even if it enhanced security.

SOURCES: G. Rivlin, 'The Sniffer vs. the Cybercrooks', *New York Times*, Section 3, p. 1, col. 2, 31 July 2005; www.msbit.com/mis.html, 2005

silicon.com

Case study **13.2**
Plugging and preventing data leaks

BY ANTHONY PLEWES

In today's knowledge economy, getting the right information at the right time can make the difference between success and failure. However, companies need to put adequate controls in place before sharing information freely. Anthony Plewes investigates how to ensure confidential data do not fall into the wrong hands.

Before sharing information across the organization, companies need to put in place a comprehensive scheme that allows for the correct level of control over data. Simply having base-line security in place is not good enough: if security is set too high, it will impede the business, and if the bar is set too low, then confidential information may be at risk.

While most large organizations have given some thought to safeguarding their data, it's an area many SMEs have yet to confront. So while the following advice should be useful to businesses of any size, it's particularly suited to those smaller companies forming their initial data security scheme.

Information ownership

The best way to understand the security or confidentiality implications of any information is to identify its owner. Floris van den Dool, head of

The dashboard of an RBAC system from ConSentry.

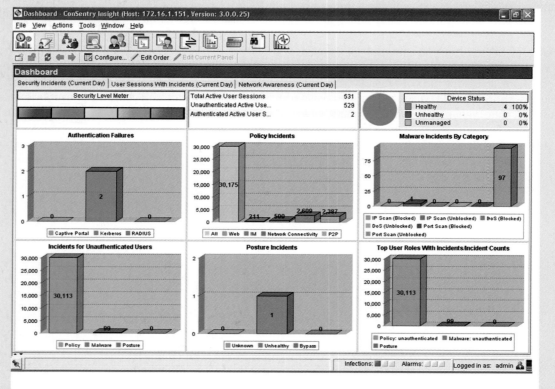

Accenture's European security practice, explains: 'Many smaller organizations consider that data ownership is the responsibility of the IT department but it is not – it is the business's responsibility.'

In some cases this will be obvious, such as the finance department taking ownership of the financial data, but in others the owner of the information may be more difficult to ascertain.

Building a classification scheme

Once the owner of the data has been identified, companies need to set up an information classification scheme. This practice is common in military and other security-conscious industries, but it should be used across all types of organization. A typical information classification scheme consists of four levels, such as external, company-confidential, client-confidential and classified.

The lowest level of classification is 'unclassified' information, which can be shared across the organization and with third parties. The second level should consist of all internal-use information, while the third level contains client-confidential information that can't be shared with all employees in the organization. Finally, the highest level needs to be information that very few people in the organization should have access to – such as legal matters or dealing with the security services.

This four-level classification scheme is just a starting point and it can vary widely across different companies. Applying information classification is difficult in retrospect, but fortunately companies will find it much easier to apply these rules to any new information created.

Mike Small, director of security strategy at CA, says: 'Information classification is difficult because companies built applications to solve certain business needs and the developers did not consider the requirements of data classification and compliance.' This is particularly true when classifying structured information stored in databases.

Identity management

Once the information has been classified, the next step is to enforce the scheme and the best way to do this electronically is through identity management. While it is possible to assign access rights to individuals, it is much more effective to do it based on the individual's role in the company. Role-based access control (RBAC) software packages help

companies automate access control but as CA's Small points out, the tools alone are no magic bullet.

He says: 'Technology is only part of the process and projects will succeed or fail because of the soft side. Role-based access control tools only work if companies have got clear information on job roles. For example, there needs to be a single personnel system, single definition of job functions and a process to track people who change jobs. If these things are not in place, then the software will not work properly.'

It's also important to consider all possible situations whereby information could wind up in the wrong hands – and they're not all digital.

As Dave Martin, managing consultant at Logica-CMG, cautions: 'Role-based access helps companies keep electronic information secure, but companies also need to address other potential sources of information leaks, such as paper left on the printer and flipcharts.'

Access control

To make sure data is secure even if it does fall into the wrong hands, companies should encrypt files. Different information will probably require different encryption policies, but typically only encrypting the data when it is stored on the server will cut down on the processing overhead. It is possible to keep files encrypted even when they are being transmitted over the network, but this will require all end-user devices to have a decryption capability.

Access to specific information can even be embedded directly in documents by using DRM. This approach also allows users to take classified information out of the organization on laptops or PDAs and still manage to control who has access to certain information.

Third parties

Companies also need to think about how they can share confidential information with third parties, and this is where federated identity management comes into play. Although federated identity is still relatively unknown in smaller organizations, it will become important as supply chains become increasingly fragmented.

In a nutshell, federated identity allows companies to match job roles and trust another organization's ID management systems. They can then give access to shared information to the correct people, without having to have any knowledge about the partner company's security infrastructure.

Companies also need to consider the issue of staff working closely with outsiders. The increasing level of outsourcing often means that businesses share data with specialists such as design companies, consultants or advertising agencies who may have other customers who are competitors to your organization. Some of the information the consultants handle can be extremely sensitive and must not fall into the hands of their colleagues who are working with your competitors.

It's worth it

Securing data may seem like a lot of work but it's clearly worth it. Businesses can still benefit from sharing information across an organization, as long as they have proper information classification and identity management in place – and keep security measures commensurate with the value of the information.

In this age of strict regulations on information storage, a good information security scheme will also help companies ensure regulators that only the right people are allowed access to data.

Thinking about the case

1   Why is it so difficult to apply 'information classification' retrospectively? Are there ways of making it less difficult?

2   Will the measures outlined in the passage above deal with a situation where an employee leaves his laptop in the back of a taxi?

Glossary

access controls Hardware and software measures, such as user IDs and passwords, used to control access to information systems.

access point (AP) An arrangement consisting of a device connected to the Internet on one end and to a router on the other end. All wireless devices link to the Internet through the router.

affiliate programme An arrangement by which a website promotes sales for another website through a link to the seller's site, and for which the affiliate is compensated. There are various schemes of compensation to affiliates.

agile methods Software development methods that emphasize constant communication with clients (end users) and fast development of code, as well as modifications as soon as they are needed.

antivirus software Software designed to detect and intercept computer viruses.

applet A small software application, usually written in Java or another programming language for the Web.

application service provider (ASP) A firm that hires the use of software applications through an Internet link.

application software Software developed to meet general or specific business needs.

application-specific software A collective term for all computer programs that are designed specifically to address certain business problems, such as a program written to deal with a company's market research effort.

arithmetic logic unit (ALU) The electronic circuitry in the central processing unit of a computer responsible for arithmetic and logic operations.

assembly languages Second-generation programming languages that assemble several bytes into groups of characters that are human-readable to expedite programming tasks.

asymmetric (public key) encryption Encryption technology in which a message is encrypted with one key and decrypted with another.

atomic transaction A transaction whose entry is not complete until all entries into the appropriate files have been successfully completed. It is an important data entry control. (Atom = Indivisible)

audit trail Names, dates and other references in computer files that can help an auditor track down the person who used an IS for a transaction, legal or illegal.

authentication The process of ensuring that the person who sends a message to or receives a message from another party is indeed that person.

B2B Business-to-business, a term that refers to transactions between businesses, often through an Internet link.

B2C Business-to-consumer, a term that refers to transactions between a business and its customers, often through an Internet link.

backbone The network of copper lines, optical fibres and radio satellites that supports the Internet.

backup Periodic duplication of data in order to guard against loss.

backward compatibility Compatibility of a device with another device that supports only an older standard. For example, USB 2.0 is backward-compatible with computers that support only USB 1.1 devices.

bandwidth The capacity of the communications channel, practically its speed; the number of signal streams the channel can support, usually measured as number of bits per second. A greater bandwidth also supports a greater bit rate, i.e., transmission speed.

banners Advertisements that appear on a web page.

baseband A communications channel that allows only a very low bit rate in telecommunications, such as unconditioned telephone twisted pair cables.

benchmarking The measurement of time intervals and other important characteristics of hardware and software, usually when testing them before a decision to purchase or reject.

beta site An organization that agrees to use a new application for a specific period and report errors and unsatisfactory features to the developer in return for free use and support.

beta version A pre-release version of a software application that is given to a company for extensive testing prior to the full release.

bill of materials (BOM) A list showing an explosion of the materials that go into the production of an item. Used in planning the purchase of raw materials.

biometric A unique, measurable characteristic or trait of a human being used for automatically authenticating a person's identity. Biometric technologies include digitized fingerprints, retinal pictures and voice. Used with special hardware to uniquely identify a person who tries to access a facility or an IS, instead of a password.

bit Binary digit; either a zero or a one. The smallest unit of information used in computing.

bits per second (bps) The measurement of the capacity (or transmission rate) of a communications channel.

blackouts and brownouts Periods of power loss or a significant fall in power. Such events may cause computers to stop working, or even damage them. Computers can be protected against these events by using proper equipment, such as UPS (uninterruptible power supply) systems.

bleeding edge The situation in which a business fails because it tries to be on the technological leading edge.

blog A contraction of 'web log'. A website where participants post their opinions on a topic or set of related topics; these postings are listed in chronological order.

Bluetooth A personal wireless network protocol. It enables wireless communication between input devices and computers and among other devices within 10 metres.

brainstorming The process of a group collaboratively generating new ideas and creative solutions to problems.

bricks-and-mortar A popular term for companies that use physical structure for doing business directly with other businesses and consumers, such as stores. Often used to contrast with businesses that sell only online.

bridge A device connecting two communications networks that use similar hardware.

broadband High-speed digital communication, sometimes defined as at least 200 kbps. T1, cable modem and DSL provide broadband.

broadband over power lines (BPL) A broadband service provided over electric power lines.

bus The set of wires or soldered conductors in the computer through which the different components (such as the CPU and RAM) communicate. It also refers to a data communications topology whereby communicating devices are connected to a single, open-ended medium.

business intelligence (BI) Information gleaned from large amounts of data, usually a data warehouse or online databases; a BI system discovers not-yet-known patterns, trends and other useful information that can help improve the organization's performance.

business recovery plan Organizational plan that prepares for disruption in information systems, detailing what should be done and by whom, if critical information systems fail or become untrustworthy; also called business recovery plan and disaster recovery plan. Also known as business continuity plan.

byte A standard group of 8 bits.

C2C Consumer-to-consumer business. The term usually refers to web-based transactions between two consumers via the servers of an organization, such as auctions and sales. eBay is an example of a C2C site.

cash management system (CMS) Information system that helps reduce the interest and fees that organizations have to pay when borrowing money and increases the yield that organizations can receive on unused funds.

cathode-ray tube (CRT) A display (for a computer or television set) that uses an electronic gun to draw and paint on the screen by bombarding pixels on the internal side of the screen.

central processing unit (CPU) The circuitry of a computer microprocessor that fetches instructions and

data from the primary memory and executes the instructions. The CPU is the most important electronic unit of the computer.

certificate authority (CA) An organization that issues digital certificates, which authenticate the holder in electronic business transactions.

character The smallest piece of data in the data hierarchy.

chief information officer (CIO) The highest-ranking IS officer in the organization, usually a vice president, who oversees the planning, development and implementation of IS and serves as leader to all IS professionals in the organization.

chief security officer (CSO) Also called chief information security officer (CISO), the highest-ranking officer in charge of planning and implementing information security measures in the organization, such as access codes and backup procedures.

chief technology officer (CTO) A high-level corporate officer who is in charge of all information technology needs of the organization. Sometimes the CTO reports to the chief information officer, but in some companies this person practically serves as the CIO.

ciphertext A coded message designed to authenticate users and maintain secrecy.

circuit switching A communication process in which a dedicated channel (circuit) is established for the duration of a transmission; the sending node signals the receiving node; the receiver acknowledges the signal and then receives the entire message.

clickstream tracking The use of software to record the activities of a person at websites. Whenever the person clicks a link, the activity is added to the record.

clock rate The rate of repetitive machine cycles that a computer can perform; also called frequency. Measured in GHz.

closed system A system that stands alone, with no connection to another system.

coaxial cable A transmission medium consisting of thick copper wire insulated and shielded by a special sheath of meshed wires to prevent electromagnetic interference. Supports high-speed telecommunication.

co-location The placement and maintenance of a web server with servers of other subscribers of the service provider. The servers are co-located in the same facility.

competitive advantage A position in which one dominates a market; also called strategic advantage.

compiler A program whose purpose is to translate code written in a high-level programming language into the equivalent code in machine language for execution by the computer.

composite key In a data file, a combination of two fields that can serve as a unique key to locate specific records.

computer-aided design (CAD) Special software used by engineers and designers that facilitates engineering and design work.

computer-aided manufacturing (CAM) Automation of manufacturing activities by use of computers. Often, the information for the activity comes directly from connected computers that were used for engineering the parts or products to be manufactured.

consumer profiling The collection of information about individual shoppers in order to know and serve consumers better.

control unit The circuitry in the CPU that fetches instructions and data from the primary memory, decodes the instructions, passes them to the ALU for execution and stores the results in the primary memory.

controls Constraints applied to a system to ensure proper use and security standards.

conversion The process of abandoning an old information system and implementing a new one.

conversion rate In marketing, the proportion of shoppers who end up buying from the organization. The term also applies to online shopping.

cookie A small file that a website places on a visitor's hard disk so that the website can remember something about the visitor later, such as an ID number or username.

cost/benefit analysis An evaluation of the costs incurred by an information system and the benefits gained by the system.

custom-designed (tailored) software Software designed to meet the specific needs of a particular organization or department; also called tailored software.

customer relationship management (CRM) A set of applications designed to gather and analyse information about customers.

cut-over conversion (direct changeover) A swift switch from an old information system to the new.

dashboard A graphic presentation of organizational performance. Dashboards display in an easy-to-grasp visual manner metrics, trends and other helpful information that is the result of processing of business intelligence applications.

data Facts about people, other subjects and events. These may be manipulated and processed to produce information.

data dictionary The part of the database that contains information about the different sets of records and fields, such as their source and who may change them.

data flow diagram (DFD) A graphical method to communicate the data flow in a business unit. Usually serves as a blueprint for a new information system in the development process. The DFD uses four symbols for entity, process, data store and data flow.

data integrity Accuracy, timeliness and relevance of data in a context.

data mart A collection of archival data that is part of a data warehouse, usually focusing on one aspect of the organization such as sales of a family of products or daily revenues in a geographic region.

data mining Using a special application that scours large databases for relationships among business events, such as items typically purchased together on

a certain day of the week, or machinery failures that occur along with a specific use mode of the machine. Instead of the user querying the databases, the application dynamically looks for such relationships.

data modelling The process of charting existing or planned data stores and flows of an organization or one of its units. It includes charting of entity relationship diagrams.

data processing The operation of manipulating data to produce information.

data redundancy The existence of the same data in more than one place in a computer system. Although some data redundancy is unavoidable, efforts should be made to minimize it.

data warehouse A huge collection of historical data that can be processed to support management decision-making.

data word The number of bits that a CPU retrieves from memory for processing in one machine cycle. When all other conditions are equal, a machine with a larger data word is faster.

database A collection of shared, interrelated records, usually in more than one file. An approach to data management that facilitates data entry, update and manipulation.

database administrator (DBA) The individual in charge of building and maintaining organizational databases.

database approach An approach to maintaining data that contains a mechanism for tagging, retrieving and manipulating data.

database management system (DBMS) A computer program that allows the user to construct a database, populate it with data and manipulate the data.

decision support system (DSS) Information system that aids managers in making decisions based on built-in models. DSSs comprise three modules: data management, model management and dialogue management. DSSs may be an integral part of a larger application, such as an ERP system.

dedicated hosting An arrangement in which a web hosting organization devotes an entire server to only the website of a single client organization, as opposed to having multiple clients' sites share one server.

denial of service (DoS) The inability of legitimate visitors to log on to a website when too many malicious requests are launched by an attacker. Most DoS attacks are distributed (DDoS).

dial-up connection A connection to the Internet through a regular telephone and modem. Dial-up connections are slow, as opposed to broadband connections.

digital certificates Computer files that serve as the equivalent of ID cards.

digital signature An encrypted digest of the text that is sent along with a message that authenticates the identity of the sender and guarantees that no one has altered the sent document.

digital subscriber line (DSL) Technology that relieves individual subscribers of the need for the conversion of digital signals into analogue signals between the telephone exchange and the subscriber jack. DSL lines are linked to the Internet on a permanent basis and support bit rates significantly greater than a normal telephone line between the subscriber's jack and the telephone exchange.

dimensional database A database of tables, each of which contains aggregations and other manipulated information gleaned from the data to speed up the presentation by online processing applications. Also called multidimensional database.

direct access The manner in which a record is retrieved from a storage device, without the need to seek it sequentially. The record's address is calculated from the value in its logical key field.

direct changeover *See* cut-over conversion.

disaster recovery plan *See* business recovery plan.

distributed computing The connection of several (relatively) small computers to give the processing power of one larger computer.

distributed denial of service (DDoS) Multiple log-in requests from many computers to the same website, so that the website is jammed with requests and cannot accept enquiries of legitimate visitors.

DMZ Demilitarized zone, a network of computers and other devices connected to the Internet where visitors are not allowed direct access to other resources connected to the DMZ. DMZs are used to serve visitors while minimizing risk of unauthorized access.

DNS (domain name system) Hardware and software making up a server whose purpose is to resolve domain names (converting them back to IP numbers) and routing messages on the Internet.

domain name The name assigned to an Internet server or to a part of a server that hosts a website.

downtime The unplanned period of time during which a system does not function.

drill down The process of finding the most relevant information for executive decision-making within a database or data warehouse by moving from more general information to more specific details, such as from performance of a division to performance of a department within the division.

dynamic IP number The IP number assigned to a computer that is connected to the Internet intermittently for the duration of the computer's connection.

dynamic web page A web page whose contents change while the visitor watches it.

e-commerce Business activity that is electronically executed between parties, such as between two businesses or between a business and a consumer.

economic order quantity (EOQ) The optimal (cost-minimizing) quantity of a specific raw material that allows a business to minimize overstocking and save cost without risking understocking and missing production deadlines.

effectiveness The measure of how well a job is performed.

efficiency The ratio of output to input; the greater the ratio, the greater the efficiency.

electronic funds transfer (EFT) The electronic transfer of cash from an account in one bank to an account in another bank.

electronic product code (EPC) A product code embedded in a radio frequency identification (RFID) tag. Similar to the older UPC.

employee knowledge network Software that facilitates search of relevant knowledge within an organization. The software points an employee with a need for certain information or expertise to co-workers who might have such information or expertise.

encapsulation In an object oriented data model, the combined storage of both data and the procedures that manipulate them.

encryption The conversion of plaintext to an unreadable stream of characters, especially to prevent a party that intercepts telecommunicated messages from reading them. Special encryption software is used by the sending party to encrypt messages, and by the receiving party to decipher them.

enterprise application An application that fulfils a number of functions together, such as inventory planning, purchasing, payment and billing

enterprise resource planning (ERP) system An information system that supports different activities for different departments, assisting executives with planning and running different interdependent functions.

entity Any object about which an organization chooses to collect data.

entity relationship diagram (ERD) One of several conventions for graphical rendition of the data elements involved in business processes and the logical relationships among the elements.

ergonomics The science of designing and modifying machines to better suit people's health and comfort.

Ethernet The design, introduced and named by Xerox, for the contention-based data communications protocol.

European Article Number (EAN) A European standard of product code, similar to UPC but containing more information.

expert system (ES) A computer program that mimics the decision process of a human expert in providing a solution to a problem. Current expert systems deal with problems and diagnostics in narrow domains. An ES consists of a knowledge base, an inference engine and a dialogue management module.

external data Data that are collected from a wide array of sources outside the organization, including mass communications media, specialized newsletters, government agencies and the Web.

external memory Any non-RAM memory, including internal and external hard disks, flash memory and optical discs.

extranet A network, part of which is the Internet, whose purpose is to facilitate communication and trade between an organization and its business partners.

feasibility studies A series of studies conducted to determine if a proposed information system can be built, and whether or not it will benefit the business;

the series includes technical, economic and operational feasibility studies.

field A data element in a record, describing one aspect of an entity or event. Referred to as an attribute in relational databases.

file A collection of related records, such as a customer file containing details of all customer names, billing addresses, delivery addresses, credit limits and so on.

File Transfer Protocol (FTP) Software that allows the transfer of files over communications lines.

firewall Hardware and software designed to control access by Internet surfers to an information system, and access to Internet sites by organizational users.

first mover A business that is first in its industry to adopt a technology or method.

fixed wireless A network of fixed transceivers to facilitate connection to the Internet. Requires line of sight between transceivers.

flash drive A storage device containing flash memory. Flash drives are used in numerous electronic devices and often are designed to connect to a computer through a USB port.

flash memory A memory chip that can be rewritten and can hold its content without electric power. Thumb drives, as well as ROM, are made of flash memory.

foreign key In a relational database: a field in a table that is a primary key in another table. Foreign keys allow association of data between the two files.

frame relay A high-speed packet switching protocol used on the Internet.

fulfilment Picking, packing and shipping after a customer places an order online.

general-purpose application software Programs that serve varied purposes, such as developing decision-making tools or creating documents; examples include spreadsheets and word processors.

geographic information system (GIS) Information system that exhibits information visually on a computer monitor with local, regional, national or international maps, so that the information can easily be related to locations or routes on the map. GISs are used, for example, in the planning of transportation and product distribution, or the examination of government resources distributed over an area.

Gigabit Ethernet A network protocol often used in local area networks (LANs) supporting up to 1 Gbps.

global information system Any information system that crosses national borders.

Global Trade Item Number (GTIN) A number that uniquely identifies products and services. The GTIN is a global standard succeeding the EAN and UPC.

glocalization The planning and designing of global websites so that they also cater to local needs and preferences.

groupware Any of several types of software that enable users of computers in remote locations to work together on the same project. The users can create

and change documents and graphic designs on the same monitor.

hard disk A stack of several rigid aluminum platters coated with easily magnetized substance to record data. Usually installed in the same box that holds the CPU and other computer components, but may be portable.

hardware All physical components of a computer or computer system.

hijacking In the context of networks, when computers are remotely taken advantage of by people who are not authorized to do so by the lawful owner. The computer is 'hijacked' after a controlling application is surreptitiously installed on the computer's hard disk. Hijacked computers are exploited to participate in spamming or DDoS attacks.

honeypot A duplicate database on a server connected to the Internet to trace an intruder. The server is dedicated specifically for detection of intrusions and is not productive. The honeypot is there to be attacked in lieu of a productive server. The traces can be used to improve security measures and possibly catch the intruder.

honeytoken A bogus record in a database on a honeypot or productive server that is likely to draw an intruder's attention. If the intruder changes the record, the security officers know that the server has been attacked and can fix vulnerabilities.

host A computer that contains files and other resources that can be accessed by 'clients', computers linked to it via a network.

hot site A location where a client organization hit by a disaster can continue its vital operations. The structure – often underground – is equipped with hardware and software to support the client's employees.

hotspot An area, usually of 300-feet radius, in which a wireless device can connect to the Internet. The hotspot is created by installing an access point consisting of a device connected to the Internet on one end and to a router on the other end. All wireless devices link to the Internet through the router.

HTTPS The secure version of HTTP.

hub In networking, a device connecting several computers or other electronic devices.

Hypertext Markup Language (HTML) A programming language for web pages and web browsers.

Hypertext Transfer Protocol (HTTP) Software that allows browsers to log on to websites.

Hypertext Transfer Protocol Secure See HTTPS.

identity theft The criminal practice of obtaining enough personal information to pretend to be the victim, usually resulting in running up that person's credit cards or issuing new credit cards under that person's name.

IEEE 802.11 A standard for wireless communication. Several other IEEE 802.x standards have been approved by the Institute of Electrical and Electronics Engineers.

imaging The transformation of text and graphical documents into digitized files. The document can be electronically retrieved and printed to reconstruct a copy of the original. Imaging has saved much space and expense in paper-intensive business areas.

impression In web advertising, the event of an ad displayed on a surfer's monitor.

information The product of processing data so that they can be used in a context by human beings.

information map The description of data and information flow within an organization.

information system (IS) A computer-based set of hardware, software and telecommunications components, supported by people and procedures, to process data and turn it into useful information.

information technology (IT) Refers to all technologies that collectively facilitate construction and maintenance of information systems.

inheritance The ability in object-oriented structures to create a new object automatically by replicating all or some of the characteristics of a previously developed object.

input Raw data entered into a computer for processing.

input device A tool, such as a keyboard or voice recognition system, used to enter data into an information system.

instant messaging (IM) The capability for several online computer users to share messages in real time; also called chatting online.

internal data Data collected within an organization, typically by transaction-processing systems, for example the number of sales per month, the value of outstanding credit owed to the organization.

internal memory The memory circuitry inside the computer, communicating directly with the CPU. Consists of RAM and ROM.

Internet Protocol (IP) number A unique number assigned to a server or another device that is connected to the Internet for identification purposes. Consists of 32 bits.

Internet service provider (ISP) An individual or organization that provides Internet connection, and sometimes other related services, to subscribers.

intranet A network using web browsing software that serves employees within an organization.

join table In relational database manipulation, a table created by linking – that is, joining – data from multiple tables.

just-in-time (JIT) The manufacturing strategy in which suppliers ship parts directly to assembly lines, saving the cost of warehousing raw materials, parts and subassemblies.

key A field in a database table whose values identify records either for display or for processing. Typical keys are part number (in an inventory file) and National Insurance number (in a human resources file).

keystroke logging Automatically recording the keystrokes of a computer user. The logging is done by special software, usually surreptitiously with the intention of later using secret access codes.

knowledge base The collection of facts and the relationships among them that mimic the decision-making process in an expert's mind and constitute a major component of an expert system.

knowledge management The combination of activities involved in gathering, sharing, analysing and disseminating knowledge to improve an organization's performance.

late mover An organization that adopts a technology or method after competitors have adopted it.

leased lines Point-to-point dedicated digital circuits provided by telephone companies.

load balancing The transfer of visitor enquiries from a busy server to a less busy server.

local area network (LAN) A computer network confined to a building or a group of adjacent buildings, as opposed to a wide area network.

logic bomb A destructive computer program that is inactive until it is triggered by an event taking place in the computer, such as the deletion of a certain record from a file. When the event is a particular time, the logic bomb is referred to as a time bomb.

machine cycle The steps that the CPU follows repeatedly: fetch an instruction, decode the instruction, execute the instruction and store the result.

machine language Binary programming language that is specific to a computer. A computer can execute a program only after the program's source code is translated to object code expressed in the computer's machine language.

magnetic disk A disk or set of disks sharing a spindle, coated with an easily magnetized substance to record data in the form of tiny magnetic fields.

magnetic-ink character recognition (MICR) A technology that allows a special electronic device to read data printed with magnetic ink. The data are later processed by a computer. MICR is widely used in banking. The bank code, account number and the amount of a cheque are printed in magnetic ink on the bottom of cheques.

magnetic tape Coated polyester tape used to store computer data; similar to tape recorder or VCR tape.

mainframe computer A computer larger than a midrange computer but smaller than a supercomputer.

management by exception A method of management whereby managers review only exceptions from expected results that are of a certain size or type, assuming that smaller deviations are immaterial.

management information system (MIS) A computer-based information system used for planning, control, decision-making or problem-solving.

manufacturing resource planning (MRP II) The combination of MRP with other manufacturing-related activities to plan the entire manufacturing process, not just inventory.

many-to-many relationship In databases, a relationship between two tables whereby every record in a table can be associated with several records in the other table.

master production schedule (MPS) The component of an MRP II system that specifies production capacity to meet customer demands and maintain inventories.

material requirements planning (MRP) Inventory control that includes a calculation of future need.

m-commerce Mobile commerce, enabled by advances in technology for mobile communications devices.

metadata Information about the data in a database, often called data dictionary.

microcomputer The smallest type of computer; includes desktop, laptop and handheld computers.

microprocessor An electronic chip that contains the circuitry of either a CPU or a processor with a dedicated and limited purpose, for example a communications processor.

microwaves Short (high frequency) radio waves. Used in telecommunications to carry digital signals.

midrange computer A computer larger than a microcomputer but smaller than a mainframe.

MIPS Millions of instructions per second; an inaccurate measure of computer speed.

mirror An Internet server that holds the same software and data as another server, which may be located thousands of miles away.

mission-critical applications Applications without which a business cannot conduct its operations.

mobile broadband wireless access (MBWA) IEEE 801.20 standard to support continuous wireless connection while moving in vehicles.

modem (modulator/demodulator) A communications device that transforms digital signals to analogue telephone signals, and vice versa, for data communications over voice telephone lines. The term is widely used for all devices that connect a computer to a wide area network, such as the Internet, even if the device does not modulate or demodulate.

modulation The modification of a digital signal (from a computer) into an analogue signal (for a phone line to transmit).

mouse An input device that controls an on-screen pointer to facilitate the point-and-click approach to executing different operations.

multidimensional database *See* dimensional database.

multiprocessing The mode in which a computer uses more than one processing unit simultaneously to process data.

network A combination of a communications device and a computer or several computers, or two or more computers, so that the various devices can send and receive text or audiovisual information to each other.

network administrator The individual who is responsible for the acquisition, implementation, management, maintenance and troubleshooting of computer networks throughout the organization.

network interface card (NIC) Circuitry embedded or installed in a computer to support proper linking of the computer to a network.

node A device connected to at least one other device on a network.

notebook computer A computer as small as a book, yet with computing power similar to that of a desktop microcomputer.

object-oriented database model A database, in which data are part of an object, that is processed using object-oriented programs.

object-oriented programming (OOP) language A programming language that combines data and the procedures that process the data into a single unit called an 'object', which can be invoked from different programs.

OC (optical carrier) A family of several very high-speed technologies using optical fibres. Usually, the standard is marked as OC-3, OC-12, OC-48, etc.

offshoring Outsourcing work to employees in other countries.

one-to-many relationship In a database, a relationship between two tables such that each record in the one table can be associated with several records in the other table, but each record in the other table can be associated with only one record in the first table.

online analytical processing (OLAP) A type of application that operates on data stored in databases and data warehouses to produce summary tables with multiple combinations of dimensions. An OLAP server is connected to the database or data warehouse server at one end and to the user's computer at the other.

open source software Software whose source code can be accessed by the general public.

open system A system that interfaces and interacts with other systems.

operating system (OS) System software that supports the running of applications developed to utilize its features and controls peripheral equipment.

optical disc A disc on which data are recorded by treating the disc surface so it reflects light in different ways; includes CD and DVD.

organizational culture An umbrella term referring to the general tone of a corporate environment.

output The result of processing data by the computer; usually, information.

output device A device, usually a monitor or printer, that delivers information from a computer to a person.

outsourcing Buying the services of an information service firm that undertakes some or all of the organization's IS operations.

packaged software General-purpose applications that come ready to install from a magnetic disk, CD, or file downloaded from a vendor's website.

packet Several bytes that make up a part of a telecommunicated message.

packet switching A telecommunications method whereby messages are broken into groups of fixed amounts of bytes, and each group (packet) is transmitted through the shortest route available. The packets are assembled at the destination into the original message.

PAN (personal area network) A network of devices typically within a small radius that enables a user to use two or more devices wirelessly, such as wireless keyboard and mouse.

parallel conversion Using an old information system along with a new system for a predetermined period of time before relying only on the new one.

parallel processing The capacity for several CPUs in one computer to process different data at the same time.

peer-to-peer (P2P) file sharing Software applications that enable two Internet users to send and receive to each other. The technology is highly objectionable to organizations that sell copyrighted materials because the software promotes violation of copyrights.

peer-to-peer LAN A local area network (LAN) in which no central device controls communications.

personal digital assistant (PDA) A small handheld computer. Many PDAs require the use of a special stylus to click displayed items and to enter handwritten information that is recognized by the computer. An increasing number of PDAs also serve as mobile phones, music players and GPS devices.

phased conversion Implementing a new information system one module at a time.

phishing The criminal practice of luring Internet users to provide their personal information via email or the Web. Phishing almost always results in fraud or identity theft.

piloting A trial conversion in which a new information system is introduced in one business unit before introducing it in others.

pixel The smallest picture element addressable on a monitor, short for 'picture element'. In an LCD monitor, it is a triad of three transistors controlling the colours of red, green and blue that can be switched on and off and kept on with varying amounts of electricity to produce various colours and hues. In a CRT monitor, the triad is made of phosphorous dots that are excited by an electron gun.

plaintext An original message, before encryption.

podcasting The practice of posting sound files at a website for automating downloading and playing by subscribers.

port A socket on a computer to which external devices, such as printers, keyboards and scanners, can be connected. Also, software that enables direct communication of certain applications with the Internet.

primary key In a file, a field that holds values that are unique to each record. Only a primary key can be used to uniquely identify and retrieve a record.

process Any manipulation of data, usually with the goal of producing information.

productivity Efficiency, when the input is labour. The fewer labour hours needed to perform a job, the greater the productivity.

programming The process of writing software.

programming languages Sets of syntax for abbreviated forms of instructions that special programs can translate into machine language so a computer can understand the instructions.

proprietary software Software owned by an individual or organization. The owner can control licensing and usage terms of the software. Non-proprietary software is not owned by anyone and is free for use.

protocol A standard set of rules that governs telecommunication between two communications devices or in a network.

prototyping An approach to the development of information systems in which several analysis steps are skipped, to accelerate the development process. A 'quick and dirty' model is developed and continually improved until the prospective users are satisfied. Prototyping has evolved into agile development methods.

proxy server A computer that serves as an intermediary between two servers on the Internet, often for the purpose of security or filtering out certain information.

public-key encryption Encryption technology in which the recipient's public key is used to encrypt and the recipient's private key is used to decrypt.

pure-play A business operating with clients only via the Web, as opposed to operating via stores or other physical facilities.

radio frequency identification (RFID) Technology that enables identification of an object (such as product, vehicle, or living creature) by receiving a radio signal from a tag attached to the object.

radio frequency interference (RFI) The unwanted reception of radio signals that occurs when using metal communication lines. Optical fibres are not susceptible to RFI.

RAID (Redundant Array of Independent Disks) A set of magnetic disk packs maintained for backup purposes. Sometimes RAIDs are used for storing large databases.

RAM (random access memory) The major part of a computer's internal memory. RAM is volatile; that is, software is held in it temporarily and disappears when the machine is unplugged or turned off, or it may disappear when operations are interrupted or new software is installed or activated. RAM is made of microchips containing transistors. Many computers have free sockets that allow the expansion of RAM.

rapid prototyping Using software and special output devices to create prototypes to test design in three dimensions.

reach percentage The percentage of web users who have visited a site in the past month, or the ratio of visitors to the total web population.

record A set of standard field types. All the fields of a record contain data about a certain entity or event.

reengineering The process by which an organization takes a fresh look at a business process and reorganizes it to attain efficiency. Almost always, reengineering includes the integration of a new or improved information system.

relational database model A general structure of database in which records are organized in tables (relations) and the relationships among tables are maintained through foreign keys.

relational operation An operation that creates a temporary table that is a subset of the original table or tables in a relational database.

repeater A device that strengthens signals and then sends them on their next leg towards their next destination.

request for information (RFI) A request to vendors for general, somewhat informal, information about their products.

request for proposal (RFP) A document specifying all the system requirements and soliciting a proposal from vendors who might want to bid on a project or service.

resolution The degree to which the image on a computer monitor is sharp. Higher resolution means a sharper image. Resolution depends on the number of pixels on the screen and the dot pitch.

return on investment (ROI) A financial calculation of the difference between the stream of benefits and the stream of costs over the life of an information system; often used as a general term to indicate that an investment in an information system is recouped or smaller than the cost the system saves or the increase in revenue it brings about.

reverse auction (name-your-own-price auction) An online auction in which participants post the price they want to pay for a good or service, and retailers compete to make the sale; also called a name-your-price auction.

ROM (read-only memory) The minor part of a computer's internal memory. ROM is loaded by the manufacturer with software that cannot be changed. Usually, ROM holds very basic system software, but sometimes also applications. Like RAM, ROM consists of microchips containing transistors.

router A network hub, wired or wireless, that ensures proper routing of messages within a network such as a LAN and between each device on that network and another network, such as the Internet.

RSS Really Simple Syndication, a type of application using XML for aggregating updates to blogs and news posted at websites.

Safe Harbor A list of US corporations that have agreed to conform to European Union data protection laws with regard to EU citizens. The arrangement enables the corporations to continue to do business with European companies.

scalability The ability to adapt applications as business needs grow.

schema The structure of a database, detailing the names and types of fields in each set of records, and the relationships among sets of records.

search advertising Placing ads at search engine websites.

sequential storage A file organization for sequential record entry and retrieval. The records are organized as a list that follows a logical order, such as ascending order of ID numbers, or descending order of part numbers. To retrieve a record, the application must start the search at the first record and retrieve every record, sequentially, until the desired record is encountered.

server A computer connected to several less powerful computers that can utilize its databases and applications.

service-level agreement A document that lists all the types of services expected of an outsourcing vendor as well as the metrics that will be used to measure the degree to which the vendor has met the level of promised services. Usually, the client makes the list.

shared hosting An arrangement by which the websites of several clients are maintained by the hosting vendor on the same server.

social engineering Deceptive methods that hackers use to entice people to release confidential information such as access codes and passwords. Often, the crooks misrepresent themselves as technicians who need one's password for fixing a problem in a network.

software Sets of instructions that control the operations of a computer.

software as a service (SaaS) An alternative to developing or licensing software, which enables the client to hire the software through communication lines, usually over the Internet, from an application service provider (ASP).

solid state disk (SSD) Flash memory that serves as external storage medium as if it were a hard disk.

source code An application's code written in the original high-level programming language.

source data input device A device that enables data entry directly from a document without need for human keying. Such devices include bar-code readers and optical character readers.

speech recognition The process of translating human speech into computer-readable data and instructions.

spyware A small application stored surreptitiously by a website on the hard disk of a visitor's computer. The application tracks activities of the user, including visits to websites, and transmits the information to the operator's server.

SSO (single sign-on) Enabling employees to access several information systems by using a single password.

static IP number An Internet Protocol number permanently associated with a device.

storage The operation of storing data and information in an information system.

storage service provider (SSP) A firm that rents storage space for software through an Internet link.

strategic information system Any information system that gives its owner a competitive advantage.

Structured Query Language (SQL) The data definition and manipulation language of choice for many developers of relational database management systems.

stylus A pen-like marking device used to enter commands and data on a computer screen.

subsystem A component of a larger system.

suite A group of general software applications that are often used in the same environment. The strengths of the different applications can be used to build a single powerful document. Current suites are usually a combination of a spreadsheet, a word processor and a database management system.

supercomputer The most powerful class of computers, used by large organizations, research institutions and universities for complex scientific computations and the manipulation of very large databases.

supply chain The activities performed from the purchase of raw material to the shipping of manufactured goods and collecting for their sale.

supply chain management (SCM) The coordination of purchasing, manufacturing, shipping and billing operations, often supported by an enterprise resource planning system.

support The maintenance and provision for user help on an information system.

switch In networking, a device that is able to direct communications to certain devices on the network. Compare with a hub which broadcasts to all connected devices.

switching costs Expenses that are incurred when a customer stops buying a product or service from one business and starts buying it from another.

symmetric (secret or private key) encryption Encryption technology in which both the sender and recipient of a message use the same key for encryption and decryption.

synergy From Greek 'to work together'. The attainment of output, when two factors work together, that is greater or better than the sum of their products when they work separately.

system An array of components that work together to achieve a common goal or multiple goals.

system requirements The functions that an information system is expected to fulfil and the features through which it will perform its tasks.

system software Software that executes routine tasks. System software includes operating systems, language translators and communications software. Also called 'support software'.

systems analysis The early steps in the systems development process, to define the requirements of the proposed system and determine its feasibility.

systems analyst An IT professional who analyses business problems and recommends technological solutions.

systems design The evaluation of alternative solutions to a business problem and the specification of hardware, software and communications technology for the selection solution.

systems development life cycle (SDLC) The oldest method of developing an information system, consisting of several phases of analysis and design, which must be followed sequentially.

systems integration Interfacing several information systems.

table A set of related records in a relational database.

tablet computer A full-power personal computer in the form of a thick writing tablet.

targeted marketing Promoting products and services to the people who are most likely to purchase them.

TCP/IP (transmission control protocol/Internet protocol) A packet-switching protocol that is actually a set of related protocols that can guarantee packets are delivered in the correct order and can handle differences in transmission and reception rates.

technology convergence The combining of several technologies into a single device, such as mobile phone, digital camera and web browser.

telecommunications Communications over a long distance, as opposed to communication within a computer, or between adjacent hardware pieces.

throughput A general measure of the rate of computer output.

time to market The time between generating an idea for a product and completing a prototype that can be mass-manufactured; also called engineering lead time.

touch screen A computer monitor that serves both as input and output device. The user touches the areas of a certain menu item to select options, and the screen senses the selection at the point of the touch.

trackball A device similar to a mouse, used for clicking, locking and dragging displayed information; in this case, the ball moves within the device rather than over a surface.

trackpad A device used for clicking, locking and dragging displayed information; the cursor is controlled by moving one's finger along a touch-sensitive pad.

transaction A business event. In an IS context, the record of a business event.

transaction processing system (TPS) Any system that records transactions.

transmission rate The speed at which data are communicated over a communications channel.

Transport Layer Security (TLS) The successor of Secure Sockets Layer (SSL), the software in the web browser responsible for secure communication.

Trojan horse A malicious piece of software hidden with a benign and legitimate software that one downloads or agrees to otherwise accept and install on one's computer. The Trojan horse then causes damage.

twisted pair cable Traditional telephone wires, twisted in pairs to reduce electromagnetic interference.

Unicode An international standard to enable the storage and display of characters of a large variety of languages – such as Asian, Arabic and Hebrew – on computers.

Unified Modelling Language (UML) An extensive standard for graphically representing elements of programming, specifically accommodating programming in object-oriented languages and web technologies.

Uniform Resource Locator (URL) The address of a website. Always starts with *http://* but does not have to contain *www*.

uninterruptible power supply (UPS) A device that provides an alternative power supply as soon as a power network fails.

Universal Product Code (UPC) A code usually expressed as a number and series of variable width bars that uniquely identifies the product by scanning.

universal serial bus (USB) A ubiquitous socket that enables the connection of numerous devices to computers.

uptime The percentage of time (so much time per year) that an information system is in full operation.

USB drive Any storage device that connects to a computer through a USB socket, but especially flash drives.

user application development Development of corporate applications by employees rather than IT professionals.

utilities Programs that provide help in routine user operations.

value-added network (VAN) A telecommunications network owned and managed by a vendor that charges clients periodic fees for network management services.

videoconferencing A telecommunication system that allows people who are in different locations to meet via transmitted images and speech.

virtual private network (VPN) Hardware and software installed to ensure that a network path that includes the Internet enables employees of the same organization or employees of business partners to communicate confidentially. The hardware and software create an impression that the entire communication path is private.

virtual private server Part of a server that serves as an Internet server for a client of a web hosting company, while other clients share the same physical server.

virus Destructive software that propagates and is activated by unwary users; a virus usually damages applications and data files or disrupts communications.

visual programming language A programming language that provides icons, colours and other visual elements from which the programmer can choose to speed up software development.

VoIP (Voice over Internet Protocol) Technologies that enable voice communication by utilizing the Internet instead of the telephone network.

web hosting The business of organizations that host, maintain and often help design websites for clients.

Webmaster The person who is in charge of constructing and maintaining the organization's website.

wide area network (WAN) A network of computers and other communications devices that extends over a large area, possibly comprising national territories. Example: the Internet.

Wi-Fi A name given to the IEEE 802.11 standards of wireless communication. Wi-Fi technologies are used in hotspots and in home and office networks. Wi-Fi is usually effective for a radius of 300 feet.

WiMAX The IEEE 802.16 standard for wireless networking with a range of up to 50 km (31 miles). (WiMAX stands for the organization that promotes that standard, Worldwide Interoperability for Microwave Access.)

wireless LAN (WLAN) A local area network that uses electromagnetic waves (radio or infrared light) as the medium of communication. In recent years almost all WLANs have been established using Wi-Fi.

workstation A powerful microcomputer providing high-speed processing and high-resolution graphics. Used primarily for scientific and engineering assignments.

worm A rogue program that spreads in a computer network.

XHTML A standard that combines HTML standards and XML standards.

XML (Extensible Markup Language) A programming language that tags data elements in order to indicate what the data mean, especially in web pages.

Name and company index

Subject index